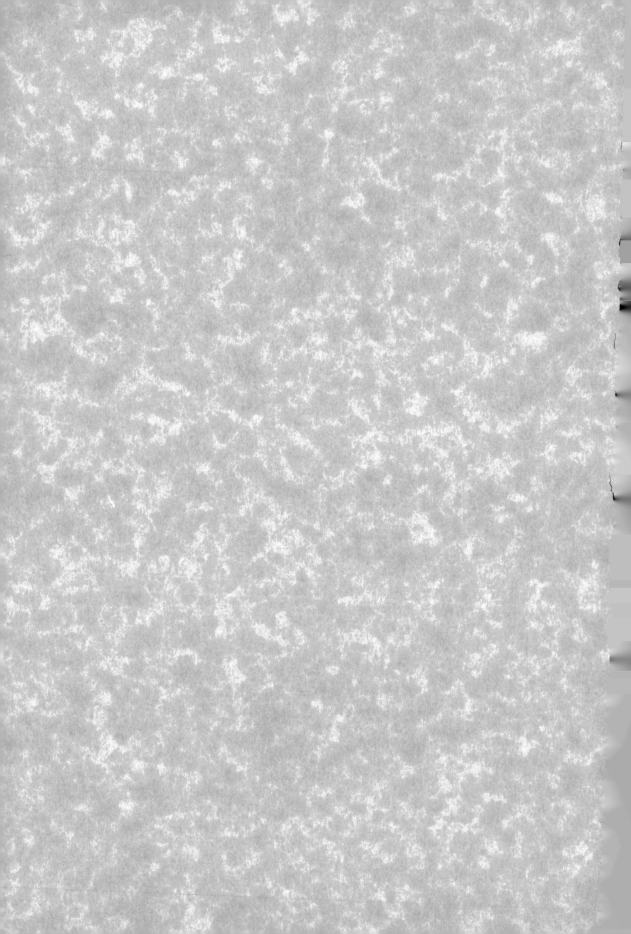

Also translated by Everett Fox

The Five Books of Moses:
Genesis, Exodus, Leviticus, Numbers, Deuteronomy

Give Us a King! Samuel, Saul, and David

THE EARLY PROPHETS

Nathan Admonishing David, *by Rembrandt van Rijn, c. 1655, pen and brown ink, heightened with white gouache. Copyright © The Metropolitan Museum of Art, New York. Source: Art Resource, N.Y.*

In this memorable study, one of four he drew of the scene in II Sam. 12, the artist presents a chastened King David, scepter pointed downward, listening to the prophet's rebuke. The theme of divine word versus kingly power is a major one in the books of Samuel and Kings.

THE
EARLY PROPHETS

Joshua, Judges, Samuel, and Kings

A New Translation with Introductions,

Commentary, and Notes by

Everett Fox

Schocken Books, New York

All rights reserved. Published in the United States by Schocken Books, a division of
Random House LLC, New York, and in Canada by Random House of Canada Limited,
Toronto, Penguin Random House companies.

Schocken Books and colophon are registered trademarks of Random House LLC.

The text of I and II Samuel, appearing here in substantially different form, is taken from
Give Us A King!: Samuel, Saul, and David. Copyright © 1999 by Everett Fox. Published by
Schocken Books, a division of Random House LLC, New York.

"On the Shimshon Cycle" first appeared in different form as "The Samson Cycle
in an Oral Setting" in *Alcheringa: Ethnopoetics* 4:1 (1978).

Grateful acknowledgment is made to Augsburg Fortress Publishers for permission to
reprint the maps on pages 2, 126, 266, 548, and 550 from *Introduction to the Hebrew Bible,* by
John J. Collins, copyright © 2004 by Augsburg Fortress Press. Reprinted by permission.

Library of Congress Cataloging-in-Publication Data
The early prophets : Joshua, Judges, Samuel, and Kings / translated by Dr. Everett Fox.
Pages cm.—(The Schocken Bible ; volume 2)
Includes bibliographical references and index.
ISBN 978-0-8052-4181-5 (hardback)   ISBN 978-0-8052-4323-9 (eBook)
I. Bible. Former prophets—Commentaries. I. Fox, Everett, author, translator. II. Bible.
Former Prophets. English. Fox. 2014.
BS1286.5.A3F695   2014   222'.077—dc23   2013027428

www.schocken.com

Jacket design by Kathleen DiGrado

Printed in the United States of America
First Edition
2 4 6 8 9 7 5 3 1

For Cherie
Proverbs 31:29
and
Akiva, Leora, and Ezra
Proverbs 23:25a

Contents

Translator's Preface ix

Acknowledgments xiii

On Using This Book xvii

General Introduction xxi

An Approximate Biblical Chronology xxix

Joshua

Map of the Twelve Tribes of Israel 2

Introduction 3

Part I. Preparations for Conquest (1–5) 13

Part II. Waging War (6–12) 33

Part III. Allotting the Land (13–22) 69

Part IV. Last Words (23–24) 113

Judges

Map of Israelite Settlement 126

Introduction 127

Part I. Opening the Bracket (1–3:6) 135

Part IIa. Early Leaders: Israel Delivered (3:7–8:32) 149

Part IIb. Later Leaders: Decline (8:33–16:31) 185

On the Shimshon Cycle 207

Part III. Closing the Bracket (17–21) 233

Appendix: The Sound and Structure of a Biblical Tale 261

Samuel

Map of the Kingdoms of David and Shelomo 266

Introduction 267

Part I. The Last "Judges": Eli and Shemuel (I 1–7) 279

Part II. The Requested King (I 8–15) 311

Part III.   The Rise of David and the Fall of Sha'ul (I 16–II 1)   351

Part IV.   David's Rule Consolidated (II 2–8)   431

Part V.   David in Control and Out of Control (II 9–12)   463

Part VI.   The Great Rebellion (II 13–20)   481

Part VII.   Final Matters (II 21–24)   527

Kings

Map of Israel and Judah   548

Map of Jerusalem in the Times of David, Shelomo, and Hizkiyyahu   549

Map of the Assyrian Empire   550

Introduction   551

The Kings of Israel in the Book of Kings   559

Part I.   Shelomo and His Kingdom (I 1–11)   561

   On the Temple   563

Part II.   The Split: Kings North and South (I 12–16:22)   631

Part III.   Omrides and Prophets (I 16:23–II 13)   657

   On Eliyyahu and Elisha (I Kings 17–II Kings 13)   659

Part IV.   Southern and Northern Kings: Destruction I (II 14–17)   763

Part V.   Judah as Vassal and Rebel: Destruction II (II 18–25)   785

   On Three Kings of Judah   787

Recurring Names in The Early Prophets   829

Bibliography   835

TRANSLATOR'S PREFACE

By nature, translation is a slow and painstaking process marked by constant rethinking and revision. Published works give an impression of finality, but in truth there is no end point for the translator, either in concept or in execution— only the ongoing attempt to draw nearer to the source. And like the experience of the performer on the stage or in the concert hall, the translator's perception of the source alters with time. It is therefore only natural that I have made changes in my work over the years, from certain aspects of the overall approach to the rendering of individual words and phrases. The publication of this book gives me the opportunity to briefly explain some of them.

I remain convinced that the best way to translate biblical texts is to try to reflect their aural quality. Whatever the Bible's origins, it is clear that most writing in antiquity was read aloud, and so to experience the Bible in its spokenness is a vital way to draw nearer to it. This was one of the chief goals of the German Buber-Rosenzweig translation (1925–1962), which served as the initial model for my work. Attempting a translation to be read aloud means paying close attention to the shape and length of phrases, the sounds of words, and the rhythmic aspect of the text. It also involves trying to reflect conventions of biblical literature such as meanings of proper names, repetition of key ("leading") theme words, allusions to other places in the text, and wordplay. Focusing on these aspects of the text constitutes a method for reading the Bible; they are fully explained in the Preface to my *Five Books of Moses* (1995), and are cited and explicated frequently in the Commentary and Notes to the present volume. My translation, therefore, aims to highlight features of the Hebrew text that are not always visible or audible to Western audiences.

At the same time that I have persevered in my fundamental approach, however, a number of other issues have come to the fore in my thinking. One is, simply, readability. Martin Buber (1878–1965) and Franz Rosenzweig (1886–1929), preparing for the publication of their entire Five Books of Moses several years after the appearance of the initial individual volumes, made substantial changes in their work, and Buber, resuming the project alone after World War II, incorporated further revisions. These changes toned down the at times strident innovations of the original project, derided by some early critics as "Expressionist" or even "Wagnerian," in favor of what Kabbalah scholar Gershom Scholem called a more urbane language—but without sacrificing core principles. I have sought to do the same, trying to preserve what I can in English of the Bible's unique flavor, while at the same time advocating for "the poor reader's case," as Buber wrote of his task in the face of Rosenzweig's sometimes difficult ("Hebraized") German. The Bible is not twenty-first-century English literature, but neither is a mechanical reproduction of biblical Hebrew in English desirable or even possible. Several other recent attempts in that direction have, to my mind, foundered.

Hence I have made some changes. First, I have reduced the number of hyphenated words, which were a major feature in *The Five Books of Moses.* While biblical Hebrew is quite compact, often requiring two or three English words to express one Hebrew one, I do not wish hyphenation, one approach to this problem, to be such an oddity that it detracts from the text's flow, even visually. Thus I have eliminated it from constructions such as "be strong," "turn back," and "reign as king," all of which represent a single Hebrew word. At the same time, I have chosen to retain hyphens in instances such as "rant-like-a-prophet" and "sacrificial-altar," where I felt that it was important to keep the root meaning of the verb in view. I hope the reader will not experience this as too confusing or inconsistent.

Similarly, I have cut down on the number of words in brackets, which in *The Five Books of Moses,* in parenthesis form, served to indicate English words not found in the Hebrew. I have found some of these to be unnecessary and replaced others with an occasional hyphen. Again, my goal here is, within the limits of my method, to allow the text to flow unimpeded.

I have retained my previous renditions of a particular Hebrew form which uses the infinitive absolute, often to intensify the concept. Thus, in the Garden of Eden story in Gen. 2, the human is told not to eat from the Tree of Knowledge, or he will "die, yes, die." Most translations utilize an adverb, treating the phrase as "you shall *surely* die." Like Buber-Rosenzweig, I wanted to convey something of the doubled force of the Hebrew (in this case, *mot yumat*); I considered bracketing my use of "yes," since it does not appear in the text, but decided in the end to keep things simple.

Turning to a larger issue, I have spent considerable time mulling over the Bible's "lovely eloquence of coordinated clauses," in literary critic and translator Robert Alter's phrase. This refers to the use of the recurring prefix *vav* in biblical Hebrew, which often introduces narrative verbs and helps to maintain the steady and suggestive flow of a story. Alter has rightly criticized earlier translations for excessive breaking of the text into subordinate clauses (e.g., "When . . ."). Hence his almost obsessive use of "and" in most cases to connect the action. While I agree that *vav* is often important syntactically, I am frankly not sure that it is always heard—it often recedes into the background—and it is well established that its meaning can vary from "and" to "so" or "but" or "thus" more than Alter will permit it to do. So in the end, while I have sought to limit subordinate clauses when the original does not use them, I have striven for a middle ground, trying to reflect the plastic character of the *vav,* using other (usually one-syllable) words besides "and," and in reading the text aloud have looked for other aural ways to maintain the flow of the narrative.

In terms of language, over the years I have tried to be open to constructive suggestions and criticisms by both colleagues and general readers. I have accordingly changed my translation of some words. Most notably, I have substituted "sacrificial-altar" or simply "altar" for the earlier "slaughter-site" (Heb. *mizbe'ah*) in the interests of both correct philology and the way the term is used in the Bible. The result is a less jarring text and a relief from what had become a distraction. Similarly, I have changed most occurrences of "New-Moon" to the more normal "month," feeling that the original meaning of the Hebrew *hodesh* is not always consciously retained by the reader.

In the same spirit, I have subjected my translations as a whole to a rigorous rereading of earlier drafts. This means, in many cases, revisiting previous choices and looking for either more accurate or more felicitous translations, or both. In this, I have not felt tied to either Buber-Rosenzweig's philology or their practice of mining earlier forms of the target language to reflect Hebrew usage. It goes without saying that the changes I have made from *The Five Books of Moses* will be reflected in a new edition of that book, in both electronic and print form.

Finally, to a greater extent than I did in *The Five Books of Moses,* I have included in the apparatus that accompanies the text information on Hebrew words, history, and archaeology. The nature and content of the Early Prophets dictate that issues such as the development of the text from different source material, the relationship of the Bible to historical events, and the way in which the past is represented in the text cannot be ignored. Within reason, therefore, I have referred to relevant findings of scholarship in the Introductions, Notes, and Commentary. While neither I nor anyone else will fully settle the question of the Bible's precise relationship to factual history, the tools of scholarship in recent decades have made possible a richer and more complex view of the text than has previously been possible, and I have tried to reflect some of the considerable debate about these issues. Readers may consult the major works in the Bibliography, and their bibliographies in turn, for more detailed arguments.

Franz Rosenzweig famously wrote that "to translate is to serve two masters." In this volume I have had to serve many more. I have by and large sought to present the text as we have it, but with the cognizance that it underwent significant alteration in the course of time. I have been and am constantly seduced by the earthiness and directness of biblical Hebrew, and have sought to create an English that, while not reproducing it—an impossible task—echoes it. I have remained committed to weighing the multifaceted findings of scholarship, whose development is never-ending. Finally, I have kept my eye firmly on the concept of *performance,* which reexperiences and reinvents the Bible every time it is read or heard—even when there is a printed text.

This last point is crucial. The translator of the Hebrew Bible is confronted with a work that turns multiple faces to the audience, and one could question how all of them could adequately be integrated, from sources to multiple reworkings, and from the earliest interpreters to those who continue to wrestle with it. How, indeed, is it possible to fully grasp the chameleon that is the Bible, the text that, more than any other, means all things to all people in the Western world? I freely admit that this cannot readily be done. My task, therefore, has been primarily to present the text anew, echoing the admonition of twenty-year-old Gershom Scholem almost a century ago, who wrote in his diary that "to translate the Bible, a person needs to write it all over again from scratch." My work reflects the hope that by fostering a real rehearing, something fresh will reach the public ear, which will encourage and facilitate the time-honored process of grappling with weighty ancient words. Perhaps that process will be of some help in the difficult world in which we find ourselves in the twenty-first century.

Thus, this is not a book to be encountered passively, nor is it a performance to be merely viewed or heard. On the contrary, to what is on the printed page you will have to add your own voice and your own struggles. That is the way the Bible was encountered through the ages, and that mandate of entering into the spirit of the text as part of a dialogue is still very much the point of translating the Bible.

ACKNOWLEDGMENTS

I AM HAPPY TO ACKNOWLEDGE THE HELP OF MANY PEOPLE, ON MANY DIFFERENT levels, in bringing this volume to completion. Foremost is Allen M. Glick, whose continuing kindness and generosity in funding my chair and my research have enabled me to travel to conferences and to more readily obtain the book and computing resources needed for a project of this type. The amount of material that has appeared on Joshua-Kings over the past decade alone, in the fields of history writing, philology, and archaeology, has been immense, with these books coming under detailed and often revised scrutiny. Hence, access to the pulse of research has been critical.

I am grateful to my dear colleagues at the Department of Language, Literature, and Culture at Clark University. Over the years, our conversations both informal and formal, and team teaching in the department's signature course, The National Imagination, have informed my thinking about a host of matters including identity and its representation. I am especially indebted for the atmosphere of good cheer that has pervaded these discussions.

At various early stages of this work a number of scholars read drafts and responded, sometimes in great detail, with helpful criticism and suggestions: Murray Lichtenstein on Joshua and Judges, and Michelle Kwitkin-Close, Ed Greenstein, and Marc Brettler on early drafts of Judges, Samuel, and Kings, respectively. Professor Lichtenstein in particular was of immeasurable assistance in matters of philology and translation, especially in poetic passages such as Judg. 5. I deeply value his learned, judicious, articulate, and often witty observations and suggestions. Professor Greenstein has been a treasured colleague and crucial sounding board over many years, from *The Five Books of Moses* and beyond; he has sharpened my thinking and saved me from many errors. Most recently, thanks go to Dr. Eve Feinstein, who read over selected passages and essays and provided helpful comments; to Bonny Fetterman, friend and erstwhile editor at Schocken, for her keen observations; and to Professor Jacob L. Wright, whose stylistic and substantive suggestions regarding the Introductions were extremely valuable. Of course, as the usual disclaimer has it, all final decisions are mine alone.

Reaching back to graduate days, I would also like to thank my fellow students (and now professors) David Roskies and George Savran, for stimulating my early work on the Samson cycle. That experience was eye-opening for me as an entry into biblical narrative art and its possible oral roots.

The responses of many readers who have written me over the years about my translations, from places as unlikely as mountaintops in Oregon, a convent in

Bavaria, and an elementary school in Malawi, have been a treat and an inspiration. Faculty and students at universities and members of congregations before whom I have presented material, attendees at conferences, and students in my adult education classes in Hebrew College's Me'ah program, have also contributed signally to my ongoing translation work, opening my eyes and ears to many issues in the text and its reception. I am particularly grateful to the many study groups that have used *The Five Books of Moses* in different settings, who demonstrate that the shared experience of studying the text can build community, foster intergroup understanding, and create an atmosphere of shared delight and profundity in encountering the wisdom and artistry of the past.

In acknowledging past influences, I must correct an omission from earlier volumes. In 1959, Abba Eban, then Israel's permanent representative to the United Nations, recorded excerpts from the Psalms and Ecclesiastes in both the King James Version and the Hebrew, in order to raise money for a chair in American drama and literature at the Hebrew University. I received the LP as a present when I was a teenager and a few years later happened to turn to it. Eban's classic English diction was indelible. But also notable, thanks to his training in Middle Eastern languages at Cambridge, was the way his Hebrew reading conveyed both the distinctive rhythms of biblical language and the importance of Hebrew grammar in reading aloud. That experience, along with encountering the Buber-Rosenzweig translation, sent me back to the Hebrew text, which for the first time became an aural document for me. I remain grateful to Eban, who surely could not have known the impact of his accepting an academic fund-raising venture on a future Bible translation.

Several other "performers" of the Bible have exerted a strong influence on my work. First, I would like to draw attention to the recordings of the entire Bible by Shlomo Bertonov, made decades ago for the visually impaired in Israel but now available in MP3 form. These have proven helpful and illuminating in the process of my checking English drafts against the Hebrew.

Second, I invite the reader to find a copy of MGM's 1936 film *Rembrandt,* in which Charles Laughton, featured in the title role, has occasion to read some biblical passages. His performance of excerpts from Ps. 77, some forty minutes into the film, is a lesson in English diction and emotional depth, and serves as a fictional but accurate insight into the place of the Bible in the hearts of generations.

Finally, I want to invoke the enduring memory of my teacher at Brandeis University, Nahum N. Glatzer. It was he who, as a graduate student in Frankfurt in the twenties, provided research materials for the paralyzed Franz Rosenzweig in his translation work; who, as reader of the Buber-Rosenzweig proofs in those early days, served as a critical eye and ear; and who, as mentor in my undergraduate and graduate years in the late sixties and early seventies, gave me encouragement and criticism when I needed them. He also led by example, in his published linear presentations of Jewish sources such as Midrash and liturgy, and equally in his reading aloud of the Bible in the classroom. Almost fifty years later, the sonorities with which he read passages from the book of Job, both in King James English and a finely enunciated Hebrew, still reverberate vividly in my ear.

Since the bulk of this volume was finished, two friends who deserve special mention have died. Both were free spirits who loved the Bible. American-Israeli artist Ivan Schwebel was an unforgettable personality who drank deeply of life. For me he was a consummately devoted artist, loving friend, and guide, whose monumental work on the David stories bespoke a love of the land of Israel and of the profoundly human aspects of biblical narrative, and renewed and inspired much of my own work. He died peacefully while walking in Nahal Sorek, where, we are told, Samson fell in love with Delilah. It was what Schwebel called his "Safe Place." I share with his family and friends the reality of an irreplaceable loss.

Peter Stark was tragically killed in a traffic accident in the early days of 2012. We knew each other from Brandeis days. Peter was a man of many talents— a wonderfully devoted son, a Jewish activist, a linguist, an actor, a director, a lover of Toscanini and the Golden Age of Opera in the early twentieth century, and, especially, a memorable teacher of Bible to older children. He is remembered by all who came in contact with him, onstage and in the classroom, and the impact of his knowledge, good humor, and dedication to Jewish education will continue to be felt.

The dedication of this book is to my long-suffering family. As always, I am grateful to my wife, Rabbi Cherie Koller-Fox, for her love and her moral and intellectual support. This project would not exist without her faith and steady encouragement. She has notably asked probing questions about the language of the text, kept me focused on the needs and questions of readers, and, through decades of teaching the Bible to both children and adults, demonstrated how the translation may be used to teach even beginners to be careful readers of the biblical text. Our own children, Akiva, Leora, and Ezra, now grown to thoughtful adulthood, have contributed much emotional support and helpful observations on language, literature, performance, and biblical narrative, as well as closely reading portions of my drafts. Together with my wife, they have helped to fill my life with seriousness, playfulness, and love.

Newton, Massachusetts
November 2014

ON USING THIS BOOK

THE HEART OF THIS VOLUME IS THE BIBLICAL TEXT ITSELF. THE READER SHOULD begin there, reading aloud slowly and, preferably, more than once. Attention should be paid to repeating words, wordplays, and other forms of rhetoric in the text.

NOTES

THE NOTES, FOUND AT THE BOTTOM OF TEXT PAGES, ARE DESIGNED TO ANTICI-pate some of the reader's questions, clarify odd expressions, explain technical terms and pertinent cultural data, indicate the location of places mentioned in the text, and provide other useful information. Sometimes they cite the Hebrew original, in order to give a sense of what I am trying to echo in English; at other points, they give pertinent readings of ancient versions and translation proposals of modern scholars. They also point out some of the connections between passages, either within the same book or further afield. A small percentage of the material in the Notes repeats from book to book in order to make it easier to read the books separately, if desired; there is occasional repetition in the Commentary as well.

COMMENTARY

THE FUNCTION OF THE COMMENTARY, WHICH APPEARS OPPOSITE THE TEXT, IS TO focus on each chapter's place in the narrative, to set out specific themes and especially key words that point to them, and to point out other features of style and imagery. It also includes observations on character development, and occasional comments on the possible historical development of the text. The reader may wish to read the text of a chapter first and turn to the Commentary afterward, or do the opposite as preparation for what is coming.

ABBREVIATIONS IN THE COMMENTARY AND NOTES

MT   Masoretic text type, the standard traditional Hebrew text represented by the Leningrad Codex (ca. 1000 C.E.), published in *Biblica Hebraica Stuttgartensia (BHS)* (Stuttgart, 1977).

LXX   Septuagint, pre-Christian translation of the Hebrew Bible into Greek, existing in several manuscripts.

4QS^a An important Hebrew manuscript of the book of Samuel, discovered at Qumran (Cave IV) near the Dead Sea.

JPS The New Jewish Publication Society version (1985 and later).

B-R *Bücher der Geschichte,* Joshua-Kings in the German translation of the Bible by Martin Buber and Franz Rosenzweig (Cologne, 1955).

Kimhi David Kimhi, twelfth-to-thirteenth-century Bible commentator and grammarian who lived in Provence.

Ketiv A word in the Hebrew text as "written," as distinct from the *Qere,* an alternate rendering, usually in the margin, to be "read." This may reflect different traditions.

Qere See *Ketiv.*

INTRODUCTIONS

EACH OF THE FOUR BOOKS IN *THE EARLY PROPHETS* BEGINS WITH AN INTRODUCtion, intended to elucidate important issues, explore some possibilities for when the texts might have been composed, and discuss the relationship of the text to history. I have treated all of these aspects in wider perspective in the General Introduction.

DIVISIONS

IN ORDER TO AID THE READER IN NAVIGATING THE BIBLICAL TEXT, WHICH IN ITS ancient form had neither chapter numbers, verse numbers, nor section headings, I have also divided the books into major divisions (labeled "Part I," etc.) and given them brief introductions within the body of the text. My divisions are for convenience only, and different scholars will find alternate ways to elucidate structure. But I hope that the overall layout and the remarks in these short introductions will aid the reader in following major themes and their development within the books.

THE TEXT

THIS TRANSLATION IS BASED MAINLY ON THE MASORETIC TEXT TRADITION. I have, in some difficult passages, occasionally adopted another reading, either from ancient versions or proposed scholarly emendations, and have indicated this in the Notes, but I have not sought to reconstruct an "original" text, believing, as I state in the General Introduction, that the Bible evolved in many stages and versions. I have therefore done my best to provide a reading—a performance, as it were—that is reasonably close to a traditional one. It should be said that some of the Hebrew texts in *The Early Prophets* are in better shape than others; Samuel, for example, is notoriously defective. The reader may consult more detailed scholarly commentaries such as Nelson, Niditch (2008), McCarter (1980 and 1984), Cogan/Tadmor, and Sweeney (2007) for extended discussions on how LXX and other versions, including the Dead Sea Scrolls, bear on the texts of these books.

Names

The biblical names most familiar to English speakers come originally from ancient Greek translations. They have survived because, by and large, they are well-known and comfortable to pronounce (for example, Joshua, Samson, Solomon), and many are still in use in English-speaking families. Despite this, in the present translation I encourage the reader to adopt Hebrew usage such as Yehoshua, Shimshon, and Shelomo. In the Bible, most of these names have meanings important to the story; they are often used in plays on words, which are clarified in both my English text and the Notes in this volume. I hope that using Hebrew forms will also introduce a freshness to the reader's experience of the biblical text, so often necessary when one reads familiar material.

Pronunciation is described in the section below called "Guide to Pronouncing Hebrew Names"; at the same time, pronunciation of individual names is given in the Notes, whenever a character or place makes its first appearance, and at the end of the volume ("Recurring Names in *The Early Prophets*").

On the Name of God and Its Translation

We do not know exactly how ancient Hebrew was pronounced, and this especially applies to the name of God. By late antiquity, Jews had become wary of articulating that name in speech, feeling a need to preserve its power and holiness. For at least the last two millennia, Jewish convention has been to pronounce the name, written with the consonants "Yhwh," by using the euphemism "My Lord" (*Adonai*)—hence the usual "the Lord" found in most early modern translations. The Buber-Rosenzweig German translation, which served as a major model for *The Early Prophets,* represented God's name by uppercase personal pronouns (e.g., "HE said to David . . ."), but while this is philosophically and artistically powerful, it is probably incorrect, and somewhat more gendered than the Hebrew as well.

In the end, I have followed current scholarly practice in reproducing what is *seen* in the text—namely, "Yhwh"—and the reader will substitute what feels comfortable to him or her in actual reading. Choices might range from "the Lord" or "the Eternal" to the aforementioned *Adonai* or *Ha-Shem* ("the Name"). Some readers are content with the scholarly (but not certain) "Yahweh," although that form is never used in a religious Jewish context, and rarely in a Christian one.

Guide to Pronouncing Hebrew Names

The following guide uses a standard of pronunciation which is close to that of modern Hebrew and which will serve for the purpose of reading the text aloud.

> *a* (e.g., Rahav, Yiftah, Naval, David) as in f*a*ther (never as in s*a*t)
> *i* (e.g., Lakhish, David, Elisha) generally as *ee*

> *o* (e.g., Yehoshua, Eglon, Moav, Shelomo) as in st*o*ne (never as in h*o*t)
> *u* (e.g., Yehoshua, Ehud, Sha'ul, Yehu) as in r*u*ler (never as in s*u*n)

When *e* occurs in both syllables of a name (e.g., Shemesh), it is generally pronounced as the *e* in t*e*n. In such cases the first syllable is the accented one; otherwise, generally speaking, biblical Hebrew stresses the last syllable.

When *e* is the first vowel of a name (e.g., Shemuel, Shelomo), it is most often lightly pronounced, as the *a* in *a*go.

> *kh* (e.g., Akhish, Mikhal) is to be sounded like the *ch* in Johann Sebastian Ba*ch*.
>
> *h* (e.g., Hanna, Hanun) most often indicates the Hebrew letter *het,* pronounced less heavily than *kh* but not as lightly as English *h*. This is difficult to reproduce in English, and I have not sought to do so. I have, however, removed the *h* at the end of names such as Hanna to avoid confusion with *het*.

The system I have used for transcribing Hebrew words follows the above model rather than standard scholarly convention (e.g., *shofar* rather than *šopār*), to better serve the general reader. For this reason, I also do not distinguish between the Hebrew letters *alef* and *ayin* in transcription, even though technically speaking their pronunciations originally differed. I have, however, added an apostrophe when the lack of one might lead the reader to otherwise mispronounce the word (for example, Be'er, Sha'ul). Note also that in the case of some names, which would more accurately be transcribed as, for instance, "Eilyyahu," I have sought a simpler transliteration, as in "Eliyyahu." This means that the Hebrew sounds *eh* and *ei* are not readily distinguishable in English.

Some well-known names in the text have been transcribed here in their familiar English spelling. These include Egypt (Heb. *Mitzrayim*), Israel (*Yisrael*), Jordan (*Yarden*), Gaza (*'Azza*), Jerusalem (*Yerushalyim*), Assyria (*Ashur*), and Judah (*Yehuda;* I use the latter when it refers to the tribe alone and not to the Southern Kingdom as a whole). The reader will note that many endings of personal names are rendered here as *-el,* even though strict practice would dictate *-eil* or *-ayl*. All this has been done to make the transition to Hebrew forms a little less jarring.

General Introduction

Influence

THE BOOKS TRANSLATED HERE AS *THE EARLY PROPHETS*—JOSHUA, JUDGES, SAMuel, and Kings—make up over one fifth of the Hebrew Bible. While they progress chronologically, stretching from the Israelites' settlement in Canaan to the destruction of the surviving kingdom of Judah some six centuries later, they constitute much more than a dry historical chronicle. For these books recount the past in a way that reverberates with meaning. They look at a long series of events, including wars, tribal rivalries, dramatic changes in leadership, and the intrusion of great empires, through the prism of a divine-human relationship. Joshua is presented not merely as the report of a conquest but as a careful demonstration of how the Promised Land is a conditional gift from YHWH, the God of the Bible. Judges presents object lessons in good and bad leadership, and links the people's fortunes to whether they worship YHWH alone. Samuel paints full and complex portraits of enormously talented yet flawed founding kings and their relationship to divinely ordained standards. And Kings plays down the worldly accomplishments of dynasties in favor of a view of the past in which the ancient covenant between God and the people of Israel is the chief criterion for worldly success.

Over the centuries, the faithful have read these books as demonstrations of the perils of disobeying God's will, and time and again found that they spoke to their own situation. The momentous events of Jewish life in late antiquity under Hellenistic and Roman domination, which included cultural assimilation, rebellions, destruction, and the reformulation of identity, ensured that the Early Prophets, in which such issues are played out frequently and pointedly, would continue to be read and pondered by Jews well beyond the periods in which the books are set. They have had an equally indelible impact on generations of Christians, who have seen in many of the stories strong foreshadowings of the life and death of Jesus, as well as models for their own lives and the careers of their leaders. Both traditional Jewish and Christian communities have read the Early Prophets as emblematic: just as the Israelites had suffered destruction and exile, surely catastrophe would await those in the contemporary world whose community or leaders did not follow divine dictates.

Yet that is by no means the whole story. In these books, as so often in the Hebrew Bible, theological reflection goes hand in hand with artistic craft. Thus, beyond its importance as a major portion of a foundational religious document, the text of the Early Prophets has been and continues to be read as a great work of literature, whose power lies in the gripping nature of many of its stories. The personalities who appear on its pages, and the political and moral dilemmas their stories powerfully illuminate, are part of the living consciousness of the Western world. The narratives recount critical moments in the life of a nation, encompassing oppression, invasion, and rescue. They meditate on what constitutes good leadership, tracing the successes and failures of military men, kings, and prophets, and on how the good society should be constructed. And along the way, they tell some extraordinary tales, presenting unforgettable characters and their entanglements. They are filled with an array of striking images, from the tumbling walls of Jericho to Samson tearing apart the lion with his bare hands, from the barren Hannah's plea for a child to David's slaying of the terrifying Goliath, from the building of Solomon's grand Temple to the prophet Elijah leaving this life in a fiery chariot. These images and many more are deeply etched into Western culture and have become beloved over the centuries largely because they so beautifully encapsulate recognizable human experience. They have attracted not only the pious but also the rebellious—including artists and writers who, whatever their religious leanings, have been unable to resist the lure of these stories that speak so poignantly to the human condition. Thus, audiences over the centuries have come to echo Horace's ancient words: *de te fabula narratur*—"the story is about you."

ORIGINS

WHILE THE POWER AND INFLUENCE OF THE EARLY PROPHETS ARE INDISPUTable, the exact origins of its four books (familiar in English as six, with "I" and "II" Samuel and Kings) are much more difficult to determine. As a defined series of scrolls, they were probably completed by the sixth or fifth century B.C.E. Scholarly attempts at identifying more precise dates range widely, with some insisting that large pieces of the text are quite early, not far removed from the events they portray, and others opting for a date as late in the biblical period as the fourth or third century B.C.E., when Israelite (now Jewish) rule in Palestine had long since crumbled to dust. Still others posit a more gradual process, a "rolling corpus," stretching over centuries in different locales, including both monarchic Israel and Babylonian Exile.

Nor is date the only problem. We have no evidence that these books were conceived of as a collection early on. Their style is not uniform, their ideology varies, and scholars disagree on the extent to which they can be read as a single long work. And the books include a wide variety of genres: chronicles, poems, stories, architectural descriptions, and territorial boundaries, all of which suggest multiple sources from different time periods.

Additionally, the standard Hebrew text of the Early Prophets cannot be shown conclusively to be, word for word, the version that was transmitted to its early audiences. The evidence of the Dead Sea Scrolls and of the early Greek versions reveal a text that was still in flux.

Finally and most important, the books rarely explain themselves directly. They contain, for instance, no thoughtful prologue such as can be found in the works of Greek historians such as Herodotus and Thucydides. The absence of such explanatory prologues may be an advantage, inasmuch as it makes the narratives more engaging and requires the reader to do the work. Yet there is another feature that is more unsettling. The books are riddled with contradictions, so many that at times it is difficult to say anything definitive about them. Who exactly slew Goliath—the renowned David or a certain Elhanan? Which biblical attitude toward monarchy is correct, wariness or overflowing praise? In which period does the text seem to fit best—the Jerusalem of the late seventh century, emerging for a while from foreign domination; the sixth-century B.C.E. Babylonian Exile, with its quiet despair; or the fifth, with its hope for further restoration back in the homeland? Once again, the contradictions force the reader to probe the text more deeply, and we can be sure that the final redactors intentionally avoided the temptation to create a perfectly consistent work.

In twentieth-century Bible scholarship, a unified theory of composition was put forth by Martin Noth. His formulation of the issues still exerts a strong influence in the field. Noth accepted the Bible's implied scheme of a retrospective history of Israel on its land, from the conquest through two destructions (of the northern Israelite kingdom by Assyria in 722 B.C.E. and of the southern by Babylonia in 587) and on to the Babylonian Exile. He viewed this great work as encompassing Joshua through Kings, with the fifth book of the Torah, Deuteronomy, as the prologue. In Noth's view, this "Deuteronomistic History" (known ever since in the scholarly world as DH or Dtr) served to explain to the exiled Israelites why they had arrived at such a sorry state. He envisioned these books as a single piece of work, based on key ideas and phraseology from Deuteronomy—especially that their god YHWH alone should be worshipped and that sacrifices should be offered to him only at the Temple in Jerusalem. Noth's DH clearly attributed Israel's ills to the apostasy of the people and their kings. In breaking the covenant with YHWH, they had forfeited the land that they had been given only conditionally to begin with.

Noth's treatment of the Early Prophets has undergone numerous challenges and refinements in the more than half a century since its appearance. One major revision was proposed by Frank Moore Cross. Like other modern Bible scholars, Cross found the idea of a single edition too simplistic. He located DH in two editions, one in the waning days of the Southern Kingdom of Judah under King Josiah in the late seventh century B.C.E. and a final one, decades later, in the Babylonian Exile, by an editor who incorporated allusions to destruction and exile in the texts. Cross was led to this overall conclusion by the strongly positive portrayal of Josiah in the book of Kings, the marked emphasis on the Northern Kingdom's sins and its destruction in 722, and its comparison with the faithful and successful House of David, from which Josiah sprang. The Southern Kingdom still appears viable in this early edition—in other words, the core of DH predated the Babylonian Exile.

The many alternatives to such models, involving minute dissections of large and small units of text, have run the gamut from postulating multiple editions to rejecting the idea of a unified DH outright, claiming that the four books simply do not hold together. But a few things have become clearer, thanks to recent research on the nature of biblical texts and their composition. It is increasingly evident that it is a mistake to speak of "original texts" in the Bible. Much of ancient literature, including the Bible, evolved over time; earlier forms of text were replaced by more complex "performances." Historical and social circumstances changed, as did audiences; in societies where oral influences continued to be felt in literature, there was a continuous process of addition and reformulation that to an extent renders the idea of a primal, original text moot. Thus, in the case of the Early Prophets, traditions about Israel's beginnings, up through the monarchy and exile, would have received varied treatments, expressing not one but multiple points of view. In Jacob L. Wright's (2009) words, "the inherent resistance of biblical literature to clear authorial identification is its hallmark, and speaks volumes to its agenda of representing the 'people' as a whole . . . rather than defending a particular institution or social class."

What might have propelled this evolution of the texts? While parts of the books of the Early Prophets resemble other ancient Near Eastern literature in some of their forms and concerns (such as accounts of military campaigns and royal propaganda), they seem to be largely concerned with other issues. These texts focus on reaching a wide-ranging understanding of who the people of Israel are, by narrating how they arrived at the land and their subsequent life in it under chieftains and kings. This emphasis on Israel's collective identity would likely have begun early on, as the fledgling Israelites sought to differentiate themselves from their immediate neighbors. But it would have become more acute as history brought them into conflict with great empires.

It is in the eighth and seventh centuries b.c.e., with the reigns of Judean kings Hezekiah and Josiah, that we may find a reasonable starting time for the writing down of many biblical texts. A growing number of scholars (see Schniedewind 2004 for a cogent presentation) point to this era as one in which, thanks to urban growth especially in Jerusalem, capital of the Southern Kingdom of Judah, literacy became more widespread. More important, in the face of long-term oppression by the resurgent and expanding Assyrian Empire, there would have been a deep need to counter the imperial claims of the invaders. At this point in Israelite history, older traditions would have served to clarify national self-definition, and their casting in written form, probably by elites, would have given impetus to a process that would reach fruition in the exilic and postexilic periods in the sixth century b.c.e., when building a renewed sense of community would have been paramount.

What is notable here is that, as Wright (2011) points out, texts like the books of the Early Prophets (and the Torah which precedes it) are not nationalistic in the sense of aggressively talking up the glories of the state. True, the trappings of the state—kings, armies, and temples—are viewed as necessary in the Bible, but this text is also (and primarily) designed to focus on the *people*—an entity in which political institutions are secondary to the covenant idea. In the Bible as we have it, allegiance to God is the source of Israel's national identity, and the people's main task is to uphold the divine-human relationship. In keeping with a pattern known among subjugated peoples throughout the centuries, the idea of this covenant may in fact be partly a subversive recasting of Assyrian political treaties, just as other moments in the Bible seem to play off other aspects of Assyrian and Meso-potamian culture (see Carr 2010 and his citations).

Such a view appears to have grown out of the realization, beginning at least with the rise of Assyria, that Israel was not destined to hold a prominent position in the ancient Near Eastern world. A perceptive reader can sense a strong under-current of anxiety in the way Israelite traditions are presented in many key texts. In Genesis, for example, one of the key motifs threading throughout the text seems, on the surface, to be a heroic one—the triumph of the younger brother over the older, from Isaac to Jacob to the climax with Joseph. Yet the book is full of so many close calls along the way, with the continuity of the family and the divine mission threatened at every turn, that it is difficult not to feel nervousness, along with relief, at the outcome. The message that emerges is that while God will always rescue Israel, it will not be a pleasant experience, with the possibility of extinction ever present.

This is not a conventional way to write or sing about ancestors, nor is it the usual manner in which court scribes, employed by kings, go about their work. Rather, it is more compatible with the views of the prophets, those ancient Israelite gadflies who spoke truth to power. As Rabbi Alan Miller notes, it was eighth-century figures such as Amos and Hosea who sensed the fateful and fatal direction in which, in the midst of prosperity, the Northern Kingdom was head-ing. Southern prophets such as Isaiah and Micah, living somewhat later, sounded similar notes of warning. For the precarious situation in which Israel found itself would not resolve easily. The prophets' task thus became to refocus the people in preparation for a time when the state would be suspended, at least temporarily, in favor of a more enduring sense of nationhood. This developing of inner commu-nal strength amid powerlessness and defeat would become, in Babylonian Exile and in the many later experiences of Jewish Diaspora, an unbreakable legacy, one which has inspired many other cultures as well. It is, then, no accident that an old Jewish tradition came to dub these books the Early Prophets.

The concern over the casting and preservation of national identity also fits within the Persian period that followed the exile, beginning in 539 B.C.E., when the surviving Jewish community had some autonomy but not full self-rule. The compilers thus promoted the old view of a world in which God was the only legitimate ruler, in which the covenant between God and Israel was still operative, and in which the ideas and laws laid down in the Torah were to become the guiding principles for a functioning society.

The end process of these many centuries of recounting, transmitting, and writing was the first half of the Hebrew Bible, Genesis through Kings, which some scholars call the "Primary History." In the form in which it was preserved, probably since the Persian era, this nine-book complex uses Deuteronomy as its center, with the narratives and laws of Genesis through Numbers as one wing and the patterned memories of Joshua through Kings as the other. Deuteronomy functions to update and complete the Torah, with dramatic rhetorical flourishes; at the same time, it serves as a powerful introduction to the Early Prophets, setting out key details of the covenant which would ultimately be broken and then restored. It is a testament to the genius of the Bible that within this overarching structure, there is room for variations and for the development of the memorable portrayals of personalities and predicaments that are so characteristic of the Hebrew text. The variations made it possible for different communities to see themselves in the text over the centuries. The deeply human portrayals have likewise remained imprinted on the hearts of readers down to our own day.

HISTORY AND METAHISTORY

THE FACT THAT THE TEXT OF JOSHUA THROUGH KINGS FOCUSES SO PROMINENTLY on community and identity through its recounting of Israel's past raises the question of the text's precise relation to what we conventionally call history. The Early Prophets is set in the Iron Age, a period for which we have many documents and inscriptions from the empires of the ancient Near East. Yet the question of how to evaluate historically Israel's surviving textual and archaeological data has spawned furious debates in recent decades. An extensive scholarly literature has been written about these books and the way they approach history. Most agree that ancient peoples in general were not interested in what we would term history for its own sake, in the sense of creating a factual account of events. The Bible in particular represents a choice, or, more properly, a series of choices, as to how and what to remember concerning Israel's past. In Marc Brettler's (2001b) words, it "suggests that the Israelites were agnostic toward the real past."

It has come to be widely accepted that for human beings, whether individuals or collective groups, there is no such thing as strictly objective reporting. Recent research on the structure of the brain suggests that memory is not composed of discrete facts; rather, it functions through the making of connections. Hence, memory and meaning are inseparable. Both as individuals and as groups, we all compose our versions of who we are, what has happened to us, and what we have done. These versions turn on issues of conscious or unconscious repression and the desire to leave behind something of value for the future. In the case of the Bible, as stressed above, the writers' focus on identity answered different needs over time, beginning with Israel's early communities vis-à-vis their immediate neighbors, to the overwhelming threat posed by imperial armies, to defeat and exile, and, finally, to building a new society on the land under Persian domination.

Given this shifting quest for Israel's identity, the biblical authors were not concerned merely to report historical facts, so that the Bible's approach would best be termed "metahistory." Alternatively, one might call it "history with an attitude." My approach in this volume is thus consonant with that of many other contemporary scholars. I regard these books as reflective of history or in dialogue with it. I believe that they recall aspects of an actual past, yet one that has been retold and rethought, in a manner lying somewhere between what we would call history and story. The texts constitute a remarkable collection of multiple voices from ancient Israel, gathered over time and in ways that are still not entirely clear to us. Sometimes these voices are in harmony, sometimes in conflict, but always they bear witness to an active consciousness that is reexamining and reexperiencing Israel's past.

Where does all this leave the modern historian? For a good part of the twentieth century, many biblical scholars, operating consciously or unconsciously out of a religious belief in the factual truth of the text, regarded the Bible as basically historical. Over time, with the lack of archaeological support, such certainty began to fade. From Abraham to the Exodus, from Joshua's conquest to the heroes of the book of Judges, from the accounts of David and Solomon with their wealth of court detail to the portrayal of the Israelite and Judean rulers in the book of Kings, most of the sacred cows of biblical history have been put through the analytical ringer by modern scholars, with often major unanswered questions as a result. In the end, however historical any or all of these figures might have been, it is clear that the biblical text evaluates them using mainly its own, metahistorical criteria.

We are thus thrown back on the text as it stands, with its stirring stories of success and failure. This is not necessarily to be regarded as a loss, although it may disappoint those whose view of truth is confined to brute facts. The Bible is interested in a different kind of truth, one that focuses on our group experience as members of religious communities and on our individual experiences of transcendent meaning, expressed through faith or great art—or both. Such truth shines from many moments in the text of the Early Prophets and continues to evoke strong reader reactions. It reflects what Martin Buber (1967) called "the great dialogue between heaven and earth," the inner conversation through which humanity struggles to understand its place in the world and in the universe. In the Early Prophets, as in all great texts, that conversation is carried on within the experience of one specific group of people, but it resonates well beyond.

The community that transmitted these books consisted of a small Persian province, with limited political independence and little impact on the geopolitical stage. But it was a community that felt itself and indeed all history to be moved by a larger force, that viewed the past as not merely a string of events but as bearing the meaning of those events. Israel had failed to keep God's covenant and had been punished by being exiled. But the punishment was nearing an end, and ultimate restoration was on the horizon. To use the imagery of the classical prophets, Israel had been in a marriage that had ended unhappily but now was returning to its lover in order to enter into an eternal union.

A memorable work of literature spanning many centuries, an evolving search for group identity, a powerful and distinctive reading of history that seeks meaning in the midst of national catastrophe—all these and more are woven together in the composition of the Early Prophets. An attentive reader may experience some or all of these facets but in the end will extract mainly what is valuable for his or her own life. On a larger scale, religious communities will continue to find direction and fellowship in these texts through study and worship. It is in that spirit of ongoing dialogue with the past that I extend to you an invitation to enter the world of the Early Prophets.

AN APPROXIMATE BIBLICAL CHRONOLOGY

I. THE PERIOD COVERED IN *The Early Prophets*

c. twelfth century B.C.E.	Settlement in Canaan
c. eleventh century B.C.E.	Period of the "Judges"
tenth century B.C.E.	Early Monarchy: Sha'ul/Saul, David, Shelomo/Solomon; First Temple
c. 920 B.C.E.	Kingdom splits
ninth century B.C.E.	Dynasty of Omri in the North; period of Eliyyahu/Elijah and Elisha
eighth century B.C.E.	Domination by Assyria; Northern Kingdom falls (722)
seventh century B.C.E.	Domination of Southern Kingdom by Assyria and Babylonia
596, 586 B.C.E.	Babylonian invasion and exile; Southern Kingdom falls
561 B.C.E.	The Judean king Yehoyakhin/Jehoiachin is released from prison in Persia

II. AMONG LATER EMPIRES

539–538 B.C.E.	Persian hegemony; Jewish exiles return
c. 515 B.C.E.	Second Temple completed
c. mid-fifth century B.C.E.	Period of Ezra and Nehemiah
332 B.C.E.	Conquest by Alexander the Great
165 B.C.E.	Maccabean revolt and eventual Jewish independence
63 B.C.E.	Conquest by Rome

III. IN THE COMMON ERA

c. 29 C.E.	Crucifixion of Jesus
66 C.E.	First Jewish revolt against Rome
70 C.E.	Destruction of Jerusalem and Second Temple
132–135 C.E.	Second Jewish revolt against Rome
second century C.E.?	Possible final editing of Hebrew Bible
c. 200 C.E.	Redaction of Mishnah, first postbiblical Jewish canonical document

יהושע

JOSHUA

The Twelve Tribes of Israel

INTRODUCTION

The Forging of Joshua

As the book that directly follows the Five Books of Moses, Joshua narrates the conquest of Canaan, ancient Israel's homeland, and the subsequent allotting of the land to the Israelite tribes. Thanks to its location in the text, the book plays an important transitional role in the first half of the Hebrew Bible. It serves as a bridge between the repeated promises of an abundant land in the Torah and the long saga of Israel's life in that land in the books that follow. Its tone is both triumphant and cautionary: the land is understood to have been given, through a war of conquest, by God, who can equally take it away if his conditions—the "covenant" with Israel, as presented in the Torah—are not faithfully observed.

The book is thus overtly theological in its presentation of events. As with all the books in the Early Prophets, there is only one criterion for the nation's success. Any concept of national history based on pride, glorifying warlike ancestors for their legendary deeds, is severely limited in Joshua. Everything depends on the keeping of the covenant.

The central ideas of that covenant are exclusive worship of Yhwh, the God of Israel, and fidelity to his laws. Beyond those general stipulations, however, there are specific rules pertaining to the book of Joshua. First, Israel is to be faithful to the symbols of its identity, especially circumcision and the observance of the festival of Passover. These covenant symbols provide continuity in the relationship between God and Israel and acknowledge his intervention on their behalf in the past. Joshua's final speeches in Chaps. 23–24 will warn against betrayal of this relationship; both the letter and spirit of such warnings occupy a good deal of the narrative territory of the Early Prophets.

Second, Israel is to adhere to laws of war, principally those having to do with the spoils of battle. They are to be "devoted" for God and not appropriated by the victorious troops, as was the standard practice in ancient and later warfare. The one time this rule is violated, in Chap. 7, the Israelite army is predictably routed. It is their only direct defeat in the book.

A third area crucial to the covenant idea is proper leadership. From the opening lines of the book, Joshua himself is charged not only with leading the troops but also with following in the footsteps of his master, Moses. He is not to depart from Moses's example of faithfulness and adherence to God's laws, and from the book's first chapter to its last, he does not disappoint.

The direct result of Israel's adherence to God's covenant in Joshua is the gift of the land, which is articulated through a large block of text devoted to detailed tribal boundaries. Chaps. 13–21 read almost like a flyover or, in the comfort of one's own chair, an exploration of the land using a map program. The reader gets to savor the lay of the land and to revel, not in conquest, but in a kind of pioneer experience. That the boundaries listed combine historical memories with clearly idealized ones, with the people of Israel represented as a largely pious generation, only adds to the audience's sense of satisfaction and wonder.

Surely this is more than what we conventionally call history, more than a recitation of factual data. And scholars who try to rely solely on the text of Joshua to reconstruct the reality of early Israelite settlement find themselves beset by vexing problems. Simply stated, the events reported in the book, and the geographical boundaries set forth there, do not always fit comfortably in the period in which they are set, generally understood to have been the twelfth century B.C.E. Among other difficulties, the surviving data do not seem to support as extensive a conquest as the Bible portrays. The opening of Judges, the book that follows Joshua, will demonstrate that there is still much left to do in that regard.

Archaeology plays a critical role in the discussion. On the basis of the available information, there appears to be a historical disconnect between the account of key cities said to have been destroyed in Joshua and the evidence on the ground. A number of these cities, such as Jericho and Ai, had long been in ruins by the period in which Joshua would have lived, and the existence of some of the others which the book characterizes as walled cities also does not neatly fit the chronology. And while there is indeed material indication of destruction in the period in which Joshua is set, there is often no way to identify the agent(s) of that destruction, leaving the overall picture clouded.

These contradictions strongly suggest that what is really at work in our text is selective and creative memory. I do not believe that it consciously sets out to falsify the past; rather, from early traditions, embedded images, stories, and reactions to past events and experiences, often preserved only in echoes, it formulates what is most helpful and illuminating for the present. Thus, books like Joshua—and here we may include all the books of the Early Prophets, as discussed in the General Introduction—would have mainly provided biblical Israelites with a blueprint for understanding their own world centuries later, a world in which great empires swept through their country and eventually forced them into decline and exile. Joshua, invoking old traditions and still-visible ancient ruins, would have painted the picture of a time when, by keeping the covenant, Israel had reaped the benefits of their loyalty. By implication, the reverse—betrayal of the divine-human relationship—would have the direst consequences for the nation.

As Peter Machinist (1994) has noted, the conquest of Canaan, and especially the identification of the Israelites as outsiders presented in Joshua and in other biblical texts, reverberates with a number of different periods in biblical history. The period of settlement itself would have necessitated clear differentiation from the locals (more on this below). The eighth-century era of the prophet Amos, reacting to the growing threat of Assyria, as well as the sixth-century B.C.E. period of Babylonian Exile, would also have found meaning in the portrayal of Israel as outsiders. So the composition of Joshua would likely have taken place over several centuries at the least, with the text undoubtedly built up from multiple layers.

For many contemporary scholars, a likely key moment in this process would have been the reign of King Josiah of Judah (c. 640–609 B.C.E.), whom the Bible characterizes as a major religious reformer. As part of its description of Josiah's program, I Kings 22 reports the finding of a scroll, "the Record of the Instruction of Moses," by officials cleaning out the Temple. The public appearance of this scroll, which was probably the core of Deuteronomy, provided textual impetus for Josiah's reform efforts, whose goals included the extirpation of idolatry, the centralization of worship in Jerusalem, and a strict separation from the surrounding nations.

It has long been recognized that the book of Joshua uses much of the same language as, and agrees with much of the ideology of, Deuteronomy. Many of the phrases with which Joshua opens fit this description (see Commentary to Chap. 1). In addition, the portrayal of Joshua himself, using pious Deuteronomic phrases, is strongly similar to that of Josiah, three books and five centuries later. And the fact that much of Joshua is set in the north, and is connected to northern traditions, may well reflect not only Deuteronomy's suspected northern origins but also Josiah's aggressive attempt to extend his religious and political reforms to that part of the land of Israel.

Joshua's northern slant suggests to some scholars several other options for the setting of the book's composition. For one thing, the book may have actually originated in the north. Additionally, northern traditions may have been preserved after the fall of the north in 722. A century earlier than Josiah, the Bible's previous reformer king in the south, Hezekiah, had to deal with the immediate and deadly presence of Assyria. During his reign, the armies of that great empire destroyed the Northern Kingdom, and much of the Southern Kingdom as well, with Jerusalem barely escaping disaster. This period saw the increased presence of northern refugees in Jerusalem, and so the prominence of northern Israel in the text of Joshua, in the view of some, may reflect a desire in Hezekiah's time to include their traditions in Israel's growing account of itself and to recall a time in the distant past when God protected Israel in the midst of war. The territorial descriptions that take up much of the second half of Joshua could also be seen as a reaction to the fall of the north, allowing the people "to gain in textual form what may have been otherwise lost in experience" (Smith).

Finally, it should be noted that some pieces of the conquest description in Chaps. 1–12 appear to mimic what is found in some Neo-Assyrian royal war accounts, proving that imitation is either the sincerest form of flattery or an effective means of protest. In the case of the Bible, the narrative would serve to glorify God, and not the Assyrian kings.

In the light of the above possibilities, we can agree with Nelson that Joshua is "a historical witness to what later generations believed had happened to their ancestors," a text that speaks to an audience concerned with their own problems rather than one interested in history for its own sake. Indeed, as he stresses, "every conquest story in Joshua is a territorial claim or an assertion of national identity." It is a text with one eye focused on the past and one on the present, or on several different "presents," in a process quite typical of the development of biblical texts.

At the same time, one should not discount the presence of authentic traditions that are well-rooted in their setting. As Meyers (2004) points out, most of the non-Israelite names in the book, such as Rahav, are attested in the very period in which Joshua is set.

THE ISRAELITE SETTLEMENT

IF THE BOOK OF JOSHUA IS NOT A FULLY ACCURATE ACCOUNT OF ISRAEL'S HIStory in the twelfth century B.C.E., it is nevertheless well placed in that time period. Put another way, there is definitive evidence of a dramatic rise in the population of Israel's highlands during that century. While we are not able to identify the population as Israelites—to date, little has been found to differentiate between Israelites and Canaanites in material culture such as pottery and architecture—it is quite plausible that Israel's literary traditions reflect this era of new growth. And such a development would fit the general situation of the wider eastern Mediterranean world at that time. For reasons that are not entirely clear, at the end of the second millennium B.C.E. older civilizations experienced what some scholars term a considerable downturn and others characterize as a full-blown collapse. Cultures and armies which had previously dominated Syro-Palestine were weakened to such an extent that a successful incursion of newcomers is quite plausible. At the same time, Egyptian and other records report widespread invasions by the so-called Sea Peoples, either from the Aegean area or perhaps from Anatolia (modern Turkey). In the books of the Early Prophets, these groups are represented by Israel's great enemy, the Philistines, whose control of the coastal area adds another piece to the puzzle, for it might well have made it easier for other settlers to achieve a foothold in the highlands of Canaan.

Viewed as a whole, then, the evidence we have does not rule out the rise of premonarchic Israel in its traditional region of settlement, but rather confirms it, albeit in the most general way. While the book of Joshua may have been strongly influenced by later developments and perceptions, the period it portrays was no fantasy. And, as noted above, some of the material in its pages gives clear evidence of rootedness in their historical setting.

Considering that Joshua has strong ideological underpinnings, and that the archaeological findings thus far are somewhat ambiguous, what else can be said about the historical process of Israelite settlement? This issue has become a major bone of scholarly contention over the past several decades, with countless books, articles, and symposia devoted to untangling the real or imagined knots. Theories include that of the German scholar Albrecht Alt in the 1920s, according to which the Israelite settlement was a long process of gradual incursion by pastoral semi-nomads who came into conflict with the more settled peoples of the area; the work of renowned American archaeologist William F. Albright, who interpreted the archaeological record as strongly confirming the biblical account of the conquest; and, decades later, influenced by the politically charged 1960s and 1970s, the approach of George Mendenhall and Norman Gottwald, which held that Israelite settlement was the direct outgrowth of strong dissatisfaction among Canaanite peasants, who then rebelled and formed new communities of their own in the hills.

All of these theories have weaknesses. In more recent years there has been a growing, if tentative, scholarly consensus that the Israelite settlement may have been a combination of various factors: basic origins in Canaanite city-states, a move up into the highlands owing to generally poor economic circumstances across the eastern Mediterranean, and an encounter with a variety of other groups in the highlands, including a band of escaped slaves from Egypt which may have included various ethnic elements. The pastoral/agricultural settlers, it has been theorized, might well have found the Exodus traditions brought in by others to be meaningful, and formed a new community. That community's struggle to understand itself and its place in the world, centering around its God, YHWH, is what informs much of the Hebrew Bible.

Of course, this composite view is not the one taken by Joshua itself. As we have seen, this book views the settlement through a strongly theological perspective, in which Israel clearly enters Canaan from the outside and is given the land as a conditional grant from God.

WRITING ABOUT WAR

CHRONICLING, CELEBRATING, OR LAMENTING WAR IS A COMMON ACTIVITY IN ALL periods of human history. But it is rarely an objective act. Wars are usually occasions for profound changes in society, and their aftereffects may not be understood until years have passed. At the same time, they may, in retrospect or reconstruction, evoke central aspects of a society's self-image: strength, heroism, or, alternately, a strong sense of having been betrayed. In any event, they do not lend themselves to dispassionate recall.

Accounts of war in the literature of the ancient world confirm this. In such classics as Homer's *Iliad,* Xenophon's *Anabasis,* and Julius Caesar's *The Gallic Wars,* we learn what it is to be a Greek or a Roman. These accounts set forth the characteristics of great men, who are taken as role models, and the idealized standards which they present for their audience.

In ancient Mesopotamia and Egypt, in periods preceding the Greek and Roman ones, monumental inscriptions describing wars are most often propaganda pieces, created to display the power of the warrior king and to enable him to boast about his conquests in great detail. That this is an ideological enterprise rather than a journalistic or historical one is demonstrated, first, by the use of kings' first person voices in the narrating and, second, by the fact that rulers frequently claimed victory when the actual outcome was less than clear. An example contemporary with the biblical world is the Assyrian account of the battle of Qarqar in 853 B.C.E., in which the inscription by Shalmaneser III mischaracterizes what was probably a draw or maybe even a defeat. Thus, narrating military events in writing, in the ancient Near East as today, was fraught with issues beyond the simple facts of the battles themselves.

With this standard in mind, the book of Joshua emerges as a document that is striking for its deviations from the usual presentation. It embeds war reports in a larger context, tying the acquisition of the land to Israel's faithfulness and thus, in a way, playing down the centrality of the fighting itself. Although Joshua himself is featured, he is glorified less for his exploits on the battlefield than for the way he faithfully fits the leadership pattern established by his predecessor Moses. Chap. 1 opens with no reference to any qualities Joshua already possesses as a warrior; he is basically assured of God's support, the key to Moses's success, and exhorted to follow God's laws. As the narrative unfolds, there is a surprisingly limited time spent on the actual fighting, with barely any description of any individual's military deeds (compare the subsequent books of Judges and Samuel, which are full of the bloody accomplishments of military heroes). A section of Joshua, notably Chaps. 10–12, does resemble other ancient Near Eastern battle accounts in its use of regular and patterned vocabulary, but by and large, the text of the book seems interested more in faithfulness and obedience to God, and a detailed description of tribal borders, than in celebrating the exploits of heroes. The classical manly virtues of bravery, self-sacrifice, and comradeship, so much a part of war epics around the world, are muted, passed over quickly, or even omitted in the biblical account found in Joshua.

THE IDEOLOGY OF CONQUEST

IMAGES OF WAR AND CONQUEST RAISE ANOTHER THORNY QUESTION FOR TWENTY-first-century readers. Current sensibilities, tempered by a century of world wars, genocides, and hate language about the "Other," may well find upsetting overtones in the simple view espoused by many generations of Jews and Christians that the book of Joshua stood for fighting the good fight—that is, God's—and for the near-total annihilation of idolaters. For on its face, Joshua presents an account of a war without pity under divine sanction. Already a century ago, British historian Arnold Toynbee expressed horror at the book, holding the opinion that the Bible has God give Israel "possession of a land that was neither his to give nor Israel's to take . . . . Yahweh's supreme value to them [the Israelites] lay in his military prowess."

One approach modern scholars have taken on this issue is to point out that ancient warfare was by nature extremely cruel, and it would not have been unusual for a conqueror to have totally wiped out his enemies. The so-called Moabite Stone, for instance, uses the same destruction terminology (h-r-m, to "devote-to-destruction") found in Joshua. Another attempt at an answer relates to what we saw above, where the book of Joshua was viewed as the product of a period much later than the one it portrays. Josiah's time—and conditions a century later, when Jews returning from exile in Babylonia sought to rebuild their community in Jerusalem—reflected concerns over who now constituted the true community. The need to delineate who is an insider and who an outsider often leads to an ideology and a literature of separation and exclusion, and the book of Joshua plays out that exclusion in the starkest terms possible. In the view of many scholars, the Canaanites in our text may well be a stand-in for internal, not external, enemies of these later centuries, as "indigenous outsiders" (Stulman) or "insiders who pose a threat to the hierarchy" (Rowlett). The historical reality of a brutal conquest thus becomes suspect, allowing modern readers to write it off as a projection backward from a later era.

But at the same time that scholars propose mitigating theories and revised historical reconstructions, it cannot be denied that, whatever its origin or original purpose, the book of Joshua has been used over the ages in the West to justify the wiping out of enemies. From King Louis IX of France, leader of the two thirteenth-century Crusades, to the Spanish conquistadores, to the Puritans of Massachusetts, and on to the nineteenth-century American practitioners of Manifest Destiny, many groups have viewed their own military struggles through the lens of the text of Joshua (see Hawk 2010 for an extended discussion).

Such historical examples make reading this book a difficult and sobering experience for many modern readers, especially for those who seek direct moral guidance from the biblical text or whose goal is to live in a "biblical" way. For communities and individuals whose understanding of the Bible is flexible and adaptive—those who embrace a reading that departs from the plain meaning of the text when changed circumstances or new ideas call for it—Joshua will represent only one stage in biblical thinking. For those who take the text directly at its word, the problem of extreme violence, even genocide, in Joshua will remain.

THE STRUCTURE OF THE BOOK

JOSHUA IS CLEARLY DIVIDED INTO TWO LARGE SECTIONS, WITH THE FIRST recounting the conquest itself and the second dealing with the parceling out of the newly won territory. The message that emerges from this structure is spelled out clearly: the land is nothing less than a gift from God. But while the twofold division holds, a slightly more complex structure might be laid out:

I   Preparations for Conquest (1–5)
   1 Yehoshua's Commissioning and God's Reassurance
   2 The Spies in Jericho
  3–4 Crossing the Jordan, Physically and Ceremonially
   5 Becoming Israelite: Circumcision and Passover

II   Waging War (6–12)
   6 Jericho (main character: Rahav)
   7 Betrayal at Ai (main character: Akhan)
   8 The Victory at Ai
   9 The Gibeonite Ruse
  10 Canaanites Fight Back; Southern Campaign
  11 Northern Campaign
  12 The List of Vanquished Kings

III   Allotting the Land (13–22)
  13 Introduction; Eastern Tribes
  14 Calev of Yehuda's Territory
  15 Yehuda's Territory
  16 Efrayim's Territory
  17 Menashe's Territory
  18 Assembly at Shilo; Binyamin's Territory
  19 Territory of the Remaining Six Tribes; Territory of the Leaders
  20 Towns of Asylum
  21 Levite Towns
  22 Civil War Averted

IV   Last Words (23–24)
  23 Final Words of Yehoshua
  24 Final Ceremony

Israel's beginnings as a self-governing entity in Canaan are thus presented in blocks of ideas, each with a clear goal. In Part I, God establishes the rules under which the conquest is to proceed, and guides the Israelites across the river and into nationhood. Fully five chapters are devoted to these matters, before actual battles are joined. And central here as well is the evoking of Yehoshua's predecessor, Moshe, who is recalled in name (six times in the book's first seven verses) and deed (the sending of spies in Chap. 2 and the observance of Passover in Chap. 5) (Fishbane).

Part II presents, first, some detailed stories of conquest, centered in Benjaminite territory, in which victory depends completely on adhering to God's instructions, and second, a systematic geographical account of the invasion, culminating in a list of vanquished kings. Like Part I (in 2:9–11 and 5:1), it is unified by the repetition of the verb "hear," especially in Chaps. 9 and 10; most of these occurrences trace the reaction of the soon-to-be-conquered peoples to reports of YHWH's doings in Egypt and Canaan (Mitchell).

Part III is both a bird's-eye and a closely detailed view of the parceling out of the land, beginning with the major southern and northern tribes and ending with the specialized cases of asylum and Levite towns. Borders are traced along natural features, such as rivers and wadis, mountain ridges, and valleys. Innumerable towns are mentioned, many as satellite villages of larger settlements.

Finally, Part IV contains the formal ratification of the covenant and Yehoshua's final words of blessing and warning. The latter are couched in terms that suggest an awareness of the sixth-century B.C.E. destruction of Jerusalem and Babylonian Exile, thus casting the conquest account of Joshua as part of a larger understanding of Israel's history.

Overall, then, Joshua can be said to move "between dream and reality" (Mitchell), reflecting distant memories, more recent catastrophes, and hopes for the future stemming from the experience of multiple generations, each of which added to and revised the text as it was transmitted over a long period of time. In its studied portrayal of the past, its focus on covenant, and its devotion to the topographical features of the land of Israel, this book forms a fitting beginning to the Early Prophets.

PART I

PREPARATIONS FOR CONQUEST

(1–5)

THE BOOK OF JOSHUA IS OBVIOUSLY CONCERNED WITH HOW THE ISRAELITES came into the land of Canaan and, conquering its territory in battle, settled in it. But the writers had choices open to them, and elected to set the stage rather elaborately. The book begins by bringing leadership to the fore, through YHWH's charge to Yehoshua, in terms that vividly recall his predecessor, Moshe. The language is intensely Deuteronomistic, preparing the way for the entire four-book account of Israel's history on its land. Also of immediate concern is the anomaly of two and a half tribes choosing to remain on the east side of the Jordan River, a problem solved, at least in the text, by their agreeing to fight with their brothers until the general conquest is over.

The text then appears to launch into military matters, with the account of the spies in Chap. 2. But this in fact serves as an opportunity to introduce two other important themes of the book: the natives' terror of the Israelite God, whose reputation stemming from the events in the Exodus story has preceded him, and the survival of some Canaanites after the conquest, here in the person of the prostitute Rahav and her family.

What remains in this section is a series of events designed to bring the Israelites fully into the land as members of a newly created nation. It accomplishes this initially by means of a kind of ritual crossing of the Jordan, which is parted before the Israelites as the Reed Sea was in Exodus, minus the drowning enemy. Significantly, this narrative focuses on the holy Coffer (Ark) borne by the priests. Once the people as a whole have crossed over, a monument of stones is set up as a lasting memorial to the event. The people's physical presence on the soil of the Promised Land, however, is not enough. The text proceeds to describe two dramatic acts which the people must accomplish in order to be fully Israelite. First, the new generation of males must be circumcised, and second, the people must observe the festival of Passover. With these prerequisites for inclusion in the nation fulfilled, the business of conquest may now proceed, with our attention initially turned back to the commander in chief. So the section ends with a fragmentary recommissioning of Yehoshua by a divine messenger, once again echoing the experience of Moshe in its language and imagery.

Chapter 1. *Setting the Stage:* The opening chapter is a fitting beginning to the book, focusing as it does on key themes to come but also purposely linking up with the ideas and vocabulary of the previous book, Deuteronomy. For example, as Polzin (1980) and others have noted, vv.3–7 contain almost literal citations of Deut. 11:24–25 and 31:7–8. And just as in an earlier example of this phenomenon, where the opening words of Leviticus take us back to the book of Exodus, thus aligning itself within the Five Books, so Joshua's beginning assures us that the words of Deuteronomy will be fulfilled. This is further reinforced by the vocabulary in Chap. 1, featuring such Deuteronomic phrases as "the servant of YHWH" (v.1), "Be strong and courageous" (v.6), and the obvious multiple repetitions of "give" and "land," which support both YHWH's long-standing promise to the Israelites and Yehoshua's worthiness to succeed Moshe. Nelson likens the chapter to the account of a "royal installation," not that of a general's commissioning, and thus it is, appropriately, societal leadership which stands at the center here, as indeed it will throughout the four-book sequence of *The Early Prophets.* So what could have been a time of instability—the predicted outcome of succession after a great leader has died—is treated by the text in a manner that gives weight to the new leader.

The boundaries cited here are at best ideal borders as conceived at a later period. They do not correspond to any known historical reality, in the Bible or elsewhere. But the language is reminiscent of Assyrian imperial thinking, an influence that appears throughout the first half of the Bible. The generalities of the boundaries—wilderness, mountains ("the Levanon"), river, and sea—are typically used in Assyrian records to indicate a king's vast rule (see Wazana 2003).

The simple word "all" recurs throughout this chapter, signifying alternately the whole people, the army, the land to be conquered, and the sum total of God's stipulations and teachings. Clearly the text wishes to impress on the audience that following "all" of God's laws will lead to possession of "all" the land.

From v.12 to the end of the chapter, the text introduces an issue that will never fully be resolved in Joshua. Two and a half tribes out of the twelve request permission to remain on the east bank of the Jordan, in the fertile region known as Gil'ad. On condition that they aid the others in conquering the west bank of Canaan, Yehoshua grants their wish. It is fulfilled in the first part of Chap. 12, but, as the opening of Chap. 22 demonstrates, biblical Israel was apparently ambivalent about the occupation of the eastern territory.

1:1 Now it was, after the death of Moshe, the servant of YHWH,
that YHWH said to Yehoshua son of Nun, the attendant of Moshe,
saying:

2 Moshe my servant is dead.
So-now, arise, cross this Jordan,
you and all this people,
into the land that I am giving to them, to the Children of Israel.

3 Every place that the sole of your foot shall tread,
to you I have given it,
as I promised Moshe;

4 from the Wilderness and this Levanon up to the Great River, the
River Euphrates,
all the land of the Hittites as far as the Great Sea, toward the
coming in of the sun,
shall be your territory.

5 No man will stand up before you, all the days of your life;
as I was with Moshe, I will be with you,
I will not desert you, I will not abandon you!

1:1 **Moshe:** Pronounced *mo-SHEH;* traditional English "Moses." **YHWH:** As explained above in "On Using This Book," the name of God in the Hebrew Bible, whose pronunciation is not precisely known, is traditionally transcribed as "the Lord." Here it is printed according to the way it appears in the Hebrew text, and the reader may choose how to say it (other possibilities include "the Eternal," *"Adonai,"* etc.). **the servant of YHWH:** The use of this title links the beginning of Joshua to the conclusion of Deuteronomy (34:5), emphasizing the unbroken continuity between Moshe and his successor. The term is also attached to David and some of the kings of Judah who followed him, indicating the concept of the sacred task of the biblical leader (Gray 1986). Regarding Moshe it is used fourteen times in the book of Joshua, a significant patterned number (two times seven). **Yehoshua:** Pronounced *yeho-SHOO-ah;* trad. English "Joshua." **the attendant of Moshe:** Yehoshua's title already when we first meet him in Exod. 24:13.

2 **arise, cross:** Kimhi understands this (starting with Heb. *q-y-m*) in the spirit of "go cross," or "go ahead and cross."

3 **Every place . . . to you I have given it:** This probably reflects an ancient legal practice of walking out a boundary to establish ownership of territory; see also Gen. 13:14–17, where God has Avraham do the same (Fishbane). The repetition of "give" in the chapter emphasizes that, in ancient legal language, this is a land grant.

4 **this Levanon:** Pronounced *leh-vah-NOHN;* trad. English "Lebanon," the "white" mountain range to the north of Israel, from which the present-day country derives its name. **the land of the Hittites:** Most of the references to "Hittites" in the Bible, and Assyrian documents, seem to refer to a localized Canaanite group, which may or may not be related to the more prominent Hittite kingdoms farther north. **the Great Sea:** The Mediterranean. **territory:** Heb. *gevul* can also, as often throughout the book, mean "border, boundary."

5 **No man will stand up before you:** No one will be able to stand against you. **not desert you . . . not abandon you:** A new expression of God's reassurance; Moshe had been told on several occasions that "I will be with you."

Chapter 2. *The Spies and Their Hostess:* Instead of launching into details about the beginning of a military campaign, as ancient Near Eastern battle accounts conventionally do, the Bible here presents a dramatic story with multiple interests. By focusing on a central character, the prostitute Rahav, who is the only named personality in the narrative (Nelson), the text is able to convey the fear in which the citizens of Jericho hold the Israelites, the practical problems and tensions of conquest, and, above all, the hand of God in what is to come. Rahav's humanity, unexpected as it is, moves the narrative from a dry reconnaissance account to one of emotional depth.

The story also introduces a key theme in Joshua: trying to explain why some Canaanites are still living among the Israelites in the audience's time. And since loyalty to God is to be a major factor in the Israelites' coming military actions, it makes sense to start with a story about Rahav's and the soldiers' loyalty to one another.

Fishbane draws attention to the repetition of "send" in the narrative, which marks both "principal actions . . . and the main spatial units." But there is more. The repeating vocabulary of the chapter emphasizes, on the one hand, what one would expect—"spies," "look over," "search out," and "seek"—but also the aforementioned "loyalty" (*hesed*), and, most notably, a verb which in the Torah is often connected to acknowledgment of God's power by foreigners: "know" (see v.9). In addition, as McCarthy has shown, the vocabulary of fear in vv.9 and 11—"dread," "quivering," and "our hearts melted"—recalls phraseology used in the ancient Near East of a common and potent image, the Divine Warrior.

The Israelites achieve their first, and perhaps most stunning, victory, then, not through advanced strategy but via the hand of God, and it is typically manifested through an actor of low social status, Rahav. Liberation from bondage in the book of Exodus began with decisive action taken by women (the midwives, Moshe's mother and sister, and Pharaoh's daughter); the conquest of the Promised Land opens similarly.

6 Be strong and courageous,
   for you yourself will cause this people to inherit the land
   that I swore to your fathers to give them.

7 Only: be exceedingly strong and courageous
   to take care to observe exactly the Instruction that Moshe my
      servant commanded you;
   do not turn aside from it, right or left,
   in order that you may prosper wherever you go.

8 This Record of the Instruction is not to depart from your mouth—
   you are to recite it day and night,
   in order that you may take care to observe
   exactly what is written in it;
   for then you will make your way prosper,
   then you will excel.

9 Have I not commanded you:
   be strong and courageous!?
   Do not be terrified, do not be dismayed,
   for with you is YHWH your God, wherever you go!

10 So Yehoshua commanded the officials of the people, saying:

11 Cross through the midst of the camp and command the people,
      saying:
   Prepare yourselves provisions,
   for in another three days, you will be crossing this Jordan
   to come to take possession of the land that YHWH your God is
      giving you to possess.

12 Now to the Re'uvenites and to the Gadites and to the half tribe of
      Menashe, Yehoshua said, saying:

6 **Be strong and courageous:** Heb. *hazak ve-ematz*. As God has already said to Moshe in Deut. 31:6; Moshe, in turn, similarly exhorts both people and Yehoshua in 31:7 and 23.

7 **to take care to observe:** Another phrase which echoes Deuteronomy (for example, in 31:6).

8 **Record of the Instruction:** Heb. *sefer ha-tora*. It is not clear what is meant here; at this point in the Bible, the phrase does not refer to the Five Books of Moses, as it commonly does later. The word *sefer*, used to mean "book" in later centuries, in the Bible can cover all kinds of written documents. **recite:** Heb. *h-g-h* indicates a low murmur, in the oral style of ancient study (see also Ps. 1:2).

9 **be dismayed:** Or "be shattered."

11 **three days:** The same period of preparation, known in Canaanite texts, preceded the meeting between God and Israel at Mount Sinai in Exod. 19. **take possession:** This verb (Heb. *y-r-sh*), which can sometimes mean "dispossess," weaves throughout the book. In simplest form, it underlines "the juridical right to land by virtue of conquest" (Mitchell).

12 **Re'uvenites . . . Gadites . . . half tribe of Menashe:** "Re'uven" (pronounced re-oo-VANE) is trad. English "Reuben," while "Menashe" (pronounced me-nah-SHEH) is "Manasseh." These three groups, back in Num. 32, had requested that they be permitted to settle on the east bank of the Jordan. There they agreed to participate with their fellow Israelites in the conquest of Canaan (on the West Bank).

◆

13 Be mindful of the word that Moshe the servant of YHWH
   commanded you, saying:
YHWH your God is granting you rest, and will give you this land;

14 your wives, your little-ones, and your livestock will stay
   in the land that Moshe gave them across the Jordan,
   while you cross over, fully-armed, before your brothers,
   all the mighty-men of valor,
   and help them

15 until YHWH grants rest to your brothers like you,
   and they too take possession of the land
   that YHWH your God is giving them,
   and you return to the land of your possession and possess it,
   which Moshe the servant of YHWH gave you across the Jordan,
   at the rising-place of the sun.

16 They answered Yehoshua, saying:
Everything that you have commanded us, we will do,
everywhere that you send us, we will go—

17 just as we hearkened to Moshe, so we will hearken to you!
Only: may YHWH your God be with you, as he was with Moshe!

18 Every man who defies your orders, and does not hearken to your
   words exactly as you command him, shall be put to death.
Only: be strong and courageous!

2:1 Yehoshua son of Nun sent twelve men, spies, from Shittim secretly,
   saying:
Go, look over the land, especially Jericho!

---

13 **the word:** Although the text reflects the gist of
Num. 32, the words attributed to Moshe here do not
appear verbatim in Numbers.

14 **wives . . . little-ones . . . livestock:** The usual components taken as the spoils of war; see Deut. 20:14.
"Little-ones," Heb. *taf,* may also have the wider connotation of "stragglers," thus including the infirm
and the aged.

15 **at the rising-place of the sun:** A common biblical
idiom for "in/toward the east."

16 **we will do:** Echoing, once again, the scene at Sinai
in Exod. 19:8. Note the portrayal of Israel as a unified nation.

18 **your orders:** Literally, "your mouth."

2:1 **Shittim:** The word, pronounced *shee-TEEM,* denotes
acacia trees. **Jericho:** Heb. *yeriho.* One of the oldest

cities in the world, it lies near the Dead Sea, with the
surrounding hills rising several thousand feet toward
the central plateau of Judah. **whore:** Traditional
commentaries, following the Targum, have sought
to soften this word, understanding it as "innkeeper,"
but its usual meaning in the Bible is indeed "prostitute," and that interpretation is more in keeping
with the common motif of God working through
less-than-heroic types (see Commentary). In the real
world of the ancient Near East, as recorded in the
much earlier Hammurabi Code, the location of an
inn/brothel in a defensive wall was mentioned as a
security risk (Weinfeld 1993). **Rahav:** Pronounced
rah-HAV); trad. English "Rahab." The name resembles a verb that means "to widen."

18

They went and they came to the house of a whore woman—her
    name was Rahav—
and they lay down there.

2 The king of Jericho was told, saying:
Here, some men have come here tonight from the Children of
    Israel to search out the land!

3 So the king of Jericho sent to Rahav, saying:
Bring out the men who came to you, who came to your house,
for it is to search out the entire land that they have come!

4 But the woman took the two men and concealed them;
then she said:
Certainly, the men came to me,
but I do not know where they were from.

5 And it was, as the gate was about to be closed at dark, that the men
    went out
—I do not know where the men went.
Pursue quickly after them,
for you may overtake them!

6 Now she had brought them up to the roof
and had hidden them in the stalks of flax, the ones arranged by her
    on the roof.

7 Now the men pursued after them by way of the Jordan at the river-
    crossings,
and they closed the gate, after the pursuers had gone out after
    them.

8 As for them, scarcely had they lay down when *she* came up to them
    on the roof.

9 She said to the men:
I know
that YHWH has given you the land,
and that the dread of you has fallen upon us;
all the settled-folk of the land are quivering before you!

---

2 **The king . . . was told:** Possibly by guards, who
would be observing the traffic in and out of the city,
or else by one of Rahav's customers.
4 **then she said:** To the king's men.
6 **flax . . . roof:** The flat roof, a useful work space in
biblical-era houses, was often used for drying and
processing grain.

7 **the men:** The king's men. **they closed:** The
townspeople.
8 *she:* The emphasis points out her energy (Hawk
2000).
9 **dread of you:** Foreigners' fear of the Israelites is a
favorite motif in the Five Books of Moses; see, for
example, Exod. 15:14–16.

10 For we heard about [how] YHWH dried up the waters of the Sea of
     Reeds before you when you went out of Egypt,
  and what you did to the two Amorite kings who were across the
     Jordan, to Sihon and to Og,
  whom you devoted-to-destruction.
11 We heard, and our hearts melted [in fear],
  and no life-breath rose within anyone because of you,
  for YHWH your God, he is God in the heavens above and on the
     earth beneath!
12 So-now, pray swear to me by YHWH, that since I have acted toward
     you with loyalty,
  you also will act toward my Father's House with loyalty
  and will give me a trustworthy sign;
13 you will keep alive my father and my mother and my brothers and
     my sisters, and all those belonging to them,
  and save our lives from death!
14 The men said to her:
  Our life [shall be] in place of yours, to die, as long as you do not tell
     this business of ours!
  And it will be, at YHWH's giving the land to us,
  that we will act toward you in loyalty and faithfulness.
15 Then she let them down by a rope through the window
  —for her house was on the outer-part of the wall, and in the wall
     she dwelt—
16 and she said to them:
  To the highlands go, lest the pursuers encounter you,

---

10 **Amorite:** Used here to denote Israel's neighbors east of the Jordan, but more often referring to the inhabitants of Canaan in general, or occasionally to those dwelling in the highlands. **Sihon . . . Og:** Pronounced *see-HONE* and *OG* (with "o" as in "old"). See Num. 21:21–35, where the Israelites encounter and defeat these two kings east of the Jordan. They are subsequently used as examples in narrating God's great deeds on Israel's behalf. **devoted-to-destruction:** This term (Hebrew root *h-r-m*), used frequently in Joshua, indicates people, animals, or objects set aside exclusively for God, often meaning wholesale destruction or death. Israel's Moabite neighbors also spoke of *herem* in respect to their national god Kemosh, in the Mesha Stele ("Moabite Stone," discovered in Jordan in 1868). The

word appears in Arabic and has entered English as "harem," signifying a group of women set apart for one man.

11 **our hearts melted [in fear]:** JPS: "we lost heart."

12 **Father's House:** A social unit in ancient Israel, much like an extended family.

12–13 **swear to me . . . :** Rahav's motivation in all this seems to be her safety and that of her family.

15 **in the wall she dwelt:** The location of Rahav's house made it the perfect entry and escape spot for the spies. A casemate structure, featuring double walls (note the two different words for "wall" in the text) that allowed soldiers to be posted inside, was an architectural feature known to generations of Israelites in biblical times.

and hide yourselves there for three days, until the pursuers' return;
afterward you may go on your way.

17 The men said to her:
We are clear of this your sworn-oath which you have had us swear:

18 here, when we come to the land,
this cord of scarlet thread you are to tie in the window through
which you let us down,
while your father and your mother and your brothers and all your
Father's Household you are to gather to yourself into the house;

19 and it shall be: whoever goes out of the doors of your house,
outside,
his blood will be on his head,
and we will be clear,
while whoever will be with you in the house,
his blood will be on our head, if [any] hand be against him!

20 Now if you tell this business of ours, we will be clear from your
sworn-oath that you have had us swear.

21 She said:
In accordance with your words, so be it!
So she sent them off, and they went,
and she tied the scarlet cord through the window.

22 They went off and came to the highlands, and stayed there for
three days,
until the pursuers returned;
the pursuers sought them all along the way, but did not find [them].

23 The two men came down again from the highlands;
they crossed over and came to Yehoshua son of Nun, and
recounted to him all that had befallen them:

24 they said to Yehoshua:
Indeed, Yhwh has given the entire land into our hand,
and also all the settled-folk of the land are quivering before us!

---

17 **We are clear:** Meaning, "We will be guiltless if you violate the terms of our agreement, and you'll die like all the other inhabitants of Jericho."

18 **cord:** As Hawk (2000) notes, Heb. *tikva* also means "hope." **scarlet thread:** Clearly noticeable from a distance, this is analogous to the blood marking the Israelites' doors in the Exodus story. It is used

elsewhere in purification rituals (see Lev. 14:4, 6, and Num. 19:6).

21 **In accordance with your words, so be it!:** Her words seal the deal.

23 **Yehoshua son of Nun:** His full name had appeared in v.1, and thus brackets the whole story nicely (Meyers 2004).

Chapter 3. *The Crossing:* Now comes the crucial moment of transition from one state of being (wandering) to another (conquest). Not surprisingly, the chapter contains a strong sense of boundaries, as if to foreshadow the entire second half of the book (Hess).

If we had any doubts as to Yehoshua's leadership capabilities, they are dispelled by his Moshe-like act of splitting the waters of the Jordan—although Yehoshua himself does not stretch out a staff as Moshe and Aharon had done; this time, the act of cleaving the river is portrayed as coming directly from God. Only once will such a splitting of waters occur again, with Eliyyahu (Elijah) in II Kings 2. He too is presented as a kind of second Moshe, in acknowledgment of another great crisis in Israel's history.

The motif of a religious object such as the Coffer (Ark) leading troops into battle is known all over the ancient and medieval world. Although the present chapter involves no fighting per se, it seems wholly appropriate that the Coffer, borne by priests, spearheads the long-awaited fording of the Jordan and thus inaugurates the conquest of Canaan.

Despite the dramatic moment in our text, the narrative is confusing at points. This has already been the case in previous accounts, such as the description of the revelation at Sinai (Exod. 19), and such confusion will also occur in Chaps. 4 and 6 below, as Nelson notes. This lack of clarity may stem from a complicated history of writing or transmitting the text, or from the desire to include all relevant traditions, no matter how inconsistent or contradictory.

Key words in the chapter include, not surprisingly, "cross" and "people," with clusters of "carry," "Coffer," and "priests," and "waters" and "stand." In the end, the crossing of the Jordan, in contrast to the cosmic upheaval at the Sea of Reeds in Exodus, is orderly and hierarchical. Once again, ceremony and what it stands for—bonding the social unit together—trump historical reporting.

Those who seek a "scientific" explanation for the events of this chapter have noted the existence of clay riverbanks in the area, a soil composition that could lead to a temporary blockage (Rainey, following Aharoni). The text itself is wholly uninterested in such an approach.

◆   3:1 Yehoshua started-early in the morning;
        they marched on from Shittim and came to the Jordan, he and all
           the Children of Israel,
        and they spent the night there, before they crossed over.

    2 Now it was at the end of three days
        that the officials crossed into the midst of the camp

    3 and commanded the people, saying:
        When you see the Coffer of the Covenant of Yhwh your God
        with the priests and the Levites carrying it,
        you yourselves are to march on from your place
        and walk behind it.

    4 However—let it be far between you and it, about two thousand
          cubits in measure;
        do not come near it,
        in order that you may know the way that you are to go,
        for you have not crossed that way yesterday [or] the day-before.

    5 Yehoshua said to the people:
        Make yourselves holy,
        for tomorrow Yhwh will perform wonders in your midst!

    6 And Yehoshua said to the priests, saying:
        Carry the Coffer of the Covenant
        and cross over before the people!
        So they carried the Coffer of the Covenant
        and walked before the people.

    7 Yhwh said to Yehoshua:
        Today I will begin to make you great in the eyes of all Israel,
        that they may know
        that as I was with Moshe, I will be with you!

3:3 **Coffer of the Covenant:** Ancient Israel's central cultic object, this chest (trad. English "Ark") contained the tablets on which the Ten Commandments (Exod. 20) were written. See Exod. 25:1–22 for a full description. **the priests and the Levites:** Others, "the Levitical priests." The term is problematic; given that it is hardly used in the subsequent books of the Early Prophets, it may indicate a southern (Jerusalem) writer's bias against Levites (Boling 1982).

4 **let it be far:** Proper distance from holy objects must be observed, lest one incur divine wrath. **two**

thousand cubits: Biblical cubits measured from eighteen to twenty-two inches, so the distance in question would have been half a mile or more. **go:** Or "walk." **yesterday [or] the day-before:** An idiom meaning "the past."

5 **Make yourselves holy:** That is, put yourselves in a state of ritual purity, by washing yourselves and abstaining from sexual relations. The same had been required of the people at Sinai (Exod. 19).

6 **Carry . . . Coffer . . . Covenant:** The Hebrew is not alliterative.

Chapter 4. *Memorializing the Crossing:* Here, as Nelson notes, recounting the act of "crossing" (once again a key word in the narrative) attains the identity-forming position suggested in the last chapter. In his words, the "act of retelling . . . would perform the function of reinforcing peoplehood." The account of river fording described in the text is thus as much a rite of passage for Israelite audiences, as well as for Jewish and Christian ones of later periods, as it is a dramatic moment in the text itself. As typically laid out in Deuteronomy, historical events are prized mainly for their later meaning; here, all-important is the issue of children asking their parents, "What are these stones?" Only when we get to v.12 is there finally a mention of war. But even this does not overshadow the elevation of Yehoshua's status as leader, despite the fact that no swords have yet been drawn and no arrows have yet flown.

In v.24 there is a reiteration of the verb "know," which had been so meaningfully used in Chap. 2.

8 And you, command the priests, those carrying the Coffer of the
Covenant, saying:
When you come to the edge of the waters of the Jordan,
in the Jordan you are to stand-still.

9 Yehoshua said to the Children of Israel:
Approach here and hearken to the words of YHWH your God.

10 Then Yehoshua said:
By this you shall know
that the Living God is in your midst,
and that he will dispossess, yes, dispossess from before you
the Canaanite, the Hittite, the Hivvite,
the Perizzite, the Girgashite, the Amorite, and the Yevusite:

11 here is the Coffer of the Covenant;
the Lord of All the Earth is crossing over before you into the
Jordan!

12 So-now, take yourselves twelve men from the tribes of Israel,
one man, one man [apiece] per tribe.

13 It will be, when the soles of the feet of the priests, those
carrying the Coffer of YHWH, the Lord of All the Earth, come to
rest in the waters of the Jordan,
the waters of the Jordan will be cut off;
as for the waters coming down from above—
they will stand as one heap!

14 So it was, at the people's marching from their tents to cross the
Jordan,
with the priests, those carrying the Coffer of the Covenant, before
the people:

---

8 **you are to stand-still:** Or "stop." The reader does not yet know why, but it clearly anticipates something dramatic.

10 **By this you shall know:** A dramatic phrase, used elsewhere only in the story of Korah (Num. 16:28) (Boling 1982). **the Living God:** Heb. *elohim hayyim.* The phrase probably carries the connotation of "active," "vital"; I could not find an adequate English translation. **the Canaanite . . . :**

An enumeration of indigenous "nations" which, in one form or another, occurs frequently in the Five Books of Moses. See Gen. 15:19 for the first such list. **Yevusite:** Trad. English "Jebusite."

13 **coming down:** Heb. *ha-yoredim,* echoing the name of the river Jordan (Heb. *Yarden,* "The Descender"). **heap:** Used elsewhere only regarding the crossing of the Sea of Reeds in Exod. 15:8 (Meyers 2004).

◆ 15 that when those carrying the Coffer came to the Jordan, and the
feet of the priests, those carrying the Coffer, dipped in the edge
of the water
—the Jordan being full to its banks, all the days of the harvest-
cutting—

16 the waters stood still, those coming down from above;
they rose as one heap, very far away, at Adam, the town that is
beside Tzaretan,
while those going down to the Sea of the Plain, the Sea of Salt,
were completely cut off,
and the people crossed over, opposite Jericho.

17 And the priests, those carrying the Coffer of YHWH's Covenant,
stood fast on dry-ground, in the middle of the Jordan,
while all Israel crossed over onto dry-ground,
until the entire nation had completed crossing over the Jordan.

4:1 Now it was, when the entire nation had completely crossed over
the Jordan,
that YHWH said to Yehoshua, saying:

2 Take yourselves from the people twelve men: one man, one man
[apiece] per tribe,

3 and command them, saying:
Lift you up from here, from the middle of the Jordan, from the
firmstanding-spot of the priests' feet,
twelve stones;
have them cross over with you
and place them at the night-lodging where you will lodge tonight.

4 So Yehoshua called for twelve men whom he had confirmed, from
the Children of Israel,
one man, one man [apiece] per tribe,

5 and Yehoshua said to them:
Cross over before the Coffer of YHWH your God, into the middle of
the Jordan,

---

15 **the days of the harvest-cutting:** In the spring, after
the yearly rains have stopped, and extending into
early summer. The waters would then be high, making the crossing more difficult and thus miraculous.

16 **Adam . . . Tzaretan:** Location unclear.   **the Sea of
the Plain, the Sea of Salt:** The Dead Sea.

17 **nation:** A term (Heb. *goy*) rarely used of Israel;
more common is the kinship-based term "people"
(*'am*). Its usage here suggests that the crossing of the
Jordan is an act of nation-founding.

4:3 **firmstanding:** Not connected in Hebrew to the
recurring "stand [still]."

and raise yourselves, each one, a stone onto his shoulder,
corresponding to the number of tribes of the Children of Israel,

6 in order that this may be a sign in your midst:
when your children ask you on the morrow, saying:
What are these stones to you?

7 you are to say to them
that the waters of the Jordan were cut off before the Coffer of the
Covenant of YHWH;
when it crossed into the Jordan, the waters of the Jordan were
cut off.
And these stones are to be a reminder to the Children of Israel, into
the ages!

8 The Children of Israel did thus, as Yehoshua had commanded:
they lifted up twelve stones from the middle of the Jordan,
as YHWH had spoken to Yehoshua,
corresponding to the number of tribes of the Children of Israel,
and had them cross over with them to the lodging-place, and
deposited them there.

9 And the twelve stones Yehoshua erected in the middle of the
Jordan, beneath the firmstanding-spot of the priests' feet, those
carrying the Coffer of the Covenant;
they are there until this day.

10 Now the priests, those carrying the Coffer, were standing fast in the
middle of the Jordan,
until all the matter that YHWH had commanded Yehoshua to speak
to the people was completed,
exactly as Moshe had commanded Yehoshua;
the people went quickly, and they crossed over.

11 And it was, when all the people had completed crossing over,
that the Coffer of YHWH and the priests crossed over before the
people.

---

6 **What are these stones to you?:** That is, what do
they mean to you?

7 **these stones are to be a reminder:** This function is
a common one in the Bible; see Gen. 28:18, where
the stone that serves as Yaakov's pillow becomes
a "standing-pillar," marking a holy or memorable
spot.

9 **until this day:** An important phrase in DH, occurring fully fifteen times in Joshua. Some scholars see
it as confirming that such traditions are preexilic (see
Geoghegan).

Chapter 5. *The Transition to Canaan:* The saga of passage across the Jordan now comes to its completion. The river itself has been crossed, but the people are somehow not yet fully Israelite. To accomplish this, the text first recounts the circumcision of the new, non-slave generation of males, which in biblical terms must now slough off its desert persona and become "civilized" as Israelites. The other ethnic marker described in the chapter is the observance of Passover, not so much as a holiday that recalls the dramatic events of deliverance from Egypt, but as a primarily agricultural festival, tied inextricably to the land, with the noticeable substitution of the "yield of the land" for the manna that had sustained the people in the wilderness. Israel is thus initiated into its full identity at the very moment that it physically sets foot on the soil of Canaan. The pairing of circumcision and Passover had already occurred at a parallel moment in Exod. 12, as Fishbane notes; and Hamilton nicely observes that "it is vital at this point to demonstrate that Israel belongs to Yahweh and not to Egypt. They are not Pharaoh's property."

Finally, just as Moshe was addressed by God at the start of Israel's earlier nation-becoming, Yehoshua encounters a divine messenger, at least briefly. The appearance of the mysterious figure, sword drawn in hand, recalls the victorious divine stance often portrayed in ancient Near Eastern iconography. At this point, the path to war has been properly paved. A people and its leader are ready.

In sum, the conquest reiterates the "prototype" of earlier days, as "the great paradigms of the past are renewed for future generations" (Fishbane). This statement could apply to the entire four-book collection that has come down to us as the Early Prophets.

12 And the Children of Re'uven, the Children of Gad, and the half
    tribe of Menashe crossed over, armed, before the Children of
    Israel,
    as Moshe had spoken to them;
13 about forty units of specially-drafted [men] from the armed-forces
    crossed over in the presence of YHWH to battle,
    to the Plains of Jericho.
14 On that day YHWH made Yehoshua great in the eyes of all Israel;
    they held him in awe, just as they had held Moshe in awe,
    all the days of his life.

15 Then YHWH said to Yehoshua, saying:
16 Command the priests, those carrying the Coffer of the Testimony,
    that they should come up from the Jordan.
17 So Yehoshua commanded the priests, saying:
    Come up from the Jordan!
18 And it was, upon the coming up of the priests, those carrying the
    Coffer of YHWH's Covenant, from the middle of the Jordan,
    —the soles of the priests' feet were drawn up onto the dry-
      ground—
    that the waters of the Jordan returned to their place
    and went on as yesterday [and] the day-before, to all their banks.

19 Now the people came up from the Jordan on the tenth of the first
    month,
    and encamped at Gilgal/Circle, at the sunrise edge of Jericho.
20 And these twelve stones that they had taken from the Jordan,
    Yehoshua erected at Gilgal.
21 He said to the Children of Israel, saying:
    When your children ask their fathers on the morrow, saying:
    What are these stones?

12 **armed:** Boling (1982): "in battle array."
13 **units:** Agreeing with a number of scholars, Boling (1982) included, who understand the word *elef* as a military "contingent," thus reducing the numbers drastically in these stories. The same reduction may be true for the Torah's enumeration of those who left Egypt, which at first blush indicates over six hundred thousand warriors. **specially-drafted:** Possibly, selected (Heb. *h-l-tz*, "removed") from among the normal soldiers.

16 **Testimony:** Another word for the covenant.
19 **on the tenth:** This seems to be an intentional allusion to the fact that the Israelites in Exodus had been commanded to take a lamb on the tenth day of the same month, in celebrating the first Passover (Fishbane). **the first month:** Corresponding to March or April. **Gilgal:** Likely located not far from Jericho (although a number of biblical towns have the same name), this was an important cultic center in early biblical times.

22 You are to make known to your children, saying:
   On dry-land did Israel cross this Jordan,

23 when Yhwh your God dried up the waters of the Jordan before
      you, until your crossing over,
   just as Yhwh your God had done at the Sea of Reeds, which he
      dried up before us, until our crossing over—

24 in order that all the peoples of the earth might have knowledge of
      the hand of Yhwh, how strong it is,
   in order that you might hold Yhwh your God in awe, all the days
      [to come].

5:1 Now it was, when they heard—all the Amorite kings who were
      across the Jordan seaward,
   and all the Canaanite kings who were by the Sea,
   that Yhwh had dried up the waters of the Jordan before the
      Children of Israel, until they had crossed over,
   their heart melted [in fear],
   and they were left breathless before the Children of Israel.

2 At that time, Yhwh said to Yehoshua:
   Make yourself knives of flint
   and again circumcise the Children of Israel, a second time.

3 So Yehoshua made himself knives of flint
   and circumcised the Children of Israel, at the Hill of Foreskins.

4 And this is the matter concerning which Yehoshua circumcised
      them:
   all the people coming out of Egypt, the males, all the men of
      battle,
   had died in the wilderness, on the way,
   upon their going out of Egypt.

5 For they had been circumcised, all the people who had gone out,
   while all the people who were born in the wilderness on the way,
      upon their going out of Egypt, had not been circumcised.

---

24 **hold . . . in awe:** Trad. "fear." Boling (1982) posits a more political meaning to the phrase: "give allegiance." See v.14 above.
5:2 **knives:** The Hebrew word usually means "swords." Flint may be used here because of its primitive, i.e., nontechnological, associations. It may be more precisely identified as obsidian, a stone known for smoothness and sharpness (Hess). **a second time:** Meaning the new generation, as explained in the subsequent verses.
4 **matter:** JPS (following Kimhi): "reason."

6 For the Children of Israel had traveled forty years in the wilderness,
    until the entire nation was gone, the men of battle, who had come
        out of Egypt,
    who had not hearkened to the voice of YHWH,
    those to whom YHWH swore that he would not let them see the
        land
    that YHWH had sworn to their fathers to give them,
    a land flowing with milk and honey.
7 But their children whom he had raised up in their place,
    them Yehoshua circumcised, for they were foreskinned,
    since they had not been circumcised on the way.
8 Now it was, when the entire nation was done being circumcised,
    that they stayed in their place in the camp, until their recovery.
9 And YHWH said to Yehoshua:
    Today I have rolled the disgrace of Egypt from off you!
    So the name of that place has been called Gilgal/Rolling, until
        this day.

10 The Children of Israel encamped at Gilgal,
    and they performed the Passover offering on the fourteenth day of
        the month, at sunset,
    in the Plains of Jericho.
11 They ate from the yield of the land on the morrow of Passover:
        unleavened cakes and parched grain,
    on this very day.
12 And the *mahn* ceased on the morrow, when they ate the yield of the
        land;
    there was no more *mahn* for the Children of Israel,
    and they ate from the produce of the land of Canaan in that year.

6 **them:** So several manuscripts; MT (the standard Hebrew text) reads "us." **flowing with milk and honey:** The land's richness is so described for the first time in Exod. 3:8. The milk is likely that of goats; while it was long considered that the "honey" referred to the syrup of dates, recent discoveries point to some domestication of bees in ancient Israel. In Canaanite poetry, the parallel phrase is "fatness and honey."
8 **recovery:** Lit., "living [again]," "reviving."
9 **the disgrace of Egypt:** Usually understood as the stigma of slavery; Hess sees it as symbolizing the disobedience of the slave generation.

10–11 **sunset . . . Plains . . . yield:** Hawk (2000) notes the Hebrew play on words of the three nouns: *'erev . . . 'arevot . . . 'avur.* The main root signifies "crossing."
11 **parched grain:** Typifying simple, easily obtained food. The list here anticipates the bounty of the Promised Land, in a kind of "down payment" (Hess). **this:** We might expect "that" here; it sounds like an audience is being addressed.
12 ***mahn:*** The miraculous food sent by God in Exod. 16:14, which sustained the Israelites in the wilderness. Trad. English "manna."

13   Now it was, when Yehoshua was at Jericho,
that he lifted up his eyes and saw:
now here, a man standing opposite him,
with his sword drawn in his hand!
Yehoshua went toward him and said to him:
Are you for us or for our foes?

14   He said: No,
rather, I am the commander of Yhwh's forces.
Now I have come!
Yehoshua flung himself on his face to the ground and bowed low,
and said to him:
What does my lord have to speak to his servant?

15   The commander of Yhwh's forces said to Yehoshua:
Put off your sandal from your foot,
for the place on which you are standing—it is holy!
And Yehoshua did thus.

---

13 **at:** Or "by."

14 **No:** Boling (1982) understands the Hebrew as "Neither one." Another possibility is "[He said] to him," as Heb. *lo'* and *lo* are homonyms. **bowed low:**

Here, as often, biblical characters prostrate themselves "nostrils to the ground."

15 **Put off your sandal . . . holy:** Echoing God's words to Moshe at the burning bush (Exod. 3:5).

PART II

WAGING WAR

(6–12)

ANCIENT NEAR EASTERN KINGS TYPICALLY INSCRIBED INFLATED ACCOUNTS OF their conquests on monuments and tablets. In the section of Joshua that is devoted to actual fighting, the book limits such language principally to one chapter (10), although traces appear in Chaps. 9 and 11–12, resembling what is found, for instance, in Assyrian inscriptions. More significantly, as I discussed in the Introduction, our text tends to play down the conquering role of the Israelites and their commander, keeping God and the covenant at the center of consciousness. Consequently, the vanquishing of Jericho does not come about as a result of the force of arms, and the victory at Ai can be won only after an Israelite offender has been punished for violating YHWH's rules of war, which had caused an initial defeat. Thus, of the seven chapters in this section, three focus directly on Israel's relation to YHWH instead of on straight military matters.

The route taken thus far in Joshua moves due west, from the Jordan River crossing through Jericho to Ai, near modern Betin. At this point (Chap. 9), before the conquest moves forward, the Israelites are approached by the inhabitants of Giv'on, southwest of Ai, in a ruse that attempts to keep them out of armed conflict. Once the claim that they are poor and from far away is uncovered as deceit, and their future status as a subjugated people is established, the text turns to a major threat from an alliance of Canaanite kings (Chap. 10) who attack Giv'on. They are routed by the Israelite armies and driven west and then south all the way to Makkeda, a town probably to the west of Hevron. In the process, the text portrays the very heavens as aiding the Israelites (vv.12–14), with the sun and moon delaying their transit across the sky in order to allow time for the victory to take place. And the grisly death of the five enemy kings, normal enough in ancient Near Eastern practice, serves to presage the conquest that will follow.

From here (v.29), the narrative settles into formulas, utilizing phrases such as "Yehoshua and all Israel crossed over," ". . . and did battle with X," "And YHWH gave X into the hand of Israel," "he struck it with the mouth of the sword," "he left no survivor," "just as he had done to the king of Y." The geographical sequence in this extended part of Chap. 10 has been termed the "Southern Campaign" and involves towns situated principally in the lowlands (Heb. *shefela*) of Judah, with a swing at the end up into the highlands around Hevron.

Chaps. 11 and 12 round out the picture, beginning with a victory in Upper Galilee (the "Northern Campaign"), continuing with an explanation of how, as YHWH had done to Pharaoh in the book of Exodus, he makes the Canaanites' heart "strong-willed" in order to hasten their destruction. It ends with an appropriate stylistic break: a list of conquered kings. Thus the account of the conquest is hardly uniform, and appears to have been composed from various sources.

As scholars have pointed out, most of the action in the first twelve chapters of Joshua occurs in the territory of what became Benjamin, along with the sanctuary at Gilgal. Such geographic placement would seem to support the idea that northern traditions are principally at work here.

––––––––––

Chapter 6. *The Fall of Jericho:* The first military action recorded in the book of Joshua is also the most memorable. While a historian of warfare might remark on the strategic genius of the siege of Jericho—troops silently marching around a city for six days might well be completely unnerving and demoralizing to its captive population—tactics and psychology are probably not the point of the narrative. Once again we have what looks like a ritual procession, almost as if an audience, by being receptive to the story, is experiencing the events as part of a communal festival of some sort (and Hawk 2000 notes the use of both *shofar* and shouting, integral to the story, in other biblical ritual contexts). In addition, there is a magical element, given that many ancient and later stories speak of a taking-possession by means of drawing a circle. In the present context, these devices, including the famous blowing of the *shofars,* have the effect of moving the credit for the victory away from the armies and squarely toward God. The way is cleared for the Israelite troops, and the actual conquest is easily accomplished.

The vocabulary of the chapter naturally centers around circling, sounding blasts on the *shofars,* and shouting; at the same time, a major theme in the book, that of "devoting-to-destruction," a holy war concept, makes its first pointed appearance here. Notably, the Coffer also makes its last appearance (Auld 1998), suggesting once again that the present version of the story is ritually based.

Nelson points out that vv.18–19 foreshadow the next story, about Akhan, in their use of "desire," "silver and gold," and "disaster." But as Chap. 4 did, this one chapter at least ends with a notice about Yehoshua's greatness.

◆ 6:1 Now Jericho closed up and was closed-up-tight before the Children
        of Israel;
      no one went out and no one came in.
  2   YHWH said to Yehoshua:
      See, I have given into your hand
      Jericho and her king, [and] the mighty-men of valor.
  3   You are to go around the city, all the men of battle,
      circling the city one time;
      thus you are to do for six days,
  4   while seven priests are to carry seven *shofars* of rams ahead of the
        Coffer.
      But on the seventh day, you are to go around the city seven times,
      while the priests sound blasts on the *shofars*.
  5   And it shall be, at the drawing out of the ram's horn:
      when you hear the sound of the *shofar,*
      that all the fighting-people are to shout a great shout,
      and the wall of the city will fall down from below;
      then the fighting-people are to go up, each one [straight] in front
        of him!
  6   Yehoshua son of Nun called for the priests
      and said to them:
      Carry the Coffer of the Covenant,
      while seven priests carry seven *shofars* of rams ahead of the Coffer
        of YHWH.
  7   And he said to the fighting-people:
      Cross over and go around the city;
      as for the vanguard, it shall cross over ahead of the Coffer of
        YHWH.
  8   And it was, as soon as Yehoshua talked to the fighting-people,
      with the seven priests carrying the seven *shofars* of rams in the
        presence of YHWH,
      that they crossed over

6:1 **closed up and was closed-up-tight:** Heb. *sogeret
u-m'suggeret.*
  2 **into your hand:** A parallel expression exists in Akkadian (Boling 1982).
  3 **You:** Plural.
  4 **seven priests . . . seven *shofars* . . . seventh day . . .**

seven times: Throughout the ancient Near East,
this number connotes completeness and perfection.   **shofars:** Rams' horns, which have both military and religious functions in the Bible.
  5 **from below:** Collapsing by its own weight.

◆ and sounded blasts on the *shofars,*
with the Coffer of Yʜwʜ's Covenant going after them.

9 Now the vanguard was going ahead of the priests, those sounding blasts [on] the *shofars,*
while the gathering-up [unit] was going after the Coffer, going and sounding blasts on the *shofars.*

10 As for the fighting-people, Yehoshua commanded them, saying:
You are not to shout, you are not to make your voice heard,
not a word is to go out of your mouth
until the time of my saying to you: Shout!
Then you are to shout.

11 He had the Coffer of Yʜwʜ go around the city,
circling one time;
then they came back to the camp
and spent the night in the camp.

12 Yehoshua started early in the morning,
and the priests carried up the Coffer of Yʜwʜ,

13 while the seven priests carrying the seven *shofars* of rams ahead of the Coffer of Yʜwʜ
were going, going along and sounding blasts on the *shofars,*
with the vanguard going ahead of them
and with the gathering-up [unit] going ahead of the Coffer of Yʜwʜ,
going along and sounding blasts on the *shofars.*

14 They went around the city on the second day, one time,
and then they returned to the camp.
Thus they did for six days.

15 Now it was, on the seventh day,
that they started early, at the coming up of dawn;
they went around the city in this manner seven times—
only on this day did they go around the city seven times.

---

9 **the gathering-up [unit]:** Those who "mop up."   13 **going, going along:** As in a procession (Boling 1982).
Others, "rearguard."

16 And it was, at the seventh time,
   that the priests sounded blasts on the *shofars,*
   and Yehoshua said to the fighting-people:
   Shout!
   For YHWH has given you the city!

17 The city will be devoted-to-destruction,
   it and all who are in it, for YHWH;
   only Rahav the whore shall live,
   she and all who are with her in the house,
   for she hid the messengers whom we sent.

18 And you, only be careful regarding the devoted-things,
   lest you feel desire and take from the devoted-things
   and render the camp of Israel devoted-to-destruction,
   and bring disaster upon it.

19 For all silver and gold and vessels of bronze and iron—
   they are holy to YHWH;
   into the treasury of YHWH they are to come!

20 So the fighting-people shouted and sounded blasts on the *shofars;*
   and it was, at the people's hearing the *shofar* sound,
   that the people shouted a great shout,
   and the wall fell down from below,
   and the people went up to the city, each one [straight] in front
      of him,
   and captured the city.

21 And they devoted-to-destruction everyone who was in the city,
   from man to woman, from young lad to old man,
   to ox and sheep and donkey,
   with the mouth of the sword.

22 But to the two men, those spying out the land, Yehoshua said:
   Go to the house of the whore woman
   and bring out from there the woman and all who belong to her,
   as you swore to her.

---

18 **devoted-things:** These were to be quarantined for God, as it were, and hence not subject to human use. See the note to 2:10, above. Nelson uses of the term "taboo," and notes how a kind of contagion is involved. **feel desire:** MT has "devoted-to-destruction" (Hebrew root *h-r-m*) here; more likely is the root *h-m-d* (the "covet" or "desire" of the tenth commandment), as reflected in LXX. The letters *resh* and *dalet* are easily confused in Hebrew script, and the switching of two adjacent letters (*dalet* and *mem*) is a common scribal error, termed metathesis. **disaster:** Such a violation would anger God.

22 **the two men, those spying:** Whom we met in Chap. 2.

Chapter 7. *Breaking Faith; The Valley of Disaster:* All has gone well so far. The Israelites, led by a pious and faithful general, have crossed the boundary into the Promised Land, secured the memory of the event for future generations, and recovered and renewed some of the most significant and symbolic ritual practices of their ancestors. Crowning this sequence, they have witnessed and participated in the miraculous destruction of an ancient and heavily fortified city. Now, however, disaster strikes, not for lack of effort or strategy, but for one reason only: the committing of sacrilege against God. One of the troops that took Jericho is unable to suppress the common soldier's craving for plunder and tries to conceal his theft. The seriousness of the offense is indicated by the repeated use of the verb "take," which will later (I Sam. 8) be highlighted in the text's warning about the perils of kingship. Interestingly, the perpetrator Akhan stems from Yehuda (Judah), the southern tribe and region so often preferred in *The Early Prophets.* This might further support a northern authorship for the story.

The drama of the narrative is heightened by the drawing of lots, with the confession coming only after their "capture," as Hebrew usage has it. Akhan's fate is execution by stoning, and, as in the case of Korah in Num. 16, includes all of his family and possessions. This serves to emphasize the seriousness of violating the rule of *herem,* plunder which is to be set aside ("devoted") for God. In general it reinforces the book's concept that ownership, of land as well as of movable goods, is ultimately God's. To forget this is to incur a wrath so great that it results in unexpected military defeat, and thus the episode is a helpful reminder in the text that the conquest is a privilege, not a foregone conclusion.

23 So the lads, the spies, went
and brought out Rahav and her father and her mother and her
brothers and all who belonged to her
—all her clan they brought out—
and they placed them outside the camp of Israel.

24 As for the city, they burned it with fire, along with everything that
was in it;
only the silver and the gold and the vessels of bronze and iron did
they place in the treasury of the house of YHWH.

25 As for Rahav the whore, and her Father's House, and all who
belonged to her, Yehoshua let [them] live;
she settled in the midst of Israel, until this day,
for she had hid the messengers whom Yehoshua had sent to spy out
Jericho.

26 And Yehoshua had [an oath] sworn at that time, saying:
Doomed be the man before YHWH
who arises and rebuilds this city, Jericho:
with his firstborn he will found it,
and with his youngest he will set up its doors!

27 And YHWH was with Yehoshua,
and report of him went throughout all the land.

7:1 But the Children of Israel committed sacrilege, yes, sacrilege
regarding the devoted-things:
Akhan son of Carmi son of Zavdi son of Zerah, of the tribe of
Judah, took from the devoted-things,
and the anger of YHWH flared up against the Children of Israel.

2 Meanwhile, Yehoshua sent men from Jericho to Ai/The Ruin,
which is beside Bet-Aven, east of Bet-El,
and said to them, saying:

---

23 **clan:** Following LXX; MT uses the plural. **outside the camp of Israel:** This isolation of Rahav and her family seems to be only temporary, since in v.25 they come to reside "in the midst of Israel."

24 **the house of YHWH:** Although in the Bible this phrase usually refers to Shelomo's (Solomon's) Temple, here it undoubtedly means a tent-sanctuary, specifically the one at Shilo (see I Sam. 1:24).

26 **with . . . with:** Most interpreters understand this "with" as meaning that the builder will pay with the lives of his sons. The prophecy is fulfilled in I Kings 16:34.

27 **report:** From the Hebrew verb that means "to hear."

7:1 **Akhan:** Pronounced *ah-KHAN;* trad. English "Achan."

2 **Ai/The Ruin:** Usually identified as Et-Tell, just southeast of Bet-El. **Bet-Aven:** All names beginning with Heb. "Bet" (house), pronounced "bayt," in this translation are "Beth" in trad. English.

◆

Go up and spy out the land.
So the men went up and spied out Ai;

3 then they returned to Yehoshua and said to him:
Not all the fighting-people need go up.
Let about two thousand men or three thousand men go up and
strike Ai—
do not exhaust all the fighting-people there, for they are few.

4 So there went up there, from the fighting-people, about three
thousand men,
but they fled from before the men of Ai:

5 the men of Ai struck down of them about thirty-six men
and pursued them in front of the gate, to the Broken-Places;
they struck them at the descent,
and the heart of the fighting-people melted [in fear] and turned to
water.

6 Yehoshua tore his clothes
and flung himself on his face on the ground before the Coffer of
YHWH, until sunset, he and the elders of Israel,
and they tossed earth on their heads.

7 Yehoshua said:
Alas, YHWH God,
why did you bring this people across, yes, across the Jordan,
to give us into the hand of the Amorite, to have us perish?
Would that we had resolved that we should stay across the Jordan!

8 Please, O my Lord,
what can I say after Israel has turned the back-of-its-neck to its
enemies?

9 When the Cannanites hear, along with all the settled-folk of the
land,
they will reverse course against us and cut off our name from the
earth—
then what will you do about your great name?

---

3 **they are few:** The inhabitants of Ai.
5 **Broken-Places:** Probably remains created by repeated destructions of the site. **melted:** Used previously to describe the fear felt by the Canaanites at the Israelites' advance.
6 **tore his clothes . . . tossed earth:** Israelite mourning practices; see, for instance, Gen. 37:34.

8 **turned the back-of-its-neck:** A gesture of submission.
9 **reverse course against us:** Turn and be able to defeat us. **name:** Meaning "reputation."

◆ 10 YHWH said to Yehoshua:
Arise;
now why are you fallen on your face?

11 Israel has sinned:
yes, they have crossed my covenant that I commanded them,
yes, they have taken from the devoted-things,
yes, they have stolen,
yes, they have lied,
yes, they have put it among their vessels!

12 So the Children of Israel will not be able to rise before their
enemies;
the back-of-the-neck they will turn to their enemies,
for they have become liable-to-destruction—
I will not continue to be with you
if you do not wipe out the devoted-things from your midst!

13 Arise, hallow the people—
you are to say:
Hallow yourselves for tomorrow,
for thus says YHWH, the God of Israel:
Devoted-things are in your midst, O Israel;
you will not be able to stand before your enemies
until your removing the devoted-things from your midst!

14 You are to come near in the morning by your tribes,
and it shall be: the tribe that YHWH captures-by-lot
shall come near by clans;
and the clan that YHWH captures
shall come near by houses;
and the house that YHWH captures
shall come near by the males.

---

10 **Arise:** Meant quite literally here; "Get up!"
11 **yes:** The repetition of Heb. *gam* builds up the effect of the crime in a wave of sound. **among their vessels:** Thus hiding them.

12 **liable-to-destruction:** By stealing from what was banned, they themselves have become banned.
14 **captures-by-lot:** The same Hebrew root (*l-k-d*) frequently used in the book to indicate conquest.

Chapter 8. *The Conquest of Ai:* This is the longest battle scene in the book. It mostly concerns the strategy of ambush and its execution; but significantly, the chapter ends (vv.30–35) with a covenant scene in which the divine "Instruction" is renewed in the manner prescribed by Moshe (see Deut. 27). Thus, despite the long description of strategy, which is of great interest to future military minds, and the geographically accurate details of the story, the chapter is really about the resolution of the Akhan debacle and the return to the original state of affairs in which God protects the Israelites in battle. To underscore this, in vv.8 and 27 the Israelites are first commanded to and then described as hearkening to "the word of YHWH"; in v.35, the assembled nation hears the word of Moshe read aloud (Nelson). Thus it is confirmed that the successful battle plan derives not from the general himself, but from the divine word. From now on, there will be no more question about how to defeat the Israelites, and in the very next chapter, a group of fearful Canaanites will have to resort to a ruse in order to simply survive.

Vv.30–35 read like an interruption in the war account, but they seem to have been placed here to reestablish the distinctive relationship between Israel and YHWH, which had been ruptured. In that sense, this little story is reminiscent of the regiving of the divine tablets in Exod. 34, which occurs after a parallel breach of the covenant. It is also an example of the book of Joshua faithfully carrying out Mosaic law, in this case the requirement of renewing the covenant as set forth in Deut. 27. Indeed, the language in vv.30–35 is constructed from phrases in Deuteronomy (Rösel).

It has often been noted that Ai, "the Ruin," was almost certainly not inhabited in the time of Yehoshua and that it was perhaps the very ruins that became entwined in popular imagination with the events recorded in our chapters.

15 And it shall be: the one captured-by-lot regarding the devoted-
   things is to be burned with fire,
   he and all who belong to him,
   because he crossed the covenant of YHWH,
   because he did a vile-thing in Israel!

16 So Yehoshua started early in the morning;
   he brought Israel near, by their tribes,
   and the tribe of Judah was captured-by-lot.

17 He brought near the clans of Judah,
   and the Zarhite clan was captured;
   he brought near the Zarhite clans, by the males, and Zavdi was
   captured;

18 he brought near his house, by the males,
   and Akhan son of Carmi son of Zavdi son of Zerah, of the tribe of
   Judah, was captured.

19 Yehoshua said to Akhan:
   My son, now give glory to YHWH, the God of Israel,
   and make confession to him;
   now tell me: What have you done?
   Do not conceal it from me!

20 Akhan answered Yehoshua and said:
   In truth, I did sin against YHWH, the God of Israel;
   like this and like that I did:

21 I saw among the spoils a goodly Shin'ar mantle, and two hundred
   weights of silver,
   and an ingot of gold, fifty weights its weight;
   I desired them and I took them—

---

15 **all who belong to him:** A man's household—his family and possessions—was considered an extension of his person.   **crossed:** Broke, violated; the English "transgressed" (from Latin) is an exact equivalent.   **a vile-thing:** A term (Heb. *nevala*) used to describe a terrible deed, often (but not necessarily) rape (see Gen. 34:7).

17 **Zarhite:** Descended from one named Zerah.

18 **house:** Denoting an extended family, sometimes called a "Father's House" in the Bible.

19 **now give glory:** Gray 1986 suggests "acknowledge the weightiness [of your crime]."   **make confession to him:** As JPS; others, "give him praise."

20 **like this and like that:** Meaning "as follows."

21 **Shin'ar:** Babylonia. It is not clear what kind of robe the text is describing. Such geographical names for clothing appear elsewhere in the ancient Near East.   **ingot:** The English word has a parallel derivation to the Heb. *lashon,* "tongue."   **hidden:** The concealment makes the crime all the worse—and in a parallel sense, the name / identity "Canaan" (k-n-'-n) is hidden in Akhan's own name ('-k-n)! (Hawk 2000).

and here they are, hidden in the ground, within my tent, along with
the silver beneath it.

22 Yehoshua sent messengers;
they ran to the tent,
and here, [it was] hidden in his tent, with the silver beneath it!

23 They took them from amid the tent and brought them to Yehoshua
and to all the Children of Israel,
and they emptied them out in the presence of YHWH.

24 Then Yehoshua took Akhan son of Zerah
and the silver, and the mantle, and the ingot of gold, and his sons,
and his daughters, and his ox, and his donkey, and his sheep, and
his tent, and all that belonged to him,
—all Israel was with him—
and they brought them up to the Valley of Akhor/Disaster.

25 Yehoshua said:
How you have brought-disaster-on us!
YHWH will bring-disaster-on you this day!
And all Israel pelted him with stones;
they burned them with fire
and stone-heaped them with stones,

26 and erected over him a large mound of stones, until this day.
So YHWH turned back from his flaming anger.
Therefore the name of that place is called the Valley of Disaster,
until this day.

8:1 YHWH said to Yehoshua:
Do not be frightened, do not be dismayed;
take all the people of battle with you
and arise, go up to Ai.
See: I have given into your hand the king of Ai, his people, his city,
and his land!

2 You are to do to Ai and to its king
as you did to Jericho and to its king;

---

24 **Then Yehoshua took Akhan:** The "taking" is now, ironically, a sign of Akhan's impending death (Mitchell). **Akhor/Disaster:** Or "trouble," which in current English seems too mild. JPS uses "calamity."

25 **pelted him with stones:** A well-known ancient form of execution.

8:1 **do not be dismayed:** Back to the confidence level of Chap. 1 (see v.9 there).

◆ only its spoils and its animals may you plunder for yourselves.
Set yourself an ambush for the city, behind it.

3 So Yehoshua arose, along with all the people of battle, to go up
against Ai.
And Yehoshua chose thirty thousand men, mighty-men of valor,
and sent them off at night;

4 he charged them, saying:
See: you are setting an ambush for the city, behind the city;
do not go exceedingly far from the city,
but all of you be ready.

5 As for me and all the fighting-people who are with me,
we will come near to the city,
and it shall be:
when they come out to meet us, as at the beginning,
we will flee before them.

6 But when they come out after us, until we have drawn them away
from the city,
—for they will think: They are fleeing before us as at the beginning!
and we flee before them—

7 then *you* are to arise from the ambush
and take possession of the city;
YHWH your God will give it into your hand!

8 And it will be, when you seize the city,
that you are to ignite the city with fire;
in accordance with the word of YHWH you are to do.
See: I have charged you!

9 Yehoshua sent them off, and they went to the [place of] ambush
and stayed between Bet-El and Ai, seaward from Ai,
and Yehoshua spent the night on that night amid the fighting-
people.

10 Yehoshua started early in the morning and mustered the fighting-
people;
then he went up, he and the elders of Israel, ahead of the fighting-
people to Ai,

3 **thirty thousand:** Or perhaps, as earlier, thirty units or groups.
5 **as at the beginning:** The first battle, recounted in Chap. 7.

7 **take possession:** Heb. *yirash;* LXX has "approach" (*yiggash*).
9 **seaward:** Westward, in the direction of the Mediterranean.

11 while all the people for battle who were with him went up and
        approached, coming opposite the city,
    and encamped north of Ai,
    with a ravine between them and Ai.

12 He took about five thousand men
    and set them in ambush between Bet-El and Ai, seaward of the city,

13 while the fighting-people set up the entire camp that was north of
        the city,
    as well as its rearguard, seaward of the city.
    And Yehoshua lodged that night in the middle of the valley.

14 Now it was, when the king of Ai saw,
    that they went quickly and started-early, and the men of the city
        came out to meet Israel in battle,
    he and all his fighting-people, to the appointed place in front of the
        plain
    —but he did not know that there was an ambush for him behind
        the city.

15 And Yehoshua and all the fighting-people acted as if beaten before
        them;
    they fled by way of the wilderness.

16 Then all the fighting-people who were in the city were summoned
        to pursue after them,
    and they pursued after Yehoshua and let themselves be torn away
        from the city,

17 so that not a man remained in Ai or in Bet-El who had not gone out
        after Israel;
    they left the city open
    and pursued after Israel.

18 Then YHWH said to Yehoshua:
    Stretch out the scimitar that is in your hand toward Ai,
    for into your hand I give it!
    So Yehoshua stretched out the scimitar that was in his hand toward
        the city,

---

11 **people for battle:** The English is as awkward as
the Hebrew. Some scholars omit "for battle," since
"people" here, as often, can mean "soldiers" (see
"fighting-people" in v.10).

13 **fighting-people:** Reading *ha-'am* for MT *ha-'emek*
("the valley"). **lodged:** Most manuscripts read
"went" here.

15 **of the wilderness:** Or "to the wilderness."

17 **remained:** Or "was left," but changed here so as
not to be identical to the different verb in the next
phrase, "they left the city open."

18 **scimitar:** A curved sword. **it:** The city.

19 and the ambush quickly arose from its place
and ran, at the stretching out of his hand;
they came to the city and captured it,
and quickly ignited the city with fire.

20 The men of Ai faced about behind them and saw:
now here, the smoke of the city went up to the heavens!
But they had no [place] at hand to flee to here or to there.
And the fighting-people who had fled to the wilderness turned back
upon the pursuers.

21 Now Yehoshua and all Israel saw
that the ambush had taken the city,
and that the smoke of the city was going up,
so they returned and struck down the men of Ai.

22 These went out of the city to meet them,
and they were, regarding Israel, in the middle: these were on this-
side and those were on that-side,
and they struck them down
until they left them no survivor or fugitive.

23 As for the king of Ai, they seized [him] alive
and brought him near to Yehoshua.

24 Now it was, when Israel had finished killing all of the settled-folk
of Ai, in the open-field and in the wilderness where they had
pursued them,
—all of them fell by the mouth of the sword, until they were
gone—
that all Israel returned to Ai and struck it with the mouth of the
sword.

25 And all those falling on that day, from man to woman,
were twelve thousand, all the inhabitants of Ai.

26 Now Yehoshua did not turn back his hand with which he had
stretched out the scimitar
until he had devoted-to-destruction all the settled-folk of Ai.

27 Only the animals and the spoils of that city did Israel plunder for
themselves,
in accordance with the word of YHWH which he had commanded
Yehoshua.

---

20 **turned back upon:** Alternatively, "turned into" (Friedman).

22 **These:** The men of the city.

24 **gone:** In the sense of "finished off."

Chapter 9. *The Unexpected Treaty:* After the long and detailed battle narrative of the previous chapter, this text provides a colorful break. It also serves to demonstrate how the Israelites have returned to following God's commands. The Giv'onites fulfill the legal role of a city that surrenders in Deut. 20; as a result, they are not destroyed by the invaders but become subject to forced labor.

The text opens with a deception occasioned by fear, just as Rahav in Chap. 2 had begun the account of the Jericho campaign with an acknowledgment of God's power. It is also the classic treatment of a recurring theme in Joshua and Judges: the conquest was not quite complete.

A key word in the chapter is "far," an ironic usage here. Giv'on was in fact close to Jerusalem, and also not a great distance from what the text represents as the recently destroyed Ai. More significant is the location of the region on major trade routes to the Mediterranean coast. No wonder that in the next chapter, Jerusalem spearheads a coalition to attack Giv'on (Rainey/Notley).

The scenario of a terror-stricken group surrendering as slaves to an invader rather than being slaughtered has many ancient Near Eastern parallels. In those cases, the purpose of the account seems to be to boost the fame of the conquering king (Younger).

28 And Yehoshua burned down Ai;
he made it into an everlasting mound, a wasteland, until
this day.

29 As for the king of Ai, he hung him on a wooden-stake, until the
time of sunset,
and when the sun came in, Yehoshua commanded that they take his
corpse down from the stake,
and they threw it by the entrance to the city gate
and erected over it a large mound of stones, until this day.

30 Then Yehoshua built a sacrificial-altar to YHWH, the God of Israel,
on Mount Eval,

31 as Moshe, the servant of YHWH, had commanded the Children of
Israel,
as is written in the Record of the Instruction of Moshe,
an altar of complete stones, upon which no iron had been raised,
and they sent up upon it offerings-up to YHWH,
and sacrificed *shalom*-offerings.

32 And he wrote there upon the stones
a copy of the Instruction of Moshe,
which he had written before the Children of Israel.

33 Now all Israel and its elders and its officials and its judges were
standing on this-side and on that-side,
by the Coffer, opposite the Levitical priests, those carrying the
Coffer of YHWH's Covenant:
as the sojourner, so the citizen,
half of them opposite Mount Gerizim and half of them opposite
Mount Eval,
as Moshe, the servant of YHWH, had commanded [them] to bless
the people of Israel at the beginning.

---

28 **an everlasting mound:** Like Jericho, Ai was not to be rebuilt. "Mound" implies a ruined heap.

29 **hung him on a wooden-stake:** This practice, possibly impalement, would take place after the actual killing, and was intended to further humiliate the victim. **until . . . sunset:** In accordance with the law in Deut. 21:23, a criminal's body was not to be left out overnight.

30 **Then:** or "This was when" (Rösel). **Mount Eval:** Pronounced *ay-VAHL*; trad. English "Ebal," the northern of the two large hills which overlook the city of Shekhem (modern Nablus). The other was Mount Gerizim, mentioned in v.33 below.

31 **complete:** Unhewn, not cut by metal. **no iron:** Continuing the traditional avoidance of iron. ***shalom*-offerings:** Scholars disagree about the meaning of Heb. *shelamim*. Some see the sacrifice as a "gift-of-greeting," others as a "peace-offering"; equally possible is a "sacrifice of solidarity," since the *shelamim* usually involve a sacred meal. I have kept *shalom* (peace, greeting, wholeness), to leave all of these possibilities open.

33 **the sojourner:** The noncitizen or foreigner.

34 After that, he read aloud all the words of the Instruction, the
blessing and the curse,
exactly as was written in the Record of the Instruction.

35 There was not a word from all that Moshe had commanded
that Yehoshua did not read aloud opposite the entire assembly of
Israel,
and the women, and the little-ones, and the sojourner who was
going in their midst.

9:1 Now it was, when all the kings who were across the Jordan heard
—in the highlands and in the lowlands, and on all the shore of the
Great Sea, opposite the Levanon,
the Hittites, the Amorites, the Canaanites, the Perizzites, the
Hivvites, and the Yevusites—,

2 that they gathered together to do battle with Yehoshua and with
Israel, [under] one command.

3 But the settled-folk of Giv'on heard about what Yehoshua had done
to Jericho and to Ai,

4 so they acted, for their part, with cunning, and went and supplied
themselves:
they took worn-out sacks on their donkeys,
and worn-out wineskins, split and sewn up,

5 with worn-out and patched sandals on their feet,
and worn-out clothes upon themselves,
while all the bread of their supplies was dry [and] had become
crumbs.

6 And they went to Yehoshua, to the camp at Gilgal,
and said to him and to the men of Israel:
From a far-off land we have come;
so-now, cut a covenant with us!

---

34 **the blessing and the curse:** A reenactment from
Deut. 27.
9:1 **across the Jordan:** West of the river.
2 **[under] one command:** Following Boling (1982); lit.,
"with one mouth."
3 **Giv'on:** Pronounced *giv-OHN;* trad. English
"Gibeon."
4 **for their part:** So JPS; others, "they too," which is

unclear. **supplied themselves:** MT has "went as a
delegation," but see v.12 in the text.
6 **cut a covenant:** See Gen. 15:10 for a memorable
example of taking the verb literally. In a practice that
is attested in the Aramaic Sefire treaty, the parties
to such an agreement would walk between cut-up
animals, implying a similar fate if one of them were
to break the agreement in the future.

7 The men of Israel said to the Hivvites:
Perhaps you are settled in my midst,
so how can I cut a covenant with you?

8 They said to Yehoshua:
We are your servants!
Yehoshua said to them:
Who are you, and from where have you come?

9 They said to him:
From a land exceedingly far off your servants have come,
because of the fame of YHWH your God,
for we have heard the heard-report of him
and of all that he did in Egypt,

10 and of all that he did to the two Amorite kings who were across the
Jordan,
to Sihon king of Heshbon and to Og king of Bashan who was at
Ashtarot.

11 So our elders and all the settled-folk of our land said to us, saying:
Take in your hand supplies for the way,
and go meet them
and say to them:
We are your servants.
So-now, cut a covenant with us!

12 This our bread—[while it was] warm, we supplied ourselves with it,
from our houses,
on the day of our setting out to go to you,
but now, here, it is dry [and] has become crumbs!

13 And these wineskins that we filled new:
here, they have split open;
and these our clothes and our sandals have worn out
from this very great journey.

14 The men took from their supplies, but did not inquire of YHWH's
mouth.

---

7 **how can I cut . . . :** Given the command to annihilate the locals (Deut. 7:1–2), such a treaty would be impermissible.

8 **We are:** Or "we will be."

12 **This our bread:** A northern idiom (Rendsburg 2003).

14 **The men:** The Israelites. **took from their supplies:** There are several possibilities here. Boling (1982) suggests the context of a covenant meal; JPS reads "took [their word] because of their provisions." **did not inquire:** Did not consult an oracle.

Chapter 10. *The Defense of Giv'on; Southern Victories:* The peace treaty concluded in the last chapter provokes a strong reaction from the neighboring "kingdoms" (actually city-states). Just as Israel seeks to obliterate the Canaanites, the latter will have no truck with those who attempt to make peace with them. In a war reminiscent of another wide-ranging one in Gen. 14 ("the four kings against the five"), in which Avraham had intervened as warrior, Yehoshua engages the coalition led by the ruler of Jerusalem and defeats them with, of course, the help of God. This time the divine intervention is more directly miraculous. As the stars will later be said to fight on the Israelites' behalf in Judg. 5:20, so God hurls hailstones down upon the hapless enemy here. Also connected to this event in the final form of our text, though perhaps not originally, is the memorable fragment about the sun and the moon "standing still" for Yehoshua. As Nelson notes, the verb may actually indicate something else (such as "remaining dark" or "being silent"), but in any case, Yehoshua is once again magnified as army commander, one who can enlist even the forces of nature in the cause of victory.

The fate of the vanquished kings in vv.16–28 serves to set the tone for the conquest to follow. By focusing on such details at the beginning of the sequence of conquest, we are not left in any doubt as to the eventual outcome. Thus the passage functions, once again, as a literary rather than as an annalistic introduction.

After v.28, the text proceeds with the blow-by-blow campaign of conquest, with this chapter focusing on the south and thus once again pointing to the eventual primacy of Yehuda. At long last, the book begins to resemble other conquest accounts from the ancient Near East, using a stock vocabulary for each paragraph and town conquered ("battle," "strike [down]," "capture," "sword," "devote-to-destruction," and "he left no survivor"). As Hess points out, from Chap. 10 on, the conquest will proceed at an ever-quickening pace, heightening the drama.

Notable from this point through 12:1 are multiple occurrences of the word "all"—some forty-five of them, according to Hawk's (2000) count. He rightly takes this as a sign of "Israelite integrity, comprehensive conquest, and obedience to YHWH and the commands of Moses." I have been unable to reproduce the repetition without undue violence to English; the reader will have to be content with noting "all" and "every [person]."

◆ 15   And Yehoshua made peace with them:
he cut a covenant with them, letting them live,
and the exalted-leaders of the community swore [an oath] to them.

16   But it was, at the end of three days after they had cut a covenant
with them,
that they heard that they [dwelt] near to them,
and that it was in their midst that they were settled!

17   So the Children of Israel marched out and came to their towns on
the third day
—now their towns were Giv'on and Kefira and Be'erot and Kiryat-
Ye'arim.

18   But the Children of Israel did not strike them down, since the
leaders of the community had sworn to them by YHWH, the God
of Israel,
so the entire community grumbled against the leaders.

19   And all the leaders said to the entire community:
We ourselves swore to them by YHWH, the God of Israel,
so now we are not able to harm them!

20   This [is how] we must act toward them:
let them live,
that there not be fury against us regarding the sworn-oath that we
swore to them!

21   And the leaders said to them:
They may live.
So they became hewers of wood and drawers of water for the
entire community,
as the leaders had spoken concerning them.

22   But Yehoshua called for them and spoke to them, saying:
Why did you deceive us, saying:
We are exceedingly far from you,
when you are settled in our midst?

---

15 **letting them live:** Paralleling Rahav in 6:25.
17 **Giv'on . . . :** Indeed, not far away, just five and a half
miles from Jerusalem.
18 **the entire community:** Probably referring to a kind
of representative body.   **grumbled:** The verb (l-w-n)

is otherwise used mainly in the rebellion stories of
the book of Numbers, beginning with Chap. 11.
19 **harm:** Or "attack, touch."
20 **fury:** Here describing divine anger over the breaking
of a solemn agreement.

◆ 23 So-now, doomed are you:
never shall a servant be cut off from you
either as hewers of wood or drawers of water for the house of
my God!
24 They answered Yehoshua and said:
It was because it was told, yes, told to your servants
that Yнwн your God had commanded Moshe his servant
to give you all the land
and to wipe out all the settled-folk of the land before you—
so we were very afraid for our lives before you,
and we did this thing.
25 But now, here we are in your hand;
as is good, as is right in your eyes to do with us, do.
26 So he did thus with them:
he rescued them from the hand of the Children of Israel, so that
they did not kill them,
27 but Yehoshua made them on that day hewers of wood and drawers
of water for the community,
and for the sacrificial-altar of Yнwн, until this day,
at the place that he chooses.

10:1 Now it was, when Adoni-Tzedek, king of Jerusalem, heard
that Yehoshua had captured Ai, and had devoted-it-to-destruction,
—as he had done to Jericho and to its king, so he had done to Ai
and to its king—
and that the settled-folk of Giv'on had made peace with Israel
and were remaining in their midst,
2 he was exceedingly afraid,
for Giv'on was a large city, like one of the royal cities
—indeed, it was larger than Ai, and all its men were mighty ones.

23 **never . . . cut off . . . :** That is, there will always be a servant. **servant:** See above note to 1:1. The Heb. *'eved* has a broad range of meanings, also including "vassal," "slave," and "worshipper" of a deity. **house of . . . God:** See note to 6:24, above.
27 **at the place that he chooses:** A classic Deuteronomic phrase, taken by many to refer to Jerusalem.

10:1 **Adoni-Tzedek:** The name means "My Lord Is Tzedek" (an Amorite god) or, more literally, "My Lord is Legitimacy," as opposed to being a usurper. **Jerusalem:** The original meaning is likely "City of [the god] Shalem." The name later came to be understood as "City of Peace" or "Safety" (*shalom*).
2 **mighty ones:** Boling (1982): "knights."

3 So Adoni-Tzedek king of Jerusalem sent [word]
   to Hoham king of Hevron, and to Pir'am king of Yarmut, and to
      Yafia king of Lakhish, and to Devir king of Eglon, saying:
4 Come up to me and help me,
   that we may strike Giv'on,
   for they have made peace with Yehoshua and with the Children of
      Israel!
5 They gathered together and went up, the five Amorite kings—
   the king of Jerusalem, the king of Hevron, the king of Yarmut, the
      king of Lakhish, and the king of Eglon,
   they and all their camps,
   and they encamped against Giv'on, and did battle with it.
6 The men of Giv'on sent [word] to Yehoshua, to the camp at Gilgal,
      saying:
   Do not let your hand slacken from your servants;
   come up to us quickly
   and deliver us, help us,
   for all the kings of the Amorites, the settled-folk of the highlands,
      have gathered against us!
7 So Yehoshua went up from Gilgal,
   he and all the people of battle with him,
   and all the mighty-men of valor.
8 And Yhwh said to Yehoshua:
   Do not be afraid of them,
   for into your hand I have given them;
   no man among them will be able to stand up before you!
9 Yehoshua came against them, suddenly,
   having gone up all night from Gilgal.

---

3 **Hevron:** Pronounced *hev-RONE.* Trad. English "Hebron," it was located about nineteen miles southwest of Jerusalem. **Yarmut:** A town located a few miles north of Hevron. It and Eglon later in the verse are not mentioned again in the book. **Lakhish:** Pronounced *lah-KHEESH;* trad. English "Lachish," the important Judean city about fifteen miles west of Hevron. It has been identified with Tell ed-Duweir. **Eglon:** A town in the lowlands; site identification not clear.

7 **and all the mighty-men:** Can also be read as "namely, all the mighty-men."

8 **them:** The five Amorite kings.

10　And Yhwh panicked them before Israel,
　　　so that they struck them, a great striking-down, at Giv'on,
　　　and pursued them by way of the Bet-Horon Pass;
　　　they struck at them as far as Azeka and as far as Makkeda.

11　Now it was, when they were fleeing before Israel,
　　　—they were at the descent of Bet-Horon—
　　　that Yhwh threw down upon them large stones from the heavens,
　　　　as far as Azeka, and they died;
　　　[there were] more who died by the stones
　　　than those whom the Children of Israel killed with the sword.

12　Then Yehoshua spoke to Yhwh
　　　on the day of Yhwh's giving the Amorites before the Children of
　　　　Israel;
　　　he said before the eyes of Israel:
　　　　O sun, at Giv'on be still,
　　　　O moon, in the Valley of Ayyalon!

13　So the sun was still, and the moon stood fast,
　　　until a nation was avenged on its enemies.
　　　—Is it not written in the Record of the Upright:
　　　The sun stood fast in the midst of the heavens;
　　　it did not hasten to come in as on a whole day?

14　There has been none like that day before it or after it,
　　　for Yhwh to hearken to a man's voice,
　　　since Yhwh was fighting for Israel.

15　Then Yehoshua and all Israel with him returned to the camp at
　　　Gilgal.

10　**panicked:** A term often used of God's fighting on behalf of the Israelites by inducing a kind of mass hysteria (e.g., Exod. 14:24, Deut. 7:23). The same verb is used in other ancient Near Eastern war accounts, with the warrior kings as the subject (Younger). **Pass:** Lit. "Ascent." **Azeka . . . Makkeda:** Pronounced *ah-zay-KAH . . . mah-kay-DAH.*

11　**large stones from the heavens:** Hailstones are mentioned in other ancient Near Eastern battle accounts as having been sent by storm gods. "Large," interestingly, does not appear in the extant Dead Sea Scroll manuscript of Joshua.

12　**still . . . Ayyalon:** The Hebrew is assonant (*dom . . . ayyalon*); for poetic effect in English, one could use

"be still [as stone]," were it not for the presence of stones already in the chapter. The Hebrew verb (*d-m-m*) can connote both silence and immobility. Ayyalon was near Bet-Horon Pass.

13　**was avenged on:** The Hebrew nuance is difficult. Boling (1982) translates as "defeated," but it may well indicate "getting satisfaction through the defeat of one's enemy," as in Judg. 16:28. **Record of the Upright:** Trad. English "the Book of Jashar." The poetic form of the quotation from this lost work (see also II Sam. 1:18) suggests that it was an epic/poetic rendition of Israel's history.

14　**Yhwh to hearken to a man's voice:** In order to intervene in nature.

16 And these five kings fled
    and hid themselves in a cave at Makkeda.

17 And Yehoshua was told, saying:
    The five kings have been found hiding in a cave at Makkeda!

18 Yehoshua said:
    Roll large stones over the mouth of the cave,
    and assign men over it to watch them.

19 As for you, do not stand around—
    pursue after your enemies, attack-their-tail;
    do not allow them to come back to their cities,
    for YHWH your God has given them into your hand!

20 So it was, when Yehoshua and the Children of Israel had finished
        striking them, a very great striking-down, until they were gone,
    while the survivors had escaped from them and had come back to
        the fortified towns—

21 that all the fighting-people returned to the camp, to Yehoshua at
        Makkeda, safely;
    not a man wagged his tongue against the Children of Israel.

22 And Yehoshua said:
    Open the mouth of the cave
    and bring out these five kings to me from the cave!

23 They did thus:
    they brought out these five kings to him from the cave,
    the king of Jerusalem, the king of Hevron, the king of Yarmut, the
        king of Lakhish, the king of Eglon;

24 and it was, upon their bringing out the kings to Yehoshua,
    that Yehoshua called for all the fighting-men of Israel and said to
        the chiefs of the men of battle who had gone with him:
    Come near, put your feet on the necks of these kings!
    So they came near and put their feet on their necks.

---

16 **And:** In the sense of "meanwhile" (JPS). **Makkeda:** Location unknown.
18 **watch:** Or "guard."
19 **attack-their-tail:** Boling (1982): "Cut off their retreat!" The Heb. verb derives from the noun "tail."
20 **survivors had escaped:** The Heb. uses one root here.

21 **wagged his tongue:** Some, "sharpened." The image is used regarding the Exodus in Exod. 11:7, with a canine flavor.
24 **put your feet on the necks:** A known gesture of conquest in the ancient Near East. The Heb. 'oref technically is the back of the neck, as I have put in translation elsewhere.

◆ 25 Yehoshua said to them:
Do not be frightened, do not be dismayed;
be strong and courageous,
for thus will YHWH do to all your enemies with whom you do battle!

26 And Yehoshua struck them down after that, and put them to death;
he hung them on five stakes,
and they were hung on the stakes until sunset.

27 Now it was, at the time of the sun coming in,
that Yehoshua commanded [them] and they took them down from
the stakes,
and they threw them into the cave where they had hidden.
Then they put large stones over the mouth of the cave,
[there] until this very day.

28 As for Makkeda, Yehoshua captured [it] on that day;
he struck it with the mouth of the sword, along with its king,
and he devoted-it-to-destruction, along with every person that was
in it—
he left no survivor.
And he did to the king of Makkeda as he had done to the king of
Jericho.

29 Yehoshua and all Israel with him crossed over from Makkeda to
Livna
and did battle with Livna.

30 And YHWH gave it too into the hand of Israel, along with its king;
he struck it with the mouth of the sword,
along with every person that was in it—
he left in it no survivor.
And he did to its king as he had done to the king of Jericho.

31 Yehoshua and all Israel crossed over from Livna to Lakhish;
they encamped against it and did battle against it.

32 And YHWH gave Lakhish into the hand of Israel,
so that he captured it on the second day;

27 **until this very day:** See note to 4:9, above.
28 **as he had done to the king of Jericho:** That, however, is *not* recounted in the text. This kind of omission is often found in biblical narrative.
28–32 **as he had done ... exactly as he had done:** The

idea, using either one of these phrases, occurs seven
times in this part of the text, stressing the campaign's success (Meyers 2004).
29 **Livna:** Another town of undetermined location,
probably in the lowlands area.

◆   he struck it with the mouth of the sword,
   along with every person who was in it,
   exactly as he had done to Livna.

33   Then Horam king of Gezer went up to help Lakhish,
   but Yehoshua and his fighting-people struck him,
   until he left him no survivor.

34   Yehoshua and all Israel with him crossed over from Lakhish to
      Eglon;
   they encamped against it and did battle with it
35   and captured it on that day.
   They struck it with the mouth of the sword,
   while every person who was in it on that day devoted-to-
      destruction,
   exactly as he had done to Lakhish.

36   Yehoshua and all Israel with him went up from Eglon to
   Hevron, and did battle with it;
37   they captured it
   and struck it with the mouth of the sword,
   along with its king and all its towns and every person that was
      in it—
   he left no survivor,
   exactly as he had done to Eglon:
   he devoted-it-to-destruction, and every person who was in it.

38   Yehoshua returned, and all Israel with him, to Devir, and did battle
      with it;
39   he captured it along with its king and all its towns,
   and struck them with the mouth of the sword and devoted-to-
      destruction every person that was in it—
   he left no survivor;
   as he had done to Hevron, thus he did to Devir and to its king,
   as they had done to Livna and to its king.

40   So Yehoshua struck the entire land:
   the highlands, the Negev, the lowlands, and the slopes,
   along with all of their kings—
   he left no survivor,

Chapter 11. *Northern Victories:* The account of conquests in the north begins with a list of Canaanites who ally themselves against the Israelites from all over the country and ends with a tallying of the conquests themselves. The wording is striking; for the first time, we hear about the extermination of "anyone breathing." In fact, the chapter comprises an entire vocabulary of verbal warfare, with "strike," "destruction," "wipe out," "sword," "take" "burn," and "battle" all prominently featured. In a way, the whole chapter is a kind of summary of the conquest. It also parallels many structural elements of the previous chapter: a coalition of enemy kings, divine reassurance, the verb "give" as a promise of victory from God, Israelite triumph and summary (Hamilton).

Nelson sees an idealized past predominating over the strictly historical here as before, as demonstrated by the mention of Hatzor. The Bronze Age ruins of that city must have made a great impression on the writers, and since Hatzor was prominent and powerful for centuries, it makes sense for it to dominate the narrative here. In general, the Upper Galilee was not settled until centuries later.

◆ while all those breathing he devoted-to-destruction,
    as YHWH, the God of Israel, had commanded.

41 Yehoshua struck them from Kadesh-Barne'a to Gaza,
    and all the region of Goshen and as far as Giv'on.

42 All these kings and their land, Yehoshua captured at one time,
    since YHWH, the God of Israel, was doing battle for Israel.

43 Then Yehoshua returned, and all Israel with him, to the camp at
    Gilgal.

11:1 Now it was,
    when Yavin king of Hatzor heard,
    that he sent to Yovav king of Madon and to the king of Shimron
      and to the king of Akhshaf,

2 and to the [other] kings that were in the north,
    in the highlands and in the plain south of the Kinneret and in the
      lowlands
    and in the Heights of Dor, toward the Sea,

3 the Canaanites toward sunrise and toward the Sea,
    and the Amorites and the Hittites and the Perizzites and the
      Yevusites in the highlands,
    and the Hivvites beneath Hermon, in the region of Mitzpa.

4 They went out, they and all their camps with them,
    an abundance of fighting-people, like the sand that is on the
      seashore in abundance,
    and horse and chariot, an exceedingly abundant [number].

5 All these kings met;
    they came and encamped together at the Waters of Merom, to do
      battle with Israel.

---

41 **Kadesh-Barne'a:** Pronounced *kah-DAYSH bar-NAY-ah,* a site frequented by the Israelites during their earlier wilderness treks. It was the very southern boundary of Judah, the later Southern Kingdom. **Goshen:** Not to be confused with the Goshen of Exodus, the Israelites' "neighborhood" in Egypt.

11:1 **Yavin:** He appears again in Judg. 4. **Hatzor:** The large and important fortress city in the north of ancient Israel. **Madon . . . Shimron . . . Akhshaf:** Three other important towns in the north.

2 **in the north, in the highlands:** Or "in the north part of the highlands." **south:** Hebrew uses the term

Negev, the "arid" southland of Judah, as a directional term. **the Kinneret:** MT has "Kinarot." In modern Israel it remains the name for the "lyre"-shaped Sea of Galilee. **the Heights of Dor:** A coastal town which has a long and distinguished history; in the later monarchy, it was eventually a district capital. Today it is the site of major ongoing archaeological excavations.

3 **toward sunrise and toward the Sea:** That is, east and west.

4 **horse and chariot:** In contrast to the inferior Israelite foot soldiers (Meyers 2004).

5 **Merom:** In the vicinity of Tzefat (Safed).

6 And Yhwh said to Yehoshua:
Do not be afraid before them,
for tomorrow at this same time I myself will make all of them
    slain-ones before Israel;
their horses you will maim,
and their chariots you will burn with fire!

7 So Yehoshua came, and all the people of battle with him, against
    them by the Waters of Merom, suddenly,
and they fell upon them.

8 Yhwh gave them into the hand of Israel, and they struck them
and pursued them as far as Greater Sidon and up to Misrefot-
    Mayim and as far as the Cleft of Mitzpe, toward sunrise—
they struck them until they had left them no survivor.

9 Yehoshua did to them as Yhwh had said to him:
their horses he maimed, and their chariots he burned with fire.

10 And Yehoshua turned back at that time and captured Hatzor,
while its king he struck down with the sword,
for Hatzor in former-times was the head [city] of all of these
    kingdoms.

11 They struck down every person who was in it, with the mouth of
    the sword;
he devoted-them-to-destruction
—no one breathing remained—
while Hatzor he burned with fire.

12 And all the towns of these kings, along with all their kings,
    Yehoshua captured and struck them with the mouth of the
    sword;
he devoted-them-to-destruction,
as Moshe, the servant of Yhwh, had commanded.

13 However: all the towns that were standing on their mounds, Israel
    did not burn;
only Hatzor alone did Yehoshua burn.

---

6 **maim:** Usually taken to mean cutting the ham-string muscle; by the time of David, a less perma-nent maiming may have taken place (see note to II Sam. 8:4).

7 **fell upon them:** At this point LXX adds "from the mountain."

8 **Greater Sidon:** The important port city, still promi-nent in today's Lebanon.

13 **standing on their mounds:** Implying that the Israel-ites did not destroy some towns, but settled in them instead.

14 Now all the spoils of these towns, and all the cattle, the Children of
   Israel plundered for themselves;
   only all the humans did they strike down with the mouth of the
   sword, until they had wiped them out—
   they left no one breathing.
15 As YHWH had commanded Moshe his servant,
   thus had Moshe commanded Yehoshua,
   and thus Yehoshua did;
   he did not omit a thing of all that YHWH had commanded Moshe.

16 So Yehoshua took all this land:
   the highlands, all the Negev, and all the region of Goshen,
   the lowlands, and the Plain,
   the highlands of Israel and its lowlands,
17 from Mount Halak that goes up toward Se'ir
   as far as Baal-Gad in the Cleft of the Levanon, beneath Mount
      Hermon.
   All their kings he captured;
   he struck them down and put them to death.
18 For many years Yehoshua engaged all these kings in battle.
19 There was not a town which had concluded peace with the
      Children of Israel
   except for the Hivvites, the settled-folk of Giv'on;
   all were taken in battle.
20 For it was from YHWH, to make their heart strong-willed toward
      battle with Israel,
   in order to devote-them-to-destruction,
   without there being any compassion toward them;
   indeed, it was to wipe them out,
   as YHWH had commanded Moshe.

15 **he did not omit a thing:** The text goes out of its way to establish the continuity in Joshua's actions.
16 **the highlands of Israel and its lowlands:** Referring here to the northern region, later the kingdom of Israel; the "highlands" earlier belonged to Judah, the south.
17 **Mount Halak:** The name connotes "smooth."

18 **years:** Often the meaning of Heb. *yamim*, conventionally "days." See, for instance, I Sam. 1:3, *mi-yamim yamima*, "from year to year" (annually).
20 **it was from YHWH:** It was YHWH's plan. **to make their heart strong-willed:** To make them stubborn, just as God had done to Pharaoh in the Exodus story.

Chapter 12. *The Vanquished Kings:* This brief chapter may serve as a summary of either what has come or what will follow. Indeed, many such lists in the Bible function as textual dividers. While the precise names in lists of this kind are notoriously susceptible to error, the overall effect is rhythmic and hence fitting as a literary marker. The fact that the movement is basically from south to north supports what has gone before. Auld (1998) suggests that the fate of these kings hints at a view often found in this part of the Bible: that there is something problematic in the institution of kingship itself.

21 Yehoshua came at that time
and cut off the Anakites from the highlands, from Hevron, from
Devir, from Anav—
from all the highlands of Judah and from all the highlands of Israel;
along with their towns, Yehoshua devoted-them-to-destruction.

22 There were no Anakites remaining in the land of the Children of
Israel—
only in Gaza, in Gat, and in Ashdod were they left.

23 So Yehoshua took all the land,
exactly as YHWH had promised to Moshe,
and Yehoshua gave it as hereditary-property to Israel, according to
their divisions by their tribes.
And the land was quiet from war.

12:1 Now these are the kings of the land
whom the Children of Israel struck down and of whose land they
took possession,
across the Jordan, toward the rising of the sun,
from the Wadi Arnon to Mount Hermon, and all the Plain toward
sunrise:

2 Sihon king of the Amorites, who sat [enthroned] at Heshbon,
ruling from Aro'er—which is by the bank of Wadi Arnon—and the
middle of the wadi, and half of Gil'ad to Yabbok the Wadi, the
border of the Children of Ammon,

3 and the Plain as far as the Sea of Kinneret, toward sunrise, and as
far as the Sea of the Plain, the Sea of Salt, toward sunrise, by way
of Bet-Yeshimmot,
and southward, beneath the slopes of Pisga,

---

21 **Anakites:** They were taken to be a race of giants and are referred to a number of times in relation to the conquest. **Judah . . . Israel:** Reflecting the later political division of the country into two kingdoms; here, it is either anachronistic or purely geographical.

22 **Gaza . . . Gat . . . Ashdod:** Three of the five cities that come to be connected with the Philistines; the others were Ekron and Ashkelon.

23 **as hereditary-property:** Boling (1982): "in fief," using a term from medieval Europe. The Hebrew root, *n-h-l*, has wider connotations than the generational transfer of property; it is closer to a prop-

erty *claim* and is frequently paralleled with "share / allotment" (Hawk 2000, who suggests "legitimate share").

12:1 **Wadi Arnon:** A stream which empties into the Dead Sea and creates a deep gorge; it served as a boundary between Re'uven in the north and Moav in the south. **all the Plain toward sunrise:** JPS: "The eastern half of the Arabah."

2 **Gil'ad:** Trad. English "Gilead." The territory across the Jordan, northeast of the Dead Sea. **Yabbok:** Pronounced *yah-BOKE;* trad. English "Jabbok," the tributary of the Jordan which historically separated Ammon and the Gil'ad region.

4 as border-territory,
  [and] the territory of Og king of Bashan, from the remnant of the
    Refa'im/Shades, who sat [enthroned] at Ashtarot and at Edre'i,
5 ruling over Mount Hermon and over Salkha and over all of Bashan,
  as far as the border of the Geshurites and of the Maakhatites,
  and half of Gil'ad, [to] the border of Sihon king of Heshbon.
6 Moshe, the servant of YHWH, and the Children of Israel had struck
    them down,
  and Moshe, the servant of YHWH, had given it as a possession to
    the Re'uvenites, to the Gadites, and to the half tribe of Menashe.

7 Now these are the kings of the land whom Yehoshua and the
    Children of Israel struck down across the Jordan, seaward,
  from Baal-Gad in the Levanon Cleft as far as Mount Halak that goes
    up toward Se'ir;
  Yehoshua gave it to the tribes of Israel as a possession, in
    accordance with their divisions,
8 in the highlands and in the lowlands, in the Plain and in the slopes-
    region, in the wilderness and in the Negev—
  the Hittites, the Amorites, and the Canaanites,
  the Perizzites, the Hivvites, and the Yevusites:
9 the king of Jericho, one,
  the king of Ai, which is beside Bet-El, one,
10 the king of Jerusalem, one,
  the king of Hevron, one,
11 the king of Yarmut, one,
  the king of Lakhish, one,
12 the king of Eglon, one,
  the king of Gezer, one,
13 the king of Devir, one,
  the king of Geder, one,
14 the king of Horma, one,
  the king of Arad, one,

---

4 **southward:** Here, and in 13:4, the text uses a different term for "south" (*teiman*). **Pisga:** "Peak," overlooking, from the east, the Jordan and indeed much
of the land of Israel. The Bible marks it as the site
of Moshe's death. **the Refa'im/Shades:** Both in
biblical and ancient Canaanite literature, the term
refa'im refers to the spirits of dead ancestors, who
in popular thinking are not only still active but quite
powerful. Some scholars, on the other hand, simply
understand them as huge, mighty warriors.

6 **Moshe, the servant of** YHWH: The same Deuteronomistic phrase used of him at the beginning of
the book.

15 the king of Livna, one,
  the king of Adullam, one,
16 the king of Makkeda, one,
  the king of Bet-El, one,
17 the king of Tappu'ah, one,
  the king of Heyfer, one,
18 the king of Afek, one,
  the king of Lasharon, one,
19 the king of Madon, one,
  the king of Hatzor, one,
20 the king of Shimron Meron, one,
  the king of Akhshaf, one,
21 the king of Ta'nakh, one,
  the king of Megiddo, one,
22 the king of Kedesh, one,
  the king of Yokne'am at the Carmel, one,
23 the king of Dor in the Height of Dor, one,
  the king of Goyim in Gilgal, one,
24 the king of Tirtza, one;
  all the kings, thirty-one.

18 **Lasharon:** Or "in Sharon"; LXX, on the other hand, reads the whole phrase as "Afek of the Sharon," which parallels v.22's "Yokne'am of the Carmel" (Rainey / Notley).
20 **Shimron Meron:** These may be two separate names.

21 **Megiddo:** The important strategic site at the western side of the Jezreel Valley, overlooking the road to the coastal plain, and hence the site of innumerable battles in antiquity.
23 **Gilgal:** LXX reads "Galil" (Galilee) here.

PART III

ALLOTTING THE LAND

(13–22)

As mentioned earlier, the boundaries laid out in the following chapters appear to be idealized ones, painting a rosy picture of a twelve-tribe unity. The order of presentation is telling. After a general statement about land distribution, the text deals with the Philistine threat in the west and the trans-Jordanian territory to the east. The allotments of important tribes (Yehuda and Yosef), the respective bases of the future Southern and Northern Kingdoms, are then enumerated (Chaps. 14–15). This is followed by distribution for seven landowning tribes, then by the special case of the priestly tribe, Levi, and finally by a return to the troublesome issue of the land occupied east of the Jordan.

As the placement of these boundaries in the time of settlement is difficult to determine from the archaeological evidence, other scholars, such as Rainey / Notley, have suggested that in their present form they correspond to Shelomo's (Solomon's) administrative districts, some centuries after the events portrayed in Joshua. They also allow that such boundaries, at least in part, probably reflect older, established ones. More important is the fact that the text in this section of the book concentrates mainly on six tribes: Efrayim, Menashe, Binyamin, Zevulun, Asher, and Naftali—which, as Rainey / Notley notes, are the very ones summoned for battle by Devora (Deborah) in Judg. 6. So once again, the decidedly northern perspective in Joshua comes into play.

In the process of looking at the larger picture, we should not ignore the detailed description of boundaries that are so tempting for most modern readers to race through. These are significant not only for what they may tell us about ancient borders, but especially as a kind of legal language. Real estate deeds are always necessarily precise, and the seeming minutiae of land description in Joshua, even though they are incomplete in their present form (see below), may have had a similar function—staking out a claim, as it were, for later generations.

Alternatively, Hawk (2000), in an extensive discussion of the latter part of this section of Joshua, sees the boundaries as sometimes fragmentary and indistinct, as if to suggest an undercurrent of incompleteness in the conquest. By Chap. 21, he posits, YHWH has held fast to his promises, but Israel's actions in carrying out its task, especially in dividing up the northern part of the land, are less than ideal. This tension will be taken up again in the opening chapters of the next book, Judges, and permeates the Hebrew Bible in general.

The section begins by noting that Yehoshua is "old, advanced in years." After the boundaries have been enumerated, the same theme and phrase will resume at the end of the book, in 23:1. Thus, almost half the Joshua text, Chaps. 13–22, presents itself as an insertion into the narrative. This is a common occurrence in the Bible (see, for example, Exod. 25–31, which is bracketed by passages laying out laws of the Sabbath) and is further evidence of a complex history for our texts.

Finally, it should be noted that the style of this half of the book seems to reflect different kinds of ancient, perhaps archival lists, with some including names of towns, as in the case of the two and a half Transjordanian tribes, and others, notably Efrayim and Menashe, mentioning borders only (Wazana 2011). And the tenses are sometimes "timeless" (Nelson).

––––––––––

Chapter 13. *Introduction to the Allotment; Eastern Lands:* The book of Joshua began with the centrality of Yehoshua and the mention of the two and a half tribes who settled on the east bank of the Jordan. We now start the account of land allotment, at the book's midpoint, with the same cast of characters (Nelson). The inclusion of the Transjordanian tribes is at best idealistic for later audiences, as their region was not a part of Israelite territory past the ninth or eighth century B.C.E. Structurally, each section regarding the two and a half tribes ends (vv.14 and 33) by alluding to another anomalous situation: the allotment of land to the Levites (Hamilton). And looking ahead, the reference to Yehoshua's old age will return at the end of the book (23:1).

According to many scholars, vv.2–6 are a later, perhaps even exilic or Persian, insertion. As Wazana (2011) proposes, these verses may be here to confirm the returnees' claim to the land. Such a strategy appears elsewhere in the Bible through the use of genealogies, which tend to validate present power structures rather than accurately report ancient realities.

The vocabulary of the chapter is composed of virtually all the previous verbs pertinent to the conquest theme: "possess," "settle," "give," "apportion," and "inherit."

Mitchell points out that from 13:1 on, all references to the indigenous population that remained in the land are to individual, isolated groups and no longer to the generic "Canaanites."

13:1   Now Yehoshua was old, advanced in years,
and Yhwh said to him:
You, you are old, advanced in years,
but the land is left with exceedingly much to possess.

2   This is the land that is left:
all the districts of the Philistines and all the Geshurite [region],

3   —from the Shihor, that is facing Egypt, as far as the territory of
Ekron northward, reckoned to the Canaanites—
five Philistine overlords: the Gazite and the Ashdodite, the
Ashkelonite, the Gittite, the Ekronite, and the Avvites, in the
south;

4   all the land of the Canaanites
including from 'Ara, which belongs to the Sidonians, to Afek, to the
territory of the Amorites,

5   the Giblite region and all of the Levanon, toward the rising of
the sun,
from Baal-Gad beneath Mount Hermon to Levo-Hamat.

6   As for all of the settled-folk of the highlands, from the Levanon to
Misrefot-Mayim—all of the Sidonians,
I myself will dispossess them before the Children of Israel.
Only: have it fall to Israel as hereditary-property, as I have
commanded you.

7   So-now, divide up this land as hereditary-property to the nine tribes
and to the half tribe of Menashe.

8   Along with it, the Re'uvenites and the Gadites had taken their
hereditary-property
that Moshe had given them across the Jordan, toward sunrise,
just as Moshe, the servant of Yhwh, had given them:

13:2 **Geshurite [region]:** A small, often independent kingdom to the northeast of Israel (in today's Golan Heights).

3 **the Shihor:** The word means "lagoon" in Egyptian. **overlords:** The name used for Philistine rulers and, by extension, their cities.

4 **from 'Ara:** Location unknown, perhaps early on, leading to MT *me'ara,* "cave," and LXX "from Gaza" (reflecting *me-'azza*).

5 **the Giblite region:** Belonging to the Gebalites. The name refers to Byblos, a Phoenician seaport north of Sidon. **the Levanon:** JPS understands this as "the Valley" (of the Levanon).

6 **fall:** By lot.

7 **Menashe:** LXX follows this with "from the Jordan to the Great Sea in the west you shall give it, the Great Sea being the border."

8 **it:** The other half of the tribe of Menashe.

◆

9 from Aro'er which is at the shore of Wadi Arnon, and the town
     that is in the middle of the wadi [valley], and all the plateau of
     Medeva, as far as Divon,

10 and all the towns of Sihon king of the Amorites, who reigned as
     king in Heshbon,
    as far as the territory of the Children of Ammon,

11 and Gil'ad, and the territory of the Geshurites and the Maakhatites,
     and all of Mount Hermon, and all of Bashan, as far as Salkha,

12 and all the kingdom of Og in Bashan, who reigned as king in
     Ashtarot and in Edre'i
    —he was the one left of the remnant of the Shades—:
    Moshe had struck them and had dispossessed them,

13 but the Children of Israel did not dispossess the Geshurites and the
     Maakhatites;
    Geshur and Maakha have remained settled in the midst of Israel,
     until this day.

14 Only to the tribe of Levi did he not give hereditary-property;
    the fire-offerings of YHWH, the God of Israel, are its hereditary-
     property, as he promised it.

15 Moshe had given to the tribe of Re'uven, according to their clans:

16 now the territory for them was
    from Aro'er which is at the shore of the Wadi Arnon, and the town
     that is in the middle of the wadi [valley], and all the plateau
     around Medeva,

17 Heshbon and all its towns that are on the plateau:
    Divon, Bamot-Baal, and Bet-Baal Me'on,

18 Yahtza, Kedemot, and Mefaat,

19 Kiryatayim, Sivma, and Tzeret-Shahar on the mountain of the
     valley,

---

9 **middle of the wadi [valley]:** And not in the wadi itself, which at certain times of year would be running with water. **Medeva:** Pronounced *may-de-VAH;* trad. English "Medaba," an oft-conquered town in Moabite territory, it is famous as the site of much later (sixth century C.E.) church mosaics that represent the earliest known map of sites in the land of Israel. NOTE: The many place-names that follow in these chapters are given in Hebrew forms, generally without traditional English equivalents in the Notes.

14 **fire-offerings:** Or "gifts." In this verse the word is awkward, and probably a later insertion, since it is lacking in the exact parallel verse in 13:33. **it:** Or "concerning them" (JPS).

16 **territory:** This is the same Hebrew word (*gevul*) that usually means "boundary, border" in Joshua. See also v.25, 18:11, and 19:18.

19 **Kiryatayim:** Meaning "twin cities."

20 Bet-Pe'or, the Pisga Slopes, and Bet-Ha-Yeshimmot:
21 including all the towns of the plateau, and all the kingdom of Sihon
 king of the Amorites, who reigned as king in Heshbon,
 whom Moshe had struck along with the leaders of Midyan:
 Evi, Rekem, Tzur, Hur, and Reva, the chiefs of Sihon, those settled
 in the land,
22 while Bil'am son of Be'or, the soothsayer, the Children of Israel
 killed with the sword, in addition to their slain.

23 And the border of the Children of Re'uven was the Jordan, and the
 bordering-territory.
 This was the hereditary-property of the Children of Re'uven for
 their clans,
 the towns and their farmsteads.

24 Moshe had given to the tribe of Gad, for the Children of Gad, for
 their clans:
25 now the territory for them was:
 Ya'zer and all the towns of Gil'ad, half the land of the Children of
 Ammon, as far as Aro'er, which faces Rabba,
26 and from Heshbon as far as Ramat Ha-Mitzpe and Betonim, and
 from Mahanayim as far as the territory of Lo-Devar,
27 and in the Valley, Bet-Haram, Bet-Nimra, Sukkot, and Tzafon,
 the remnant of the kingdoms of Sihon king of Heshbon,
 the Jordan and the bordering-territory, as far as the edge of the Sea
 of Kinneret,
 across the Jordan toward sunrise.
28 This was the hereditary-property of the Children of Gad, for their
 clans,
 the towns and their farmsteads.

---

20 **Bet-Ha-Yeshimmot:** "The House of Wastelands," an appropriate name for a location at the Dead Sea (Boling 1982).

21 **chiefs:** Some understand as "vassals."

22 **while Bil'am . . . :** See the famous story of Bil'am (Balaam), who was hired to curse the Israelites, in Num. 22–24. Here he is dismissed as a mere "sooth- sayer" (Heb. *kosem*), as part of the negative reassess- ment of him in such passages as Num. 31:8, 16, Deut. 23:5–6, and Josh. 24:9–10.

23 **farmsteads:** Others, "villages."

26 **Lo-Devar:** As per II Sam. 9:4 and 17:27; MT has "Lid- vir," "belonging to Devir."

Chapter 14. *Calev of Yehuda:* Instead of launching immediately into the tribal apportioning of land, Chap. 14 presents, first, a general statement (vv.1–5), and then a personalized account of how Hevron was given to Calev, the only "good" spy of Num. 13 besides Yehoshua. It makes sense, perhaps, to start the allotments with one whose loyalty to God could be held up as a model for Israelite behavior and whose Judahite affiliation fits the general thrust of this section of the Bible.

Additionally, the order of allotments begins with, first, the tribe of Yehuda, and then Yosef—the two tribes that represent the later Southern Kingdom and Northern Kingdom, respectively.

29 Moshe had given to the half tribe of Menashe,
 for the half group of the Children of Menashe, according to their
  clans:
30 now their territory was
 from Mahanayim, all of Bashan, all the kingdom of Og king of
  Bashan,
 and all the tent-villages of Ya'ir that were in Bashan, sixty towns;
31 half of Gil'ad,
 Ashtarot and Edre'i, towns of the kingdom of Og in Bashan,
 to the Children of Makhir son of Menashe—to half the Children of
  Makhir—for their clans.
32 These it was that Moshe had given-as-hereditary-property in the
  Plains of Moav, across the Jordan [at] Jericho, toward sunrise.
33 But to the tribe of Levi, Moshe had given no hereditary-property;
 YHWH, the God of Israel—he is their hereditary-property,
 as he promised them.

14:1 Now these were what the Children of Israel received-as-hereditary-
  property in the land of Canaan,
 which El'azar the priest and Yehoshua son of Nun and the heads
  of the Fathers of the tribes among the Children of Israel
  distributed-as-property to them
2 by the lot as their hereditary-property,
 as YHWH had commanded by the hand of Moshe
 for the nine tribes and the half tribe.
3 For Moshe had given the hereditary-property of the two tribes and
  the half tribe across the Jordan,
 but to the Levites he had not given hereditary-property in their
  midst.
4 For the Children of Yosef were two tribes, Menashe and Efrayim,
 but they had not given a portion to the Levites in the land,
 except for some towns to settle in and their pasture-lands for their
  cattle and their acquisitions.

---

29 **for the half group:** Here a different word (*matteh*) is used than the usual one for "tribe" (*shevet*).
32 **Moav:** Trad. English "Moab."
14:1 **these:** The parcels of land. **El'azar:** Trad. English "Eleazar," the High Priest and son of Aharon (Aaron). The book will end with his death and burial. **Fathers:** In this context, the word indicates clans or extended families.
3 **Levites . . . not given hereditary-property:** As specified in the Torah, for instance in Deut. 18:1–2.
4 **pasture-lands:** Or "grazing lands." **acquisitions:** Other livestock.

Chapter 15. *Yehuda's Territory:* The bulk of what was to become the Kingdom of Judah for three and a half centuries lies within the borders enumerated here. Interestingly, the list ignores the presence of the contiguous Philistines (Auld 1998). The fact that this list is the longest and richest of all indicates the importance of Yehuda/Judah in Israelite history and historiography. Its boundaries may reflect actual districts established during the monarchy (Meyers 1998).

Before the many towns of Yehuda are listed, the role of Calev is reprised, with the additional little story of his wife, Akhsa, that will be retold in Judg. 1.

Some of the conquest details enumerated in this chapter suggest later composition, principally the mention of coastal areas (vv.45–47) and the Dead Sea, where either historical circumstances or lack of archaeological evidence pushes the text beyond the time of Yehoshua.

The chapter ends with an admission of failure. Jerusalem is not captured, and indeed was to remain outside the Israelite sphere (see the Levite's fateful reluctance to stay overnight there in Judg. 19) until the text reports its conquest and building up by David in II Sam. 5:6–9.

5 As YHWH had commanded Moshe, thus the Children of Israel did;
   so they divided up the land.

6 The Children of Yehuda approached Yehoshua at Gilgal,
   and Calev son of Yefunneh the Kenizzite said to him:
   You yourself know the word that YHWH spoke to Moshe the man
      of God
   regarding me and regarding you, at Kadesh-Barne'a.

7 Forty years old was I when Moshe the servant of YHWH sent me
      from Kadesh- Barne'a to spy out the land,
   and I brought him back word, just as was in my heart.

8 But my brothers who went up with me melted the heart of the
      people [with fear],
   while I fully-followed after YHWH my God.

9 So Moshe swore on that day, saying:
   If the land on which your foot has tread does not become
      hereditary-property for you and for your children, into the
      ages . . . !
   since you have fully-followed after YHWH your God.

10 So-now, here, YHWH has kept me alive, as he promised, these forty-
      five years,
   from when YHWH spoke this word to Moshe,
   when Israel was going through the wilderness.
   And now, here, today I am eighty-five years old;

11 I am still as strong today
   as on the day of Moshe's sending me—
   as my might was then, so my might is now for battle,
   for going out and for coming in.

---

6 **Yehuda:** Pronounced *ye-hoo-DAH;* trad. English "Judah." **Calev:** Pronounced *kah-LAVE;* trad. English "Caleb." Along with Yehoshua, he was the only other optimistic spy of Num. 14. They alone survive of the generation whose lack of trust in YHWH resulted in their dying out in the wilderness, before the book of Joshua begins. **Kenizzite:** A non-Israelite group later absorbed into the tribe of Yehuda (Meyers 2004). **regarding you:** Plural.

7 **just as was in my heart:** Heb. "with my heart"— a true, honest report, along with that of Yehoshua himself, unlike the panic-stricken account of the ten other spies.

8 **melted the heart of the people [with fear]:** That is, discouraged them from going up to conquer the land. **fully-followed after:** The verb stem connotes "fullness"; JPS: "was loyal to."

9 **If the land . . . does not . . . :** This "incomplete oath" construction, common in biblical Hebrew, implies that if something is not true, "may such and such happen to me."

11 **for going out and for coming in:** A biblical expression often denoting leading the troops.

12 So-now, give me these highlands, which YHWH promised me on
that day,
—for you yourself heard on that day—
though Anakites are there, and great and fortified towns;
perhaps YHWH will be with me, and I will dispossess them,
as YHWH promised.
13 So Yehoshua blessed him
and gave Hevron to Calev son of Yefunneh as hereditary-property.
14 Therefore Hevron is hereditary-property for Calev son of Yefunneh
the Kenizzite, until this day,
because he was fully-true to YHWH, the God of Israel.
15 Now the name of Hevron formerly was Kiryat-Arba;
he was the greatest man among the Anakites.
And the land was quiet from war.

15:1 Now the allotment for the tribe of the Children of Yehuda, for their
clans, was:
to the border of Edom, at the Wilderness of Tzyn, toward the
south, as the rightmost edge.
2 The border for them, on the south, was from the edge of the Sea of
Salt, from the "tongue" that faces the south.
3 Then it goes out south of Scorpions' Pass, and crosses over to Tzyn.
Then it goes up south of Kadesh-Barne'a
and crosses over to Hetzron and went up to Addar, swinging
around to Karka.
4 Then it crosses over to Atzmon and goes out to the Wadi of Egypt;
and the outer-reaches of the border are at the Sea
. . . this will be the border for you on the south.
5 And the border on the east: the Sea of Salt, as far as the edge of the
Jordan;
and the border on the north side:
from the "tongue" of the Sea, from the edge of the Jordan.

---

15 **he was:** Namely, Arba.
15:1 **Edom:** The area south and slightly east of the Dead
Sea, it is in southwestern Jordan today. **Wilderness of Tzyn:** In northeastern Sinai, south of the
Negev.
2 **the "tongue":** The bay.
3 **Then:** Multiple times in this chapter I have rendered
Heb. *vav* as "then" rather than as "and," to convey

the running descriptive flavor of the drawing of borders. **south of:** Heb. *negev;* LXX reads "opposite"
(*neged*). **Scorpions' Pass:** Lit. "Scorpions' Ascent."
See Num. 34:4.
4 **Wadi of Egypt:** The present-day Wadi El-Arish,
south of Gaza.
5 **edge:** The mouth of the Jordan, at the Dead Sea.

6 Then the border goes up to Bet-Hogla, and crosses north of Bet-
 Arava.
 Then the border goes up to the Stone of Bohan son of Re'uven.
7 Then the border goes up to Devir from the Valley of Disaster and
 faces toward Gilgal,
 which is opposite Red Pass, which is south of the wadi.
 Then the border crosses over to the waters of the Sun Spring;
 its outer-reaches are at Rogel Spring.
8 Then the border goes up the Ravine of the Son of Hinnom, along
 the shoulder of the Yevusite, on the south—that is Jerusalem.
 Then the border goes up to the top of the hill that faces the Ravine
 of Ben Hinnom, seaward,
 which is at the edge of the Valley of the Shades, northward.
9 Then the border diverges from the top of the hill at the Spring
 of the Waters of Neftoah and goes out to the towns of Mount
 Efron.
 Then the border diverges toward Baala—that is Kiryat-Ye'arim.
10 Then the border swings around from Baala seaward to Mount Se'ir,
 and crosses to the shoulder of Mount Ye'arim, northward—that is
 Kesalon—
 and goes down to Bet-Shemesh and crosses over by Timna.
11 Then the border goes out to the shoulder of Ekron, northward.
 Then the border diverges toward Shikkeron and crosses to Mount
 Baala.
 Then it goes out to Yavne'el;
 the outer-reaches of the border are at the Sea.
12 And the seaward border
 is the Great Sea, and the [adjacent] territory.
 This is the border of the Children of Yehuda, all around, for their
 clans.

6 **Stone of Bohan:** Possibly meaning a "thumb-shaped" stone.
7 **Valley of Disaster:** See Chap. 7, above. **Gilgal:** Not necessarily the prominent Gilgal of earlier in the book. A number of place-names are used for multiple sites in the Bible; another example would be Afek.
8 **the Ravine of the Son of Hinnom:** Or "of Ben Hinnom." This valley, immediately south of today's Old City of Jerusalem, came to be associated with the once-burning fires of child sacrifice (see II Kings 23:10). Jeremiah (7:31–32) saw it as the place of ultimate punishment, and in this sense, the Hebrew name for the valley, *Gei-Hinnom,* passed into later Judaism (and Christianity and Islam as well) as *Gehinnom* or *Gehenna,* "Hell." **shoulder:** This anatomical term connotes "ridge."
9 **diverges:** or "veers off." The syntactic form of the Hebrew verb, which itself occurs only in Joshua, suggests a late usage (Rainey/Notley). **Waters of Neftoah:** 'Ain Lifta, near the northwestern edge of Jerusalem today. **towns:** LXX has "ruins."

13 Now to Calev son of Yefunneh he gave a portion amid the Children
of Yehuda, at Yhwh's order to Yehoshua:
Kiryat-Arba, the father of the Anakites—that is Hevron.

14 And Calev dispossessed from there the three sons of Anak—
Sheshai, Ahiman, and Talmai, those born of Anak.

15 He went up from there against the settled-folk of Devir
—now the name of Devir formerly was Kiryat-Sefer.

16 And Calev said:
The one who strikes Kiryat-Sefer and captures it,
I will give him Akhsa my daughter as a wife!

17 Otniel son of Kenaz, Calev's brother, captured it,
so he gave him Akhsa his daughter as a wife.

18 And it was when she came, that she induced him to request a field
from her father.
When she alighted from the donkey, Calev said to her:
What [ails] you?

19 She said:
Give me a gift-of-blessing!
Indeed, you have given me arid land;
you should give me pools of water!
So he gave her the Upper Pools and the Lower Pools.

20 This is the hereditary-property of the tribe of the Children of
Yehuda, for their clans:

21 the towns at the edge of the tribe of the Children of Yehuda
toward the border of Edom, in the Negev:
Kavtze'el, Eider, and Yagur,

22 Kina, Dimona, and Ad'ada,

23 Kedesh and Hatzar-Yitnan,

24 Zif, Telem, and Be'alot,

25 Hatzor-Hadatta and the hamlets of Hetzron—that is Hatzor,

26 Amam, Shema, and Molada,

---

14 **those born of:** Boling (1982) theorizes that this
indicates not biological ties but rather some form
of military initiation. JPS, on the other hand, uses
"descendants of."

15 **Kiryat-Sefer:** "City of Documents/Records."

17 **brother:** The word can carry the meaning of kinsman as well as sibling. **Akhsa:** Pronounced *akh-
SAH*; trad. English "Achsah."

18 **she induced him:** LXX indicates that he is the active

party, but see the repeated story in Judg. 1:14, where
MT (with Akhsa as the active chief actor) makes
more sense. **field:** A fertile one.

19 **arid land:** Or "the Southland" (Heb. *negev*). JPS
understands the expression as referring to Akhsa
herself, namely, a woman without a dowry.

23 **Hatzar-Yitnan:** MT has "Hatzar and Yitnan," but
the former grammatically needs to be connected
with the latter, as in the examples from vv.27 and 28.

27 Hatzar-Gadda, Heshmon, and Bet-Pelet,

28 Hatzar-Shual, Be'er-Sheva, and Bizyotya,

29 Baala, Iyyim, and Etzem,

30 Eltolad, Kesil, and Horma,

31 Tziklag, Madmanna, and Sansanna,

32 Levaot, Shilhim, and Rimmon Spring—
all the towns: twenty-nine, and their farmsteads.

33 In the lowlands:
Eshtaol, Tzor'a, and Ashna,

34 Zanoah and Gannim Spring,
Tappu'ah and Enam,

35 Yarmut and Adullam,
Sokho and Azeka,

36 Shaarayim and Aditayim,
Gedera and Gederotayim—
towns, fourteen, and their farmsteads;

37 Tzanan, Hadasha, and Migdal Gad,

38 Dil'am, Mitzpe, and Yokte'el,

39 Lakhish, Botzkat, and Eglon,

40 Kabbon, Lahmas, and Kitlish,

41 Gedeirot, Bet-Dagon, Naama, and Makkeda—
towns, sixteen, and their farmsteads;

42 Livna, Eter, and Asham,

43 Yiftah, Ashna, and Netziv,

44 Ke'ila, Akhziv, and Maresha—
towns, nine, and their farmsteads;

45 Ekron and its daughter-towns, and its farmsteads,

46 from Ekron seaward
all those near Ashdod, and their farmsteads,

47 Ashdod, its daughter-towns and its farmsteads,
Gaza, its daughter-towns and its farmsteads,
as far as the Wadi of Egypt, up to the Great Sea and the border-
territory;

28 **Bizyotya:** LXX reads this as *u-v'noteha*, "and its daughter-towns," a common term in these texts for "dependencies" (Boling 1982).

32 **Rimmon Spring:** Again following LXX, which reads *'Ayin Rimmon* as *'En Rimmon*, "Pomegranate Spring."

36 **fourteen:** The list from vv.33 to 36 actually includes fifteen towns; medieval Jewish commentators attempted to solve the problem by reducing two of the towns to one.

Chapter 16. *Efrayim's Territory:* With an opening section (vv.1–4) that speaks of the allotment to Yosef (and hence in the northern section of the country), that designation immediately splits off into its two historical tribal components, with Efrayim the subject of the rest of this brief chapter. Note that this chapter too ends with an admission of failure, in the survival of the Canaanite population of Gezer. It and Chap. 17 also constitute a much fuzzier account than that of Yehuda, perhaps for editorial/ideological reasons.

The hereditary region of Efrayim contained a number of towns important in biblical narrative, including Shilo (see Chap. 18 and the first four chapters of Judges) and Bet-El (see, for instance, I Kings 13).

48 in the highlands:
   Shamir, Yattir, and Sokho,
49 Danna, Kiryat-Sanna—that is Devir,
50 Anav, Eshtemo, and Anim,
51 Goshen, Holon, and Gilo—
   towns, eleven, and their farmsteads;
52 Arav, Duma, and Esh'an,
53 Yanum, Bet-Tappuah, and Afeka,
54 Humta, Kiryat-Arba—that is Hevron—and Tzi'or—
   towns, nine, and their farmsteads;
55 Ma'on, Carmel, Zif, and Yutta,
56 Yizre'el, Yokde'am, and Zanoah,
57 Kayin, Giv'a, and Timna—
   towns, ten, and their farmsteads;
58 Halhul, Bet-Tzur, and Gedor,
59 Maarat, Bet-Anot, and Eltekon—
   towns, six, and their farmsteads;
60 Kiryat-Baal—that is Kiryat-Ye'arim—and Rabba—
   towns, two, and their farmsteads;
61 in the wilderness:
   Bet-Arava, Middin, and Sekhakha,
62 Nivshan, Salt City, and En-Gedi—
   towns, six, and their farmsteads.
63 Now as for the Yevusites, the settled-folk of Jerusalem,
   the Children of Yehuda were not able to dispossess them,
   so the Yevusites are settled with the Children of Yehuda in
       Jerusalem, until this day.

16:1 And the allotment for the Children of Yosef went out from Jordan
       [at] Jericho, to the waters of Jericho, toward sunrise, into the
       wilderness,
   going up from Jericho through the highlands to Bet-El.
2 Then it goes out from Bet-El to Luz,
   and crosses to the border of the Arkites at Atarot.

---

59 **and their farmsteads:** This phrase is followed in LXX by a list of eleven towns situated south of Jerusalem.
16:1 **Yosef:** Pronounced *yo-SAYF*; trad. English "Joseph."

2 **Arkites:** A group belonging to the tribe of Bin-yamin.

Chapter 17. *Menashe's Territory:* The boundaries of this tribe are preceded by a retelling in summary form of the Daughters of Tzelofhad story from Num. 27, in which inheritance played the key role. In that instance, a man died without male heirs, and Moshe was prevailed upon, by God as well as by the women themselves, to pass the family land on to females.

The territory of Menashe comprised the largest and biblically most significant region in the north, extending from the Mediterranean to the Jordan, and included the key towns of Megiddo, Bet-She'an, and Shekhem, among others.

For a third time in our text, the Israelites cannot dispossess the Canaanites from some areas (vv.12–13).

The allotment of the Children of Yosef is rounded out in vv.14–18, with a kind of pioneer movement into forested hill-country encouraged by Yehoshua.

3 Then it goes down seaward to the border of the Yafletites, as far as
the border of Lower Bet-Horon and as far as Gezer;
its outer-reaches are at the Sea.

4 Thus were the Children of Yosef, Menashe and Efrayim, given
hereditary-property.

5 Now the boundary of the Children of Efrayim, according to their
clans, was:
the border of their hereditary-property was, toward sunrise, from
Atarot-Addar as far as Upper Bet-Horon.

6 Then the border goes out seaward to Mikhmetat on the north.
Then the border swings around toward sunrise to Taanat Shilo,
and crosses by it, sunrise to Yanoah.

7 Then it goes down from Yanoah to Atarot and to Naara and
touches Jericho, and goes out to the Jordan;

8 from Tappuah the border goes seaward, to the Wadi Kama,
and its outer-reaches are at the Sea.
This is the hereditary-property of the Children of Efrayim, for their
clans,

9 with the towns set apart for the Children of Efrayim amid the
hereditary-property of the Children of Menashe,
all the towns and their farmsteads.

10 But they were not able to dispossess the Canaanites, those settled in
Gezer,
so the Canaanites remained settled amid Efrayim, to this day;
they became laboring serfs.

17:1 And the allotment for the tribe of Menashe was—since he was the
firstborn of Yosef—
for Makhir firstborn of Menashe, father of Gil'ad, since he was a
man of battle,
and Gil'ad and Bashan belonged to him [already].

---

3 **Yafletites:** An unknown group living on the border
between Efrayim and Binyamin.
7 **touches:** The verb is used in these texts to describe
the meeting of borders; some use "impinges on."

17:1 **a man of battle:** JPS: "a valiant warrior." God is so
described in the Song at the Sea, Exod. 15:3.

2 So it was for the rest of the Children of Menashe, according to their clans:
for the Children of Avi'ezer, for the Children of Helek, for the Children of Asriel, for the Children of Shekhem, for the Children of Heyfer, for the Children of Shemida—
these were the Children of Menashe son of Yosef, the males for their clans.

3 Now Tzelofhad son of Heyfer son of Gil'ad son of Makhir son of Menashe—he had no sons, but rather daughters,
and these were his daughters' names:
Mahla, No'a, Hogla, Milka, and Tirtza.

4 They came before El'azar the priest and before Yehoshua son of Nun and before the exalted-leaders, saying:
YHWH commanded Moshe to give us hereditary-property amid our brothers!
And they were given, by the order of YHWH, hereditary-property amid their father's brothers.

5 The measured-areas falling to Menashe [were] ten,
aside from the land of Gil'ad and Bashan, which are across the Jordan,

6 for the daughters of Menashe inherited hereditary-property amid their brothers,
while the land of Gil'ad was for the rest of the Children of Menashe.

7 And the border of Menashe was:
from Asher to Mikhmetat, which faces Shekhem,
then the border goes to the right/the south, toward Yashuv [and] En Tappuah,

8 —belonging to Menashe was the region of Tappuah, but Tappuah is on the border of Menashe, belonging to the Children of Efrayim—

---

4 **our brothers:** Meaning "kin," since they clearly had no brothers.
5 **measured-areas:** Boling (1982): "shares." The Hebrew is related to the word for "rope," hence the idea of measuring.

7 **to the right/the south:** The general orientation here is toward the east, so to face right is to face the south. **Yashuv:** Either a place name (LXX) or, following MT, *yoshevei*, "the settled-folk of."

9   then the border goes down to the Wadi Kana.
South of the wadi, these towns belonged to Efrayim amid the
    towns of Menashe;
the border of Menashe was north of the wadi,
and all their outer-reaches are at the Sea.

10   The southland belongs to Efrayim and the north belongs to
    Menashe, and the Sea is its border;
Asher they touch on the north, and Yissakhar toward sunrise.

11   There belonged to Menashe in Yissakhar and Asher:
Bet-She'an and its daughter-towns, Yivle'am and its daughter-
    towns,
along with the settled-folk of Dor and its daughter-towns,
the settled-folk of En Dor and its daughter-towns, the settled-
    folk of Ta'nakh and its daughter-towns, and the settled-folk of
    Megiddo and its daughter-towns, the Three Heights.

12   But the Children of Menashe were not able to dispossess these
    towns;
the Canaanites persisted in remaining-settled in this land.

13   It was, when the Children of Israel grew strong, that they put the
    Canaanites into forced-labor,
but dispossess, they could not dispossess them.

14   Now the Children of Yosef spoke to Yehoshua, saying:
For-what-reason have you given me as hereditary-property [only]
    one allotment, one area?
For I am a numerous people,
since until now YHWH has blessed me greatly!

15   Yehoshua said to them:
If you are [such] a numerous people,
go you up into the forest
and clear [ground] for yourself there in the land of the Perizzites
    and of the Refaites,
since the highlands of Efrayim are too confining for you!

---

9 **these towns . . . :** Boling (1982) understands the
whole phrase as a question, "Do these belong to
Efrayim, amidst towns of Menashe?"

11 **There belonged to Menashe . . . :** The text here is
in a somewhat garbled state; see the discussion in
Nelson.   **Three Heights:** Denoting a region.

15 **the forest:** Hinting at the extensive forestation of
Canaan in biblical times. Already by the Roman
period, some centuries later, the clearing of the
countryside was quite advanced.

Chapter 18. *The Shilo Conference; Binyamin's Territory:* Here begins the allotment of territory for the remaining tribes. The text over the next two chapters has an almost ceremonial ring to it, as it commences with the people's assembly at the holy city of Shilo and introduces the practice of registering the territories in writing. Israel's coming-of-age as a community had been heralded with the writing down of the covenant in Exod. 19–24; now that it becomes a full-fledged people with the acquisition of a land, writing appears once again. The text starts with Binyamin, seemingly as a logical next step in the march from south to north, but more likely based on the concept of traditional familial order, with Yaakov's main wives' sons first, and then those of the maidservants (Gen. 30; Nelson).

Binyamin's region contained Jerusalem, hence the text's detailed interest here. It also descended several thousand feet to Jericho on the east.

16 The Children of Yosef said:
　There is not [enough] for us in the highlands,
　　but iron chariots are everywhere among the Canaanites who are
　　　settled in the valley region,
　　those in Bet-She'an and its daughter-towns and those in the Valley
　　　of Yizre'el.
17 Yehoshua said to the House of Yosef, to Efrayim and to Menashe,
　　saying:
　You are a numerous people,
　and you have great might;
　you shall not have [just] one allotment,
18 for the highlands shall be yours, since it is forest—
　you are to clear it, and its outer-reaches will be yours,
　for you will dispossess the Canaanites,
　though they have iron chariots,
　though they are strong.

18:1 Now the entire community of the Children of Israel assembled at
　　Shilo
　and they set up there the Tent of Appointment,
　since the land was subdued before them.
2 And there remained among the Children of Israel, whose
　　hereditary-property had not been divided up, seven tribes.
3 So Yehoshua said to the Children of Israel:
　Until when will you show yourselves slack
　in coming, in settling the land that YHWH, the God of your Fathers,
　　has given you?
4 Provide yourselves three men per tribe, that I may send them out
　Let them arise and walk about in the land,
　　that they may write it up according to their hereditary-property;
　　then let them come back to me.

---

16 **There is not:** Heb. "There is not found." **iron chariots:** The vaunted military superiority afforded by the Canaanite iron chariots is made more explicit in Judg. 4:7, 13, and 5:28. The use of iron seems to have been mainly in the chariots' fittings (Hess).

17 **the House of Yosef:** As Meyers (2004) notes, "the Children of Yosef" would be more common here, but the text wishes to emphasize the northern tribes.

18 **outer-reaches:** Understood in this case by Boling (1982) as "approaches."

18:1 **Shilo:** Pronounced *shee-LO*, this site houses the Coffer and is thus an important religious center in the traditions of Judges and Samuel. **Tent of Appointment:** Following its installation at Shilo in Yehoshua's days, the tent shrine itself figures very little in later accounts of Israelite worship, especially contrasted to its centrality in the Torah's account of the early wanderings.

3 **Until when:** Or "how long."

4 **write it up:** Others, "describe" (which, appropriately, is related to "inscribe" in English).

5   They are to divide it among themselves into seven divisions:
Judah will be situated on his territory in the Negev,
while the House of Yosef will be situated on their territory in the
    north.

6   As for you, you are to write up the land as seven portions and have
    it come to me here,
that I may cast the lot for you here, in the presence of YHWH
    our God.

7   For the Levites have no portion in your midst,
since the priesthood of YHWH is their hereditary-property,
and Gad, Re'uven, and the half tribe of Menashe have taken their
    hereditary-property across the Jordan, toward sunrise,
which Moshe, the servant of God, gave them.

8   The men arose and were about to go,
and Yehoshua commanded those who were going to write up the
    land, saying:
Go, go about through the land and write it up, and return to me;
it is here that I shall cast lots for you in the presence of YHWH at
    Shilo.

9   The men went and crossed through the land,
and they wrote it up, regarding the towns, as seven portions, in a
    record;
then they came back to Yehoshua in the camp at Shilo.

10 And Yehoshua cast lots for them at Shilo, in the presence of YHWH,
and Yehoshua divided up the land there for the Children of Israel,
    according to their divisions.

11 The lot came up of the tribe of the Children of Binyamin, for their
    clans:
the territory of their allotment went out between the Children of
    Judah and the Children of Yosef;

12 the border for them, on the northern side, [starting] from the
    Jordan.

5 **Judah:** Elsewhere I use the Hebrew form, "Yehuda,"
referring to the tribe; but here it signifies the later,
larger Southern Kingdom.

Then the border goes up to the shoulder of Jericho on the north
and goes up into the highlands, seaward;
its outer-reaches are at the Wilderness of Bet-Aven.

13 Then the border crosses from there to Luz, on the shoulder of Luz,
toward the Negev
—that is Bet-El.
Then the border goes down toward Atarot-Addar,
on the hill that faces Lower Bet-Horon.

14 Then the border diverges and swings around on the seaward side,
toward the Negev, from the hill that faces Bet-Horon, toward the
Negev;
its outer-reaches are at Kiryat-Baal—that is Kiryat-Ye'arim, a town
of the Children of Yehuda—
that is the seaward side.

15 And on the Negev side, from the edge of Kiryat-Ye'arim,
the border goes seaward, and then goes out to the Spring of the
Waters of Neftoah.

16 Then the border goes down to the edge of the hill that faces the
Ravine of the Son of Hinnom, that is in the Valley of the Shades,
northward.
Then it goes down in the Ravine of Hinnom to the Yevusite
shoulder, toward the Negev,
and goes down to Rogel Spring.

17 Then it diverges from the north
and comes out at the Spring of the Sun.
Then it goes out Gelilot, that is opposite Red Pass.
Then it goes down to the Stone of Bohan son of Re'uven.

18 Then it crosses to the shoulder opposite the Plain, northward,
and goes down to the Plain.

19 Then the border crosses to the shoulder of Bet-Hogla, on the
north;
the outer-reaches of the border are at the tongue of the Sea of Salt,
on the north,

---

13 **that is Bet-El:** Referring to Luz.
18 **the Plain:** LXX: "to Bet-Arava." The phrase indicates the Jordan Valley.

Chapter 19. *The Other Six Tribes:* From here the text branches out to include Shim'on, whose territory lies wholly within Yehuda's, and a group of five northern tribes, including Dan, who migrates in Judg. 18, as a latecomer in the extreme north. The chapter ends basically as the book itself will, with Yehoshua and his inheritance (parallel to his burial in Chap. 24), and mention of the High Priest, El'azar, whose death will adorn the entire book's last lines. Yehoshua's inheritance also closes a bracket: what began in 14:6ff. with Calev's inheritance here rounds out the parceling out of land to the tribes west of the Jordan (Hess).

at the edge of the Jordan, on the south-side
—that is the border on the south.

20 And the Jordan borders it on the eastern side.
This is the hereditary-property of the Children of Binyamin, for
their clans, according to its borders all around, for their clans.

21 And the towns that were the tribe of the Children of Binyamin's,
for their clans, are:
Jericho, Bet-Hogla, and Emek Ketzitz,

22 Bet-Arava, Tzemarayim, and Bet-El,

23 Avvim, Para, and Ofra,

24 Kefar-Ammona, Ofni, and Geva—
towns, twelve, and their farmsteads;

25 Giv'on, Rama, and Be'erot,

26 Mitzpe, Kefira, and Motza,

27 Rekem, Yirpael, and Tar'ala,

28 Tzela, Elef, the Yevusite—that is Jerusalem,
Giv'at and Kiryat__—
towns, fourteen, and their farmsteads.
This was the hereditary-property of Binyamin, for their clans.

19:1 The second lot came out for Shim'on, for the tribe of the Children
of Shim'on, for their clans;
their hereditary-property was amid the hereditary-property of the
Children of Yehuda.

2 They had in their hereditary-property:
Be'er-Sheva, Sheva, and Molada,

3 Hatzar-Shual, Bala, and Etzem,

4 Eltolad, Betul, and Horma,

5 Tziklag, Bet-Markavot, and Hatzar-Susa,

6 Bet-Levaot, and Sharuhen—
towns, thirteen, and their farmsteads;

---

28 **Kiryat__:** The Hebrew form of the name is incomplete (lit. "city of . . . ," similar to "___ville" in English). JPS proposes "Kiryat-Ye'arim," following the "Kiryat-'Arim" of Ezra 2:25.

19:1 **Shim'on:** Pronounced *shim-OHN;* trad. English "Simeon."

2 **Be'er-Sheva:** Trad. English "Beersheba."

6 **thirteen:** The count is again wrong—a mistake by either a scribe or in our understanding of separate names on the list.

7 Ayin, Rimmon, Eter, and Ashan—
   towns, four, and their farmsteads;

8 and all the farmsteads that are around these towns, as far as Baalat-
   Be'er, [and] Ramat Negev.
   This is the hereditary-property of the tribe of Shim'on, for their
   clans.

9 From the area of the Children of Yehuda was the hereditary-
   property of the Children of Shim'on,
   for the portion of the Children of Yehuda was too large for them,
   so the Children of Shim'on received hereditary-property amid their
   hereditary-property.

10 The third lot came up for the Children of Zevulun for their clans;
   the border of their hereditary-property is as far as Sarid.

11 Their border goes up toward the Sea and Mar'ala, touching
   Dabbeshet,
   and touches the wadi that faces Yokne'am.

12 Then it turns from Sarid eastward, toward the rising of the sun, to
   the border of Kislot-Tavor,
   and goes out at Dav'rat, going up to Yafi'a;

13 from there it crosses eastward, toward sunrise, to Gat-Heyfer and
   to Et-Katzin.
   Then it goes out to Rimmon, diverging to Nei'a.

14 Then the border swings around it, north to Hannaton;
   its outer-reaches are the Ravine of Yiftah-El,

15 with Kattat, Nahalal, Shimron, Yid'ala, and Bet-Lehem—
   towns, twelve, and their farmsteads.

16 This is the hereditary-property of the Children of Zevulun, for
   their clans,
   these towns and their farmsteads.

17 For Yissakhar the fourth lot came out,
   for the Children of Yissakhar, for their clans;

---

9 **amid their hereditary-property:** Yehuda's.
10 **Zevulun:** Pronounced *ze-voo-LOON;* trad. English "Zebulun." **Sarid:** LXX: "Sadud."
13 **Gat-Heyfer . . . Et-Katzin:** So many interpreters, although MT seems to indicate four names, not two.

15 **Bet-Lehem:** Not the well-known town south of Jerusalem, but one in the north, situated east of the Carmel ridge.
17 **Yissakhar:** Pronounced *yi-sah-KHAR;* trad. English "Issachar."

18 their border was
    toward Yizre'el: Kesulot, Shunem,
19 Hafarim, Shi'on, and Anharat,
20 Rabbeet, Kishon, and Evetz,
21 Remet, En-Gannim, En-Hadda, and Bet-Patzetz.
22 The border touches Tavor, Shahatim, and Bet-Shemesh;
    the outer-reaches of their border are at the Jordan—
    towns, sixteen, and their farmsteads.
23 This is the hereditary-property of the tribe of the Children of
        Yissakhar, for their clans,
    the towns and their farmsteads.

24 The fifth lot came out for the tribe of the Children of Asher, for
        their clans.
25 Their border was
    [along] Helkat, Hali, Beten, and Akhshaf,
26 Alamelekh, Am'ad, and Mish'al;
    it touches Carmel seaward, and Shihor Livnat.
27 Then it returns toward the rising of the sun, to Bet-Dagon, and
        touches Zevulun and the Ravine of Yiftah-El, northward, to Bet-
        Emek and Ne'iel,
    and goes out toward Cavul on the left / the west,
28 and Evron, Rehov, Hammon, Kana, as far as Greater Sidon.
29 Then the border turns to Rama, and as far as the fortified city of
        Tyre.
    Then the border turns to Hosa;
    and its outer-reaches are at the Sea, Mahalav, Akhziv,
30 and Umma, Afek, and Rehov—
    towns, twenty-two, and their farmsteads.
31 This is the hereditary-property of the tribe of the Children of
        Asher, for their clans,
    these towns and their farmsteads.

18 **was:** More with the sense "included" here, since we have a list of towns.
27 **northward:** LXX here has "the border went northward."
28–29 **Sidon . . . Tyre:** The inclusion of these key cities of Phoenicia (Heb. *Tzidon* and *Tzor*) betrays ideal rather than real boundaries on the part of the writer, as often happens in Joshua (Meyers 2004).

29 **fortified city of Tyre:** The LXX reads "the spring ['*ayin*] of the fortress of Tyre," different from '*ir*, "city." The second "returned" in this verse may be a scribal error here, and hence unnecessary. **Mahalav:** The Hebrew is unclear; many read as here, similar to the "Ahlav" of Judg. 1:31.

Chapter 20. *Towns of Asylum:* An integral part of the plans for occupying the land, as already laid out in Num. 35:6, 9–34 and Deut. 19:1–13, is the setting aside of six towns on either side of the Jordan as safe havens for those who commit unintentional murder (manslaughter). Unlike the brief chapter here, the text in Numbers goes into great detail, both in laying out hypothetical variations on manslaughter and in specifying the punishment and its time period. But our text has also added aspects of Deut. 19:1–10, in a move that foreshadows how Rabbinic law will handle different biblical texts (Meyers 2004). Once again, we can observe an active and fluid attitude to texts on the part of the transmitters and editors.

While one could compare this institution, which is a cut above the age-old practice of family vengeance, to other ancient Near Eastern societies' solutions to the problem, in the context of Yehoshua it functions to cap the account of precisely how the land was to be allotted, continuing into the next chapter, which deals with another unusual case: the landless Levites.

32 For the Children of Naftali the sixth lot came out,
   for the tribe of Naftali, for their clans;

33 their border was
   from Helef, from the Oak in Tzaananim, Adami-Nekev and
      Yavne'el, as far as Lakkum;
   its outer-reaches are at the Jordan.

34 The border turns seaward to Aznot-Tavor, and goes out from there
      to Hukkok.
   Then it touches Zevulun on the south and touches Asher seaward,
      and Yehuda, [with] the Jordan toward the rising of the sun,

35 along with the fortified towns—
   Tziddim, Tzer, Hammat, Rakkat, and Kinneret,

36 Adama, Rama, and Hatzor,

37 Kedesh, Edre'i, and En Hatzor,

38 Yir'on and Migdal-El,
   Horem, Bet-Anat, and Bet-Shemesh—
   towns, nineteen, and their farmsteads.

39 This is the hereditary-property of the tribe of the Children of
      Naftali, for their clans,
   the towns and their farmsteads.

40 For the tribe of the Children of Dan, according to their clans,
   the seventh lot came out;

41 and the territory of their hereditary-property was:
   Tzor'a, Eshtaol, and the city of Shemesh,

42 Shaalabin, Ayyalon, and Yitla,

43 Eilon, Timna, and Ekron,

44 Eltekei, Gibbeton, and Baalat,

45 Yehud, Benei Berak, and Gat-Rimmon,

46 Mei Yarkon and Rakkon, with the territory opposite Yafo.

---

33 **Oak:** Oak trees are apparently notable enough as a natural feature to be used in identifying a given locality, here and elsewhere in the Bible (see Gen. 12:6, 13:18, 35:8; Judg. 9:6, 37; I Sam. 10:3). **Adami-**

Nekev: Or "Red Passage," not to be confused with the "Red Pass" (*Maalei Adummim*) of 15:7.

34 **and Yehuda, [with] the Jordan:** Heb. unclear.

40 **Dan:** Pronounced as *Don*.

◆

47 But the territory of the Children of Dan got away from them,
 so the Children of Dan went up and did battle with Leshem, and
 took it,
 they struck it with the mouth of the sword
 and dispossessed it and settled in it.
 And they called Leshem: Dan, in accordance with the name of
 Dan, their ancestral-father.
48 This was the hereditary-property of the tribe of the Children of
 Dan, for their clans,
 these towns and their farmsteads.

49 So they had finished providing-inheritance in the land, according to
 its borders.
 Then the Children of Israel gave hereditary-property to Yehoshua
 son of Nun in their midst—
50 in accordance with the order of YHWH, they gave him the town he
 had requested, Timnat-Serah in the highlands of Efrayim;
 he built up the town and settled in it.

51 These are the hereditary-properties that El'azar the priest and
 Yehoshua son of Nun and the heads of the Fathers of the
 tribes distributed-as-hereditary-property to the Children of
 Israel by lot,
 at Shilo, in the presence of YHWH, at the entrance to the Tent of
 Appointment.
 Thus they finished dividing up the land.

20:1 And YHWH spoke to Yehoshua, saying:
 2 Speak to the Children of Israel, saying:
 Provide for yourselves the Towns of Asylum of which I spoke to
 you by the hand of Moshe,
 3 for fleeing to by an [accidental] murderer, one who strikes down a
 life in error, without forethought,
 that they may be asylum for you from the blood redeemer.

---

47 **the territory of . . . Dan got away from them:**
Or "went out of their (control)"; RSV: "was lost to
them." A fuller version of the Danite migration is
recounted in Judg. 18. LXX also has a longer text
here. **Leshem:** Modern Tel Dan, where in 1993 an
inscription was found that is believed to contain the
words "House of David," the primary material wit-

ness for the historicity of the biblical king to date.
Leshem is called "Layish" in Judg. 18.
20:2 **Towns of Asylum:** Others, "cities of refuge."
 3 **[accidental] murderer:** Or "manslayer" (JPS).
blood redeemer: A member of the family who, in
ancient practice, is duty bound to avenge his relative's slaying. The Western religious term "re-

4 He shall flee to one of these towns
and stand at the entrance to the town gate
and speak his words in the hearing of the elders of that town.
They shall receive him into the town, to themselves,
and give him a place, that he may settle beside them.

5 And if the blood redeemer pursues after him,
they are not to hand over the murderer—
for without foreknowledge did he strike down his neighbor;
he did not hate him from yesterday [or] the day-before.

6 Let him stay in that town until he stands before the community in
judgment,
until the death of the Great Priest that is there in those days;
then the murderer may return and come into his town and into his
house, to the town from which he fled.

7 So they hallowed Kedesh in the Galilee, in the highlands of Naftali,
and Shekhem in the highlands of Efrayim,
and Kiryat-Arba—that is Hevron—in the highlands of Judah;

8 and across from the Jordan [at] Jericho, toward the rising of the sun,
they provided Betzer in the wilderness, on the Plateau, from the
tribe of Re'uven,
and Ramot in Gil'ad, from the tribe of Gad,
and Golan in Bashan, from the tribe of Menashe.

9 These were the Towns of Appointment for all the Children of
Israel and for the sojourner who sojourns among them,
to which might flee anyone striking down a person in error,
so that he might not die at the hands of the blood redeemer,
until his standing before the community.

---

deemer," often used to characterize God as liberator, thus actually involves the restoration of a previously existing condition, such as freedom (redemption from slavery) or the ownership of land (redemption from a buyer).

4 **receive:** Or "admit" (JPS); lit. "gather." **a place:** Often referring to a sacred spot (e.g., Jer. 7:12).

5 **hand over:** To the avenging relative; lit. "close him up in his hand."

6 **in judgment:** Or "on trial." **death:** The death of

the High (Heb. "Great") Priest ends his general role in atoning for Israel's guilt, and thus the manslayer's need for "atonement" as well (Murray Lichtenstein, written communication).

7 **hallowed:** Set apart, especially for some ritual or other sacral purpose.

8 **provided:** Or "designated" (Boling [1982], who also understands this clause as referring to the past ["already"]).

9 **until his standing:** That is, he will be protected.

Chapter 21. *The Levite Towns:* In these closing chapters related to the parceling out of the land, the text treats the somewhat unusual cases—here, the Levites, who do not receive a broad territory like the other tribes, and in the next chapter, the two and a half tribes that settle on the east side of the Jordan.

The long account of Levitical towns by clan, with its patterned number of forty-eight (twelve times four), introduces a further note of order into the measured lines of territory recounted thus far.

Vv.41–43 provide a grand conclusion to the whole account of apportioning the land that started in Chap. 13. In just three verses, repetition ("give" three times and "all" six) and a potent set of ideas—the oath to the ancestors, the helplessness of the people's enemies, and the fulfillment of the divine word—summarize the idealistic, ideological vision of the book.

◆ 21:1 The heads of the Levite Father's [Houses] approached El'azar the
priest and Yehoshua son of Nun
and the heads of the tribal Father's [Houses] of the Children of
Israel

2 and spoke to them at Shilo, in the land of Canaan, saying:
Yhwh commanded by the hand of Moshe to give us towns to settle
in, and their pasture-lands for our animals!

3 So the Children of Israel gave the Levites [land] from their
hereditary-property, by order of Yhwh,
these towns and their pasture-lands.

4 The lot came out for the Kehatite clans;
for the Children of Aharon the Priest, from the Levites were:
from the tribe of Yehuda, from the Shim'onite tribe, and from the
tribe of Binyamin, by lot—
towns, thirteen;

5 and for the Children of Kehat who remained from the clans of the
tribe of Efrayim and from the tribe of Dan and from the half
tribe of Menashe, by the lot—
towns, ten;

6 and for the Children of Gershon:
from the clans of the tribe of Yissakhar and from the tribe of Asher
and from the tribe of Naftali and from the half tribe of Menashe,
in Bashan, by lot—
towns, thirteen;

7 and for the Children of Merari, for their clans:
from the tribe of Re'uven and from the tribe of Gad and from the
tribe of Zevulun—
towns, twelve.

8 The Children of Israel gave the Levites these towns and their
pasture-lands,
as Yhwh had commanded by the hand of Moshe, by lot.

9 They gave, from the tribe of the Children of Yehuda and from the
tribe of the Children of Shim'on, these towns which they called
by name;

21:1 **Father's [Houses]:** Capitalized in English to convey
that these were social units in ancient Israel, rather
like extended families.

4 **Kehatite:** Kehat, like Gershon in v.6 and Merari in

v.7, was a son of Aharon.　**Aharon:** Pronounced *ah-hah-RONE;* trad. English "Aaron."　**Binyamin:** Pronounced *bin-yah-MEEN;* trad. English "Benjamin."

◆

10 it was for the Children of Aharon, from the Kehatite clans from the
  Children of Levi,
  for theirs was the first lot:

11 they gave them Kiryat-Arba, the father of Anak—that is Hevron, in
  the highlands of Judah, with its pasture-lands all around it,

12 while the open-field of the city and its farmsteads they gave to
  Calev son of Yefunneh as his holding;

13 to the Children of Aharon the Priest they gave a town of asylum
  for the [accidental] murderer—
  Hevron and its pasture-lands,

14 Livna and its pasture-lands,
  Yattir and its pasture-lands,

15 Eshtemoa and its pasture-lands,
  Holon and its pasture-lands,

16 Devir and its pasture-lands,
  Ayin and its pasture-lands,
  Yutta and its pasture-lands,
  Bet-Shemesh and its pasture-lands—
  towns, nine, from these two tribes;

17 and from the tribe of Binyamin:
  Giv'on and its pasture-lands,
  Geva and its pasture-lands,

18 Anatot and its pasture-lands,
  and Almon and its pasture-lands—
  towns, four;

19 all the towns of the Children of Aharon, the priests—
  thirteen towns and their pasture-lands.

20 Now for the clans of the Children of Kehat, the Levites who
  remained from the Children of Kehat,
  the towns of their allotment were from the tribe of Efrayim.

21 They gave them a town of asylum for the murderer—
  Shekhem and its pasture-lands, in the highlands of Efrayim,

---

10 **theirs was the first lot:** Yehuda's and Shim'on's. As
Boling (1982) points out, the theme of "Judah first"
is central to the structure of the subsequent book of
Judges.

21 **the murderer:** The "accidental" murderer, who
commits manslaughter, as in the previous chapter.

22 Gezer and its pasture-lands,
Kivtzayim and its pasture-lands,
and Bet-Horon and its pasture-lands—
towns, four;

23 and from the tribe of Dan:
Eltekei and its pasture-lands,
Gibbeton and its pasture-lands,

24 Ayyalon and its pasture-lands,
Gat-Rimmon and its pasture-lands—
towns, four;

25 and from the half tribe of Menashe:
Ta'nakh and its pasture-lands
and Yivle'am and its pasture-lands—
towns, two;

26 all the towns were ten, and their pasture-lands, according to the
clans of the Children of Kehat who remained.

27 And for the Children of Gershon, from the Levite clans:
from the half tribe of Menashe,
a town of asylum for the murderer—
Golan in Bashan and its pasture-lands,
and Be'eshtera and its pasture-lands—
towns, two;

28 from the tribe of Yissakhar,
Kishyon and its pasture-lands,
Dav'rat and its pasture-lands,

29 Yarmut and its pasture-lands,
and En-Gannim and its pasture-lands—
towns, four;

30 and from the tribe of Asher,
Mish'al and its pasture-lands,
Avdon and its pasture-lands,

31 Helkat and its pasture-lands,
and Rehov and its pasture-lands—
towns, four;

---

25 **Yivle'am:** MT has "Gat-Rimmon" here as in previous verse; it must be an error, and I follow LXX as a result.

27 **Be'eshtera:** Called "Ashtarot" in I Chron. 6:56.

Chapter 22. *Finishing Business: The Two and a Half Tribes:* The final three chapters of Joshua are concerned with the community of the past and the community of the future. In that context, the long story in Chap. 22 both poses and solves the potentially dangerous problem of what constitutes proper worship of YHWH. The opening five verses are strongly Deuteronomistic in language, suggesting a resolution of the entire conquest story, with the last pieces of territory (albeit east of the Jordan) being allotted to Israelites tribes. But beginning in v.11, a major rift seems in the offing, with the bulk of the Israelite tribes, those west of the Jordan, seriously misunderstanding the construction of a gigantic altar by their eastern counterparts. They take this act as a major violation of the worship of YHWH, and hence of the covenant itself, even likening it to two major biblical stories of treachery: the account in Num. 25 of how the Israelites "went whoring" after foreign gods, and Akhan's violation of the Israelite rules of war earlier in Joshua (Chap. 7), after which the wording here is perhaps modeled. In addition, as Hamilton notes, a specific verb for "rebel" (*m-r-d*, "revolt") uses up a fifth of its appearances in the entire Bible in this chapter.

The two and a half tribes' impassioned reply in vv.22–29 is a stirring testament to their group loyalty and to their faithfulness to YHWH. For them, the huge altar is supposed to act as a kind of giant flag or similar symbol, to signal to the Israelites and to others that they have by no means forgotten YHWH's sanctuary, where the Coffer is situated. The resolution that follows, sanctioned by the very priest (Pin'has) who had violently stemmed the tide of idolatry in Num. 25, lets the aggregate Israelite community breathe easier (vv.30 and 33, "it was good in their eyes"), and civil war is averted. Conflicts between tribes will not be so peacefully resolved in the next book, Judges. For the moment, though, Joshua can at least move toward its conclusion on a tranquil and idealizing note.

Not all readers will accept this "happy ending"; for them, the reality of two and a half tribes existing in a geographically ambiguous situation is still cause for concern, as the continued presence of Canaanites among the new settlers had been earlier. Israelite identity is still in question on some level (Hawk 2000).

32 and from the tribe of Naftali,
a town of asylum for the murderer—
Kedesh in the Galilee and its pasture-lands,
Hammot Dor and its pasture-lands,
and Kartan and its pasture-lands—
towns, three.

33 All the towns of the Gershonites were, according to their clans—
thirteen towns and their pasture-lands.

34 And for the clans of the Children of Merari, the Levites who
remained:
from the tribe of Zevulun,
Yokne'am and its pasture-lands,
Karta and its pasture-lands,

35 Rimmon and its pasture-lands,
Nahalal and its pasture-lands—
towns, four;
[and from the tribe of Re'uven,
Betzer and its pasture-lands,
Yahtza and its pasture-lands,
Kedemot and its pasture-lands,
and Meifaat and its pasture-lands—
towns, four;

36 and from the tribe of Gad,
a town of asylum for the murderer—
Ramot in Gil'ad and its pasture-lands,
and Mahanayim and its pasture-lands,

37 Heshbon and its pasture-lands,
Ya'zer and its pasture-lands—
all the towns, four.

38 All the towns for the Children of Merari, according to their
remaining clans from the Levite clans,
their allotment was towns, twelve.

---

32 **Kartan:** Called "Rakkat" in 19:35 and "Kiryatayim" in I Chron. 6:61.

35 **Rimmon and its pasture-lands . . . :** It appears that some material has been lost here; see LXX and I Chron. 6:63. The rest of the verse in the present text, in brackets, is based on some ancient biblical manuscripts. **Rimmon:** Following LXX: "Rimmon," as the spelling in I Chron. 6:62. MT has "Dimna."

◆ 39 All the towns of the Levites amid the holdings of the Children of
Israel,
[were] towns, forty-eight, and their pasture-lands;
40 these towns were, town by town, [considered] along with its
pasture-lands all around it,
thus for all these towns.

41 So YHWH gave to Israel all the land that he had sworn to give to
their fathers;
they took possession of it and settled in it.
42 And YHWH gave rest to them round about,
just as he had sworn to their fathers,
so that no man was able to stand up before them among all their
enemies—
all their enemies, YHWH gave into their hand.
43 There did not fail one thing of all the good things
that YHWH had promised to the House of Israel;
all of it came-to-pass.

22:1 Then Yehoshua called the Re'uvenites, the Gadites, and the half
tribe of Menashe
2 and said to them:
You yourselves have kept all that Moshe, the servant of YHWH,
commanded you,
and you have hearkened to my voice in all that I have commanded
you:
3 you have not abandoned your brothers these many years, until this
day,
but you have kept the keeping
of the commandment of YHWH your God.

40–41 **these towns were . . . :** LXX adds text here about
Yehoshua's territory and the flint knives used for circumcision in Chap. 5.

41–43 **all:** As previously in 11:16–23, the translation retains
the use of the Hebrew term *kol*, emphasizing
the strong (if historically dubious) view that the
conquest was total (Meyers 2004). In this usage, it
echoes the first chapter of the book.

42 **no man was able to stand:** RSV: "not one . . . had
withstood them."

43 **fail:** Lit., "fall." **thing . . . things . . . promised:**
Heb. *davar . . . ha-davar . . . dibber.*

22:3 **kept the keeping / of the commandment:** Boling
(1982): "scrupulously kept."

4 But now, YHWH your God has given rest to your brothers, as he
    promised them.
  So-now, face about and go you forth to your tents, to the land of
    your holdings
  which Moshe, the servant of YHWH, gave to you across the Jordan.
5 Only: be very careful to observe the commandment and the
    Instruction that Moshe, the servant of YHWH, commanded you:
  to love YHWH your God,
  to walk in all his ways, to keep his commandments, to cleave to him
    and to serve him
  with all your heart and with all your being!
6 So Yehoshua blessed them and sent them off, and they went back to
    their tents.
7 Now to the half tribe of Menashe, Moshe had given [a share] in
    Bashan,
  and to its [other] half Yehoshua had given-share beside their
    brothers, across the Jordan, seaward.
  And also, when he had sent them off to their tents, he had blessed
    them
8 and had said to them, saying:
  With much wealth return to your tents, and with exceedingly many
    livestock,
  and with silver and with gold and with bronze and with iron and
    with clothing, exceedingly much;
  portion out your enemies' spoils with your brothers!
9 So they returned and went, the Children of Re'uven, the Children
    of Gad, and the half tribe of Menashe, from among the Children
    of Israel,
  from Shilo which is in the land of Canaan,
  to go to the land of Gil'ad, to the land of their holding which they
    had made-as-their-holding
  in accordance with the order of YHWH, by the hand of Moshe.

---

4 **But now . . . :** The wording here resembles that of
1:15, thus drawing the conquest and allotment of the
land to a close (Mitchell).
5 **commandment:** Including the entire covenant (Boling 1982, quoting Aryaprateep).   **love . . . walk . . .
cleave . . . serve . . . with all your heart and with**

all your being: The covenant vocabulary of Deuteronomy (see Chap. 6 there).
7 **Bashan:** Pronounced *bah-SHAHN,* it was the prized
fertile plateau east of the Sea of Galilee and north of
Gil'ad.

10 They came to the districts of the Jordan which are in the land of
      Canaan,
    and the Children of Re'uven and the Children of Gad and the half
      tribe of Menashe built a sacrificial-altar there, by the Jordan,
    an altar large to see.
11 Now the Children of Israel heard it said:
    Here, the Children of Re'uven and the Children of Gad and the
      half tribe of Menashe have built an altar opposite the land of
      Canaan,
    in the districts of the Jordan, across from the Children of Israel—
12 the Children of Israel heard [it], and so they assembled, the entire
      community of the Children of Israel, at Shilo,
    to go up against them in force.
13 And the Children of Israel sent Pin'has son of El'azar the priest
    to the Children of Re'uven, to the Children of Gad, and to the half
      tribe of Menashe, in the land of Gil'ad,
14 and ten exalted-leaders with him—one leader, one leader [apiece]
      per Father's House among all the tribes of Israel,
    each one a head of his Father's House were they, among the
      thousands of Israel.
15 They came to the Children of Re'uven, to the Children of Gad, and
      to the half tribe of Menashe, in the land of Gil'ad
    and spoke to them, saying:
16 Thus says YHWH's entire community:
    What is this sacrilege by which you have committed sacrilege
      against the God of Israel,
    by turning today from [following] after YHWH
    by building yourselves an altar
    for transgressing today against YHWH?!
17 Was the iniquity of Pe'or too little for us
    from which we have not become purified until this day,
    —a plague was upon the community of YHWH!—

10 **large to see:** Boling (1982): "conspicuously large."
13 **sent:** JPS includes "[first]," implied by the context.   **Pin'has:** Trad. English "Phineas."
14 **one leader, one leader:** Biblical Hebrew expresses the idea of a leader per tribe by simply repeating the word.   **thousands:** Boling (1982), again, understands Heb. *elef* as "village-unit" or "militia"; others, "contingents."

16 **sacrilege:** The same Hebrew root (*m-'-l*) as the one used to describe Akhan's actions in Chap. 7. See v.20 in the text.
17 **the iniquity of Pe'or:** In Num. 25, an Israelite marries a Midyanite woman, leading to idolatry.

18   that you turn today from [following] after YHWH?
     It will be:
     should you revolt today against YHWH,
     tomorrow, he will be furious against the entire community of
        Israel!

19   Surely, if the land of your holdings is polluted, cross you over to the
        land of YHWH's holding, where the Dwelling of YHWH dwells,
        and get holdings in our midst—
     but against YHWH, do not revolt!
     And against us, do not revolt by building yourselves an altar
     apart from the altar for YHWH our God!

20   Did not Akhan son of Zerah commit sacrilege, yes, sacrilege
        regarding the devoted-things,
     so that there was fury against the entire community of Israel?
     And he did not perish as [just] one man for his iniquity?

21   The Children of Re'uven and the Children of Gad and the half
        tribe of Menashe answered;
     they spoke to the heads of the thousands of Israel:

22   God of gods is YHWH!
     God of gods is YHWH!
     He knows, and Israel itself will know:
     if [it was] in revolting or in committing sacrilege against YHWH
     —do not deliver us on this day!—

23   by building ourselves an altar to turn from [following] after YHWH,
     or if by offering up offerings-up and grain-gifts,
     or if by performing on it sacrifices of *shalom,*
     may YHWH himself examine it!

24   . . . if it was not out of deep-concern over a matter that we have
        done this, saying:
     On the morrow your children might say to our children, saying:
     What is between you and YHWH, the God of Israel?

---

18 **he will be furious:** God.

19 **polluted:** In Leviticus, the term carries a ritual connotation; here, it has a less charged meaning, tied to what the Israelites consider improper worship.

20 **Akhan . . . iniquity:** The strong reference to the story in Chap. 7 demonstrates how much the Israelites believe in their fellows' guilt (Mitchell).

22 **God of gods is YHWH!:** The phrase is not entirely clear; JPS renders it as "God, the LORD God!" **He knows, and Israel . . . will know:** Boling (1982) takes this as "Let him make known . . . let Israel learn."

23 **may YHWH himself examine it!:** Or "May the LORD Himself demand [a reckoning]" (JPS).

24 **. . . if it was not out of deep-concern . . . :** Namely, it *is* out of concern that we've done this.

25 As a border between us and you, O Children of Re'uven and
  Children of Gad, Yhwh made the Jordan;
  you have no portion in Yhwh!—
  Your children would cause our children to cease holding Yhwh in
  awe!
26 So we said:
  Let us act for ourselves to build an altar,
  not for offerings-up, not for sacrifices,
27 but rather as a witness let it be between us and you, and between
  our generations after us,
  [for us] to serve the service of Yhwh in his presence,
  through our offerings-up, through our sacrifices, and through our
  shalom-offerings,
  so that your children will not say on the morrow to our children:
  You have no portion in Yhwh!
28 And we said:
  It will be,
  if they say [thus] to us and to our generations on the morrow,
  then we will say:
  See the replica of the altar of Yhwh that our fathers made,
  neither for offering-up nor for sacrifice;
  rather, it is a witness between us and you!
29 [Heaven] forbid for us to revolt against Yhwh, to turn today from
  [following] after Yhwh
  by building an altar for offering-up, for grain-gift, and for sacrifice
  aside from the altar of Yhwh our God that is in front of his
  Dwelling!
30 Pin'has the priest and the leaders of the community and the heads
  of the thousands of Israel who were with him heard
  the words that the Children of Re'uven, the Children of Gad, and
  the Children of Menashe spoke,
  and it was good in their eyes;

28 **replica:** The Hebrew is from the key root of the
chapter, *b-n-h*, "build."

31   so Pin'has son of El'azar the priest said to the Children of Re'uven,
to the Children of Gad, and to the Children of Menashe:
Today we know that YHWH is in our midst,
in that you did not commit sacrilege against YHWH with this act-of-
sacrilege;
so then, you have rescued the Children of Israel from the hand of
YHWH!

32   So Pin'has son of El'azar the priest and the leaders returned from
the Children of Re'uven and from the Children of Gad,
from the land of Gil'ad, to the land of Canaan, to the Children of
Israel,
and returned word to them.

33   The word was good in the eyes of the Children of Israel,
so the Children of Israel blessed God,
and they decided not to go up against them in force,
to wreak ruin on the land in which the Children of Re'uven and the
Children of Gad were settled.

34   And the Children of Re'uven and the Children of Gad called the
altar [:Witness],
for it is a witness between us
that YHWH is God!

31 **from the hand of YHWH:** From God's punishment.
33 **word:** Or "matter."
34 **called the altar [:Witness]:** So JPS, following
ancient versions. It appears that the name given the
altar has been omitted here, unlike normal Hebrew
usage.

PART IV

LAST WORDS

(23–24)

In the spirit of Deuteronomy (see Moshe's final speeches to the Israelites, Chaps. 32–33) and also of Genesis (Chaps. 49–50, which include the words of the dying Yaakov and Yosef), an aged leader here has final wisdom to impart. In the case of Joshua, there is likewise a double ending, and there will be another poetic one at the end of Samuel. Our Chap. 23 uses concentrated language drawn from Deuteronomy (see the comment to the chapter) as part of Yehoshua's personal plea for the Israelites to remain faithful to God, including a warning at the end that the penalty for violating the pact is exile, the most feared of all punishments in the Bible.

In Chap. 24 Yehoshua appropriately summarizes Israel's journey from earliest days, i.e., the period of Avraham the patriarch, for the purpose of exhorting the Israelites to keep their covenant with Yhwh.

As so often happens in the Bible, the book ends with a death notice, here not only of Yehoshua but also of the last priestly representative of the older generation, El'azar. The wanderings are over, and the Israelites are home at last.

Chapter 23. *Yehoshua's Parting Speech:* The text now picks up, as it were, from the narrative in 13:1, using the same formula ("Now Yehoshua was old . . ."). We are at the end of Yehoshua's life. In the first of two extended speeches to the Israelites, he gathers the people in order to personally plead with them to understand the importance of this moment. Hamilton notes three exhortations in this speech: (1) for the leaders of the people to be faithful to God's "Instruction"; (2) for them to maintain separation from the Canaanites; and (3) for them to love God as loyal vassals. Not surprisingly, Yehoshua uses classic Deuteronomistic words, including such terms as "strengthen," "keep," "observe," "Instruction," "[do not] turn aside," "serve," "cleave to," "love," "dispossess," and "cross." The sum total of this vocabulary is simply expressed: you are to love God and keep his commandments; do not turn aside from them, or else you will be dispossessed from the land. Or: having now received God's gift of the land, do not turn to idolatry, or you will wind up in exile.

Another notable verbal feature of the chapter is the repetition fourteen times (a doubling of the "perfect" seven) of the phrase "YHWH your God." It too recalls Deuteronomy, where it occurs some twenty-two times. So Yehoshua is once again linked to his predecessor Moshe.

23:1 It was, many years after YHWH had given Israel rest from all their
      enemies round about
  —now Yehoshua was old, advanced in years—

2 that Yehoshua called all Israel: its elders, its heads, its judges, and its
      officials,
  and said to them:
  I have become old, I am advanced in years.

3 Now you yourselves have seen
  all that YHWH your God did to all the nations before you,
  for YHWH your God,
  he is the one who does battle for you!

4 See, I cast [lots] for you from these nations that were left, as
      hereditary-property for your tribes, from the Jordan
  —including all the nations that I cut down—and [from] the Great
      Sea, toward the coming in of the sun.

5 YHWH your God, he will push them out before you
  and will dispossess them from before you,
  so that you will possess their land,
  as YHWH your God promised you.

6 You are to be very strong,
  in keeping and in observing all that is written in the Record of the
      Instruction of Moshe,
  so as not to turn aside from it, right or left,

7 so as not to come in among these nations that are left beside you;
  the name of their gods you are not to invoke, you are not to swear
      [by them],
  you are not to serve them, you are not to bow down to them.

8 Rather, to YHWH your God you are to cleave, as you have done, to
      this day!

9 YHWH your God has dispossessed before you nations great and
      numerous,
  while as for you, no man has stood up before you, to this day.

23:1 **many years after:** Or "a long time afterward."
given . . . rest: This Deuteronomistic phrase appears a number of times in Judges as well. **advanced in years:** Used, for instance, of Avraham and Sara in Gen. 18:11.

5 **dispossess . . . possess:** As elsewhere, the Hebrew uses different forms of the verb (*y-r-sh*).

7 **these nations that are left beside you:** Now Israel's way of dealing with them will be cultural separation and no longer extermination (Hawk 2000). **invoke:** More than merely "remember."

Chapter 24. *Parting Ceremony:* In contrast to the previous speech, this long chapter has some of the earmarks of a covenant-making or covenant-renewal ceremony. All the Israelites and their various leaders are "stationed" before God at the important city of Shekhem. The speaker begins with an extended history lesson, tracing Israel's lineage to idol-worshippers living beyond the Euphrates and proceeding through the gift of the land to the Patriarchs, the enslavement and liberation from Egypt, and God's guidance to the Promised Land. The wording reveals the emotional underpinnings: "give" occurs six times in thirteen verses at the chapter's beginning, just as it was central in Chap. 1. "Serve," another key verb that figured in Chap. 1, occurs here some fourteen times. God, as the prime subject of the speech, is connected to numerous verbs of action throughout ("took," "led," "gave," "sent," "smote," "took out," "brought," "rescued"), in order to emphasize that everything flows from what he has done for the Israelites. Beginning in v.14, Yehoshua, with the repeated, rhetorically significant "So-now," launches into the official, ceremonial request, urging the people to serve God as "I and my household" do. There ensues a kind of scripted dialogue (vv.16–24), in which the leader basically goads the people to affirm and reaffirm their intention to follow YHWH, and they respond positively. All is sealed with a written document and a great stone as unshakable witnesses.

As has often been pointed out, many of these elements are common to ancient Near Eastern treaty formulas, especially from Hittite documents. Missing from the usual covenant ceremony, as Nelson notes, are the pointed threats leveled at potential violators, such as we find in Lev. 26 and Deut. 27. So this chapter, while it uses common conventions, may be a dramatic device, intended to impress upon audiences the seriousness not only of the end of the book but of the whole sequence that began with the promises of Genesis. It should also be noted that vv.2–4 of the chapter were used later, by the Rabbis before the third century C.E., as part of the family Passover meal text (Haggadah), and they still have that function today.

Both chapter and book end with three notices related to dying or death. First, Yehoshua himself dies; then comes the final burial of Yosef's bones, which had been brought up from Egypt at the time of the Exodus (Exod. 13:19), in conformity with his wishes in Gen. 50:24–25; and finally we are told of the death of the High Priest, El'azar. All of these leaders find their resting place on northern soil, traditions that were ultimately incorporated into the final version of the book. That the priestly figure is the last to be mentioned may suggest a priestly editor, or at least one for whom cultic matters were central. At any rate, the death notices signal that the long journey, both literal and figurative, that was begun in the book of Exodus is now over. And "the reader is left with the sense of a perfected past . . . for now all is well" (Fishbane).

There has long been debate about this chapter among scholars, starting from the premise that it and the previous one are slightly redundant. Indeed, the openings of both are so similar in their convoking of the people and their leaders that one cannot help but think that one chapter or the other is a later addition.

10 One man among you pursues a thousand,
    for YHWH your God, he is the one who does battle for you, as he
        promised you.
11 Take care with your very being
    to love YHWH your God,
12 for if you should turn, yes, turn away and cleave to the rest of these
        nations, the ones left alongside you,
    and marry among them, so that they come among you and you
        among them,
13 you must know, yes, know that YHWH your God will not continue
        to dispossess these nations from before you;
    they will become for you a trapping-net and a snare,
    a whip in your sides and barbs in your eyes,
    until your perishing from off this good ground that YHWH your
        God has given you.
14 Here, I am going today the way of all the earth;
    you know with all your heart and with all your being
    that not one thing has failed of all the good things that YHWH your
        God promised you;
    everything has come-to-pass for you—
    not one thing of it has failed!
15 But it shall be,
    just as there has come upon you every good thing that YHWH your
        God promised you,
    so can YHWH your God cause to come upon you every evil thing,
    until he has wiped you from off this good ground that YHWH your
        God has given you:
16 if you cross the covenant of YHWH your God which he commanded
        you,
    and you go and serve other gods and bow down to them,
    YHWH's anger will flare against you
    and you will perish quickly from off the good land that he has
        given you!

12 **cleave to:** Connoting "be in alliance with." **come among:** The Hebrew is possibly a pun; "come in to," an alternate translation here, can often mean "to have sexual intercourse with" in the Hebrew Bible.

13 **a trapping-net and a snare:** These hunting devices are regularly applied to the moral/ethical sphere in such books as Proverbs. Here the connotation is the hidden but lethal danger of being seduced into acts of infidelity to God.

14 **going . . . the way of all the earth:** As Meyers (2004) points out, this phrase, a poetic description of death, is otherwise employed only of David (I Kings 2:2); here it reinforces the royal tone with which Joshua opened in Chap. 1.

The location of the ceremony at Shekhem, first capital of the Northern King-dom (tenth century), is seen by some as an indication that the hope of recover-ing the north, destroyed by Assyria in 722, remained a live issue in ancient Israel and perhaps influenced the composition of Joshua (Schniedewind 2004). Others have viewed our chapter as coming out of exile many centuries hence, given its troubled portrait of a "zealous" God, whom "you will not be able to serve" (v.19). But the people's assent to staying in the covenant resonates with the desire of the Bible's writers to remain faithful to a long-standing heritage and mission. The doubling effect created by linking Chaps. 23 and 24 serves to confirm this direction.

The book of Joshua, however, ends with a paradox: a people mostly united and a land mostly conquered, with a leader dying (and no successor in sight) and Canaanites still living among them. It will be up to Judges, which picks up at Yehoshua's death, to see if unity and proper leadership will ultimately prevail.

◆ 24:1 Yehoshua gathered all the tribes of Israel at Shekhem;
he called together all the elders of Israel, their heads, their judges,
and their officials,
and they stationed themselves in the presence of God.

2 And Yehoshua said to all the people:
Thus says YHWH, the God of Israel:
Across the River were your fathers settled in former ages
—Terah father of Avraham and father of Nahor—
and they served other gods.

3 But I took your father Avraham from Across the River
and I had him go throughout all the land of Canaan;
I made his seed many and gave him Yitzhak.

4 And I gave to Yitzhak—Yaakov and Esav,
I gave to Esav Mount Se'ir for him to possess,
while Yaakov and his children went down to Egypt.

5 Then I sent Moshe and Aharon,
and I dealt blows to Egypt, with what I did in its midst,
and afterward I brought you out.

6 I brought your fathers out from Egypt, and you came to the Sea,
and Egypt pursued after your fathers with chariots and riders at the
Sea of Reeds.

7 They cried out to YHWH, and he put deep-darkness between you
and the Egyptians,
and brought down the Sea upon them, so that it covered them.
Your [own] eyes saw what I did in Egypt!
And you stayed in the wilderness for many years;

24:1 **Shekhem:** Pronounced *sheh-KHEM;* trad. English "Shechem," a city featured in a number of biblical narratives (for example, Gen. 34). It was situated near present-day Nablus, about forty miles north of Jerusalem, and was not part of the territories prominent in the conquest account in the first half of the book. **stationed themselves:** JPS: "presented themselves." The phrase recalls another seminal moment, Israel standing at Sinai to make the covenant (Exod. 19:17).

2 **Avraham:** The "a's" are pronounced as "ah," with the accent on the last syllable of the name; trad. English "Abraham."

3 **Across the River:** The Euphrates—either in Mesopotamia or west of the river, i.e., Harran, as would

be indicated by Assyrian and Persian terminology (Nelson). Some connect "across" (Heb. *mei-eiver*) with the term "Hebrews" (Heb. *ivriyyim*).

4 **Mount Se'ir:** Southeast of the Negev, in today's Jordan. It was considered the home of the Edomites, Esav's descendants, and is frequently connected to YHWH in the Bible. **down to Egypt:** LXX adds here, parallel to Deut. 26:5b, "There they became a large, numerous, and powerful nation, and the Egyptians oppressed them."

5 **dealt blows:** Or "plagued"; the present translation is more literal. **with what I did:** The plagues.

8 then I brought you to the land of the Amorites, who were settled
across the Jordan, and they did battle with you,
but I gave them into your hand, so that you took possession of their
land,
and I wiped them out from before you.

9 Then Balak son of Tzippor arose, king of Moav, and he waged
battle against Israel:
he sent and called for Bil'am son of Be'or to curse you,

10 but I was not willing to hearken to Bil'am,
so he blessed, yes, blessed you,
and I rescued you from his hand.

11 Then you crossed the Jordan and came to Jericho,
and they waged battle against you, the landowners of Jericho,
the Amorites, the Perizzites, the Canaanites, the Hittites, the
Girgashites, the Hivvites, and the Yevusites,
but I gave them into your hand.

12 I sent the hornet before you
and it drove them out before you,
[like the] two Amorite kings—not with your sword and not with
your bow.

13 And I gave you a land for which you did not labor,
towns which you did not build, in which you settled,
vineyards and olive-groves which you did not plant, [and from
which] you are eating!

14 So-now,
hold YHWH in awe and serve him in integrity and trust;
remove the gods whom your fathers had served across the River
and in Egypt
and serve YHWH!

15 But if it be evil in your eyes to serve YHWH,
choose yourselves today whom you wish to serve—

9 **waged battle:** Not reported or even suggested in Num. 22; Boling (1982) thinks that this statement may be tongue in cheek. But it might also mean "set out to fight" (Nelson).

10 **he blessed, yes, blessed you:** Gray (1986): "he went on blessing you."

11–12 **they waged battle . . . :** Note that here, in contrast to the famous story in Chap. 6, the residents of Jericho put up a fight. So, as often happens in the Bible,

two versions or traditions about an event appear in the same book.

12 **hornet:** An image already used in Exod. 23:28 and Deut. 7:20. Some understand it as a remnant of a hoary practice of letting insects loose in war by catapulting them in clay vessels. **two Amorite kings:** The aforementioned Sihon and Og. **not with your sword . . . not with your bow:** See Yaakov's words in Gen. 48:22.

whether the gods whom your fathers who were Across the River
   served
or the gods of the Amorites, in whose land you are settled.
But as for me and my household, we will serve YHWH!

16 The people answered and said:
[Heaven] forbid for us, from abandoning YHWH
to serve other gods!

17 Rather, YHWH our God,
he is the one who brought up us and our fathers from the land of
   Egypt, from a house of serfs,
and who performed before our eyes these great signs
and kept-us-safe on all the way that we went
and among all the peoples through whose midst we crossed—

18 YHWH has driven out all the peoples, the Amorites, the settled-folk
   of the land, before us.
We too will serve YHWH,
indeed, he is our God!

19 And Yehoshua said to the people:
You will not be able to serve YHWH,
for he is a holy godhead;
he is a zealous God,
and will not bear your transgression and your sins!

20 When you abandon YHWH and serve foreign gods,
he will turn and do evil to you and will finish you off,
after having done good to you.

21 But the people said to Yehoshua:
No, rather, it is YHWH we will serve!

22 So Yehoshua said to the people:
You are witnesses against yourselves
that you on your part have chosen YHWH for yourselves, to
   serve him.
They said:
Witnesses!—

---

19 **a holy godhead:** A rare case of Heb. *elohim* accompanied by a plural adjective; the meaning seems to be "divine power." **zealous:** Heb. *kanno'*. In the form *kanna'*, God is so described in Exod. 20:5 and 34:14, and Deut. 4:24, 5:9, and 6:15. Woudstra describes the concept as "God's zeal for the maintenance of his honor"; it is a form of anger. It is often mistranslated as "jealous." **your transgression and your sins:** The pronoun is in the plural.

◆ 23 So-now, remove the foreign gods that are in your midst,
and incline your heart to YHWH, the God of Israel!

24 The people said to Yehoshua:
It is YHWH our God we will serve;
to his voice we will hearken!

25 So Yehoshua cut a covenant with the people on that day;
he made them a law and a judgment at Shekhem.

26 And Yehoshua wrote down these words in the Record of God's
Instruction.
Then he took a large stone and erected it there,
beneath the tamarisk that was in the Holy-Place of YHWH.

27 And Yehoshua said to all the people:
Here, this stone shall be against us as a witness,
for it has heard all the statements of YHWH which he spoke with us;
it will be against you as a witness, lest you deny your God!

28 Then Yehoshua sent the people away, each one to his hereditary-
property.

29 Now it was some time afterward
that Yehoshua son of Nun, the servant of YHWH, died, a hundred
and ten years old;

30 they buried him in the territory of his hereditary-property, at
Timnat-Serah that is in the highlands of Efrayim, north of
Mount Gaash.

31 And Israel served YHWH all the days of Yehoshua
and all the days of the elders who [lived] long years after Yehoshua,
who had known all the deeds of YHWH that he had done for Israel.

32 And the bones of Yosef, which the Children of Israel had brought
up from Egypt,

---

23 **remove the foreign gods:** Yaakov makes the same request in Gen. 35:2.

25 **a law and a judgment:** Boling (1982): "a legal precedent."

26 **the Record of God's Instruction:** Not the usual "Record of the Instruction of Moshe," but of God. **tamarisk:** Heb. *elon*, related to the "oak" (*ela*) in 19:33, above. **the Holy-Place:** The "Dwelling" (Tabernacle), but some others suggest "sacred precinct."

27 **spoke with us:** Boling (1982): "negotiated with us."

29 **servant of YHWH:** Yehoshua, at death, finally merits the title of his master Moshe. **a hundred and ten years old:** The same life span as Yosef, another northern figure.

32 *kesitas:* See Gen. 33:19. The term may indicate a weight or measure of some kind. Some render it as "lambs' worth."

they buried in Shekhem, in the portion of open-ground that Yaakov
   had acquired from the Children of Hamor father of Shekhem,
   for a hundred *kesitas;*
it had become hereditary-property for the Children of Yosef.

33 And El'azar son of Aharon died;
   they buried him on the hill of Pin'has his son, which had been
   given to him in the highlands of Efrayim.

שׁוֹפְטִים

JUDGES

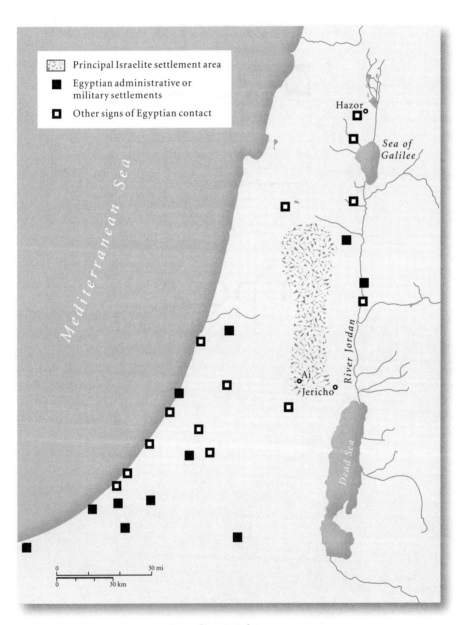

Israelite Settlement

INTRODUCTION

A Diverse and Curious Collection

> You may imagine, then, that this book of Judges is not pleasant to read—
> much of it is quite ghastly. You must not go to it for any details of life, or
> to learn anything about your own duty at the present time, except as you
> can see that it is your duty not to imitate the ways of most of the people
> of whom you read in it.
>
> —Rev. T. Rhondda Williams,
> *Old Testament Stories in Modern Light* (1911)

THIS ASSESSMENT OF JUDGES, QUOTED BY DAVID GUNN IN HIS ILLUMINATING treatment of how the book has been read over the past two millennia, will ring true to many modern readers. Of the four books that make up *The Early Prophets,* Judges is certainly the most bizarre. It is not, like Joshua, centrally concerned with establishing Israel's claim to the land, nor is it a sustained masterpiece of characterization like Samuel. Neither does it contain the world-historic interest of Kings, in which the actions and cultures of ancient superpowers intrude on Israel's story. Instead, in its wealth of violent detail, Judges is probably the goriest book in the Hebrew Scriptures. As has long been noted, in some respects it feels like the Bible's version of the American Wild West, for it presents a scenario of instability and violence in which civil society is threatened by both internal and external forces. Its heroes, tasked with restoring some semblance of order, are themselves frequently morally flawed. Women, who appear quite often in its pages, are frequently victims of violence—but they crop up as bloody heroines as well. And the book does not follow a clear or realistic chronological pattern, but rather is laid out in tribal and geographic terms, with no anchoring in the history of older, neighboring civilizations. In short, much like literary and cinematic representations of the American frontier period, in which qualities of self-reliance, bravery, and violence take precedence over historical accuracy, and in which certain locales are emphasized while others are omitted, Judges is an ideology-driven portrait of an age in transition.

Our best chance to understand the book is therefore to take it on its own terms and to approach it thematically. First, as in the books that precede it, the story line in Judges mainly concerns Israel's relationship to YHWH. More specifically, the people's security is seen as depending entirely upon its faithfulness to God. Chap. 2 lays out the pattern in stark terms: keep the covenant (that is, do not worship other gods), and despite the precariousness of your life on the land, you will prosper and be at peace. Fail to worship YHWH alone, and you will be subject to the laws of history, vulnerable to control by others. This message is especially striking in light of the book's opening, where, in what appears to be a departure from the picture presented in Joshua, the recent conquest of Canaan is viewed as having been only partially successful. The framework of Chap. 2, probably imposed on the book at a late stage by so-called Deuteronomistic hands (those responsible for much of the overall thrust of the books of Deuteronomy through Kings), tries to represent the period of Judges not from the viewpoint of an un-biased chronicler but rather by the idea that the past is driven by an underlying meaning.

Second, in its broad sweep, the book of Judges suggests that Israel cannot survive without the institution of monarchy. Despite the timely intervention of YHWH, who regularly sends a "judge-leader" to militarily extract Israel from its predicament, their loose tribal system—what scholars today call a segmented society—appears too fragile to have any staying power. Story after story portrays charismatic warriors who are unable to provide for stable government beyond their own lifetime. There is no central authority which can adequately deal with growing external threats such as the Philistines, or with the burgeoning eco-nomic needs of an expanding population. By the end of Judges—which repeats the refrain "In those days there was no king in Israel, / each one would do what was right in his eyes"—the people of Israel have been presented as an essentially leaderless nation, fragmented by conflict, who have yet to realize the harmonious life under the covenant with God that had been envisioned (or at least hoped for) in Deuteronomy. In the simplest terms, then, Judges appears to demonstrate how badly Israel needed a king.

A third theme, the primacy of the tribe of Judah, which later became the core of the surviving Southern Kingdom, is brought out in Judges through the narra-tive structure. At the beginning of the book, Judah's battles succeed; at its end, the failures occur specifically in the north, which was Judah's counterpart and sometime rival. As many have noted, Chap. 19, the ultimate example of moral and societal decay in Judges, contains numerous veiled allusions to Saul, Israel's first king, whose power base was the north; he was replaced by the talented and suc-cessful Judahite David. While David's southern base succeeded, with one dynasty in power for the next three and a half centuries, the north, which broke off after his son Solomon's death, is chronicled in the book of Kings as living under numer-ous dynasties and is evaluated quite harshly for its violation of the covenant.

All these considerations reveal that Judges makes use of violence mainly to convey a series of religious and political messages. There appears to be no inter-est in or attempt at true historical reportage. While on the one hand, the book is consonant with what we know both about pre-state societies in general and the premonarchic period in Israel in particular, it represents a kind of literature that simply does not lend itself to historical reconstruction. As previously mentioned, chronology is not followed closely; the final chapters of the book seem to hearken back to the time period represented at the beginning. Characters often sport symbolic names, such as Cushan-Rish'atayim ("Nubian Double-Wickedness") in 3:8, and the sites of stories sometimes have an ideological basis (as in the aforementioned case of Chap. 19, whose setting of Gibeah is the birthplace of the later, rejected king Saul). Thus everything about Judges pushes the reader away from the stark recounting of historical facts, toward what we typically find in the Bible—a narrated version of the past that is designed to speak to a present time.

When could that "present" have been? Some recent scholars have pointed to the time of Josiah, king of Judah in the late seventh century B.C.E., who is idealized in Kings and who then would be the real object of Judges' desire, so to speak. But that theory may be too simple. A composition process in stages, such as is typical of biblical texts, might have seen an original core of northern local hero tales, enhanced and expanded by Deuteronomists to include the later judges, then finally framed by the opening and concluding chapters to form a bridge between Joshua and Samuel-Kings perhaps as late as the exilic period of the mid-sixth century B.C.E. or the postexilic one of decades later (see Mobley 2011 and Carr 2010 for recent discussions).

JUDGES AND HISTORY: AN IN-BETWEEN ERA

THAT SAID, CAN WE RECOVER ANYTHING ABOUT THE PERIOD IN WHICH JUDGES is set? The often obsessive desire on the part of modern scholars to understand Israel's early history "as it really was" (to use German historian Leopold von Ranke's famous phrase) has led to a flurry of archaeological and textual spadework in recent decades. Somewhat predictably, these efforts have not turned up a great deal of useful detail. As with the period of the "Conquest" (see the Introduction to the book of Joshua, above), material evidence about this time has been hard to come by. This is not at all surprising, given the relative dormancy of surrounding cultures in that era, as well as the lack of centralized state control in Israel. Thus we are left to tease out a general portrait of a period that lacks the panache of a monarchy, and which instead must be seen as a time of growth and change featuring a lower-level, decentralized society. What might Israelite life have been like in the era between settlement and the age of David and Solomon?

One possible source for answering this question lies in the Bible itself. Despite later editing of Judges, which may have specifically sought stories or traditions that fit its messages, the book does appear to preserve some authentic details of a time of change. The Deborah/Barak narrative in Chaps. 4–5, for example, portrays a not-yet-unified Israel, where some tribes fight against a common enemy while others refrain. In Chap. 12, Jephthah, having just rescued the Gileadites (on the east bank of the Jordan), fights their countrymen on the west bank, the men of Ephraim. Chap. 18 describes the migration of one tribe (Dan) well to the north. These examples strongly suggest the reality of a fragmented Israel in this period. Not only is there no central authority to raise an army for common defense, but serious conflict, even approaching the level of civil war (see Chap. 20), is an ever-present possibility.

The type of leadership found in Judges also fits a time of transition. The leaders tend to be local, occasionally serving as unifying forces, but their success is tied to personal talent, and they are frequently described in the text as being filled with "the rushing-spirit of YHWH." In a word, they are charismatic, not dynastic; the sole attempt by the son of a leader to succeed his father, that of Abimelech in Chap. 9, comes to a disastrous end.

The Hebrew word used to describe the judges themselves, which also gives the book its name, comes from a widely found Semitic root (sh-p-t) which can mean both "judge" in the juridical sense and "leader, chieftain" in a broader one. Basically speaking, the job of a biblical *shofet* is to restore and maintain order in society. While such a leader can be colorful in literature and undoubtedly in life, he or she is hardly a model to rely on for permanent political stability. The American West once again comes to mind, with its celebrated but sometimes morally questionable lawmen. So the book's description of its era likely preserves some aspects of historical reality.

To the portrait painted in our text, archaeology can contribute a general assessment of Israelite communities during the twelfth to tenth centuries B.C.E. Scholars have found strong evidence of a dramatic upturn in population during this period, especially in the traditional areas of Manasseh, Ephraim, and Benjamin (collectively known as the "Highlands of Ephraim"). They are able to confidently posit small farming communities, in which groups of extended families resided in a few houses arranged around a central courtyard. These houses were typically, as elsewhere in Canaan, two- to four-room structures, with food preparation and storage areas and stalls for animals on the first floor and sleeping quarters on the second, topped by a flat roof that could be used for processing grain. Notably absent in the region are the trappings of a centralized state, such as walled cities, royal buildings, a standing army, and bureaucratic officials. Interpersonal conflicts would have been handled locally, usually by the immediate family ("Father's House") or elders; larger problems would have been resolved by the clan or even the full tribe. To propose that there was a more extensive form of government is probably a mistake; there is no evidence to support earlier theories such as that of Noth, who theorized that Israel had a full-blown twelve-tribe league unified by a central shrine, parallel to an institution found in ancient Greece.

In the sphere of religion, both text and archaeology reflect the reality that ancient Israelites in this era worshipped Canaanite gods such as Baal, often alongside YHWH. We have seen that the text is deeply concerned with what it regards as Israel's apostasy in this period, and material remains from Israelite settlements include numerous figurines of the very deities whose worship is banned in Judges. Few central religious sites are mentioned in the book, and we do not encounter either important priests or the Coffer (the Ark of the Covenant), outside of a brief mention in 20:27, until the beginning of the next book, Samuel.

To summarize, Israel in the period of the Judges is a developing but still small-scale society, trying to eke out a living in the central highlands of Canaan. The glory days lie ahead.

LITERARY ASPECTS

As Niditch (2008) and others have pointed out, Judges is a memorable piece of literature and contains a good many recognizably literary traits, including strains of folklore, epic poetry, and humor. Folkloric aspects include the clever if grisly assassination of the enemy king in Chap. 3, the scene of the enemy general's mother waiting for him to return from battle in Chap. 5, Gideon's fleece and the dream he overhears in Chaps. 6–7, the sacrifice of Jephthah's daughter in Chap. 11, and many moments in the Samson cycle, including the prominence of animals, riddles, feats of astounding strength, and deep secrets. In the area of epic poetry, the Song of Deborah in Chap. 5 contains much that is characteristic of that genre, in its sweep, vivid descriptions, and use of "older" poetic forms. Theodor Gaster compared it to the Scottish highland ballads millennia later, which similarly celebrate great deeds in battle. Indeed, many of the traditions preserved in Judges undoubtedly reflect ancient memories of colorful local heroes, with all their deeds and foibles on display. And finally there are the flashes of humor, often difficult to identify in long-gone cultures but unmistakably present in a few of these stories. One might, for example, cite Samson's astounding feat of strength in Chap. 16, where he carries the town gates of Gaza on his shoulders for forty miles—uphill!—as the ambush waiting to pounce on him looks on in mute stupefaction. This brand of humor often appears among oppressed groups, and includes reveling in the enemy's downfall through stealth and glorifying in his suffering, especially at the hands of noncombatants such as women (see the tale of Jael in Chap. 4).

Other interpreters have perceived different emphases. Yairah Amit (1999a), one of the contemporary experts on Judges, finds that the book is shot through with examples of "signs" designed to assure the Israelites of God's ongoing power and protection. She also notes an internal arrangement pairing heroes together for structural purposes: Ehud/Shamgar's weapons are specifically mentioned (a short sword and an oxgoad, respectively); Barak and Gideon are initially cowed, and God is pointedly involved in the battles they wage; and Jephthah and Samson experience direct contact with God through vows and being infused with the divine "rushing-spirit."

For later generations of Jews and Christians, especially throughout the Middle

Ages, Judges provided both sheer entertainment and important symbolism. Jews, as a tiny oppressed minority in Europe, found some escape and solace in tales of ancient, warlike heroes. Christians, for their part, related to both what they saw as foreshadowing the Jesus story (for instance, Samson) and mirroring political developments in their own time (see Milton's appropriation of the figure of Samson in his *Samson Agonistes*). Indeed, the stories in Judges became a popular subject for artists in the Renaissance and beyond, appearing in major works by Dürer, Caravaggio, and Rembrandt, to cite some of the most memorable examples. In sum, the deeds of the heroes in Judges "continue to amaze, inspire, and confound readers" (Mobley 2011).

WOMEN IN JUDGES

AS MANY RECENT FEMINIST CRITICS HAVE NOTED, WOMEN PLAY AN IMPORTANT role in Judges, to an extent not seen in the Bible since the early chapters of Exodus. While they barely appear in Joshua, in Judges they are present in every major narrative save that of Ehud (Chap. 3). And the way they are painted seems to act as a moral barometer for the state of Israelite society as it was conceived of by the writers. Some female characters show strength and independence (Achsah, Deborah, Jael, and Abimelech's killer), but others appear as the victims of violence within and beyond the patriarchal system (Jephthah's daughter, the concubine at Gibeah, and the Benjaminite women at the end of the book—all of whom are unnamed!), and even as the enemy or corrupt figures (Delilah and the Levite's mother).

These narratives do not merely reflect a patriarchal society. More often than not, they serve to set the male characters in relief, demonstrating the shortcomings of the leaders in Judges. Achsah is not shy about asserting her rights; Deborah has the self-assurance that Barak does not; Jael succeeds in the absence of her husband; Jephthah's nameless daughter survives in cultural memory despite her early end; Delilah outsmarts the superhumanly strong Samson; and the numberless female victims in the last three chapters of the book serve to indict first a single Levite, then the tribe of Benjamin, and finally the entire people, for their crimes of abandonment, murder, rape, and abduction. If Samson and his ilk symbolize a badly faltering Israel, the female characters in the book function to sharply etch the consequences of the people's actions.

THE STRUCTURE OF THE BOOK

GIVEN THE DIFFERENT SOURCES, STYLES, AND PLOTS IN JUDGES, ONE COULD question whether it displays any kind of unity. Nevertheless, here is one possible outline:

I Opening the Bracket
    Introduction: Conquest II (Chap. 1)
    The Pattern (2–3:6)

II The Leaders Themselves
    A Early Leaders: Israel Delivered
    Othniel; Ehud (3:7–31)
    Deborah and Jael: A Twofold Victory (4–5)
    Gideon (6–8:32)
    B Later Leaders: Decline
    Abimelech (8:33–9:27)
    Tolah/Jair (10)
    Jephthah; Ibzan/Elon/Abdan (11–12)
    Samson (13–16)

III Closing the Bracket
    The Levite and the Danites (17–18)
    Trouble in Benjamin: Gibeah and Civil War (19–21)

Setting out the general structure of the book does not, at least initially, reveal the inner connections. That work has been done by a number of interpreters. Zakovitch has pointed to two important features in the narratives: first, a frame structure using the motifs of the tribe of Judah ascending to fight and the troops eventually returning home in both Chap. 1 and in the book's last two chapters; and second, the frequent linking of adjacent stories by means of words and ideas, a technique which he calls "associative arrangement." One illustration of the latter would be the eleven hundred pieces of silver that appear both in Chap. 16, as Delilah's reward money for betraying Samson, and Chap. 17, as the money the young Levite had "borrowed" from his mother.

For Malamat, the book also unfolds in two patterns, one geographical and one "judgmental." In this view, as the narrative ascends from the "good" south to the problematic north, the morals descend. The anomalous tribe Benjamin, which straddles the border between the two, is dealt with through an initial "good" story (Ehud) toward the beginning of the book and a "bad" one (the concubine at Gibeah) toward the end. Further, the last sections of Judges reveal a not-so-subtle attitude toward two later rulers: Saul, Israel's first king, who will hail from Benjamin, suggesting that he is a tainted choice, and Jeroboam I of the tenth-century Northern Kingdom, who, like the Danites in Chap. 18, institutes his own forms of Israelite religion, to be roundly condemned by the book of Kings (see Sweeney 1997). By the time Judges closes, Jephthah and Samson, who are defective enough as models, have been eclipsed by the lies and violence attributed to the northern tribes. The way is being prepared for a southern king—David, from Bethlehem in Judah.

Given the wide range of stories and tones in Judges, its final form would seem to be the work of creative editors. This also holds true for subunits in the book, such as the Samson cycle, in which narratives of differing lengths and emphases have been combined into a work that is remarkably unified in vocabulary (see the Appendix to Judges). While the early traditions about individual judges probably did not have such focused direction, the book has been edited in such a way that the conclusion is unmistakable: Israel, a chaotic society (especially in the north), is in desperate need of a stable political system, and kingship offers the only way out (although it too has its problems). Stories that may have originally concerned only individual tribes have been recast or reinterpreted to encompass Israel as a whole, with the warrior leaders coming to symbolize the entire people.

But for all the schematizing tendency noted above, Judges leaves us with an unanswered question. Why, amid all the flawed human behavior exhibited in the book, from group apostasy to individual acts of questionable judgment, does the God of Israel still stand by this people? This question will persist in the coming books, and indeed will become an unabating one in the Hebrew Bible as a whole. The answer, for the writers, centers around divine promises, made earlier to the Patriarchs and Moses, and later to David. Beneath all the chaos and uncertainty manifest in the book of Judges—and indeed in the books to come—the text testifies to the ongoing resiliency of Israel. Apparently, the troubled experience of the world at different historical moments by the people who wrote and transmitted the Hebrew Bible could not mute their ultimate hope and faith in the covenant with YHWH. Despite the looming presence of conquering empires, and eventually the traumas of destruction and exile, they understood God and Israel to be bound in a permanent relationship which could never be sundered. In this perspective, and in its pattern of estrangement from God, rescue, backsliding, and looking to the future, the book of Judges is another important link in the unfolding central plot of the Hebrew Bible.

PART I

OPENING THE BRACKET

(1–3:6)

WHILE JUDGES OPENS BY INVOKING THE NAME OF YEHOSHUA, WHOSE DEATH IN the previous book sealed the conquest of Canaan, it unexpectedly launches into an account of fighting and, more tellingly, a list of which territories the Israelites had *not* conquered. Immediately, then, the reader is plunged into a narrative situation of instability. Gone is the assurance of peaceful settlement and security, and the Israelites can expect military and cultural conflict, which is exactly what ensues throughout the book. Only the success of the tribe of Yehuda (Judah) at the beginning points to eventual ascendancy; the rest of the stories will oscillate among oppression, deliverance, and the recurrence of chaos.

This is made clear in the pattern introduced by Chap. 2, undoubtedly the creation of a later editor in the Deuteronomistic mold. The sequence of Israel's apostasy, God's handing them over to enemies, his eventual sending of a dynamic leader, a period of peace, and then a relapse by the people, sets the stage for the action to follow.

Once again, echoes from the past are understood not by invoking social, economic, or military causes, but through the lens of the covenant, especially as expressed in the language of Deuteronomy. And this message is delivered by a prophetic-type "messenger" of YHWH. In contrast, the "judges" themselves will by and large be military types, who are more tied to strategy than ideology.

Chapter 1. *The Link to Joshua:* The book of Joshua, capped by two long speeches by the dying Yehoshua, narrated the conquest and partitioning of the land of Canaan. Judges opens by in effect questioning the full realization of that process. We are dealing, possibly, with an alternative tradition, or with an admission that the conquest was not as total as we had thought. This ambiguous success and its result, that Canaanites will continue to live among the Israelites, set the stage for the confrontations and trials to follow in the book.

It is significant that Yehuda (Judah) is the tribe with which the chapter opens; as indicated in the Introduction, a major thrust of the book is to set up the coming of the monarchy. Although the first king will come from the tribe of Binyamin (Benjamin), the favored and permanent dynasty of David will stem from Yehuda. Thus there is a strong ideological overlay to Judges.

A small episode in this chapter, little discussed by earlier commentators but more emphasized recently, may have wider implications. Vv.12–15 repeat a story that had been recounted in Josh. 15:16–19 about Akhsa, the wife of Calev, who requests landed property as part of her marriage. Klein notes how in the context of Judges, a woman in a legally stable and approved relationship (the couple are from the same tribe, and he "earns" her hand) asking for fertile land might be seen as a sign of healthy normality, parallel to Israel receiving the fertile land of Canaan from God. In stark contrast are the troubled male-female relationships in the book's final chapters, indeed in its entire second half. Of course, it is no accident that the Akhsa episode is told about a family from the tribe of Yehuda.

Embedded in the long sequence of the chapter's second half is another brief piece (vv.22–25), this time about spies who obtain information from a watchman in return for sparing his life and that of his family in the coming battle. The tale parallels the prostitute Rahav's in Josh. 2, creating a certain symmetry between the books.

◆ 1:1 Now it was after the death of Yehoshua
that the Children of Israel inquired of YHWH, saying:
Who among us will go up first against the Canaanites to wage
battle against them?

2 YHWH said:
Yehuda will go up;
here, I have given the land into his hand.

3 Yehuda said to Shim'on his brother-tribe:
Go up with me into my allotted-territory, and let us wage battle
against the Canaanites,
and I will go with you as well into your allotted-territory.
So Shim'on went with him.

4 Yehuda went up,
and YHWH gave the Canaanites and the Perizzites into their hand,
so that they struck them down in Bezek,
ten thousand men.

5 They found Adoni-Vezek in Bezek, and waged battle against him,
and they struck the Canaanites and the Perizzites.

6 And Adoni-Vezek fled, so they pursued after him,
and they seized him and chopped off the thumbs of his hands and
of his feet.

1:1 **Yehoshua:** Pronounced *ye-ho-SHOE-ah;* trad. English "Joshua." **inquired:** Consulted God through an oracle. **YHWH:** As explained above in "On Using This Book," the name of God in the Hebrew Bible, whose pronunciation is not precisely known, is traditionally transcribed as "the Lord" and the like. Here it is printed according to the way it appears in the Hebrew text, and the reader may choose how to say it.

2 **Yehuda:** Pronounced *ye-hoo-DAH.* The Hebrew name for the largest and politically most significant Israelite tribe, from which the favored dynasty of David sprang. Where it refers to the Southern Kingdom in Samuel and Kings, I use "Judah" to distinguish it from the single tribe.

3 **Shim'on:** Pronounced *shim-OHN;* trad. English "Simeon." **brother-tribe:** Contiguous to Yehuda, in the south, around Be'er-Sheva (Beersheba).

4 **the Canaanites and the Perizzites:** Indigenous peoples of Canaan; in lists elsewhere (see, for instance, Gen. 15:19–21), a number of other "nations" are mentioned (see also 3:5, below). **ten thousand:** Some scholars take the word for "thousand" (Heb. *elef*) as a military division, so the number would be smaller in that case.

5 **Adoni-Vezek:** "Adoni" means "my lord/master," a divine epithet often found in the ancient Near East. The "v" in "Vezek" is due to a long vowel at the end of "Adoni." **Bezek:** Pronounced *BEH-zek;* either a site northeast of Shekhem or one between that city and Jerusalem.

6 **chopped off the thumbs:** Either to render him unfit to lead troops or simply to humiliate him (Burney).

◆   7   Adoni-Vezek said:
           Seventy kings, the thumbs of their hands and of their feet
               chopped off,
           used to gather [crumbs] under my table;
           as I did, so has God paid me back!
           They brought him to Jerusalem, and he died there.
      8   Then the Children of Yehuda waged battle against Jerusalem:
           they captured it, they struck it with the mouth of the sword,
           and the city they sent up in fire.
      9   Afterward, the Children of Yehuda went down to wage battle
               against the Canaanites,
           those settled in the highlands, the Negev, and the lowlands.
      10   And Yehuda went against the Canaanites, the ones settled in
               Hevron,
           —now the name of Hevron in former times was Kiryat-Arba—
           and he struck Sheishai and Ahiman and Talmai.
      11   He went from there against those settled in Devir
           —now the name of Devir in former times was Kiryat-Sefer.
      12   Now Calev said:
           Whoever strikes Kiryat-Sefer and captures it,
           I will give him Akhsa my daughter as a wife!
      13   Otniel son of Kenaz captured it,
           a brother of Calev younger than he,
           and he gave him Akhsa his daughter as a wife.
      14   Now it was, when she came,
           that she induced him to request fielded-property from her father.
           She alighted from on the donkey,
           and Calev said to her:
           What [ails] you?

7 **Seventy:** Commonly signifying "many" in the Bible. **Jerusalem:** Along with the next verse, this contradicts the later account in II Sam. 6, where it is David who conquers the city from the Jebusites.

9 **lowlands:** Heb. *shefela*, the low foothills that rise out of the coastal plain toward the central highlands.

10 **Hevron:** Pronounced *hev-ROHN*; trad. English "Hebron." **Arba:** Or "of the Four (Clans)." **Shei-shai and Ahiman and Talmai:** Descendants of Anak, and understood to have been giants. In modern Hebrew, *anak* means "gigantic."

11 **Devir:** Southwest of Hevron. **Sefer:** Denoting "writing" or an "inscribed document."

12 **Calev:** Pronounced *kah-LAVE;* trad. English "Caleb." He seems to appear out of nowhere, but this section is apparently an established tradition (see Josh. 15:13–19). **Akhsa:** Pronounced *akh-SAH;* trad. English "Achsah." See the version of this little story that appears in Josh. 15:16ff.

13 **Otniel:** Pronounced *aught-nee-AYL;* trad. English "Othniel," possibly meaning "God Is My Strength" or "God Is My Protection."

14 **she induced him:** Some ancient versions, here and in Josh. 15:18, have "he induced her."

15 She said to him:
Get me a blessing-gift,
for you have given me arid land—
you should give me pools of water!
So Calev gave her the Upper Pools and the Lower Pools.

16 Now the Children of the Kenite, Moshe's father-in-law, went
up from the Town of Date-Palms, along with the Children of
Yehuda,
into the Wilderness of Yehuda that is south of Arad;
they went and settled with the people.

17 And Yehuda went with Shim'on his brother;
they struck the Canaanites settled in Tzefat, and devoted-it-to-
destruction,
so they called the name of the town Horma / Destruction.

18 Then Yehuda captured Gaza and its territory
and Ashkelon and its territory
and Ekron and its territory.

19 Now YHWH was with Yehuda, so that he took possession of the
highlands,
but he was not [able] to dispossess the settled-folk of the valley,
for they had chariotry of iron.

20 And they gave Hevron to Calev, as Moshe had promised,
and he dispossessed the three sons of Anak from there.

---

15 **arid land:** Or "the Southland" (Heb. *negev*). JPS understands the expression as referring to Akhsa herself, namely, a woman without a dowry.

16 **the Kenite:** A tribe of smiths (the literal meaning), associated with the Midyanites and inhabiting the region between southern Israel and the Sinai Peninsula. Moshe's (Moses's) father-in-law Yitro (Jethro) belongs to this group (see Exod. 18), and some older scholarly theories saw the origins of Mosaic religion there. **the Town of Date-Palms:** Probably not Jericho; possibly Tzo'ar (Zoar) (Soggin). **they went:** MT (the standard Hebrew text) has the singular. **the people:** It is not clear what is meant here; one LXX text reads "the Amalekites."

17 **Tzefat:** Pronounced *tze-FAHT*. A town in the Negev region, not the later famous hill town (modern Safed) in the Galilee. **devoted-it-to-destruction:** Heb. verb *haram*, as in English "harem," something or someone set apart. Here it reflects a war concept that the spoils belong to God, not to the conquerors.

18 **captured:** But LXX reads "did not capture." **Gaza** (Heb. *'Azza*) **. . . Ashkelon . . . Ekron:** Three cities settled by the Philistines, invaders from the sea and subsequently Israel's great enemy (see note to 13:1, below).

19 **[able]:** Missing in MT but present in some manuscripts. The restored text would then correspond to, for instance, Josh. 15:63, *lo' yakhelu le-horisham*. **the valley:** Or "the plain." **iron:** The period of settlement/Judges roughly marks the beginning of the Iron Age. For another textual comment on the Philistines' possession of iron, and the Israelites' need of it, see I Sam. 13:19.

20 **sons of Anak:** See note to 1:10, above.

21 But the Yevusites, those settled in Jerusalem, the Children of
    Binyamin did not dispossess;
the Yevusites are settled along with the Children of Binyamin in
    Jerusalem until this day.

22 Now the house of Yosef went up, they too, to Bet-El,
and YHWH was with them.

23 The house of Yosef scouted out Bet-El
—now the name of the town in former times was Luz—

24 and the watchmen saw a man going out of the town,
so they said to him:
Pray let us see the way to enter the town, and we will show you
    loyalty.

25 He let them see the way to enter the town, and they struck the city
    with the mouth of the sword,
but the man and his entire clan they sent free.

26 The man went to the land of the Hittites and built a town;
he called its name Luz
—that is its name until this day.

27 Menashe did not take possession of Bet-She'an and her daughter-
    towns,
or of Ta'nakh and her daughter-towns,
or of the settled-folk of Dor and her daughter-towns,
or of the settled-folk of Yivle'am and her daughter-towns,
or of the settled-folk of Megiddo and her daughter-towns;
the Canaanites were determined to remain settled in this region.

28 And it was, when Israel became strong, that they put the
    Canaanites under forced-labor,
but dispossess, they did not dispossess them.

---

21 **Yevusites:** Trad. English "Jebusites," the inhabitants of Yevus, the Bible's chief name for pre-Israelite Jerusalem. They do not appear to have been there for an extended period. **Binyamin:** Pronounced *bin-yah-MEEN;* trad. English "Benjamin."
22 **Yosef:** Pronounced *yo-SAYF;* trad. English "Joseph." **Bet-El:** Pronounced *bayt ayl;* trad. English "Beth-El."
24 **loyalty:** Others, "kindness," but the biblical term *hesed* often denotes adherence to a treaty or agreement.

26 **the land of the Hittites:** See note to Josh. 1:4. **this day:** Here, as in v.21 above, it is the narrator's era which is being referred to, the actual date of which cannot be determined.
27 **Bet-She'an:** Trad. English "Beth-Shean," the important northern city in the Jordan Valley, not far from the Jezreel Valley. **daughter-towns:** Satellite towns. **Ta'nakh . . . Dor . . . Yivle'am . . . Megiddo:** The text takes us westward through the fertile Jezreel Valley; these sites were fortresses (Gray 1986).

29 Now Efrayim did not dispossess the Canaanites, those settled in
Gezer,
and so the Canaanites remained settled in their midst, in Gezer.

30 Zevulun did not dispossess the settled-folk of Kitron, or the settled-
folk of Nahalol,
and so the Canaanites remained settled in their midst,
and went into forced-labor.

31 Asher did not dispossess the settled-folk of Akko, or the settled-folk
of Sidon,
or of Ahlav, or of Akhziv, or of Helba,
or of Afik, or of Rehov.

32 So the Asherites settled amid the Canaanites, the settled-folk of the
land,
for they did not dispossess them.

33 Naftali did not dispossess the settled-folk of Bet-Shemesh
or the settled-folk of Bet-Anat,
so they settled amid the Canaanites, the settled-folk of the land,
and the settled-folk of Bet-Shemesh and of Bet-Anat went into
forced-labor for them.

34 And the Amorites pressed the Children of Dan into the highlands,
indeed, they did not give them [leave] to go down into the valley.

35 The Amorites persisted in remaining settled in Mount Heres, in
Ayyalon and in Shaalvim,
yet the hand of the House of Yosef grew heavy [against them], so
that they went into forced-labor.

36 Now the territory of the Amorites was from Scorpions' Pass, to the
Crag and further.

---

29 **Gezer:** An important city at the junction of the northern lowlands and the Judean hills, on the southwest border of Efrayim.
30 **Zevulun:** Pronounced *zeh-voo-LOON;* trad. English "Zebulun." **Kitron . . . Nahalol:** Identification uncertain.
31 **Akko . . . Sidon:** On the northern seacoast; present-day Acre (in Israel) and Sidon (in Lebanon). **Ahlav . . . :** See Josh. 19:29, where it is "Mahalav."
33 **Bet-Shemesh:** Not the more prominent Bet-

Shemesh west of Jerusalem, but one far to the north, near the eventual territory of Dan.
34 **Amorites:** Often a general term for the Canaanites.
35 **Mount Heres . . . :** North of Bet-Shemesh. **the House of Yosef:** A term for the northern tribes.
36 **Amorites:** LXX manuscripts read "Edomites," which is more likely, given the geography. **Scorpions' Pass:** A pass linking Mediterranean areas with the Jordan Valley. **the Crag:** Possibly the famous site of Petra, in today's Jordan.

Chapter 2. *The Pattern:* Having made the transition from Joshua in Chap. 1, the book proper begins with a harsh message from God: Israel will not occupy the land exclusively, and this means that they will have to deal somehow with the "foreign gods" worshipped by the local population. What ensues is a causational view of history, seeking to explain what happened to the Israelites and why. It begins as the book of Exodus did, with a new generation that has forgotten the past (in Exod. 1:8, it was the Pharaoh who was thus described). The text proceeds to lay out a pattern which will serve as a general outline for what is to follow. The elements are: (1) The Israelites "abandon" God by worshipping local gods (vv.11–13); (2) God reacts in anger, abandoning them to the power of their enemies and leading them to be distraught (14–15); (3) God has pity on them and sends a "judge," almost always a military leader, who delivers them (16, 18); over time, they rebel against God again, starting the cycle once more (17, 19); this leads to a reprise of God's anger (20–23) and his decision to leave the Canaanites in the land as a permanent test among the Israelites.

This very negative scheme would seem to lock the entire book into an ironclad pattern, but the skill of the authors and compilers varies it constantly and introduces other themes as well. And typically for the Bible, the presence of a global view does not detract from the text's ability to portray intriguing situations and memorable characters.

In the second half of the chapter, the recurrence of central words points to the key issues, as frequently happens in biblical texts. From vv.11–14, there is a chiastic (ring) structural pattern, created by the brackets of "served . . . abandoned" and "abandoned . . . served." Six times toward the end of the chapter, the word "hand" echoes, indicating that the crucial question is one of power: Which group will control the land?

◆ 2:1 A messenger of Y<small>HWH</small> went up from Gilgal to Bokhim
and said:
I had you go up from Egypt,
and I brought you to the land that I swore to your fathers;
I said:
I will not annul my covenant with you for the ages!

2 While you,
you are not to cut a covenant with the settled-folk of this land—
their altars you are to demolish!
But you did not hearken to my voice.
Now what have you done!

3 So I also say:
I will not drive them out before you;
they will be traps to you,
and their gods will be a snare to you!

4 It was, when the messenger of Y<small>HWH</small> had spoken these words to all
the Children of Israel,
that the people lifted up their voice and wept.

5 So they called the name of that place Bokhim/Weepers,
and they sacrificed there to Y<small>HWH</small>.

6 Yehoshua had sent the fighting-people off,
and the Children of Israel had gone off, each one to his hereditary-
property, to take possession of the land.

7 And the people had served Y<small>HWH</small> all the days of Yehoshua
and all the days of the elders who had prolonged years after
Yehoshua,
who had seen every great deed of Y<small>HWH</small> that he had done for Israel.

2:1 **messenger:** This is the actual meaning of Heb. *mal'akh.* Even the traditional rendering "angel" does not necessarily imply a supernatural creature, as the English word itself reflects the Greek *angelos,* "messenger," human or otherwise. **Gilgal:** An important political and cultic center, near Jericho. The name seems to indicate some kind of circular structure, of stones, perhaps a platform (Rainey/ Notley). **Bokhim:** The name is interpreted in v.5, below. Gray (1986) raises the possibility that this refers to the "Oak of Weeping" of Gen. 35:8, which may originally reflect a Canaanite mourning or fasting ritual.

2 **cut a covenant:** The expression derives from the idea of cutting up sacrificial animals, to imply that one who violates the agreement will wind up like them. See Gen. 15. **altars:** Where sacrifices were offered up. Pulling down pagan altars is an important covenant theme in Deuteronomy, and again in Kings.

3 **traps:** Heb. unclear; Josh. 23:13 suggests that *tziddim* ("sides") here may be short for "a whip in your sides" (Kimhi). **snare:** A trap for catching birds, and, more figuratively, foolish, wicked, or simply unwary human beings.

4 **wept:** As they will do at the end of the book, in 21:2 (Boling 1975).

7 **prolonged years:** I.e., survived (Moore).

◆ 8 And Yehoshua son of Nun, the servant of YHWH, had died,
a hundred and ten years old;

9 they had buried him in the territory of his hereditary-property,
in Timnat-Heres in the highlands of Efrayim, north of the
highlands of Gaash.

10 Now also that entire generation was gathered to its fathers,
and another generation arose after them, that did not know YHWH,
as well as the deed[s] that he had done for Israel.

11 And the Children of Israel did what was evil in the eyes of YHWH:
they served the Baals,

12 they abandoned YHWH, the God of their fathers,
the one who brought them out of the land of Egypt,
and they walked after other gods, from among the gods of the
peoples who were around them;
they bowed down to them
and so provoked YHWH—

13 they abandoned YHWH
and served Baal and the Astartes.

14 So YHWH's anger flared up against Israel,
and he gave them into the hand of pillagers, so that they pillaged
them,
and sold them into the hand of their enemies round about,
so that they were no longer able to stand up before their enemies.

15 Whenever they went out [to war], the hand of YHWH was against
them for evil,
as YHWH had promised,

8 **a hundred and ten:** An ideal life span, as in the case of Yosef (Joseph) in Gen. 50:22.

9 **Timnat-Heres:** In Josh. 19:50 and 24:30, it is spelled "Timnat-Serah."

11 **the Children of Israel did what was evil in the eyes of YHWH:** This phrase acts as a unifying refrain in the stories about the judges, occurring seven times in Chaps. 2–3. **Baals:** The use of the plural here probably refers to the multiple forms and manifestations of the god in Canaanite worship. Baal ("master" or "lord"; pronounced *BAH-ahl*) was the powerful thunderstorm/fertility god of the area, whose mythic exploits are preserved on clay tablets from the ancient city of Ugarit on the Syrian coast, fifteenth–thirteenth centuries B.C.E. Judges and Samuel give evidence of the strong attraction of this Canaanite god for Israelite farmers. Some of

YHWH's characteristics echo Baal's; both, for example, are referred to in their respective literatures as "Rider on the Clouds."

12 **provoked:** Or "exasperated" (Moore).

13 **Astartes:** Heb. *Ashtarot*, goddesses usually identified with well-known divine figures such as the Babylonian Ishtar. Here the plural is probably meant to include various local goddesses.

14 **sold them:** A more figurative way of expressing "handed them over," possibly also connoting finality or legitimacy associated with the concept of a sale. Conversely, physically "handing over" something can symbolically indicate the performance of an actual sale (see Ruth 4:7).

15 **they were exceedingly distressed:** Or, with LXX, "he (God) afflicted them" (Soggin).

as Yhwh had sworn to them,
and they were exceedingly distressed.
16 Then Yhwh raised up judge-leaders;
they delivered them from the hand of their plunderers.
17 But also to their judges they did not hearken:
indeed, they went whoring after other gods
and bowed down to them;
they quickly turned aside from the way that their fathers had
    walked, hearkening to the commands of Yhwh—
they did not do thus.
18 Now whenever Yhwh raised up judges for them,
Yhwh would be with the judge,
and would deliver them from the hand of their enemies
all the days of the judge,
for Yhwh would feel regret at their moanings, because of their
    oppressors and their persecutors.
19 But it would be, upon the death of the judge:
they would return and do ruin, more than their fathers,
by walking after other gods,
by serving them and by bowing down to them;
they would not let any of their actions or their stubborn path fall
    away.
20 So Yhwh's anger flared up against Israel,
and he said:
Because this nation has crossed my covenant that I commanded
    their fathers,
and has not hearkened to my voice,
21 for my part, I will not continue to dispossess any before them
from the nations that Yehoshua left behind when he died—
22 in order to test Israel through them,
whether they will keep the way of Yhwh, to walk in it,
as their fathers kept, or not.

---

16 **judge-leaders:** As noted in the Commentary, *shafat* often means "to lead" or "to govern"; I have sought to retain both senses, at least this first time. See the passage in 3:10, below.
17 **went whoring after:** A common biblical expression for idolatry.   **thus:** Follow God's commands.

19 **do ruin:** Or "behave badly" (Moore).
20 **crossed:** As in the literal meaning of "transgressed," that is, "trans" (cross) + "gressed" (went over), in the sense of violating laws or norms.

Chapter 3:1–6. *The Neighbors:* Continuing from Chap. 2, we are told who Israel's neighbors are, ending with the oft-repeated idea that intermarriage with them will lead to the worship of other gods.

23 So Yhwh let these nations stay
and did not dispossess them quickly,
neither did he give them into the hand of Yehoshua.

3:1 And these are the nations that Yhwh let remain
to test Israel through them,
all those who knew nothing of all the battles over Canaan,
2 only for the sake of knowledge of the Children of Israel's
generations,
to teach them war
—only those who previously had not known them:
3 the five Philistine overlord [cities]
and all the Canaanites and the Sidonians and the Hivvites, the
settled-folk of the highlands of the Levanon,
from the mount of Baal Hermon to Levo-Hamat.
4 They were to test Israel through them,
to know whether they would hearken to the commandments of
Yhwh
which he had commanded their fathers, by the hand of Moshe.
5 So the Children of Israel settled amid the Canaanites,
the Hittites, the Amorites, and the Perizzites,
the Hivvites, and the Yevusites;
6 they took their daughters for themselves as wives,
while their own daughters they gave to their sons,
and they served their gods.

3:1 **all those:** The Israelites.
3 **overlord:** A word used exclusively of Philistine nobles. Some relate the word (Heb. sing. *seren*) to the Greek *tyrannos,* from which English "tyrant" is derived. **Sidonians:** From the important Phoenician port city. **Levanon:** Trad. English "Leba-non." **from . . . Baal Hermon to . . . Hamat:** Israel's northern border.
5 **Yevusites:** Trad. English "Jebusites."
6 **took their daughters . . . :** This, in the eyes of the writers, was the cardinal sin, since it was understood as leading directly to idolatry.

EARLY LEADERS: ISRAEL DELIVERED

(3:7–8:32)

THE FIRST LEADERS WHOSE DEEDS ARE DESCRIBED IN THE BOOK STRIKE A GENER-
ally positive note. Judges' account of the human "deliverers" of Israel begins with
a surprisingly brief example, that of Otniel. But his inclusion at this point is significant. The three verses which describe his activities are enough to establish his
identity as a member of the tribe of Yehuda and to attribute his prowess in battle
to the "rushing-spirit of YHWH" which infuses him.

With Ehud, the twin aspects of bold human strategy and savage humor make
their appearance. Apparently both are compatible with biblical literature, despite
the divine overlay. It is almost as if the serious business, the message of YHWH's
protection and the primacy of Judah, has been taken care of, and the audience can
now enjoy a brief but fully fleshed out tale of triumph. This narrative also makes
it clear that in Judges, violence, sometimes extreme, will be used unhesitatingly
to extract Israel from its local and regional struggles. That it will spill over into
Israelite private life in the second half of the book is not yet apparent.

The Devora / Barak leadership, recounted in both a narrative account (Chap. 4)
and a poetic version (Chap. 5), provides a high point in this section of Judges. The
first telling, as it were, combines the dialogue of the leaders, focused on establishing divine credit for the coming victory, in a dramatic geographic setting, and
concludes with the grisly story of the enemy general's death. The ensuing poem
takes up themes of ancient warriors, cosmic battle, and the contrast between
triumphant females and bereaved ones. By the end of the two-chapter sequence,
God is fully ensconced as the Divine Warrior who defeats Israel's enemies by
enlisting both the climate and the human agencies of sword and stealth. It is hard
to imagine what can go wrong for Israel at this point.

But as Chap. 2 posited, it is the Israelites themselves who consistently upset
the delicate balance. By once again doing "what was evil in the eyes of YHWH"
as Chap. 6 opens, a long cycle of stories pertaining to the next judge, Gid'on,
begins. These form an important fulcrum in the book in the eyes of many interpreters. After the militarily effective Ehud and the stalwart leadership of Devora,
Gid'on introduces notes of doubt, contention, and even, it seems, a form of idolatry. While in the opening scene the new judge conventionally portrays himself

as unworthy for the task, as Moshe before him had done, his questioning goes beyond personal qualifications to challenge God's deliverance. Further, a number of times in the narrative, townspeople and other Israelites are portrayed in conflict with Gid'on; once, he even sneaks around them at night out of fear. True, he rejects the crown offered to him with the emblematic words, "*I will not rule over you,* / *my son will not rule over you—* / YHWH *will rule over you!*" (8:23), but he follows this important gesture with a concession to Baal worship, the very thing that had caused God to turn his back on the Israelites several times already in the book.

So the wheel in Judges begins to turn. On the one hand, there is a military rout, complete with a prophetic dream and psychological strategy, but on the other, the hero ends by building an image which winds up leading the Israelites astray. The book is heading in a dangerous direction.

––––––––

Chapter 3:7–11. *First Judge: Otniel:* The first of the military leaders whom God sends as a response to Israel's cries is, not surprisingly, from the tribe of Yehuda. Though brief, the story displays the necessary skeletal elements of Chap. 2's outline: idolatry, oppression (by an enemy king with a stereotyped name), the Israelite outcry, a leader who is possessed of God's "spirit," a quick victory, and a land that remains tranquil for a defined period. As Amit (1999a) notes, it also contains "the largest concentration of formulaic phrases in the book" (fifteen of them, such as "And the people of Israel did what was evil in the eyes of YHWH," "served the Baals and the Astartes," "YHWH sold them into the hand of . . . ," "YHWH raised up a deliverer," and "the land was quiet for *x* years"). The pattern is deceptively simple; from now on, a good deal of color, variation, and ambiguity will be added.

Chapter 3:12–30. *Bravery and Burlesque: Ehud:* Without much breathing room, the text immediately deviates from the standard Judges pattern represented by Otniel, as we are introduced to satire as a biblical form (Brettler 2001a). The story of Ehud and King Eglon reads like the ultimate crowd-pleaser for an oppressed people: the enemy ruler is ridiculed in scatological terms and dies an incredibly violent death, with the hero escaping easily. While we do not possess much information about humor in the Bible, and it is always tricky to divine what is amusing to an ancient culture, one can nevertheless imagine Israelite audiences enjoying the picture of the enemy king wallowing in his own filth and blood, while his hapless servants cannot figure out what is taking him so long in the "cool upper-chamber." The means of killing is described in a well-thought-out and clever plot, and while a modern nonviolent reader may recoil at the particulars, we are served notice by

3:7 And the Children of Israel did what was evil in the eyes of Yhwh;
they forgot Yhwh their God
and served the Baals and the Ashera-poles.

8 So the anger of Yhwh flared up against Israel,
and he sold them
into the hand of Cushan Rish'atayim / Nubian Double-Wickedness,
king of Aram of the Two Rivers,
and the Children of Israel served Cushan Rish'atayim for eight
years.

9 And the Children of Israel cried out to Yhwh,
so Yhwh raised up a deliverer for the Children of Israel, and he
delivered them:
Otniel son of Kenaz,
brother of Calev, one younger than he.

10 Now there [came] upon him the rushing-spirit of Yhwh;
he led Israel as judge and went out to battle,
and Yhwh gave into his hand Cushan Rish'atayim king of Aram,
and his hand was powerful against Cushan Rish'atayim.

11 The land was quiet for forty years;
then Otniel son of Kenaz died.

12 But the Children of Israel continued to do what was evil in the eyes
of Yhwh,
and so Yhwh strengthened Eglon king of Moav over Israel,
since they had done what was evil in the eyes of Yhwh.

13 He gathered the Children of Ammon and Amalek to him;
then he went and struck Israel,
and he took possession of the Town of Date-Palms.

3:7 **Ashera-poles:** The name is pronounced *ah-shay-RAH*. The term for this goddess is often interchangeable here with a cult object. However, it is more probable that the name in this passage should be read as "Astarte," who is more commonly paired with the Baals.

8 **Cushan Rish'atayim / Nubian Double-Wickedness:** Probably a deliberate play on a more conventional name, or one with a more conventional etymology. **Aram of the Two Rivers:** Syria, with the Tigris and Euphrates mentioned. The Hebrew is pronounced *ah-RAHM*.

9 **Otniel:** Already mentioned in 1:13.

10 **came:** Lit. "was." **the rushing-spirit:** God's spirit is viewed as something almost physical; the same word also means "wind, breath." Sometimes the infusion of the divine leads to an increase in physical strength, as with Shimshon's, while in other cases it is connected to prophetic or artistic inspiration. **led . . . as judge:** Or "assumed leadership" (Rainey / Notley).

12 **Eglon:** pronounced *egg-LOHN*. **Moav:** Trad. English "Moab," the territory on a plateau east of the southern half of the Dead Sea (in today's Jordan). In the Bible, the Moabites are one of Israel's traditional enemies.

the text that this is a heroic age, in which details of death in battle and assassination are matters of intense interest and detailed description.

As Brettler (2001a) and others have noted, the narrative uses multiple terms for sacrifice, beginning with the name of the king himself. "Eglon" carries the connotation of a calf or bull, ready for the slaughter. The term for "gift" or "tribute" (Heb. *minha*), while normal in this context, can also indicate a sacrifice of grain. The verb "bring near" (*k-r-b*), similarly, is the conventional one for offering a sacrifice.

Another cluster of images is sexual: doors and locking, "hand" (sometimes in the Bible a euphemism for male genitalia), and the phrase "come [in]to" (v.20), a common biblical expression for intercourse. Such imagery is undoubtedly used in this chapter to humiliate the enemy king, similar to the English language usage of overtly sexual terms in anger or humor not always directly related to sexuality. It is also worthy of note that we are dealing here with a Moabite king, and the Bible is unabashed in its negative (and sexual) portrayal of that nation, from its putative origins in incest in Gen. 19 to its causing Israel to go "whoring" after other gods in Num. 25.

The text progressively isolates the two characters. Tribute is usually delivered in public, in a crowd; but here we have, first, Ehud's men retiring, then Eglon's, until the two principals are left alone in the "cool upper-chamber" of the palace. There will be only one who will exit the room. It will take the courtiers' unlocking the door to unlock the mystery of what has happened.

Eglon's is the kind of downfall that will happen to many of Israel's enemies in the book: defeat and death through stealth and daring, understood as aided primarily by God. The story is thus a good example of what Brettler (2001a) calls an "ideological" text, and its actual historical value is probably moot.

◆ 14 And the Children of Israel served Eglon king of Moav for eighteen
years.

15 And the Children of Israel cried out to YHWH,
so YHWH raised up a deliverer for them:
Ehud son of Gera, a Binyaminite,
a man restricted in his right hand.
And the Children of Israel sent a tribute-gift by his hand to Eglon
king of Moav.

16 Ehud made himself a sword;
it had two mouths, a *gomed* its length,
and he strapped it under his garb, over his right thigh.

17 Then he brought near the tribute-gift to Eglon king of Moav
—now Eglon was an exceedingly well-nourished man—

18 and it was, when he had finished bringing near the tribute-gift,
that he sent away the people, those bearing the tribute-gift,

19 while he himself returned from the carved-images, those near
Gilgal,
and said:
I have a secret message for you, O King!
He said:
Hush!
And they went out from him, all who were standing [in attendance]
around him.

---

15 **Ehud:** Pronounced *ay-WHO'D*. **Gera:** Pronounced *gay-RAH*. **restricted:** This probably refers to their training, leading to the capability of fighting with either hand (Halpern). The Binyaminites are known in the Bible as talented warriors.

16 **it had two mouths:** Two-edged. ***gomed:*** Pronounced *GO-med*. It measured a little over a foot long, corresponding to what the ancients called a "short sword." **garb:** An outer garment, often part of military or priestly dress (see Lev. 6:3). Ehud is wearing his sword under his garment to avoid detection. **over his right thigh:** Presumably the king's soldiers would not think to frisk him on the side opposite from where a sword is usually drawn (by a right-handed person).

17 **now Eglon was . . . well-nourished:** The word *bari'*, often understood as "fat" and hence playing up the burlesque aspects of the story, here may be meant to contrast the victorious Moabites with the oppressed Israelites. The same word was also used to describe the hale and healthy cows of the Pharaoh's dream in Gen. 41:2,4,18, and 20.

19 **the carved-images:** Apparently Ehud leaves the king's presence with the other tribute bearers, accompanying them to the border marked by these images. Ehud then doubles back for his audience with Eglon, having made sure that his countrymen are safely across. **a secret message:** Or secret word (Heb. *davar*). **Hush!:** The command seems aimed at Ehud, so that others will not hear the "secret" message. But the courtiers vacate the room.

Chapter 3:31. *Shamgar the Brief:* A fragment has been placed at this point, with enigmatic names at its core. "Shamgar" is manifestly a non-Hebrew name, while "Anat" recalls a well-known Canaanite goddess. Further, this leader is mentioned later, in the Song of Devora (5:6), and thus appears out of place here. Perhaps, as Brettler (2001a) suggests, this brief notice was inserted after the core of Judges was written. In any event, Shamgar anticipates Shimshon (Samson) in his wielding an unusual, animal-related weapon. His presence also reinforces the Judahite emphasis of the book.

◆ 20   When Ehud came to him, he was sitting in the cool upper-chamber
           that he had, alone.
        And Ehud said:
        I have a message from God for you!
        He arose from his throne,
   21   and Ehud stretched out his left hand,
        and took the sword from on his right thigh
        and thrust it into his belly.
   22   Even the grip entered after the flashing-blade,
        so that the fat closed up behind the blade,
        for he did not draw the sword from his belly,
        and the feces came out.
   23   Then Ehud went out toward the porch
        and closed the doors of the upper-chamber after himself, and
           bolted them.
   24   Once he had gone out, his servants came back,
        and they saw that here, the doors of the upper-chamber were
           bolted,
        so they said:
        Surely he is "covering his feet" in the cool inner-room!
   25   They waited-anxiously until it was shamefully-late,
        and here, he was not opening the doors of the upper-chamber,
        so they took the key and opened [them] up—
        and here was their lord, fallen on the ground, dead!
   26   As for Ehud, he had escaped while they tarried;
        he crossed by the carved-images, and escaped to Se'ira.

---

20 **upper-chamber:** A room built on top of the house with air-admitting windows (Burney). **message from God:** Ehud's choice of words ups the stakes and causes the king to rise from his seat. It may also be ironic, since the "message from/word of God" often predicts or precipitates a catastrophe in the Bible. **throne:** Heb. *kissei,* which in modern Hebrew means "chair," rarely has such an everyday usage in the Bible.
21 **his belly:** Eglon's.
22 **grip:** And not "hilt," as often understood (Stone). **feces:** Others understand this obscure word (Heb. *parshedona*) as "vestibule," through which Ehud exited.

23 **porch:** Heb. *misderona;* note the rhyme with the rare word in the previous verse, which gives the story a distinct tone.
24 **his servants:** Eglon's. **bolted:** From the inside. **"covering his feet":** A biblical euphemism for defecating (see I Sam. 24:3 for another example).
25 **until it was shamefully-late:** Or "as long as shame demanded" (Gray 1986). **fallen . . . dead!:** Anticipating "fallen dead" in 4:22 and "fallen, ravaged" in 5:27, both of which refer to another enemy of the Israelites, Sisera.
26 **Se'ira:** Location unknown, not to be confused with "Mount Se'ir" in other biblical texts.

Chapter 4. *Devora and Barak; Ya'el and Sisera:* In another shift from the norm established in Chap. 2, the text here presents multiple heroes, two of them women (unexpected in a book recounting violent exploits). The character of Devora broadens and deepens the question of leadership, introducing a "judge" who indeed sits and governs the people in a way that most of the male judges do not, and who is even described as a "prophet."

Coming as it does after the stunning deeds of several warrior-judges, the chapter serves to warn the audience that victory ultimately comes from God alone. It accomplishes this by tying the triumph to circumstances unusual for a war: the Israelite commander depends closely on a woman's counsel, stressing the idea that "it will not be your glory" (v.9), and the enemy general is slain by a noncombatant, also a woman. Indeed, the use of the typical phrase "I will give the enemy into your hand" (here in vv.7 and 14) is nicely counterbalanced by "hand," referring twice to Ya'el (vv.9 and 21).

The battle scene itself utilizes stock biblical battle language ("panic" in v.15, "not even one was left" in v.16) and is typically brief, preferring to shift the chapter's focus to the interaction between the characters before and after the actual fighting.

As in the Ehud story, the narrative uses stealth as a major feature. We do not expect betrayal from a covenant partner, nor murder at the hands of a woman, especially one who acts in so maternal a manner: Ya'el covers Sisera (tucks him in!), gives him milk, and stands guard in the tent. Her utter single-mindedness and fearlessness contrast with Barak's initial hesitation in v.8.

The result echoes Israel's deliverance at the Reed Sea (Exod. 15); the prose account there ended with "So YHWH delivered on that day / Israel from the hand of Egypt . . . ," while our story similarly reads, "So God humbled on that day / Yavin king of Canaan, before the Children of Israel."

◆ 27 Now it was, when he came [there],
that he gave a thrusting-blast on the *shofar,* in the highlands of
Efrayim,
and the Children of Israel went down with him from the highlands,
with him ahead of them.
28 He said to them:
Come down after me,
for YHWH has given your enemies, Moav, into your hand!
They went down after him
and took the Jordan crossings from Moav;
they did not let a man cross.
29 And they struck Moav at that time—
about ten thousand men,
all stout ones, all men of valor;
not a man escaped.
30 Thus Moav was humbled at that time under the hand of Israel.
And the land was quiet for eighty years.

31 After him was Shamgar son of Anat:
he struck the Philistines, six hundred men, with an ox-goad;
thus he too delivered Israel.

4:1 But the Children of Israel again did what was evil in the eyes of
YHWH,
and Ehud was dead.
2 So YHWH sold them into the hand of Yavin king of Canaan, who
reigned as king in Hatzor;
the commander of his armed-forces was Sisera.
Now he sat [enthroned] at Haroshet of the Nations.

27 **thrusting-blast:** I have tried to keep the connection between this and Ehud's action in v.21. ***shofar:*** The ram's horn, usually sounded in battle.
28 **Come down:** Reading *redu,* with LXX, for MT *ridfu,* "pursue." **crossings:** Others, "fords."
29 **stout:** Perhaps with double meaning, first, as "stalwart men," and second, repeating the "grotesque" fat motif from earlier in the story (Amit 1999a).
30 **humbled:** Or "subdued" (Moore).
31 **ox-goad:** From Heb. *l-m-d,* a root that usually means "to learn" or, in another form, "to teach." Klein understands its usage here as suggesting the thought "I'll teach the enemy a thing or two."
4:1 **Ehud was dead:** Different traditions seem to be at work here; Shamgar is not mentioned as he is in 5:6.

2 **Yavin:** Pronounced *yah-VEEN;* trad. English "Jabin." **king of Canaan:** As Amit (1999a) notes, Canaan had no centralized authority; the characterization is probably meant to aggrandize the victory. **Hatzor:** pronounced *hah-TZOHR;* trad. English "Hazor," the strategically and economically important city in the north of Israel, above the Sea of Galilee. An alternate tradition recounts the city's destruction in Josh. 11:1–11. **Sisera:** A foreign name of uncertain origin; it may be a play on *saris,* "official" or "eunuch." **Haroshet:** Meaning "farmland" and indicating the plain to the east of Megiddo (Rainey / Notley).

◆

3 And the Children of Israel cried out to YHWH,
  for he had nine hundred iron chariots,
  and he had been oppressing the Children of Israel strongly for
      twenty years.

4 Now Devora was a prophet woman, wife of Lappidot/Torches;
  she was judging Israel at that time.

5 She was sitting [as judge] under the Palm of Devora, between
      Rama and Bet-El, in the highlands of Efrayim,
  and the Children of Israel would come up to her for judgment.

6 She sent and called for Barak/Lightning son of Avino'am, from
      Kedesh in Naftali,
  and she said to him:
  Has not YHWH, the God of Israel, charged you?
  Go deploy at Mount Tavor,
  and take with you ten thousand men from the children of Naftali
      and from the Children of Zevulun;

7 I will deploy against you, at Wadi Kishon, Sisera, the commander
      of Yavin's forces, along with his chariotry and his throng,
  and I will give him into your hand.

8 Barak said to her:
  If you go with me, I will go,
  but if you do not go with me, I will not go!

9 She said:
  I will go, yes, go with you;
  but it will not be your glory on the way that you are going.

3 **iron:** See note to 1:19, above.
4 **Devora:** Pronounced *de-vo-RAH*; trad. English
  "Deborah." The name means "bee" but is also
  reminiscent of *davar*, "[divine] word"—appropriate
  for a prophet. See also 5:12, "speak forth [*dabberi*]
  a song." **Lappidot:** Pronounced *lah-pee-DOHT*;
  "torches" is sometimes metaphorical for lightning
  flashes. The fiery connotations of this word have led
  some to identify him with the general Barak ("Lightning"). The phrase "wife of Lappidot" has been read
  by some as "a fiery woman," but the form here generally calls for a proper name.
5 **She was sitting [as judge]:** A counter to the enemy
  king in v.2, "who sat [enthroned]." **between Rama
  and Bet-El:** Later known as the area of the prophet
  Samuel's activity.
6 **Kedesh in Naftali:** Not to be confused with one

of the other towns named Kedesh. **deploy:** The
Hebrew denotes "drawing out" or "extending" a
battle line. **Tavor:** Trad. English "Tabor," a significant and imposing mountain centrally located in
the Galilee near major roads. Gray (1986) points out
that, as a forested area, it would provide good cover
for the Israelites.
7 **Wadi Kishon:** Pronounced *kee-SHOHN*, an east-
west brook which empties into the Mediterranean,
east of today's Haifa. In I Kings 18:40 Eliyyahu (Elijah) will slaughter the prophets of Baal there.
9 **I will go, yes, go:** Others express the repetition of
the verb by "I *will* go." **a woman:** That is, a non-
soldier. See 9:54, below. Here, the text does not yet
reveal the identity of the woman, whom one might
assume to be Devora herself.

◆ Rather, it is into the hand of a woman
that Y<small>HWH</small> will sell Sisera!
And Devora arose and went with Barak to Kedesh.

10 So Barak called up Zevulun and Naftali to Kedesh,
and behind him came up ten thousand men,
while Devora came up with them.

11 —Now Hever the Kenite had parted from the Kenites,
from the Children of Hovav, Moshe's father-in-law;
he had spread his tent as far as the oak in Tzaananim, which is near
Kedesh.—

12 And Sisera was told that Barak son of Avino'am had come up to
Mount Tavor,

13 so Sisera summoned all his chariotry, nine hundred iron chariots,
and all the fighting-people who were with him,
from Haroshet of the Nations to Wadi Kishon.

14 Devora said to Barak:
Arise, for this is the day that Y<small>HWH</small> is giving Sisera into your hand!
Does not Y<small>HWH</small> go out [to war] before you?
So Barak came down from Mount Tavor,
with ten thousand men behind him.

15 And Y<small>HWH</small> panicked Sisera and all the chariotry and all the camp,
with the mouth of the sword, before Barak,
and Sisera got down from the chariot and fled on foot.

16 Now Barak was pursuing after the chariotry and after the camp, as
far as Haroshet of the Nations,
while all the camp of Sisera fell by the mouth of the sword;
not even one was left.

17 Now Sisera had fled on foot, to the tent of Ya'el, the wife of Hever
the Kenite,
for there was peace between Yavin king of Hatzor and the house of
Hever the Kenite.

---

10 **behind him:** Lit. "in his footsteps."

11 **Hever the Kenite . . . :** See the notes to 1:16 on the Kenites and 3:17 on the intrusion of seemingly irrelevant information in biblical stories, above. The meaning of the name, "confederate," is appropriate for a treaty partner. **Hovav:** An alternative name for Yitro, for reasons that are unclear (a separate tradition?). **Tzaananim:** Following the *Qere*.

14 **go out [to war]:** Applied to leadership, this common verb frequently has a military connotation.

15 **panicked:** A standard biblical expression for God's routing the enemy (see, for instance, Exod. 14:24).

17 **Ya'el:** Pronounced *yah-AYL;* trad. English "Jael." Like some other biblical names, especially of women, this refers admiringly to an animal, the ibex or mountain goat.

Chapter 5. *The Song of Devora:* The victory recounted in Chap. 4, probably based on some kind of historical incident, clearly played a key role in Israel's later vision of itself. Set as it is after the prose account, the poem in the present chapter is parallel, as previously mentioned, to the events of Exod. 14, which similarly is followed by an archaic-sounding poem.

Cross/Freedman and others have maintained that Chap. 5 is one of ancient Israel's oldest texts, dating perhaps to the period when the event is to have taken place. It contains a number of constructions characteristic of early Hebrew. Brettler (2001a), however, summarizing several decades of recent scholarship, concludes that the bulk of the chapter's language is "standard biblical Hebrew" and that we can actually draw no conclusions about a composition date. It has long been known that oral literature—if that is what is at play here, as some scholars who make claims for the poem's historical authenticity maintain—is not actually preserved unaltered for centuries. But if Judg. 5 is not, then, an accurate rehearsal of historical events, or such events are not fully recoverable, what exactly is it, at least as it now appears in the Bible? Brettler's proposal in this regard is an intriguing one: that the poem may have been used in ancient Israel to rally troops to battle. While he floats this as only a theory, I would add that there exists a more modern American parallel, familiar to schoolchildren of past generations: "Paul Revere's Ride" by Longfellow. Many, perhaps most, of those made to memorize its famous lines grew up convinced that this was precisely the way events had unfolded in 1775. But the poet composed his piece in 1861, shortly before the first shots were fired on Fort Sumter, and it was dragged out again two years later, at the height of Lincoln's attempt to get reluctant northerners to enlist in the Union army. Thus the poem, like its ancient relative, was written, or at least used, in Brettler's words, to "persuade and convince." In the case of Judg. 5, then, as so often in biblical texts, the events of the past, however accurate their portrayal, may here serve primarily to illuminate some present situation.

The chapter contains memorable imagery, from the distinctive descriptions of the tribes, YHWH as warrior, the gathering soldiers, and the involvement of the very cosmos (in the person of the stars) in the battle. Vv.4 and 21 in fact point to a rainstorm as a key element in Israel's victory. Finally, the theme of voluntarism which is emphasized in the poem, lauding those who participated and castigating those who did not, parallels early heroic poetry in other cultures.

Of particular note is the description of Sisera's assassination in v.27. On the surface, its rhythms are significant, with the repetitions in v.26 reminiscent of slow-motion death scenes in film. But more than that: as feminist readers of the Bible have pointed out, the verbal imagery is actually sexualized. The traditional "at her feet" can quite reasonably be rendered "between her legs," and the verb "crouched" (Heb. *kara'*) is used with sexual meaning in Job 31:10. Thus our narrative brilliantly paints Ya'el as a many-faced figure, much as in fairy tales— nurturing mother, potential or actual lover, and finally, of course, gruesome killer. The images do double duty: the milk is a symbol of motherhood, but is also effective in putting Sisera to sleep; the netting/blanket serves to cover him as

18	Ya'el came out to meet Sisera
	and said to him:
	Do turn aside, my lord, do turn aside to me, do not be afraid!
	So he turned aside to her, to the tent,
	and she covered him with a blanket.

19	He said to her:
	Now let me drink a little water, for I am thirsty!
	She opened a skin of milk, gave him drink, and covered him.

20	Then he said to her:
	Stand at the entrance to the tent,
	and let it be: if anyone comes and asks you, and says:
	Is there anyone here?
	you are to say: Nobody.

21	Then Ya'el, the wife of Hever, took a tent peg, and put a hammer in
	her hand,
	and came to him silently
	and thrust the peg into his temple, so that it went down into the
	ground
	—now he had been sound asleep, for he was weary—
	and he died.

22	Now here, Barak was pursuing Sisera,
	and Ya'el came out to meet him and said to him:
	Come, I will show you the man whom you are seeking.
	He came to her, and here was Sisera fallen dead, with the peg in his
	temple!

23	So on that day God humbled Yavin king of Canaan before the
	Children of Israel.

24	And the hand of the Children of Israel went harder [and harder]
	against Yavin king of Canaan,
	until they had [completely] cut off Yavin king of Canaan.

5:1	And Devora sang, along with Barak son of Avino'am, on that day,
	saying:

---

18 **do not be afraid:** Why would he have reason to be afraid of her or of her husband, with whom, as the text tells us in the previous verse, his lord has a pact of friendship? The phrase seems to be hinting at what is to come. **blanket:** Some understand this as a fly net.

20 **Nobody:** Sisera has been reduced to the status of a nonperson, or shortly will be (Fokkelman 1999).

one would a child, but also ultimately functions as a covering for a corpse; and the tent peg and mallet, which normally betoken domesticity, are transformed into murder weapons, with unavoidably phallic imagery.

In fact, as many interpreters have noted, there are multiple images of the mother here: Devora, described as a "mother in Israel," is a classic "good mother" figure, whereas Ya'el melds the nurturing and dangerously erotic images of mothering in the strongest way, as mentioned above. The last of the triad of women, Sisera's mother, combines the picture of parental concern with a condoning reference to rape by the expected victors (v.30, "a lass [literally, 'a womb'] . . . for each warrior chief"). Thus conflicting images, which could be understood as varying sides of the same coin, coalesce to express the ambivalence of the Bible's male writers. Historically speaking, this is not unusual in male-female relations, but its expression is particularly notable in this story.

Most striking of all in the poem, however, is the inclusion at the end of the episode regarding Sisera's mother, whom we have not met previously, and whose passivity contrasts with Ya'el's activism. The wrenching image of women helplessly waiting and watching for their husbands, brothers, or sons to return safely from battle, which can be found in the ballads of many cultures up to our own time, is used here to maximum effect. The poet masterfully contrasts the mother's natural fears, occasioned by her son's lateness, with her self-delusion, which is punctuated by literally colorful visions of captive women and scarves. These serve only to set up the fiercely triumphant moment of v.31: "So perish all your enemies, O YHWH!"

2   When war-loosened [hair] is loose in Israel,
        when fighting-people present themselves—
        bless YHWH!

3   Hearken, O kings,
        give ear, O princes—
        I, to YHWH I will sing,
        I will give praise to YHWH, the God of Israel!

4   YHWH, in your going out from Se'ir,
        in your striding forth from the Steppes of Edom,
        the earth quaked, the heavens too dripped,
        the clouds too dripped water,
5   the mountains shook before YHWH, the One of Sinai,
        before YHWH, the God of Israel!

6   In the days of Shamgar son of Anat,
        in the days of Ya'el, the caravans ceased,
        those who walked on roads
        walked on twisting paths.

7   The villagers ceased,
        they ceased in Israel,
        until you arose, Devora,
        you arose, a mother in Israel!

8   He chose new gods
        —then there was battle in the gates.
        Was shield seen, or spear,
        among forty thousand in Israel?

5:2 **When war-loosened [hair] is loose:** Heb. Not entirely clear; others, "When leaders took the lead," or Brettler's attractive paraphrase, "When all hell breaks loose" (2001a).

4 **Se'ir . . . Edom:** The plateau territory southeast of Israel, in the southern part of today's Jordan. Some have taken this to point to the region as a geographical source of early Israelite religion. Or does it simply suggest sunrise (see Deut. 33:2)? The name "Edom" denotes "red," possibly mirroring the color of the sandstone mountains in the area. The Edomites and Israelites frequently fought, although a kinship is recognized in the Patriarchal stories of Genesis, where Edom is an alternative name for Esav (Esau), older brother of Yaakov (Jacob). **the earth quaked:** Although there are traditions about Baal, and equally about YHWH, as a god who thunders and causes the earth to shake, the Heb. verb z-l-l with this meaning is attested only in Arabic; it may instead connote something closer to the watery images to follow.

5 **the One of Sinai:** A title for God.

6 **caravans:** Reading *orehot* for *orahot* (paths).

8 **He chose new gods:** Reflecting the deteriorating economic and political situation (Boling 1975).

◆

9   My heart was toward the decree-makers in Israel,
those presenting themselves among the people,
bless YHWH!

10   O those who ride on white she-asses,
those who sit on cloths,
those who walk on the way,
report [it]!

11   At the sound of the trumpets by the water-drawers,
there they retell the righteous-acts of YHWH,
the righteous-acts for his villagers in Israel.

Then they went down to the gates,
the fighting-people of YHWH.

12   Bestir, bestir yourself, Devora!
Bestir, bestir yourself, speak forth a song!
Arise, Barak,
and capture your captives, O son of Avino'am!

13   Then the remnant went down against the powerful,
the fighting-people of YHWH went down for me against the
    mighty!

14   From Efrayim, their root in Amalek,
after you, Binyamin, among your people!
From Makhir, the decree-makers went down,
and from Zevulun, leaders with the census-counter's staff.

15   Rulers in Yissakhar beside Devora,
as Yissakhar, so Barak,
in the valley, sent out behind him.

---

9 **decree-makers:** Rulers.
10 **those who ride on white she-asses,** / **those who sit on cloths:** The wealthy, as opposed to "those who go on the way."
11 **trumpets . . . water-drawers:** Emending *mhtztzym* to a common root for "trumpet," and likewise reading the other noun as coming from the verb for drawing water (*sh-'-b*), understanding it with LXX as representing the lowest rung of society.
14 **their root in Amalek:** The tribe of Efrayim stays put, choosing not to participate in the battle (Bol-

ing). Amalek was viewed in the Bible as a traditional foe of Israel; the bad feelings stemmed from their behavior in attacking the Israelites at the time of the Exodus (Exod. 17:8–13; see also I Sam. 15:2). **Makhir:** A clan from the tribe of Menashe.
15 **Yissakhar:** Pronounced *yi-sah-KHAR;* trad. English "Issachar." Amit (2004) notes the likelihood that this should read "Naftali," given the connection to Barak and other factors. **behind him:** NRSV "at his heels," implying "at his command." **soul searching:** In a negative sense; indecision.

In the tribal divisions of Re'uven
was great soul searching:

16 why did you sit between the sheepfolds,
hearkening to whistling for flocks?
At the tribal divisions of Re'uven
was great soul searching.

17 In Gil'ad, across the Jordan he dwelt,
and Dan—why did he sojourn in ships?

Asher sat by the shore of the sea,
by his landing-place he dwelt.

18 Zevulun—a people risking life amid dying;
Naftali—upon the risen terraces of the field.

19 Kings came, they waged battle,
then they waged battle, the kings of Canaan,
at Ta'nakh, by Megiddo's waters—
profit of silver they took none.

20 From the heavens the stars waged battle,
from their courses they waged battle with Sisera.

21 The Wadi Kishon swept away [the foe],
the ancient wadi, the Wadi Kishon.
—May my being bless them with strength!

22 Then the horses' hooves pounded
from the dashing, the dashing of their war-steeds!

23 Doomed be Meroz, says YHWH's messenger,
doomed, yes, doomed be her settled-folk,
because they did not come to the help of YHWH,
to the help of YHWH among the mighty!

---

16 **whistling for flocks:** Perhaps the traditional pipe-playing of shepherds.

18 **risking life amid dying:** That is, with no regard to their own safety, as opposed to those tribes who did not volunteer (see Ehrlich).

19 **Ta'nakh:** Five miles south of Megiddo. **Megiddo:** The crucial pass which permits entry to the coastal plain. Because of its strategic importance, it was frequently the site of major battles. The English form "Armageddon," denoting a final cataclysmic battle, derives from the Greek transcription of the name *Har* (Hill of) *Megiddo*.

20 **the stars waged battle:** In Ugaritic texts, rain originates in the stars, so the image reinforces the connection between cosmic forces and the flooding which seems to play such a large part in the Israelite victory (Gray 1986).

21 **bless:** Emending MT *d-r-k* to *b-r-k*, "bless," more in keeping with the singer's reflective pauses in the poem (e.g., vv.2, 9, 16).

23 **Meroz:** Exact location unknown.

Chapter 6. *Gid'on I: The Commission:* This first full cycle of stories about a hero in Judges opens by utilizing an important category of religious texts: the "call." A hero is addressed by God or his messenger and is charged with leading the people out of oppression or danger. Here it is prefaced, like the call of Moshe in Exod. 3, by a description of Israel's sufferings, this time under the Midyanites (vv.2–6). The variation on the classic Judges pattern of Chap. 2 here appears in vv.8–10, where God responds to the Israelites' usual outcry with the moral equivalent of "What do you expect, given your idolatrous behavior?" Only then can the deliverer be sent.

The call narrative in Judg. 6 looks forward as well as backward. The image of divine fire consuming a sacrifice, and the realization that what appeared to be a man is actually a messenger from God, are both elements of the Shimshon (Samson) birth story in Chap. 13. And the use of "signs" here and elsewhere in the story introduces that major motif into the book (Amit 1999a) as a whole.

There are other variations from the Chap. 2 paradigm in this chapter. The oppression, in this case wrought by the Midyanites, is much more detailed than before; Israel's very food supply is threatened, and the size of the enemy hordes is vividly described. Then too, instead of directly launching a war of liberation against the Midyanites, vv.25ff. establish Gid'on as a fighter against idolatry, although they also indicate further weakness of character: he is unwilling to risk the wrath of the locals by tearing down the altar to Baal in the daylight hours. The little story here is an etiology, a narrative that explains an important name (in this case "Yerub-baal" for Gid'on). Whereas in the account of Ehud idolatry was on the periphery (suggested only by the mention of "carved images," or a name with similar meaning), here it becomes central, and surfaces again in Chap. 8. Judges will not let us forget the core issue of the people's apostasy.

Vv.33–40 return to Gid'on's need for proof through "signs," a doubling that suggests not only the hero's need for reassurance but also that of the audience.

24 May she be blessed among women, Ya'el,
 wife of Hever the Kenite,
 among women in tents may she be blessed!

25 Water he asked for, milk she gave,
 in a bowl for the valiant, she brought near cream.

26 Her hand to the peg she stretched out,
 her right-hand to the workmen's pounder.
 She pounded Sisera, smashed his head,
 she shattered and passed it through his temple.

27 [?] Between her legs he bent down, he fell, he lay,
 between her legs he bent down, he fell,
 where he bent down, there he fell, ravaged!

28 Through the window she peered,
 Sisera's mother wailed through the lattice:
 For-what-reason comes his chariot [so] shamefully-late?
 For-what-reason are the beats of his chariots tardy?

29 The wisest of her attendants gives answer,
 yes, she sends back her words to her:

30 Are they not finding, dividing the spoils—
 a lass, two lasses for each warrior chief?
 Spoils of dyed cloths has Sisera,
 spoils of dyed embroidered cloth;
 dyed [tunics], embroidered at the neck,
 he is taking-as-spoils . . . .

31 So perish all your enemies, O YHWH,
 but let those who love you
 be like the emergence of the sun in its might!

 And the land was quiet for forty years.

---

25 **for the valiant:** With the meaning of "fit for the valiant."

27 [?] **bent down:** Others "sank." Note that Heb. *k-r-'* can also indicate worship. **ravaged:** The word is perhaps parallel to the underworld term "wasted" (in the homicidal, not the alcoholic sense). The Hebrew root (*sh-d-d*) can carry the suggestion of rape along with plunder, appropriate in the sexual role reversal of this story, hence the resemblance between "ravaged" and "ravished."

29 **attendants:** Not lowly maidservants, but women of higher status.

30 **lass:** Parallel to Moabite usage, along with a Ugaritic cognate meaning "girl." Some read the Heb. *rehem* literally as "womb" and understand it as contemptuous of women. **neck . . . taking-as-spoils:** Redividing the text from *tzavarei shalal* to form *tzavar yishlol* at the end of the phrase.

6:1 But the Children of Israel did what was evil in the eyes of YHWH,
so YHWH gave them into the hand of Midyan, for seven years.

2 And the hand of Midyan was powerful against Israel;
[in fear] of Midyan, the Children of Israel made use for themselves
of the dens that were in the highlands,
as well as the caves, as well as the strongholds.

3 It would be, whenever Israel would sow seed,
that Midyan would go up, along with Amalek and the Children of
the East;
they would go up against it,

4 they would encamp against them and would lay ruin the yield of
the ground, as far as where-you-come to Gaza,
and they would not leave anything sustaining-life in Israel
for sheep, or for ox, or for donkey.

5 For they and their acquired-livestock would go up, along with their
tents,
and they would come like locusts in abundance
—[what was] theirs and their camels' was innumerable—
and they came into the land to bring it to ruin.

6 So the Children of Israel became exceedingly impoverished before
Midyan,
and the Children of Israel cried out to YHWH.

7 And it was, when the Children of Israel cried out to YHWH, on
account of Midyan,

8 that YHWH sent a man, a prophet, to the Children of Israel;
he said to them:
Thus says YHWH, the God of Israel:
I myself brought you up from Egypt,
and took you out of a house of serfs,

9 and rescued you from the hand of Egypt
and from the hand of all your oppressors;
I drove them out from before you
and gave you their land.

6:1 **Midyan:** Pronounced *mid-YAHN;* trad. English "Midian," a region and a people whose primary location was the Hejaz (northwestern Arabia), but who also were found in the Sinai and the Jordan Valley.

2 **dens:** The Arabic cognate is *minhara,* a place hollowed out by water (Burney).

5 **like locusts:** In the Bible's imagery, the largest number possible (see Exod. 10:5, where locusts "covered the eye of the earth").

8 **I myself brought you up . . . :** A typical Deuteronomistic passage of admonition (Burney brings parallels from Josh. 24:2ff. and I Sam. 12:7ff.).

10 And I said to you:
I am YHWH your God;
you are not to hold in awe the gods of the Amorites, in whose land
you are settling—
but you did not hearken to my voice!

11 Now a messenger of YHWH came and sat under the oak that is in
Ofra, that belonged to Yoash the Avi'ezrite,
while Gid'on/Hewer his son was beating down wheat in the
winepress,
to whisk it away from before Midyan.

12 And YHWH's messenger was seen by him;
he said to him:
YHWH is with you, O mighty-man of valor!

13 Gid'on said to him:
Please, my lord,
if YHWH is with us,
why has all this found us?
Where are all the wonders which our fathers recounted to us,
saying:
Was it not from Egypt that YHWH brought us up?
Yet now, YHWH has forsaken us
and has given us into the grasp of Midyan!

14 YHWH faced him and said:
Go forth in this strength of yours
and deliver Israel from the grasp of Midyan!
Have I not sent you?

15 He said:
Please, O Lord,
whereby shall I deliver Israel?
Here, my family is the weakest in Menashe,
and I am the youngest in my Father's House!

11 **Ofra:** A location in Manasseh, where the Avi'ezrite clan lived. **Yoash:** "YHWH Has Given"; trad. English "Joash." **Gid'on:** Pronounced *gid-OHN;* trad. English "Gideon." **Hewer:** More felicitous English would be "Hacker," but that has very different associations in the age of technology. **in the winepress:** In a less conspicuous place than an open-air threshing floor.

13 **found:** Or "happened to." **grasp:** Lit. "palm."
15 **O Lord:** Some manuscripts have "my lord," which makes more sense given that Gid'on does not know that his visitor is divine. A parallel occurs in Chap. 13 with Shimshon's father, Manoah. **family:** Indicating an extended family or clan.

◆ 16 YHWH said to him:
   Indeed, I will be with you;
   you will strike down Midyan as [if they were] one man!
17 He said to him:
   Now if I have found favor in your eyes,
   make me a sign that it is you speaking to me:
18 now do not depart from this-place until I come back to you
   and have brought out my gift and placed it before you!
   He said:
   I will stay until your return.
19 So Gid'on came out
   and made ready a goats' kid with an *efa* of unleavened meal:
   the meat he put in a basket, while the broth he put in a boiling-pot,
   and he took them out to him beneath the oak, and brought them
      close.
20 And God's messenger said to him:
   Take the meat and the unleavened bread and place them on this
      boulder,
   and the broth, pour out.
   He did so.
21 And YHWH's messenger stretched out the tip of the crook that was
      in his hand
   and touched the meat and the unleavened bread;
   and fire went up from the rock
   and consumed the meat and the unleavened bread,
   while YHWH's messenger went away from his eyes.
22 Gid'on saw that he was YHWH's messenger,
   so Gid'on said:
   Alas, my Lord YHWH,
   for now I have seen YHWH's messenger face to face!

16 **Indeed, I will be with you:** Recalling God's assurances to Moshe in Exod. 3 (Boling 1975).
18 **gift:** In other contexts, *minha* can mean a sacrifice of grain; perhaps it appears in a double sense here, given Gid'on's unawareness of his guest's true identity. In 3:17 it is the same term used to describe the tribute paid to Eglon, king of Moav.
19 *efa:* Pronounced *ay-FAH,* it was a dry measure, equaling perhaps a bushel. **took them out ... brought them close:** In both cases, "them" does not appear in the text, but biblical Hebrew often omits the object pronoun. **brought them close:** I.e., presented them (Moore). The verb (*k-r-b*) is frequently used regarding sacrifices.
21 **crook:** A shepherd's implement. The Hebrew word (*mish'an*) is used in Ps. 23:4 (in KJV, "Thy rod and Thy *staff,* they comfort me").
22 **Alas . . . :** As often in the Bible (see again in Chap. 13 below), a person who "sees God" has good reason to fear for his life. Another example occurs with Yaakov in Gen. 32:31.

23 YHWH said to him:
Peace be to you—do not be afraid; you will not die.

24 Gid'on built there a sacrificial-altar to YHWH,
and he called it: YHWH of Peace.
Until this day, it is still in Ofra of the Avi'ezrites.

25 It was on that night that YHWH said to him:
Take an ox bull that belongs to your father,
a second-born bull, seven years old:
you are to tear down the altar of Baal that belongs to your father,
and the Ashera-pole that is next to it you are to cut down,

26 and you are to build an altar to YHWH your God
on the top of this stronghold in an arrangement [of stones];
then you are to take the second-born bull
and are to offer it up as an offering-up, with the wood of the
    Ashera-pole that you cut down.

27 Gid'on took ten men from his servants
and did as YHWH had spoken to him.
Now it was, because he was too afraid of his Father's House and of
    the men of the town to do it during the day,
that he did it during the night.

28 The men of the town started-early in the morning,
and here, the altar of Baal had been demolished,
and the Ashera-pole that was next to it had been cut down,
and the second-born bull had been offered up upon the rebuilt altar!

29 They said, each one to his fellow:
Who did this thing?
They made inquiry and searched,
and they said:
Gid'on son of Yoash did this thing!

30 So the men of the town said to Yoash:
Bring out your son, that he may die,
because he demolished the altar of Baal,
and because he cut down the Ashera-pole that was next to it!

---

23 **you will not die:** But typically in the Bible, the hero who comes into direct contact with God *does* survive.

24 **Peace:** Or "Well-being."

25 **Ashera-pole:** The name of this goddess and her cult object, representing a tree, are accentuated in this verse by the repeated occurrences of "sh" sounds in Hebrew: *shor* (ox), *asher* (that), and *Ashera,* and secondarily by *u-far ha-sheni sheva' shanim* ("second-born bull, seven years old").

27 **afraid:** Another indication of a character weakness in Gid'on.

Chapter 7. *Gid'on II: The Battle Against Midyan:* On the heels of Gid'on's doubts, God counters, emphasizing that there must be no illusion that the Israelite victory could be due to the prowess of its warriors (see a similar sentiment in 4:9, above, using the same key word, "glory"). While the meaning of the symbolism of the soldiers drinking from the stream is elusive, it is clear that Gid'on will succeed militarily, as Yehoshua did, only through God's intervention, although in the coming battle there are elements of strategy as well.

The dream of the Midyanite soldiers (vv.13–14) functions as a further sign that God will supply the victory. It is tempting to see in this scene one of the sources of Shakespeare's famous prebattle dream sequences. A nice touch is supplied by the fact that it is not the hero who has the dream here, but an enemy soldier, who recounts it secondhand.

We do not get to the battle itself until v.17. The victory is quite unorthodox—upside down, as the dream has it: instead of the Israelites doing the slaughtering, it is the confused Midyanites who put each other to the sword. Only the fierce and symbolically named enemy commanders are cited as direct victims of the Israelites, although obviously many of their soldiers would have died in the Israelites' pursuit.

31 But Yoash said to all who were standing [in attendance]
      around him:
   Will you yourselves strive for Baal?
   Or will you yourselves deliver him?
   Whoever strives for him will be put to death by daybreak!
   If he is a god, let him strive for himself
   when someone demolishes his altar!
32 So they called him from that day on: Yerub-baal/Let-Baal-Strive,
      saying:
   Let Baal strive with him,
   because he demolished his altar!

33 Now all Midyan and Amalek and the Children of the East gathered
      together;
   they crossed over and camped in the Valley of Yizre'el.
34 But the rushing-spirit of YHWH clothed Gid'on;
   he gave a blast on the *shofar* and the Avi'ezrite-clan was summoned
      after him.
35 He sent messengers to all of Menashe,
   and they rallied to the summons, they too, after him,
   and he sent messengers to Asher, to Zevulun, and to Naftali,
   and they went up to meet them.
36 Gid'on said to God:
   If you wish to deliver Israel by my hand, as you have spoken,
37 here: I am setting a clipping of wool on the threshing-floor;
   if dew is on the clipping alone, but on all the ground [it is] dry,
   then I will know
   that you will deliver Israel by my hand, as you have spoken.

31 **deliver him:** Others, "defend his cause."
32 **Yerub-baal/Let-Baal-Strive:** Or "Let-Baal-Sue." Trad. English is "Jerubbaal." In actuality the name probably means "May Baal Plead [for Me]"; the story, however, understands it otherwise, in a classic case of folk etymology. Normally, later scribes polemically substituted *boshet,* "shame," for the Baal part of such names (see also "Ish-Boshet" for "Ish-Baal" in II Sam. 2:8, 10). Here, though, they did not, because of the centrality of the name Baal in this episode (Burney).

33 **Children of the East:** Or "easterners," denoting other nomadic groups (Rainey/Notley) **Yizre'el:** Pronounced *yiz-reh-AYL;* trad. English "Jezreel," the large, fertile valley in the northern part of Israel.
34 **the rushing-spirit of YHWH clothed Gid'on:** An unusual description which demonstrates how physical the concept of "spirit" is in the Bible. Yet it is not a magical talisman to be used at will, like a helmet conferring invisibility; the text does not say "Gid'on clothed himself in it."
37 **clipping:** Others, "fleece."

38 And it was so.
He started-early on the morrow;
he wrung out the clipping
and drained the dew from the clipping—
a bowl full of water.

39 Then Gid'on said to God:
Do not let your anger flare up against me,
but let me speak just one [more] time:
pray let me make a test only one [more] time with the clipping;
pray let there be dryness on the clipping alone,
but on all the ground let there be dew.

40 And God did so on that night:
here was dryness on the clipping alone,
but on all the ground there was dew.

7:1 Now Yerub-baal—that is Gid'on—and all the fighting-people who
were with him started-early;
they camped by En Harod/Spring of Trembling,
while the camp of Midyan was north of it,
at Giv'at Ha-Moreh/Hill of the Sage, in the valley.

2 YHWH said to Gid'on:
Too many are the fighting-people who are with you
for me to give Midyan into their hand.
—lest Israel honor itself over me, saying:
My [own] hand delivered me!

3 So-now,
pray call out in the hearing of the people, saying:
Who is fearful and trembling?
Let him turn back and depart from Mount Gil'ad!
So there turned back from the people twenty-two thousand, while
ten thousand remained.

7:1 **Trembling:** Anticipating the people's feelings in v.3. **Sage:** Or "oracle."
2 **honor itself:** Take the credit.
3 **Who is fearful and trembling?:** The concern is that the fearful soldier will demoralize his comrades; see Deut. 20:8. **depart:** Heb. *tz-p-r,* a verb with uncertain meaning. Some emend to *'-v-r,* "cross over," among others. On the other hand, it sounds like the word for "bird/sparrow," and so possibly suggests "fly away like a sparrow," or even "Let him turn back twittering." **Gil'ad:** Possibly with the connotation of "fright" (Burney traces it to Babylonian *gadalu,* "to be afraid"), given that no "Mount Gil'ad" is attested in the Bible.

4 YHWH said to Gid'on:
Still the people are too many!
Lead them down to the water,
that I may refine them for you there:
it will be, [the one] about whom I say to you: This one shall go
with you,
he shall go with you,
and [the one] about whom I say to you: This one shall not go
beside you,
he shall not go.
5 So he led the people down to the water,
and YHWH said to Gid'on:
Whosoever licks with his tongue from the water, as a dog licks,
set him aside,
but whosoever crouches on his knees to drink . . .
6 Now the number of those who licked, from their hand to their
mouth,
was three hundred men,
while all the rest of the people crouched on their knees to drink
water.
7 YHWH said to Gid'on:
By the three hundred men, those who were licking, I will deliver
you;
I will give Midyan into your hand,
and then all the people will go, each one back to his place.
8 So they took the people's provisions in their hand, along with their
shofars,
while all the fighting-men of Israel he sent away, each to his tents,
but of the three hundred men he kept hold.
Now the camp of Midyan was beneath him, in the valley.

4 **refine:** The Heb. *tz-r-f* is a metallurgical term for "smelt, test the mettle." It may also be a play on the *tz-p-r* of v.3, since *p* and *f* are the same root letter in Hebrew (Boling 1975).
5 **licks . . . crouches:** In Burney's view, lapping the water on the stomach means that they are vulnerable to attack, and hence God is clearly the only one who can deliver them. The traditional explanation

is that the alternative posture, on the knees, implies idolatry.
6 **three hundred:** Mobley (2005) memorably compares this number to other celebrated small groups of fighters such as the three hundred Spartans, the Seven Samurai, and the Dirty Dozen.
7 **place:** Home.

◆ 9 And it was on that night
that Yнwн said to him:
Arise, go down against the camp,
for I have given it into your hand!
10 And if you are afraid to go down [to attack],
go down, you along with Pura your serving-lad, to the camp,
11 and hearken to what they are saying;
afterward your hands will be strengthened, so that you may go
down against the camp.
So he went down, he and Pura his serving-lad, to the edge of the
armed men who were in the camp.
12 Now Midyan and Amalek and all the Children of the East were
sprawled out in the valley, like locusts in abundance,
and their camels had no number,
like the sand that is on the shore of the sea in abundance.
13 And Gid'on came, and here, a man was recounting a dream to his
fellow;
he said:
Here, I have dreamt a dream,
and here, a loaf of barley bread was turning over in the camp of
Midyan.
It came as far as the tent and struck it, and it fell;
it overturned it, upward,
and the tent fell down!
14 His fellow spoke up and said:
This is none other than the sword of Gid'on son of Yoash, the man
of Israel!
God has given Midyan into his hand, yes, the entire camp!
15 It was, when Gid'on heard the recounting of the dream and its
interpretation,
that he bowed low;
then he returned to the camp of Israel

9 **the camp:** Of the enemy.
11 **go down:** In force.
12 **like locusts:** The same image had been used in 6:5.
13 **barley bread:** A symbol of the Israelite farmers, in contrast to the nomadic Midyanites (Gray 1986). The Hebrew word for "bread," *lehem*, also recalls the verb *l-h-m*, "to fight/battle"; as Niditch (2008)

notes, such word associations are characteristic of dreams. **turning over:** And over. **overturned it . . . fell:** Words used elsewhere in the Bible to connote destruction. **upward:** Or "upside down." **and the tent fell down!:** Earlier in the line, after "it struck it," MT has "it fell down," which is omitted in LXX and appears to be superfluous.

and said:

Arise, for Yhwh has given into our hand the camp of Midyan!

16 He split up the three hundred men into three companies,
and he placed *shofars* in everyone's hand along with empty jugs, and
torches inside the jugs,

17 and said to them:
Look at me and do thus:
when I come to the outskirts of the camp,
let it be: as I do, so you are to do:

18 I will sound a blast on the *shofar,* I and all who are with me,
and then you are to sound a blast on the *shofars,* you as well, all
around the entire camp,
and you are to say:
For Yhwh and for Gid'on!

19 So Gid'on came, along with the hundred men who were with him,
to the outskirts of the camp,
at the beginning of the middle watch
—they had just installed, installed the watchmen—
and they sounded blasts on the *shofars,* with the jugs that were in
their hand [ready to be] shattered.

20 And the three companies sounded blasts on the *shofars,* and broke
the jugs;
they gripped the torches in their left hands,
and in their right hands, the *shofars,* to sound blasts,
and called out:
A sword for Yhwh and for Gid'on!

21 Then they stood still, each one in his position all around the camp,
and the entire camp was on the run;
they shouted and they fled.

22 The three hundred *shofars* were sounded,
and Yhwh put each one's sword against his fellow, that is, against
the entire camp,

16 **companies:** Lit. "heads."
19 **middle watch:** The biblical night was divided into three- to four-hour watches, so this would be around ten P.M. **just installed . . . the watchmen:** The new detail, which was thus not fully settled in yet.
21 **they shouted:** Boling (1975) suggests that the verb (Heb. *r-w-tz*) can have the meaning "jump up," hence he uses "awoke with a start."

22 **against his fellow:** In other words, the enemy were so confused and panicked that they killed one another. **Bet-Shitta:** Location unknown; pronounced *bayt shee-TAH.* **border:** Lit. "lip," used elsewhere for banks and shores.

Chapter 8. *Gid'on III: Aftermath and Climax:* The battle against the Midyanites is not yet over: Gid'on must pursue two of their kings across the Jordan. Before this, however, there is a brief moment of "strife" (recalling the meaning of the name Yerub-baal) with the men of Efrayim—the kind of intertribal problems that will plague the Israelites numerous times in Judges. Gid'on's treatment of both his fellow Israelites and the enemy is harsh: he ends up threshing and killing the men of Sukkot, and he slays the enemy kings with his own hands.

The chapter caps a turning point in the book, as Schneider comments. Gid'on is the first man to whom the crown is offered, but his rejection of it, while noble-sounding and providing a catchphrase for the entire span of the Early Prophets, is followed immediately by his constructing of a semi-idolatrous image which becomes a "snare" for his whole family. And despite Gid'on's positive death notice in v.28, the moment he dies, the Israelites go back to "whoring after the Baals." So the mere suggestion of kingship leads to trouble, paralleling Moshe's experience: even when God is acknowledged as the true king, the people still feel compelled to search for a concrete symbol to worship (Amit 1999a). In addition, the classic Judges pattern has been broken, for the people no longer "cry out" to God for deliverance, and the new, chosen leader is flawed (Schneider). A full reckoning will come in the form of a curse acted out in the next generation.

and the entire camp fled as far as Bet-Shitta, toward Tzerera, to the
    border of Avel- Mehola, near Tabbat.

23   The men of Israel were mustered from Naftali, from Asher, and
    from all of Menashe,
and they pursued after Midyan.

24   Now Gid'on had sent messengers throughout all the highlands of
    Efrayim, saying:
Go down to meet Midyan [in battle], and take the water from
    them, as far as Bet-Bara and the Jordan!
So all the men of Efrayim were mustered, and they captured the
    water, as far as Bet-Bara and the Jordan.

25   And they captured the two commanders of Midyan, Orev / Raven
    and Ze'ev / Wolf;
they killed Orev at Raven's Rock, while Ze'ev they killed at
    Wolf's Vat
—for they had pursued as far as Midyan—
and the heads of Orev and Ze'ev they brought to Gid'on, from
    across the Jordan.

8:1   Then the men of Efrayim said to him:
What is this thing you have done to us, not calling for us
when you went to do battle against Midyan?
And they strove with him strongly.

2   He said to them:
What now have I done against you?
Are not the gleanings of Efrayim better than the vintage of
    Avi'ezer?

3   Into your hand God has given the commanders of Midyan, Orev
    and Ze'ev;
what have I been able to do compared to you?
And their spirit [of anger] subsided from upon him, when he spoke
    these words.

---

24 **the water:** The significance of this is unclear here. **Bet-Bara:** Location unclear.

25 **heads:** The Hebrew, true to its idiom, has the singular; similarly with "grasp" (from lit. "palm") in 8:6.

8:1 **strove:** Returning to the pun in the hero's name of Yerubbaal (see 6:31–32 above).

2 **gleanings:** Of grapes. The point of God's ques-tion is that the Efrayimites should be content with capturing the Midyanite commanders, even though they did not participate in the major part of the battle (Burney).

3 **[of anger]:** The word "spirit" (Heb. *ru'ah*) can include a range of emotional meanings.

4 Gid'on came to the Jordan,
   crossing over, he and the three hundred men who were with him,
   weary and in pursuit.

5 He said to the men of Sukkot:
   Now give some round-loaves of bread to the fighting-people who
      are behind me,
   for they are weary,
   while I will pursue after Zevah and Tzalmunna, the kings of
      Midyan.

6 The commanders of Sukkot said:
   Is the grasp of Zevah and Tzalmunna now in your hand,
   that we should give your forces bread?

7 Gid'on said:
   Therefore,
   when God gives Zevah and Tzalmunna into my hand,
   I will tread over your flesh with wilderness thorns and with nettles!

8 He went up from there to Penuel, and spoke to them like this,
   and the men of Penuel answered him
   as the men of Sukkot had answered.

9 So he said also to the men of Penuel, saying:
   Upon my return in peace,
   I will demolish this tower!

10 Now Zevah and Tzalmunna were in Karkor,
   and their camps were with them, about fifteen thousand,
   all who were left from the entire camp of the Children of the East,
   for those fallen were a hundred and twenty thousand men drawing
      the sword.

11 And Gid'on went up by the Road of the Tent Dwellers, east of
      Novah and Yogbeha,
   and he struck the camp, while the camp was feeling-secure.

---

4 **in pursuit:** Or, with LXX and other versions, "hungry."

5 **Zevah . . . Tzalmunna:** Pronounced *ZEH-vah* and *tzahl-mu-NAH;* trad. English "Zebah and Zalmunna."

6, 8 **Sukkot . . . Penuel:** Near the Yabbok (Jabbok) River, east of the Jordan.

6 **grasp . . . in your hand:** This may refer to the ancient Near Eastern practice of cutting off the vanquished enemy's hand (Gray 1986; see also 1:6 above).

7 **tread:** Usually signifying the process of threshing (Burney).

10 **Karkor:** East of the Dead Sea, near the Moabite base of operations (Boling).

11 **Road of the Tent Dwellers:** Or "Nomads," probably the main north-south track (Burney).

12 Zevah and Tzalmunna fled, but he pursued after them,
and he captured the two kings of Midyan, Zevah and Tzalmunna,
and made the entire camp tremble.

13 Gid'on son of Yoash returned from the battle, from Heres Pass,

14 and he captured a lad from the men of Sukkot, and
questioned him,
and he wrote out for him [the names of] the commanders of
Sukkot and its elders,
seventy-seven men.

15 Then he came to the men of Sukkot
and said:
Here are Zevah and Tzalmunna, with whom you mocked me,
saying:
Is the grasp of Zevah and Tzalmunna now in your hand,
that we should give your weary men bread?

16 So he took the elders of the town, and the wilderness thorns and
the nettles,
and trod over the men of Sukkot with them,

17 while the tower of Penuel he demolished, and killed the men of the
town.

18 Then he said to Zevah and Tzalmunna:
What about the men whom you killed at Tavor?
They said:
Like you were they,
every one like the appearance of the king's sons.

19 He said:
They were my brothers, the sons of my mother!
By the life of Yhwh,
if [only] you had let them live,
I would not have to kill you!

20 And he said to Yeter his firstborn:
Rise up, kill them!

---

12 **made . . . tremble:** Heb. *heherid*. Some emend, to
better effect, to "devoted-to-destruction" (*heherim*)
or "put-to-the-sword" (*heheriv*).

13 **Heres Pass:** Pronounced *HEH-ress*. The location is
unclear, but scholars discount that it is identical with
Mount Heres in 1:35 or Timnat-Heres in 2:9. The
word itself means "sun."

14 **he wrote:** The lad.

16 **trod over:** So ancient versions; MT has "caused to
know" (*va-yadosh* changed to *va-yoda'*).

18 **at Tavor:** The reference is obscure (Boling 1975).

20 **Yeter:** Similar to the "Yitro" of Exodus (Moses's
father-in-law). The name means "excellence."

◆ But the lad would not draw his sword,
for he was afraid,
for he was still a lad.

21 Then Zevah and Tzalmunna said:
Rise up, you yourself, and attack us,
for as the man is, [so] is his might!
So Gid'on arose and killed Zevah and Tzalmunna,
and he took the crescent-ornaments that were on their camels'
necks.

22 Now the men of Israel said to Gid'on:
Rule over us—so you, so your son, so your son's son,
for you have delivered us from the hand of Midyan!

23 Gid'on said to them:
I will not rule over you,
my son will not rule over you—
Yhwh will rule over you!

24 Then Gid'on said to them:
I have a request to request of you:
Give me, each one, a ring from his spoils!
—for they had gold rings, for they were Yishmaelites.

25 They said:
We will give, yes, give [them] over.
So they spread out a cloth
and threw there, each one, a ring from his spoils.

26 Now the weight of the gold rings that he requested
was a thousand and seven hundred [weights of] gold,
aside from the crescents and the pearl-drops and the purple
garments that were on the kings of Midyan,
and aside from the collars that were around their camels' necks.

---

21 **as the man is . . . :** An adult warrior, as opposed to the "lad" or "squire," will be able to carry out the sentence of vengeance. **Gid'on arose:** The "Hewer" now does the killing himself.

24 **ring:** Not for the fingers, but for the ear (men) or the nose (women). **for they were Yishmaelites:** The "they" in this verse refers to the Midyanites, who are here identified with the Ishmaelites of Northern

Arabia, a group presumably more well known to the text's audience (JPS). The Ishmaelites were camel breeders who were heavily involved in the incense trade.

25 **We will give, yes, give:** Repeating the verb here is the biblical Hebrew equivalent of saying "We agree."

26 **pearl-drops:** Or "pendants."

27 And Gid'on made it into an *efod;*
he set it up in his town, in Ofra,
and all Israel went whoring after it there.
It became a snare for Gid'on and for his house.

28 And Midyan was humbled before the Children of Israel,
so that they could no longer lift up their head.
And the land was quiet for forty years in the days of Gid'on.

29 Yerub-baal son of Yoash went and settled down in his house.
30 Now Gid'on had seventy sons issuing from his loins,
for he had many wives.
31 As for his concubine, who was in Shekhem, she too bore him a son;
he appointed his name Avimelekh / Father-is-King.

32 And Gid'on son of Yoash died at a good ripe age,
and was buried in the burial place of Yoash his father,
in Ofra of the Avi'ezrites.

27 **made it into:** Or "used it for" (Burney). So the text must be describing some kind of idol itself, given the large amount of material (Burney). **efod:** Pronounced *ay-FODE*, this was an outer garment worn by the High Priest (see Exod. 28), perhaps in the shape of an apron. It was used in consulting God (see I Sam. 23:9-12), since in ancient Near Eastern contexts it seems to describe an adornment of divine statues, and was hence a means of contact with the gods. **snare:** See note to 2:3, above.

29 **Yerub-baal:** The change of name probably indicates a change in the source of the text.
31 **appointed his name:** Buber (1967) points to the only other occurrences of this odd expression, II Kings 17:34 and Neh. 9:7, to assert that it means "giving a new name" and suggests that Avimelekh renames himself. Ironically, the name can also mean "God (Father) Is King," so Avimelekh is immediately identified as a usurper of both his own father, who had refused the crown, and God.

LATER LEADERS: DECLINE

(8:33–16:31)

AS NOTED ABOVE, ALTHOUGH GID'ON PROVIDES LONG-LASTING LEADERSHIP, and properly turns down the tribes' offer of a crown, his actions in connection with the worship of the *efod* at the end of Chap. 8 are troubling. Immediately upon his death, the Israelites turn back to Canaanite gods, and the usual cycle begins again. This time, however, the oppressor is one of their own, illegitimate though his birth may be. The long and violent tale of Gid'on's son Avimelekh foreshadows Shakespeare's Richard III as a monarch who seizes power violently and lives by the sword. The biblical villain meets an ignominious end, and the text makes no bones about his receiving his just deserts. Here, amid a book which elsewhere is clearly calling for the establishment of a monarchy, Chaps. 8 and 9 pose a negative lesson and imply an alternate vision, perhaps closer to the traditional Israelite one, in which God alone is to rule.

Moving forward, the middle part of this section of the book is studded with brief references to "minor judges," figures whose exploits are barely outlined but who perhaps provide a welcome breather between major stories. More important, their appearance also allows the compiler of the book to include all of the tribes of Israel.

The last two judges spring from the realm of folklore—unlikely heroes because of birth or demeanor, whose deeds have been woven into Judges with an eye to explaining Israel's decline. Yiftah is a rough figure of lowly origins whose dreadful miscalculation tarnishes his heroic image. Like Avimelekh the son of a concubine, he fits the classic pattern of exile, recall by kinsmen, leadership of a band of outcasts à la Robin Hood, and return to rescue his beleaguered countrymen, a pattern also remarked in the ancient stories of kings Idrimi of Alalakh and David of Israel (see Greenstein/Marcus). He also strikes an enigmatic and troubling note with the sacrifice of his daughter. Yiftah foreshadows the next judge, Shimshon, in that his general motivation is personal, a need to avenge his having been cast out of his society, rather than a desire to help to the people (Fewell).

Shimshon himself, the ultimate trickster figure, breaks every rule in the book while still managing to kill thousands of Israel's great enemy, the Philistines. Buber aptly characterized him as a "berserker," a warrior whose rages lead him to perform superhuman feats. While Shimshon's story is an entertaining one, his extreme individualism strikes an anomalous chord in a communal society. So by the time his cycle of stories ends in Chap. 16, we have fully experienced the rough-and-tumble of this transitional era, with strong signs of God's intervention but also the crying need for a more centralized earthly authority.

———

Chapter 9. *Avimelekh the Usurper:* The rambling three-chapter account of Gid'on is followed by the long one-chapter cautionary tale of his son Avimelekh. If leadership is indeed a theme central to Judges, as Amit (1999a) contends, then this chapter represents a decisive moment in the book. The people had requested a king in 8:22, only to see their wish rejected in the recognition that YHWH is to be Israel's sole ruler. This is now reinforced by example, as the villain's name suggests (see the note to 8:31, above). Despite the chapter's protestations that its main subject is Avimelekh's payback for his crime of killing all save one of his brothers, the clear implication is that kingship, at least when it is not sanctioned fully by God, will lead to violence and ruin. In this exploration of power and character, one in which, for a change, idolatry is not the issue, Avimelekh points ahead, as suggested above, to Shakespeare, and the story is appropriately studded with ominous features: the would-be leader is the son of a second-level wife, and he gets his power initially from the gentry of Shekhem, the very city that had been the scene of a notorious rape and murder in earlier times (see Gen. 34), and that would one day witness the coming apart of the united kingdom of Israel (I Kings 12). And, of course, Avimelekh seizes power by the wholesale slaughter of his own brothers.

The story's moral is doubled, with the first warning coming after the murder. Using a common folklore motif, the survival of the youngest of many brothers (see, for example, the Norse story of Sigmund in the *Volsunga Saga*), we are told what the inevitable outcome will be through Yotam's famous parable of the trees (vv.8–15). Israel in its normal state is symbolized by vegetation that supplies the treasured staples of figs, olive oil, and wine. And the governing alternative of concentrating power in the hands of one man is likened to dealing with a troublesome indigenous tree, the *atad* (see the note to v.15, below), which is powerful enough to destroy even the mighty cedars of Lebanon.

As in *Richard III,* the decline of the usurper takes a while to unfold, fueled by jealousies and "ill will." Along the way he proves himself a cruel but effective warrior. The introduction of fire into the last of his victories (v.49) foreshadows the end that Yotam had predicted in v.20. Avimelekh's fate has elements of what has gone before (Sisera's death at the hands of a woman), and of what will happen to Israel's first legitimate king, Sha'ul, who will also kill himself once he has been seriously wounded in a losing battle. As mentioned before, Avimelekh's end is attributed by the text to his crime of fratricide, but the very next verse (57) notes how the men of Shekhem are punished as well, having chosen a king, and a bad one at that.

8:33 Now it was, when Gid'on died,
    that the Children of Israel returned and went whoring after the
        Baals;
    they made Baal Berit a god for themselves.
  34 The Children of Israel did not keep YHWH their God in mind,
    the one rescuing them from the hand of all their enemies round
        about,
  35 and they did not act in loyalty with the house of Yerub-baal Gid'on,
    in accordance with all the good things that he had done for Israel.

9:1 Avimelekh son of Yerub-baal went to Shekhem, to his mother's
        brothers
    and spoke to them and to the entire clan of his mother's Father's
        House, saying:
   2 Now speak in the hearing of all the landowners of Shekhem:
    What is better for you—
    for seventy men to rule over you, all of Yerub-baal's sons,
    or for one man to rule over you?
    And keep in mind
    that I am your bone and your flesh!
   3 So his mother's brothers spoke concerning him, in the hearing of
        all the landowners of Shekhem,
    all these words,
    and their heart inclined after Avimelekh,
    for they said: He is our brother!
   4 So they gave him seventy pieces of silver from the temple-house of
        Baal Berit,
    and with them Avimelekh hired some empty and impetuous men;
    they went [following] after him.

8:33 **Baal Berit:** "Baal of the Covenant."
35 **Yerub-baal Gid'on:** It is not clear why both names are used here, as this does not happen elsewhere in the story.
9:1 **Avimelekh:** Pronounced *ah-vee-MEH-lekh;* trad. English "Abimelech." **his mother's brothers:** As the son of a concubine, his legal standing would be diminished in his father's house. **Father's House:** A social unit in ancient Israel, much like an extended family.
2 **landowners:** Heb. *be'alim,* the plural of *Baal,* but here used in its human Hebrew meaning of "master, owner." **bone and . . . flesh:** Idiomatically in English, "flesh and blood."

5 He came to his Father's House, to Ofra,
and killed his brothers, Yerub-baal's sons,
seventy men on one stone;
but Yotam son of Yerub-baal, the youngest, was left,
for he had hidden himself.

6 Then gathered all the landowners of Shekhem and all of Bet-Millo
and went and kinged Avimelekh as king,
alongside the oak of the monument that is in Shekhem.

7 Yotam was told [about it],
so he went and stood on the top of Mount Gerizim
and lifted up his voice and called out;
he said to them:
Hearken to me, O landowners of Shekhem,
that God may hearken to you!

8 The trees went, they went to anoint a king over themselves.
And they said to the olive:
Reign as king over us!

9 The olive said to them:
Should I be made to leave my luxuriant-oil
through which gods and men honor themselves,
that I should go and hold sway over the trees?

10 So the trees said to the fig:
You go, reign as king over us!

11 The fig said to them:
Should I be made to leave my sweetness and my good produce,
that I should go and hold sway over the trees?

12 So the trees said to the grapevine:
You go, reign as king over us!

13 The grapevine said to them:
Should I be made to leave my new-wine,

---

5 **on one stone:** In Gray's view (1986), so portrayed to concentrate the blood, with the effect of bringing down a curse of the land on the perpetrator. Some see the act as a ritual killing. **Yotam:** Pronounced *yo-TAHM;* trad. English "Jotham."

6 **Bet-Millo:** Pronounced *bayt mee-LO.* The name signifies "earth-fill," possibly describing the supporting structure for a city wall. **of the monument:** Following the suggestion of LXX; MT has "propped up." Klein notes the man-made and hence profane nature of this tree, as opposed to, for example, Deborah's palm tree.

7 **Mount Gerizim:** Pronounced *ge-ree-ZEEM,* one of the two large hills overlooking Shekhem; ironically, in Deut. 27 it is the site of the blessing of Israel.

8 **The trees went, they went:** The equivalent of "Once, the trees went," in a fairy-tale tone.

9 **luxuriant-oil . . . honor:** Olive oil in ancient Israel was a sign of plenty and pleasure; mourners avoided its use (see Isa. 61:3). **through which:** Following LXX; MT has "with which, through me."

13 **new-wine:** The first product of the treading of the grapes, which seems to have had intoxicating properties (Burney).

which gives joy to gods and men,
that I should go and hold sway over the trees?

14   So all the trees said to the *atad:*
You go, reign as king over us!

15   The *atad* said to the trees:
If [it is] in faithfulness you are anointing me as king over you,
come, take refuge in my shade;
but if not—
then let fire come forth from the *atad*
and devour the cedars of the Levanon!

16   So-now, if you acted in truth and integrity
when you made Avimelekh king,
and if you acted in good-faith with Yerub-baal and with his house,
and if you acted in accordance with the dealings of his hands

17   —[seeing] that my father did battle for you
and threw aside his own life and rescued you from the hand of
Midyan,

18   yet you, you have risen up against my Father's House today
and have killed his sons, seventy men on one stone,
and have made Avimelekh, son of his maid, king over the
landowners of Shekhem, because he is your brother—

19   so if you have acted in truth and integrity with Yerub-baal and his
house this day,
may you rejoice in Avimelekh, and may he rejoice in you!

20   But if not,
may fire come forth from Avimelekh
and devour the landowners of Shekhem and Bet-Millo,
and may fire come forth from the landowners of Shekhem and Bet-
Millo
and devour Avimelekh!

---

14 **all the trees:** The "all" feels like a stylistic flourish, coming as it does at the end of the sequence.   *atad:* This appears to be a large, wild-looking tree (*Zizyphus spina-christi*) whose roots destroy those of other fruit trees and whose wood burns well (Hareuveni). It is thus a fine choice as a symbol of the powerful but destructive Avimelekh. Others understand it as a thorny bush such as the boxwood.
15 **to the trees:** A departure from the usage "to them,"

which characterized the previous three answers; this heightens the gravity of the *atad's* answer.   **shade:** Heb. *tzel,* as Gray (1986) reminds us, can also mean "protection."
16 **integrity:** Or "wholeness." Note how Yotam adds this word to Avimelekh's "faithfulness" in the previous verse.
17 **threw aside:** I.e., risked.

21 Then Yotam fled:
   he ran away and went to Be'er and settled there,
   away from the face of Avimelekh his brother.

22 Avimelekh governed Israel for three years.
23 Then God sent a spirit of evil between Avimelekh and the
      landowners of Shekhem,
   and the landowners of Shekhem broke faith with Avimelekh,
24 so that the wrong [done] the seventy sons of Yerub-baal, and their
      bloodguilt, might come
   to be placed on Avimelekh their brother, who had killed them,
   and on the landowners of Shekhem,
   who had strengthened his hands to kill his brothers.
25 So the landowners of Shekhem set up ambushers against him on
      the summits of the mountains,
   and they robbed all those who were crossing them on the road.
   And it was told to Avimelekh.

26 Then Gaal/Loathing son of Eved/Slave came, along with his
      brothers,
   and they crossed through Shekhem.
   And the landowners of Shekhem put [their] trust in him.
27 So they went out into the open-field, amassed their vineyards'
      [grapes], and trod [them] out,
   and they made jubilation;
   then they entered the temple-house of their god, and ate and
      drank,
   and made light of Avimelekh.
28 Gaal son of Eved said:
   Who is Avimelekh, and who is Shekhem, that we should serve him?
   Is he not the son of Yerub-baal, and Zevul is his adjutant?
   The men of Hamor, Shekhem's father, should serve him,
   but why should we serve him ourselves?

---

21 **Be'er:** Pronounced *beh-AYR*. Some suggest modern El-Bireh, south of the Sea of Galilee, but the name is a common one.
23 **evil:** Burney compares it to God's hardening of Pharaoh's heart in the Exodus narrative.

24 **come:** To fruition. **strengthened his hands:** Encouraged him.
26 **put [their] trust in:** Or "relied on."

29 O who would give this people into my hand, that I might remove
  Avimelekh,
  that someone would say to Avimelekh:
  Drive off your forces and go away!

30 But Zevul the commander of the city heard the words of Gaal son
  of Eved,
  and his anger flared up,

31 so he sent messengers to Avimelekh at Aruma, saying:
  Here, Gaal son of Eved and his brothers have come to Shekhem,
  and here, they are besieging the town against you!

32 So-now, arise at night,
  you and the fighting-people who are with you,
  and wait in ambush in the open-country;

33 and it will be in the morning, when the sun rises:
  start-early and spread out against the city,
  and here, [when] he and the fighting-people who are with him go
    out to you,
  you may do with him whatever your hand finds.

34 So Avimelekh arose, and all the fighting-people who were with
  him, at night;
  they lay in ambush against Shekhem, in four companies.

35 Gaal son of Eved went out and stood at the entrance to the town
  gate,
  and Avimelekh and all the people who were with him arose from
  the ambush.

36 Gaal saw the people, and he said to Zevul:
  Here, fighting-people are coming down from the mountains!
  Zevul said to him:
  It is the shadow of the mountains that you see as men!

37 But Gaal continued further to speak and said:
  Here, fighting-people are coming down from the Navel of the
    Land,
  and one company is coming by way of the Soothsayers' Oak!

29 **would say:** The Hebrew text has "he said."
31 **Aruma:** A location a few miles from Shekhem; MT: "Torma" is possibly a corruption. **besieging:** But the syntax might indicate "alienating" (Boling 1975).
33 **spread out against:** Gray (1986) has "deploy." **finds:** Or "finds-possible."

37 **Navel of the Land:** A term for the Shekhem area, where north-south and east-west roads cross (Gray 1986).

38 Zevul said to him:
   Where, now, is your mouth that was saying:
   Who is Avimelekh, that we should serve him?
   Isn't this the people whom you rejected?
   Pray go out now and wage battle against them!

39 So Gaal went out before the landowners of Shekhem
   and waged battle against Avimelekh.

40 And Avimelekh pursued him, so that he fled from his face,
   and many wounded fell, up to the entrance of the gate.

41 Avimelekh stayed in Aruma,
   and Zevul drove out Gaal and his brothers from being settled in
      Shekhem.

42 Now it was on the morrow
   that the people went out to the open-country and told Avimelekh.

43 So he took the fighting-people and split them into three companies
   and waited in ambush in the open-country.
   And he saw that here, the fighting-people were going out of the
      town,
   so he arose against them and struck them.

44 Now Avimelekh and the companies that were with him spread out
   and took their stand at the entrance to the town gate,
   while the two [other] companies spread out against all those who
      were in the open-country, and struck them.

45 Avimelekh was waging battle against the town all that day,
   and he captured the town,
   and all the people who were in it, he killed;
   then he demolished the town, and sowed it with salt.

46 And all the landowners of the Tower of Shekhem heard,
   so they came to the underground-chamber of the Temple-House
      of El-Berit.

47 And it was told to Avimelekh that all the landowners of the Tower
      of Shekhem had gathered,

48 so Avimelekh went up the Mount of Tzalmon,
   he and all the fighting-people who were with him,
   and Avimelekh took axes in his hand

---

45 **sowed it with salt:** Preventing future growth, hence
utterly destroying the town.

48 **Tzalmon:** "The shady one," obviously well stocked
with trees (see what follows in the text).

and cut down tree branch-clumps;
he lifted them up, put them on his shoulder
and said to the fighting-people who were with him:
What you see me do—quickly, do like me!

49   So all the fighting-people also cut down, each one, a branch,
and they went [following] after Avimelekh;
they put them on the underground-chamber and kindled the
     cavern over them with fire,
so that also all the men of the Tower of Shekhem died, about a
     thousand men and women.

50   Avimelekh went to Tevetz
and encamped against Tevetz, that he might capture it.

51   Now there was a strong tower in the midst of the town,
and they fled there, all the men and women, that is, all the
     landowners of the town;
they shut it upon themselves
and went up on the roof of the tower.

52   And Avimelekh came up to the tower and waged battle against it,
but when he approached the entrance of the tower to burn it with
     fire,

53   a woman threw a riding millstone onto Avimelekh's head
and crushed his skull.

54   Quickly he called out to his serving-lad, his weapons bearer,
and said to him:
Draw your sword and dispatch me,
lest they say of me: A woman killed him!
So his serving-lad pierced him through, and he died.

55   When the fighting-men of Israel saw that Avimelekh was dead,
they went [home], each one to his place.

56   Thus God returned the evil of Avimelekh
that he had done to his father, by killing his seventy brothers,

50   **Tevetz:** Trad. English "Thebez," presumably not far
from Shekhem.
53   **riding millstone:** The detached round upper millstone used in grinding grain. Archaeologists have
uncovered examples of these loaf-shaped stones,
which sometimes weighed as much as ten pounds,

making them both portable and capable of inflicting
serious damage when thrown down from a height.
54   **Draw your sword . . . :** The scene is a foreshadowing of Sha'ul's (Saul's) death in I Sam. 31.   **dispatch:**
An intensive form of Heb. *m-w-t*, "die," meaning
"deal the death blow."

Chapter 10. *Interlude:* After the long sequence of stories relating to Gid'on, and before the dramatic ones to come, there seems to be a need for a respite. This is provided by accounts of two "minor" judges, both of which involve wordplays. Ya'ir is from Gil'ad, east of the Jordan; the action will resume there beginning in v.17. From v.6 to v.16, however, there interposes what feels like a reprise of material from Chap. 2: a laying out of the pattern of idolatry, divine anger, foreign oppression, Israelite outcry, and, this time, God's initial refusal to rescue them. For a change (v.16), the Israelites heed God's rebuke in vv.11–14 and actually reject their "foreign gods."

◆
57 while all the evil of the men of Shekhem, God returned on their
    heads,
    and the curse of Yotam son of Yerub-baal came upon them.

10:1 There arose after Avimelekh, to deliver Israel,
    Tola / Scarlet son of Pua son of Dodo, a man of Yissakhar.
    Now he was settled in Shamir, in the highlands of Efrayim.

2 He led Israel as judge for twenty-three years;
    then he died, and was buried in Shamir.

3 There arose after him Ya'ir the Gil'adite;
    he led Israel as judge for twenty-two years.

4 He had thirty sons riding on thirty foals,
    and they had thirty towns;
    those they call the Tent-Villages of Ya'ir until this day, that are in
        the land of Gil'ad.

5 Then Ya'ir died, and was buried in Kamon.

6 But the Children of Israel continued doing what was evil in the eyes
        of YHWH;
    they served the Baals and the Astartes
    and the gods of Aram, the gods of Sidon, the gods of Moav,
    the gods of the Children of Ammon, and the gods of the Philistines;
    they abandoned YHWH, and did not serve him.

7 So YHWH's anger flared up against the Children of Israel,
    and he sold them into the hand of the Philistines and into the hand
        of the Children of Ammon;

8 they shattered and battered the Children of Israel from that year on
        for eighteen years—
    all the Children of Israel who were across the Jordan in the land of
        the Amorites, which is in Gil'ad.

10:1 **Pua:** A different name (and spelling) than that of the famous midwife (Pu'a) of Exod. 1:15ff. "Tola son of Pua" means literally "Worm son of Madder" (a plant), both of which yield a reddish dye. **Dodo:** Pronounced *doe-DOE*. Meaning "uncle" or "beloved" (like the name "David"), it has an unfortunate ring in English. Hebrew, happily, places the accent on the last syllable.

3 **Ya'ir:** Trad. English "Jair"; "He Gives Light."

4 **foals . . . towns:** The two words are similar in MT; ancient versions vocalize the second as *'irim* (towns) rather than *'ayarim*. JPS nicely renders them "bur-ros . . . boroughs." The listing of possessions here undoubtedly stresses wealth; not all of these leaders are simple men of the people.

6 **Sidon:** Standing not only for the celebrated port city (Sidon in today's Lebanon) but also for the surrounding region.

8 **shattered . . . battered:** Following JPS, for Heb. *va-yir'atzu vayrotzetzu*. **Gil'ad:** The large area across the Jordan to the east (north of Ammon), often occupied by the Israelites. The name appears to mean "rugged," an apt description.

Chapter 11. *Yiftah:* Tracing the precipitous decline that marks the second half of the book, Judges now turns to the first of two problematic figures, Yiftah the Gil'adite. While he is remembered in Western thought and art exclusively for one incident which spans only eleven verses, the ill-fated vow regarding his daughter, the chapter in which this tale is embedded is fully forty verses long, in addition to another seven that round out his story in the next chapter. So it is important to examine the larger setting.

Like the villain Avimelekh, Yiftah is born to a mother of low social status. He obtains leadership not through being commissioned by God (as was, for instance, Gid'on) but by human agency. The Gil'adites elect him as leader, just as Avimelekh had been chosen by the Shekhemites (Schneider). Schneider also points out the connections between Yiftah and King Sha'ul (Saul), who similarly fights the Ammonites and is chosen at Mitzpa (in I Sam. 10; that location appears in v.11 here). It will also be the site of the Israelites' gathering immediately after the terrible events of Chap. 19.

As part of his leadership role, Yiftah negotiates with the Ammonites, recounting along the way some of Israel's traditions relating to the Exodus from Egypt. At that time, several peoples to the east of Israel had refused to grant the ex-slaves passage through their territory, leading directly to the Israelites' God-given victory over them and the possession of their land. Ironically, the Ammonites were not among them; they seem to have been put into this chapter at a later date. In any event, the wordplay, in Yiftah's speech, on "possess/dispossess" eight times in four verses (21–24) highlights God's role. The repetitions are perhaps also reflective of the warrior's forceful, maybe even stubborn, personality, with v.25 witnessing three separate double verb formulations (using "be better . . . strive . . . do battle").

Thus righteously armed, Yiftah commits his fatal error, reflected in the narrative's wording. First, he vows to sacrifice whatever "goes out" to greet him upon his return from defeating the Ammonites, if God should grant him victory. When that turns out to be his daughter, his only child, he has no choice, according to his culture, but to go through with the pledge that had "gone out" of his mouth (v.36). Second, his harping on the verb "possess" foreshadows the loss of his most treasured possession, his daughter. Finally, we should note that the name Yiftah, while probably originally signifying the divine opening of the womb, may be subtly playing on the idea of opening the mouth.

The motif of sacrificing a child to the gods to ensure success in war is widespread, and the Greeks used it most famously in the Iphigenia story (see Marcus 1986). But whereas that tale is but the beginning of a chain reaction of events stretching over many years—the arrival of the Greeks at Troy, victory after a ten-year war, Agamemnon's triumphant homecoming, his murder by his wife and her lover, and *her* murder by their son, who must then wander condemned and tormented for years—the Yiftah story is a single incident about an unmarried woman and an obscure festival. To be sure, it is embedded in the book of Judges as an example of the ongoing decline of Israel and its leadership, but the effect

9   And the Children of Ammon crossed the Jordan to wage battle also
against Yehuda, and against Binyamin, and against the House of
Efrayim,
and Israel was exceedingly distressed.

10 So Israel cried out to Yhwh, saying:
We have sinned against you!
For we have abandoned our God
and have served the Baals!

11 Yhwh said to the Children of Israel:
Did not [I deliver you] from Egypt and from the Amorites and from
the Children of Ammon and from the Philistines?

12 And when the Sidonians and Amalek and Midyan oppressed you,
you cried out to me,
and I delivered you from their hand;

13 but you have abandoned me, and served other gods—
therefore I will not continue to deliver you.

14 Go cry out to the gods whom you have chosen,
let *them* deliver you at the time of your distress!

15 The Children of Israel said to Yhwh:
We have sinned!
Do, you yourself, to us
according with whatever is good in your eyes,
only: just rescue us this day!

16 So they removed the foreign gods from their midst
and served Yhwh,
and he became short-tempered with the travails of Israel.

17 The Children of Ammon mustered [troops] and encamped in Gil'ad,
while the Children of Israel gathered and encamped in Mitzpa.

18 The fighting-people, the commanders of Gil'ad, said each one to
his fellow:
Who is the man that will be first to do battle against the Children
of Ammon?
He shall be head of all the settled-folk of Gil'ad!

11 [**I deliver you**]: Implied by the somewhat corrupt
Hebrew text.   **the Children of Ammon . . . the
Philistines:** The historical subjugation of these peoples lay in the future, suggesting that these lines are
a later addition.

12 **Midyan:** MT: "Ma'on"; I follow LXX here.

17 **Mitzpa:** Lit. "lookout."

18 **the commanders:** Usually taken as either a gloss
or an indication that two traditions have been
merged.   **Who . . . will be first:** Echoing the opening of the book.

is hardly the same as in the Greek example. Nevertheless, the story's focus on leadership is crucial. Yiftah is best understood in the biblical context by way of comparison, as so often is the case in this literature, both forward and backward (see Schneider). He certainly recalls Avraham, the faithful one who was willing to sacrifice even his "only one" to God (Gen. 22)—but who, in the end, was emphatically not required to do so. And he anticipates Sha'ul, whose rash vow in I Sam. 14 invokes a nominal death sentence on his son Yonatan, but who likewise is prevented from going through with the threat, in this instance by his indignant troops. Additionally, in the text's focus on a domestic crisis, Yiftah prepares the ground for Shimshon; despite the military triumphs of both men, they are compromised by private events. By way of summary, one could almost agree with Schneider, who sees in this judge "no qualities, no deeds, no crisis, no God."

Not surprisingly in a narrative about a vow, language plays a central role in the text. Yiftah is overly wordy with the Ammonites, with the rhetorical flourishes noted above, but it is a single sentence that creates the ultimate disaster in his own family. And it is the family name, the ultimate language marker, which will now die with him, although in long-range perspective, it *will* survive in later literature and art.

The character of Yiftah's unnamed daughter deserves some attention. She strangely does not protest her father's obligation to carry out his vow, either by direct refusal to play the victim or by simply running away. The way in which she retains dignity in the face of a clearly patriarchal text is to request and receive a two-month reprieve to mourn the loss of her sexual maturity in the company of female companions. As Exum (1993) notes, this secures her immortality, if nothing else. But she remains the quintessential anonymous female victim, in a book whose male figures are anything but idealized.

For a more positive treatment of the daughter's fate as tied to a rite of passage for females in ancient Israel, see Niditch (2008).

11:1 Now Yiftah the Gil'adite was a mighty-man of valor,
    but he was the son of a whore woman;
    Gil'ad begot Yiftah.
2 And Gil'ad's wife bore him sons,
    but when the wife's sons grew up,
    they drove Yiftah away and said to him:
    You shall not get hereditary-property in our Father's House,
    for you are the son of a different woman!
3 So Yiftah ran away from the face of his brothers
    and settled in the land of Tov/Good.
    And there gathered around Yiftah empty men;
    they went out [to war] beside him.

4 Now it was after some years
    that the Children of Ammon did battle with Israel,
5 and it was, when the Children of Ammon did battle with Israel
    that the elders of Gil'ad went to fetch Yiftah from the land of Tov.
6 They said to Yiftah:
    Come now and become chief for us,
    that we may wage battle against the Children of Ammon!
7 Yiftah said to the elders of Gil'ad:
    Is it not you who spurned me
    and drove me away from my Father's House?
    So for-what-reason have you come to me now,
    when you are in distress?
8 The elders of Gil'ad said to Yiftah:
    Agreed, [but] now we have returned to you, so that you may go
      with us
    and wage battle against the Children of Ammon,
    that you may be headman for us,
    for all the settled-folk of Gil'ad!

11:1 **Yiftah:** Pronounced *yif-TAH;* trad. English "Jeph-thah." Ironically for the story of a father and a daughter, with no mother mentioned, the name denotes God "opening" the womb.
2 **different:** Or "another," with the flavor, perhaps, of "another kind of."
3 **Tov/Good:** The region northeast of Gil'ad. The "good" part may refer to the rich soil of the area. **empty men:** As with David in I Sam. 22:2, Yiftah gathers outcasts to him. Gray (1986) translates as "destitute."
6 **chief:** Heb. *katzin;* an Arabic cognate means "one who renders judgment"—hence, parallel to "judge" (*shofet*), another leadership title.
8 **Agreed:** Lit., "this being so."

9 Yiftah said to the elders of Gil'ad:
If you reinstate me, yourselves, to wage battle against the Children
   of Ammon,
so that YHWH gives them before me,
I will be headman for you.

10 The elders of Gil'ad said to Yiftah:
May YHWH be hearer between us:
if we do not do so, in accordance with your word . . . !

11 So Yiftah went with the elders of Gil'ad,
and the people set him as headman and as chief over them;
and Yiftah spoke all his terms in the presence of YHWH at Mitzpa.

12 Then Yiftah sent messengers to the king of the Children of
   Ammon, saying:
What is there [between] me and you,
that you come to me, to wage battle against my land?

13 The king of the Children of Ammon said to Yiftah's messengers:
Because Israel took away my land when they came up from Egypt,
from the Arnon as far as the Yabbok, as far as the Jordan.
So-now, return it peaceably!

14 Yiftah once again sent messengers to the king of the Children of
   Ammon;

15 he said to him:
Thus says Yiftah:
Israel did not take away the land of Moav or the land of the
   Children of Ammon;

16 rather, when they came up from Egypt,
Israel went through the wilderness, near the Sea of Reeds, and
   came to Kadesh.

17 And Israel sent messengers to the king of Edom, saying:
Now let me cross through your land.
But the king of Edom did not hearken,

9 **reinstate:** Yiftah had been driven out and basically disinherited, given his social status; his acceptance of leadership now hinges on his restoration (Marcus 1989).
10 **hearer:** The concept is a legal one; God is witness to an oath.
11 **in the presence of** YHWH: Usually indicating a sacred location such as a sanctuary in the Bible. **Mitzpa:** Klein notes the ironic use here; Yiftah doesn't "look

out" very well, for either the making or carrying out of his oath.
13 **from the Arnon as far as the Yabbok:** These two wadis mark the territory from the northern half of the Dead Sea well up to the mountains of Gil'ad (east of the Jordan). Yabbok, pronounced *yah-BOHK,* is trad. English "Jabbok." **it:** Ancient versions make more sense here; MT has "them."
16 **when they came up . . . :** See Num. 20–21.

◆ and they sent also to the king of Moav, but he was not willing,
so Israel stayed at Kadesh.

18 Then they went through the wilderness and circled around the land
of Edom and the land of Moav,
and they came to the sun-rise [side] of the land of Moav, and
encamped across the Arnon,
but they did not come into the territory of Moav,
for the Arnon is the territory-border of Moav.

19 And Israel sent messengers to Sihon king of the Amorites, king of
Heshbon;
Israel said to him:
Now let me cross through your land, to my place.

20 But Sihon did not trust Israel to cross through his territory;
Sihon gathered all his fighting-people and encamped at Yahatz,
and did battle with Israel.

21 But YHWH the God of Israel gave Sihon and all his fighting-people
into the hand of Israel, and they struck them,
so Israel came to possess the entire land of the Amorites, the
settled-folk of that land.

22 They took possession of the entire territory of the Amorites,
from the Arnon as far as the Yabbok and from the wilderness as far
as the Jordan.

23 So-now,
YHWH the God of Israel dispossessed the Amorites before his
people Israel—
and you, you would take possession of it?

24 Is it not: what Kemosh your god dispossesses, of *that* you may take
possession,
and whatever YHWH our God dispossesses before us, of *that* we
may take possession?

25 So-now, are you better, yes, better than Balak son of Tzippor, king
of Moav?

---

24 **Kemosh:** Trad. English "Chemosh." This denotes the Moabite (not Ammonite!) god Kamish; the name appears on the extra-biblical Moabite Stone. **Kemosh . . . YHWH:** Reflecting the ancient concept that a god's control is limited to his territory (Gray 1986).

25 **Balak:** Pronounced *bah-LAHK;* he appears more famously in the Bil'am (Balaam) story of Num. 22–24.

◆   Did he strive, yes, strive with Israel,
      or wage battle, yes, battle against them?

26   When Israel remained-settled in Heshbon and its daughter-towns,
        and in Ar'or and its daughter-towns,
      and in all the towns that are along the Arnon,
      for three hundred years,
      for-what-reason did you not rescue [them] during that time?

27   As for me, I have not sinned against you,
      yet you do me evil by waging battle against me!
      May Yhwh the judge render judgment today between Israel and
        the Children of Ammon!

28   But the king of the Children of Ammon did not hearken to Yiftah's
        words which he had sent to him.

29   Now there came upon Yiftah the rushing-spirit of Yhwh;
      he crossed over to Gil'ad and Menashe,
      and he crossed over to Mitzpe of Gil'ad, and from Mitzpe of Gil'ad
        he crossed over to the Children of Ammon.

30   And Yiftah vowed a vow to Yhwh and said:
      If you will give, yes, give the Children of Ammon into my hand,

31   it will be: the one going out who goes out of the doors of my
        house to meet me, when I return in peace from the Children of
        Ammon
      shall be Yhwh's
      and shall be offered up by me as an offering-up!

32   So Yiftah crossed over to the Children of Ammon, to wage battle
        against them,
      and Yhwh gave them into his hand;

33   he struck them from Aro'er as far as where-you-come to Minnit,
      twenty towns, and as far as Avel-Keramim,
      an exceedingly great striking down,
      and the Children of Ammon were humbled before the Children of
        Israel.

---

26 **Heshbon . . . Ar'or:** Moabite cities; versions render the second by the more familiar form of "Aro'er."

28 **Yiftah's words:** As Mobley (2011) notes, in this chapter and the next, words have the power of life and death.

31 **the one going out who goes out:** Though some domestic animals lived inside Israelite houses, Yiftah probably means a person here. **offered up by me:** Following NJPS, so as not to prejudice the gender; the Hebrew suggests "I shall offer it up."

33 **Avel-Keramim:** "Meadow of the Vineyards."

◆ 34   Yiftah came back to Mitzpa, to his house,
        and here, his daughter was going out to meet him, with timbrels
            and with dancing
        —yet she was a lone-child, he had no son or daughter beside her.

35   It was, when he saw her,
        that he tore his garments
        and said:
        Alas, my daughter! You have cast, yes, cast me down,
        you have become my disaster—
        for I myself opened my mouth to Yhwh,
        and I am not able to turn it back!

36   She said to him:
        Father, you opened your mouth to Yhwh;
        do with me as has gone out of your mouth,
        since Yhwh has wrought for you acts of vengeance against your
            enemies, from the Children of Ammon!

37   And she said to her father:
        Let this thing be done for me:
        let me be for two months,
        so that I may go down upon the highlands
        and weep for my womanhood, I and my companions.

38   He said:
        Go.
        He sent her off for two months,
        and she went, she and her companions,
        and wept for her womanhood upon the hills.

39   It was at the end of two months
        that she returned to her father,
        and he wrought upon her his vow that he had vowed.
        Now she had never known a man.
        And it became a rule in Israel:

34 **a lone-child:** And so his name would die with her (Gray 1986). In actuality the name would be carried on by a son, so in this case, it would have to be her son.
35 **cast, yes, cast me down:** The Hebrew words (*hakhre'a hikhra'tani*) are an anagram of *'okhri*, "my disaster," recalling the Akhan story in Josh. 7. Consequently the LXX emends the first phrase accordingly: "You have brought disaster . . ." **opened my mouth:** Took an oath, made a promise.

37 **go down:** or "wander free" (Burney), reading *ve-radti* for MT *ve-yaradti*. But see JPS on Isa. 15:3, where *y-r-d* and weeping occur together. **weep . . . womanhood:** The Hebrew is not assonant. **womanhood:** That is, marriageable state (or "nubility"), naturally congruent with virginity in that society, but not necessarily identical to it (Wenham).
39 **he wrought upon her:** Mobley (2011) notes how the fate of this young woman, even in a book filled with violence, is "literally unspeakable."

Chapter 12. *Civil Strife; More Minor Judges:* This chapter is an example of how, often, the biblical chapter numbers do not fully correspond to natural divisions in the text (they were, after all, developed millennia later, probably by Bishop Stephen Langton, Archbishop of Canterbury, d. 1228). It begins with the final episodes of the Yiftah story—first, with a minor civil war, which reprises the Efrayimites' unhappiness of 8:1 and anticipates the strife-filled final chapters of the entire book. Here the Yiftah motif of language returns; this time, it is neither a pun, a doubled verb, nor a hasty vow that grabs our attention, but rather the pronunciation of a single word (*shibbolet*) which marks the dividing line between life and death.

The summary of Yiftah's career includes notice of his anomalous six-year term as judge. There now follow three new figures in quick succession, combining regional or tribal interests and descriptions of wealth, as measured in children and animals.

40 from year-day to year-day, the daughters of Israel go to
retell [the tale] of the daughter of Yiftah the Gil'adite,
four days a year.

12:1 The men of Efrayim were mustered;
they crossed over to Tzafon
and said to Yiftah:
For-what-reason did you cross over to wage battle against the
Children of Ammon,
but *us* you did not call to go with you?
Your house we will burn down over you with fire!
2 Yiftah said to them:
I was a man in strife, I and my people and the Children of Ammon,
exceedingly much;
I summoned you, but you did not deliver me from their hand,
3 so when I saw that you were not acting-as-deliverer,
I put my life in my palm and crossed over to the Children of
Ammon,
and YHWH gave them into my hand.
So why have you come up against me this day, to wage battle
against me?
4 And Yiftah gathered all the fighting-men of Gil'ad and did battle
with Efrayim,
and the men of Gil'ad struck Efrayim,
for they had said:
Fugitives of Efrayim are you, [men of] Gil'ad;
[being] among Efrayim is [like being] among Menashe!
5 And Gil'ad took the Jordan crossings of Efrayim.
Now it would be, when [one of] the fugitives of Efrayim would say:
Let me cross!
that the men of Gil'ad would say to him:
Are you an Efratite?
He would say:
No.

40 **retell:** Others "bewail." But see note to 5:11, above.
12:1 **mustered:** Lit. "cried out to," an obvious image of being summoned for war. **Tzafon:** Perhaps near Tell Deir 'Alla, east of the Jordan.
2 **strife:** Boling (1975) makes a case for Heb. *riv* here connoting diplomacy, not warfare.
5 **Efratite:** Efrayimite.

6 Then they would say to him:
   Now say *"shibbolet,"*
   and he would say *"sibbolet"*
   —he did not understand how to speak correctly—
   so they would grab him and slaughter him, at the Jordan crossings;
   there fell from Efrayim at that time forty-two thousand.
7 And Yiftah led Israel as judge for six years;
   then Yiftah the Gil'adite died
   and was buried in his town, [in] Gil'ad.

8 After him, Ivtzan from Bet-Lehem led Israel as judge;
9 —he had thirty sons,
   and thirty daughters he sent away outside,
   while thirty daughters he brought for his sons from the outside—
   and he led Israel as judge for seven years.
10 Then Ivtzan died
   and was buried in Bet-Lehem.

11 After him, Elon the Zevulonite led Israel as judge,
   and led Israel as judge for ten years.
12 Then Elon the Zevulonite died
   and was buried in Ayyalon, in the region of Zevulun.

13 After him, Avdon son of Hillel the Pir'atonite led Israel as judge
14 —he had forty sons and thirty sons' sons, riding on seventy ass-
      colts—
   and led Israel as judge for eight years.
15 Then Avdon son of Hillel the Pir'atonite died
   and was buried at Pir'aton in the region of Efrayim, in the
      Amalekite highlands.

---

6 *shibbolet:* The word, Heb. *shee-BOH-let,* means either "ear of grain" or "stream," but that is less important than the pronunciation issue. Gray (1986) points to the differing Hebrew and Arabic pronunciations of one letter as a parallel (e.g., Heb. *shalom* and Arabic *salaam*). The word itself has entered English in the form "shibboleth," meaning a password or test word. **understand:** The reading adopted by some manuscripts (*yavin*) for MT *yakhin* ("prepare"). **correctly:** Or at least according to Gil'adite pronunciation. **forty-two thousand:** The number forty-two occurs several times in the Early Prophets (e.g., the number of boys slain by bears in II Kings 2:24, and of those massacred by Yehu [Jehu] in II Kings 10:14). It is (three plus three) times seven, utilizing patterned numbers such as we find elsewhere in the Bible.

8 **Ivtzan:** Meaning "Swift." **Bet-Lehem:** Pronounced *bayt-LEH-hem,* usually denoting the familiar town (Bethlehem) just south of Jerusalem, but Boling suggests here another site far to the north, near Lebanon.

9 **from the outside:** Or "abroad."

11 **Zevulonite:** From the tribe of Zevulun.

13 **Avdon:** "Servile." **Pir'atonite:** From a town not far from Shekhem.

ON THE SHIMSHON CYCLE

Of all the narratives in Judges, the cycle which features its last great figure, Shimshon, is the most puzzling at first blush. While the immediately preceding judge, Yiftah, was presented as flawed, he at least fit the book's standard leadership profile by leading Israelite troops against their enemies. Shimshon, on the other hand, makes no inspiring speeches and heads no armies. The hero's "call" in Chap. 13 consists mainly of a revelation to Shimshon's parents before his birth, and his consciousness of any kind of broader mission in life seems severely limited. And what are we to make of the bizarre, even burlesque elements of the cycle, which include an angel who disappears in sacrificial fire, an enigmatic riddle about strength and sweetness, the hero's slaughtering of a thousand Philistines with an ass's jawbone, his over-the-top feat of strength after a visit to a prostitute, a seduction scene followed by the most famous haircut of all time, and a final violent spectacle that seems tailor-made for opera or film? Simply put, there is nothing quite like it in the Bible.

Thanks to such entertaining elements, audiences have delighted in these stories for centuries. At the same time, interpreters have struggled mightily with them. In the late nineteenth century it was fashionable to read the cycle as a "solar myth," based, first, on the fact that the name Shimshon resembles *shemesh,* "sun," and, second, that various motifs in the text, not to mention the name of the local town of Beit Shemesh, suggest an origin in pagan tales about the sun or sun god. Another school of interpretation has sought to locate the story in Greek traditions about Herakles (Hercules), whom Shimshon resembles in many respects, from his anger to his weakness for women, and in some of the details of the story. But these kinds of comparisons, while initially attractive, do not explain the distinctively Israelite character of the Shimshon tales. As so often happens, it may be more fruitful to look at the narrative through the Bible's own thematics and wording.

Initially, the overarching theme of the cycle appears to be the breaking of the Nazirite vows laid out in Num. 6 and indicated in the opening lines of our story. In this biblical practice, a person could take on a special vow for a certain period, necessitating abstention from consuming alcohol, haircutting, and contact with the dead. Shimshon's actions, however, systematically violate every Nazirite rule; by the end of the story, the reasons for his downfall are manifest. The theme of Naziriteship thus suggests that Shimshon is an individual in control of his own destiny. But despite the trappings of a hero story, the narrative makes it clear from the beginning that, as usual, it is really God who is at the center of events. All of Shimshon's inappropriate behavior—his violations of the vow, his rages, his lust-ing after foreign women—serve in this text as vehicles for fulfillment of a divine plan. In what amounts to a classic biblical pattern, people act upon their own impulses and emotions, but the end result is what God, not they, had intended. Our text points to God's hand behind the scenes: "Now his father and his mother did not know that it was from YHWH, / for he was seeking a pretext from the Philistines" (14:4). Even more strikingly, as has often been noted, the hero's selfish reasoning in 14:3, "Take *her* for me, for she is right in my eyes," is integrated into the larger theme of Judges, premonarchical chaos, which appears several times in the subsequent, final chapters of the book, and notably at its very end (21:25): "In those days there was no king in Israel; / each one would do what was right in his eyes."

This tension between the divine and the human is maintained by the theme of secrecy, which permeates the entire narrative and holds it together. Everything points toward two dramatic revelations: uncovering the secret of Shimshon's strength to Delila and its final fatal revelation to the assembled Philistines. On an ongoing basis, the thread of secrecy is underscored by the use of three major leading words in the text: "tell," "know," and "see." Secrets are withheld from every major character at some point or other, from parents to women to enemies. Dominating them all is the muscle-bound figure of the hero, ironically the most unaware character in the entire cycle. Significantly, the narrator rarely uses the verb "know" in relation to Shimshon himself, preferring instead to utilize "seeing" as the central metaphor.

To stress "see" as a key word is to make a loaded choice. The "seer" in the Bible is usually the man of God (see Avraham and Moshe), one who is perfectly and painfully aware of what God wants of him. But Shimshon is more voyeur than visionary, rarely seeing beyond his anger or his lust. Not surprisingly, Talmudic interpreters felt that Shimshon's downfall was connected to his sight; in their words, "he who was led astray by his eyes, lost them" (B. Sotah 9b).

So Shimshon is the perfect antihero, largely unconcerned with his obligations to his people or his God. Like Herakles, he is motivated chiefly by his sexual drive and his anger. But the quality of Shimshon's obliviousness to the Bible's main concern, the covenant between Israel and God, may be a clue to something else that is going on below the surface of the text. Greenstein (1981), in a perceptive analysis, has focused on Shimshon as a figure who mirrors the people of Israel as a whole. Like Shimshon with his Nazirite regulations, Israel has a defined series of rules. Just as Shimshon repeatedly breaks his vows, Israel is characterized in both the Torah and the Early Prophets as constantly backsliding and breaking the covenant. Indeed, notes Greenstein, the name "Shimshon," so often linked to the Hebrew term for the sun, may also be punning on *shem*, "name," and suggesting that Israel's *identity* is the key issue of the story.

Also noteworthy in the vocabulary of the narrative, as suggested above, is the repetition of the verb "bind" (Heb. *'-s-r*), which first appears in the jawbone episode and is prominent in the Delila story. Not only is it used in the Bible to indicate physical restraint, but it also frequently carries the connotation of prohibition or the setting of rules. Viewed from that perspective, the Shimshon cycle is very much about a classic "wild man" who breaks society's rules and lives by his own. If Greenstein (1981) is right, then the Bible has transformed an ancient hero into a symbol for the book's "wild society," which it will indeed prove to be in the chapters that follow Shimshon and conclude the book.

One last aspect of Shimshon is striking, already noticed by scholars such as Wellhausen. True to the chapters of Judges that follow it, the Shimshon cycle indirectly indicts a major character in the upcoming book of Samuel: King Sha'ul (Saul). Like Shimshon, he does not possess the character traits necessary for true and successful leadership. He can only lay the groundwork for the eventual defeat of the Philistines and the rise of a unified kingdom (similarly, Shimshon can only "begin" to defeat the Philistines). Both men, at least, are granted a heroic death, yet it is striking how similarly they are portrayed—a picture of the divine spirit gone awry. Neither man has control over his overwhelming gift, and both suffer personal tragedy. In Shimshon's case, it is not the tragedy portrayed by later Western interpreters; as he appears in Judges, he is neither a symbol of despair turned into faith and resistance (Milton's *Samson Agonistes*), nor a national liberator who sadly forgets himself in the bedroom (Saint-Saëns's opera *Samson et Dalila*). Instead, he functions in the end as the symbol of the straying, suffering, and, for the biblical writer, ultimately redeemed folk from which he stems. With the cycle of stories around Shimshon, the book of Judges is almost ready to draw to a close.

For a detailed look at the uses of verbal and thematic repetition in the Shimshon cycle, see "Appendix: The Sound and Structure of a Biblical Tale" at the end of Judges.

Chapter 13. *The Birth of Shimshon:* The narrative now moves on to a second impulsive character. But the story opens in leisurely and formulaic fashion, utilizing repeating words and phrases and allowing the dramatic and entertaining action to properly build up.

The significance of the Shimshon story, which ends the core narratives about individual judges, is signaled by the appearance and involvement of a divine messenger, whose exit is miraculous and pyrotechnic, and by the repetition of rules regarding both the mother's pregnancy and the hero's future life. The announcement of conception to a previously barren woman is something we have encountered many times before in Genesis, where it always signifies the birth of a hero, but it receives its most elaborate treatment here. In its representation of Nazirite regulations—detailed in Num. 6 as a person taking on a special vow not to drink wine or beer, cut his/her hair, or come into contact with a corpse or carcass—there are several twists: the *mother* is given parallel rules, and, more specifically, the "Consecrated One's" status will be lifelong and not confined to a limited time frame. It should be noted that the next book will open with a similarly lifelong devotee, Shemuel (Samuel).

We have encountered an angel before in Judges, in the Gid'on story of Chap. 6, but the recipient of revelation here is a woman (with an absent husband), reinforcing the importance of women throughout the book and especially in the Shimshon cycle. The parallel annunciation account in the New Testament became a key scene in medieval Western art, and for this and other reasons, Shimshon was often regarded in early and later Christianity as a prefiguring ("type") of Jesus.

From the outset, the story (and the cycle) involves secrets and mysteries. The woman is befuddled by the appearance of a stranger who looks like a messenger of God (v.6); her husband will likewise have no clue as to the angel's identity until the angel does something out of the ordinary (v.19). The revelation of the messenger's secret, far from having a salutary effect, strikes fear into Manoah's heart, which can only be calmed down after his wife reassures him. The chapter ends with the note of the birth, naming, and one-phrase childhood and adolescence of Shimshon, but what YHWH's spirit "stirring him up" will mean remains to be fully discovered. For Gid'on and Yiftah it had signified the charismatic ability to lead the troops, but that will not be the pattern here.

The presence of secrets reminds us that the narrative is studded with folklore motifs. Besides the birth of a hero to a previously barren mother, the text begins with the fairy-tale-like opening, "There was a man" (see also, as other examples, I Sam. 1:1 and 9:1). And the angel disappears in the flame of the altar, another classic "sign" of God's acts of deliverance (Amit 1999a). Additionally, the verbal repetitions betoken the world of folklore, as well as the Bible's use of repetition, with "see" as a verb seven times, and "guard," three.

Almost lost in the details of the chapter is the notice that Shimshon "shall begin to deliver Israel from the hand of the Philistines" (v.5). He thus anticipates the monarchy or, more specifically, King David, who will finish the job. As is typical in Judges, Shimshon's victory will be only a temporary one.

13:1   The Children of Israel again did what was evil in the eyes of Yhwh,
        so Yhwh gave them into the hand of the Philistines for forty years.

    2   There was a man from Tzor'a, from a Danite clan;
        his name was Manoah.
        Now his wife was barren, she had not given birth.

    3   And Yhwh's messenger was seen by the woman;
        he said to her:
        Now here,
        you are barren, you have not given birth,
        but you shall conceive, you shall give birth to a son.

    4   So-now, pray guard yourself:
        do not drink wine or beer,
        do not eat anything *tamei,*

    5   for here, you are about to conceive, you shall give birth to a son.
        A razor must not go up on his head,
        for One Consecrated to God shall the lad be from the womb on;
        he shall begin to deliver Israel from the hand of the Philistines!

    6   The woman came and said to her husband, saying:
        A man of God came to me,
        the sight of him like the sight of a messenger of God,
        exceedingly awe-inspiring.
        I did not ask him where he was from,
        and his name he did not tell me,

13:1 **Philistines:** This group, whose area of settlement lay largely on the coast of Israel, appears to have been one of the "Sea Peoples" who invaded the Near East from somewhere in the Mediterranean in the twelfth century B.C.E. Unsuccessful in gaining a foothold in Egypt, the Philistines became Israel's principal foe in Judges and Samuel—technologically advanced through possession of iron weapons, and militarily powerful. Little is known of their language and religion; their pottery, however, has affinities with that of the Aegean. They quickly adopted Canaanite culture and, despite being decisively defeated by King David, survived for centuries. Ironically, their name, vocalized as "Palestine," became that of the country after biblical kings were long gone, and is today used as the name of a proposed Arab state in the West Bank/Gaza.

2 **Tzor'a:** A town fifteen miles west of Jerusalem, near Bet-Shemesh. The story opens not far from the border with Philistia.   **a Danite clan:** Had the body of the tribe already migrated far to the north, as in Chap. 18?   **Manoah:** Pronounced *mah-NO-ah;* the name connotes a "secure resting place."   **barren:** A sure sign in the Bible that a significant figure is about to be born.

4 *tamei:* Ritually polluted, and so forbidden (see, for instance, the list in Lev. 11).

5 **One Consecrated:** Others, transcribing the Hebrew, render as "Nazirite." See Commentary.

In true biblical fashion, there is no childhood in the story. Shimshon does not have to display prodigious feats of strength, as the infant Herakles does in strangling snakes sent by a jealous Hera. The text need only note that God blesses him (v.24), and that Shimshon feels the beginnings of his strength on home ground. The rest will follow soon enough.

7 but he said to me:
Here, you are about to conceive, you shall give birth to a son;
so-now,
do not drink wine or beer,
do not eat anything *tamei,*
for One Consecrated to God shall the lad be
from the womb until the day of his death!
8 Manoah entreated YHWH, he said:
O my Lord,
as for the man of God whom you sent, pray let him come again
to us
and instruct us: What are we to do for the boy who will be born?
9 God hearkened to the voice of Manoah,
and God's messenger came again to the woman
—now she was sitting in the open-field, while her husband Manoah
was not with her.
10 Quickly the woman ran and told it to her husband; she said to him:
Here, he has made himself seen by me, the man who came in the
day to me!
11 Manoah arose and went after his wife;
he came to the man and said to him:
Are you the man who spoke to the woman?
He said:
I am.
12 Manoah said:
So-now, should your words come to pass,
what will be the rule for the boy and what-we-do for him?
13 YHWH's messenger said to Manoah:
From all that I said to the woman she is to guard herself,
14 from all that goes out from the vine of wine she is not to eat,
wine and beer she must not drink,
all [things] *tamei* she must not eat;
all that I have commanded her, she is to guard.

---

7 **until the day of his death:** The woman has changed
the messenger's words of v.5, foreshadowing the
events of Chap. 16. The omission of the usual
Nazirite prohibition against haircutting (also in v.14)
is surprising, given Manoah's request for detailed

information. Perhaps this is another instance of the
theme of secrecy in the story.
12 **rule:** In the sense of "a set of rules," also referring to
one's regular or customary practice.

Chapter 14. *Shimshon's Marriage:* Before the hero is able to do any "delivering," his first contact with the Philistines characteristically involves a woman. Strikingly, the text emphasizes *seeing* (vv.1–2, and "eyes" in v.3) instead of using the term "love," which will take its time to appear.

Shimshon's first superhuman act is the slaying of a lion, parallel to Herakles's killing the Nemean lion. Normally an occasion for wonderment, in the context of the cycle it signals the first breaking of Nazirite restrictions, contact with the dead. It also introduces the hiding of secrets in this particular chapter, which is accomplished by having the parental escort mysteriously disappear in vv.5–6. This is followed by the account of how Shimshon's wife betrays the secret of his riddle, against the background of yet another violation of his vows, as the term "drink-fest" in v.10 hints.

Verbal repetitions here include "take," "my people," "riddle a riddle," "not telling," and the rhythmic fivefold mention of the place name Timna. And Shimshon's act of "breaking off" (*r-d-h*) honey supplies the chapter's seventh occurrence of sounds suggested by the family's movement of "going down" (*y-r-d*) to Philistine territory.

The whole chapter utilizes folk motifs: Shimshon's slaying of the lion (a favorite subject in Western art), the honey in the carcass, the riddle, the use of numbers three and four, the pressure from the wife, and the substitution of armor for festive garments. It sets a precedent for the climactic Delila story of Chap. 16, which describes the use of feminine wiles in almost identical terms. Once the first woman has talked Shimshon into revealing his first secret, we know that the last woman will have no trouble prying the crucial one out of him in the end.

The inclusion of a riddle in this chapter is another one of Klein's examples of irony in Judges; often in folklore, solving a riddle leads to winning, not losing, the bride.

15 Manoah said to Yhwh's messenger:
Now let us detain you,
that we may make ready a goats' kid for you.

16 Yhwh's messenger said to Manoah:
If you detain me, I will not eat of your food,
but if you wish to make ready an offering-up to Yhwh, you should
offer it up
—for Manoah did not know that he was Yhwh's messenger.

17 Manoah said to Yhwh's messenger:
What is your name,
so that when your words come to pass, we may honor you?

18 Yhwh's messenger said to him:
Now why do you ask about my name?
For it is wondrous!

19 Manoah took the goats' kid and the gift-offering
and offered them up on the rock to Yhwh.
He did wondrously, while Manoah and his wife saw it:

20 it was,
as the flame was going upward from the altar to the heavens,
that Yhwh's messenger went up in the flame of the altar.
When Manoah and his wife saw it,
they flung themselves upon their faces to the ground.

21 Yhwh's messenger was not seen again by Manoah or by his wife,
so Manoah knew that he was Yhwh's messenger.

22 Manoah said to his wife:
We are going to die, yes, die,
for it is a god that we have seen!

23 But his wife said to him:
Had Yhwh desired to have us die
he would not have taken an offering-up and a grain-gift from our
hand,
he would not have let us see all these,
and at that moment, he would not have let us hear such things.

---

18 **wondrous:** Or "Wondrous One." The sense is of
something removed from the ordinary and natural
world.

22 **die:** See note on 6:22 above.

24 The woman gave birth to a son;
   she called his name Shimshon.
   The boy grew up, and Yʜwʜ blessed him.
25 And Yʜwʜ's rushing-spirit began to stir him up in Mahaneh-Dan,
   between Tzor'a and Eshtaol.

14:1 Shimshon went down to Timna,
   and he saw a woman in Timna from the daughters of the
      Philistines.
2 He came up and told it to his father and to his mother;
   he said:
   A woman have I seen in Timna from the daughters of the
      Philistines.
   So-now, take her for me as a wife!
3 His father and his mother said to him:
   Is there not among your brothers' daughters or among all my
      people a woman,
   that you must go to take a woman from the Philistines, the
      Foreskinned Ones?
   Shimshon said to his father:
   Take *her* for me, for she is right in my eyes!
4 Now his father and his mother did not know that it was from
      Yʜwʜ,
   for he was seeking a pretext from the Philistines
   —now at that time the Philistines were ruling over Israel.
5 Shimshon went down along with his father and his mother to
      Timna;
   they had come as far as the vineyards of Timna
   when here, a full-maned roaring lion, [coming] to meet him!

24 **Shimshon:** pronounced *shim-SHOHN;* trad. English "Samson." See the discussion of the name in the essay "On the Shimshon Cycle," above.
25 **stir him up:** A Hebrew homonym is related to the idea of "beating" or "throbbing." **Mahaneh-Dan:** "The camp of Dan." The mention of this and Tzor'a at the chapter's end forms a framework for the chapter; similarly, the names return at the very end of the whole cycle. **Eshtaol:** Just a few miles from Tzor'a.
14:1 **Timna:** Also close to Tzor'a.
2 **take her for me:** As would have been the ancient custom.
3 **brothers:** Kinsmen. **my people:** LXX reads "your people." **Foreskinned:** Circumcision seems to have been widely practiced in the ancient Near East, making the Philistines noticeably different from their neighbors. **she is right in my eyes:** Others: "she pleases me." The phrase anticipates the book's final section (Chaps. 17–21), where in the form, "each one would do what was right in his eyes," it is a refrain.
4 **a pretext:** Creating the right conditions for an Israelite victory, so to speak. **at that time:** The text here distances itself from the era of the Judges.
5 **along with his father and his mother:** Yet they do not witness his great feat of strength in v.6.

6 YHWH's spirit advanced upon him
and he tore it apart as one tears apart a kid,
without a thing in his hand.
But he did not tell his father and his mother what he had done.

7 Then he went down and spoke to the woman—
she was right in Shimshon's eyes.

8 He returned after a year to take her;
he turned aside to see the fallen lion,
and here: a swarm of bees in the lion's corpse, and honey!

9 He broke it off into his hands,
and went along, going and eating.
Then he went back to his father and to his mother,
and gave some to them, and they ate.
But he did not tell them that it was from the lion's corpse that he
had broken off the honey.

10 His father went down on account of the woman,
and Shimshon made a drinkfest there, for that is what young
men do;

11 and it was when they saw him, that they fetched thirty feasting-
companions [who] remained with him.

12 Shimshon said to them:
Now let me riddle you a riddle!
If you can tell, yes, tell me its [answer] during the seven days of the
drinkfest
and can find it out,
I will give you thirty linen garments and thirty changes of clothes;

13 but if you are not able to tell me,
you will have to give me, yourselves, thirty linen garments and
thirty changes of clothes.

---

6 **without a thing in his hand:** Like two other ancient heroes, Herakles/Hercules fighting the Nemean lion, and the Mesopotamian Gilgamesh (Burney).

8 **to take her:** To actually marry her. **honey:** Associated with restoration of energy, as in I Sam. 14, where Yehonatan is reenergized following a fast imposed by his father, King Sha'ul. There may also be a hidden pun here; it is theorized that there was an older Hebrew word (still used in Arabic) for honey, *ari,* which in our story signifies the lion.

9 **broke it off:** "It" here probably refers to a piece of honeycomb. Scraping it off, as some translations

have it, would be rather a messy procedure. The use of the rare *r-d-h* here may be for the sake of punning with the theme word *y-r-d,* "go down" (Boling).

10 **His father went down:** Shimshon appears to have taken the woman as a wife in the meantime; the events are hazy here. **drinkfest:** By participating, Shimshon would be breaking another one of the Nazirite vows.

11 **when they saw:** Some ancient versions have "because they feared" (the Hebrew spelling is quite close).

12 **clothes:** Most likely festival garments.

Chapter 15. *Shimshon with Philistines and Judahites:* The troubled wedding feast gives way to revenge on all sides (v.10: "to do to him as he did to us"; v.11: "As they did to me, so I did to them"). Shimshon's wife is given to another, so he counters with the colorful episode of the fox tails and the fire, in which the Philistine crops are destroyed. This results in another fire, causing the death of Shimshon's wife and father-in-law, which is followed by Shimshon's taking revenge by slaughtering more Philistines.

The story in the second half of the chapter (vv.9ff.) witnesses the hero's first reported contact with other Israelites. It also introduces the symbolically important theme of binding, already implied by the same verb in the Nazirite restrictions. For a third straight chapter, an animal plays a role in the narrative, this time in the form of a donkey's jawbone. Shimshon's victims are legion; a fitting illustration of the scene is Gustave Doré's classic etching, found in many Bibles, which features innumerable tiny figures falling into the gorge. While the text then presents an etiological passage, with two names (Ramat Lehi and En Ha-Korei) receiving folk etymologies, its real significance lies in Shimshon's calling upon God—something he will not do again until his final moments. The hero, like Eliyyahu (Elijah) in I Kings 17, is nourished by God, but, unlike the prophet, the strong man gives no indication of his true calling. The "great deliverance" for which he pleads is thus only his personal one, and he does not view the slaying of a thousand Philistines as an act undertaken on behalf of an oppressed people. All the more jarring, then, is the editorial note that has been inserted in v.20, characterizing Shimshon as a "judge."

◆ They said to him:
Riddle your riddle, and we will hear it!

14 He said to them:
   Out of the eater came food-to-eat,
   out of the strong one came something sweet.
They could not tell him [the answer to] the riddle for three days;

15 so on the fourth day it was that they said to Shimshon's wife:
Seduce your husband, that he may tell us [the answer to] the riddle,
lest we burn you and your Father's House with fire—
is it to dispossess us that you have invited us here?

16 Shimshon's wife wept on him, she said:
You surely hate me, you do not love me;
should you riddle a riddle to the sons of my people,
and not tell [the answer] to me?
He said to her:
Here, I haven't told it to my father or to my mother—
so should I tell it to you?

17 She wept on him for the seven days in which they held the
      drinkfest,
and then it was, on the seventh day, that he told it to her, for she
      kept pressing him,
and she told the riddle's [answer] to the sons of her people.

18 So the men of the city said to him on the seventh day, before the
      daystar set:
   What is sweeter than honey?
   What is stronger than a lion?
He said to them:
   If you hadn't plowed with my heifer,
   you wouldn't have found out my riddle!

19 And Yhwh's spirit advanced upon him;
he went down to Ashkelon

15 **fourth:** So LXX; MT has "seventh." **Seduce:** The verb, *p-t-h,* may also connote "deceive," taking advantage of his gullible nature. This will happen with another woman in 16:5. **dispossess:** Or "impoverish." **here:** Heb. corrupt; I follow ancient manuscripts.

18 **before the daystar set:** That is, just before the sun came in, an element common to folktales. Some emend the rare Hebrew word for "sun"

here, *heres,* to *heder,* "inner-room," suggesting that the marriage is about to be consummated. **If you hadn't plowed . . . :** The image of plowing had sexual connotations throughout the ancient world. **heifer . . . riddle:** Heb. *'eglati . . . hidati.*

19 **Ashkelon:** One of the five major Philistine cities, situated on the Mediterranean coast. **sashes . . . changes:** Heb. *halitzot . . . halifot.*

◆ and struck down thirty fighting-men of them,
took their sashes
and gave them as clothing-changes to those who had told the
riddle's [answer].
His anger flared on,
and he went up to his father's house.

20 Now Shimshon's wife was [given] to one of his feasting-
companions, who had been his [own] companion.

15:1 Now it was [after] a year, in the days of the wheat cutting,
that Shimshon visited his wife with a goats' kid;
he said: I will come in to my wife, in the inner-room!
But her father did not give him [leave] to come in.

2 Her father said:
I said [to myself], said:
Indeed, you bear hatred, yes, hatred toward her,
so I gave her to your companion.
Isn't her sister more good-looking than she?
Let her be yours in her place!

3 Shimshon said to them:
This time I will be clear of blame from the Philistines,
if I do evil with them!

4 So Shimshon went
and captured three hundred foxes,
and took [some] torches
and faced tail to tail,
and placed each torch between two tails, in the middle,

5 and ignited fire in the torches,
and sent them free in the standing-stalks of the Philistines;
he ignited from sheaf-stacks to standing-stalks, to vineyards [and]
olive-trees.

15:1 **the days of the wheat cutting:** Late spring. **come in to:** The verb often refers to sex in the Bible, and probably does here as well.
3 **evil with them:** In the sense of "to them."
4–5 **So Shimshon went . . . :** The long string of verbs here, and in passages like 16:3, seems to reflect the hero's precipitous action, so much a part of his character. **foxes:** It is not clear whether these or jackals are meant, as the distinction, sadly for me, is not always made in the Bible. Jackals, as social animals, would be more catchable in a naturalistic setting, whereas foxes, whose behavior is more solitary, suggest a miraculous, folktale background, perhaps more appropriate here.

6 The Philistines said:
Who has done this?
They said:
Shimshon, the Timnite's son-in-law,
for he took away his wife and gave her to his companion!
So the Philistines went up and burned her and her father with fire.

7 Shimshon said to them:
If you do [things] like this,
surely when I have avenged myself upon you, [only] afterward will
I stop!

8 And he struck them down, hip over thigh, a great striking down;
then he went down and stayed in the gorge of Etam's Crag.

9 The Philistines went up and camped in Yehuda;
they were spread out at Lehi.

10 And the fighting-men of Yehuda said:
Why have you come up against us?
They said:
To bind Shimshon have we come up,
to do to him as he did to us!

11 Three thousand fighting-men from Yehuda went down to the gorge
of Etam's Crag
and said to Shimshon:
Don't you know that the Philistines are ruling us?
Now what have you done to us?
He said to them:
As they did to me, so I did to them!

12 They said to him:
We have come down to bind you, to give you into the hand of the
Philistines.
Shimshon said to them:
Swear to me, lest you attack me yourselves!

---

6 **her father:** Many manuscripts read "her Father's House," thus including more people. "Household" is the same word in Hebrew; see the Philistines' threat in 14:15 (Gray 1986).

7 **avenged:** Usually the prerogative of God in the Bible (Boling 1975). It is also used to describe Shimshon's final emotion and act in 16:28.

8 **hip over thigh:** Burney likens the phrase to a wrestler's term. It may also be a realistic description of the scene, with numerous body parts tangled up. **Etam's Crag:** Identification unknown.

9 **Lehi:** Pronounced *LEH-hee;* somewhere in the Judean lowlands.

Chapter 16:1–3. *The Gates of Gaza:* Here is another tale which may have had a humorous flavor for ancient audiences. God has just slaked Shimshon's thirst, but the hero's insatiable desire for women takes him right back to the enemy camp, in this case one of the five major Philistine cities. To all appearances he is about to be trapped, as the natives set an ambush (a motif which will reappear in the next episode). But the contrast between pursuers and pursued takes an unexpected turn: the Philistines' quiet and patience are overcome by Shimshon's impulsiveness and overwhelming strength. Like a mythical giant, he uproots the huge doors of the city gate, bolt and all, and carries them off to Hevron, which is not only many miles away from Gaza but also three thousand feet up in the hills. The Philistines' response is stunned silence, and they simply disappear from the text. One imagines them with mouths agape at the spectacle before them, and the text's audience shaking their heads with a smile, or more.

13 They said to him, saying:
    No,
    rather, we want to bind, yes, bind you, and give you into their hand,
    but death, we will not cause your death!
    So they bound him with two new ropes
    and led him up from the Rock.

14 He had come as far as Lehi,
    when the Philistines shouted [in triumph] meeting him;
    YHWH's spirit advanced upon him,
    and the ropes which were on his arms became
    like [threads of] flax which are ignited with fire;
    his bonds melted off his hands.

15 He found the fresh jawbone of a donkey
    and stretched out his hand and took it,
    and with it he struck down a thousand men.

16 Then Shimshon said:
        With the jawbone of a donkey,
        one donkey, two donkeys,
        with the jawbone of a donkey
        I've struck down a thousand men!

17 It was, when he had finished speaking,
    that he threw the jawbone from his hand
    —so they called that place Ramat Lehi/Jawbone Height.

18 He became exceedingly thirsty, so he called out to YHWH and said:
    You yourself have given into your servant's hand
    this great deliverance,
    so-now, shall I die of thirst
    and fall into the hand of the Foreskinned Ones?

19 So God split open the cavity that was at Lehi,
    and water came out of it, and he drank;
    his spirit returned, and he revived.

---

15 **fresh:** Lit. "moist." If it had been dry, it would have been brittle and thus might well have cracked (Gray 1986). Shimshon's touching the remains of an ass here is another example of his violation of Nazirite rules.

16 **With the jawbone of a donkey . . . :** Heb. difficult; some have understood h-m-r to mean "heap," thus: "With the jawbone of an ass, / heaping mass upon mass . . ." Boling (1975) likens the phrase *hamor hamortayim* to *raham rahamatayim* ("a lass, two lasses")

and *rikma . . . rikmatayim* ("embroidered cloth . . . embroidered") in 5:30.

17 **Ramat . . . Height:** Heb. *r-m-h* may also denote "toss away," fitting the action in the previous verse.

19 **spirit:** Or "life-breath," although "spirit" has been a force earlier in the story. **Ha-Korei:** This can also mean "the partridge," likely the original significa-tion of the name. The whole name is pronounced *AYN ha-ko-RAY*.

Chapter 16:4–22. *The Woman of the Night:* Although it is not the final story in the cycle, the Delila episode is a climax of sorts. Carefully constructed of repeating phrases (for example, "Now the ambush was sitting [for her] in the inner-room"; "Philistines upon you, Shimshon!"), it reprises most of the words and motifs that have appeared up to this point (see "Appendix: The Sound and Structure of a Biblical Tale") and welds them into a tight whole. Folk motifs return, in the person of the nagging lover, the new, fresh ropes, and the number of Delila's attempts to get at the truth—the classic 3+1 pattern of folklore. The tension is palpable, with the ambush lying in wait and Delila inching ever closer to the truth (on the third try, Shimshon brings his "locks" into the picture). The text is punctuated by the repeated "I'd become weak, I'd become like [Heb. *ve-hayyiti ve-haliti*] any man," culminating in the slightly altered "all men" in v.17. Shimshon is, of course, the last to know about his newly weakened state, and his lack of knowledge contin-ues the broader theme of secrets withheld (note that the word "tell" occurs seven times in the episode).

Shimshon's punishment is twofold. First, he temporarily loses his strength, and second, more permanently, he loses his sight.

◆ Therefore they called its name En Ha-Korei/Spring of the Caller,
which is in Lehi,
until this day.

20 He led Israel as judge in the days of the Philistines, for twenty
years.

16:1 Shimshon went to Gaza;
he saw there a whore woman, and came in to her.

2 Among the Gazites it was said:
Shimshon has come here!
They circled about and set an ambush for him the whole night at
the town gate,
and they plotted the whole night, saying:
Until the light of daybreak—then we will kill him!

3 Shimshon lay until the middle of the night;
he arose in the middle of the night
and seized the doors of the town gate, along with the two posts,
and pulled them up, together with the bolt
and put them on his shoulders
and brought them up to the top of the hill that faces Hevron.

4 Now it was [some time] after this
that he fell in love with a woman in the Wadi of Sorek/Vines;
her name was Delila.

5 The Philistine overlords went up to her and said to her:
Seduce him and see
whereby his might is so great,
whereby we can overcome him,
so that we can bind him, to subdue him,
and we ourselves, each one, will give you a thousand and a hundred
pieces of silver!

---

20 **He led Israel as judge:** See Commentary.
16:1 **Gaza:** Heb. *'Azza,* another major Philistine city
along the coast.
2 **plotted:** Often read as "kept silent," but the verb
may be a homonym which is used several times in
Proverbs.
3 **lay . . . arose . . . :** Once again, the rush of verbs
seems to indicate swift, almost breathless, action.
doors: From archaeological indications of Iron Age
gates, these must have been quite large.   **brought
them up . . . Hevron:** A distance of some forty
miles, with a rise of close to three thousand feet!

4 **Sorek:** A few miles south of Tzor'a.   **Delila:** Pronounced *de-lee-LAH;* trad. English "Delilah." Many
meanings have been theorized for the name, including "vine" (alluding to Shimshon's violation of his
vows), "flirt" (Arabic), and "dangling curls" (Niditch
2008; the hair motif again). Most significant, in
my view, is the name's resemblance to Heb. *layla,*
"night," evocative of seduction and a fitting contrast
to Shimshon's name's connection to "sun."
5 **overlords:** See note to 3:3 above.

6 Delila said to Shimshon:
Pray tell me,
whereby is your might so great,
whereby can you be bound, to subdue you?

7 Shimshon said to her:
If they were to bind me with seven fresh gut-strings, that have not
been dried,
I'd become weak, I'd become like
any man!

8 The Philistine overlords brought up to her seven fresh gut-strings,
that had not been dried,
and she bound him with them.

9 Now the ambush was sitting for her in the inner-room.
She said to him:
Philistines upon you, Shimshon!
He snapped the strings
as hempen cord bursts when it smells fire,
and his might was not made known.

10 Delila said to Shimshon:
Here, you've taunted me,
you've been speaking lies to me—
but now, pray tell me:
whereby can you be bound?

11 He said to her:
If they were to bind, yes, bind me with new ropes,
with which no work has been done,
I'd become weak, I'd become like
any man!

12 So Delila took new ropes
and bound him with them,
and said to him:
Philistines upon you, Shimshon!

---

6 **whereby:** What's the cause (of your strength)?

7 **gut-strings:** Bowstrings, which would be well-nigh impossible to break with bare hands. **I'd become weak, I'd become like:** Heb. *ve-haliti ve-hayyiti,* which feels like a deliberate rhyme. It recurs twice here, and suggests the rhythm of a folktale. The usual translation is "I will become as weak as any other man," but that misses the style.

9 **inner-room:** A place of concealment or intimacy, often descriptive of a bedroom.

11 **new ropes:** In folklore, unused objects often have pristine, magical powers. Thus, animals described as "having not yet yielded to a yoke" are sometimes used in special rituals (Num. 19:2, I Sam. 6:7).

◆ —Now the ambush was sitting in the inner-room.—
He snapped them from off his arms like a thread.

13 Delila said to Shimshon:
Until now you've taunted me,
you've been speaking lies to me—
tell me:
whereby can you be bound?
He said to her:
If you were to weave the seven locks of my head in a warp . . .

14 She drove them tight with the pin,
and said to him:
Philistines upon you, Shimshon!
He awoke from his sleep
and pulled out the pin, the weaver's-bobbin, and the warp.

15 Then she said to him:
How can you say: I love you,
when your heart is not with me?
Three times now you've taunted me,
yet you haven't told me
whereby your might is so great!

16 And it was,
when she had pressed him with her words all the time
and had prodded him, so that he became short-tempered to [the
    point of] death,

17 that he told her all his heart;
he said to her:
No razor has gone up on my head,
for One Consecrated to God have I been from my mother's
    womb on:
if I were to be shaven,
my might would leave me;

---

13 **tell me:** Some manuscripts add the "pray" of vv.6 and 10. **head:** The allusion to Shimshon's hair is a fine narrative strategy for getting us closer to the truth; Shimshon is clearly growing tired of this game and is ready to reveal all. **warp . . . :** Of a loom. The text appears to be defective, and is appropriately filled in by LXX, along the pattern of the previous trials. I have left it here as it appears in MT.

14 **pulled out the pin . . . :** The same verb (*n-s-'*) was used to describe Shimshon's "pulling up" the gates of Gaza in v.3, above.

16 **short-tempered to [the point of] death:** Again foreshadowing the end. The idiom seems to indicate literal shortness of breath as an indicator of impatience.

17 **all men:** Most translations from LXX on have "corrected" "all" to read "any" (*kol* to *ke-ahad*) as in the previous occurrences of the phrase. But the slight shift in wording here may give Delila a hint that Shimshon has cracked at last (see the double "*all his heart*" in the next verse).

Chapter 16:23–31. *Grand Finale:* The stage is set for Shimshon's last triumph, in a scene that is truly cinematic, with literally a cast of thousands. The sequence of humiliation and over-the-top revenge is an old favorite among audiences in many cultures; a modern example would be the classic cult film *Carrie*. Here, however, it is not totally unexpected, as we have been slipped a hint at the time of Shimshon's capture and imprisonment that his hair is growing again (v.22). But he will have to invoke God once more in order to enable the deed to take place.

The image of a man, however strong, pulling down an entire temple with his bare hands has typically been considered the ultimate fairy-tale element. But excavations at Tell Qasile in coastal Israel have unearthed a Philistine structure in which two wooden pillars served as major supports for the building—although not, to be sure, side by side. So we get to enjoy both the miraculous and a sense of the real world simultaneously.

Similar to the end of Chap. 15, Shimshon's feat at his death, while taking an enormous toll on the enemy and thus fulfilling his destiny, is ambiguously represented as a spectacular deed of personal vengeance. The hero's plea to God in v.28 shows no recognition of any kind of leadership role, or indeed of any reality much beyond his various body parts. With the collapse of the Philistine temple, the core quest of Judges, Israel's dreams of competent, covenant-based human leadership, ends up in a heap of ruins as well.

♦ I'd become weak, I'd become like
all men!

18 Delila saw that he had told her all his heart,
so she sent and called for the Philistine overlords, saying:
Come up this time,
for he has told me all his heart!
The Philistine overlords went up to her,
and they brought up the silver in their hand.

19 She lulled him to sleep upon her knees,
and she called for a man and he shaved off the seven locks of
his head;
she began to subdue him,
and his might left him.

20 Then she said:
Philistines upon you, Shimshon!
He awoke from his sleep,
and he said [to himself]:
I'll get away as time after time,
I'll shake myself free!
But he did not know that YHWH had left him.

21 The Philistines grabbed him and gouged out his eyes;
then they brought him down to Gaza and bound him with double-
bronze,
and he had to grind [grain] in the prison house.

22 But the hair of his head began to sprout again, as soon as it had
been shaven off.

23 Now the Philistine overlords gathered together to sacrifice a great
sacrifice to Dagon their god
and for [a feast of] rejoicing.
They said:
Given has our god
into our hand
Shimshon our foe!

---

21 **Gaza:** The very site of his great triumph earlier in the chapter. **double-bronze:** Chains.
23 **Dagon:** Pronounced *dah-GOHN,* a Semitic fertility god, the worship of whom was adopted by the Philistines. See I Sam. 5 for a further story regarding the god's statue.

23–24 **our:** Each Hebrew phrase ends with the suffix *-einu,* "our," creating a kind of rhyme (rare in the Bible). See II Sam. 12:11 for a similar scheme, based on *-ekha,* "your."

24 The people saw him
and praised their god,
indeed, they said:
> Given has our god
> into our hand
> [Shimshon] our foe,
> destroyer of our land,
> who made many our slain!

25 Now it was, since their heart was in good-humor,
that they said:
Call for Shimshon, that he may provide-amusement for us!
They had Shimshon called out of the prison house,
and he provided-amusement before them.
They stood him between the standing-columns,

26 and Shimshon said to the serving-lad who held him by the hand:
Let me rest;
let me feel the columns on which the house is founded,
so that I may support myself on them!

27 Now the house was full of men and women;
all the Philistine overlords were there,
and upon the roof were about three thousand—man and woman—
who were seeing Shimshon provide-amusement.

28 And Shimshon called out to Yhwh;
he said:
My Lord, Yhwh,
now be mindful of me,
now strengthen me,
just this one time;
O God,
I would take revenge, a single revenge for my two eyes
from the Philistines!

---

24 **saw him:** JPS posits that this fits better after v.25.
26 **the house:** Presumably Dagon's temple; the Bible uses "house" (*bayit*) for such diverse meanings as "home," "palace," "temple," and "dynasty."

28 **a single revenge . . . :** MT has "revenge for one of my two eyes"; I follow LXX here as being more intelligible.

29　Shimshon clasped the two middle columns on which the house was
　　　founded;
　　he put-his-weight on them,
　　one with his right [hand], and one with his left,
30　and Shimshon said:
　　Let me die with the Philistines!
　　He inclined with might,
　　and the house fell down on the overlords,
　　on all the people who were in it.
　　Now the dead whose death he caused at his death
　　were more than those whose death he had caused in his life.
31　His brothers and all his Father's House went down,
　　they lifted him, brought him up and buried him
　　between Tzor'a and Eshtaol, in the burial place of Manoah his
　　　father.
　　Now he had led Israel as judge for twenty years.

29　**put-his-weight on:** Boling (1975) understands this as "reached around."

30　**me:** Lit. "my (very) being." Others, "soul." In biblical Hebrew, *nefesh* almost always means "life" or "life force," or "breathing/swallowing organs," and not "soul" in the later sense of an entity distinct from the body.　**with might:** Mentioned so often earlier in the chapter, Shimshon's strength now returns full bore.　**Now the dead . . . :** The multiple repetition of the root *m-w-t* ("dead, death") highlights the importance of this statement, summarizing Shimshon's militarily effective career.

31　**between Tzor'a and Eshtaol:** The mention of the place names with which the story began provides a classic aural signal that the story has come to an end.

PART III

CLOSING THE BRACKET

(17–21)

THE LAST SECTION OF JUDGES, WHICH CONSTITUTES ALMOST A QUARTER OF THE book, does not fit the pattern established in Chap. 2, nor does it recount the great deeds of heroes, even ambiguous ones. For these reasons, interpreters sometimes consider it an appendix that has been tacked on to the book at a later date. From a more global point of view, this view is erroneous. These chapters constitute an appropriate and coherent ending to Judges, portraying a society in disarray and advancing some major ideological agendas.

On the surface, Chaps. 17–18 are a series of narratives involving bad-faith dealings in finance, worship, hospitality, and tribal relations. A closer look, however, reveals a detailed description of priestly illegitimacy: first, a Levite conducting his own local form of worship, with an idol, and second, an entire tribe setting up its own sanctuary with that priest, whom they have hired away from the family with whom the section began. We may well be dealing here with a condemnation of worship outside of Jerusalem—an issue of more relevance to the time of King Josiah in the seventh century B.C.E. than to the period in which Judges is set—and a graphic portrayal of the idolatrous practices against which Deuteronomy and earlier passages in Judges had warned.

Chaps. 19–21, as we shall see, appear aimed at Israel's first king, Sha'ul (Saul), who will make his entrance in the very next book, through condemning his home tribe of Binyamin. In a series of extremely violent narratives, involving the violation of the sacred rules of hospitality as well as a gang rape, dismemberment, civil war, and mass abduction, we are left with the strongest possible expression of a society that has reached its nadir. The career of a single judge would not have sufficed to paint this portrait. Chaps. 17–21 betoken a complete breakdown of the leadership which had at least tentatively enabled Israel to survive, with, once again, variations on the refrain that echoes throughout these chapters: "In those days there was no king in Israel; / each one would do what was right in his eyes." It will take a good chunk of the next book, Samuel, to set matters aright.

Chapter 17. *Mikha and the Levite:* The final section of Judges begins with a brand-new story ("There was a man . . ."). A family crime, a son's theft of a large sum of money from his mother, leads ultimately to another one, idolatry, with implications for all Israel. The text demonstrates not only the defective leadership we have traced over the past chapters, but a systemic religious decline that will be confirmed in subsequent chapters. Mikha gives living proof of the refrain that will resound so often throughout this final section—"each one would do what was right in his eyes"—by making an idol and appointing a Levite as his own personal priest.

In the absence of any kind of effective leadership, the text presents us with three characters of dubious distinction: a thieving son, a parsimonious and idolatrous mother, and a wandering young Levite who is all too happy to serve as a priest in an idol-worshipping household. The text itself, however, applies no adjectives to them; they are known only through their actions (Schneider).

The story's vocabulary, especially as the Levite is hired, is consistent: "Levite" six times, "sojourn" twice, and "lad" three times. And, lest it seem jarring after so many stories about military leaders, it contains at least several links to the Shimshon cycle: an active mother, the phrase "right in his/their own eyes," and a sum of money identical to what was promised to Delila by the Philistines.

17:1 There was a man from the highlands of Efrayim;
his name was Mikhayehu.

2 [Once] he said to his mother:
The thousand and a hundred pieces of silver that were taken from you,
and you yourself put an oath-curse [on it], and even said it in my
hearing—
here, the silver is with me,
I myself took it!
His mother said:
Blessed is my son of YHWH!

3 He has returned the thousand and a hundred pieces of silver to his
mother!
And his mother said:
I render the silver holy, yes, holy to YHWH,
from my hand, for my son,
to make a carved and molten [idol].
So-now, I return it to you.

4 He returned the silver to his mother,
and his mother took two hundred pieces of silver and gave it to a
smelter;
he made it into a carved and molten [idol],
and it remained in the house of Mikhayehu.

5 Now the man Mikha had a house of God;
he had made an *efod* and *terafim*
and had given-mandate to one of his sons, so that he had become a
priest for him.

17:1 **Mikhayehu:** Pronounced *mee-KHA-y'hu;* trad. English "Micaiah." It means "Who Is Like YHWH?" (ironic in a story about idolatry) and is sometimes shortened to "Mikha" in the narrative that follows. A more familiar variation of the name is "Mikhael" (Michael).

2 **thousand and a hundred:** A sum identical to the reward promised to Delila in the previous chapter, leading some commentators to identify the mother here with that more famous lady. Or it may simply have a connecting function, enabling the editor(s) to juxtapose the two stories (and note too the reappearance in vv.8 and 11 of the place-names cited previously in 13:25 and 16:31). **oath-curse:** Invoked when human punishment cannot be brought to bear (Gray 1986). In this story it makes Mikhayehu's nonpayment to his mother an occasion for divine punishment. **Blessed is my son:** She effectively removes the curse (JPS note).

3 **for my son:** Heb. *li-vni;* LXX reads "alone" (*levaddi*). **a carved and molten [idol]:** The figure would be made from molten metal poured into a mold carved in the desired shape. This emphatically violates the Israelites' covenant with YHWH (see Exod. 20:2). **to you:** To God.

4 **two hundred pieces:** What did she do with the other nine hundred? Is this a hint of misappropriation or of stinginess?

5 **house of God:** Some read as "house of gods," which the Hebrew allows; most translations simply use "shrine." *efod:* See note to 8:27 above. *terafim:* usually understood as household idols or figurines; see Gen. 31:19ff. **given-mandate:** Lit. "filled the hand," installing him as a priest. **one of his sons:** Since he was not a Levite, this is quite illegal (Amit 2004).

235

Chapter 18. *The Danite Migration and Its Consequences:* What in several scholars' estimation is the original end of the book of Judges is a mixture of a small-scale story (continued from the previous chapter) and a larger event rooted in some kind of historical memory, the northward migration of the tribe of Dan. But those elements have been transformed into an ideological text, the main purpose of which seems to be (as Brettler 2001a emphasizes; see above) to condemn the future northern rebellion during the reign of King Rehav'am (Rehoboam) some centuries later. The need to convey such a message is so strong that it does not seem to matter to the editors that the migration, chronologically speaking, should really have appeared much earlier in the book.

The Danites are portrayed here as cruel, thieving, and idolatrous—they destroy a peaceful and "secure" city, echoing the destruction of Shekhem in Gen. 34, they steal Mikha's personal idols and his priest, and they keep the idols and the priest not just for the moment but permanently ("until the time of the exile of the land," v.30). Three times, in vv.11, 16, and 17, they are menacingly described as "girded in battle gear." As the book began with conquest, so this initial transitional section ends as well, along with a ringing condemnation of the north for practices that in II Kings 17 will lead to the permanent end of the kingdom.

This negativity is borne out by vocabulary in the middle of the chapter (vv.14–24) which concentrates on words connected to idolatry: "carved-image," "gods," "*efod*" (see 8:27), "*terafim*," and "molten-image." To top it all off, a scribe has even sneaked into a story about the north the name of the most hated king in southern (Judean) history, by substituting the name "Menashe" (Manasseh; see II Kings 18) for "Moshe" (Moses) in v.30, in what is outwardly an attempt to disassociate the great lawgiver's family from any connection to later idolatrous events.

6 In those days, there was no king in Israel;
each one would do what was right in his eyes.

7 There was a lad from Bet-Lehem [in] Yehuda, from a clan of Yehuda
—now he was a Levite, and he was sojourning there.

8 And the man went from the town, from Bet-Lehem [in] Yehuda to
sojourn wherever he could find,
and he came to the highlands of Efrayim, to the house of Mikha, to
make his way.

9 Mikha said to him:
From where have you come?
He said to him:
I am a Levite,
from Bet-Lehem [in] Yehuda,
and I am going to sojourn wherever I can find.

10 Mikha said to him:
Come stay with me, and be for me a "father" and a priest,
and I myself will give you ten pieces of silver a year, an outfit of
garments, and your living needs.
So the Levite went;

11 the Levite agreed to settle with the man,
and the lad became for him like one of his sons.

12 Mikha gave-mandate to the Levite,
and the lad became a priest for him
and remained in Mikha's house.

13 Mikha said:
Now I know
that YHWH will do good for me,
for a Levite has become a priest for me!

7 **lad:** Or "young man." **sojourning:** Living there temporarily.

8 **to make his way:** Or, parallel to Akkadian usage, "to pursue his endeavors."

10 **"father":** Although the Levite is still a "lad" and thus probably under twenty, the term "father" here can connote "technical adviser," in the same spirit as Yosef in Gen. 45:8 is called a "Father to Pharaoh." **ten pieces of silver:** This yearly sal-ary makes clear how enormous a sum the original amount was.

10–11 **So the Levite . . . the Levite:** The Hebrew text seems corrupt here, if only because of the awkward repetition of the subject.

13 **that YHWH will do good for me:** Mikhayehu seems to feel that his new idol and shrine will be accepted and even favored by God.

◆ 18:1   In those days, there was no king in Israel.

And in those days, the Danite tribe was seeking for itself a
    hereditary-property to settle in,
for there had not fallen [any land] to it until that day among the
    tribes of Israel as a hereditary-property.

2   So the Children of Dan sent from their clan five men from [all]
        their quarters, valiant men from Tzor'a and from Eshtaol,
to spy out the region and to explore it.
They said to them:
Go, explore the region!
So they came to the highlands of Efrayim, to the house of Mikha,
that they might spend the night there.

3   They were near the house of Mikha
when they recognized the voice of the Levite lad,
so they turned aside there and said to him:
Who brought you here?
And what are you doing in this [place]? And what [business] do you
    have here?

4   He said to them:
Like this and like that has Mikha done for me;
he has hired me, and so I have become a priest for him.

5   They said to him:
Pray inquire of God,
that we may know whether it will succeed, our way on which we
    are going.

6   The priest said to them:
Go in peace—
straight before YHWH is your way on which you are going!

18:1   **there had not fallen [any land] to it . . . hereditary-
property:** That is, they had not gained a solid foothold in the area between Israelite and Philistine
territory.
   3   **voice:** Or "accent, dialect."   **turned aside:** A verb

that often indicates moral failing ("turning aside
from the way") in the Bible (Klein).
   6   **straight before:** Lit. "in front of"; it connotes
"acceptable."

7   So the five men went and came to Layish,
    and they saw the men who were in its midst, settled in security in
        the manner of the Sidonians, quiet and secure,
    with no one humiliating anyone in the region [or] barring an heir;
    they were far from the Sidonians, and had no dealings with anyone.

8   They came back to their brothers in Tzor'a and Eshtaol,
    and their brothers said to them:
    What do you [think]?

9   They said:
    Arise and let us go up against them,
    for we have seen the region, and here, it is exceedingly good.
    But you are silent—
    do not be sluggish to go, to enter and take possession of the region!

10 When you come [there], you will be coming to a people feeling-
        secure,
    while the region is as broad as [outstretched] hands;
    indeed, God will give it into your hands,
    a place where there is no lack of anything that is in the region.

11 So they marched from there, from the Danite clan, from Tzor'a and
        from Eshtaol,
    six hundred men, girded in battle gear,

12 and they went up and encamped at Kiryat-Ye'arim, in Yehuda
    —therefore they called that place Camp of Dan, until this day;
    here, it is behind Kiryat-Ye'arim.

13 They crossed through the highlands of Efrayim from there
    and came as far as the house of Mikha;

14 then the five men spoke up, the ones going to spy out the region of
        Layish,
    and said to their brothers:
    Do you know that there are in these houses an *efod* and *terafim,*
    and a carved and molten [idol]?
    Now, know what you must do!

7   **Layish:** Meaning "lion." The town was located at the northern border of ancient Israel (today's Tel Dan). **in security:** Or "unafraid," as in Ps. 78:53, Prov. 3:23–26, and Job 11:18–19. **the Sidonians:** The inhabitants of Tyre on the Mediterranean coast. **no one humiliating anyone . . . [or] barring an heir:** Heb. unclear. "Barring an heir," if correct, would denote preventing a person from receiving his rightful inheritance. **dealings:** Or "communication" (Rainey/Notley). **anyone:** Heb. *adam,* for which versions read, perhaps with better sense, *Aram* (Syria).
9   **good:** Fertile, prosperous.
12 **Kiryat-Ye'arim:** With the meaning of "wooded town," west of Jerusalem. It lay on the Judah/Binyamin border. **behind:** West of.

15 So they turned aside there and came to the house of the Levite lad,
   the house of Mikha,
   and inquired after his welfare.

16 Now six hundred men girded in battle gear were standing at the
   entrance to the gate, the ones from the Children of Dan,

17 while the five men going to spy out the region went up and they
   came there
   [and] took the carved-image, the *efod*, the *terafim*, and the molten-
   image,
   while the priest was standing at the entrance to the gate,
   along with the six hundred men girded in battle gear.

18 When these came to the house of Mikha and took the carved *efod*,
   the *terafim*, and the molten-image,
   the priest said to them:
   What are you doing?

19 They said to him:
   Be still!
   Put your hand over your mouth, and go with us,
   and become a "father" and a priest for us!
   Is it better, your being a priest for the house of one man,
   or your being a priest for a tribe and a clan in Israel?

20 The heart of the priest was disposed-for-good,
   so he took the *efod*, the *terafim*, and the carved-image, and came
   amid the fighting-people;

21 they faced about and went off,
   and put the families and the livestock and the weighty-wealth in
   front of them.

22 They had gone far from the house of Mikha
   when the men who were in the houses that were near Mikha's
   house mustered themselves and caught up with the Children of
   Dan;

23 they called out to the Children of Dan, and they turned their faces
   and said to Mikha:
   What [ails] you, that you have mustered yourself?

16 **six hundred:** LXX adds the definite article to "men."
20 **heart:** Frequently with the connotation of "mind"
   in biblical texts.

24 He said:
My gods that I made, you have taken, along with the priest, and
   you have gone off!
What do I have anymore?
So why, now, do you say to me: What [ails] you?

25 The Children of Dan said to him:
Don't make your voice heard among us,
lest men of bitter feelings attack you
and you have to lose your life-breath and the life-breath of your
   household!

26 So the Children of Dan went on their way;
and Mikha saw that they were stronger than he,
so he faced about and returned to his house.

27 Now they took what Mikha had made and the priest that he had,
and came against Layish,
against a people quiet and secure,
and struck them with the mouth of the sword,
while the town they burned with fire.

28 Now there was no rescuer, for it was far from Sidon,
and they had no dealings with anyone;
it was in the valley that belongs to Bet-Rehov.
They rebuilt the town and settled in it,

29 and they called the name of the town Dan, after the name of Dan
   their ancestral-father, who had been born to Yisrael;
however, Layish was the name of the town in former times.

30 And the Children of Dan erected the carved-image for themselves,
while Yehonatan son of Gershom son of Moshe, he and his sons
   were priests for the Danite tribe, until the time of the exile of the
   land;

---

24 **gods that I made:** Emphasizing the pagan nature of the situation (Amit 1999a).

25 **feelings:** Or "temperament."

28 **anyone:** Or, as suggested for v.7, "Aram."

29 **Yisrael:** Israel, the patriarch Yaakov (Jacob).

30 **Yehonatan:** Pronounced *ye-ho-nah-TAHN;* trad. English "Jonathan." **Moshe:** MT has inserted a small *n*-letter in the middle of the name, turning it into "Menashe" (Manasseh). A scribe, unable at this point to erase the name and substitute another, clearly sought to remove any reference to Moshe as the ancestor of idolatrous priests, and came up with this "solution." **exile of the land:** Kimhi reads *ha-aretz*, "land," as *ha-aron*, "the Coffer," referring to the capture of the Ark of the Covenant by the Philistines in I Sam. 4. But the phrase probably indicates the destruction of the Northern Kingdom, Israel, in 722 B.C.E., and thus is yet another condemnation of the north in these texts.

Chapter 19. *The Nightmare at Giv'a:* This notorious narrative, surely the most horrific nonmilitary story in the Hebrew Bible, launches the final three-chapter section of Judges. As we indicated above, it appears to be motivated by two factors: a desire to (1) demonstrate the sorry state of Israel's polity in that era and (2) establish a link with the later House of Sha'ul (Saul), implying its own moral bankruptcy. Several editorial devices are used to connect this section to the previous one: first, the appearance of another Levite, whose character proves to be even worse than that of his predecessor. Yee sees these chapters as a polemic against "country Levites," continuing the trend begun in Chap. 17. We will shortly encounter more corrupt priests, Eli's sons, in I Sam. 2. A second possible link lies in the image of the nobles at the door, reminiscent of the six hundred Danites in the previous chapter, whose ominous presence at the town gate led to the appropriation of Mikha's idols.

In order to portray moral decay, the chapter patterns itself after the Lot story of Gen. 19, but goes well beyond that narrative, which itself had a chilling outcome: the destruction of the cities of Sedom and Amora (Sodom and Gomorrah). Whereas in the earlier story the host also offered to surrender his women, here (v.24) he goes so far as to suggest rape ("force them or do to them whatever is good in your eyes"; the first two words are an addition to what appeared in Genesis), and the Levite actually pushes his concubine out the door. That, and the absence of protecting angels, would be enough to differentiate these two texts, but the telling detail is neither the comportment of the natives nor of the host, but rather the callous and self-centered behavior of the Levite himself. Despite his quest to get his concubine back at the beginning of the chapter, once he arrives at his father-in-law's house he rarely acknowledges her existence; he is contemptuous of foreigners, and so declines to stay in Yevus for the night; he is complicit in the rape by pushing his concubine outside; and he never bothers to check if the violated body on the threshold is dead or alive. In contrast to the text's mention of "refresh/humor the heart" multiple times in describing his father-in-law's and his later host's hospitality, the Levite is a man virtually without a heart. In the end we are left with a descendant of Aharon (Aaron) who, in a parody of priestly sacrificial behavior, "sections" (see Lev. 1:6) the abused woman whose bed he shared.

Klein notes that the Levite is anonymous and comes from the outlying area of his region. In addition, neither he nor the concubine's father calls her to task for her sexual straying, unusual behavior for biblical males. And the purported host, who has seemed generous until now, and who is the Levite's countryman, commits the unforgivable act of offering not only his daughters but also the Levite's concubine to the mob.

In the end, the deeds done to the concubine are so vile that the writer feels compelled to break into a poetic rhetoric: "Never has there been, / never has been seen [anything]" like this act in all of Israelite history (v.30). It signals the collapse of societal standards, violating at one swoop the rules of hospitality and the proper sexual treatment of both men and women. Such a low point may be

31 they set up for themselves the carved-image of Mikha which he had
made, all the days that the house of God was at Shilo.

19:1 Now it was in those days,
when king there was none in Israel:
there was a Levite man, sojourning on the flanks of the highlands
of Efrayim.
He took himself a concubine woman, from Bet-Lehem [in] Yehuda.

2 But his concubine whored against him;
she went from him to her father's house, to Bet-Lehem [in] Yehuda,
and she remained there for a period of four months.

3 And her husband arose and went after her,
to speak to her heart, to have her return
—his serving-lad was with him, along with a brace of donkeys.
She brought him into her father's house,
and when the girl's father saw him,
he rejoiced meeting him;

4 his father-in-law, the girl's father, prevailed upon him,
so that he stayed with him for three days,
and they ate and drank and spent the night there.

5 Now it was on the fourth day
that they started-early in the morning, and arose to go,
but the girl's father said to his son-in-law:
Refresh your heart with a bit of bread;
afterward you may go!

6 So they stayed and ate, the two of them together, and they drank.
And the girl's father said to the man:
Now consent to spend the night, so that your heart may be in good-
humor!

31 **all the days . . . at Shilo:** The Danite shrine, as rival
to the ("legitimate") sanctuary at Shilo, parallels the
idolatrous one just mentioned, which was set up in
opposition to the Jerusalem Temple.
19:1 **Now it was in those days . . . :** Here the refrain,
which occurred already in 17:6 and 18:1, introduces the consequences of political anarchy on
moral behavior, not in social or cultic matters as
before. **flanks:** The remote parts. **Efrayim:** The
name connotes fertility, but there will be none in this
story (Klein). **concubine woman:** Not quite the
status of a wife; see similarly II Sam. 5:13, 19:6, and
II Chron. 11:21.
2 **whored:** Some read as a homonym of z-n-h, based
on LXX, meaning "felt repugnance against" or
"became angry with."
3 **She brought him:** MT; LXX has "he came."

subtly hinted at by the description of the hours in vv.9–11: the day is "weakening," "declining," and "low," a fitting characterization of Israel as well. But it is the dismembering of the concubine that ultimately suggests what has happened to Israel. The book of Samuel too will be replete with examples of bodily harm, and its accumulated tally of stricken body parts will also point to an unhealthy society (see the Introduction to Samuel later in this volume).

Perry tellingly notes that the narrative here embodies something further, which continues into the subsequent two chapters: the rejection of male warrior-based ideology. In his words, "God tries to teach the callous male union the hard way, at the expense of forty thousand dead, to hesitate, to be remorseful, to weep and have brotherly feelings toward the 'enemy,' to 'play the woman' (20:19–28)." The rare unification of the tribes takes place through gang rape and subsequent dismemberment.

Finally, as hinted at previously, attributing such behavior to the tribe of Binyamin, at the town of Giv'a, clearly implicates Sha'ul by association in the future. In addition, Israel's first king begins his career by cutting up a brace of oxen and sending them all around the tribes, in order to rally them to battle. It is almost as if the subliminal message of the text is "In those days there was no king in Israel (17:6, 18:1, 19:1, 21:25), and Saul wouldn't be much better either!" (Brettler 2001a).

7 The man arose to go,
but his father-in-law pressed him,
so that [once] again he spent the night there.

8 He started early on the morning of the fifth day to go,
but the girl's father said:
Now refresh your heart
and tarry until the lengthening of the day!
So the two of them ate.

9 Then the man arose to go, he and his concubine and his
serving-lad,
but his father-in-law, the girl's father, said to him:
Here now, the day is weakening toward sunset;
now spend the night,
[for] here, the day is declining!
Spend the night here, so that your heart may be in good-humor;
you may start early on the morrow on your way, so that you may
go back to your tent.

10 But the man would not spend the night;
he arose and went and arrived at [a place] in front of Yevus—that is
Jerusalem—and with him was a brace of loaded donkeys,
and his concubine was with him.

11 They were near Yevus, and the day was exceedingly low,
so the serving-lad said to his lord:
Come now, let us turn aside to this Yevusite town and spend the
night in it!

12 But his lord said to him:
We will not turn aside to a foreign town
in which none of the Children of Israel are here;
we will cross over as far as Giv'a.

13 And he said to his serving-lad:
Come, let us go near one of the places
and spend the night in Giv'a or in Rama.

---

7 **pressed him:** The same verb is used in the companion story in Gen. 19 (vv.3 and 9).
8 **the lengthening of the day:** Later in the day.
10 **Yevus:** Pronounced *yeh-VOOS.* This was the earlier name for Jerusalem; see 1:21 above. **was with him:** Versions read "and his serving-lad" (*ve-naaro*) instead of the MT's *ve-'immo.*

11 **was exceedingly low:** Or lit. "had gone down exceedingly."
12 **Giv'a:** Pronounced *giv-AH;* trad. English "Gibeah," a town located a few miles north of Jerusalem, on the way to Shekhem.
13 **Rama:** Just north of Giv'a.

14 So they crossed over and went,
and the sun came in on them alongside Giv'a, which belongs to
Binyamin.

15 They turned aside there, to come in to spend the night in Giv'a,
and they came and sat in the town square,
but no one was gathering them into the house to spend the night.

16 Now here, an old man came in from his work, from the fields, at
sunset
—the man was from the highlands of Efrayim, and he was
sojourning in Giv'a,
while the men of the place were Binyaminites—

17 and he lifted up his eyes and saw the man, the wayfarer, in the town
square;
the old man said:
Where are you going, and from where do you come?

18 He said to him:
We are crossing from Bet-Lehem [in] Yehuda as far as the flanks of
the highlands of Efrayim
—I am from there;
I went to Bet-Lehem in Yehuda,
and to my house I am going back,
but no one will gather me into the house!

19 Yes, there is straw, yes, fodder for our donkeys, and yes, there
are bread and wine for me and for your handmaid and for the
serving-lad with your servants;
there is no lack of anything.

20 The old man said:
Peace be to you!
Surely whatever you lack shall be on me,
for sure do not spend the night in the square!

---

15 **square:** Or more literally, "broad place, market-place." **no one was gathering them . . . :** There was no hospitality for these travelers.

16 **work . . . fields:** JPS renders as "property outside the town." **he was sojourning:** So it takes another stranger, not a native, to aid the travelers. And he is, not accidentally, one of their fellow Efrayimites.

18 **my house:** MT has "the House of YHWH," probably a mistake. The possessive Hebrew letter *yod*, added to *bayit*, "house," may simply have been misunder-stood, since *yod* could also serve as an abbreviation for YHWH.

19 **Yes, there is straw . . . :** The guest modestly requests only shelter here, not food for himself or for his animals. See similarly Num. 20:17, 19, and 21:22.

20 **for sure do not spend the night in the square!:** The old man evidently knows a thing or two about the locals.

21 He brought him into his house
and provided for the donkeys;
they washed their feet
and ate and drank.

22 They were putting their hearts in good-humor
when here, the men of the city, base men, encircled the house;
they kept on beating against the door
and said to the man, the old house owner, saying:
Bring out the man who came into your house—
we want to know him!

23 But the man, the house owner, went out to them and said to them:
No, my brothers! Do not do evil, now!
Since this man came into my house,
do not do this vile thing!

24 Here are my nubile daughter and his concubine;
now let me bring them out—force them or do to them whatever is
good in your eyes,
but to this man, do not do this vile thing!

25 But the men would not hearken to him,
so the man took hold of his concubine and pushed [her] out to
them, outside,
and they knew her and abused her all night, until daybreak;
then they sent her away when the dawn came up.

26 The woman came back toward daybreak
and fell down at the entrance of the house of the man where her
lord was,
until [it was] light.

27 Her lord arose at daybreak;
he opened the doors of the house and went out to go on his way—

22 **putting their hearts in good-humor:** NRSV "enjoying themselves." The protagonist has yet another
drinkfest! **to know him:** Their request, and their
action in v.25, has a sexual tone (as in the "biblical
sense" of "know").

23 **Since this man came into my house:** Emphasizing
the host's solemn responsibility for the safety of his
guest. **this vile thing:** Another sexual crime, the
rape of Dina, is similarly described in Gen. 34:7, as
well as the rape of Tamar in II Sam. 13:12.

24 **nubile daughter:** As elsewhere in the Bible, Heb.
betula means a girl of marriageable age, not necessarily a virgin.

27 **with her hands on the threshold:** A powerful and
pathetic image of a victim who is unable to escape
her tormentors and get inside the house, with no
help forthcoming. Note that the text is reticent to
reveal whether the woman is dead or alive at this
point.

Chapter 20. *Civil War:* For once, Israel acts as a body (vv.1 and 11, "as one man"), but it is a unity born out of outrage and results in a near genocide. The narrative gathers steam from the Levite's speech to the assembled men, and goes on to describe first the Israelites' mustering and then that of the Binyaminites. The battle sequence is a long one, involving two successive defeats for the Israelites, who twice are also reduced to tears, just as at the beginning of the book (2:4). The third, and finally successful, attempt recalls the conquest of Ai in Josh. 8, both in the ambush tactics and in the initial delay. Since the victory in Joshua follows a major breach of faith (the Akhan story of Chap. 7), our text here might be suggesting that Israel needs to acknowledge God before they can proceed. The vocabulary of the chapter, which uses "turn around" twice and "face about" three times, literally reflects the turnaround in the events. As for the Binyaminites, whose reputation in war is cited a number of times in the Bible (see, for instance, Gen. 49:27), they might be seen as counterbalancing Chap. 3's Ehud, another and more successful left-handed warrior.

and here, the woman, his concubine, was fallen down at the
    entrance to the house,
with her hands on the threshold!

28 He said to her:
Get up, let's go!
But no one was answering.
So he took her up on the donkey,
and the man arose and went back to his place.

29 He came to his house
and took a knife
and lay hold of his concubine
and chopped her up, into her limbs, into twelve chopped-pieces,
and sent her off throughout all the territory of Israel.

30 And it was that all who saw it would say:
Never has there been, never has been seen [anything] like this
from the day of the Children of Israel's going up from the land of
    Egypt until this day!
Take it [seriously] for yourselves, get counsel, and speak out!

20:1 So the Children of Israel went out
and the community assembled as one man, from Dan to Be'er-
    Sheva, including the land of Gil'ad, to YHWH at Mitzpa.

2 And the "cornerstones" of all the people, all the tribes of Israel,
    stood forth,
in the assembly of the people of God,
four hundred thousand fighting-men, foot-soldiers drawing the
    sword.

---

28 **Get up:** Elsewhere, I use "arise" for this verb, but that feels too formal here. This is the most repulsive line in the whole story; can he think of nothing else to say after she has been raped and abused all night?

29 **knife:** Specifically, a large knife or a cleaver. It derives from the verb "to eat/devour," which is also found in the common biblical idiom for destruction by the sword (and which uses "mouth" for "edge"). The same word describes Avraham's knife, intended for his son's throat in Gen. 22:6, 10. **chopped her up . . . sent her off:** Sha'ul does the same thing with an ox (I Sam. 11:7) in order to rally the Israelites to battle. The narrator here, unlike the husband, chooses to retain the last shred of the woman's dig-

nity by referring to the cut-up pieces as "her." Or it may be bitterly ironic—what of "her" is left?

30 **Never has there been**, **never has been seen:** Heb. *lo nihyeta ve-lo nir'ata*.

20:1 **from Dan to Be'er-Sheva:** The classic expression of Israel's ideal boundaries (see I Kings 5:5), it is the moral equivalent of America's "from sea to shining sea." **Mitzpa:** Trad. English "Mizpah," the site of a centralized shrine to YHWH a few miles from Giv'a. It became important mainly after the Babylonian Exile in the sixth century.

2 **"cornerstones":** A metaphorical term for "chieftains." **four hundred thousand:** Clearly an exaggeration, as often in biblical and other ancient texts.

◆

3   And the Children of Binyamin heard that the Children of Israel had
        gone up to Mitzpa.
    The Children of Israel said:
    Speak:
    how did this evil come to be?

4   Then answered the Levite man, the husband of the murdered
        woman;
    he said:
    To Giv'a, which is in Binyamin, I came, I and my concubine, to
        spend the night,

5   but the landowners of Giv'a arose against me
    and encircled the house against me at night;
    me they intended to kill,
    and my concubine they forced, so that she died.

6   And so I grabbed my concubine,
    I chopped her up
    and sent her off throughout all the open-country of Israel's
        hereditary-property,
    for they did a lewd and vile [thing] in Israel!

7   Here, all of you, O Children of Israel:
    give yourselves word and advice here!

8   And all the people arose as one man, saying:
    We will not go back, anyone to his tent,
    nor will we turn aside, anyone to his house!

9   Now: this is the thing that we will do to Giv'a:
    [Go] against it by lot!

10 We will take ten men per hundred, for all the tribes of Israel,
    and a hundred per thousand, and a thousand per myriad,
    taking provisions for the fighting-people, to make ready to go
        against Giv'a of Binyamin,
    in accordance with all the vileness that they have done in Israel!

11 So all the fighting-men of Israel gathered together against the
        town, as one man, confederates.

---

5 **intended:** The Hebrew denotes "conceiving an image" (Gray 1986). **my concubine they forced:** He conveniently leaves out his act of pushing her out to them (Klein).

6 **lewd . . . [thing]:** The Hebrew word (*zimma*) is used in reference to incest and other sexual crimes in Lev. 18–20.

7 **give yourselves word and advice:** JPS: "produce a plan of action." See also 19:30, above: "get advice."

10 **myriad:** Ten thousand. **Giv'a:** MT reads "Geva."

12 And the tribes of Israel sent men among the entire tribe of
Binyamin, saying:
What is this evil that came-about among you?

13 So-now, give over the men, the base ones, who are in Giv'a, that we
may put them to death,
that we may eradicate evil from Israel!
But the Children of Binyamin would not hearken to the voice of
their brothers, the Children of Israel,

14 and the Children of Binyamin gathered together from the towns to
Giv'a
to go out for battle with the Children of Israel.

15 And the Children of Binyamin were counted-for-war on that day,
from the towns:
twenty-six thousand fighting-men drawing the sword;
aside from the settled-folk of Giv'a, seven hundred chosen men
were counted,

16 from all these fighting-people, seven hundred chosen men,
restricted in their right hand;
each of these could sling a stone at a hair and not miss.

17 Now the fighting-men of Israel were counted, aside from
Binyamin:
four hundred thousand men drawing the sword,
each of these a man of battle.

18 They arose and went up to Bet-El, and inquired of God;
the Children of Israel said:
Who will go up for us first in battle with the Children of Binyamin?
YHWH said:
Yehuda first.

19 The Children of Israel arose at daybreak
and encamped against Giv'a.

20 And the fighting-men of Israel went out to battle with Binyamin;
the men of Israel arranged their ranks with them for battle at Giv'a.

---

15 **chosen:** Or "choice."
16 **restricted in their right hand:** See note to 3:15
above. **not miss:** This verb, Heb. *h-t-'*, most frequently appears in the biblical vocabulary as the
common term for "to sin," namely, "to (morally)
miss the mark/target." It can also mean "to give
offense" when used in an inter-human context.

18 **Who will go up for us first . . . Yehuda:** Echoing
the opening of the book. Ironically and ominously,
what began there as a battle for survival ends here in
a civil war.

21 And the Children of Binyamin went out from Giv'a;
on that day they brought to ruin among Israel: twenty-two
thousand men to the ground.

22 But the fighting-people, the men of Israel, strengthened
themselves,
and they again arranged ranks for battle
in the place where they had arranged [them] on the first day.

23 And the Children of Israel went up
and wept in the presence of YHWH, until sunset;
they inquired of YHWH, saying:
Shall I again approach for battle with the Children of Binyamin my
brother?
YHWH said:
Go up against him.

24 So the Children of Israel drew near to the Children of Binyamin on
the second day,

25 and when Binyamin went out to meet them from Giv'a on the
second day,
they brought to ruin among the Children of Israel another eighteen
thousand men, to the ground,
all of these drawing the sword.

26 Then all the Children of Israel went up, and all the fighting-people,
and came to Bet-El;
they wept and sat there, in the presence of YHWH,
and they fasted on that day until sunset
and offered up offerings-up and *shalom*-offerings, in the presence of
YHWH.

27 And the Children of Israel inquired of YHWH
—now the Coffer of God's Covenant was there in those days,

28 and Pin'has son of El'azar son of Aharon was standing [in
attendance] before it in those days—
saying:
Shall I once again go out for battle with the Children of Binyamin
my brother,

21 **brought to ruin:** Burney understands Heb. *sh-h-t* by means of Akkadian *shahatu*, "felled."
22 **strengthened themselves:** Or "took courage."
26 **offerings-up:** Others, "burnt offerings," the most common type of biblical sacrifices. **shalom-offerings:** The idea seems to be of a sacrifice that creates reconciliation and solidarity within the community. JPS has "offerings of well-being."
28 **Pin'has:** Pronounced *pin-HASS*, and meaning "dark-skinned" in Egyptian. Trad. English "Phineas."

or shall I hold back?

YHWH said:

Go up,

for on the morrow I will give him into your hand!

29 So Israel set ambushes against Giv'a all around.

30 And the Children of Israel went up against the Children of
Binyamin on the third day,

and arranged-ranks against Giv'a as time and time [before];

31 and when the Children of Binyamin went out to meet the fighting-
people,

they were torn away from the town

and began to strike down some of the people, [leaving] slain as time
and time [before] on the highways

—of which one goes up to Bet-El and one to Giv'a, in the open-
country—

about thirty men in Israel.

32 The Children of Binyamin said:

They are beaten before us, as at the beginning!

But the Children of Israel said:

Let us flee and tear them away from the town, onto the highways!

33 Now when all the fighting-men of Israel had risen from their place

and had arranged-ranks at Baal Tamar,

the ambush of Israel burst forth from its place, from the Giv'a
Cave,

34 while from opposite Giv'a came ten thousand men, chosen ones
from all Israel.

Now the battle was heavy,

but they did not know that evil-fortune was [already] reaching
them.

35 So YHWH defeated Binyamin before Israel,

and the Children of Israel brought to ruin among the Children of
Binyamin on that day

twenty-five thousand and a hundred men,

all of these drawing the sword.

---

31 **torn away:** Others: "lured away."
33 **Cave:** LXX reads *mi-maarav le-,* "to the west of," for
MT *mi-maarei.*

34 **opposite:** Manuscripts read "south of."

Chapter 21. *The Replenishing of Binyamin:* Using the Wild West analogy I drew in the Introduction to Judges, a possible subtitle to this chapter might be "700 Brides for 700 Brothers." According to one view, Judges ends, appropriately, in a state of confusion. In short order, the text has moved from the gang rape of one woman to the near extermination of a tribe, and on to the abduction of hundreds of women. The nation, such as it is, has been saved, but at the cost of massive violence of several kinds. Fathers and husbands are unable to give women even the most basic protection (Schneider). Thus the dismembered concubine remains as a symbol of Israel's body politic, an observation borne out by the final two verses of the chapter, in which we hear the Hebrew word/English phrase "each [one]" (as opposed to the group) three times.

While on the surface Israel is made whole again (see Niditch 2008 for this positive view on the tone of the chapter), we know that this cannot possibly last. The two subsequent books, Samuel and Kings, will portray an Israel that is irrevocably split, with the contentious tribe of Binyamin containing Jerusalem at the center of the land.

The chapter's links to future texts are major geographical ones. The Yavesh-Gil'ad of v.9 is the town that appeals to Israel for help in I Sam. 11 and is rescued by Sha'ul, while Shilo (v.12) will be the site of events in the very next chapter (I Sam. 1). The appearance of Shilo also functions as a preparation for the "questionable events" that occur with Eli's sons (Amit 1999a).

Amit also notes the bracketing effect of this chapter: both here and in Chap. 2, Yevus (Jerusalem) is mentioned, along with weeping and sacrifices, and "each [one] to his hereditary-property" (2:6 and 21:25). She attributes this to the final editor's desire to smooth over the rough edges created by the interpolation of Chaps. 17–21.

◆
36   The Children of Binyamin saw that they were defeated,
       and the fighting-men of Israel gave ground to Binyamin,
       for they were secure regarding the ambush that they had set at
            Giv'a.
37   Now the ambush they hurried along and spread out against Giv'a,
       and the ambush drew out
       and struck the entire city with the mouth of the sword.
38   Now the arrangement for the men of Israel with the ambush had
            been
       to send up a rising-mass of smoke from the city;
39   then the men of Israel were to turn around in battle.
       And Binyamin had begun to strike, [leaving] slain among Israel
            about thirty men;
       indeed, they said:
       Surely, he is defeated, yes, defeated before us, as in the beginning
            battle!
40   But the rising-mass began to go up from the town—a column of
            smoke;
       Binyamin faced about behind him
       and here, the whole of the town went up [in smoke] to the heavens!
41   The men of Israel turned around,
       and the men of Binyamin were terrified,
       for they saw that evil-fortune was reaching them.
42   So they faced about before the men of Israel toward the way of the
            wilderness,
       but the battle caught up with them;
       whoever was from the town, they brought him to ruin in its midst:
43   they encircled Binyamin and they pursued him
       —to Menuha they forced him along—
       up to [a spot] opposite Giv'a, toward the rising of the sun.
44   And there fell of Binyamin eighteen thousand men,
       all these, men of valor.

---

37   **drew out:** Deployed (Burney).
38   **arrangement:** According to prearranged plan.
     a rising-mass of smoke: As a signal (see Jer. 6:1).
42   **faced about:** In retreat.
43   **encircled:** Some suggest emending *kitteru* to *kittetu*

("crushed to pieces"). **and they pursued him:**
MT has, probably erroneously, "they had them pursued." **Menuha:** Location unknown; Boling suggests Noha. **Giv'a:** Usually emended to "Geva," as
in Boling.

45 They faced about and fled to the wilderness, to the Rimmon Crag,
but they picked them off on the highways,
five thousand men;
they caught up with them as far as Gid'om/Hewing Them,
and struck down from them two thousand men.

46 And all those who fell from Binyamin were twenty-five thousand
men drawing the sword on that day,
all these, men of valor.

47 They faced about and fled to the wilderness, to the Rimmon Crag:
six hundred men,
and they stayed at the Rimmon Crag for four months.

48 Now the men of Israel returned to the Children of Binyamin and
struck them with the mouth of the sword,
from the men of the town to the cattle and to all that was found,
and also all the towns that were found they sent up in fire.

21:1 Now the men of Israel had sworn in Mitzpa, saying:
Let no man among us give his daughter to Binyamin as a wife!

2 And the fighting-people came to Bet-El,
and sat there until sunset, in the presence of God;
they lifted up their voices and wept, a great weeping,

3 and they said:
Why, O YHWH, God of Israel, did this happen in Israel,
for one tribe to be accounted [missing] today from Israel?

4 So it was on the morrow that the people started early
and built a sacrificial-altar there,
and they offered up offerings-up and *shalom*-offerings.

5 And the Children of Israel said:
Who is it that did not go up among the assembly from all the tribes
of Israel to YHWH?
For the great sworn-oath was against anyone who did not go up to
YHWH at Mitzpa, saying:
He shall be put to death, yes, death!

---

45 **picked them off:** Following JPS's ingenious reflection of Heb. *'-l-l,* "glean." Another colloquial possibility would be "cleaned them up." **Gid'om:** The
name is otherwise unattested; many suggest emending to "Geva."

48 **Children of Binyamin:** Nonmilitary personnel
(Burney).

21:5 **the great sworn-oath:** See the beginning of Chap. 20.

6 And the Children of Israel felt regret toward Binyamin their
    brother;
they said:
Hewn off today is one tribe from Israel!

7 What can we do for them, for those left, regarding wives?
For we ourselves have sworn by YHWH
not to give them any of our daughters as wives!

8 And they said:
Which is the one from the tribes of Israel that did not go up to
    YHWH at Mitzpa?
Now here, not a man had come to the camp from Yavesh-Gil'ad, to
    the assembly.

9 The people were counted,
and here, there was not a man there from the settled-folk of Yavesh-
    Gil'ad.

10 So the community sent there twelve thousand men of the valiant
    ones,
and they charged them, saying:
Go and strike down the settled-folk of Yavesh-Gil'ad with the
    mouth of the sword,
along with the women and the little-ones!

11 And this is the thing that you are to do:
every male, and every woman [who] has known lying with a male,
    you are to devote-to-destruction.

12 They found among the settled-folk of Yavesh-Gil'ad four hundred
    nubile girls
who had not known a man by lying with a male,
and they brought them to the camp at Shilo, which is in the land of
    Canaan.

13 And the entire community sent
and spoke to the Children of Binyamin who were at Rimmon Crag;
they called out to them: Peace!

---

6 **Hewn off:** Some manuscripts read "subtracted, missing" (*nigra'* for *nigda'*).

8 **Yavesh-Gil'ad:** Trad. English "Jabesh Gilead," a town across the Jordan in northwest Gil'ad. It too is bound up with the life and reign of Sha'ul in the next book.

11 **devote-to-destruction:** See note to 1:17, above.

12 **nubile girls:** See note to 19:24, above.   **which is in the land of Canaan:** This designation does not say much for all the conquests enumerated in Joshua and Judges; instability still reigns (Boling 1975).

14 So the Children of Binyamin returned at that time,
and they gave them the women whom they had kept alive among
the women of Yavesh-Gil'ad;
but they did not find enough for them thus.

15 Now the people had felt regret toward Binyamin,
since YHWH had made a breach among the tribes of Israel,

16 so the elders of the community said:
What are we to do with those left, for wives?
—for [the] women were wiped out from Binyamin!

17 They said:
[There must be] a surviving possession for Binyamin,
so that a tribe in Israel not be wiped out!

18 Now as for us, we are not able to give them wives from our
daughters,
—for the Children of Israel had sworn, saying:
Doomed be the one giving a wife to Binyamin!—

19 so they said:
Here, there is the pilgrimage-festival of YHWH at Shilo—year after
year—
that is north of Bet-El, toward the rising of the sun from the
highway that goes up from Bet-El to Shekhem, and south of
Levona.

20 So they charged the Children of Binyamin, saying:
Go and lie in wait in the vineyards,

21 and see: here, if the daughters of Shilo go out to dance in the
dances,
you are to go out from the vineyards
and are to catch for yourselves, each one, his wife from the
daughters of Shilo;
then you may go back to the land of Binyamin.

22 So it will be, when their fathers or their brothers come to complain
to us
that we will say to them:
Be gracious to them,

---

17 **a surviving possession:** Heb. unclear.
19 **north:** Lit. "toward Tzafon," an impressive mountain (today called Jebel Aqra') near the Mediterranean coast in Syria. **toward the rising of the sun:**
In contrast to the previous example, I have stayed
with Hebrew usage here as more immediately
understandable, meaning "east." **Levona:** A few
miles from Shilo.

◆

for haven't we taken, each one, his wife in battle?
For if you yourselves had given [them] to them,
[then] at that time you would have incurred-guilt.

23 So the Children of Binyamin did thus:
they took up wives according to their number
from the dancers whom they kidnapped;
then they went and returned to their hereditary-property
and rebuilt the towns, and settled in them.

24 And the Children of Israel went off from there at that time,
each one to his tribe and to his clan,
and each one went out from there to his hereditary-property.

25 In those days, there was no king in Israel;
each one would do what was right in his eyes.

---

23 **took up:** Boling renders "took enough."
24 **went off:** More idiomatically, as in JPS, "dispersed."

APPENDIX: THE SOUND AND
STRUCTURE OF A BIBLICAL TALE

THE STORIES ABOUT SHIMSHON CONSTITUTE AN OUTSTANDING EXAMPLE OF NAR-
rative art in the Bible. Although Judg. 13–16 has sometimes been viewed as a
loosely gathered series of tales about the hero (Brettler 2001a), it in fact exhibits
a verbally tight structure, possibly indicating oral origins. More than perhaps any
other cycle of stories in the Bible, it is built architectonically on the repetition of
words and motifs. I have presented a list of these below. More could be adduced,
but this sampling of thirty-nine elements will, I think, be sufficient to make the
point that the entire cycle of stories has been carefully built up and knit together
by means of repetition.

This technique, as many have observed, is one of the classic building blocks of
biblical narrative, but the Shimshon material goes beyond its conventional use.
Here, instead of simply using several key words or phrases to suggest important
concerns in the text, we are treated to a stunning piece of ancient literary architecture. The storyteller, or, just as likely, a series of storytellers and creative "redactors," has connected different episodes in a dizzying set of combinations. The
fourth episode, for example, picks up twelve elements that have already appeared
in the previous sections, but it also introduces three new ones of its own. Almost
half of the words/ideas in the cycle make their first appearance in episode I; but it
is episode VI, the Delila story, that contains the most of any single section in the
text: twenty-four.

What this means is that the story of Shimshon and Delila, arguably the most
famous section of the cycle and one that is unforgettable in its tension and dia-
logical richness, is constructed overwhelmingly out of pieces that have already
been given to the audience. The previous five episodes have, as it were, paved the
way for what is to come, contributing their building materials to the most important edifice. In the Delila account, everything comes together: strength, secrets,
women, and enemies, but something new appears as well. For the first time,
Shimshon himself acknowledges his special status as a "Consecrated One" (*nazir*).

The example of the Shimshon cycle is an important one for understanding biblical narrative, for it demonstrates that, whatever the origin of the discrete pieces
of the story, its present form has been tightly and beautifully woven together
by means of sound. An ancient audience would no doubt have appreciated the
story's artistry, in conjunction with its humor, its irony, and its didactic intent.

The episodes in the chart below are as follows: I Birth = 13:2–25, II Wedding =
14:1–20, III Foxes = 15:1–8, IV Jawbone = 15:9–20, V Gaza = 16:1–3, VI Delila = 16:4–22,
VII Death = 16:23–31.

I Birth	II Wedding	III Foxes	IV Jawbone	V Gaza	VI Delila	VII Death
Tzor'a						Tzor'a
Manoah						Manoah
see	*see*				*see*	*see*
drink	*drink*		*drink*			
razor					*razor*	
Consecrated					*Consecrated*	
begin					*begin*	
deliver			*deliver*			
tell	*tell*				*tell*	
death	*death*	*death*	*death*		*death*	*death*
woman	*woman*	*woman*		*woman*	*woman*	*woman*
vine	*vineyards*	*vineyards*			Sorek/*Vines*	
goats' kid	*goats' kid*	*goats' kid*				
up	*up*	*up*	*up*	*up*	*up*	*up*
know	*know*		*know*		*known*	
flame	*fire*	*fire*			*fire*	
spirit	*spirit*		*spirit*			
fall	*fall*		*fall*			*fall*
	Foreskinned		*Foreskinned*			
		fresh		*fresh*		
	eyes				*eyes*	
	rule		*rule*			
	down	*down*	*down*		*down*	
	30/3	*300*	*3000*		*3*	*3000*
	7				*7*	
	seduce				*seduce*	
	don't love				*don't love*	
	press hard				*press hard*	
	inner-room	*inner-room*			*inner-room*	
	hate	*hate*				
	call		*call out*			*call out*
		this-time			*this-time*	*this-time*
		avenge				*avenge*
			bind		*bind*	
			new ropes		*new ropes*	*avenge*
			led as judge			*led as judge*
				ambush	*ambush*	
				Gaza	*Gaza*	
					overlords	*overlords*

The basic structural characteristic of the cycle is that scene by scene, new elements are consistently added, while a liberal selection of older ones is retained. Episode II adds eleven; episode III, two; episode IV, three; episode V, two; and episode VI, likewise one. The final two scenes reprise thirty-one out of the thirty-nine elements, and even most of the missing ones (for instance, "deliver," "spirit," "Foreskinned Ones"/ Philistine rule) are implied. They serve to bring together all the great facets of the farce-drama that is the Shimshon cycle: seeing and enticing, knowing and telling, deliverance and death. Thus viewed, Chap. 16, far from being a separate set of tales, integrates what has come before in a sophisticated and spectacular display of the Hebrew Bible's narrative artistry.

שמואל

———◦◦◦———

SAMUEL

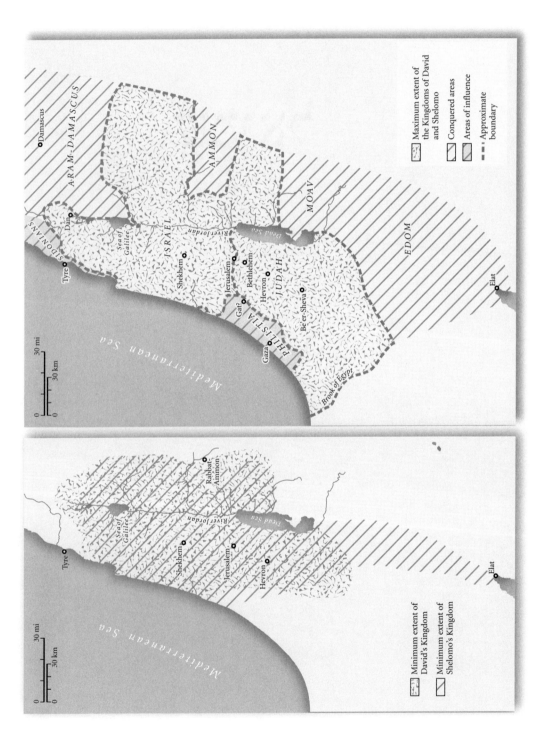

The Kingdoms of David and Shelomo

INTRODUCTION

Approaching Samuel

Of the four books included in the Early Prophets, the long book of Samuel is the most satisfying in its richness. For millennia, audiences have been drawn to its complex characters and struck by the fateful implications of their actions as leaders and as human beings. Their stories have become deeply integrated into the consciousness of the Western world, expressed in literature, art, music, and politics.

The book aims to portray the origins of Israelite kingship. It moves from the lifetime of Samuel the prophet, who functions as Israel's last "judge," through the dramatic and sometimes enigmatic careers of Saul and David, the first kings in a long sequence of rulers in what became separate kingdoms of north and south.

Among the many possible entryways into this book, I would like to initially single out three which have figured in my introductions to the previous two books: historical, ideological, and literary. The historical approach seeks to recover the "real" Saul and David in the setting of their era—that is, to establish the text's relationship to historical facts. The ideological view looks at the influence of particular political and religious interests that may be embedded in the text. And the literary approach focuses on the book as a story and on the ways in which the writer's palette enhances the narrative's appeal to the inner world of the audience.

We begin with the historical. As of this writing, archaeologists have uncovered little direct trace of the period of Saul and David. This may change, but conditions both material (the many centuries of destruction and reconstruction of Jerusalem) and political (the Arab-Israeli conflict) will probably prevent major archaeological breakthroughs. But regardless of future finds, the stories in Samuel do appear to reflect major trends that fit its eleventh- and tenth-century B.C.E. setting. Material evidence indicates continued demographic growth in the Israelite highlands, especially in the north. In many societies, reaching a critical point of population necessarily produces a change from a small-scale agricultural way of life to one that requires a more bureaucratically developed structure. So the rise of a monarchy against this backdrop is eminently realistic. There is also the telling fact that within a century of the time generally ascribed to David, archaeological evidence reveals monumental structures in a number of Israelite cities. And by the ninth century B.C.E., outside written records such as the Black Obelisk of Assyria's Shalmaneser III give evidence of bona fide Israelite monarchs.

These historical developments are mirrored in the biblical texts of Samuel and Kings. The plotlines paint a memorable and detailed picture of the origins and development of Israelite kingship, while underlying motifs point to a long and difficult adjustment period, in which the old ideals of the countryside (government by elders and tribal leaders) sometimes clash with new realities (kings, capitals, armies, and bureaucrats). There are major shifts in power, sometimes involving assassinations; palaces and temples are built; armies are raised; there is evidence of centralized economic planning; and a royal ideology arises, intimately connected to the Temple and to the all-important city of Jerusalem. We are given putative names of court officials and military leaders, royal cities, and royal spouses and children.

Such details suggest real data out of which historians could begin to fashion a narrative history of the period. But scholars are still engaged in bitter arguments over the Bible's usefulness in that regard, with one camp finding the picture painted in the text largely reliable, and another finding little corroboration with the historical facts as they must have been. Most are agreed that on the basis of the available evidence, the biblical David and his son Solomon are not likely to have ruled over a large and powerful empire. Additionally, as has often been observed, the tone and style of Samuel, played out through dramatic personal stories, seem more consonant with the conventions of historical fiction than those of factual reporting. All that can definitively be said, then, is that Samuel grew out of a generally plausible historical context, and that the traditions concerning David point to the impact of a real personality.

Further clouding the historical path to Samuel is the issue of ideology. Many scholars have characterized the book as an apologia for the House of David. He is, after all, its central human figure, one from whom a permanent, "blessed" dynasty will spring (II Sam. 7). There is also the matter of the text's forceful, and at times forced, attempts to exonerate David from virtually all of the murders in the narrative, deeds from which he nevertheless ultimately profits. Overall, Samuel, as well as parts of Judges and Kings, goes a long way toward justifying the legitimacy of David's dynasty, understandable in a Bible in which that dynasty ruled for over three centuries.

But the book also contains some strong ideological counter-material. As presently constituted, it is far from being a whitewash of its central character. The narratives in Samuel which portray David the king turn on the troubling Bathsheba episode (II Sam. 11–12), with its double crimes of adultery and murder, and culminate in Absalom's rebellion (13–20)—traditions that at least blunt the generally approving tone that the book creates around David. This negative valuation is more in line with prophetic ideas, wherein God is seen as the primary king of Israel, a viewpoint which appears not only in Samuel but prominently in Kings as well. So the text's portrayal of David, rightly described by interpreters as a deeply human one, reflects prominent strains of ideology within biblical Israel that take both positive and negative positions toward kingship.

The literary approach to Samuel, which elevates aesthetic and humanistic values (see "Imagery and Language," below), is perhaps closest to the manner in which the text has been read throughout the ages in Western culture. After all, no book of the Bible, with the possible exception of Genesis, displays the depth and variety of characterization found here. A range of personality types, transcending their deceptively simple categories, appears in the book: Hannah the barren woman, Eli the failing priest/leader, Samuel the man of God, Saul the tragic first king, David the romantic hero turned morally compromised monarch, and Absalom the rebel—to cite only the most notable among them. Then, too, there are the contrasting pairs of characters who people the book, and whose interplay reveals so much about each individual: Hannah and Eli, Eli and Samuel, Samuel and Saul, Saul and Jonathan, and David with a host of individuals—Saul, Jonathan, Michal, Joab, Abigail, Nathan, Bathsheba, and Absalom. Here as well, a short list exemplifies but cannot exhaust the possibilities presented by the narrative.

Viewed thus, Samuel is primarily a book about human beings, specifically leaders, and their trials, seen partially through a theological lens. Whatever our religious beliefs, it takes us in through the sheer force and artistry of its portrayals and its utterly true-to-life character. As in all great literature, the reader will frequently see himself or herself in the characters' physical and spiritual journeys.

The three paths to Samuel I have suggested so far are all legitimate and rewarding, and raise important questions of interpretation. But one can go further. The book of Samuel in its final form, in the context of the Early Prophets in which it is now embedded, forms the core of ancient Israel's profound meditation on its identity and on its concepts of leadership and power. Using historical references, ideological statements, and literary art as its raw materials, it occupies an important position in the ongoing story of the relationship between a God of history and a people upon whom he mysteriously chooses to shower his attention. That relationship is presented in story form, meaning above all that it is intended to *instruct*.

In Samuel, Israel's identity is expressed through family position and boundaries. The portrayal of David as a youngest son suggests a self-awareness of Israel's political place within the ancient Near East. In contrast to the hoary civilizations of Egypt and Mesopotamia, the Israelites knew themselves to be latecomers and relatively insignificant players on the world stage. The striking use in Samuel of the "Younger Son Triumphant" motif which appears so often in Genesis is at least partly an expression of this self-image, and equally of Judah's position as the later and initially less prosperous of the two kingdoms into which Israel was divided for a good deal of its independent existence.

The geographical setting of Samuel, on the other hand, cleaves to the ideal in its tracing of a Davidic kingdom with extensive boundaries, to an extent probably never reached in reality. Indeed, one could argue that the entire picture of the days of the "United Kingdom" of David and Solomon is itself an idealized portrait, designed at least partially to evoke a sense of nostalgia for the "good old days" when the Israelites regularly defeated their enemies and were not seduced by idol worship (at least until the end of Solomon's reign). Both of these conditions would change in the story told in the subsequent book of Kings.

As for Samuel's exploration of leadership and power, here the Bible's presentation frequently stands in contrast to what we know of the older civilizations of the region. The rulers of ancient Egypt and Mesopotamia were often portrayed as semidivine or even divine, and their power was viewed as an important foundation for their societies as a whole. The book of Samuel, on the other hand, while conceding that real-world conditions demand a strong person such as a monarch at the helm of the country, also makes clear that the king is a human being, and that society and its leaders cannot ignore the abiding principles they are obligated to serve. The biblical authors saw ancient Israel as bound to a covenant, a formal agreement between the people and God. One important aspect of this pact was the expectation that Israel would espouse justice in personal relations and among larger social units, and this extended to kings themselves, who in the Deuteronomistic view were expected to uphold and embody the stipulations of the covenant. Deut. 17:14–20 reflects this viewpoint, mandating that the king was supposed to have "this Instruction" (Heb. *tora;* conventionally spelled *torah*) by his side and "not turn aside from what is commanded" in it. That these societal and kingly ideals were bound to be unattainable does not detract from their power. Their breach will figure prominently in Kings' explanation of the eventual defeat and exile of both the Northern and the Southern Kingdoms.

In treating issues of identity and leadership, Samuel also raises the question of how divinely ordered destiny and human free will interact. What, it asks, does it mean to have been chosen by God from birth, as Samuel was? What does it mean to have been chosen like Saul, only to fall out of favor and experience his successor's triumph in his own (and his popular son Jonathan's) lifetime? And finally, what does it mean to have been chosen in the heralded manner of David, but to have to bear the full consequences of that chosenness, which may include, depending on his faithfulness to the task, severe personal loss and even exile from the throne? In the answer to these questions lies the biblical journey as a whole. Through this literature, ancient Israel was striving for survival and legitimacy, to be sure, but its struggle also encompassed a restless vision of an ideal which is still with us.

Ultimately, one can only marvel at the extent to which Samuel is able to accommodate so many different levels of discourse. The book's ability to integrate message and characterization—or, to put it another way, to let the divine and the human operate simultaneously, with neither eclipsing the other—is a phenomenon which has already appeared to profound effect earlier in the biblical text, in Genesis. Just as God's plan for Jacob to be the father of a multitude is accomplished mainly through the very human rivalry that burns between two sisters; just as the divine plan to bring the Israelites down to Egypt, so that they may fulfill their destiny, is carried out mainly through the familial convolutions of the Joseph story; so too do the stories of Samuel unfold within the parameters of recognizable human concerns and passions, with no spectacular "biblical miracles" in sight. It is thus the task of the reader, listening with what Martin Buber called "perfect attentiveness," to follow these developments down the tortured path which the characters of Samuel must walk to find out what God demands of them.

THE WRITING OF SAMUEL

AS IS THE CASE WITH EVERY OTHER BOOK OF THE HEBREW BIBLE, WE DO NOT know who authored Samuel. From the Persian-era book of Chronicles, we know that some Jews assumed it was the prophet himself, at least for the first part of the book. In recent times, it has been surmised that Samuel was written by someone with access to David's or Solomon's court, a later scribe who used court records, a member of prophetic circles, or a writer in the Persian period, lobbying for the restoration of the Davidic dynasty—to mention a few of the possibilities. Rost (1926) discerned blocks of tradition in Samuel, especially an "Ark Narrative" (a series of stories about ancient Israel's sacred object) in I Sam. 4–6 and II Sam. 6, and a "Succession Narrative" about how Solomon came to be the next king, stretching from II Sam. 9–20 to I Kings 1–2. Noth's (1943) theory of a Deuteronomistic History, consisting of Joshua through Kings and spanning the period from the Conquest (c. twelfth century B.C.E.) to the fall of Jerusalem in 587, subsumed Samuel as part of the larger work of Joshua through Kings, and subsequent research, for those who accept his premise, has identified two or possibly three redactions of the four-book unit as part of this process. Others now view Samuel and Kings as a history of the *monarchy,* parallel to a *people's* history in the preceding books.

But Samuel does not feature Deuteronomistic phraseology as extensively as do the other books in the Early Prophets, and a composition date remains elusive. The old argument that the details of court life and conversations in Samuel must reflect a source very close to the actual events is no longer entirely persuasive. Neither is Samuel likely to have stemmed directly from a standard royal chronicle, given its novelistic form. At the same time, arguments for a very late date make little sense, given that we have a clearly revisionist history of David, which omits some of the more troubling episodes that appear in Samuel, in the book of Chronicles, written in the fifth or fourth century B.C.E. More likely, the wellsprings of Samuel lie in a combination of influences and sources, developed over time. Early material might have included archival lists (see Na'aman 1996) and folk traditions. Texts justifying David's reign seem also to move us in the direction of his own time or shortly thereafter. But literacy in Israel, beyond the purview of the elite, seems to have been rather late, perhaps not until the eighth century B.C.E. or later. As it stands, Samuel appears to have been put into final form by a great artist or artists in the waning days of Judah or perhaps even during the sixth-century Babylonian Exile. It is clearly a southern document, given its Davidic slant, yet one wonders whether the warts-and-all portrayal of the hero and the not entirely unsympathetic picture of Saul might not be a concession to northern sympathies, which survived for centuries. In any event, the final version displays a remarkable freedom in its combination of multiple views of David's character, with the sensitivity and concerns of both artists and prophets. It seems to combine traditions from various periods and points of view, as is characteristic of a good deal of biblical literature.

The book of Chronicles covers much of the same ground historically, but with the very different purpose of stressing the Temple in Jerusalem, and consequently the positive aspects of David and Solomon's reigns. In contrast, Samuel presents a skeptical look at the origins of kingship, something close to what Israeli literary critic Meir Sternberg might call "the whole truth." David's charm and fighting ability contrast with the extermination of the House of Saul by David's henchmen; his brilliant political moves, such as the establishment of previously non-Israelite Jerusalem as the country's capital, are followed by his disastrous personal behavior in the Bathsheba incident and beyond. The characters in the book of Samuel are not cardboard figures: Samuel is not as successfully pious, nor Saul as unremittingly evil, as we would prefer to think, and the text's attitude toward the monarchy is not a knee-jerk, "Long live the king!" response. The audience of Chronicles may well have hoped for the monarchy's restoration, but the audience of Samuel was undoubtedly an earlier one, for whom kingship was still a living reality, and a reality to be taken with a grain of salt. For the book of Samuel, kings are indeed chosen by God (although the choice is changeable), but they are fickle creatures who may choose not to listen to God and his demands, and instead to follow their own political and material instincts. King Saul is chastised by the prophet Samuel; King David is rebuked by the prophet Nathan; and it is in the direct confrontation between these two representatives of different kinds of power that the drama and significance of the book are to be found. The king, whose word is always law, comes up against the word of God, and it is the divine demands which, for the writer, ultimately carry the greater weight. In contrast to the typical ancient Near Eastern royal chronicle, this book therefore may well be the product of circles for whom the old memories were tempered with prophetic ideas. And Samuel in its final form is a text that mirrors many of the concerns of Israel's great prophets, whose activity begins in the ninth century B.C.E.

An additional issue in the composition of Samuel concerns parallels between it and the book of Genesis, from plot structure (especially the above-mentioned similarities between David and Jacob) to many specific examples of verbal correspondence. These have led scholars such as Joel Rosenberg, Edward Greenstein (1990), and Gary Rendsburg (1986) to posit a strong relationship between the writing of the two books. Richard Friedman has taken the bold step of suggesting that the author of "J" (the theorized core narratives that form the backbone of Genesis, Exodus, and Numbers) and the author of much of Samuel are one and the same. While these scholars have rendered an important service in pointing out the intimate relationship between these literatures, I am not prepared, as Friedman is, to see the two books as arising from the same hand. All we can say for certain is that one literature has played off the other. Some would take this to indicate that Genesis is a late product, composed under the shadow of David's remarkable career, while others, in a more traditional approach, would suggest that the author of the core of Samuel was familiar with Genesis, whose stories may well have been in circulation already in the monarchic period.

Of course, a relatively early date for the writing of Samuel does not rule out later reworking, and it is striking the degree to which its stories prefigure the concerns of a people in exile or on the verge of it. In the case of the Northern Kingdom, Israel, the trauma of destruction would point to the late eighth century B.C.E.; for the south, Judah, it would indicate the early sixth. It is telling that the last surviving member of Saul's dynasty, Mephibosheth, is portrayed in Samuel as "eating regularly" at David's table (II Sam. 9:10–13), succored but also a virtual prisoner—precisely the situation and description of the last survivor of David's own line, Jehoiachin, in the very last verses of Kings, where he eats at the king of Babylonia's table but does not himself rule. The final editor here has had the last word, but it is a word compatible with much of what appears in the book of Samuel. The refrain of divine approval in II Sam. 7—the repeated promise that David's dynasty shall sit on the throne in Jerusalem "for the ages"—is countered by the ominous "So-now— / the sword shall not depart from your house for the ages" (12:10), both conveyed by the same prophet, Nathan. As Fewell acutely presents it, the good-and-bad David ultimately belies the simple Deuteronomistic scheme of reward and punishment, instead reflecting a community in trauma, attempting to make sense of what has happened to a nation destroyed and in exile.

IMAGERY AND LANGUAGE

THE BOOK OF SAMUEL TRANSMITS ITS PROPHETIC MESSAGE OF SOCIAL AND political criticism through the life situations of its characters. But it also conveys it by means of another familiar aspect of literature: the evocative power of imagery. It is here that translation, if done carefully, has much to contribute. I will present only one set of images to illustrate what I mean.

Robert Polzin, in his thought-provoking study of II Samuel (1993), draws our attention to the way in which a number of major and minor characters in the book die. Not only are they assassinated or killed in battle, but on quite a few occasions they literally lose their heads. Thus David decapitates Goliath (I 17), Saul is dismembered after his death by the Philistines (I 31), Saul's son Ish-Bosheth's head is brought to David for reward (II 4), the rebel Absalom meets his death as the result of his head becoming stuck in a tree, and the head of the rebel Sheba son of Bichri is flung off the battlements of Abel, effectively ending the last threat to David's throne (II 20). Polzin sees the use of head imagery as an important symbolic clue to the book as a whole:

> However clearly we see this seizing of the head as stylized imagery for
> the grasping of kingship, the semantic fullness of "head" here is scarcely

exhausted. For from the beginning of his career to the end, David's character zone is intimately connected with the head as a locus of guilt and death. For one thing, David, wittingly or unwittingly, is constantly associated with the contemplated or actual beheading of his enemies . . . the head (also) functions as the locus of the guilt and sin of David's enemies . . . the heady bloodshed surrounding David still remains a significant means by which he rose to become "head of the tribes of Israel" (1 Samuel 15:17) and "head of nations" (2 Samuel 22:44).

But Polzin's point may be expanded, for the head is not the only body part to hold interpretive value in Samuel. The heart too comes into play, particularly in the memorable cycle of stories that recounts Absalom's rebellion against his father, David (II Sam. 13–20; see the Introduction to that section below). And the use of body symbolism does not stop there. Samuel is a book that talks about deep emotions, but the text is quite visceral in a wider and quite literal way. From head to foot (see II Sam. 14:25), bodily images absorb a good deal of the book's energy. We move from hair (Absalom's), the cause of his pride and perhaps of his death, to failing eyes (Eli's); ears (Saul's) are avoided out of fear; hearts weaken and are stirred; hands are ready to close in on David; abdomens are pierced in revenge and assassination; feet (Mephibosheth's) are lame; and, not least, genitalia, notably David's, become the cause not only of personal but also of national disaster. The Bible, like other ancient Semitic literatures, frequently makes reference to human anatomy in both its narratives and its poetry, but Samuel uses it to a remarkable and meaningful degree.

What could be at work in this literary onslaught of body parts? Polzin's initial observation, that the text is concerned with the leaders ("heads") of Israel, and that this bodes ill for those who keep their heads as well as for those who lose them, is germane here. One is reminded of a passage from Isaiah (1:5–6), in which the prophet tries to convey the all-pervading corruption of Judean society several centuries after David's time:

> Every head is ailing,
> And every heart is sick.
> From head to foot
> No spot is sound:
> All bruises, and welts,
> And festering sores—
> Not pressed out, not bound up,
> Not softened with oil.
>
> (NJPS)

I believe that the same imagery is at work in Samuel. This book, conceding to Israel its heroes and its monarchy, nevertheless wishes to suggest the inherent sickness of the Israelite body politic, and uses examples of physical ailments to do so. The request for a king, and its grudging fulfillment by God, leads to a communal illness, which in one view can be cured only by the purifying fires of exile. The Judean community, ruled over by the House of David, cannot survive as a society that is ailing from top to bottom. That postexilic generations longed for a restoration of the monarchy does not eliminate these problems, but rather sharpens them into a hope for a perfect king as a representative of God.

THE STRUCTURE OF THE BOOK

AS WITH ALL BIBLICAL BOOKS, THE TEXT OF SAMUEL MAY BE VIEWED THROUGH A number of proposed section divisions. While several schemes are possible, the structure below will serve to highlight important themes in the text.

I (I Sam. 1–7) The Last "Judges": Eli and Shemuel

II (I Sam. 8–15) The Requested King

III (I Sam. 16–II Sam. 1) The Rise of David and the Fall of Sha'ul

IV (II Sam. 2–8) David's Rule Consolidated

V (II Sam. 9–12) David in Control and Out of Control

VI (II Sam. 13–20) The Great Rebellion

VII (II Sam. 21–24) Final Matters

As this outline makes clear, fully three-quarters of the book is taken up with the life and career of David. But the text encompasses a good deal more. Part I includes material about the decline of the priestly leader Eli and his sons, and narratives about the Ark ("Coffer"). As a whole, this section is a continuation of the previous book, Judges, in its portrayal of the problems of succession in leadership. Part II details the circumstances of the establishment of the monarchy in Israel, incorporating the troubled personality of Saul. Part III describes David's rise at court, and the dramatic story of Saul's unsuccessful pursuit of the young hero, culminating in the old king's death in battle. Part IV chronicles the liquidation of the House of Saul, as well as David's vanquishing of his foreign enemies and his secure establishment on the throne of both north and south. Part V serves as a bridge to the account of David's decline, with material related to Part IV leading into David's crimes in the Bathsheba episode. Part VI is an extended account of the revolt of David's son Absalom, with David driven from the throne and then restored as a shadow of his former self. Finally, Part VII collects other material about David, including battle accounts, final poems, and a story about the purchase of the future Temple site; it completes the book not, as one might expect, with the king's death, which is narrated along with Solomon's accession in the first two chapters of Kings, but with the removal of a plague that had been precipitated by David's actions, and the acquisition of ancient Israel's holiest site. Structurally, the book had opened in mirror fashion, with Hannah's successful movement from barrenness to fertility, leading into Samuel's residence at the holy place at Shiloh.

The use of poetry as marker provides a further overall structure for the book, with Hannah's thanksgiving poem near the beginning, David's dirge over Saul and Jonathan in the middle, and David's last poetic words near the end. But other schemes have been noticed, giving evidence of stages in the book's development. Brettler (1995), for instance, points to the use of bureaucratic lists at the end of I Sam. 14 and II Sam. 8, which he sees as bracketing an extended unit about "David as Proper King." What seems to have happened here, as in other collections of biblical narrative, is that later editorial orderings of the book have superseded earlier ones, with resulting structures that actually overlap.

Despite these layers, and the at times conflicting ideologies that find expression in them, it is still possible to read Samuel as a unified book. By the time it ends, with a chastened and humble King David, the audience has come, through experiencing the ups and downs of his career, to ruminate on the losing, gaining, and retention of power, and to sharpen its focus on where exactly power is to reside in ancient Israel. These questions ultimately supply the narrative with coherence.

THE EVOLVING DAVID

AFTER ALL IS SAID AND DONE, WE ARE STILL LEFT WITH THE BOOK OF SAMUEL'S greatest enigma: David himself. As recent interpreters have pointed out, he is a man whose feelings are often hidden from us, a man intensely scrutinized and loved by others but whose own motivations are often opaque. How are we to reconcile the book's complex portrait of him with what he came to mean to generations of Jews and Christians? David, after all, was already an extremely important and positive symbolic figure in the Bible. Over time he came to stand as the unshakable symbol of God's eternal promise of a political continuity and a holy city that would never disappear. This conviction, for Jews, remained firm even in the face of destruction and exile, and eventually crystallized in the image of "Messiah son of David," a future God-sent king of David's line who, unlike most of the biblical kings, would not fail, and who would usher in a final age of peace and prosperity for all humanity.

For early Christians as well, David naturally was connected with the figure of the Messiah, both as a foreshadowing of Jesus (in the person of the popular ancient symbol of the "shepherd king") and as his biological ancestor. It is no accident that the Gospel of Matthew, which opens the New Testament, begins with the phrase, "An account of the genealogy of the Jesus the Messiah, the son of David, the son of Abraham" (NRSV). David thus provides the crucial link between Christianity's literary and biological antecedents, the Hebrew Bible and the Jews, and the new community of believers.

Should we write off this posthumous David, beloved "sweet singer" and paragon of piety, as simply the product of wishful thinking? Or should we dismiss his at times problematic behavior, as portrayed in Samuel, merely as part of a critical tradition that crept its way into an otherwise unblemished account of a glorious past? To go too far in either direction is to lose the richness of David. It is more likely that Samuel's morally compromised figure of David has been prized by Jews and Christians precisely because of his depth and suitability as a mediator between the human and the divine. Like most religions, both Judaism and Christianity came to cultivate the concept of human redemption, the idea that human beings are capable of rising beyond their flaws and, through deeds and/or faith, of helping to perfect the world. David, as a man who is sincere but hardly a saint, has through the ages provided a powerful model for repentance. In the Bathsheba episode he immediately and unflinchingly admits his guilt; in the book's final story, wherein his exercise of royal power via census-taking leads to a plague among the Israelites, he accepts responsibility and places his fate in God's hands. David emerges from Samuel as a humble and humbled king, who points the way to the possibilities of genuine change (see Borgman for an extended treatment of this point).

Ultimately, like the younger son/brother Jacob, from whose God-given name the people of Israel derived its own, David and his struggles become absorbed into the Children of Israel's national character. Warrior, climber to kingship, singer of sacred songs, sinner and penitent, a man whose exploits and tribulations were celebrated by the great bards of ancient Israel, the David portrayed in Samuel is unalterably connected to the very image of how ancient Israel came to understand itself. As such, he is at the core of the complex but rewarding legacy bequeathed to us by the book of Samuel.

PART I

THE LAST "JUDGES": ELI AND SHEMUEL

(I 1–7)

THE BOOK THAT INTRODUCES THE INSTITUTION OF KINGSHIP INTO THE BIBLE begins, appropriately, with a birth. As so often happens in this literature, human continuity is initially threatened by apparent infertility, but instead of starting merely with a biological fact, Samuel introduces the first of its great human portraits by imbuing the heroine with considerable depth of feeling and, not surprisingly, a gift for poetry. Hanna makes a telling contrast to the High Priest, Eli, continuing a pattern that recurs throughout Judges and Samuel, where women provide a foil and a profound sounding board for issues of power.

It is worth noting, as many have, that Hanna's poem in Chap. 2, which is undoubtedly from an independent source, is a prelude to major themes of the book, especially the idea that God, the great Reverser, may choose to exalt the powerless. YHWH, who "brings down . . . and brings up" (v.6), will be directing the fate of Israel and its early kings, and while he will in the end "give power to his king" (v.10), he will also make it clear that "not by might does a man prevail" (v.9).

The priest-judge Eli, an ineffective leader, typifies an era that is coming to a close. His first act, mistaking Hanna's deep inner religiosity for drunkenness, sets the tone. Unlike his young charge Shemuel, he is never in direct verbal contact with God; in addition, he is incapable of providing the military leadership of his predecessors, and, most tellingly, unable to control the highly inappropriate behavior of his sons. Barely noticeable amid Eli's initial bluster in Chap. 1 is a striking detail: he sits on a kind of "throne" (Spina). The first part of this section of the book (Chaps. 1–4) will end with his death in that very seat, overturned when he hears the disastrous news of the Ark's capture. The fall of the house of Eli gives way to the leadership of his judge-prophet successor, Shemuel.

A central feature of this part of the book, in fact, is narrative emphasis on the Ark (here "Coffer"). As the great biblical symbol of the divine presence, its physical location in these chapters emphasizes the desperate situation in which the Israelites find themselves—or rather, in the eyes of the biblical writer, the situation which they themselves have created. Bereft of God's presence, the people have no chance of procuring either general blessing or military victory. The Coffer's return, on the other hand, does not provide a full solution in their eyes. That they can envision only in the establishment of a monarchy.

At the same time, there is considerable irony in the Coffer's loss in this section of the book, for it will be absent all throughout the reign of Sha'ul, the first king, strongly suggesting that God will not be with him as well (Sweeney 2012).

Shemuel himself contains elements characteristic of the prophets who will be important in subsequent books. Like Yirmeyahu (Jeremiah) centuries later, he is called by God early in life; like all the great prophets, his relationship to monarchy is highly critical. He functions, as they do, as God's mouthpiece, yet the text eventually finds room for his personal emotions, especially in his complex relationship with Sha'ul. This opening section of the book, which covers most of his career, gives only passing indication of an inner life; throughout the bulk of it, the writer seems mainly concerned with establishing Shemuel's legitimacy. In contrast to Eli, he is the one with the vision. He vicariously leads the troops, and it is on his watch that the Coffer returns to Israel. And he functions as the last of the "judges," at least judicially, in his circuit riding among central Israelite towns. We will encounter him as a character with deep feelings only in the transitional Chap. 8 and the events that follow it.

It should also be noted, as Hancock does in some detail, that aspects of Shemuel's career, especially early on, parallel that of Moshe. This is only natural in a book that takes biblical leadership as one of its great themes.

———————

Chapter 1. *The Birth of Shemuel:* "There was a man," the folktale-type wording with which Samuel opens, immediately establishes continuity with the book of Judges, as it was the same phrase that introduced several stories there (Chaps. 13, 17, and 19). But here it is a woman, Hanna, who will be the central character. As was the case with Sara, Rivka, and Rahel in Genesis, as well as with Shimshon's mother in Judges, her barrenness is a signal of something momentous to come. Yet the text takes its time, painting an intimate picture of a family and dwelling in detail on personalities in a way that sets the tone for the character-driven book of Samuel. Here are vivid portraits of a tender but clueless husband, an insensitive priest, and, above all, a woman whose desire for a child is so intense that she is willing to surrender him to the service of God well before he has grown up. This pattern of wish, fulfillment, and partial loss is also emblematic of the experience that Israel will have in the coming narratives, beginning with a new monarchy, political splendor, and military victory in Samuel but ending with the near snuffing out of the Davidic dynasty at the end of Kings.

It may seem surprising that this book, which is so much about male leadership, begins by focusing on a woman. But as I suggested previously, throughout both Judges and Samuel, the characterization of women often helps to clarify issues of leadership. Additionally, Hanna's experiences and her voice set the personal tone through which these issues will be subsequently played out. And once again,

1:1 Now there was a man from Ramatayim in Tzofim, from the
    highlands of Efrayim;
    his name was Elkana son of Yeroham son of Elihu son of Tohu son
    of Tzuf, an Efrayimite.
2   He had two wives:
    the name of one was Hanna / Grace, while the name of the second
    was Peninna / Pearl;
    now Peninna had children, but Hanna had no children.
3   And that man used to go up from his town, from year to year,
    to bow down and to sacrifice to Yhwh of the Forces-On-High, at
    Shilo
    —Eli's two sons, Hofni and Pin'has, priests to Yhwh, were there.
4   Now it was, one day,
    that Elkana was sacrificing,
    —he would give to Peninna his wife, and to all her sons and
    daughters, portions,
5   but to Hanna he would give a double portion,
    for [it was] Hanna he loved,
    although Yhwh had closed up her womb.
6   And her rival-wife would provoke her with provocation, for the
    sake of making-her-complain,
    for Yhwh had closed up her womb;

1:1 **Ramatayim:** Possibly Rama ("Height"), a location frequently associated with Shemuel in the text; it was north of Jerusalem, near the border of what became Israel, the Northern Kingdom. **Tzofim:** "Watchmen," but McCarter (1980), following Driver, judges the text corrupt here, and posits "a Tzufite," after Elkana's ancestor later in the verse. **the highlands of Efrayim:** The geographical backbone of what became the Northern Kingdom. **Elkana:** The name means "God Acquires / Creates." His son Shemuel will not grow up with his parents, perhaps hinted at here.
2 **Hanna:** Pronounced *hahn-NAH;* trad. English "Hannah." **Peninna:** Pronounced *pe-nin-NAH;* trad. English "Peninnah."
3 **from year to year** (see also v.7, "year after year"): This phrase had occurred in the last chapter of Judges; such links between adjacent texts occur from time to time in the Bible. **bow down:** This posture of worship, also used in approaching a supe-

rior, is on the knees, usually with "nostrils to the earth." **Yhwh:** As explained above in "On Using This Book," the name of God in the Hebrew Bible, whose pronunciation is not precisely known, is traditionally transcribed as "the Lord" and the like. Here it is printed according to the way it appears in the Hebrew text, and the reader may choose how to say it (for example, "The Eternal" or "*Adonai*"). **Yhwh of the Forces-On-High:** In *The Early Prophets* this title has a military ring; *tzeva'ot* may also refer to the concept of a heavenly council of gods from earlier mythological traditions. **Shilo:** Pronounced *shee-LO;* trad. English "Shiloh," one of the important pre-Jerusalem shrines, situated in the highlands of Efrayim. **Hofni . . . Pin'has:** Pronounced *hof-NEE* and *pin-HASS*. Like a number of early Israelite priestly names, these are Egyptian in origin. Pin'has is trad. English "Phineas" and means "dark-skinned."

a classic biblical pattern appears, as a person or type from whom we might not expect success—here a barren wife, elsewhere a younger brother—comes to prevail in the end.

The way in which Eli the priest is portrayed is also worthy of comment. While his heart seems to be in the right place, his failure to distinguish in this opening chapter between the true prayer of the heart and drunken babbling is already a sign of inner shortcomings. As the story progresses, we will note his failure as father and leader (the narrator equates the two), culminating in his literal blindness and his dramatic death.

The key word in this chapter is "request," which occurs seven times; it will return, doubled, in 2:20, to round out the story. Many scholars have taken this to mean that the book originally began with material about the birth of Sha'ul, the "requested one," and that something has been confused in the editing process. Others, myself included, note in the final text a deliberate and profound connection between the two men (see the discussion in Garsiel 1985). In addition, Hanna's request for a son foreshadows Israel's request for a king seven chapters hence (Polzin 1989).

7 and thus he would do, year after year:
  whenever she would go up to the House of God, thus would she
    provoke her—
  . . . and she wept and would not eat,
8 so Elkana her husband said to her:
  Hanna, why are you weeping?
  Why don't you eat?
  And why is your heart in such ill-humor?
  Am I not better to you than ten sons?
9 Hanna arose after eating at Shilo, and after drinking
  —now Eli the priest was sitting on a throne by the doorpost of the
    great-hall of Yhwh—
10 and she was bitter of feelings,
  so she prayed to Yhwh, while she wept, yes, wept;
11 she vowed a vow, and said:
  O Yhwh of the Forces-On-High,
  if you will see, yes, see the affliction of your maidservant,
  and will bear me in mind and not forget your maidservant,
  and will give your maidservant seed of men,
  then I will give him to Yhwh all the days of his life:
  no razor shall go up on his head!
12 Now it was, as she multiplied her praying in the presence of Yhwh,
  that Eli was watching her mouth:
13 now Hanna, she was speaking in her heart,
  only her lips were moving, but her voice could not be heard—
  so Eli took her for a drunkard.

---

7 . . . **and she wept** . . . : The narrative picks up from v.4, on a day that Elkana was offering sacrifices; everything in between is the background to Hanna's weeping.

8 **better . . . than ten sons:** As Alter (1999) points out, Elkana's question is both empathetic and off the mark; how could he understand a barren mother's feelings?

9 **Eli:** Pronounced *ay-LEE*. **throne:** Unlike in modern usage, Heb. *kissei* tends to mean more than a simple "chair" in the Bible. **great-hall:** Used here to denote the sanctuary.

11 **see:** The preposition used with the Hebrew verb adds an element of feeling, connoting "look sympa-

thetically." **your maidservant:** Referring to oneself in the third person is used in the Bible when one addresses a superior. **I will give him to Yhwh . . . no razor:** Hanna here alludes to the Nazirite laws of Num. 6, where in fulfillment of a religious vow, a person would not shave (there are additional provisions and prohibitions). Shemuel, like Shimshon (Judg. 13–16) before him, appears to be Nazirite for life, a concept not found in the Numbers text.

12 **in the presence of Yhwh:** This phrase usually indicates a sacred location or building.

13 **took her for a drunkard:** Praying, as well as reading and writing, was not a silent activity in the ancient world, hence Eli's mistaken assessment of Hanna.

Chapter 2. *The Song of Hanna; Eli and His Sons:* Hanna's prayer occurs earlier in Samuel than any other poem in a biblical narrative book. As mentioned above, it introduces the idea that God may reverse the expected course of events. It thus carries the repetition of an oft-rehearsed biblical theme which undoubtedly points to the people of Israel itself, in its status as a latecomer and a frequently subordinate group in the ancient Near East.

Not surprisingly, the poem is shot through with vocabulary reflecting both ends of the social spectrum. "Mighty . . . sated . . . rich . . . noble . . . might" alternate with "those who stumble . . . those once hungry . . . the barren one . . . the needy . . . the destitute," and the like. The line "The barren one has given birth to seven" (v.5) is perhaps the immediate reason for its having been chosen for the mouth of the previously childless Hanna; such verbal connections between texts, which often hinge on a single word or phrase, are fairly typical in ancient literature. But above all, it is the triumphant ending on a monarchical note, with the exalting of God's "anointed," that not so subtly indicates what we are reading: a book about the choosing of a king.

When the narrative resumes, even before we learn anything about Shemuel as Eli's successor, the text makes sure that we are aware of the state of deterioration into which the worship of Yhwh has fallen. As a prelude to the actions of Eli's sons, we are told at some length how even the servants of the priests make a mockery of the sacrifices in their zeal to extract the priests' due. Only in v.22 do we learn of the exact nature of the sons' sin, the serious act of sleeping with the serving-women at the very entrance to the shrine. Despite Eli's entreaties, his sons ignore him because Yhwh has other plans.

The long condemnation of Eli by Yhwh through an anonymous "man of God" that ends the chapter in vv.27–36 leaves no doubt about the fate of the priest and his descendants. It mirrors what will happen to Sha'ul, Israel's first king, later in the book.

14 Eli said to her:
How long will you be drunk?
Put away your wine from you!

15 But Hanna answered and said:
No, my lord,
a woman hardened of spirit am I.
Wine and beer I have not drunk,
but I have been pouring out my soul in the presence of YHWH!

16 Do not consider your maidservant a base woman,
for it is out of my great anxiety and my being provoked [that] I
have spoken until now.

17 Eli answered and said: Go in peace,
and may the God of Israel grant your request that you have
requested of him.

18 She said:
May your handmaid find favor in your eyes.
The woman went on her way, and she ate,
and her face was no longer [sad] on her.

19 They started-early in the morning:
they bowed down in the presence of YHWH;
then they returned, and came back to their house in Rama.
And Elkana knew Hanna his wife,
and YHWH kept her in mind.

20 So it was, at the turning of days,
that Hanna conceived and gave birth to a son;
she called his name: Shemuel/The One From God,
meaning: from YHWH I requested him.

21 And the man Elkana went up, along with all his household,
to sacrifice to YHWH the yearly sacrifice, and his vow-offering,

22 but Hanna did not go up,
for she said to her husband:
. . . until the lad is weaned—

15 **pouring out my soul:** An extremely strong expression; usually in the Bible, the objects of pouring are blood or anger. Here it is also a nice play on imagery, since Hanna has just rightly denied that she has been drinking. Generally I avoid "soul" for Heb. *nefesh*, which in the Bible does not mean the opposite of "body," but here, the English has the connotation of "feelings."

20 **the turning of days:** Or "the turning of the year," namely, a year later. **Shemuel:** Pronounced *sheh-moo-AYL;* trad. English "Samuel." **requested:** As noted in the Commentary, this verb, *sh-'-l,* is really associated with the name of Sha'ul (Saul) (see v.28, where "lent-on-request" is vocalized *sha'ul*).

22 **forever:** Permanently, as per her promise in v.11. **weaned:** Probably around the age of three.

◆

then I will bring him,
that he may be seen in the presence of YHWH;
he is to stay there forever.

23 Elkana her husband said to her:
Do whatever is good in your eyes:
stay until you have weaned him—
only: may YHWH fulfill his word!
So the woman stayed behind and nursed her son, until she had
weaned him.

24 She brought him up with her, when she had weaned him,
with a three-year-old bull and an *efa* of flour, and a skin of wine,
and brought him to the House of YHWH at Shilo,
though the lad was [just] a lad.

25 They slaughtered the bull,
and then they brought the lad to Eli.

26 She said:
Please, my lord, as you yourself live, my lord:
I am the woman who was standing beside you here, to pray to
YHWH.

27 It was for this lad that I prayed,
and YHWH has granted my request that I requested of him!

28 So I now lend-him-on-request to YHWH;
all the days that he lives he is lent-on-request/*sha'ul* to YHWH.
And they bowed down there to YHWH.

2:1 And Hanna prayed, she said:
My heart swells because of YHWH,
my horn is raised because of YHWH;
my mouth is wide-with-boasting over my enemies,
for I rejoice in your deliverance!

---

24 **three-year-old bull:** Following LXX; MT (the standard Hebrew text) has "bulls, three." *efa:* Pronounced *ay-FAH*. It was a dry measure, perhaps
fifteen liters. **though the lad was [just] a lad:**
The Hebrew is strange here; one manuscript of
LXX suggests a longer text, describing the family's
pilgrimage.

28 **lend-him-on-request:** Since Heb. *sh-'-l* can also mean
"lend." **they:** So ancient versions; MT has "he."
2:1 **my horn is raised:** See also v.10. McCarter (1980)
notes that "the exalted horn is . . . a visible sign of
success." See also the use of the image in Bil'am's
blessings in Num. 23:22.

◆
2   There is no one holy like YHWH,
       indeed, no one beside you,
       there is no rock like our God!

3   Do not speak so high, so high [and mighty],
       letting your mouth run free,
       for a god all-knowing is YHWH,
       by him are actions measured.

4   The bow of the mighty is shattered,
       but the stumblers are girded with strength.

5   Those once-sated must hire themselves out for bread,
       but those once-hungry will endure forever.
       The barren one has given birth to seven,
       while the one [with] many sons is dried up.

6   YHWH brings-death and bestows-life,
       brings down to Sheol and brings up.

7   YHWH makes-poor and makes-rich,
       brings low and, yes, lifts up.

8   He raises the needy from the dust,
       lifts the destitute from the dunghill,
       to seat them with the noble ones,
       and a throne of glory he has them inherit.
       For YHWH's are the molten-pillars of the earth,
       he has set the world upon them.

9   The feet of his loyal ones he guards,
       but the wicked moan in darkness—
       for not by might does a man prevail.

10   YHWH shatters those opposing him,
       from the heavens he thunders against them.
       YHWH judges to the limits of the earth;
       may he give power to his king,
       and lift up the horn of his anointed one!

---

2 **rock:** Rocks and stones appear frequently in the Bible as symbols of solidity and permanence—for instance, as monuments—and are thus appropriate images for God's dependability.

5 **endure:** LXX; MT has "cease." **seven:** The number of wholeness or perfection, in the Bible and elsewhere in the ancient Near East.

6 **Sheol:** Pronounced *sheh-OHL*. The biblical underworld. Unlike the later concepts of heaven and hell, it appears to be simply a subdued place where the dead rest (see Chap. 28 below), similar to the Greek Hades.

8 **destitute . . . dunghill:** The Hebrew is not alliterative. **world:** Or "mainland."

9 **moan:** See Levine; *d-m-m* sometimes has this meaning, as opposed to the traditional "are silent."

10 **king:** An anachronism which nicely foreshadows the major concern of the book. **anointed one:** A synonym for "king"; the verb refers to the practice of consecrating a ruler by pouring oil on his head.

11 And Elkana went to Rama, to his house,
  while the lad began to attend Y<small>HWH</small>, in the presence of Eli the
    priest.

12 Now the sons of Eli were base fellows;
  they did not know Y<small>HWH</small>.

13 And the norm of the priests with the people [was]:
  whoever sacrificed a sacrifice,
  the priest's serving-lad would come while the flesh was boiling
  with a fork of three teeth in his hand

14 and would strike at the pot or the kettle or the cauldron or the
    boiling-vat;
  everything the fork would bring up, the priest would take for
    himself.
  Thus they would do to all Israel who were coming there, at Shilo.

15 Even before they would turn the fat into smoke,
  the serving-lad of the priest would come and say to the person
    sacrificing:
  Give over some flesh for roasting, for the priest,
  for he will not take boiled flesh from you—only raw!

16 And if the person said to him:
  Let them first turn the fat into smoke, yes, smoke,
  then take for yourself whatever your appetite craves—
  he would say to him:
  No, but give it over right-now;
  if not, I'll take it by force!

17 Now the sin of the serving-lads was exceedingly great in the
    presence of Y<small>HWH</small>,
  for the men scorned the gift [intended] for Y<small>HWH</small>.

18 Shemuel was attending in the presence of Y<small>HWH</small>,
  as a lad girded with a linen *efod*.

---

12 **base fellows:** It is difficult to find an appropriate modern English translation for the phrase; "ne'er-do-wells," "lowlifes," or "scoundrels" are older equivalents. Some later scholars have translated the term *beliyaal* as a devil figure, "Belial." **know:** In a deep sense. In solely human contexts, it can refer to sexual relations.

13 **fork:** Others, "flesh hook."

14 **and would strike . . . :** He would plunge the fork into the vat.

15 **not . . . boiled flesh . . . only raw:** By not burning away the fat first, as was the ritual requirement, the lads were committing an act of sacrilege (see Lev. 3:16–17).

18 **efod:** Pronounced *ay-FODE,* an apron-like priestly garment which covered the torso, described in Exod. 28:6ff.

19   Now a small cloak his mother used to make him
        and used to bring it up from year to year, when she went up with
            her husband to sacrifice the yearly sacrifice.
20   And Eli would bless Elkana and his wife;
        he would say:
        May YHWH give you seed from this woman
        in place of the requested-one who was lent-on-request to YHWH!
        Then they would go back to their place.
21   Indeed, YHWH took account of Hanna,
        and she conceived and gave birth to three sons and two daughters;
        but the lad Shemuel grew up in the presence of YHWH.

22   Now when Eli became exceedingly old,
        he heard about all that his sons were doing to all Israel:
        how they were lying with the women who were acting-as-a-
            workforce at the entrance to the Tent of Appointment.
23   He said to them:
        Why do you act in accordance with these words that I hear—
        evil accounts of you from all of these people?
24   Don't, my sons!
        Indeed, it is no good, the report that I hear YHWH's people
            spreading.
25   If a man sins against [another] man, God will mediate for him,
        but if it is against YHWH [that] a man sins, who will intercede for
            him?
        Yet they did not hearken to their father's voice,
        for YHWH desired to have them die.
26   But the lad Shemuel went on growing greater and more pleasing,
        so with YHWH, so with men.

19 **cloak:** Shemuel's adult cloak will play an important
    role in his relationship with Sha'ul, the king whom
    he will later anoint.
20 **their:** So ancient versions; MT has "his."
21 **Indeed:** 4QS[a] has, more likely, "And." **took ac-
    count:** The same expression is used regarding the
    previously barren Sara in Gen. 21:1. **in the pres-
    ence of:** Reading *lifnei,* as in 4QS[a] and LXX, in place
    of MT's *'im,* "with."
22 **to all Israel:** Thus stressing the serious nature of
    their offenses. **they were lying with the women:**

Alter notes the appetite parallels between food and
sex which are roundly condemned in this chapter. **acting-as-a-workforce:** That is, serving at various tasks at the sanctuary. **Tent of Appointment:**
A pre-Temple sanctuary, identified here with the one
the Israelites carried around in the wilderness after
the Exodus.
25 **YHWH desired to have them die:** Here, as elsewhere, the book is moving toward the establishment
of the monarchy, so Eli's sons have to be removed
from the picture.

Chapters 3:1–4:1. *The Call of Shemuel:* There are numerous other "call" scenes in the Bible, where a prophet or leader such as Moshe (Moses) or Yesha'yahu (Isaiah) is chosen, but the present story is unique in both its location and cast of characters. At a time when the word of God is rare (v.1), Shemuel, who is either a child or a teenager, hears the voice of God in the very sanctuary at Shilo. Both he and the aging priest mistake what is happening, but Eli finally realizes that it is God himself speaking, and so he prepares the lad for the inevitable revelation. The divine message confirms what we saw in the previous chapter: Eli, who has failed as a father of priests, is rejected by God, and his sons will not succeed him. No future sacrifices or rituals can change that. Strikingly, nevertheless, his reaction to this news is to humbly accept God's will.

The reader will note that God's words to Shemuel do not, as so often in biblical "call" narratives, require answer and dialogue. Young Shemuel appears in this chapter as one through whom God speaks, and is thus a prophet, but there is none of the usual tension between the one called and the burden he is asked to carry—at least for the moment—that we find elsewhere in the Bible.

27 A man of God came to Eli and said to him:
Thus says YHWH:
Did I not reveal, yes, reveal myself to your Father's House when
they were in Egypt, [belonging] to Pharaoh's house,
28 and choose it from all the tribes of Israel for myself, to act-as-
priests—
to ascend upon my sacrificial-altar, to send up smoking-incense, to
wear the *efod* in my presence?
And I gave to your Father's House all the fire-offerings of the
Children of Israel.
29 Why have you kicked away my sacrifices and my cereal-gifts that I
commanded, with a grudging-eye?
And you have honored your sons more than me,
by letting them grow fat from the premier-part of all the gifts of
Israel, in my presence!
30 Therefore,
the Utterance of YHWH, God of Israel:
I had said, yes, said:
Your house and your Father's House will walk in my presence for
the ages;
but now, the Utterance of YHWH:
[Heaven] forbid for me!
For those who honor me, I honor,
but those who despise me will be cursed!
31 Here, the days are coming
when I will hew off your arm and the arm of your Father's House,
so that [no man] will grow old in your house;
32 you will look with a grudging-eye on all his doing-good for Israel,
and there will be no elder in your house, all the days [to come].
33 Yet I will not cut off everyone belonging to you from my sacrifices,
[but] to consume your eyes and exhaust your breath,
in all of the greater-part of your house, men will die.

---

27 **Father's House:** A social unit smaller than a tribe, similar to an extended family.
29 **kicked away . . . :** The entire passage is unclear, especially the two occurrences of Heb. *ma'on* ("habitation," here and v.32), which, following others, I have emended to *'ayin*, "eye." **premier-part:** The portion of the sacrifices intended for God.

30 **Therefore, the Utterance:** The usual introductory formula when a prophet speaks in the name of God.
31 **hew off your arm:** The idiom perhaps refers to disabling one's capacity to shoot an arrow.
32–33 **you will look . . . :** The text is unclear and difficult to reconstruct.

34 And this is the sign for you that it will come-to-pass for your two
    sons, for Hofni and Pin'has:
on a single day the two of them will die!

35 But I will establish for myself a trusted priest
who will do [what is] in my heart and in my being;
I will build him a trustworthy household,
and he will walk in the presence of my anointed one all the days [to
    come].

36 And it will be
that whoever is left in your house—
he will come to bow low to him
for payment of silver and a round-loaf of bread;
he will say:
Pray appoint me to one of the priestly-offices,
[for me] to eat a bit of bread!

3:1 The lad Shemuel was attending Yhwh in the presence of Eli.
Now the word of Yhwh was precious in those days;
visions were not widespread.

2 It was on that day
that Eli was lying down in his place
—his eyes had begun to dim, [so that] he was not able to see—

3 and the lamp of God had not yet gone out,
while Shemuel was lying down in the great-hall of Yhwh, where
    the Coffer of God was.

4 And Yhwh called to Shemuel.
He said:
Here I am.

5 And he ran to Eli
and said:
Here I am, for you called me!

---

35 **a trusted priest:** Many scholars such as McCarter (1980) identify him as Tzadok, founder of the dominant priestly line in Jerusalem under David. **trustworthy:** Or "secure" (see II Sam. 7:6). **my anointed one:** Once again referring to the future king.

36 **[for me] . . . :** Namely, the priests will be desperate for food.

3:3 **Coffer:** Others, "Ark"; this was Israel's most sacred cultic object, the chest in which the tablets of the Ten Commandments were kept in the center of the Tabernacle.

5 **return, lie down:** Or "lie down again."

But he said:
I did not call;
return, lie down.
He went and lay down.
6 But YHWH called yet again: Shemuel!,
and Shemuel arose and went to Eli,
and said:
Here I am, for you called me!
But he said:
I did not call, my son!
Return, lie down.
7 Now Shemuel did not yet know YHWH;
not yet had the word of YHWH been revealed to him.
8 And YHWH called again: Shemuel! a third time,
and he arose and went to Eli,
and said:
Here I am, for you called me!
Then Eli understood
that YHWH was calling the lad.
9 Eli said to Shemuel:
Go, lie down,
and it shall be, if he calls you, you are to say:
Speak, O YHWH, for your servant hearkens!
So Shemuel went and lay down in his place.
10 And YHWH came and stood [there]
and called as time and time [before]: Shemuel! Shemuel!
Shemuel said: Speak, for your servant hearkens!
11 YHWH said to Shemuel:
Here, I am about to do a thing in Israel
such that everyone who hears of it—their two ears will ring!
12 On that day, I will fulfill upon Eli all that I spoke concerning his
house,
from beginning to end!

---

10 **and stood [there]:** This very human description of God made later readers somewhat uncomfortable, but a physical presence of God is alluded to a number of times in biblical texts (see Gen. 3 and Exod. 33 for examples). **Shemuel! Shemuel!:** Such doubling occasionally occurs at an important biographical moment in the text (see Gen. 22:11 and Exod. 3:4).

11 **ring:** The customary "tingle" hardly seems adequate to describe a reaction of horror.

12 **all that I spoke:** See vv.30–36 above.

Chapter 4:2–22. *Defeat, Disaster, and the Death of Eli:* The course of the last two books, Joshua and Judges, made clear that victory in battle would depend solely on Israel's faithfulness to YHWH. Given that Chaps. 2–3 have convincingly demonstrated that leadership is failing badly, the outcome of the brewing battle in Chap. 4 is a foregone conclusion. The military encounter itself takes only one verse, and the defeat causes the Israelites to believe that they have only one recourse. As Hamilton notes, they do not even think of consulting Shemuel. Instead, as in many cultures, they decide to bring their great national and religious symbol, in this case the Coffer (Ark) of the Covenant, with them into battle, to afford protection and victory. Initially, the Philistines are overcome by fear of YHWH, but they rally themselves to "be men" (v.9) and the Israelites are defeated once again. This time a triple catastrophe occurs: military defeat, the capture of the Coffer, and the death of Eli's sons.

Beginning in v.12, a classic scene unfolds. Accounts of ancient battles always include the bringing of the news to wives, mothers, and fathers; one need only recall the pathos of the Greek story of Jason's father, Aegeus, awaiting his son's return from Colchis. The present text contains interesting variations on the old theme. Eli anxiously awaits word of the fate of the Coffer, having apparently written off his sons, but unexpectedly, the text gives new bits of information about him: he is ninety-eight, blind, and heavy. All these seemingly superfluous details come together in the vivid description of his death that follows, where his life comes crashing down as he sits in his seat of power. It is the literal downfall of an aged leader who lacks vision, whose office weighs him down, and who cannot survive the loss of the cult object whose purpose he has served his whole life.

As if to reinforce the negative message, the chapter ends with an ill-boding birth, that of Eli's grandson. In the mother's dying moments, she is compelled to give her child the fateful name of "Where-is-Glory," which betokens the capture of the Coffer.

Thus in the overall opening section of the book of Samuel the normal course of events is reversed, and a shadow is temporarily cast over the future. But we also know that with Shemuel, future leadership is in place, and it appears to be of a higher quality than what preceded it.

This chapter witnesses the introduction of the Philistines into biblical narrative. In Judges and Samuel, the Philistines are the archenemies of Israel, a powerful people resident mostly on or around the country's southern coast, and technologically superior through their possession of iron. Their portrayal in the Bible is entirely negative, and almost no useful cultural details are given about them except for their being uncircumcised. Similarly, the archaeological record about the Philistines is spotty, but thanks to the work of the Dothans and others, we can now piece together a tentative picture. This group may well have been one of the "Sea Peoples" who invaded the Middle East in the twelfth century. The Bible gives Crete (or possibly Cyprus) as their point of origin, but they may have

13 I have told him
that I am passing judgment on his house, for the ages,
for the iniquity about which he has known,
because his sons were treating God lightly, yet he did not condemn
   them.

14 Therefore I swear concerning the house of Eli:
Should the iniquity of the house of Eli be purged away
through sacrifices or grain-gifts, for the ages . . . !

15 Shemuel lay down until daybreak,
and he opened the doors of the House of Yhwh,
but Shemuel was afraid of reporting the seen-vision to Eli.

16 Eli called Shemuel;
he said:
Shemuel, my son!
He said:
Here I am.

17 He said:
What is the word that he spoke to you?
Now do not conceal it from me . . .
Thus may God do to you and thus may he add,
if you conceal from me any word
from all the word[s] that he spoke to you!

18 So Shemuel reported to him all the words, and he did not conceal
   [anything] from him.
And he said:
He is Yhwh;
whatever is good in his eyes, may he do!

19 Shemuel grew up, and Yhwh was with him;
he did not let any of his words fall to the ground.

20 So all Israel knew, from Dan to Be'er-Sheva,
that Shemuel was trustworthy as a prophet to Yhwh.

---

13 **God:** Following LXX; MT has "them" (Heb. *lhm,* as opposed to *'lhym*). **condemn:** The same word in v.2 ("be dim") refers to Eli's failing eyesight; its use points to Eli's "lack of insight" (Polzin 1989).

14 **Should . . . :** Namely, the iniquity will *not* be purged away.

17 **Thus may God do to you . . . :** Shemuel will be punished if he does not reveal the results of his encounter with God.

18 **He is Yhwh . . . :** Eli humbly accepts God's judgment, despite the horrific consequences for him personally.

20 **from Dan to Be'er-Sheva:** From one end of the country to the other, north to south.

come from Asia Minor or the Aegean. Some Canaanite element is also possible. The visual records from Egypt, which successfully repulsed their attack, show warriors with plumed helmets, although they were not the only group to be so attired. In those texts, the Philistines are referred to as Peleshet or Tjekker. Distinctive cultural elements include the coloring and decoration of pottery, which was red and black with birds and other figures, a double ax of bronze, and a floor plan of temples which is closer to that of Aegean models than of Canaanite ones. Nevertheless, the Philistines appear to have been extremely adaptable, quickly absorbing Canaanite language and gods (including the aforementioned Dagon). Sadly, none of their texts has survived.

The Philistines are portrayed as having settled in five coastal or near-coastal cities: Ashdod, Ashkelon, Ekron, Gat, and Gaza. Their reach, however, was greater. There is evidence of Philistine presence in Bet-She'an, just west of the Jordan River, and battles with them as reported in the Bible range throughout the central and northern parts of the land. David is credited with ending their dominance in the area.

It is ironic that Israel's classic enemy ultimately gave their name to the country itself. The Greeks and Romans dubbed it Palestine, the Land of the Philistines, and the name has been used for centuries as a neutral term by scholars, but the past few decades of Middle Eastern politics have given it a more charged connotation.

21 And YHWH was seen again at Shilo,
for YHWH had revealed himself to Shemuel at Shilo, in accord with
the word of YHWH.
4:1 And the word of Shemuel came-to-pass for all Israel. . . .

And all Israel went out to meet the Philistines for battle;
they encamped at Even Ha-Ezer/The Stone of Help,
while the Philistines encamped at Afek.
2 The Philistines arrayed-ranks to meet Israel,
and the battle was spread out, so that Israel was defeated before the
Philistines—
they struck them in ranks in the open-field: about four thousand
men.
3 The people came back to the camp, and the elders of Israel said:
Why has YHWH defeated us today before the Philistines?
Let us take ourselves, from Shilo, the Coffer of YHWH's Covenant,
that he may come into our midst
and deliver us from the grasp of our enemies!
4 So the people sent to Shilo,
and carried from there the Coffer of the Covenant of YHWH of the
Forces-On-High, [The One] Seated on the Winged-Sphinxes
—Eli's two sons were there with the Coffer of the Covenant of
God, Hofni and Pin'has.
5 And it was
when the Coffer of the Covenant of YHWH came into the camp
that all Israel shouted with a great shout,
so that the land was in panic.
6 The Philistines heard the sound of the shouting
and said:
What is this great sound of shouting in the Hebrews' camp?
Then they knew
that the Coffer of YHWH had come into the camp.

4:1 **Afek:** The Philistine border, northeast of Joppa, and a starting point for their campaigns northward.
3 **defeated:** Or, more literally, "beaten." **grasp:** Lit., "palm," often used in Samuel in place of "hand."
4 [**The One**] **Seated on the Winged-Sphinxes:** The Coffer serves as God's footstool, an image found elsewhere in the ancient Near East. The "winged-

sphinxes" (Heb. *keruvim*), mythical guardians of ancient Near Eastern palaces and temples, should not be confused with the later image of "cherubim," the naked, chubby little angels of Western art.
6 **Hebrews:** A term used in the Bible when foreigners are talking about the Israelites; see the early chapters of Exodus.

7 And the Philistines were afraid,
for they said [to themselves]:
A god has come into the camp!
And they said:
Woe to us,
for it was not like this yesterday [and] the day-before,

8 woe to us—
who will rescue us from the hand of this mighty god?
This is the god who struck down Egypt with every kind of blow in
the wilderness!

9 Strengthen yourselves and be men, O Philistines,
lest you have to serve the Hebrews, as they have served you!
Be men and wage battle!

10 So the Philistines waged battle,
and Israel was defeated, so that they fled, each to his tent.
The striking-down was exceedingly great:
there fell from Israel thirty thousand foot-soldiers.

11 Moreover the Coffer of God was taken,
and Eli's two sons died, Hofni and Pin'has.

12 A Binyaminite man ran from the ranks;
he came to Shilo on that same day
with his garb torn and earth on his head.

13 He came, and here: Eli was sitting on a throne, beside the road,
waiting-anxiously,
for his heart was trembling for the Coffer of God.
And when the man came to tell it in the town,
the whole town cried out;

14 Eli heard the sound of the outcry
and said:
What is this sound of panic?
The man quickly came and told it to Eli,

---

7 **yesterday [and] the day-before:** A biblical idiom for "in the past," "recently."

8 **This is the god . . . :** The Bible likes to portray non-Israelites' awe and terror of YHWH. **blow:** Lit., "stroke."

10 **thirty thousand:** Like many ancient troop and casualty numbers, this figure is certainly exaggerated.

12 **Binyaminite:** The tribe of Binyamin's territory was in the center of the country. **his garb torn and earth on his head:** Standard signs of mourning in ancient Israel.

15 —Now Eli was ninety-eight years old;
his eyes were set so that he could not see—

16 the man said to Eli:
I am the one who comes from the ranks,
I myself—from the ranks I fled today!
He said:
How did the matter go, my son?

17 The newsbringer answered;
he said:
Israel has fled before the Philistines,
and also there has been a great defeat of the people,
and also your two sons died, Hofni and Pin'has,
and the Coffer of God has been taken!

18 Now it was,
at his making mention of the Coffer of God,
that he fell from on the throne backward, alongside the gate,
and his neck was broken, so that he died,
for he was an old man, and heavy.
He had led Israel as judge for forty years.

19 Now his daughter-in-law, the wife of Pin'has, was pregnant, about
to give birth,
and when she heard the heard-report of the taking of the Coffer of
God
and of the death of her father-in-law and her husband,
she crouched and gave birth,
for her labor-pains had turned [suddenly] upon her.

20 At the time of her dying, those [women] standing over her spoke:
Do not be afraid, for you have given birth to a son!

21 But she did not answer, nor did she pay any mind,
but she called the lad I-Khavod/Where-is-Glory, saying:
Exiled is the glory from Israel!

---

15 **ninety-eight:** As with many other biblical numbers, this one fits a "perfect" pattern, as a (double!) multiple of seven. **set:** McCarter (1980) uses "fixed."

18 **he fell:** Eli. **heavy:** Heb. *kaved*, punning with the important term *kavod* ("glory") used both earlier (2:30) and later in the narrative (Auld 2011). **led Israel as judge:** As in the book of Judges, such a person has functions beyond court procedure (especially, and often, military leadership). **forty:** Another special number, familiar from the Flood and Sinai stories, and likewise used in Judges.

21 **I-Khavod:** The "I" is pronounced as "ee." Trad. English "Ichabod."

Chapter 5. *The Philistines and the Coffer:* As if to stress that the Philistines' victory in the previous chapter was the doing of God and not strictly the result of their own military prowess, the text follows the Coffer to the Philistine town of Ashdod, where it becomes clear that possessing it brings danger. In passages that express the Bible's usual contempt for pagan culture, the very statue of the Philistine god Dagon is mysteriously destroyed by the Coffer's presence, and the inhabitants, first, of Ashdod, and then of Gat, are stricken with hemorrhoids to the point that their "cry-for-help went up to the heavens" (v.12). Clearly, the Coffer will have to be returned to Israel.

◆

concerning the taking of the Coffer of God
and concerning her father-in-law and her husband.

22 She said:
Exiled is the glory from Israel,
for taken is the Coffer of God!

5:1 Now when the Philistines took the Coffer of God,
they brought it from Even Ha-Ezer to Ashdod.

2 Then the Philistines took the Coffer of God
and brought it to the House of Dagon,
and set it next to Dagon.

3 The Ashdodites started-early on the morrow,
but here was Dagon, fallen down on his face to the ground before
the Coffer of YHWH!
So they took Dagon and returned him to his place.

4 They started-early at daybreak, on the morrow,
but here was Dagon, fallen down on his face to the ground before
the Coffer of YHWH,
with Dagon's head and the two palms of his hands cut off, on the
threshold;
only Dagon['s torso] remained on him.

5 —Therefore the priests of Dagon and all who enter the House of
Dagon do not tread on the threshold of Dagon in Ashdod,
until this day.

6 And the hand of YHWH was heavy against the Ashdodites, and he
devastated them;
he struck them with tumors,
Ashdod and its territories.

5:1 **Ashdod:** One of the five chief Philistines cities, the others being Ashkelon, Gaza, Ekron, and Gat. All are on or near the Mediterranean coast.

2 **Dagon:** Pronounced *dah-GOHN*, a long-revered fertility god of the ancient Near East, here connected with the Philistines. While no material evidence of his worship among them has been found, the Philistines are known to have adapted quickly to local cultures.

4 **fallen down on his face:** In an obvious posture of submission. **head and . . . palms . . . cut off:** A known treatment of those defeated in war; see I Sam. 31:9–10, below, and the fate of the notorious Jezebel in II Kings 9:35.

5 **Therefore the priests . . . :** Like many biblical stories, this one has an etiological function, attempting to explain an old custom or name.

6 **devastated:** Some emend Heb. *sh-m-m* to *h-m-m*, "panicked," a key word in Chaps. 4–5. **tumors:** The written text has the nastier "hemorrhoids" (*tehorim*); scribal tradition has substituted the present "tumors" (*'ofalim*). These, and the mice-related plague (see 6:4), are viewed as a further divine curse on the Philistines for their possession of the Coffer. See Alter (1999) for a discussion of the long-standing confusion in the text; he cites an old interpretation that the passage actually refers to the bubonic plague.

Chapters 6:1–7:1. *Following the Coffer:* The theme of the Coffer's potency continues, with the Philistines making elaborate preparations, including sacrifices and reparations consisting (somewhat humorously, perhaps) of five golden hemorrhoids/tumors and five golden mice. The "priests and diviners" seem not entirely convinced that the disasters that have befallen them are the work of YHWH, and so devise a test: if the cart bearing the Coffer and the payment goes straight into Israelite territory, to Bet-Shemesh, it will confirm the intervention of the divine hand.

That same hand, however, guards the Coffer from being profaned even among the Israelites, and following a peeking incident in v.19, a great plague comes upon them. This theme of what Hamilton calls "the high voltage of the supersancta," the dangerous parameters of a divine object, will return in II Sam. 6:6–7, where it will lead to a man's immediate death. Here, the Coffer has to move from Bet-Shemesh to Kiryat-Ye'arim, a border town some miles to the northeast, where it will be guarded by a man "hallowed" for the purpose.

7   The men of Ashdod saw that [it was] thus,
     so they said:
     The Coffer of the God of Israel must not stay with us,
     for his hand is hard upon us and upon Dagon our god!

8   So they sent and gathered together all the Philistine overlords to them
     and said:
     What shall we do with the Coffer of the God of Israel?
     They said:
     To Gat let the Coffer of the God of Israel be removed!
     So they had the Coffer of the God of Israel removed [there].

9   But it was, after their removing it,
     that the hand of Yнwн was against the town, [causing] an
       exceedingly great panic;
     he struck the men of the town, from small to great,
     and tumors broke out on them.

10   So they sent off the Coffer of God to Ekron,
     but when the Coffer of God entered Ekron,
     the Ekronites cried out, saying:
     They have removed to us the Coffer of the God of Israel,
     to cause our death and our people's!

11   So they sent and gathered all the Philistine overlords
     and said:
     Send away the Coffer of the God of Israel, that it may return to its
       place,
     so that it does not cause our death and our people's!
     For there was a death panic all throughout the town;
     exceedingly heavy was the hand of God there.

12   Now the men who did not die were struck with tumors,
     and the town's cry-for-help went up to the heavens.

6:1   Now the Coffer of Yнwн was in the territory of the Philistines for
     seven months;

2   then the Philistines called for the priests and for the diviners, saying:
     What are we to do with the Coffer of Yнwн?
     Let us know how we can send it back to its place!

---

11 **overlords:** Heb. *seranim,* related to the English word "tyrants" through Greek.

6:1 **for seven months:** LXX adds "and mice invaded their fields." The Hebrew text is somewhat defective in this whole story of the plague.

3 They said:

If you wish to send back the Coffer of the God of Israel, do not
  send it back empty,

rather, make restitution, yes, restitution to him with a reparation-
  offering;

then you will be healed

and it will be made known to you why his hand has not turned
  aside from you.

4 They said:

What is the reparation-offering with which we are to make
  restitution to him?

They said:

[By] the number of Philistine overlords:

five gold tumors and five gold mice,

for one plague was upon all [of you] and upon your overlords.

5 You are to make images of your tumors and images of your mice
  that are bringing the land to ruin,

and you are to give honor to the God of Israel;

perhaps he will lighten his hand from upon you,

from upon your gods and from upon your land.

6 Why do you make your heart heavy-with-stubbornness,

as Egypt and Pharaoh made their heart heavy-with-stubbornness?

Was it not when he dealt wantonly with them that he sent them
  free and they went away?

7 So-now,

fetch and make ready a new wagon and two milch cows that have
  not yet yielded to a yoke;

you are to bind the cows to the wagon,

but you are to turn back their young behind them, indoors.

---

3 **reparation-offering:** Heb. *asham*, a biblical sacrifice, explained in Lev. 5 as financial restitution for wrong-doing, including unintentional actions.

6 **he dealt wantonly with them:** Referring to God, who treated Egypt thus in Exod. 10:2. The verb can also mean "abused."

7 **new wagon:** New since it is to be used for sacred purposes. **not yet yielded to a yoke:** The alliteration (Heb. *lo 'ala 'alehem 'ol*) highlights the importance of the idea: animals in the Israelite cultic system (see Num. 19:2) must be perfect, untainted by secular use (exactly like the wagon above).

8 Then you are to take the Coffer of Yhwh
and are to put it on the wagon,
and the gold objects with which you are making restitution to him
as a reparation-offering
you are to place in a pouch, to its side;
then you are to send it off, that it may go.

9 And look [well]:
if it goes up by way of its own territory, to Bet-Shemesh,
then he did us this great evil;
but if not,
we will know that his hand did not touch us—
an accident happened to us.

10 The men did thus:
they got two milk-yielding cows and bound them to the wagon,
but their young they shut up indoors.

11 And they placed the Coffer of Yhwh on the wagon,
along with the chest and the gold mice and the images of their
tumors.

12 And the cows went-straight on the road, on the road to Bet-
Shemesh:
on one path they went, going along [and] lowing,
but they did not turn right or left,
while the Philistine overlords were walking behind them, as far as
the territory of Bet-Shemesh.

13 Now Bet-Shemesh were harvesting the wheat harvest in the valley,
and they lifted up their eyes, and saw the Coffer,
and they rejoiced seeing it.

14 When the wagon came to the field of Yehoshua the Bet-Shimshite,
and came to a stop there
—there was a great stone there—
they split the wood of the wagon,
while the cows they offered up as an offering-up to Yhwh.

---

8 **pouch:** Following McCarter (1980).
9 **Bet-Shemesh:** Just east of the major Philistine cities.   **he:** God.   **evil:** Or "misfortune."
10, 12 **their young they shut up . . . lowing:** As Alter

(1999) notes, the cows are forced to pull the Coffer
against their natural inclination, which would be to
suckle their young. Perhaps this detail underscores
the power of the Coffer.

Chapter 7:2–17. *Beating Back the Philistine Threat:* The Philistine plague is only
the beginning of Israel's restoration. If that is to happen properly, however, two
things need to occur: Israel has to "put away the foreign gods" from their midst,
and Shemuel has to intercede with God. The order is significant as, once again,
military victory depends on the people's faithfulness to God, and not solely on
effective leadership. It is likewise telling that the site of the victory is the same at
which defeat had occurred in 4:1 and 5:1 (Willis). So a narrative that began with
"sighing" (v.2) ends with a restoration of territory, peace (v.14), and a description
of Shemuel's judgeship. All would seem to be well.

15 Now the Levites had brought down the Coffer of YHWH
and the pouch that was with it, in which the gold objects were,
and had put them on the great stone,
while the men of Bet-Shemesh had offered-up offerings-up
and sacrificed sacrifices on that day to YHWH.

16 When the five Philistine overlords saw [it],
they returned to Ekron on that day.

17 And these are the gold tumors with which the Philistines made
restitution as a reparation-offering to YHWH:
for Ashdod, one;
for Gaza, one;
for Ashkelon, one;
for Gat, one;
and for Ekron, one.

18 And the gold mice
[were by] the number of all the towns of the Philistines, by the five
overlords,
from fortified town as far as rural village,
as far as the great stone on which they deposited the Coffer of
YHWH;
until this day
[it is] in the Field of Yehoshua the Bet-Shimshite.

19 But he struck down some of the men of Bet-Shemesh,
for they had looked at the Coffer of YHWH;
he struck down of the people seventy men [and] fifty thousand
men.
So the people mourned,
for YHWH had struck down the people, a great striking-down.

20 The men of Bet-Shemesh said:
Who can stand in the presence of YHWH, this holy God?
And to whom may it be brought up away from us?

21 So they sent messengers to the settled-folk of Kiryat-Ye'arim,
saying:
The Philistines have returned the Coffer of YHWH;
go down, bring it up to you!

17 **Gat:** Pronounced *got;* trad. English "Gath."
18 **[were by] . . . :** Hebrew syntax difficult.
19 **for they had looked:** Not only does the harbor-

ing of the Coffer do damage to the Philistines, but Israelites as well have to be extremely cautious in its powerful presence.

7:1   So the men of Kiryat-Ye'arim came and brought up the Coffer of
          YHWH;
      they brought it to the house of Avinadav in Giv'a,
      and El'azar his son they hallowed to watch over the Coffer of
          YHWH.

2   Now it was,
      from the time of the Coffer staying in Kiryat-Ye'arim,
      —the years became many, so that they became twenty years—
      that the whole House of Israel sighed after YHWH.

3   So Shemuel said to the whole House of Israel, saying:
      If it is with all your heart that you are returning to YHWH,
      put away the foreign gods from your midst, including the Astartes;
      direct your hearts toward YHWH, and serve him alone,
      and he will rescue you from the hand of the Philistines!

4   And the Children of Israel put away the Baals and the Astartes,
      and served YHWH alone.

5   And Shemuel said:
      Gather all Israel to Mitzpa/Lookout, so that I may intercede on
          your behalf to YHWH.

6   They were gathered to Mitzpa;
      then they drew water and poured it out in the presence of YHWH,
      and fasted on that day.
      They declared there:
      We have sinned against YHWH!
      And Shemuel acted-as-judge for the Children of Israel at Mitzpa.

7   The Philistines heard that the Children of Israel were gathered at
          Mitzpa,
      so the Philistine overlords went up against Israel;
      and the Children of Israel heard, and they became afraid before the
          Philistines.

7:1   **Kiryat-Ye'arim . . . Giv'a:** Moving ever closer to
the Jerusalem area. Trad. English for these towns is
"Kiriath-Jearim" and "Gibeah." **hallowed:** Here
connoting "appointed."

3–4   **Astartes:** The main goddesses of Canaan, often
referred to in the Early Prophets as the objects of
the Israelites' religious backsliding. They may also
be terms used to denote local pagan gods in general
(McCarter 1980).

5   **Mitzpa:** Trad. English "Mizpah," roughly between
Rama and Bet-El—again, a central location in Israel.
It was the scene of important tribal assemblies in
Judges (see 11:11 and 20:1).

6   **poured it out:** Perhaps, since it is accompanied by
fasting, this is some kind of purification ceremony
(see McCarter 1980). **fasted:** A common ancient
response to national calamity, natural or otherwise.

8 The Children of Israel said to Shemuel:
Do not be silent from us, from crying out to Yhwh our God,
that he may deliver us from the hand of the Philistines!

9 So Shemuel took a suckling lamb and offered it up as an
offering-up, a whole-offering, to Yhwh,
and Shemuel cried out to Yhwh on behalf of Israel,
and Yhwh answered him.

10 Now it was, when Shemuel was offering up the offering-up,
that the Philistines approached for battle against Israel.
And Yhwh thundered with a great sound on that day against the
Philistines;
he panicked them, so that they were defeated before Israel.

11 The men of Israel went out from Mitzpa
and pursued the Philistines,
and they struck them as far as below Bet-Kar.

12 Then Shemuel took a stone and put it between Mitzpa and Shen/
The Tooth-Rock
and called its name Even Ha-Ezer/The Stone of Help;
he said:
Near here, Yhwh helped us!

13 So the Philistines were humbled;
they no longer came anymore into the territory of Israel,
and the hand of Yhwh was against the Philistines all the days of
Shemuel.

14 The towns that the Philistines had taken away from Israel returned
to Israel,
from Ekron as far as Gat,
while their territory Israel rescued from the hand of the Philistines.
Now there was peace between Israel and the Amorites.

15 Shemuel led Israel as judge all the days of his life:

---

9 **whole-offering:** This seems to be an explanation of the preceding "offering-up," although the two terms are basically synonymous, denoting a sacrifice that is wholly burnt and not eaten by the one who brings it.

11 **Bet-Kar:** Presumably near Mitzpa.

14 **Amorites:** A general name for the indigenous Canaanite population.

◆

16 he would go year after year,
    circling about Bet-El, Gilgal, and Mitzpa,
    and would act-as-judge over Israel near all these sacred-places;
17 then his return [would be] to Rama, for there was his house,
    and there he would act-as-judge over Israel.
    He built there an altar to YHWH.

---

16 **year after year:** This phrase brackets the Samuel story, given its occurrence in 1:3 (Alter 1999). **Gilgal:** Although several biblical towns bore this name, the one mentioned here probably refers to a major Israelite religious site that was associated with important national events; it lay somewhat northeast of Rama, possibly near Jericho.

PART II

THE REQUESTED KING

(I 8–15)

THE NEXT SECTION OF SAMUEL RECOUNTS TRADITIONS ABOUT THE ORIGINS OF the monarchy in ancient Israel and, in the process, sends a series of strong messages about how kingship was to be understood. Although framed partly as a portrait of Shemuel's own frustrations, the stories that follow paint a picture of an institution which was considered necessary, even divinely sanctioned, but which was also to be regarded with reservations. Thus, before the selection of the first king can proceed, the people have to be cautioned about the possible abuses of kingship.

Shemuel's warning in Chap. 8, which reads like an indictment of later kings' behavior, forms an ominous backdrop out of which monarchy is to emerge. Many cultures' traditions tend to stress from the outset a new king's military exploits and charisma, choosing to build the monarchy on a firm popular foundation, but in the Bible, a note of misgiving is sounded before anything else happens. In this sense, Shemuel is both the last of the old-time practitioners of theocracy (rule by God) and the first of the prophetic critics of human kingship.

One of the great literary characterizations in the Bible, Sha'ul, the "Requested-One," seems doomed from the beginning. Chosen only after Shemuel's dire warning in Chap. 8, and its reiteration and expansion in Chap. 12, Sha'ul must meander about, looking for lost she-asses, until he is "found" (Chaps. 9 and 10)— and even then he is only anointed after being brought out from having "hidden himself among the gear" (10:22). Such a beginning is hardly auspicious. On the other hand, he is physically imposing and a great warrior, and even, to the surprise of his people, can at times be seized by the spirit of God "like-a-prophet" (10 and 19). It is, ironically, this latter endowment, also possessed by several of the Judges, that will eventually prove too much for him to handle: God's spirit will depart, leaving an "evil spirit" in its wake (16:14).

Sha'ul's kingship is characterized by wrong turns and tragic misperceptions. Once past his initial success against the Ammonites, he runs afoul of both people and prophet. Although God in Chap. 8 had conceded the kingship by telling Shemuel to "hearken to their [the people's] voice," Sha'ul in short order jumps the gun thrice—by inappropriately offering sacrifices (Chap. 13), almost killing the heir to the throne (14), and disobeying God's command (15), tellingly "hearken[ing] to [the people's] voice" (15:24) instead of God's. In this disobedience, according to the text, lies the reason for his family's forfeiture of the throne, similar to the fate of many of the later kings of the Northern Kingdom of Israel, although their crime almost always was the practice of idolatry. This rather harsh judgment is perhaps appropriate given Sha'ul's key position as Israel's first king and the expectations raised by Shemuel and God, as well as by the book of Judges. Another perspective emphasized in our text is the ideology of writers who sought to justify David's claim to the throne, and who thus had to portray Sha'ul as deeply flawed. Or it may, once again, be an indication of a concept of monarchy that is highly cautionary (Machinist 2000). To paraphrase Brettler (1995), in selecting Sha'ul as the first occupant of Israel's throne God seems to be saying, "You want a king? All right, I'll give you a king!"

At the same time, it should not be ignored that the Bible's presentation of Sha'ul is not the portrait of a villain (for a black-and-white presentation of such a character, see, for instance, Judg. 9). This may be due to a desire to include northern traditions in the final text, but it may also be occasioned by the artistry of a great writer, who knows that tragedy is richer than melodrama. In any event, even at his lowest moments, Sha'ul somehow engages our sympathy.

The narrative in Chaps. 9–11 is at times confusing and contradictory. As McKenzie (2000) summarizes, we may be dealing here with what were originally three separate accounts—of Sha'ul seeking lost asses and being anointed by the prophet, of a public coronation ceremony, and of his acclamation as king following a stirring military victory. They bring with them a complex picture of Sha'ul as a man with undeniable talent, even charisma, but one who somehow fails to measure up to the task.

Chapter 8. *"Give Us a King!":* It is a consistent pattern in world literature that when a great leader grows old, he either makes a long final public speech or deals with the appointment of a successor. Sometimes it is both. Like his mentor Eli, however, Shemuel is stymied in his desire for continuity in leadership by the fact that his own sons do not "walk in his ways" (vv.3 and 5). In addition to the sons' corrupt behavior as judges, violating rules stated already in Exod. 23:8, the real need of the moment is for a strong military leader, as it was earlier in the book of Judges. So the Israelites request a king who will fight their wars (v.20) and thus enable them to be a self-respecting entity (vv.5 and 20, "like all the nations").

Shemuel takes their plea as a personal rejection, but God has to remind him in v.7 that it is really a rejection of God himself as Israel's only king. Up to this point in the narratives of the Bible, the concept of divine kingship had been implied, through wilderness wanderings, conquest, and settlement. Now it appears that

◆ 8:1 Now it was, when Shemuel had grown old,
that he made his sons judges for Israel

2 —the name of his firstborn son was Yoel,
and the name of his second, Aviyya—
judges in Be'er-Sheva.

3 But his sons did not walk in his ways:
they turned aside after profit,
and they took bribes and cast aside cases-for-justice.

4 So all the elders of Israel gathered together
and came to Shemuel at Rama;

5 they said to him:
Here, you have grown old,
and your sons have not walked in your ways.
So-now,
make us a king to lead us, like all the nations!

6 The matter was evil in the eyes of Shemuel, when they said:
Give us a king to lead us!
So Shemuel prayed to YHWH,

7 and YHWH said to Shemuel:
Hearken to the voice of the people in all that they say to you;
for it is not you they have rejected,
rather, it is me they have rejected from being king over them,

8 just like all the deeds that they have done
from the day I brought them up from Egypt until this day:
they have abandoned me
and served other gods!
Thus they are doing to you as well!

9 So-now, hearken to their voice.
However, you are to warn, yes, warn them;
you are to tell them the rule of the king who will reign as
king over them.

8:1 **Now it was . . . :** The opening here is reminiscent of another story regarding continuity, Yaakov's stealing of the birthright in Gen. 27.

2 **Yoel . . . Aviyya:** Pronounced *yo-AYL* and *ah-vee-YAH;* trad. English "Joel . . . Abijah." The names are ironically pious ones, meaning "YHWH Is God" and "Father [God] Is YHWH," respectively. **in Be'er-Sheva:** As if Shemuel, realizing their faults, puts considerable distance (fifty miles) between himself and them (Hamilton). Be'er-Sheva is trad. English "Beersheba."

3 **cast aside cases:** Or "swayed decisions, 'threw' cases" (Greenstein, written communication).

9, 11 **rule:** Or "practice." I have followed Tsevat here in reproducing a pun in the Hebrew, where the stem *sh-p-t* can refer to both legal decision-making and leadership.

this cannot continue, at least not without an earthly stand-in. But to make clear the writer's opinion that monarchy must be controlled, Shemuel delivers a pointed warning to the people (vv.11–18). It unmistakably implies that kings are takers—that verb punctuates the speech four times—who will disrupt the time-honored practices of village life and spend their own time accumulating personal power and wealth. The ominous warning at the end of the speech, that God will not listen to the Israelites' predictable outcry when they are oppressed by future kings, goes unheeded, as the people refuse (Heb. root *m-'-n*) to be swayed from their obsession with security, and in essence reject (*m-'-s*) God.

In many ways this chapter is a transitional one, and could either be grouped with the stories about Shemuel alone, as some scholars have done, or placed as the introduction to what follows, as here. It may be another example of the Bible's tendency, at least in its final form, to display overlapping structures.

10 And Shemuel related all the words of Yhwh
   to the people who were requesting a king from him;
11 he said:
   This will be the rule of the king who will reign as king over you:
   your sons he will take away,
      setting them in his chariotry and among his riders,
      so that they run ahead of his chariotry,
12 to make them commanders of thousands and commanders of
      fifties,
   to plow his plowing and harvest his harvest,
   and to make his battle weapons and his chariot weapons;
13 your daughters he will take away
   as ointment-mixers, as cooks, and as bakers;
14 your fields, your vineyards, and your olive-groves, the best ones, he
      will take away
   and give to his servants;
15 your sowing-seed and your vine-fruit he will tithe
   and give to his officers and to his servants;
16 your servants, your maids, your best young-men, and your
      donkeys, he will take away,
   that they may do his work;
17 your flock he will tithe,
   and you yourselves will be slaves for him.
18 And you will cry out on that day
   because of your king whom you have chosen for yourselves,
   but Yhwh will not answer you on that day!
19 But the people refused to hearken to Shemuel's voice; they said:
   No!
   Rather, let there be a king over us

---

12 **commanders of thousands . . . fifties:** Military titles which recur throughout the books of Samuel and Kings.
14 **servants:** Royal functionaries, like vassals (Alter 1999).
15 **tithe:** Tax a tenth of its value. I have been careful not to use the idiomatic English "take a tenth," so

as not to muddle the key repetition of "take" in this passage. **officers:** The term was long translated "eunuchs," but that meaning is probably not meant literally here.
16 **young-men:** Changing one letter, LXX reads "cattle."

Chapters 9–10. *The Choosing of Sha'ul:* Israel's first king stems from the tribe of Binyamin, whose territory straddled the north-south border region of the country but which was understood to be of northern provenance. Barely have we heard of Sha'ul's qualifications for the job—solid lineage and notable physical stature—when we are introduced to him in person as, of all things, a seeker of lost she-asses. Some, such as Sweeney (2012), would see this as having a "fairy-tale" quality; others, myself included, sense something more negative: a foreshadowing of the later, "lost" Sha'ul. The meandering tale brings the young man unwittingly into the orbit of Shemuel, who, to Sha'ul's utter surprise, hails him in v.20. Indeed, geographically, Sha'ul's wanderings form an oval that partly intersects the circle of Shemuel's activities in the book—another indication of the closeness of the two characters.

The text plays out the selection of the new king, lingering on scenes of searching, asking, and, finally, declaring God's will through the prophet. Whereas in the first part of the narrative Sha'ul wanders seemingly in vain, his journey ultimately bears out Shemuel's predictions (10:2–7) of signs from God and the leader-elect's transformation (note that the key verb "find" occurs some thirteen times in eighteen of the chapter's verses). Despite all of this, however, Sha'ul does not reveal the earthshaking result of his encounter with Shemuel to his family, much like Shimshon (Judg. 14) before him. That remains, for the moment, both God's secret and a sign of Sha'ul's modesty. Likewise, when Israel is summoned to Mitzpa, the new king, who is chosen publicly by lots, is initially nowhere to be found, and is discovered only eventually amid the gear. When he is finally acclaimed by the people in v.24, what follows is a note of doubt on their part (v.27). Sha'ul weathers this little storm, in contrast to his later capitulations, but we are left to wonder why the first Israelite monarch arises under such clouded circumstances and with such hesitation. It feels less like the classic prophetic rejection of God's mission, where a figure such as Moshe at least argues with God, and more like a hint of flawed character. This may be symbolically indicated by Shemuel's use of a flask of oil to anoint the new king, as opposed to the more usual horn (Miscall).

Sha'ul's strange experience of behaving like a prophet, which is predicted in vv.5–6 and recounted in 10–11, is unique in ancient Israel's description of its kings. The "mantic" form of prophecy referred to here, comprising extreme forms of behavior, is attested throughout the ages (see the cult of Dionysus in ancient Greece, and "speaking in tongues" still today). The experiences of "later prophets" such as Yesha'yahu (Isaiah) and Yirmeyahu (Jeremiah) tend to focus (although not exclusively) on the divine word, which is usually not obscure but, on the contrary, all too intelligible. In our chapter, one may wonder whether Sha'ul's gift indicates chosenness, as in the earlier cases of judges who are seized by God's spirit, or the possession of qualities that indicate a kind of instability that may not be appropriate for the sober needs of governing (Brueggemann 1990).

◆

20 so that we, we too may be like all the nations!
Let our king lead us
and go out before us
and fight battles for us!

21 Shemuel heard all the people's words,
and spoke them in the hearing of YHWH.

22 YHWH said to Shemuel:
Hearken to their voice:
you are to king them a king!
Then Shemuel said to the men of Israel:
Go back, each to his town.

9:1 Now there was a man of Binyamin—
his name was Kish son of Aviel son of Tzeror son of Bekhorat son
of Afiakh,
the son of a [Bin]yaminite man,
a mighty-man of value.

2 He had a son—his name was Sha'ul/Requested-One:
a youth, and goodly;
now there was no man of the Children of Israel goodlier than he,
from his shoulders and upward, taller than all the people.

3 And the she-asses of Kish, the father of Sha'ul, strayed,
so Kish said to Sha'ul his son:
Pray take with you one of the serving-lads
and arise, go, look for the she-asses!

4 They crossed the highlands of Efrayim and crossed the region of
Shalisha, but they did not find them;
and they crossed the region of Shaalim, but—nothing;
and they crossed the region of [Bin]yamin, but they did not find
them.

---

20 **battles for us:** Lit. "our battles," but the Hebrew verse has a kind of rhyme which I wanted to echo.
9:1 **a man:** Some ancient versions read "a certain man," paralleling the opening of the book. **Kish son of Aviel . . . :** Hamilton points out some similarities between this genealogy and Shemuel's, as if Sha'ul's choosing parallels the earlier one of Shemuel; both are requested of God. The pronunciations of names are: *keesh . . . ah-vee-AYL . . . tze-ROHR . . . beh-kho-*

RAHT . . . ah-fee-AKH. **value:** Heb. *hayil* in these books often means "valor," as a measure of military excellence, but here, as with some other biblical terms for "strength," it can refer to high economic status as well.
2 **Sha'ul:** Pronounced *shah-OOL;* trad. English "Saul." **goodly:** Or "good-looking."
3 **strayed:** Or "were lost."
4 **Shalisha . . . Shaalim:** The locations are unclear.

◆ 5   They had [just] come to the region of Tzuf,
     when Sha'ul said to his serving-lad who was with him:
     Go, let's turn back,
     lest my father stop [caring] about the she-asses and worry about us!

6   But he said to him:
     Here, there is a man of God in this town;
     the man is honored—
     all that he speaks comes, yes, comes-to-pass.
     Now let us go there;
     perhaps he can tell us about our way on which we have gone.

7   Sha'ul said to his lad:
     But here, if we go,
     what can we bring for the man?
     For the food is gone from our vessels,
     and there is no present to bring to the man of God.
     What is with us?

8   The lad answered Sha'ul further,
     he said:
     Here, I find in my hand a quarter weight of silver;
     I will give it to the man of God, so that he may tell us about
       our way.

9   —Formerly in Israel,
     thus would a man say when he went to inquire of God:
     Go, let us go to the seer.
     For a prophet today was formerly called a seer.—

10   Sha'ul said to his lad:
     Your words are good;
     Go, let's go!
     So they went to the town where the man of God was.

---

5 **They had [just] come . . . when:** Alter (1999) notes a similarly worded sequence in vv.5, 11, 14, and 27, as a series of "coincidences" leading to the commissioning of Sha'ul. **Tzuf:** Shemuel's home district. **Go, let's turn back:** If Alter (1999) is correct that a biblical character's first words are an important indication of his character, this is not a good sign.

6 **perhaps he can tell us about our way:** As indeed he does, though not with the limited perspective that Sha'ul is expecting.

7 **we bring:** Heb. *navi*, identical in sound with the word for "prophet."

8 **a quarter weight of silver:** Coins were not yet in use throughout much of the biblical period.

9 **prophet . . . seer:** The early audience of the book would presumably already have been puzzled by the use of the old term "seer" here.

◆ 11 They were going up the ascent to the town
when they found some girls coming out to draw water;
they said to them:
Is the seer in this place?

12 They answered them and said:
He is—here, ahead of you;
go quickly now,
for just now he has come to town,
for there is a sacrificial-meal today for the people at the sanctuary.

13 As soon as you come into the town, you will find him,
before he goes up to the sanctuary to eat
—for the people will not eat until his coming,
for he must bless the sacrifice;
after that, the invited-guests may eat.
So-now, go up;
as for him, this very day you will find him.

14 So they went up to the town.
They were coming into the midst of the town,
and here, Shemuel was coming out toward them
to go up to the sanctuary.

15 Now YHWH had bared Shemuel's ear
a day before Sha'ul's coming, saying:

16 Around this time tomorrow
I will send to you a man from the region of Binyamin;
you are to anoint him as *Nagid* over my people Israel.
He will deliver my people from the hand of the Philistines—
for I have seen my people,
for their cry has come to me!

17 Now when Shemuel saw Sha'ul,
YHWH declared to him:
Here is the man about whom I said to you:
This one shall keep rein on my people!

---

15 **bared . . . ear:** Probably parallel to the English expression "to bend the ear."

16 **Nagid:** Pronounced *nah-GEED;* others, "Prince," but the term does not mean a king's son. It probably indicates a military leader specially appointed by God, a "designate." Because of ongoing debate about the term, I have left it in Hebrew. **for I have**

seen . . . for their cry: Echoing God's redemptive speech at the Burning Bush (Exod. 3:7). Some render Heb. *ki,* "for," as "indeed."

17 **keep rein on:** The use of a verb (*'-tz-r*) that usually means "restrain" is puzzling. Many understand it as something like "govern."

◆ 18   Sha'ul approached Shemuel amid the gateway
and said:
Now tell me:
Where is the seer's house?

19   Shemuel answered Sha'ul,
he said:
I am the seer.
Go up ahead of me to the sanctuary;
you are to eat with me today.
Then I will send you off at daybreak,
and all that is in your heart I will tell you.

20   As for the she-asses that were straying from you three days ago,
do not take them to heart, for they have been found—
and to whom do all the riches of Israel belong,
is it not to you and to all your Father's House?

21   Sha'ul answered and said:
Am I not a Binyaminite, from the smallest of the tribes of Israel,
and my clan is the least of all the clans of the tribe of Binyamin?
So why do you speak to me according to these words?

22   Shemuel took Sha'ul and his serving-lad, brought them to the
dining-hall
and gave them a place at the head of the invited-guests
—they were about thirty men.

23   Shemuel said to the cook:
Give over the portion that I gave you,
about which I said to you: Set it [aside] with you.

24   So the cook raised the thigh and the fat-tail and offered it up and set
it before Sha'ul.
He said:
Here is what-is-reserved;
set it before you, eat,
since for this appointed-time it has been kept for you, saying:
I have invited the people.
So Sha'ul ate with Shemuel on that day.

---

21 **words:** Heb. singular. Alternatively, "this matter."

24 **thigh . . . fat-tail:** Parts of the sacrificial animal that were usually reserved for consumption by the priests. In this chapter, Sha'ul will briefly take on both priestly and prophetic roles. **saying: I have invited the people:** Or, with JPS, "when I said I was inviting the people." The Hebrew text appears garbled.

25 Then they went down from the sanctuary to the town,
and he spoke with Sha'ul on the roof.
26 . . . they started-early;
so it was, when dawn came up,
that Shemuel called Sha'ul to the roof, saying:
Arise, so that I may send you off.
Sha'ul arose, and the two of them went forth, he and Shemuel,
outside.
27 They were going down, at the edge of the town,
when Shemuel said to Sha'ul:
Speak to the lad, that he may cross over ahead of us,
—and he crossed over—
but you stop at once,
that I may have you hear the word of God.
10:1 And Shemuel took a flask of oil and poured it on his head and
kissed him,
and he said:
Is it not [so] that YHWH has anointed you over his inheritance as
Nagid?
2 When you go today from me,
you will find two men by Rahel's burial-place in the territory of
Binyamin, at Tzeltzah;
they will say to you:
They are found, the she-asses that you went to look for!
Here, your father has left off the matter of the she-asses,
but he is worried about you, saying:
What should I do about my son?
3 So you are to move on from there, and further,
and you are to come to the Oak of Tavor;
they will find you, three men going up to [worship] God at Bet-El—
one carrying three kids,
one carrying three rounds of bread,
and one carrying a skin of wine.

25–26 **roof . . . :** The Hebrew is difficult here; once again, a chunk of text appears to be missing.
10:1 **his inheritance:** The people of Israel.
2 **Rahel's burial-place . . . Tzeltzah:** The location of the traditional tomb of Rachel in Bethlehem, built in medieval times, has long been felt to be incorrectly identified. It most probably stood near Kiryat-Ye'arim, northwest of Jerusalem. Alternatively, *Tzeltzah* may be some kind of description—"rushing" or "limping"—and not a place name. The ancient versions are confused.

♦ 4   They will ask you after [your] welfare,
and they will give you two bread-loaves;
you are to take them from their hand.

5   After that, you will come to Giv'at Elohim/The Hill of God, where
the Philistine garrison is;
and it will be, when you come there, to the town,
that you will encounter a band of prophets coming down from the
sanctuary,
and ahead of them, lyre and timbrel, flute and harp,
and they will be ranting-in-prophecy.

6   Now the rushing-spirit of YHWH will advance upon you,
so that you will rant-like-a-prophet with them,
and you will be changed into another man.

7   And it will be,
when these signs come-to-pass for you,
do for yourself whatever your hand finds [to do]!
For God is with you.

8   Then you are to go down ahead of me, to Gilgal,
and here, I will be going down to you to offer up offerings-up and
to sacrifice sacrifices of *shalom*.
For seven days you are to tarry, until I come to you;
then I will make known to you what you are to do.

9   Now it was,
when he faced about to go from Shemuel,
that God changed in him another heart,
and all these signs came-to-pass on that day.

10 They came there, to Giv'a,
and here, a band of prophets, [coming] to meet him!
The rushing-spirit of God advanced upon him,
and he ranted-like-a-prophet in their midst.

---

5 **garrison:** Others, "prefect." **ranting-in-prophecy:**
The verb "to prophesy," conventionally thought of
as predicting the future but really encompassing
speaking the word of God more generally, can also
have the earlier meaning of certain forms of ecstatic
religious behavior (see Commentary).
6 **rushing-spirit:** Heb. *ru'ah* can mean either "spirit"
or "wind," so the concept might be seen as a spiritual one with physical force.

7 **do for yourself whatever . . . :** I.e., follow your
impulse, since it's from God (McCarter 1980).
9 **changed in him another heart:** That is, altered his
mental and religious state, as if he were another person. This kind of consciousness change is familiar to
many cultures and periods down to the present.

◆ 11 It was:
all who knew him from yesterday [and] the day-before,
when they saw
that here, with the prophets he was ranting-like-a-prophet,
the people said, each one to his neighbor:
What, now, has come over the son of Kish?
Is Sha'ul too among the prophets?

12 And a man from there spoke up and said:
But who is their father?
Therefore it became a proverb:
Is Sha'ul too among the prophets?

13 He finished ranting-like-a-prophet, and came to the sanctuary.

14 Now Sha'ul's uncle said to him and to his serving-lad:
Where did you go?
He said:
To look for the she-asses.
And when we saw that [they were] not [there],
we came to Shemuel.

15 Sha'ul's uncle said:
Pray tell me:
What did Shemuel say to you?

16 Sha'ul said to his uncle:
He told, yes, told us
that the she-asses had been found.
But as for the matter of the kingship,
he did not tell him what Shemuel had said.

17 Now Shemuel summoned the people to YHWH, at Mitzpa.

18 He said to the Children of Israel:
Thus says YHWH, the God of Israel:
I myself brought Israel up from Egypt,
I rescued you from the hand of Egypt and from the hand of all the
kingdoms that were oppressing you.

---

11 **son of Kish:** Referring to a person simply as someone's son, without the person's own given name, is
considered an insult in the Bible.
12 **But who is their father?:** A strange question, but in
perhaps looking for the prophets' leader ("father"),
the text raises the larger leadership question of the
book.

16 **he did not tell him:** The reason is unclear; is it out
of modesty or inner uncertainty?
17 **Mitzpa:** Since this town did not become important
until the sixth century B.C.E., it is possible that the
material has been reworked (McKenzie 2000).

Chapter 11. *Sha'ul the Victorious:* Immediately after Sha'ul's acclamation, his leadership is put to the test. A fierce Ammonite commander threatens an Israelite town lying to the north of his territory. While in our text his words seem ominous enough, the chapter as it appears in one of the Dead Sea Scroll manuscripts of Samuel—4QS^a, probably an earlier and fuller version than MT—shows that he is a man of his word. The restored passage reads,

> Now Nahash, king of the Ammonites, had been grievously oppressing
> the Gadites and the Re'uvenites.
> He would gouge out the right eye of each of them, and would not grant
> Israel a deliverer.
> No one was left of the Israelites across the Jordan whose right eye
> Nahash, king of the Ammonites, had not gouged out.
> But there were seven thousand men who had escaped from the
> Ammonites and had entered Yavesh-Gil'ad.

In MT that has come down to us, apparently a scribe's eye wandered from the original first "Yavesh-Gil'ad" to the second, skipping several sentences.

Upon hearing the news of the Ammonite danger, Sha'ul, in contrast to his weeping countrymen, is seized with the spirit of God and, in a reminder of the horrifying concubine story of Judg. 19–20, cuts up his oxen and sends their pieces around the country. The tribes rise up "as one man," themselves gripped by a "terror of God" (an emotional state which elsewhere is usually viewed as a negative), and vanquish the brutal enemy.

Sha'ul is gracious in victory, refusing to kill those of his countrymen who had earlier doubted his abilities. In a passage that may come from an alternate source, his leadership is celebrated ("renewed") at Gilgal as the chapter draws to a close. What began with a threat of mutilation ends with "joy" (v.15) over the strength of the newfound leader.

19 But you, today: you have rejected your God,
the one delivering you from all your trials and your troubles!
You said to him:
No, rather, a king make over us!
So-now,
station yourselves in the presence of YHWH, by your tribes, by your
families.

20 So Shemuel brought near each of the tribes of Israel,
and the tribe of Binyamin was captured-by-lot.

21 Then he brought near the tribe of Binyamin by its clans,
and the Matrite clan was captured-by-lot;
then Sha'ul son of Kish was captured-by-lot.
But when they looked for him, he was not to be found.

22 So they inquired further of YHWH:
Has any other man come here?
YHWH said:
Here, he has hidden himself among the gear!

23 They ran and fetched him from there
and he stood amid the people,
and he was taller than all the people, from his shoulders and
upward.

24 Then Shemuel said to all the people:
Do you see whom YHWH has chosen?
Indeed, there is none like him among all the people!
And all the people shouted;
they proclaimed: May the king live!

25 And Shemuel spoke to the people, the rule of kingship,
and wrote it in a record,
and put it in the presence of YHWH.
Then Shemuel sent all the people off, each one to his house.

19 **your trials and your troubles:** Heb. *ra'otekhem ve-tzarotekhem.* **station yourselves:** I.e., present yourselves.
20 **captured-by-lot:** As several scholars point out, everywhere else in the Bible this procedure is used to determine the identity of a criminal. The verb (*l-k-d*) is more commonly used to describe the con-quest of territory in the Bible. See also Josh. 7:15–18 and I Sam. 14:41.
22 **the gear:** Others, "the baggage." How are we to take the behavior of the king-elect here—as humble, or as something else?
25 **record:** Heb. *sefer,* a written document. It only comes to mean "book" centuries later.

26 And Sha'ul too went to his house at Giv'a,
and there went with him the valiant ones
whose heart God had touched.

27 Now some base fellows said:
How can this one deliver us?
So they despised him
and did not bring him a gift.
But he was like one silent.

11:1 Now Nahash/Snake the Ammonite went up
and encamped against Yavesh-Gil'ad.
All the men of Yavesh said to Nahash:
Cut a covenant with us, and we will serve you!

2 But Nahash the Ammonite said to them:
On *this* [condition] I will cut [a covenant] with you—
on [condition of] gouging out every one of your right eyes!
Thus will I make it a disgrace upon all Israel!

3 The elders of Yavesh said to him:
Leave us be for seven days;
we wish to send messengers throughout all the territory of Israel.
And if there is no deliverer for us,
we will go out [to surrender] to you.

4 The messengers came to the Hill of Sha'ul
and spoke the words in the hearing of the people,
and all the people lifted up their voice and wept.

5 Now here, when Sha'ul came after the cattle, from the open-field,
Sha'ul said:
What [ails] the people, that they are weeping?
They related to him the words of the men of Yavesh.

6 And the rushing-spirit of God advanced upon Sha'ul when he heard
these words,
and his anger flared up exceedingly;

27 **he was like one silent:** McCarter (1980) emends *vayhi ke-maharish* to *vayhi kemo hodesh* ("Now it was about a month later"), thus connecting the phrase to 11:1.

11:1 **Ammonite:** The Ammonites occupied the territory east of the Jordan, between the Dead Sea and the Sea of Galilee (biblical Kinneret). **Yavesh-Gil'ad:** Trad. English "Jabesh Gilead"; on the east bank of the Jordan and so bordering on Ammonite lands. **Cut a covenant:** Make a treaty; the "cutting" part may refer to an accompanying animal sacrifice (see Gen. 15, and elsewhere in the ancient Near East).

2 **On *this* [condition]:** Following Driver.

3 **Leave us be:** Elsewhere I use "to slack" for Heb. *r-p-h,* so a colloquial equivalent would be "Cut us some slack." **[to surrender]:** Again following Driver.

7 he took a brace of cattle and chopped it up,
and he sent it off throughout all the territory of Israel by the hand
of messengers, saying:
Whoever does not go out [to war] after Sha'ul and after Shemuel,
thus shall be done to his cattle!
And a terror of Yhwh fell upon the people,
so that they went out as one man.

8 He counted them [for war] at Bezek:
the Children of Israel totaled three hundred thousand,
while the men of Judah were thirty thousand.

9 Then he said to the messengers who came:
Thus you are to say to the men of Yavesh-Gil'ad:
Tomorrow there will be victory for you, when the sun is hot!
The messengers came
and told it to the men of Yavesh,
and they rejoiced.

10 And the men of Yavesh said:
Tomorrow we will go out to you,
and you may do with us whatever is good in your eyes.

11 Now it was on the morrow
that Sha'ul put the fighting-people into three companies;
they entered the midst of the camp at the daybreak watch
and struck Ammon until the hot-part of the day.
And it was that those [who were] left—they were scattered,
so that there were not left among them two together.

12 The people said to Shemuel:
Who was it that said: Shall Sha'ul be king over us?
Give over the men, that we may put them to death!

13 But Sha'ul said:
No one is to be put to death on this day,
for today Yhwh has wrought victory in Israel!

---

7 **terror of Yhwh:** Parallel to the "panic" so often seen among Israel's enemies in the Bible, although here it refers to the Israelites themselves (McCarter 1980).

8 **Bezek:** On the west bank of the Jordan. **three hundred thousand:** See note to 4:10, above.

9 **victory:** Or "deliverance."

Chapter 12. *Shemuel's Summation:* In Chap. 8 we observed God, through Shemuel, expressing considerable reservations about the institution of kingship. Here, after the victory against the Ammonites, God reaffirms the monarchy, but in the broader context of Israelite history from Egypt to the present. After Shemuel establishes his own credibility by demonstrating that he, unlike future kings, has "taken" nothing from any Israelite, he launches into a long public oration which sounds rather like one of the farewell speeches we have come to expect at the end of biblical books (see the final chapters of both Deuteronomy and Joshua). The message is a simple one, thematically reminiscent of those earlier texts: if the Israelites will serve YHWH alone, forsaking the local gods, then all will be well; but if they "revolt," both they and their king will be lost. The speech, despite its length, is able to remain on focus by sprinkling a specific vocabulary throughout. Four words occur in varying repetitions: "sin," "evil," and "request," which denote Israel's need for a king out of weakness, and "serve," which comes to indicate their desired loyalty to YHWH. As in Chap. 8, the speech ends with a warning.

14 Shemuel said to the people:
Come, let us go to Gilgal,
and let us renew the kingship there!

15 So all the people went to Gilgal
and made Sha'ul king there, in the presence of Yhwh at Gilgal.
They sacrificed sacrifices of *shalom* there, in the presence of Yhwh,
and there Sha'ul and all the men of Israel rejoiced exceedingly.

12:1 Shemuel said to all Israel:
Here, I have hearkened to your voice, in all that you have said
to me:
I have set-a-king as king over you.

2 So-now,
here is the king, going about before you,
but I, I have grown old, and I have grown hoary,
and as for my sons—here they are with you;
but I, I have gone about before you from my youth until this day.

3 Here I am:
testify against me, before Yhwh and before his anointed one:
Whose ox have I taken? Whose donkey have I taken?
Whom have I defrauded? Whom have I crushed?
And from whose hand have I taken a ransom, that I shut my eyes
with it?
—I will return them to you!

4 They said:
You have not defrauded us, you have not oppressed us,
you have not taken a thing from anyone's hand!

5 He said to them:
Yhwh is witness before you and his anointed one is a witness
this day

---

14 **Gilgal:** An important cultic site; in Joshua, the Israelite men had been circumcised there, and the location was also associated with the "Dwelling" (Tabernacle). **renew the kingship:** Again, some see this piece of text as an alternate account of Sha'ul's elevation.

12:1 **set-a-king as king:** Heb. *va-yamlikh . . . melekh*, not an unusual construction in Hebrew.

3 **Here I am . . . :** This verse follows a pattern of legal declaration, familiar from several places in Deuteronomy (Fishbane). **taken:** The key verb from Shemuel's warning speech in Chap. 8 returns (see Garsiel 1985). **crushed:** Or "mistreated, oppressed." **ransom:** Heb. *kofer;* a related concept is that of a bribe (Heb. *shohad*). **that I shut my eyes with it:** MT is confusing; McCarter (1980), following LXX, emends to "or a pair of shoes? Accuse me"—reflecting Ruth 4:7 and an old custom of circumventing legal conventions. JPS renders the phrase "to look the other way."

5 **Witness!:** The verbatim repeating of part of a question is the biblical way to say "yes" (see Greenstein 1989).

◆

        that you have not found a thing in my hand!
        They said:
        Witness!

6   Shemuel said to the people:
        [It is] Yнwн
        who wrought-deeds with Moshe and with Aharon,
        and who brought your fathers up from the land of Egypt.

7   So-now,
        stand fast, that I may plead-in-judgment with you in the presence of
           Yнwн
        concerning all of Yнwн's righteous-acts that he has wrought with
           you and with your fathers.

8   When Yaakov came to Egypt,
        and your fathers cried out to Yнwн,
        Yнwн sent Moshe and Aharon;
        they brought your fathers out of Egypt and settled them in this
           place.

9   But they forgot Yнwн their God,
        so he sold them into the hand of Sisera, commander of the armed-
           forces of Hatzor,
        into the hand of the Philistines,
        and into the hand of the king of Moav,
        so that they waged battle against them.

10 Then they cried out to Yнwн,
        they said: We have sinned!
        For we have abandoned Yнwн and served the Baals and the
           Astartes!
        So-now, rescue us from the hand of our enemies, and we will
           serve you!

11 So Yнwн sent Yerub-baal, and Bedan, and Yiftah, and Shemuel,
        and rescued you from the hand of your enemies round about,
        so that you dwelt in security.

---

6 **[It is] Yнwн:** LXX reads "Yнwн is a witness."

8 **Moshe and Aharon:** Trad. English "Moses and Aaron."

9 **Sisera . . . Hatzor:** See Judg. 4–5. **Moav:** Trad. English "Moab."

11 **Yerub-baal . . . :** Yerub-baal is Gideon (see Judg. 7:1), while the identity of "Bedan" remains a textual mystery. LXX reads it as "Barak," from Judg. 4, while Kimhi takes it as an abbreviation for *ben Dan*, "son of Dan," namely Shimshon.

12   But when you saw that Nahash king of the Children of Ammon
      was coming against you,
  you said to me:
  No, rather, a king must reign-as-king over us
  —but Yhwh your God is your king!

13   So-now,
  here is the king whom you have chosen, whom you have requested;
  here, Yhwh has placed a king over you.

14   If you hold Yhwh in awe,
  and serve him and hearken to his voice,
  and do not revolt against Yhwh's order,
  and both you and the king who reigns as king over you [follow]
      after Yhwh your God . . . !

15   But if you do not hearken to the voice of Yhwh,
  and revolt against Yhwh's order,
  then Yhwh's hand will be against you [as it was] against your
      fathers.

16   Even now, stand fast and see this great thing
  that Yhwh is about to do before your eyes:

17   Is it not the wheat cutting today?
  I will call out to Yhwh,
  so that he gives forth thunder-sounds and rain—
  then know and take note
  that your evil is great that you have done in Yhwh's eyes
  by requesting yourselves a king!

18   So Shemuel called out to Yhwh,
  and Yhwh gave forth thunder-sounds and rain on that day.
  And all the people [stood] in exceedingly great fear of Yhwh and of
      Shemuel.

19   Then all the people said to Shemuel:
  Intercede on behalf of your servants to Yhwh your God, so that
      we do not die,

---

13 **requested:** The same verb (*sh-'-l*) previously used in reference to Shemuel here properly connected to Sha'ul's name.

15 **order:** Literally, "mouth."

16 **stand fast and see this great thing / that Yhwh is about to do:** Recalling Moshe's words at the Reed Sea, "Stand fast and see / Yhwh's deliverance which he will work for you today" (Exod. 14:13).

17 **wheat cutting . . . thunder-sounds:** The wheat harvest typically occurred in late May or early June, so here, in the dry season, there could be no question of naturally occurring rain. **know and take note:** The use of these two imperative verbs in sequence is peculiar to Samuel, Kings, and Jeremiah. I follow the translation of Cogan (2001) in I Kings.

Chapter 13. *Sha'ul Rejected I:* The narrative has given us almost no time to savor Sha'ul's victory in Chap. 11. It immediately provides an example of exactly what Shemuel had just warned against. In the midst of a back-and-forth struggle, with the Israelites attacking the Philistines in vv.2–4 and the Philistines retaliating from v.5 on, Sha'ul seeks to rally the troops again, with help anticipated from Shemuel. When the prophet is late in arriving, the king jumps the gun and offers the requisite sacrifices himself. He apparently is worried that he cannot win the battle without placating God, and he is additionally concerned about the bleeding away of the soldiers. When Shemuel finally shows up, his response to Sha'ul's behavior is to in essence fire the king and indicate that another will take his place. Curiously, we get no reaction from Sha'ul, who goes back to mustering the troops, and the text sees fit to concentrate on details regarding the Philistines' technological superiority.

◆

         for we have added evil to all our sins
         by requesting ourselves a king!

20   Shemuel said to the people:
         Do not be afraid.
         You have done all this evil,
         but do not turn aside from [following] after YHWH;
         you are to serve YHWH God with all your heart!

21   You are not to turn aside
         after the confusion-gods who will not avail, who will not prevail,
         for they are confusion!

22   For YHWH will not forsake his people
         because of his great name;
         for YHWH has ventured to make you into a people for him.

23   I too—
         [Heaven] forbid for me, sinning against YHWH,
         by holding back from interceding on your behalf!
         I will instruct you in the good and right way.

24   Only: hold YHWH in awe:
         you are to serve him in truth with all your heart,
         for see how he does-great-things with you!

25   But if you do evil, yes, evil,
         both you and your king will be swept away!

13:1   Sha'ul [was] _____ years old upon his becoming king,
         and for _____ years he reigned as king over Israel.

2   And Sha'ul chose for himself three thousand [men] from Israel;
         there were two thousand with Sha'ul at Mikhmas and at the
            highlands of Bet-El
         and a thousand were with Yonatan at the Hill of Binyamin,
         while the rest of the people he sent away, each one to his tent.

---

21 **after:** Omitting the word "because" which occurs in the Hebrew immediately before this, along with LXX. **avail . . . prevail:** Heb. *yo'ilu . . . yatzilu.* I normally translate *n-tz-l* (from which the second verb is derived) as "rescue." **confusion:** Heb. *tohu,* related to the chaos at the beginning of Creation in Gen. 1:2 (where Heb. *tohu va-vohu* can be rendered "Confusion and Chaos").

13:1 **___ years old . . . ___ years:** The MT is missing the first number here, and uses "two years" (of Sha'ul's reign) for what may have been a more reasonable number. Probably the whole phrase was inserted

later to make Sha'ul's kingship follow the usual Deuteronomistic description, but the specifics were lost or omitted.

2 **Mikhmas:** Between Mitzpa and Gilgal, hence north of Rama. **Bet-El:** An important biblical town lying between Shekhem (today's Nablus) and Jerusalem. **Yonatan:** Pronounced *yo-nah-TAHN;* trad. English "Jonathan." Sha'ul's son and heir, sometimes spelled "Yehonatan" in the text. The name means "YHWH Gives/Has Given." **Hill of Binyamin:** Or "Giv'a [Gibeah] of Binyamin."

◆ 3 And Yonatan struck the garrison of the Philistines that was in Geva,
and the Philistines heard [about it].
And Sha'ul sounded the *shofar* throughout all the land, saying:
Let the Hebrews hearken!

4 All Israel did hearken, saying:
Sha'ul has struck the garrison of the Philistines,
and also Israel reeks to the Philistines!
And the people were summoned after Sha'ul, to Gilgal.

5 Now the Philistines had gathered to do battle with Israel,
three thousand chariots and six thousand horsemen,
and fighting-people like the sand that is on the shore of the sea in
abundance;
they came up and encamped at Mikhmas, east of Bet-Aven.

6 Now the men of Israel saw that they were in [dire] straits,
for the fighting-people were pressed
—the people hid themselves
in caves, in holes, in boulder-cracks,
in tunnels, and in cisterns,

7 while [some] Hebrews crossed the Jordan, into the region of Gad
and Gil'ad.
Now Sha'ul was still in Gilgal, with all the fighting-people
trembling behind him.

8 And he waited for seven days,
for the appointed-time that Shemuel had [set],
but Shemuel did not come to Gilgal,
and the people began to scatter from him.

9 So Sha'ul said:
Bring close to me the offering-up and the *shalom*-offerings!
And he offered up the offering-up.

10 But then it was,
when he had finished offering up the offering-up,
that here: Shemuel came.
Sha'ul went out to meet him, to bless him [in greeting].

---

4 **reeks:** An oft-used biblical expression to describe
odious behavior and hence reputation (see also
II Sam. 10:6, 16:21).

11　But Shemuel said:
　　What have you done?
　　Sha'ul said:
　　When I saw that the fighting-people were scattering from me,
　　—and you, you did not come within the appointed days—
　　and the Philistines were gathering at Mikhmas,

12　I said [to myself]:
　　Now the Philistines will come down against me at Gilgal,
　　yet YHWH's face I have not soothed!
　　So I forced myself,
　　and offered up the offering-up.

13　Shemuel said to Sha'ul:
　　You have acted-foolishly!
　　If you had kept the command of YHWH your God which he
　　　　commanded you,
　　indeed now, YHWH would have established your kingship over
　　　　Israel for the ages.

14　But now, your kingship will not stand!
　　YHWH seeks for himself a man after his own heart,
　　so that YHWH may commission him as *Nagid* over his people,
　　for you have not kept what YHWH commanded you!

15　Shemuel arose and went up from Gilgal toward the Hill of
　　　　Binyamin,
　　while Sha'ul counted the fighting-people who were found with him
　　　　[for war],
　　about six hundred men.

16　Now Sha'ul and Yonatan his son and all the people who were found
　　　　with them were situated on the Hill of Binyamin,
　　while the Philistines were encamped at Mikhmas.

17　And the ruinbringers went out of the Philistines' camp in three
　　　　companies:
　　one company facing toward the road to Ofra, toward the Region of
　　　　the Jackal,

---

12 **YHWH's face I have not soothed:** I have not
appeased him.　　17 **ruinbringers:** Raiders.

Chapter 14. *Yonatan the Hero; Sha'ul Errs Again:* In strange contrast to the rejection of Sha'ul and his dynasty that has just occurred, Yonatan (full name: Yehonatan), the heir to the throne, proves his mettle by single-handedly killing twenty Philistines. This leads to what looks to be a general rout of the Philistines by his father. In the heat of battle, Sha'ul prohibits any eating until sunset, an oath which, however, is not heard by Yonatan, who unwittingly violates it. To this is added the Israelites' own breaking of rules, as they eat the animals they have slain along with the blood (a universal, not only Israelite, prohibition according to Gen. 9:4). All is forgiven with the subsequent sacrifice, but Yonatan has to be rescued from his father's wrath by the Israelites. Once again, Sha'ul has somehow misfired as king, this time within his own family.

The chapter ends with two summaries of Sha'ul's reign. Vv.47–48 describe him as the great warrior who rescued Israel from six different enemies. Vv.49–52 contain a typical summary list, in this case of Sha'ul's immediate family members and the name of his commanding general (Avner), along with a note of the ongoing struggle against the Philistines.

18 one company facing the road to Bet-Horon,
 and one company facing the road of the border which looks out
  over the Ravine of the Hyena, in the wilderness.

19 —Now no metal worker could be found throughout all the land of
  Israel,
 for the Philistines had said [to themselves]:
 Lest the Hebrews make swords or spears!

20 So all Israel had to go down to the Philistines,
 for each one to have his plowshare, his mattock, his ax, and his
  sickle forged.

21 And the sharpening-charge was a *pim* for plowshares and for
  mattocks,
 for three-pronged [forks] and for axes,
 and for setting the goads.

22 So it was on the day of the battle
 that there was not to be found sword or spear in the hand of all the
  fighting-people who were with Sha'ul and Yonatan,
 but they were found for Sha'ul and for Yonatan his son.

23 And the Philistine garrison went out to the Pass of Mikhmas.

14:1 Now one day it was
 that Yonatan son of Sha'ul said to the serving-lad, his weapons
  bearer:
 Come, let's cross over to the Philistines' garrison,
 the one that is across, over there!
 But his father he did not tell.

2 Now Sha'ul was staying at the edge of Geva,
 beneath the Pomegranate [Rock] that is in the Migron;
 and the fighting-people that were with him were about six
  hundred men,

3 while Ahiyya son of Ahituv, brother of I-Khavod, son of Pin'has
  son of Eli, priest of YHWH at Shilo, was wearing the *efod*.
 But the people did not know that Yonatan had gone.

---

20 **sickle:** Following LXX; MT seems to repeat "plow-share."

21 ***pim:*** Pronounced *peem*. Stone weights with the inscription *p-y-m* have been found by archaeologists in Israel. They were two-thirds of a silver shekel in value.

14:2 **the Migron:** Or "the threshing floor" (McCarter 1980), a place where ancient Near Eastern rulers often sat, near the city gate (see I Kings 22:10). If the name derives from *n-g-r,* "gush," it possibly refers to Wadi es-Swenit, not too far from Giv'a; the "Pomegranate" would then be the cave referred to in Judg. 20:45–47 (Arnold/Williamson).

3 **while Ahiyya . . . :** Why this detail? See v.18 below.

4 Now between the gorge-crossings that Yonatan sought to cross, to
  [get to] the Philistines' garrison,
  was a tooth-shaped cliff over here and a tooth-shaped cliff over
    there:
  the name of the one was Botzetz, and the name of the other was
    Senne.

5 The one tooth was located on the north, in front of Mikhmas,
  while the other was on the south, in front of Geva.

6 Yehonatan said to the lad, his weapons bearer:
  Come, let's cross over to the garrison of these Foreskinned Ones!
  Perhaps YHWH will act on our behalf,
  for there is nothing to constrain YHWH from delivering by the many
    or by the few!

7 His weapons bearer said to him:
  Do whatever your heart inclines to—
  here, I am with you, according to your heart!

8 Yehonatan said:
  Here, we are crossing over to the men,
  and we will be revealing ourselves to them;

9 if they say thus to us:
  Halt, until we get close to you—
  we will stop in our place, and will not go up against them.

10 But if they say thus:
  Come up to us—
  then we will go up,
  for YHWH will have given them into our hand,
  and this will be the sign for us.

11 So the two of them revealed themselves to the Philistines' garrison,
  and the Philistines said:
  Here, Hebrews are coming out of the holes where they were hiding
    themselves!

---

4 **Botzetz . . . Senne:** Pronounced *bo-TZAYTZ* and *SEN-neh;* possibly meaning "twinkler" and "thorn."
6 **Yehonatan:** An alternate spelling of "Yonatan," with no change in meaning. **Foreskinned Ones:** The Israelites' characterization of the Philistines, who were not circumcised. The term was already used in Judges. **for there is nothing to constrain . . . :** Namely, God works through the few as well as through the many.
7 **your heart inclines to:** Following LXX; MT has "your heart. Incline . . ." The idiom itself means "as you desire."

12   And the men of the garrison yelled out to Yonatan and to his
       weapons bearer,
     and said:
     Come up to us,
     and we will show you something!
     Yonatan said to his weapons bearer:
     Come up behind me,
     for YHWH has given them into the hand of Israel!

13   So Yonatan climbed up by his hands and by his feet, with his
       weapons bearer behind him.
     And they fell before Yonatan, while his weapons bearer dispatched
       them behind him.

14   Now the first striking-down that Yonatan and his weapons bearer
       struck was some twenty men,
     over about half a furrow for a brace [of oxen plowing] in a field.

15   And there was trembling in the camp, out in the open-field, and
       among all the fighting-people
     —the garrison and the ruinbringers fell-to-trembling, they too, and
       the earth shuddered;
     it was a trembling of God.

16   Now Sha'ul's watchmen saw at the Hill of Binyamin,
     and here, the throng was swaying, going and coming back there.

17   And Sha'ul said to the people who were with him:
     Pray count and see who has gone out from us!
     They counted, and here: Yonatan and his weapons bearer were not
       [there].

18   Sha'ul said to Ahiyya:
     Bring close the Coffer of God
     —for the Coffer of God was at that time with the Children of
       Israel.

---

13 **climbed up by his hands and by his feet:** Or "by
his arms and legs."   **dispatched:** A slightly different
form of the Hebrew root (*m-w-t*) from which "die"
and "put to death" are derived. Others, "deal the
death blow."
15 **a trembling of God:** Others, "very great panic,"
"panic from God."

16 **the throng was swaying, going and coming back:**
McCarter (1980): "surging back and forth."
18 **Coffer:** McCarter (1980) argues for LXX's "*efod*," an
object more likely to be used in divination.

19 And it was,
   as Sha'ul was speaking to the priest,
   that the panic that was in the Philistines' camp went on and on
      [becoming] greater;
   Sha'ul said to the priest:
   Withdraw your hand!

20 And Sha'ul cried out, and all the people that were with him;
   they came out to the battle,
   and here: each one's sword was against his neighbor,
   an exceedingly great panic.

21 Now the Hebrews [that] had been with the Philistines yesterday
      [and] the day-before,
   in that they had gone up with them to the camp all around,
   they too [turned] to be with Israel, who were with Sha'ul and
      Yonatan,

22 while all the [other] men of Israel, the ones hiding themselves in
      the highlands of Efrayim,
   heard that the Philistines had fled,
   and they too caught up with them in battle.

23 So Yhwh delivered Israel on that day,
   and the battle crossed by Bet-Aven.

24 But the men of Israel were hard-pressed on that day,
   for Sha'ul had put an oath-curse on the fighting-people, saying:
   Doomed be the man that eats food until sunset,
   that I may be avenged on my enemies!
   So all the people did not taste food.

25 Now when all the people came into the forest,
   there was honey on the surface of the open-field.

26 And when the people came into the forest,
   here: honey was running free,
   but no one reached his hand to his mouth,
   for the people were afraid of the sworn-oath.

---

19 **Withdraw your hand!:** Since we can hear the sounds of the enemy's defeat, there is no longer any need to resort to the *efod* (Alter 1999).

20 **each one's sword . . . :** Describing the Philistine panic.

25 **the people:** So manuscripts; MT has "the land."

26 **honey was running free:** Many read instead "Its bees had left" (Heb. *halakh devoro* for *helekh devash*).

◆ 27 Now Yonatan had not heard when his father had made the people
swear,
so he stretched out the edge of the staff that was in his hand
and dipped it into the honeycomb;
then he returned his hand to his mouth, and his eyes brightened.

28 A man from [among] the fighting-people spoke up and said:
Your father had the people swear, yes, swear, saying:
Doomed be the man who eats food today!
And the people grew weary.

29 Yonatan said:
My father has stirred-up-disaster for the land!
Pray see: indeed, my eyes are brightened,
for I tasted this little [bit of] honey;

30 if the people had eaten, yes, eaten today from their enemies' spoils
that they found,
indeed now, wouldn't the strike against the Philistines have been
greater?

31 They struck down the Philistines on that day from Mikhmas to
Ayalon,
and the people grew exceedingly weary.

32 So the people swooped down on the spoil
and took sheep and cattle and young-cattle, slaughtering them to
the ground,
and the people ate [them] with the blood.

33 Someone told Sha'ul, saying:
Here, the people are sinning against Yhwh, in eating with the
blood!
He said:
You have [all] broken faith!
Roll me a great stone here.

34 And Sha'ul said:
Scatter among the fighting-people;
you are to say to them:
Each one bring close to me his ox, each one his lamb;

27 **his eyes brightened:** Reflecting the life-enhancing
properties of honey claimed by the ancients.
29 **My father has stirred-up-disaster:** Alter (1999)
notes the parallel with Yiftah (Jephthah), another
rash vow-maker (Judg. 11).

32 **ate [them] with the blood:** A practice forbidden
earlier in the Bible (see Gen. 9:4). In the biblical view,
blood belongs to God alone.

you are to slaughter them here and are to eat,
and you are not to sin against YHWH by eating with the blood!
So all the people brought close each one his ox in his hand that
    night, and they slaughtered them there.

35 And Sha'ul built a sacrificial-altar to YHWH;
it was the first [that he] built as an altar to YHWH.

36 Sha'ul said:
Let us go down after the Philistines at night, and plunder among
    them until the light of daybreak,
and let us not leave a man of them!
They said:
Whatever is good in your eyes, do!
But the priest said:
Let us draw near here to God.

37 So Sha'ul inquired of God:
Shall I go down after the Philistines?
Will you give them into the hand of Israel?
But he did not answer him on that day.

38 Then Sha'ul said:
Come close to here, all the "cornerstones" of the people;
know and take note
wherein this sin occurred today.

39 For by the life of YHWH, who delivers Israel,
for even if it be Yonatan my son,
indeed, he will die, yes, die!
But no one answered him from all the people.

40 He said to all Israel:
You be on one side,
and I and Yonatan my son will be on one side.
The people said to Sha'ul:
What is good in your eyes, do!

41 Sha'ul said to YHWH, the God of Israel:
Give *tammim*!

35 **the first [that he] built:** That Sha'ul's altar build-ing occurs this late in the narrative (he has already been rejected in the previous chapter) may hint at his desperation, or simply be another indication of his fragmented communications with God.

36 **draw near:** To consult God through an oracle, as in the next verse's "inquire" (which is built on the same verb, *sh-'-l*, as Sha'ul's name).

37 **on that day:** Or any other, for that matter.

38 **"cornerstones":** Nobles; a parallel English idiom might be "pillars [of the community]."

41 **YHWH, the God of Israel:** More appropriate as a form of address, as Alter (1999) translates. **Give *tammim*!:** That is, reveal through the oracle, mak-ing use of the objects known as the *Urim* and *Tum-mim* (pronounced *oo-REEM* and *too-MEEM;* see

◆ Yonatan and Sha'ul were captured-by-lot,
and the people escaped.

42 Then Sha'ul said:
Cast [lots] between me and Yonatan my son!
And Yonatan was captured-by-lot.

43 Sha'ul said to Yonatan:
Tell me what you have done!
So Yonatan told him;
he said:
I tasted, yes, tasted with the edge of the staff that was in my hand,
a little honey.
Here I am; I will die.

44 Sha'ul said:
Thus may God do, and thus may he add,
for you shall die, yes, die, Yonatan!

45 But the people said to Sha'ul:
Shall Yonatan die, who has wrought this great victory in Israel?
[Heaven] forbid, by the life of YHWH,
if a [single] hair of his head should fall to the ground . . . !
For with God he has acted this day!
Thus the people redeemed Yonatan, so that he did not die.

46 And Sha'ul went up from [pursuing] after the Philistines,
while the Philistines went back to their place.

47 Now when Sha'ul had captured the kingship over Israel,
he waged battle all around against all his enemies:
against Moav, against the Children of Ammon, against Edom,
against the king of Tzova, and against the Philistines;
and wherever he faced, he was victorious.

48 He did valiantly: he struck down Amalek
and rescued Israel from the hand of its pillager.

Exod. 28:30). It is not exactly clear what they were; in any event, some theorize that they gave a "yes or no" answer to the petitioner. Note also that *Urim* begins with the first letter of the Hebrew alphabet, and *Tummim* with the last. The LXX gives a longer text at this point, including the *Urim* in the request. **captured-by-lot:** See 10:20 and note, above.

43 **Here I am; I will die:** Following Driver.

45 **redeemed:** Rescued.

47 **had captured:** The Hebrew verb (*l-k-d*) is often connected to the casting of lots, as in v.41 above, and also 10:20–21, as well as referring to conquest. **Moav . . . Edom:** Pronounced *mo-AHV* and *eh-DOHM*. Along with Ammon, these were traditional enemies who were understood in Genesis to come from the same stock as Israel. The Moabites inhabited the region due east of the Dead Sea, with the Edomites occupying the area to the south of that. **king:** So ancient versions; MT has "kings." **Tzova:** The area north of Damascus. **was victorious:** Reading MT's *yrsh'* ("did wrong," "was blameworthy"), which makes no sense here, as *ywsh'*, following LXX and other ancient versions.

Chapter 15. *Sha'ul Rejected II:* Chap. 13 and the present one appear to be sepa-rate accounts of Sha'ul's rejection. This is buttressed by the opening of Chap. 15, which seems oblivious to the previous events. God commands the king to utterly wipe out the Amalekites, in revenge for their treacherous actions against the Isra-elite ancestors at the time of the Exodus (see Exod. 17:8–16). Sha'ul is scrupulous here in one regard, making sure that the Israel-friendly Kenites who live among the enemy are not caught up in the destruction, but in the end he chooses to preserve both the best of the spoils and Agag, the Amalekite king, thus violating God's instructions.

When confronted by Shemuel, Sha'ul claims to have done God's will, and to have saved the best animals for sacrifice to him. Further rebuke from the prophet reveals the truth: Sha'ul was afraid of his own soldiers, fearing that they, following usual practice, would not fight without promise of a reward in the form of spoils. Such a disregard of God's honor in favor of human considerations means that Sha'ul must now forfeit his role as the founder of a dynasty, expressed through the fourfold use of "reject" in vv.23 and 26.

Despite the condemnation directed at Sha'ul, the text strikingly portrays She-muel as feeling for the king; when God first expresses regret over having made Sha'ul king, Shemuel "cried out . . . all night" (v.11), while at the end of the chap-ter (vv.30–31) he accedes to Sha'ul's request to at least accompany him as he wor-ships in the people's presence. Shemuel, of course, does not extend this kind of humanity to Agag and, as far as we can tell, executes him with his own hands. But the close association between king and prophet, which had begun in the long-ago days of running after lost donkeys, would seem to have come to an end.

49 Now the sons of Sha'ul were:
Yonatan, Yishvi, and Malki-Shua.
And the name of his two daughters:
the name of the firstborn was Merav,
and the name of the younger-one was Mikhal.

50 And the name of Sha'ul's wife was Ahinoam daughter of Ahimaatz.
And the name of the commander of his armed-forces was Aviner,
son of Ner, Sha'ul's uncle.

51 Now Kish was the father of Sha'ul, and Ner was the father of
Avner, the son of Aviel.

52 And the war was strong against the Philistines all the days of Sha'ul;
whenever Sha'ul would see any mighty man, or any valiant one,
he would gather him to him.

15:1 Shemuel said to Sha'ul:
It is I [whom] YHWH sent to anoint you as king over his people,
over Israel;
so-now, hearken to the voice of YHWH's words:

2 Thus says YHWH of the Forces-On-High:
I have taken account of what Amalek did to Israel,
how he set upon him on the journey, on his going up from Egypt.

3 Now,
go and strike down Amalek;
you are to devote-to-destruction all that is his
—you are not to spare him,
but are to put to death [everyone]
from man to woman,
from child to suckling,
from ox to sheep,
from camel to donkey!

---

49 **Merav . . . Mikhal:** Pronounced *may-RAHV* and *mee-KHAL;* trad. English "Merab . . . Michal."

50 **Aviner:** Pronounced *ah-vee-NAYR*. Usually spelled as "Avner" in the text; similar, in II Samuel, are "Aminon/Amnon" and "Avishalom/Avshalom." The name means "Father [God] Is a Light/Lamp." He is also, as indicated in the next verse, Sha'ul's cousin. Trad. English "Abner."

52 **gather him:** A term denoting the recruiting of troops.

15:2 **what Amalek did:** In Exod. 17, the Amalekites, who in Sha'ul's day inhabited the Negev, attacked the newly freed Israelites in the rear, provoking God to declare a kind of eternal war against them. The later book of Esther's hero and villain, Mordekhai and Haman, are cast as descendants of Sha'ul and Agag, the Amalekite king here.

3 **devote-to-destruction:** Some biblical war accounts describe the practice of proscribing the spoils of war—devoting them to God, which could mean confiscation for the sanctuary or, in the case of persons, death. See the famous case of Akhan in Josh. 7.

4 So Sha'ul summoned the fighting-people
and counted them [for war] in Tela'im:
two hundred thousand foot-soldiers
along with ten thousand, the men of Judah.

5 And Sha'ul came to the city of Amalek,
and lay-in-ambush in the wadi.

6 Now Sha'ul said to the Kenites:
Come, turn aside, go down from amid the Amalekites,
lest I sweep you away with them!
For you—you acted with loyalty with all the Children of Israel on
their going up from Egypt.
So the Kenites turned aside from amid Amalek.

7 And Sha'ul struck down Amalek, from Havila as far as where-you-
come to Shur, which is facing Egypt.

8 He seized Agag king of Amalek alive,
while all the people he devoted-to-destruction with the mouth of
the sword.

9 But Sha'ul and the people spared Agag
and the best of the sheep and the cattle, the fat ones, the lambs and
all that was goodly;
they would not devote them to destruction—
[only] all the property despised and rejected,
that they devoted-to-destruction.

10 Now the word of YHWH [came] to Shemuel, saying:

11 I repent
that I kinged Sha'ul as king,
for he has turned from [following] after me;
my word he has not fulfilled!
Shemuel was agitated,
and he cried out to YHWH all night.

---

4 **Tela'im:** Perhaps Telem in southern Judah, but the spelling here is identical to that of a word for "lambs" (see the language of the previous verse; the word used for lambs in v.9 is, however, different).

5 **wadi:** A dry riverbed or ravine.

6 **Kenites:** Another desert tribe, reputed to be descended from Moshe's father-in-law Yitro (Jethro). They and Amalek are seen as both descended from Esav/Edom. Here the relationship leads to their being spared in the midst of Israel's taking vengeance. See also Judg. 4.

7 **Shur:** The "wall" that served as the eastern border of Egypt.

9 **the fat ones:** Reading Heb. *ha-mishnim* ("second"?) as *ha-shemenim*.

11 **repent:** Or "regret."

12 Shemuel started-early to meet Sha'ul at daybreak,
and it was told to Shemuel, saying:
Sha'ul has gone to Carmel
—here, he is setting up a monument for himself—
so he turned about, crossed over, and went down to Gilgal.

13 Shemuel came to Sha'ul,
and Sha'ul said to him:
Blessed are you of YHWH;
I have fulfilled the word of YHWH!

14 But Shemuel said:
Then what is this sound of sheep in my ears,
and the sound of oxen that I hear?

15 Sha'ul said:
From the Amalekites they have brought them,
and what the people spared as the best of the sheep and the oxen,
in order to sacrifice them to YHWH your God;
what was left we devoted-to-destruction.

16 Shemuel said to Sha'ul:
Leave off, and I will tell you what YHWH spoke to me during the
    night.
He said to him: Speak!

17 Shemuel said:
Though you may be too small in your own eyes,
you are head of the tribes of Israel,
for YHWH has anointed you as king over Israel!

18 Now YHWH sent you on a journey;
he said:
Go, devote-to-destruction the sinners, Amalek!
You are to wage battle against them, until you have finished
    them off.

19 So why did you not hearken to the voice of YHWH?
You swooped down on the spoils
and did what was evil in the eyes of YHWH!

---

12 **Carmel:** In southern Judah, just southeast of Hev-ron, and not to be confused with the high country in and around present-day Haifa.

17 **too small:** Echoing Sha'ul's self-assessment in 9:21, when he was chosen as king (Alter 1999).

◆ 20 Sha'ul said to Shemuel:
I did hearken to the voice of YHWH!
I went on the journey on which YHWH sent me:
I brought back Agag king of Amalek,
while Amalek I devoted-to-destruction;

21 but the people took from the spoils
sheep and oxen, the premier-part of what was devoted,
to sacrifice to YHWH your God at Gilgal!

22 Shemuel said:
Is there pleasure for YHWH in offerings and sacrifices
more than in hearkening to the voice of YHWH?
Here, hearkening is better than sacrifice,
attention than the fat of rams.

23 Indeed, [like] the sin of diviners is revolt,
[like] the iniquity of *terafim* is arrogance.
Because you have rejected the word of YHWH,
he has rejected you as king!

24 Sha'ul said to Shemuel:
I have sinned;
indeed, I have crossed the order of YHWH and your words,
for I was afraid of the people,
and so I hearkened to their voice!

25 But-now,
pray bear away my sin
and return with me, so that I may bow down to YHWH!

26 Shemuel said to Sha'ul:
I will not return with you,
for you have rejected the word of YHWH,
so YHWH has rejected you from being king over Israel!

27 And Shemuel turned about to go,
but he held on to the corner of his cloak, so that it tore.

28 Shemuel said to him:
YHWH has torn the kingdom of Israel from you today
and will give it to your fellow, the one better than you!

---

23 *terafim:* Household idols (see Gen. 31:19).
24 **crossed:** Violated.
27 **he held:** Sha'ul.   **the corner of his cloak:** To hold

on to the hem of the royal garment was, in ancient
Near Eastern practice, a sign of entreaty or loyalty
(see Brauner). Tearing it here is ominous.

29 And also: the Eternal One of Israel does not speak-falsely and does
    not repent—
for he is not a human-being, to repent!

30 He said:
I have sinned—
now, pray honor me in front of the elders of my people, in front of
    Israel:
return with me, so that I may bow down to YHWH your God!

31 So Shemuel returned after Sha'ul,
and Sha'ul bowed down to YHWH.

32 Then Shemuel said:
Bring close to me Agag king of Amalek!
Agag went to him with faltering-steps;
Agag said:
Indeed, the distress of death is near!

33 Shemuel said:
    Since bereaved were women by your sword,
      may the most bereaved of women be your mother!
And Shemuel slashed Agag [to pieces] in the presence of YHWH at
    Gilgal.

34 Then Shemuel went back to Rama,
while Sha'ul went up to his house at the Hill of Sha'ul.

35 And Shemuel did not see Sha'ul again until the day of his death,
for Shemuel was mourning over Sha'ul,
while YHWH had repented that he had made Sha'ul king over Israel.

---

32 **with faltering-steps:** Following LXX; McCarter
(1980), following Kimhi, reads it as "in fetters."

33 **Since bereaved . . . :** The last word of each line
rhymes in the Hebrew, creating a more dramatic

effect. **slashed . . . [to pieces]:** Heb. unclear, but
sh-s-f fits the general category of *sh-s-x* verbs, all of
which mean something violent like "plunder" or
"cleave."

PART III

THE RISE OF DAVID AND THE FALL OF SHA'UL

(I 16–II 1)

As the central and most vital personality in the Early Prophets, David will now occupy the bulk of the text in the book of Samuel. In the half of I Samuel that remains, the audience follows the young hero's meteoric rise from the sheepfolds of Bethlehem to the court of Sha'ul, where he will excel as a musician and warrior. Although in the story of David's selection as king (Chap. 16) God constantly admonishes Shemuel and the reader to ignore what is "seen," namely, external appearance, it does not seem to hurt that David is handsome and talented. Everyone appears to fall at his feet without much exertion on his part: fearsome enemies, the crown prince, and women, including princesses. And Chap. 16 will focus on a prominent earlier theme in the Bible: the triumph of a younger or youngest son.

It is entirely appropriate that the narrative about Golyat (Goliath) in Chap. 17 has been placed at the beginning of David's achievements. Nothing less will do for the man who was to become Israel's greatest king. The leisurely account, with greater detail than most biblical narratives, has imprinted itself on audiences of all periods, and remained symbolic of conflicts of all kinds throughout the centuries (in modern America it is often invoked regarding sports and politics). While the Commentary and Notes treat the chapter in detail below, David's cutting off of the giant's head may be singled out here, as touching on an overarching theme. As Polzin (1989) points out, Sha'ul and his son Ish-Boshet will lose theirs as well, which he sees as emblematic of the leadership problem in this book (see the Introduction to Samuel, above).

The narratives in these chapters center around several themes: Sha'ul's pursuit of David (18–26); David in exile all over Judah and especially among the Philistine enemy (19–30); David's opportunities to kill Sha'ul (24 and 26); and the desperation of the king's last days (28, 31). These are heightened by the powerfully drawn emotional triangle involving David, Sha'ul, and Yehonatan, and by the appearance of a number of secondary characters who help to set David's sometimes opaque personality into sharper relief. Thus, for instance, it takes Golyat (17) to bring out his intense faith, and Avigayil (25) to blunt his not-so-restrained temper.

Key words abound and evolve in this section. As previously noted, the account of David's anointing in Chap. 16 centers around "seeing" (see Alter 1981). The oft-repeated threat of "death" in Chap. 19 will ironically be resolved by that of Sha'ul, not of David. The troubled king's attempt to catch David in his "hand" (23, 24, 26) will fail, and he knows that in the end, "the kingdom of Israel will be established in your hand" (24:21). Finally, as Dietrich has noted, the Sha'ul/David narratives contain numerous verbs for "fleeing" or "escape." The reader should pay careful attention to all of these and other repeating words within individual chapters.

As I Samuel closes, David is on the sidelines, and our attention focuses back on Sha'ul. As previously mentioned, despite his failures and his subsequent descent into a monomaniacal pursuit of David, there is a tone in the text that mutes readers' reactions. Sha'ul is to be rejected not as evil but rather as tragically marred. The final stories about him, at En Dor (28) and in battle at Mount Gilboa (31), naturally elicit sympathy, reflected in the medium's tender feeding of him in the former story and the men of Yavesh-Gil'ad's care for his body in the latter. As eulogized in David's resonant poem of II Sam. 1, Sha'ul is not a misfit but a "mighty" warrior who has fallen, surely not a cause for rejoicing.

Chapter 16. *David Chosen and at Court:* With Sha'ul now rejected and destined to be the last of his own dynasty to rule, the text turns to the anointing of his successor, the Judean David. Compared to the convoluted accounts of Sha'ul's accession to the throne in Chaps. 9–10, the story in which David makes his first appearance is almost an idyll. It also fits a classic folklore pattern which we first encountered in multiple manifestations in Genesis: the choosing or triumph of the younger brother. Here, as in many fairy tales, the youngest appears last, and, like Sha'ul, he is initially hidden.

The text makes the event a journey of discovery for Shemuel. God does not reveal the new king's name to the prophet in advance, nor is it mentioned until the very end of the chapter, after the anointing. Shemuel, like us, will have to learn the criteria for divine choice. Perhaps he is blinded by Sha'ul's failures, which he himself has taken to heart (note God's question in v.1: "Until when will you keep on mourning for Sha'ul?"). In any event, God's speech in v.7 centers around the idea of "seeing," a verb and an activity that are typically associated with prophecy in the Bible (as in 9:9, above). It is used ten times in eighteen verses of the text. So the little tale incorporates both physical and figurative aspects of seeing: appearance, foresight, and insight.

The fact that David is a shepherd resonates strongly in ancient culture. Moshe, of course, had followed the same vocation as an adult. The poetry of the Bible frequently contains shepherd imagery, most famously in Ps. 23 and the Song of Songs, and the figure of the Shepherd King, so beloved in the ancient Near East, easily survived to become a central motif in early Christianity.

16:1   YHWH said to Shemuel:
      Until when will you keep on mourning for Sha'ul,
      when I myself have rejected him from reigning as king over Israel?
      Fill your horn with oil and go:
      I am sending you to Yishai the Bet-Lehemite,
      for I have seen among his sons a king for me.

2   Shemuel said:
      How can I go?
      If Sha'ul were to hear, he would kill me!
      YHWH said:
      A she-calf of the herd you are to take in your hand,
      and you are to say:
      It is to sacrifice to YHWH [that] I have come.

3   Then you are to invite Yishai for the sacrificial-meal,
      and I myself will make known to you what you are to do:
      you are to anoint for me the one that I tell you.

4   Shemuel did what YHWH had spoken;
      he came to Bet-Lehem.
      The elders of the town trembled [going] to meet him,
      they said:
      Is it in peace, your coming?

5   He said:
      In peace—
      it is to sacrifice to YHWH [that] I have come!
      Hallow yourselves,
      so that you may come with me to the sacrificial-meal.
      So he hallowed Yishai and his sons
      and invited them to the sacrificial-meal.

6   Now it was, when they came,
      that he saw Eli'av;
      he said [to himself]:
      Surely before YHWH is his anointed one!

16:1 **Until when:** Others, "How long." **Yishai:** Pronounced *yee-SHY;* trad. English "Jesse." **seen among his sons:** Following Auld (2011). **for me:** As contrasted with "us" (Israel) in 8:5 (Kimhi).

3 **sacrificial-meal:** In the Bible, meat is rarely eaten outside of a sanctuary—hence the need for ritually purifying ("hallow" in v.5) the family in v.5.

4 **Is it in peace, your coming?:** A holy man's visit is not always a cause for rejoicing in the Bible.

5 **Hallow yourselves:** A sacrificial meal required ritual washing.

6 **Eli'av:** Pronounced *eh-lee-AHV;* trad. English "Eliab."

David starts on his biblical path with formidable tools. He is physically attractive and possessed of the "spirit of YHWH," like some of the leaders before him in the book of Judges. In addition, the end of our chapter reveals him as a string musician, a skill sometimes also associated with prophecy in the Bible (see II Kings 3:15). At the same time that this talent of David is described, we also learn of his reputation as a warrior. Clearly this is no ordinary shepherd boy.

The section already begins what will develop into an epic struggle, not only between the two men, but between two dynastic houses. Its echo was to endure long after their own deaths.

7 But YHWH said to Shemuel:
Do not look at what you see of him, or at the tallness of his stature,
for I have rejected him!
For [God sees] not as a human being sees—
for a human being sees the [outer] aspect, but YHWH sees the heart.

8 Then Yishai called Avinadav, and had him pass before Shemuel,
but he said:
Also this one, YHWH has not chosen.

9 And Yishai had Shamma pass by,
but he said:
Also this one, YHWH has not chosen.

10 Yishai had his seven sons pass before Shemuel,
but Shemuel said to Yishai:
YHWH has not chosen these!

11 Then Shemuel said to Yishai:
Are the lads at-an-end?
He said:
There still remains the youngest—
here, he is shepherding the flock.
Shemuel said to Yishai:
Send and fetch him,
for we will not sit around [the table] until his coming here.

12 He sent and had him come
—now he was ruddy, with beautiful eyes, and goodly in
   appearance.
YHWH said:
Arise, anoint him, for this is he!

13 So Shemuel took the horn of oil and anointed him amid his
   brothers.
And the spirit of YHWH advanced upon David from that day and
   onward.
Then Shemuel arose and went [back] to Rama.

---

7 **what you see of him:** His outward appearance.
12 **had him come:** The hero is not identified by name
until the next verse. It is almost as if his anointing
creates him as a person.   **goodly:** Heb. *tov,* the root
which echoes three times from vv.16–23 as "well" in
this translation.   **appearance:** Heb. *ro'i,* again from
the root "to see."

13 **the spirit of YHWH advanced upon David:** Previously, the expression had been used three times about
the mighty Shimshon (Judg. 14:6, 19, 15:14).   **David:**
Pronounced *dah-VEED.* This is the first occurrence
of the name, which means "beloved."

Chapter 17. *David and Golyat:* Perhaps the most famous story about David, this narrative appears to have its own independent history, which, however, is difficult to untangle. Unlike most other instances, here MT is much longer than LXX. Sections exclusive to the Hebrew version are vv.12–31 (the introduction of David and his reaction to Golyat's taunting), 41 and 48b (minor variations), 50, and 55–58 (Sha'ul inexplicably asking about David's identity as if he had never met him previously, Chap. 16 notwithstanding). Most scholars have concluded from this that there are two traditions at work in some form, or that an "original" has given birth to one or two later versions through expansion or contraction. Given that the LXX version reads coherently on its own, many infer that MT here is in fact an expansion. Following the model of the Sinai account in Exod. 19 (see Greenberg), our present text might be viewed as a composite, a gathering of different traditions in a manner that makes for richness and completeness, despite our Western need for total coherence (Alter 1998). In a wider sense, it reflects the Bible's general aspect of textual inclusiveness—what I would call multivocality, in which competing and even contradictory accounts are allowed to coexist for the sake of fullness.

In addition to the textual issues, a battle account near the end of the book, in II Sam. 21:19, mentions how "Elhanan son of Yaarei-Oregim the Bet-Lehemite struck down Golyat the Gittite / —now the shaft of his spear was like a weaver's beam," and the same hero is identified as having killed Golyat's brother in I Chron. 20:5. This suggests that we are dealing with an independent story which has been placed on David's shoulders, for obvious reasons.

Regardless of its various permutations, the long, leisurely David/Golyat narrative reads much like a fairy tale, and is in many respects quite accessible to many cultures. It has never lost its popularity, and the phrase "David and Goliath," used to describe everything from business competition to sporting events, is still very much in common use. The setup is classic: a huge warrior with a reputation as a champion—"the Man of the Space-Between [the armies]" (v.4)—strides forth, mocking his enemies and challenging them to a one-on-one duel. The detailed description of Golyat's armor is a departure from the usually sparse biblical landscape, but it is certainly psychologically appropriate here, as are the other rare biblical descriptions of a person's attire (Hamilton).

Of course, neither Sha'ul nor any of his soldiers dares fight the Philistine. It is left to a teenager untried in standard weaponry to face him. The text is clear about David's inexperience in formal battle, but it needs to be pointed out that, although he is not a professional warrior, he is also no slouch. His description of fighting off lions and bears in his shepherd days (vv.34–36) is not a vain or irrelevant boast; in addition, v.51 describes him deftly unsheathing Golyat's sword and finishing off the Philistine with it. Further, David's wielding of a sling to defeat Golyat should not be trivialized. In ancient warfare, a division of slingers could be quite lethal (see the Greek account in Xenophon's *Anabasis,* or, previously in the Bible, Judg. 20:16).

In addition to the detailed military descriptions, which sound more like Homer

14 Now the spirit of YHWH departed from Sha'ul,
and an evil spirit from YHWH began to torment him.

15 Sha'ul's servants said to him:
Now here, an evil spirit of God is tormenting you;

16 pray let our lord speak—your servants [stand ready] before you:
let them look for a man,
one who knows how to strum the lyre,
so that it may be, whenever there is upon you an evil spirit of God,
he may strum with his hand, and it will be well with you.

17 Sha'ul said to his servants:
Pray select for me a man who strums well,
and have him come to me!

18 One of the serving-lads spoke up and said:
Here, I have seen a son of Yishai the Bet-Lehemite, [one] who
knows how to strum;
a mighty-man of valor,
a man of battle,
skilled in words,
a man of [pleasing] form,
and YHWH is with him!

19 So Sha'ul sent messengers to Yishai, he said:
Send me David your son, who is with the flock!

20 Yishai took a donkey [laden with] bread and a skin of wine, and one
goat kid,
and sent them by the hand of David his son, to Sha'ul.

21 David came to Sha'ul, and stood before him;
he grew to love him exceedingly,
and he became his weapons bearer.

22 And Sha'ul sent to Yishai, saying:
Now let David stand [in attendance] before me, for he has found
favor in my eyes.

---

14 **an evil spirit:** That is, what was previously a gift now becomes a torment.

16 **before you:** Perhaps connoting "ready" (McCarter 1980). **look for:** In Chaps. 9–10, this verb was connected to the finding and choosing of Sha'ul as king. **strum:** The Bible uses different verbs for playing different categories of musical instruments; the present *n-g-n* applies only to stringed ones.

than the Bible, the story focuses on memorable confrontations between pairs of characters: Golyat and the Israelites (vv.8–11); David and his brother Eli'av (28–29); David and Sha'ul (32–39); and, finally, David and Golyat (42–47). The last and most significant one will vault David's prowess and fame beyond that of regular warriors, his family, and Sha'ul.

The most surprising aspect of this tale is that it is not only, as popularly understood, a case of the weak against the strong, the small against the large. Its vocabulary in fact leads in a different direction. Only here, of all the biblical texts concerning war, does the word "ranks" occur repeatedly (twelve times); the other recurring word is the verb "mock." This leads naturally to the conclusion that what is really at stake is the fact that "this foreskinned Philistine" has "mock[ed] the ranks of the Living God" (v.26). In other words, the story, splendidly illustrating the rise of David, centers around the perceived insult to YHWH and his earthly armies, which must be properly avenged. Golyat's literal downfall accomplishes this; his posture of falling "on his face to the ground" (v.49) is more reminiscent of proper respect and worship than the simple act of keeling over.

There is one other biblical text that takes up the issue of "mocking" God using this language: II Kings 18, where the Assyrian king's representatives taunt King Hezekiah and YHWH in full hearing of the Judean troops. It is thus quite plausible that an old story has here been retold in terms and vocabulary that address the needs of a later audience.

◆ 23 And so it would be:
whenever the spirit of God was upon Sha'ul,
that David would take up the lyre and strum [it] with his hand;
Sha'ul would have respite, and it would be well with him,
and the evil spirit would depart from him.

17:1 Now the Philistines gathered their encampments for battle;
they gathered themselves at Sokho, which is in Yehuda,
and encamped between Sokho and Azeka, at Efes-Dammim,

2 while Sha'ul and the men of Israel gathered and encamped in the
Valley of the Oak,
and arranged-ranks for battle to meet the Philistines.

3 Now the Philistines were stationed on a hill, on this-side,
while Israel was stationed on a hill, on that-side,
with the ravine between them.

4 And the Man of the Space-Between came out, from the Philistine
camps—
Golyat his name, from Gat:
his height was six cubits and a span;

5 a helmet of bronze was on his head,
with armor of scales he was clothed
—the weight of the armor was five thousand *shekel*-weights of
bronze;

6 greaves of bronze were on his legs,
and a scimitar of bronze was between his shoulders;

7 the shaft of his spear was like a weaver's beam,
while the flashing-point of his spear was six hundred *shekel*-weights
of iron,
and the shield bearer was walking before him.

---

23 **the spirit of God:** Obviously, in this case, an evil one. **spirit . . . respite:** Heb. *ru'ah . . . revah,* a nice punning contrast between Sha'ul's malady and the relief that David's playing provides.

17:1 **Sokho:** West of Bet-Lehem, toward Philistine territory.

2 **Valley of the Oak:** Or the "Valley of Ela."

4 **Man of the Space-Between:** A champion, to fight his opponent in what we would call No-Man's-Land. **Golyat . . . Gat:** Pronounced *gall-YAHT* and *got;* trad. English "Goliath . . . Gath." **cubits:** Biblical units of length based on a man's forearm, they varied from eighteen to twenty-two inches. At six

cubits, Golyat is folktale size. He need not be such a mythical giant, however; LXX reads the phrase as "four cubits," about six foot nine and thus tall enough to be formidable in any era.

6 **scimitar:** A curved sword.

7 **weaver's beam:** McCarter (1984), following Yadin, explains the similarity: the spear contains a thong and rings for slinging, similar to what was found in ancient Greece and Egypt. **six hundred *shekel*-weights:** Maybe as much as fifteen pounds—the equivalent of having a bowling ball at the end of his spear!

8 He stood and called out to the ranks of Israel;
he said to them:
Why do you come out and arrange-ranks in battle?
Am I not a Philistine, and you the servants of Sha'ul?
Pick yourselves a man, that he may come down to me!

9 If he prevails in doing battle with me and strikes me down,
then we will become your servants,
but if I prevail against him and strike him down,
then you will become our servants, and will have to serve us!

10 And the Philistine said:
As for me,
I mock the ranks of Israel this day—
give me a man, and let us do battle together!

11 Sha'ul and all Israel heard those words of the Philistine,
and they were dismayed and exceedingly frightened.

12 Now David was the son of this Efratite man, from Bet-Lehem in
   Judah
whose name was Yishai—he had eight sons.
And the man, in the days of Sha'ul, was old, advanced [in age]
   among men.

13 Now they had gone, the three oldest sons of Yishai,
gone after Sha'ul, into battle
—the name[s] of his three sons who had gone to battle were:
Eli'av, the firstborn,
and his second, Avinadav,
and the third one, Shamma.

14 As for David, he was the youngest,
while the three oldest ones had gone [to follow] after Sha'ul.

15 Now David would go and return from [attending] upon Sha'ul,
to shepherd the flock of his father in Bet-Lehem.

16 And the Philistine came close, early and late, and presented himself
   for forty days.

---

14 **the youngest:** A situation that recurs in folktales; in the Bible, it fits a general pattern beginning in Genesis, where the younger son always prevails.

16 **forty days:** The usual biblical measure of time, as in the Flood story and many others.

17 Yishai said to David his son:
Now take your brothers this *efa* of parched-grain, and these ten
  bread-loaves,
and run them out to the camp to your brothers,
18 and these ten cuts of milk-cheese, bring to the Commander of a
  Thousand.
As for your brothers, take account of [their] welfare,
and bring back assurance from them—
19 for Sha'ul and they and all the fighting-men of Israel in the Valley
  of the Oak are doing battle with the Philistines.
20 So David started-early in the morning;
he left the flock with a watchman,
lifted up [the food] and went, as Yishai had charged him, and came
  to the circular-camp,
as the army was going out to the ranks and was shouting in battle.
21 And Israel and the Philistines were arranged-in-ranks, rank opposite
  rank.
22 David let down the gear from him, in the hand of a watchman of
  gear,
and ran to the ranks.
When he arrived, he asked about his brothers, about [their] welfare.
23 While he was speaking with them,
here, the Man of the Space-Between was coming up, Golyat the
  Philistine his name, from Gat, from the ranks of the Philistines.
He spoke according to those words, and David heard.
24 Now all the fighting-men of Israel, when they saw the man, fled
  before him,
for they were exceedingly afraid.
25 A man of Israel said:
Do you see this man who comes up?
Indeed, it is to mock Israel that he comes up!
Now it will be: the man who strikes him down, the king will enrich
  him with great riches,
and his daughter he will give him,
and his Father's House he will make free in Israel!

25 **the king will enrich him . . . :** Once again, the
atmosphere and details resemble those of a folktale.

◆ 26 David said to the men who were standing with him, saying:
What shall be done for the man who strikes down this Philistine
and removes the mocking from upon Israel?
For who is this foreskinned Philistine
that he should mock the ranks of the Living God?

27 The people told him according to those words, saying:
Thus shall be done for the man who strikes him down.

28 Now Eli'av his oldest brother heard as he was speaking to the men,
and Eli'av's anger flared up against David;
he said:
Why now have you come down, and with whom have you left that
little flock in the wilderness?
I know your presumption and the evil-intentions of your heart—
indeed, it is in order to see the battle that you have come down here!

29 David said:
What have I done now? It was only words!

30 He went around him, facing another,
and spoke to him according to those words,
and the people answered him with words according to the former
words.

31 Now the words that David had spoken were heard;
they told them in the presence of Sha'ul, and he had him fetched.

32 David said to Sha'ul:
Do not let anyone's heart fail him;
your servant will go and do battle with this Philistine!

33 But Sha'ul said to David:
You cannot prevail in going against this Philistine, to do battle
with him,
for you are a lad,
while he has been a man of battle since his youth!

---

26 **David said . . . What shall be done . . . :** David's first biblical words reflect one of his lifelong characteristics, that of seeking political gain (Alter 1999). **mocking:** The word can also mean "disgrace," as in Josh. 5:9.
27 **those words:** See v.25.
28 **presumption . . . evil-intentions:** This characterization of the "bratty" David by a brother parallels the treatment of Yosef in Genesis.
29–30 **words:** Singular in the Hebrew.

32 **David said . . . :** There are no court niceties here; David cuts to the chase. **anyone's:** LXX suggests "the king's."
33 **lad:** The word is also used in the Bible with the meaning "squire," one who is not quite a warrior, so David could easily be eighteen or nineteen, and strong—not a child, as often seen in illustrations. **lad . . . youth:** Heb. *naar . . . ne'urav;* perhaps "squire . . . squireship" would express the military sense, but not very elegantly in English.

34 David said to Sha'ul:
Your servant was a shepherd of the flock for his father,
and whenever a lion or a bear came and carried off a lamb from the
    flock,

35 I would go out after it and strike it down, and rescue it from its
    mouth;
if it rose against me, I would take hold of it by its beard, strike it
    down, and put it to death.

36 Even the lion, even the bear did your servant strike down—
so this foreskinned Philistine will be like one of them,
for he has mocked the ranks of the Living God!

37 And David said:
Yhwh,
who rescued me from the hand of the lion and from the hand of
    the bear,
he will rescue me from the hand of this Philistine!
Sha'ul said to David:
Go, and may Yhwh be with you!

38 And Sha'ul clothed David in his military-garb:
he placed a helmet of bronze on his head
and clothed him in armor.

39 David strapped on his sword over his garb,
but he was unable to walk, since he was not used [to them].
David said to Sha'ul:
I cannot walk with these, since I am not used [to them].
So David removed them from himself.

40 He took his stick in his hand
and chose himself five smooth stones from the wadi
and put them in the shepherd's bag that he had, namely, in the
    pouch, with his sling in his hand,
and approached the Philistine.

41 The Philistine went, going along and coming nearer to David,
with the man, the shield bearer, before him.

---

37 **from the hand:** From this point on in the narrative, "hand" appears multiple times, connoting power, as often in the Bible.

39 **unable:** Reading the verb *y-'-l* as *l-'-h,* along with LXX.

◆ 42 And the Philistine looked out and saw David, and taunted him,
for he was a lad,
and ruddy, beautiful of appearance.

43 The Philistine said to David:
Am I a dog,
that you come at me with sticks?
And the Philistine cursed David by his gods.

44 And the Philistine said to David:
Come to me,
that I may give your flesh to the birds of the heavens and to the
beasts of the field!

45 But David said to the Philistine:
You come at me
with sword and spear and scimitar,
but I come at you
with the name of YHWH of the Forces-On-High,
the God of the ranks of Israel, whom you have mocked!

46 This day YHWH will turn you over into my hand,
so that I will strike you down
and will remove your head from you;
I will give your carcass and the carcass of the Philistine camp
this day
to the birds of the heavens and to the wildlife of the earth,
so that all the earth may know that Israel has a God,

47 and that all this assembly may know
that it is not with a sword or with a spear that YHWH delivers—
for the battle is YHWH's,
and he will give [all of] you into our hand!

48 And it was, when the Philistine arose and came near to meet David,
that David quickly ran toward the ranks to meet the Philistine.

49 David stretched out his hand to the bag
and took from there a stone, and slung it,

---

43 **dog:** This motif, one of insult, repeats in the following chapters. Here it contrasts nicely with David's mastery over lions and bears (vv.34–36) (Fokkelman 1993). **sticks:** Heb. *maklot*, sounding similar to the immediately following *vaykallel*, "cursed."

45 **with the name:** A more conventional rendering would be "in the name," but the Hebrew preposi-

tion is the same as the many "withs" earlier in the verse.

46 **your carcass and:** Added by LXX.

49 **forehead:** Some understand this instead as the shin or a spot on the leg not covered by armor, which would perhaps better explain Golyat's literal and forward-moving downfall.

and struck the Philistine on his forehead:
the stone sank into his forehead
and he fell on his face to the ground.

50 So David overpowered the Philistine with a sling and a stone;
he struck down the Philistine and put him to death,
yet no sword was in David's hand.

51 And David ran and stood over the Philistine
and took his sword and drew it from its sheath
and dispatched him;
he cut off his head with it.
The Philistines saw that their mighty-man was dead, so they fled,

52 and the men of Israel and Judah arose and shouted;
they pursued after the Philistines as far as where you come to the
    ravine, as far as the gates of Ekron,
and the Philistine slain fell in the road to Shaarayim/Double-Gate,
    as far as Gat, as far as Ekron.

53 The Children of Israel returned from dashing-hotly after the
    Philistines, and they pillaged their camp.

54 And David took the Philistine's head and brought it to Jerusalem,
    while his gear he put in his tent.

55 Now when Sha'ul saw David going out to meet the Philistine,
he said to Avner, commander of the armed-forces:
Whose son is this lad, Avner?
Avner said:
As you live, O king, if I know . . .

56 The king said:
Make inquiry yourself:
Whose son is this youth?

57 So when David returned from striking down the Philistine,
Avner took him and brought him before Sha'ul,
with the head of the Philistine in his hand.

---

52 **Gat . . . Ekron:** All the way back to the Philistine cities.

54 **Jerusalem:** Another anomaly in the text; it will not be an Israelite city until David himself conquers it in II Sam. 5. Similarly, as a nonwarrior, David would not have had his own tent.

55 **Whose son:** Since in the ancient Near East, kings were sometimes referred to as "sons of the gods," Sha'ul's question is not as innocent as it seems, at least to the audience. See II Sam. 7:14.

Chapter 18. *The Rise of David in Sha'ul's House I:* As if the Golyat story were not dramatic enough, the artistry of the text continues unabated in the chapters that follow. The present one highlights "love," its chief theme word: the love borne David by Yehonatan, Sha'ul's heir; by the Israelites, who are dazzled by David's military exploits; and by Sha'ul's daughter Mikhal, who not surprisingly falls for the young hero. Contrasted to this and to David's "prospering" (vv.5, 14, 15, 30) is the jealous rage into which Sha'ul's emotions propel him. Whether the "evil spirit from YHWH" (v.10, and see 16:14) is related to Sha'ul's depression over having been rejected by God, or is due to a previously existing psychological state, the rise of his young rival only magnifies it. Whereas in Chap. 16 David's lyre playing had been able to soothe the ailing king, it now spawns elaborate scheming and an outbreak of personal violence.

The precise nature of the love between David and Yehonatan has been a prime subject of speculation in recent interpretations of this text. In today's terms, the language appears strongly suggestive of a sexual relationship, although the text does not elaborate on this. Alternatively, if one reads the story in a nonsexual way, it may be reflecting a warrior society, in which male bonding has always been central. A further possibility is that the relationship is playing an ironic role in the text: the person about whom each cares the most is the one with whom he has the greatest potential political conflict.

The David-Yehonatan relationship has been explicated by Ackerman in a book-length study (2005). She notes that the text, while not explicit, does utilize vocabulary that elsewhere in the Bible is clearly sexual, and that in general Yehonatan occupies a role that is emotionally and politically subordinate to David (see I Sam. 18:4, 28:13–15, and 23:17). If one accepts these arguments, the text may be putting forward a striking, if symbolic, example of how David will triumph over the House of Sha'ul.

In any event, as with all biblical texts, readers will find multiple ways to read the same passage.

58 Sha'ul said to him:
Whose son are you, [my] lad?
David said:
The son of your servant Yishai the Bet-Lehemite.

18:1 It was, when he finished speaking to Sha'ul,
—now Yehonatan's own self became bound up with David's self,
so that Yehonatan loved him like his own self—
2 that Sha'ul took him [into service] on that day,
and did not give him [leave] to return to his Father's House.
3 And Yehonatan and David cut a covenant,
because of his love for him, like his own self.
4 Yehonatan stripped off the cloak that he had on and gave it to David,
along with his [military] garb, including his sword, including his
bow, and including his belt.

5 David went out,
and everywhere that Sha'ul sent him, he prospered.
Sha'ul placed him over the men of war,
and it was good in the eyes of all the people, and also in the eyes of
Sha'ul's servants.
6 And it was upon their coming back, upon David's return from
striking the Philistine,
that women came out from all the towns in Israel, for singing and
dances,
to meet King Sha'ul with timbrels, with joyful-sounds and with
triangles.
7 And the dancing women chanted and said:
Sha'ul has struck down his thousands,
but David—his myriads!
8 Sha'ul became exceedingly agitated,
and this matter was evil in his eyes;
he said [to himself]:
They give-credit to David for myriads,
but to me they give-credit for thousands!
There yet [remains] for him only the kingdom!

18:1 **self:** Or "being." Heb. *nefesh*, a person's life-essence
or emotions, is often mistranslated as "soul."

3 **his love for him:** Yehonatan's for David.
7 **myriads:** Units of ten thousand.

◆   9   And Sha'ul was keeping-an-eye on David from that day onward.

10   Now it was on the morrow
      that an evil spirit of God advanced upon Sha'ul, and he ranted-like-
            a-prophet in the midst of the palace-house,
      while David was strumming with his hand, as day after day.
      Now there was a spear in Sha'ul's hand,

11   and Sha'ul hurled the spear; he said [to himself]:
      I will strike David and the wall [together]!
      But David evaded him twice.

12   And Sha'ul was afraid before David,
      for YHWH was with him,
      while from Sha'ul he had turned away.

13   So Sha'ul kept him away from [being] beside him;
      he made him commander of a thousand,
      and he went out and came back before the people.

14   David was prospering in all his ways,
      and YHWH was with him.

15   And Sha'ul saw that he was prospering exceedingly, and he was in
            dread before him,

16   but all Israel and Judah loved David,
      for he was going out and coming back before them.

17   Sha'ul said to David:
      Here is my oldest daughter, Merav—
      her I will give you as a wife;
      only be a son of valor for me
      and fight the battles of YHWH!
      —For Sha'ul said [to himself]:
      Let not my own hand be against him,
      but let the Philistines' hand be against him!

18   David said to Sha'ul:
      Who am I and who are my living-relatives, my father's clan in
            Israel,
      that I should become son-in-law to the king?

11 **David and the wall [together]:** Sha'ul seeks to pin David to the wall.
13 **and he went out and came back:** David's actions are described with this idiom denoting military leadership, a role we encountered already in v.5.
17 **son of valor:** More idiomatically, a "valiant one," but the word "son" echoes throughout this text.
18 **living-relatives:** LXX from MT: "my life"; it is missing in some LXX manuscripts.

◆ 19 But it was,
at the time for giving Merav daughter of Sha'ul to David,
that she was given to Adriel the Maholatite as a wife.
20 Now Mikhal daughter of Sha'ul had fallen in love with David,
and when it was told to Sha'ul, the matter was right in his eyes.
21 Sha'ul said [to himself]:
I will give her to him,
that she may become a snare to him,
and that the Philistines' hand may be against him!
So Sha'ul said to David a second-time:
You are to become-a-son-in-law to me today!
22 And Sha'ul charged his servants:
Speak to David secretly, saying:
Here, the king is pleased with you,
and all his servants love you;
so-now, become-a-son-in-law to the king!
23 Sha'ul's servants spoke these words in David's ears.
But David said:
Is it a light-thing in your eyes, becoming-a-son-in-law to the king
—for I am a man poor and lightly-regarded!
24 Sha'ul's servants told him, saying:
According to these words did David speak.
25 Sha'ul said:
Say thus to David:
The king takes no pleasure in any bride-price except for a hundred
Philistine foreskins,
to be avenged on the king's enemies
—for Sha'ul planned to cause David's fall by the Philistines' hand.
26 His servants told David all these words,
and the matter was right in David's eyes to become-son-in-law to
the king.
Not [many] days were fulfilled

---

19 **Maholatite:** Possibly from Avel Mehola, south of Bet-She'an.
21 **snare:** Driver understands this as "the trigger of a trap" for animals. **a second-time:** The Hebrew is strange, literally "in two." Some propose "in two

years," others "two opportunities" or even "two daughters."
25 **a hundred Philistine foreskins:** Not so easy to obtain.
26 **were fulfilled:** Passed.

Chapter 19. *The Rise of David in Sha'ul's House II:* Having been entranced by David in the previous chapter, Sha'ul's children now actively take his side against their father. At first, Yehonatan's intercession works, and his friend is restored to his position at the king's side. But the "evil spirit" in Sha'ul cannot be denied, especially after another report of David's successes in battle (v.8), and he once again hurls his spear at the young musician. David's subsequent flight is the beginning of a long period of running which will end only with Sha'ul's death. He is aided in his escape by his wife, Mikhal, who, in a scene of deception that vaguely recalls Rahel's tricking of *her* father in Gen. 31:34–35, makes use of what are apparently household idols to fool the king's messengers.

But such help is not sufficient. David needs divine protection from Sha'ul, and the king's messengers are disoriented by "ranting-in-prophecy," followed by Sha'ul himself. While in Chap. 10 above, such behavior might have suggested the king's special gifts and hence leadership capabilities, here, in what is perhaps originally an alternate tradition, it reduces him to a helpless babbler, and David goes unharmed. Curiously, Shemuel never feels Sha'ul's wrath for accompanying David here.

27 when David arose and went, he and his men,
and he struck down two hundred men of the Philistines.
And David brought their foreskins and paid-them-in-full to the king,
to become-son-in-law to the king,
and Sha'ul gave him Mikhal his daughter as a wife.

28 Sha'ul took note and knew that YHWH was with David,
while Mikhal daughter of Sha'ul loved him.

29 And Sha'ul continued to be afraid of David, even more;
Sha'ul was bearing-enmity to David all the days.

30 The Philistine commanders went out [to battle],
and it was: as often as they went out, David prospered more than
all of Sha'ul's servants,
so that his name became exceedingly esteemed.

19:1 And Sha'ul spoke to Yonatan his son and to all his servants
about causing David's death,
but Yehonatan son of Sha'ul took exceeding pleasure in David,

2 so Yehonatan told David, saying:
Sha'ul my father is seeking to cause your death.
So-now, pray take care in the morning
that you stay in a secret-place and hide yourself.

3 As for me, I will go out and stand next to my father in the field
where you are;
I myself will speak about you to my father,
and whatever I see, I will tell you.

4 So Yehonatan spoke of David for good to Sha'ul his father;
he said to him:
Let not the king sin against his servant, against David,
for he has not sinned against you,
for his deeds have been exceedingly to your good!

5 He took his life in his hands and struck down the Philistine,
and YHWH wrought a great victory for all Israel
—you saw it and rejoiced.
So why would you sin against innocent blood
by causing David's death for nothing?

---

27 **two hundred:** A typical hero move—doubling the test.
19:1 **took exceeding pleasure in:** Or "was exceedingly fond of." On discussions about the possibility of a sexual relationship, see Commentary.

4 **for good:** Favorably.
5 **the Philistine:** Golyat.   **for nothing:** For no cause.

◆ 6 Sha'ul hearkened to Yehonatan's voice,
and Sha'ul swore:
By the life of YHWH, if he should be put to death . . . !
7 So Yehonatan called David,
and Yehonatan told him all these words.
Yehonatan brought David to Sha'ul,
and he was in his presence as yesterday [and] the day-before.

8 The battles continued to take place;
David went out to wage battle against the Philistines,
and he struck them down, a great striking-down,
so that they fled before them.
9 But an evil spirit of YHWH [came] upon Sha'ul:
he was sitting in his palace-house, his spear in his hand,
while David was strumming with his hand.
10 And Sha'ul sought to strike, with the spear, David and the wall
[together],
but he slipped away from Sha'ul,
so that he struck [only] the wall with his spear,
and David fled, and escaped on that night.
11 Sha'ul sent messengers to David's house, to watch out for him and
to put him to death at daybreak,
but Mikhal, David's wife, reported to him, saying:
If you don't escape with your life tonight,
tomorrow you will be put to death!
12 So Mikhal let David down through the window;
he went off, got away, and escaped.
13 Then Mikhal took the *terafim* and put it in the bed,
and a tangle of goats'-hair she put at its head,
and covered it with a garment.
14 And when Sha'ul sent messengers to take David, she said:
He is sick.
15 Then Sha'ul sent the messengers to see David, saying:
Bring him up in the bed to me, to put him to death!

12 **through the window:** Note that Mikhal will later (II 6:16) despise the man whose life she saves here, upon seeing him "through the window" dancing before the Coffer in what she deems an inappropriate manner (Fokkelman 1991).

13 *terafim:* See note to 15:23, above. **a tangle:** Following McCarter (1980). **it:** Though the word is plural in form, a single object seems indicated here.
15 **Bring him up in the bed:** With the force of "Even if you have to carry him here in his bed."

16 But when the mesengers arrived,
   here, the *terafim* were in the bed, with a tangle of goats'-hair at its
      head!
17 Sha'ul said to Mikhal:
   Why have you deceived me thus?
   You have sent my enemy free, so that he has escaped!
   Mikhal said to Sha'ul:
   He said to me: Send me free—
   why should I cause your death?
18 Now David had gotten away and escaped, coming to Shemuel at
      Rama,
   and had told him all that Sha'ul had done to him.
   He went, he and Shemuel, and they stayed at Nayot.
19 Now it was told to Sha'ul, saying:
   Here, David is at Nayot in Rama!
20 So Sha'ul sent messengers to fetch David,
   and they saw a group of prophets ranting-in-prophecy,
   with Shemuel standing [there], stationed over them.
   And there [came] upon Sha'ul's messengers the spirit of God,
   so that they ranted-like-prophets, they too.
21 They told Sha'ul,
   and he sent other messengers,
   but they ranted-like-prophets, they too.
   And Sha'ul again sent, a third [group of] messengers,
   but they ranted-like-prophets, they too.
22 So he went, he too, to Rama;
   he arrived at the great cistern that is in Sekhu,
   and made inquiry, and said:
   Where are Shemuel and David?
   They said:
   Here, in Nayot in Rama.
23 So he went there, to Nayot in Rama,
   and there [came] upon him, him too, the spirit of God;
   he went, going along and ranting-like-a-prophet, until he arrived at
      the shepherds'-camps in Rama.

17 **sent . . . free:** I.e., let go.
18 **Nayot:** Either a place-name, or possibly "pasture-settlements" where prophets lived (McCarter 1980).

20 **too:** The first of the word's eight occurrences in four verses, indicating surprise.

Chapter 20. *Final Break; The Covenant of the Friends:* In a last-ditch attempt to save his friend's life, Yehonatan offers to intercede with Sha'ul. David proposes a simple test: if Sha'ul can accept David's absence on a family matter, it will be a sign that he is once again in the king's good graces, but if Sha'ul is unconvinced and agitated by the explanation given to him, the two friends will have to concede that there is no chance to mend the rift. The story makes use of an additional character through whom David and Yehonatan can communicate, an unsuspecting young servant who is sent to fetch arrows that Yehonatan shoots. Depending on the instructions given him, he is to (unwittingly) signal to David that all is either well or ill. Appropriately, the narrative echoes with repetitions of "good" and "evil," referring to David's fate.

The scene in which the prince sets out to determine his father's attitude toward David (vv.27–33) is nicely constructed around the word "son." David is referred to derisively (by omitting his given name), as the "son of Yishai"; Sha'ul insults Yehonatan by calling him the "son of a twisted rebellion"; and then Sha'ul pronounces the death sentence on his young rival by literally terming him a "son of death."

The most significant repeating word in the story, however, is "know," occurring nine times, which highlights a central concern in the text: David wishes to convince Yehonatan that there is no hope for any kind of reconciliation. That is, through the scenes of confrontation with Sha'ul, Yehonatan finally becomes convinced of what the audience "knew" all along. The story ends with a heartfelt covenant between the two young men, which is all the more ironic given that later events in the book will witness tension and death as the chief currencies between the House of David and the House of Sha'ul.

24 And he stripped off, he too, his garments,
    and ranted-like-a-prophet, he too, before Shemuel;
    he fell down naked all that day and all night.
    Therefore they say:
    Is Sha'ul too among the prophets?

20:1 Now David had gotten away from Nayot in Rama;
    he came and said before Yehonatan:
    What have I done?
    What is my iniquity, what is my sin before your father,
    that he seeks my life?

2 He said to him:
    [Heaven] forbid!
    You will not die—
    here, my father does not do anything great or anything small
      without baring my ear.
    So for-what-reason should my father hide this matter from me?
    This cannot [be]!

3 David swore again and said:
    Your father knows, yes, knows
    that I have found favor in your eyes,
    so he has said [to himself]:
    Yehonatan is not to know about this, lest he be pained;
    but: by the life of Yhwh, and by your life,
    indeed, there is only something like a step between me and death!

4 Yehonatan said to David:
    Whatever you yourself say, I will do for you.

5 David said to Yehonatan:
    Here, the New-Moon is tomorrow,
    when I must sit, yes, sit beside the king to eat;
    send me away, and I will hide in the open-field, until the third
      sunset.

20:5 **New-Moon:** Hebrew *hodesh* generally means "month," but here retains its connection to *h-d-sh,* "new." The New Moon was a major festival in bibli-cal times. This chapter is still read by Jews in synagogue on Sabbaths when a New Moon follows on the next day.

6 Now if your father takes account, yes, account of my [absence]
and you say: David requested, yes, requested-leave for himself from
me to run back to Bet-Lehem his town,
for the yearly sacrificial-meal is there, for the entire clan—
7 if he says thus: Good!
it is well for your servant.
But if he is agitated, yes, agitated,
know that evil has been determined by him.
8 So act with loyalty toward your servant,
for you brought your servant into YHWH's covenant with you.
Now if there be any iniquity in me,
put me to death yourself,
so to your father, why then should you bring me?
9 Yehonatan said:
[Heaven] forbid for you!
If I were to know, yes, know that evil is determined by my father to
come against you,
would I not tell that to you?
10 David said to Yehonatan:
Who will tell me if your father answers you roughly?
11 Yehonatan said to David:
Come, let us go out to the field.
The two of them went out to the field.
12 And Yehonatan said to David:
By YHWH, the God of Israel,
when I have sounded out my father at this time tomorrow [or] the
third [day],
and here: good is [determined] toward David,
shall I not then send to you and bare your ear?
13 Thus may YHWH do to Yehonatan, and thus may he add:
if it seems good to my father, the evil [determined] against you,
I will bare your ear
and will send you away, that you may go in peace.
And may YHWH be with you, as he was with my father!

13 **Thus may YHWH do to Yehonatan . . . :** With the
force of "May God strike me down if . . ."

14 Will you not, while I am still alive,
   will you not deal with me in the loyalty of YHWH,
   so that I do not die?
15 You must not cut off your loyalty from my house, for the ages,
   not even when YHWH cuts off David's enemies, each one from the
      face of the ground!
16 Yehonatan has cut [a covenant] with the House of David;
   may YHWH seek it from the hand of "David's enemies"!
17 And Yehonatan swore to David again, by his love for him,
   for he loved him with the love [he had] for his own self.
   Then Yehonatan said to him:
18 Tomorrow is the New-Moon;
   you will be counted-missing, for your seat will be counted-empty.
19 When you are three-days-gone, go down exceedingly [quickly],
   and when you come to the place where you were hiding at the time
      of the incident,
   you are to sit near that stone.
20 As for me, I will shoot three arrows to the side, to send them flying
      from me at a target.
21 And here, I will send the serving-lad toward you, [saying]:
   Go, find the arrows!
   If I say, yes, say to the lad:
   Here, the arrows are [to the side] of you, over there—
   take them and come back, for it is well for you,
   there is no problem, by the life of YHWH.
22 But if I say thus to the boy:
   Here, the arrows are [to the side] of you, farther onward—go,
   for YHWH will have sent you away.
23 And as for the promise that we have spoken, I and you,
   here, YHWH will be between me and you, for the ages!

14 **Will you not:** The repetition here is strange and probably a scribal error.
15 **from my house:** From my family.
16 **Yehonatan has cut [a covenant] . . . may YHWH seek it:** LXX and McCarter (1980) read the first phrase as "If Yehonatan be cut off," but MT plays nicely here on the verb. "Seek" means "seek retribution" or "hold responsible." **"David's enemies":** As in II Sam. 12:14, later scribes have added the word "enemies" here, in order to avoid placing a verbal curse on David.
17 **with the love [he had] . . . :** Following Waltke/O'Connor.
19 **incident:** Lit. "doing, deed." **that stone:** Heb. unclear; MT has "Ezel Stone." With LXX, Rainey/Notley reads this as a corruption of "this cairn" (Heb. *ha-argov ha-lazeh*).
23 **YHWH will be between me and you:** As a witness.

24 So David hid in the open-field.
Now it was at the New-Moon, that the king sat by the food, to eat,

25 and the king sat in his seat as time and time [before],
in the seat by the wall.
Yehonatan was at-the-front, and Avner sat at the side of Sha'ul,
while David's place was counted-empty.

26 Now Sha'ul did not say anything on that day,
for he said [to himself]:
It is an accident;
he is not ritually-pure, for he has not been purified.

27 But it was on the morrow of the New-Moon, on the second [day],
that David's place was counted-empty.
So Sha'ul said to Yehonatan his son:
For-what-reason has the son of Yishai not come, even yesterday,
even today, to the food?

28 Yehonatan answered Sha'ul:
David requested, yes, requested-leave for himself from me, to Bet-
Lehem;

29 he said: Pray send me off,
for it is the sacrificial-meal of the clan for us in the town,
and my brother charged me.
So-now, if I have found favor in your eyes,
pray let me get away, that I may see my brothers.
Therefore he has not come to the king's table.

30 Sha'ul's anger flared up against Yehonatan;
he said to him:
[You] son of a twisted rebellion!
Don't I know that you have chosen the son of Yishai,
to your shame and to the shame of your mother's nakedness?

25 **at-the-front:** Following LXX (reflecting *vykdm*); MT has *vykm*, "arose."

26 **an accident . . . not ritually-pure:** The New Moon festival required ritual purity of its participants; if one had a bodily discharge of the "polluting" kind, for instance (see Lev. 12–15), one was temporarily excluded.

27 **the morrow of the New-Moon:** See Fishbane for a discussion of this difficult phrase, which historically has raised ritual calendar questions among Jews in its appearance in Lev. 23:15's "the morrow of the Sabbath."

29 **get away:** Or "free to go" (McCarter 1980); the word, though, is most often found in contexts of survival, and so its use may be a bit ironic here. Fokkelman (1981) understands it as a Freudian slip which enrages Sha'ul.

30 **[You] son of a twisted rebellion!:** Ehrlich points out that Sha'ul would not insult his lone wife as the "perverse, rebellious woman" found in most translations. Instead, he proposes that Yehonatan, in the eyes of Sha'ul, is advocating overthrowing his own father by allowing David to live—a "twisted" act. **the son of Yishai:** Once again, omitting a per-

31 For all the days that the son of Yishai is alive on the earth,
   you will not be firmly-established, you or your kingdom!
   So-now,
   send and fetch him to me,
   for he is a son of death!

32 Yehonatan answered Sha'ul his father;
   he said to him:
   Why should he be put to death? What has he done?

33 But Sha'ul hurled the spear at him, to strike him down,
   and so Yehonatan knew
   that his father had determined to put David to death.

34 Yehonatan arose from the table in blazing anger;
   he did not eat food on the second day of the New-Moon,
   since he was pained about David,
   since his father had humiliated him.

35 So it was at daybreak,
   that Yehonatan went out to the open-field to the appointment with
      David,
   a young serving-lad with him.

36 He said to his lad: Run, now find the arrows that I shoot!
   As the lad ran, he shot an arrow past him,

37 and when the lad came to the place of the arrow that Yehonatan
      had shot,
   Yehonatan called after the lad, he said:
   Isn't the arrow [to the side] of you, and farther onward?

38 And Yehonatan called after the lad:
   Quick! Hurry! Don't stand still!
   So Yehonatan's serving-lad collected the arrows and brought them
      to his lord.

39 Now the lad knew nothing;
   only Yehonatan and David knew about the matter.

40 And Yehonatan gave his weapons to the lad that he had;
   he said to him:
   Go, bring [these back] to the town.

son's given name is usually understood in the Bible   31 **firmly-established:** Or "secure."   **a son of death:**
as an insult.   Or "a dead man."

Chapter 21. *David at Nov and Gat:* David the fugitive has two pressing needs, food and weapons, as he flees from Sha'ul. Arriving at Nov, his solitary presence arouses suspicions, but he is able to allay these through his cunning (note the recurrence of the related word "know" in v.3). We, of course, know that the "matter of the king" is no secret message, but rather refers to the fact that David is on the lam from Sha'ul. In any event, he is able to obtain bread and a sword—not just any weapon, but precisely the great sword of Golyat, which symbolically suggests David's ability to prevail in the most difficult of circumstances.

Thus armed, David meets his third challenge of the chapter. He flees to the heart of enemy country, one of the Philistine towns, and is apparently recognized, exposing himself to immediate danger. In a final example of quick thinking, and perhaps an ironic reference to Sha'ul's erstwhile ranting, he pretends to be crazy, dispelling the fears of the Philistines as to his identity.

41 When the lad went off,
David arose from beside the mound,
flung himself on his nostrils to the ground, and bowed low three
times,
and each one kissed his fellow,
each one wept with his fellow, until David [had wept] a great deal.

42 Yehonatan said to David:
Go in peace,
[seeing] that the two of us, [even] we, have sworn in the name of
Yʜwʜ, saying:
May Yʜwʜ be between me and you, between my seed and your
seed, for the ages!

21:1 He arose and went away,
while Yehonatan came back to the town.

2 David came to Nov, to Ahimelekh the priest.
And Ahimelekh trembled [coming] to meet David;
he said to him:
For-what-reason are you alone, and no one with you?

3 David said to Ahimelekh the priest:
The king has charged me with a matter,
he said to me:
No one is to know anything of the matter on which I am sending
you, with which I have charged you!
And with the serving-lads I have made-appointment at such and so
a place.

4 So-now,
what do you have on hand?
Give five [rounds of] bread into my hand, or whatever is found.

5 The priest answered David and said:
There is no ordinary bread on hand,
only hallowed bread is there—
provided that the lads have kept themselves away, of course, from
women.

41 **from beside the mound:** Following LXX in reading
ha-negev, "the southland," as *ha-argov.*
21:2 **Nov:** Just northeast of Jerusalem, perhaps Mount
Scopus, today familiar as the site of the Hebrew
University of Jerusalem (Rainey/Notley). **Ahimelekh:** Pronounced *ah-hee-MEH-lekh;* trad. English
"Ahimelech."

4 **on hand:** Lit., "under your hand," also found in vv.5
and 9. **five:** A biblical way of saying "a few."
5 **hallowed bread:** See v.7 and the accompanying
note. **provided that the lads . . . :** As McCarter
(1980) reminds us, holy bread could only be eaten
in a state of ritual, and thus sexual, purity; see rules
about encountering the holy in Exod. 19:15.

Chapter 22. *David in Flight; Sha'ul's Revenge:* From Gat, David moves southeast into the Judean hill-country. Here he becomes a kind of Robin Hood figure, attracting the disenfranchised (who are described as a class in other ancient Near Eastern texts) and serving as their chief. Sha'ul, meanwhile, vents his frustration on the priests of Nov, who are aghast to learn that the David to whom they gave food and weaponry in the previous chapter, and who had hitherto been a trusted key member of the royal household, is now accounted the king's "ambusher" (v.13). Sha'ul's command to kill the priests is resisted by his servants, but as so often in literature and in life, a volunteer comes forward, in this case Do'eg the Edomite. And, true to type, there is a survivor, Evyatar, who finds secure refuge with David. Together with his son, he will later become one of David's priests (II Sam. 8:17, 20:25).

6 David answered the priest;
he said to him:
Certainly women have been held back from us, so yesterday [and]
the day-before;
whenever I went out, the lads' gear was hallowed, even [if it was]
an ordinary journey—
how much more so today the gear should be hallowed!

7 So the priest gave him hallowed [bread],
for there was no bread there except for the Bread of the Presence
that was removed from the presence of Yhwh,
for [them] to put warm bread [there] at the time of its being taken
away.

8 Now a man was there from the servants of Sha'ul that day,
held-in-custody in the presence of Yhwh;
his name was Do'eg the Edomite,
chief of the shepherds that belonged to Sha'ul.

9 David said to Ahimelekh:
Don't you have on hand here a spear or a sword?
For neither my sword nor my weapons did I take along in my hand,
for the matter of the king was urgent!

10 The priest said:
The sword of Golyat the Philistine, whom you struck down in the
Valley of the Oak—
here it is, wrapped up in a cloth, behind the *efod*.
If it is what you wish to take for yourself, take it,
for there is no other one besides it in this [place].
David said: There is none like it—give it to me!

11 And David arose
and got away on that day from before Sha'ul,
and came to Akhish king of Gat.

---

6 **gear was hallowed:** Everything connected with the men was made ritually pure.

7 **Bread of the Presence:** See Exod. 25:30, where this bread is placed in the "Dwelling" (Tabernacle); it corresponds to food set out for the gods in pagan sanctuaries, whereas here its use is purely symbolic.

8 **held-in-custody:** The reason for Do'eg's detention is not stated. **Do'eg:** Pronounced *doe-AYG*. The name derives from the verb "to worry," and he will indeed become more than cause for concern in the next chapter (v.18).

11 **Akhish:** Pronounced *ah-KHEESH*; trad. English "Achish."

◆ 12 Now the servants of Akhish said to him:
Isn't this David, the king of the land?
Isn't it about this one that they chant in [their] dances, saying:
Sha'ul has struck down his thousands,
but David—his myriads!?

13 David took these words to heart, and was exceedingly afraid in the
presence of Akhish king of Gat,

14 so he altered his demeanor in their eyes
and acted deranged [while] in their hands:
he drummed on the doors of the gate
and let his spittle run down his beard.

15 And Akhish said to his servants:
Here, look at this one acting-like-a-madman!
Why do you bring him to me?

16 Do I lack madmen
that you have brought this one to act-like-a-madman around me?
Should this one come into my house?

22:1 David went from there and escaped to the Cave of Adullam.
His brothers and his whole Father's House heard,
and they went down to him there.

2 And there gathered to him every man in straits, every man who had
a creditor, and every man of bitter feelings,
and he became commander over them.
And there were with him about four hundred men.

3 David went from there to Mitzpe / Lookout of Moav;
he said to the king of Moav:
Pray let my father and my mother stay with you
until I know what God [intends to] do with me.

4 So he led them into the presence of the king of Moav, and they
stayed with him, all the days of David's being at the stronghold.

5 But the prophet Gad said to David:
You are not to stay at the stronghold;

12 **king of the land:** The Philistines textually confirm David's selection as king (Alter 1999).
14 **drummed:** Reading *vayyatof* with ancient manuscripts; MT has the strange *vaytav*.
22:1 **Adullam:** A town in the lowlands between Bet-Lehem, south of Jerusalem, and Gat. See Gen. 38.
3 **Moav:** The territory due east of the Dead Sea, in today's Jordan. Although the Moabites were tradi-

tional enemies of Israel, the Bible records their connection to David through his ancestress Ruth in the book that bears her name.
5 **Gad:** Pronounced *god*. He is a prophet not previously mentioned; see II Sam. 24. In contrast to Sha'ul, David is in frequent contact with God, either through a prophet or alone.

384

go, come on your [way] to the land of Judah.
So David went and came to the Forest of Heret.

6 And Sha'ul heard that [the whereabouts of] David were known, and
of the men that were with him.
Now Sha'ul was staying at Giv'a, under a tamarisk at Rama, with
his spear in his hand,
and all his servants were standing-in-attendance around him.

7 Sha'ul said to his servants who were standing around him:
Now hearken, O Binyaminites:
Is it really to all of you that the son of Yishai will give fields and
vineyards?
Will he make all of you commanders of thousands and
commanders of hundreds,

8 that all of you have banded together against me?
No one bares my ear when my son cuts [a covenant] with the son
of Yishai;
none of you is concerned about me or bares my ear
[to reveal] that my son has raised up my servant against me as an
ambusher, as is this day!

9 Then Do'eg the Edomite spoke up
—he was standing around the servants of Sha'ul—
and said:
I saw the son of Yishai come to Nov, to Ahimelekh son of Ahituv;

10 he inquired for him of Yнwн, and provisions he gave him,
and the sword of Golyat the Philistine he gave him!

11 So the king sent to call Ahimelekh son of Ahituv the priest
along with all his Father's House, the priests who were at Nov,
and all of them came to the king.

12 Sha'ul said:
Now hearken, son of Ahituv!
He said:
Here I am, my lord.

---

6 **tamarisk:** A shady tree that sometimes marks a holy
site in Genesis (see, for example, 21:33).
8 **banded together:** Others, "conspired." **bares my
ear:** Meaning "informs me"; I have retained the lit-

eral idiom, which occurs three times in this chapter, to keep the reader's focus on the theme of body
parts in Samuel (see Introduction).

385

Chapters 23:1–24:1. *Cat and Mouse:* In the wilds of Judah, David zigs and zags, consulting God as to his moves (vv.2, 4, and 10–12) and staging a successful raid against the Philistines. His future is affirmed in another meeting with Yehonatan, with the latter's phrase "Even . . . my father knows this" (v. 17) recalling Chap. 20. Sha'ul continues his dogged pursuit, and at one point the two men are actually on either side of the same hill (v.26). They will in fact have contact, both intimate and distant, in the next chapter.

As JPS points out, David's exact movements in this chapter and the next are not always clear, and are partially duplicated in Chap. 26.

13 Sha'ul said to him:

Why have you banded together against me, you and the son of
  Yishai,

by your giving him food and a sword

and inquiring for him of God,

to rise up against me as an ambusher, as is this day?

14 Ahimelekh answered the king, he said:

But who among all your servants is like David—trustworthy,

the king's son-in-law,

commander over your obedient-bodyguard,

and honored in your house?

15 [Only] today I first inquired for him of God—[Heaven] forbid
  for me:

do not let the king place an accusing-word against his servant,
  against all my Father's House,

for your servant did not know about all this, anything small or
  great!

16 But the king said:

You shall die, yes, die, Ahimelekh,

you and all your Father's House!

17 And the king said to the outrunners who were standing around
  him:

Turn about and put to death the priests of Yнwн,

because their hand too is with David,

and because they knew that he was getting away and did not bare
  my ear!

But the king's servants would not stretch out their hand to attack
  the priests of Yнwн,

18 so the king said to Do'eg:

You turn about and attack the priests!

So Do'eg the Edomite turned about, and *he* attacked the priests:

he put to death on that day eighty-five men wearing a linen *efod,*

---

14 **obedient-bodyguard:** From Heb. *shamo'a,* "hearken, obey."

16 **you and all your Father's House:** Fulfilling the
curse on the line of Eli from I Sam. 2:31–34.

17 **outrunners:** The palace guard (McCarter 1980);

when in the field, they "run ahead of his chariot"
(8:11 above). Goldman notes their erstwhile function as executioners (see II Kings 10:25). **attack:** Or
"smite, strike."

19 and as for Nov, the town of the priests, he struck it with the mouth
       of the sword,
    from man to woman
    and from child to suckling,
    and ox and donkey and sheep,
    with the mouth of the sword.

20 But one son of Ahimelekh son of Ahituv escaped—his name was
       Evyatar;
    he got away to David.

21 And Evyatar told David
    that Sha'ul had killed the priests of YHWH.

22 David said to Evyatar:
    I knew that day, when Do'eg the Edomite was there,
    that he would tell, yes, tell Sha'ul.
    I myself am responsible for every life in your Father's House!

23 Stay with me, and do not be afraid,
    for they must [first] seek my life who seek your life;
    indeed, you will be under care with me!

23:1 They told David, saying:
    Here, the Philistines are waging battle against Ke'ila,
    they are pillaging the threshing-floors!

2   David inquired of YHWH, saying:
    Shall I go and strike these Philistines?
    YHWH said to David:
    Go and strike the Philistines, and deliver Ke'ila!

3   Now David's men said to him:
    Look, we are here in Judah, afraid;
    shall we really go to Ke'ila, against the Philistine ranks?

4   So David once again inquired of YHWH,
    and YHWH answered him, he said:
    Arise, go down to Ke'ila,
    for I give the Philistines into your hand!

---

20 **Evyatar:** Trad. English "Abiathar." The name appro-
    priately suggests the verb *y-t-r,* "to remain" (Garsiel
    1985).
22 **responsible:** Following LXX; MT has "turned
    about," recalling its use in v.18.

23:1 **Ke'ila:** South of Adullam, where David had fled
    from Gat.

5 So David went, along with his men, to Ke'ila,
and he waged battle against the Philistines:
he led away their livestock and struck them down, a great striking-
down.
Thus David delivered the settled-folk of Ke'ila.

6 —Now it was, when Evyatar son of Ahimelekh had gotten away to
David, to Ke'ila,
that an *efod* had come down in his hand.—

7 It was told to Sha'ul that David had come to Ke'ila, and Sha'ul said:
God has transferred him into my hand,
for he has turned himself over by entering a town with gates and
bars!

8 So Sha'ul summoned all the fighting-people for battle,
to come down to Ke'ila, to besiege David and his men.

9 And David realized that Sha'ul was concocting evil against him,
so he said to Evyatar the priest: Bring the *efod* close!

10 Then David said:
O Yhwh, God of Israel,
your servant has heard, yes, heard
that Sha'ul is seeking to enter Ke'ila, to bring-ruin to the town on
my account.

11 Will the inhabitants of Ke'ila turn me over to his hand?
Will Sha'ul come down, as your servant has heard?
O Yhwh, God of Israel,
now tell your servant . . . .
Yhwh said:
He will come down.

12 David said:
Will the inhabitants of Ke'ila turn me over, along with my men,
into the hand of Sha'ul?
Yhwh said:
They will turn [you] over.

---

6 **an *efod* had come down . . . :** In typical biblical fashion, what seems like an intrusion here will shortly
make sense (in v.9).

7 **transferred:** In legal language, "alienated" (often

regarding property). **turned himself over:** Lit.,
"closed himself up"; others, "delivered." Sha'ul is
confident that David has walked into a trap.

◆

13 So David and his men arose, some six hundred men;
   they moved out from Ke'ila, and went about wherever they could
      go about.

   Now when it was told to Sha'ul that David had escaped from Ke'ila,
      he held back from moving out.
14 And David stayed in the wilderness, in the strongholds;
   he stayed in the highlands, in the Wilderness of Zif,
   and Sha'ul sought him all the days,
   but God did not give him into his hand.
15 And David saw that Sha'ul was going forth to seek his life
   —David was in the Wilderness of Zif, in the woods.
16 But Yehonatan son of Sha'ul arose and went to David in the woods;
   he strengthened his hand in God
17 and said to him:
   Do not be afraid,
   for the hand of Sha'ul my father will not find you;
   you yourself will reign as king over Israel,
   and I myself will be second-in-command to you.
   Even Sha'ul my father knows this!
18 So the two of them cut a covenant in the presence of YHWH.
   And David stayed in the woods, while Yehonatan went back to his
      house.

19 Some Zifites went up to Sha'ul at Giv'a, saying:
   Is not David hiding himself among us in the strongholds in the
      woods,
   at the Hill of Hakhila which is to the right/south of the wasteland?
20 So-now, according to all your craving, O king, to come down—
      come down,
   and [it will be] our [task], turning him over to the king's hand.

---

13 **held back from moving out:** McCarter (1980): "gave up the march."
14 **Wilderness of Zif:** Southeast of Hevron, flanking the Judean Desert.
15 **in the woods:** Or perhaps a place-name, "Horesh." In fact much of biblical Israel seems to have been wooded.

16 **strengthened his hand:** Encouraged him. For the reverse image, see II 4:1, below.
19 **Hill of Hakhila:** Exact location unknown.
20 **craving:** Another of the many terms indicating strong desire in the David narratives.

21 Sha'ul said:
Blessed are you of YHWH,
that you have taken pity on me!

22 Now go, be determined once-again,
know and take-note of his place where his foot is [now and] who
has seen him there,
for they have said to me that he acts-shrewdly, yes, shrewdly.

23 So take-note and know
in which of all the hiding-places he hides himself,
and return to me when it is determined;
then I will go with you,
and it will be: if he is in the region,
I will search for him among all the thousands of Judah.

24 They arose and went to Zif, ahead of Sha'ul,
while David and his men were in the Wilderness of Ma'on/Abode,
in the plain to the right of the wasteland.

25 And Sha'ul and his men went to seek [him],
and it was told to David,
so he went down to a certain crag and stayed in the Wilderness of
Ma'on.
Sha'ul heard, and pursued after David, in the Wilderness of Ma'on:

26 Sha'ul went on [one] side of a hill, over-here,
with David and his men on the [other] side of the hill, over-there.
Now David was hastening to get away from Sha'ul,
while Sha'ul and his men were closing in on David and his men, to
seize them.

27 But a messenger came to Sha'ul, saying:
Come quickly,
for Philistines are sweeping down on the region!

28 So Sha'ul had to turn back from pursuing after David;
he went to meet the Philistines.
Therefore that place was called: Crag of the Parting.

24:1 And David went up from there
and stayed in the strongholds of En-Gedi.

---

24 **Ma'on:** Northwest of Masada and hence west of the
Dead Sea.

Chapters 24:2–25:1. *David Holds Back from Killing Sha'ul I:* In the midst of the stories of flight and pursuit, David has the opportunity to rid himself of his enemy once and for all. By good fortune, the king is literally exposed, vulnerable in a private moment. David's response, though short of assassination, is the still significant act of cutting off the corner of Sha'ul's cloak, equivalent in the ancient Near East to the filching of a person's wallet or passport. After the fact, David is portrayed in the text as remorseful, feeling that he has tarnished the office of the monarchy.

For the first time since Chap. 18, the two men meet and exchange words. But what a conversation it is! From a distance, David admits his originally murderous intent, but then focuses on his compassion and his innocence (vv.11–12). He does this in a speech which seven times (vv.11–16) features "hand," a word that usually denotes power and personal responsibility in the Bible. Sha'ul is forced to acknowledge his own culpability, and can only confirm David's future ascension to the throne. His one request of his successor is full of pathos and reflects good Israelite ideology: he asks that in the inevitable struggle for power, his children and grandchildren may be spared, so that his name will survive. The verb utilized, "[not] to cut off," nicely dovetails with its earlier use in the chapter, describing David's actions (Hamilton).

A final section (25:1) seals Sha'ul's fate. Shemuel, who had anointed him in the first place, finally dies. Now the king, who had already felt deserted by both his courtiers and his children, is truly alone, although he will turn to his old friend again in Chap. 28, despite the fact that at that point they occupy the separate worlds of the living and the dead.

◆ 2 Now it was, when Sha'ul returned from [chasing] after the
    Philistines,
that it was told to him, saying:
Here, David is in the Wilderness of En-Gedi!

3 So Sha'ul took three thousand men, hand-picked from all Israel,
and went to seek out David and his men, in front of the Wild-Goat
    Rocks.

4 He came to some sheep pens along the way, and there was a cave
    there,
and Sha'ul went in to "cover his feet,"
while David and his men were staying in the recesses of the cave.

5 And David's men said to him:
Here is the day about which YHWH said to you:
Here, I give your enemy into your hand!
You may do with him whatever seems good in your eyes!
And David arose and cut off the corner of the cloak that belonged
    to Sha'ul, discreetly.

6 But it was after that
that David's heart struck him,
because he had cut off the corner that belonged to Sha'ul.

7 He said to his men:
[Heaven] forbid for me from YHWH
if I should do this thing to my lord, to YHWH's anointed,
to stretch out my hand against him,
for he is YHWH's anointed!

8 David checked his men with [these] words,
and did not give them [leave] to rise up against Sha'ul,
while Sha'ul arose from the cave, and went on his way.

9 But David arose after that
and came out of the cave, and he called out after Sha'ul, saying:
My lord king!

24:2 **En-Gedi:** The name means "Spring of the Goat-
Kid." It is located near the Dead Sea, and has long
been a well-loved tourist spot noted for its lushness.
4 **"cover his feet":** A euphemism for defecating.
5 **corner of the cloak:** See note to 15:27 above. The act
of cutting off the corner was a serious and dangerous matter.

7 **for he is YHWH's anointed!:** In European history,
this passage has sometimes been used as an argument against assassinating kings.
8 **checked:** Hebrew meaning uncertain.

Chapter 25:2–44. *David Held Back from Killing Naval:* The reader, like David, could use a break from Sha'ul's relentless manhunt, but instead of some sort of humorous diversion such as we might expect in Shakespeare, we are presented with a story relating to David's wilderness years that makes some important points about his personality, romantic aspects aside. With its fairy-tale beginning (again, "[there was] a man . . ."), it features a hero with a problem, a bad-tempered villain, and a beautiful and wise problem-solver who, of course, marries the hero at the end of the story.

As he had done in Chap. 20, David requests food on his arrival in a new place, going to great lengths to demonstrate his worthiness by pointing out the exemplary behavior of his whole band. The churlish Naval's answer (vv.10–11) is not only negative but deeply offensive, with the tone equivalent to "Who do these runaway slaves think they are?!" For David the warrior and man of action there can be only one possible response: to strap on his sword and have his followers do the same. By v.22 he is vowing to wipe out Naval and his household like dogs, using a particularly colorful biblical expression.

Violence is averted only by the wisdom and timely intervention of the fair Avigayil. In a long and masterful speech (vv.24–31), she stresses how David must not act alone in this matter, "shed[ding] blood for nothing" (v.31), for that would taint his future status as the founder of a dynasty. Instead, she suggests, God will take care of the matter. Her plea and David's response bespeak prevention and restraint, and suffice to preserve his integrity and public innocence. The text draws a nice contrast between the threefold "peace" and the threefold "sword" (Hamilton). It also has Avigayil use "my lord" no less than fourteen times, a repetition that may seem overly groveling to modern ears but which serves to accomplish her purpose.

Naval's fate is sealed, and is played out in a striking way. It requires only the words of his wife, reporting her conversation with David, to induce something like a stroke in the drunken husband; he is thus killed not by the hotheaded David but by the proper judgment of God.

Only at the very end of the tale (vv.43–44) are we informed that part of its raison d'être, David's need for women, is that Sha'ul had taken away David's wife (and the king's daughter) Mikhal and given her to another.

The placement of this story precisely at this point in the larger narrative warrants some thought, bracketed as it is by the two accounts of David's opportunity to kill Sha'ul. From one point of view, the text goes out of its way to declare David's innocence in both of those chapters:

> [Heaven] forbid for me from YHWH
> if I should do this thing to my lord, to YHWH's anointed,
> to stretch out my hand against him,
> for he is YHWH's anointed! (24:7)
>
> . . . .

Sha'ul looked behind him,
and David prostrated himself, nostrils to the earth, and bowed low,

10 and David said to Sha'ul:
Why do you hearken to the words of anyone [who] says:
Here, David is seeking evil-against-you?

11 Here, this day your eyes have seen
that Yhwh gave you today into my hand, in the cave;
they intended to kill you,
but I had compassion on you:
I said [to myself]:
I will not stretch out my hand against my lord,
for he is Yhwh's anointed!

12 And Father, see too:
see the corner of your cloak in my hand—
for when I cut off the corner of your cloak,
I did not kill you!
[So] know and take-note that there is no evil or transgression in my
    hand,
nor have I sinned against you—
yet you are stalking my life, to take it!

13 May Yhwh judge between me and you,
and may Yhwh avenge me upon you—
but *my* hand shall not be against you!

14 As the proverb of the ancients says: From the wicked comes
    wickedness.
But my hand shall not be against you!

15 After whom has the king of Israel gone out?
After whom are you pursuing?
After a dead dog?
After a single flea?

16 May Yhwh be the one-who-decides, and judge between me
    and you:
when he sees, may he uphold my cause
and exact justice from your hand!

---

14 **the proverb of the ancients:** Restoring the plural,
following 4QS^a.

[Heaven] forbid for me, by YHWH,
from stretching out my hand against YHWH's anointed one! (26:11)

But Chap. 25 strongly suggests that David is not as pure-hearted and in control of himself as one might think, as he comes within a hair of taking a brutal revenge upon Naval. The bracketing chapters, in other words, may be protesting too much. These kinds of doubts will accompany many of the narratives about David and Sha'ul, extending to the untimely ends of Sha'ul's descendants and generals subsequent to the death of the king himself.

17 Now it was, when David had finished speaking these words to
 Sha'ul,
 that Sha'ul said:
 Is that your voice, my son David?
 And Sha'ul lifted up his voice and wept;
18 he said to David:
 You are in the right, more than I,
 for you have dealt with me for good, while I have dealt with you for
 evil!
19 And you have told me today
 how you have done good with me,
 how Yhwh turned me over to your hand, yet you did not kill me.
20 If a man comes upon his enemy,
 does he send him off on the way in good-condition?
 May Yhwh pay you back in-good-measure for this day,
 for what you have done with me!
21 So-now, here: I know
 that you will reign as king, yes, king,
 and that the kingdom of Israel will be established in your hand;
22 so-now, swear to me by Yhwh:
 if you should cut off my seed after me,
 if you should wipe out my name from my Father's House . . . !
23 And David swore to Sha'ul.
 Then Sha'ul went back to his house,
 while David and his men went up to the stronghold.

25:1 Shemuel died;
 all Israel gathered and beat [the breast] for him,
 and they buried him at his house in Rama.
 Then David arose and went down to the Wilderness of Ma'on.

2 Now [there was] a man in Ma'on, with his business in Carmel,
 and the man was exceedingly great [in wealth]:
 he had sheep, three thousand, and a thousand goats,
 and he was shearing his sheep in Carmel.

---

22 **seed:** Descendants.
23 **the stronghold:** Probably Masada, just west of the
 Dead Sea.
25:1 **beat [the breast]:** The literal meaning of this term

for mourning; my thanks to E. L. Greenstein (private communication) for this rendering.
2 **Ma'on:** MT has "Pa'ran"; the present reading follows ancient versions.

◆ 3 The man's name was Naval,
and his wife's name was Avigayil.
Now the woman was of good sense, and beautiful of form,
but the man was rough and evil in deeds;
he was a Calevite.

4 And David heard in the wilderness that Naval was shearing his
    sheep,

5 so David sent ten serving-lads,
and David said to the lads:
Go up to Carmel
and come to Naval, and inquire of him in my name for peace,

6 and say thus: To Life!
[May] you [be in] peace, your house [be in] peace, and all that
    belongs to you [be in] peace!

7 So-now, I have heard that you have shearers;
now: the shepherds that belong to you were with us—
we did not hurt them,
and nothing has been unaccounted for by them,
all the time of our being in Carmel.

8 Inquire of your lads, and they will tell you.
So may [my] lads find favor in your eyes,
for upon a good day we have come—
now give whatever you can find in your hand to your servant, to
    your son David!

9 So David's lads came
and spoke to Naval according to all these words, in David's name,
and then they stood-at-ease.

10 Naval answered David's servants; he said:
Who is David? Who is the son of Yishai?
Nowadays there are many servants who break away, each one from
    his lord!

---

3 **Naval:** Pronounced *nah-VAHL;* trad. English "Nabal." In some other contexts it means "fool, foolish one." A more colloquial translation here might use a word like "jerk." The name also happens to pun on *neveila,* "corpse," in anticipation of the story's end (see McKenzie 2000). Naval is also the anagram of another biblical villain, Yaakov's uncle Lavan (Laban) in Genesis. **Avigayil:** Possibly meaning "My Father [or God] Was Delighted."

Trad. English "Abigail." **Calevite:** Descended from Calev, who, with Yehoshua, was one of the "good spies" in Num. 13. More to the point here is the play on *kelev,* "dog," a negative image that recurs a number of times in Samuel.

6 **To Life!:** The Hebrew (*le-hai*) is obscure; some read "my brother" (*ahi*), but that does not seem appropriate.

11 So should I take away my bread, my water and my butchered-meat
  that I butchered for my shearers,
  and give it to men who are from I don't know where?

12 David's lads turned about, [back] on their way;
  they returned and came and told him in accordance with all these
    words.

13 Then David said to his men:
  Each one gird on his sword!
  Each one girded on his sword,
  and also David girded on his sword;
  they went up behind David, about four hundred men,
  while two hundred stayed with the gear.

14 Now Avigayil wife of Naval
  was told by a lad from among the serving-lads, saying:
  Here, David sent messengers from the wilderness to give blessing-
    of-greeting to our lord,
  but he shrieked at them.

15 Now the men were exceedingly good to us;
  we were not hurt, we did not [find] anything unaccounted for
  all the days we went about with them, during our being in the
    open-field;

16 they were a wall about us,
  even by day, even by night,
  all the days we were beside them herding the sheep.

17 So-now,
  know and take-note what you should do,
  for evil is concluded against our lord and against his entire house!
  But he is [too] base a fellow for speaking to!

18 Avigayil quickly took two hundred loaves-of-bread and two skins of
    wine,
  five sheep made ready and five *sei'as* of parched-grain
  and a hundred raisin-cakes and two hundred pressed-figs,
  and she put them on some donkeys.

19 Then she said to her lads:
  Cross on ahead of me,

---

14 **shrieked:** A rare verb related to the noun for "bird
of prey," i.e., "shrieker."
15 **all the days:** The entire time.

16 **they were a wall about us:** English idiom might
yield "they were solid as a rock to us."
18 **five *sei'as*:** About a bushel.

here, I will be coming behind you—
but her husband Naval she did not tell.

20 Now she was riding on the donkey, going down a covert in a hill:
but here were David and his men, going down toward her,
and she encountered them.

21 Now David had said [to himself]:
Surely in vain did I keep-safe all that belongs to this one in the
wilderness,
though from all that belongs to him, nothing was unaccounted
for—
he has returned to me evil in place of good!

22 Thus may God do to "the enemies of" David, and thus may he add,
if I leave from all that belongs to him, by daybreak, [even] one
pissing against the wall!

23 When Avigayil saw David,
she quickly got down from the donkey
flung herself before David, on her face,
and bowed low to the ground.

24 She flung herself at his feet and said:
On *me,* my lord, be the iniquity!
Now let your maidservant speak in your ear,
and hearken to the words of your maidservant:

25 now let not my lord pay any mind to this base man, to Naval,
for as his name is, so is he:
Naval/Vile-One is his name, and vileness is with him!
But as for me, your maidservant,
I did not see my lord's lads whom you sent.

26 So-now, my lord,
by the life of YHWH and by your life,
[given] that YHWH has prevented you from coming into blood-guilt,
namely, delivering yourself by your hand [alone]—
so-now,

---

20 **a covert:** Or "under cover of" (McCarter 1980).

22 **"the enemies of":** See note to 20:16. **one pissing against the wall:** Others, euphemistically, "a single male," but the imagery is doglike again. Unlike most modern translations, Tyndale and the King James Version got it right: "aught / one that pisseth by the wall."

26 **by your hand [alone]:** I.e., without the intervention of God. Note that the expression recurs in vv.31 and 33; it has the force of "taking the law into your own hands."

may your enemies be like Naval,
yes, those who seek evil against my lord!

27 And now,
this token-of-blessing that your handmaid has brought to my lord,
let it be given to the lads who go about in my lord's footsteps.

28 O bear-in-forgiveness the transgression of your maidservant,
for when YHWH makes, yes, makes for my lord a secure house
—for the battles of YHWH does my lord fight,
and no evil may be found in you [all] your days—

29 should anyone arise to pursue you, to seek your life,
may my lord's life be bound up in the bundle of life with YHWH
your God,
but may the life of your enemies be slung away in the hollow of a
sling!

30 And may it be,
when YHWH does for my lord in accordance with all that he
promised, the good things for you,
and he commissions you as *Nagid* over Israel:

31 then do not let this be for you an obstacle, or a stumbling-block of
heart for my lord,
to shed blood for nothing,
for my lord to find deliverance by himself [alone]!
And when YHWH does-good to my lord,
then call-to-mind your maidservant!

32 David said to Avigayil:
Blessed is YHWH, the God of Israel,
who has sent you this day to meet me!

33 And blessed is your discernment, and blessed are you,
who has prevented me this day from coming into blood-guilt,
delivering myself by my hand [alone].

34 For: by the life of YHWH, the God of Israel, who has held me back
from doing-evil to you—
indeed, had you not quickly come to meet me,
there would not have been left to Naval, by the light of daybreak,
[even] one pissing against the wall!

---

29 **bound up in the bundle of life:** "Bundle" here may
indicate a written document, as in the ancient idea
of a "Book of Life." The phrase is still used by Jews
in memorial prayers.

34 **one pissing against the wall:** See note to v.22.

Chapter 26. *David Holds Back from Killing Sha'ul II:* An alternative tradition to the one in Chap. 24 is more expansive. It is marked by multiple conversations (between David and Avishai, David and Avner, and Sha'ul and David) and more psychological detail. David's actions here are also more risk-filled than they were in Chap. 24, with Sha'ul's generals and soldiers immediately present, yet he is also clearly protected by YHWH (see v.12). The motif word "hand" returns (vv.8, 9, 11, 18, 23) to link the two accounts. Of greatest interest is the verbal connection with the Naval story of the previous chapter: David has learned his lesson—YHWH will "smite" Sha'ul, either naturally or in battle (v.10), just as he "smote" Naval in 25:38, and David will not have to bear either the guilt or the political consequences.

The abiding question is whether David acts here out of true piety and regard for the "divine right of kings" or whether he is simply politically astute. The text leaves it for the reader to decide (for a strong vote for the former, see Borgman; most recent commentators are highly skeptical of David's motives).

35 David took from her hand what she had brought him,
and to her he said:
Go up in peace to your house;
see,
I have hearkened to your voice, and have lifted up your face!

36 Avigayil went back to Naval,
and here, he was having a drinkfest in his house, like a king's
drinkfest.
Now Naval's heart was in good-humor upon him—he was drunk to
excess—
so she did not tell him a thing, small or great, until the light of
daybreak.

37 But it was at daybreak,
when the wine was going out of Naval,
that his wife told those things to him,
and his heart died within him, and he himself became [like] a stone.

38 It was about ten days [later]
that Yhwh attacked Naval, so that he died.

39 David heard that Naval was dead,
and he said:
Blessed is Yhwh,
who has upheld my cause at having been mocked at the hand of
Naval,
and his servant he has held back from evildoing!
And as for the evildoing of Naval, Yhwh has returned it on his
head.
David sent and spoke for Avigayil, to take her as a wife for him;

40 David's servants came to Avigayil, to Carmel,
and spoke to her, saying:
David has sent us to you, to take you as a wife for him.

---

35 **lifted up your face:** Granted your request, been favorable to you.
37 **the wine was going out of Naval:** A play on another meaning of *naval:* "wineskin." I regret not being able to use English "vial" here, along with "viol" for *neivel,* "harp," to go with my rendering of "vile" for

the descriptive word that occurs in v.25. **his heart died within him . . . stone:** The text appears to be describing a stroke.
39 **his servant:** David. **spoke for:** A term indicating marriage negotiations.

41 She proceeded to bow down, nostrils to the ground,
and said:
Here, your maidservant is a handmaid to wash the feet of my lord's
servants!

42 Avigayil quickly arose and mounted a donkey, with five of her girls
who went behind her;
she went after David's messengers,
and she became a wife for him.

43 Now Ahinoam [too] David had taken, from Yizre'el,
and the two of them alike became wives for him;

44 for Sha'ul had given Mikhal his daughter, David's wife,
to Palti son of Layish, who was from Gallim.

26:1 Some Zifites came to Sha'ul at Giv'a, saying:
Is not David hiding himself at the Hill of Hakhila, facing the
wasteland?

2 So Sha'ul arose and went down to the Wilderness of Zif,
and with him were three thousand men, hand-picked ones of Israel,
to seek out David in the Wilderness of Zif.

3 Sha'ul encamped at the Hill of Hakhila, which faces the wasteland,
along the road,
while David was staying in the wilderness;
and he saw that Sha'ul had come after him into the wilderness,

4 so David sent spies, that he might know that Sha'ul had come for
certain.

5 Then David arose and came to the place where Sha'ul was
encamped;
David saw the place where Sha'ul was lying, along with Avner son
of Ner, the commander of his forces,
with Sha'ul lying in the wagon-ring, and all the fighting-people
encamped around him.

---

43 **Ahinoam:** Levenson (1978) makes the case that she is Sha'ul's wife (see 14:50), thus explaining the prophet Natan's words in II Sam. 12:7–8, "I gave you . . . the wives of your lord." A son or successor stealing away / sleeping with his predecessor's wife or concubine thus established his new power base; in this passage, the process is muted but present.

44 **Gallim:** Location unknown.

26:5 **wagon-ring:** Another term for "encampment."

6 And David spoke up, he said to Ahimelekh the Hittite and to
  Avishai son of Tzeruya, Yoav's brother, saying:
 Who will go down with me to Sha'ul, to the camp?
 Avishai said:
 I will go down with you!

7 So David and Avishai went to the fighting-people at nighttime,
 and here, Sha'ul was lying asleep in the wagon-ring,
 with his spear stuck into the ground at his head
 and Avner and the fighting-people lying around him.

8 Avishai said to David:
 God has turned over your enemy today into your hand!
 So-now, just let me strike him with the spear into the ground one
  time;
 I will not [have to do it] twice to him!

9 But David said to Avishai:
 You are not to bring him to ruin!
 For who could stretch out his hand against Yʜwʜ's anointed one
  and be cleared?

10 And David said:
 By the life of Yʜwʜ,
 rather, Yʜwʜ will attack him:
 either his day will come, and he will die,
 or into battle he will go down and be swept away!

11 [Heaven] forbid for me, by Yʜwʜ,
 from stretching out my hand against Yʜwʜ's anointed one!
 So-now,
 just take the spear that is at his head, and the cruse of water,
 and let us go on our [way].

12 So David took the spear and the cruse of water at Sha'ul's head,
  and they went on their [way];
 no one saw, no one knew, and no one awoke,
 for all of them were sleeping,
 for a deep-slumber of Yʜwʜ had fallen upon them.

---

6 **Avishai:** Trad. English "Abishai." **Tzeruya:** Trad. English "Zeruiah." **Yoav:** Pronounced *yo-AHV*; trad. English "Joab." David's nephew (through his sister Tzeruya) and future commander in chief. Note that Sha'ul's commander, Avner, is also the king's kinsman.

7 **his spear stuck into the ground:** And thus easily accessible.

9 **cleared:** Of punishment.

12 **deep-slumber:** A God-induced sleep (see Gen. 2:21).

13 Then David crossed over the side-across
and stopped at the summit of the hill, afar off,
—great was the space between them—
14 and David called out to the fighting-people and to Avner son of
Ner, saying:
Won't you answer, Avner?
Avner answered and said:
Who are you, [that] you call to the king?
15 David said to Avner:
Aren't you a man?
And who is like you in Israel?
So why haven't you kept watch over your lord king?
For one of the fighting-people came to bring ruin to the king your
lord!
16 No good is this thing that you have done!
By the life of YHWH,
indeed, you are sons of death,
[seeing] that you did not keep watch over your lord, over YHWH's
anointed!
For-now, see:
where are the king's spear and the cruse of water that were at his
head?
17 Sha'ul recognized David's voice;
he said:
Is that your voice, my son David?
David said:
It is my voice, my lord king!
18 And he said:
Why now does my lord pursue after his servant?
Indeed, what have I done?
And what evil is there in my hand?
19 So-now,
pray let my lord king hearken to the words of his servant:
if it is YHWH [who] incited you against me, let him savor a gift-
offering;

19 **let him savor a gift-offering:** The smell of the
offering was understood to be pleasing to God (see
Gen. 8:21).

◆   but if it was by humans,
then let them be doomed before Yhwh,
for they have driven me away today from being attached to Yhwh's
    inheritance,
saying:
Go, serve other gods!

20   So-now,
let not my blood fall to the earth, away from the presence of
    Yhwh!
For the king of Israel has come out to seek a single flea,
as one pursues a partridge in the hills!

21   Sha'ul said:
I have sinned; return, my son David!
For I will do evil to you no more,
since my life was precious in your eyes this day.
Here, I have acted-foolishly and have been in exceedingly great
    error!

22   David answered and said:
Here is the king's spear;
let one of the serving-lads cross over and fetch it,

23   and may Yhwh return upon each one his righteousness and his
    trustworthiness,
[seeing] that Yhwh gave you into my hand
but I would not stretch out my hand against Yhwh's anointed.

24   Here, as your life has been deemed-great this day in my eyes,
so may my life grow-great in Yhwh's eyes,
and may he rescue me from every distress!

25   Sha'ul said to David:
Blessed are you, my son David;
you will do, yes, do [well],
and you will prevail, yes, prevail!
David went on his way, and Sha'ul returned to his place.

---

20 **partridge:** Homonymous with "caller," hence
McCarter's (1980) "calling bird."

Chapter 27. *David as Mercenary:* In what feels like an unlikely turn, David, at last freed from pursuit by Sha'ul (v.4), distances himself from his Israelite compatriots by becoming a vassal of the enemy (Philistine) king, Akhish of Gat. In his desire to secure the king's trust, he exercises ruthlessness toward captured populations, cleverly intimating that these include his fellow Judeans. The scenario is reminiscent of typical undercover stories.

27:1 David said in his heart:
Now
I will be swept away one day by the hand of Sha'ul;
there is nothing better for me than that I should escape, yes, escape
to the land of the Philistines—
then Sha'ul will despair of me, of seeking me again throughout all
the territory of Israel,
and I will escape from his hand.

2 So David arose and crossed over, he and the six hundred men who
were with him, to Akhish son of Maokh, king of Gat.

3 And David stayed with Akhish in Gat, he and his men, each one and
his household,
and David and his two wives,
Ahinoam, the Yizre'elite, and Avigayil wife of Naval, the Carmelite.

4 It was told to Sha'ul that David had gotten away to Gat,
and he did not continue to seek him anymore.

5 David said to Akhish:
Now if I have found favor in your eyes,
let there be given to me a place in one of the country towns, and let
me settle there;
why should your servant settle in the royal city with you?

6 So Akhish gave him Tziklag on that day;
therefore Tziklag came-to-belong to the kings of Judah, until
this day.

7 Now the number of days that David stayed in Philistine country
was a year and four months.

8 And David would go up, along with his men;
they would sweep down on the Geshurites, the Gizrites, and the
Amalekites
—for they were the settled-folk of the land who were [there] from
ages [past]—
as you come to Shur, as far as the land of Egypt.

27:5 **country:** Elsewhere translated as "open-field."
6 **Tziklag:** A town on the edge of Philistine territory, between Gaza and Beersheba. Trad. English
"Ziklag."

8 **Shur:** See note to 15:7, above.

Chapter 28. *Sha'ul and Shemuel at En Dor:* Of all the dramatic moments in Sha'ul's life—and there are many—nothing quite matches the eerie mood of this brief story, which takes place at night and involves the spirit of a dead man. It feels as if it might have been the inspiration for moments in *Hamlet* or *Macbeth*. In its devastating finality, it comprises the emotional end of the Sha'ul narratives. The account of the king's actual death, which is reported in Chap. 31, only reports the inevitable.

The story expands on the theme of God's abandonment of Sha'ul, opening with a reminder that Shemuel is gone (see 25:1) and the observation that all of the conventional means by which a king might divine God's will have proved futile (v.6). Sha'ul, who for once had followed God's law in v.2, now must break it in secret, out of desperation. In order to do so, he must circumvent the Philistine lines, disguised in "other garments" (ironically echoing his transformation into "another man" with "another heart" when he was anointed as king in 10:6 and 9), thus concealing his identity from the medium.

The consulting of spirits to learn the future was a well-known practice in the premodern world, but its appearance here is unique in the Hebrew Bible. While raising the dead and other aspects of sorcery were banned in the Bible, they were not viewed as ineffective; nevertheless, the text passes over any description of exactly how the woman works her magic and goes right to the unorthodox meeting between the two old friends. As usual, it is the face-to-face confrontation that interests the Bible rather than the background details, and so we must do without the dramatic lighting, special effects, and sinister music that would mark the presentation of such a scene in today's media.

A number of enigmatic points emerge in this narrative. First, how does Sha'ul know from the woman's laconic description of the ghost that it is indeed that of the old prophet? "An old man . . . wrapped in a cloak" would seem to reveal little in the way of identity. But we may recall that it was Shemuel's cloak that was the physical focal point of Sha'ul's rejection as king (15:27), as the ghost implies with its reuse of "torn" in v.17. Second, there is Shemuel's tantalizing suggestion about the nature of the Underworld in v.15, "Why have you disturbed me?" This tells us only that, in the biblical view, our state after death is akin to rest or sleep, and does not involve the elaborate construction of Heaven and Hell with which we are so familiar in the Western world. Finally, Shemuel's reply to the "distressed" king does not address the question asked of him until he has rehashed God's rejection of Sha'ul. His answer, in v.19, contains one of the most chilling lines in the Bible. The text could simply have said, "Tomorrow, you and your sons will die," but instead intones the memorable "tomorrow, you and your sons are with me."

What could have been the story's ending is striking enough: Sha'ul does not merely collapse, an understandable reaction to the bad news he has just received; he falls "his full stature to the ground" (v.20), providing a purposeful contrast to one of the reasons Sha'ul had been chosen king in the first place. We recall that initially he had been described as "taller than all the people" (9:2), and had been

9 And David would strike the land;
  he would leave alive no man or woman,
  but he would take sheep and oxen, donkeys and camels and
     garments,
  and then he would return and come back to Akhish.

10 And Akhish would say:
  On [whom] did you sweep down today?
  And David would say:
  Against the Negev of Judah,
  or: against the Negev of the Yerahme'elites,
  or: against the Negev of the Kenites.

11 But no man or woman would David leave alive to bring to Gat,
     saying:
  Lest they report concerning us, saying:
  Thus did David do
  and thus was his practice,
  all the days that he stayed in Philistine country.

12 So Akhish came-to-trust David, saying:
  He has made himself reek, yes, reek so to his own people, to Israel,
  so he will be servant to me for a lifetime!

28:1 It was in those days
  that the Philistines gathered their camps into an armed-force, to
     wage battle against Israel.
  Akhish said to David:
  You know, yes, know that you must go out with me in the camp,
     you and your men.

2 David said to Akhish:
  Then you yourself will know what your servant can do!
  So Akhish said to David:
  Then I will make you my chief bodyguard for all the days [to
     come]!

---

10 **the Negev of . . . :** These were subregions of the large area of southern Israel, inhabited by various raiding tribes.

11 **Lest they report . . . :** David does not want it to appear that he is anything but a good Philistine commander.

28:2 **my chief bodyguard:** Lit., "guardian of my head."

rejected with the words "Do not look at . . . the tallness of his stature" (16:7). Sha'ul has farther to fall than most.

It is at this point in the story, in a narrative that has already provided some surprises, that the unexpected happens again. If the Bible's purpose had been solely to portray Sha'ul as a villain, he might simply have slunk back to the Isra-elite camp and wept, or experienced a night of uneasy dreams in the manner of Shakespeare's Richard III. Instead, both king and reader are given a compassion-ate moment of respite. Literature abounds in less than reputable characters who demonstrate their humanity (see, for instance, Rahav, the classic "good-hearted prostitute" of Josh. 2). In this case, it is the medium who acts as a kind of stand-in for God, offering the stricken king nourishment and thus confirming his human-ity. Moving from ground to bed (v.23), Sha'ul for the moment staves off his death and, instead of receiving the promised "bit of bread" (v.22), is given a more sub-stantial meal, as befits a king. Thus the Sha'ul who exits his shattering meeting with the dead Shemuel is fortified for his heroic ordeal of the next day, when he will die leading the troops one last time against Israel's enemies. From the beginning of the story, where the king had denied both his identity and his val-ues as upholder of divine law, he emerges at the end, thanks to the medium's act, as ruler and commander in chief, prepared to die if necessary at the head of "Yhwh's armies" (see Simon 1997).

3 Now Shemuel had died,
 and all Israel had beaten [the breast] for him and had buried him in
   Rama, in his town.
 Now Sha'ul had removed [those inquiring of] ghosts and all-
   knowing ones from the land.

4 And the Philistines gathered and came, encamping at Shunem,
 while Sha'ul gathered all Israel, encamping at Gilboa.

5 Sha'ul saw the Philistines' camp
 and he became afraid, and his heart trembled exceedingly.

6 So Sha'ul made request of YHWH,
 but YHWH did not answer him,
 either through dreams, or through *Urim,* or through prophets.

7 So Sha'ul said to his servants:
 Seek for me a woman, a possessor of ghosts,
 that I may go to her, that I may inquire of [the dead] through her.
 His servants said to him:
 There is a woman, a possessor of ghosts at En Dor.

8 Sha'ul disguised himself and clothed himself in other garments,
 and he went, he and two men with him,
 and came to the woman at night.
 He said:
 Now divine for me by a ghost;
 bring up for me the one whom I will designate to you.

9 The woman said to him:
 Here, *you* know what Sha'ul has done,
 how he has cut off [those inquiring of] ghosts and all-knowing ones
   from the land.
 So why would you ensnare my life, to cause my death?

---

3 **[those inquiring of] ghosts and all-knowing ones:**
The terms here can refer to both the spirits and
those who consult them. The calling up of the dead
was illegal in biblical law (see Deut. 18:11) but, interestingly, not viewed as ineffective.
4 **Shunem . . . Gilboa:** These hills controlled the
towns of the Jezreel Valley on the way to Bet-She'an
(Beth-Shean), where there seems to have been a historical Philistine presence.
5 **saw . . . became afraid:** The two similar-sounding
verbs (Heb. *r-'-h* and *y-r-'*) echo each other throughout the narrative (twelve times in total). Both at the

beginning and the end, Sha'ul's seeing will lead to
his being afraid.
6 **made request:** Or "inquired," formally consulted
God.   **Urim:** Pronounced *oo-REEM,* this was some
sort of object used in determining the future; see
note to 14:41, above.
7 **possessor:** Following Waltke/O'Connor.   **En Dor:**
Just a few miles northeast of the Philistine camp. So
for Sha'ul, whose camp was to the south, this was a
dangerous journey.
8 **in other garments:** Reminiscent of his "becoming
another man" in 10:6, above.

◆ 10 Sha'ul swore to her by YHWH, saying:
By the life of YHWH, should any guilt befall you through this
matter . . . !
11 The woman said:
Whom shall I bring up for you?
He said:
Bring up Shemuel for me.
12 The woman saw Shemuel,
and she cried out in a loud voice;
the woman said to Sha'ul, saying:
Why have you deceived me? For you are Sha'ul!
13 The king said to her:
Do not be afraid;
rather, what do you see?
The woman said to Sha'ul:
I see a godlike-being coming up from the ground.
14 He said to her:
What is its form?
She said:
An old man is coming up,
and he is wrapped in a cloak.
Then Sha'ul knew that it was Shemuel,
and he prostrated himself, nostrils to the earth, and bowed low.
15 Shemuel said to Sha'ul:
Why have you disturbed me, by bringing me up?
Sha'ul said:
I am exceedingly distressed—
the Philistines are waging battle against me
and God has turned away from me:
he no longer answers me,
either through the hand of the prophets or through dreams.
So I have called you to make known to me what I should do!
16 Shemuel said:
But why do you make request of me?
For YHWH has turned away from you and has become your foe!

13 **a godlike-being:** The dead in Israel were seen as something other than human, but not exactly deified (Lewis).

15 **disturbed:** The same verb is used in warnings on ancient tombstones (McCarter 1980).

16 **But why do you make request of me?:** Alluding to Sha'ul's name again: *Ve-lamma tish'aleini?* **has become your foe:** Emending *'arekha* to *tzarekha.* Ancient versions read as *'im rei'ekha,* "has gone over to your fellow" (David).

17 YHWH has done to you as he promised through my hand:
   YHWH has torn away the kingdom from your hand
   and has given it to your fellow, to David

18 —as you did not hearken to YHWH's voice,
   and did not carry out his blazing anger against Amalek.
   Therefore this thing has YHWH done to you this day!

19 And YHWH will also give Israel with you into the hand of the
      Philistines;
   tomorrow, you and your sons are with me;
   also the camp of Israel YHWH will give into the hand of the
      Philistines!

20 Sha'ul quickly fell his full stature to the ground;
   he was exceedingly afraid at Shemuel's words,
   also there was no strength in him,
   for he had not eaten food all day and all night.

21 The woman came to Sha'ul,
   and she saw that he was exceedingly terrified,
   so she said to him:
   Here, your handmaid hearkened to your voice,
   and I put my life in my hand—
   I hearkened to your words which you spoke to me.

22 So-then,
   now hearken, you also, to your handmaid's voice:
   I will put before you a bit of bread—eat,
   so that there may be strength in you when you go on your way.

23 He refused, and said: I will not eat!
   But his servants pressed him, and also the woman,
   so he hearkened to their voice;
   he arose from the ground and sat down on the couch.

24 Now the woman had a stall-fed calf in the house;
   she hurried and slew it,
   took meal and kneaded it, and baked it into unleavened-cakes.

25 Then she brought it close before Sha'ul and before his servants, and
      they ate,
   and they arose and went away, that [very] night.

---

17 **to you:** So LXX and manuscripts; MT has "to him."
21 **she saw:** This time, "seeing," in its last appearance
   in the story, evokes compassion.

Chapter 29. *Philistine Suspicions About David:* As the Philistines prepare for battle against the Israelites, David accompanies them, but his loyalty is immediately questioned, despite all his efforts to prove himself in Chap. 27. The Philistine overlords are rightly concerned about the possibility that David, their former tormentor, will return to his roots and go over to the Israelite side. King Akhish is forced to reluctantly order David to head back to Philistia, forbidding him to participate in the coming battle against Sha'ul. Once again, as so often, David will be absent when his enemies are done away with.

29:1 The Philistines gathered all their encampments at Afek,
while Israel was encamped at the spring that is in Yizre'el.

2 Now the Philistine overlords were crossing over by [divisions of]
hundreds and by [divisions of] thousands,
with David and his men crossing over in the rear, beside Akhish.

3 The Philistine commanders said:
What [about] these Hebrews?
Akhish said to the Philistine commanders:
Is this not David, servant of Sha'ul king of Israel,
who has been with me for these days and these years,
yet I have found nothing [amiss] in him, from the day of his falling
in [with us] until this day?

4 The Philistine commanders became furious with him,
and the Philistine commanders said to him:
Return the man, and let him return to his place which you assigned
him,
but do not let him go down with us into battle,
so that he will not be an adversary to us in battle!
For whereby will this one make himself acceptable [again] to his
lord—
is it not with the heads of those men?

5 Is this not David,
about whom they chanted with dancing, saying:
Sha'ul has struck down his thousands,
but David—his myriads?

6 So Akhish had David called
and said to him:
By the life of YHWH,
indeed, you are upright,
and good in my eyes is your going out and your coming in with me
in the camp,
for I have not found any evil in you from the day of your coming to
me until this day—
but in the eyes of the Philistine overlords you are not good!

29:1 **Afek:** See note to 4:1 above.   **Yizre'el:** The fertile
Jezreel Valley of northern Israel.

4 **the heads of those men:** A JPS note understands
this expression as euphemistic for "our heads," with
"those men" indicating the Philistines.

6 **By the life of** YHWH**:** The Philistines, of course,
were not worshippers of YHWH, but the expression
here is a standard biblical one—or else Akhish is
showing special sensitivity to David.

Chapter 30. *David as Rescuer:* In the course of his journey away from direct confrontation in battle with Sha'ul, David discovers that the Philistine-occupied town of Tziklag has been devastated, and all its women, including his own wives Ahinoam and Avigayil, have been taken captive. A chance encounter with an Egyptian man reveals that the raiders were Amalekites, and David is subsequently able to crush them as they revel among the spoils.

The story appears to have several functions. It puts David in a similar light to the patriarch Avraham, who had rescued his nephew and family from wartime captivity (see Gen. 14); it provides a contrast to Sha'ul, who had previously failed in his battle dealings with the Amalekites (Chap. 15); it links David to a current (in the writer's time) practice of parceling out spoils even to parts of the army that have not participated in the battle proper; and, in the final verses, it gives David a means through which to eventually win back the good graces of his fellow Judeans.

As Fokkelman (1993) has carefully worked out, timewise the action of this chapter is simultaneous to Sha'ul's defeat in the next one. Thus, David's victory fittingly coincides with Sha'ul's end.

7 So-now,
turn back, and go in peace,
so that you do not do evil in the eyes of the Philistine overlords.

8 David said to Akhish:
Indeed, what have I done;
what have you found in your servant
from the day that I was [first] before you, until this day,
that I may not come and wage battle against the enemies of my
lord king?

9 Akhish answered and said to David:
I acknowledge that you are as good in my eyes as a messenger of
a god;
however, the Philistine commanders say:
He must not go up with us into battle!

10 So-now, start-early at daybreak,
and as for your lord's servants who came with you,
you are [all] to start-early at daybreak;
when it is light for you, go!

11 So David started-early, he and his men, to go at daybreak, to
return to the land of the Philistines,
while the Philistines went up to Yizre'el.

30:1 It was, when David came and his men to Tziklag, on the third
day
—now Amalekites had swept down on the Negev, on Tziklag;
they had struck Tziklag, and burned it with fire,

2 and they had taken captive the women that were in it, from
young to old.
They had not put any [of them] to death,
but had led them away and gone on their way—

3 David and his men came to the town,
and here, it was burned down with fire,
with their wives and their sons and their daughters taken captive!

4 And David and the fighting-people that were with him lifted up
their voice and wept
until there was no strength in them to weep.

5 Now David's two wives had been taken captive,
Ahinoam the Yizre'elite and Avigayil wife of Naval the
Carmelite.

◆ 6 And David was exceedingly distressed,
for the people intended to stone him,
for bitter were all the people's feelings,
each one over his sons and over his daughters—
but David found strength in YHWH his God.

7 David said to Evyatar the priest, son of Ahimelekh:
Now bring the *efod* close to me!
Evyatar brought the *efod* close to David.

8 And David inquired of YHWH, saying:
Shall I pursue after this raiding-band?
Will I overtake them?
He said to him:
Pursue,
for you will overtake, yes, overtake, and will rescue, yes, rescue
[them]!

9 So David went, he and the six hundred men who were with him,
and they came to Wadi Besor, while those left stayed behind.

10 And David gave pursuit, he and four hundred men,
while two hundred men stayed behind, who were [too] exhausted
to cross Wadi Besor.

11 They found an Egyptian man in the open-field, and took him to
David;
they gave him bread and he ate, and they had him drink water,

12 and they gave him a slice of pressed-figs and two raisin-bunches,
and he ate.
Then his spirit returned to him
—for he had not eaten bread and had not drunk water for three
days and three nights.

13 And David said to him:
To whom do you [belong]? And where are you from?
He said:
I am an Egyptian serving-lad, the servant of an Amalekite man;
my lord abandoned me, since I became sick three days ago.

30:8 **rescue [them]:** Their own wives and children.
9 **Wadi Besor:** South of Tziklag and running eastward to Bet-Lehem and beyond.
11 **an Egyptian man:** Three times in the David narra-

tives, a foreigner brings news of "a dire event" (Alter 1999). The other passages occur in II Sam. 1 (an Amalekite) and 18 (a Cushite).
12 **spirit:** Or "breath."

14 We were sweeping down on the Negev of the Kereitites,
against what belongs to Judah,
and against the Negev of Calev,
and Tziklag we burned with fire.

15 David said to him:
Will you bring me down to this band?
He said:
Swear to me by God
if you should put me to death, if you should turn me over to the
hand of my [former] lord . . . !
Then I will bring you down to this band.

16 He brought him down,
and here, they were stretched out all over the surface of the ground,
eating and drinking and celebrating
among all the great spoil that they had taken from the land of the
Philistines and from the land of Judah.

17 And David struck them from the [dawn] breeze until the morrow's
sunset;
not one of them escaped except for four hundred serving-lads who
mounted camels and fled.

18 So David rescued everything that Amalek had taken,
and his two wives David rescued [as well];

19 nothing was missing of theirs, from small to great, to sons and
daughters,
or from the spoils to anything that they took for themselves—
everything David restored.

20 David took all the flocks and all the herds;
they drove them before that livestock and said:
These are David's spoils!

21 And David came back to the two hundred men that had been too
exhausted to go after David
—they had had them stay at Wadi Besor—
and they went out to meet David and to meet the fighting-people
who were with him.
And David came close to the people, and he inquired of them for
peace,

21 **of them for peace:** Or "of their welfare."

421

Chapter 31. *The Death of Sha'ul:* The final episode in Sha'ul's tragedy, stunningly portrayed in Pieter Brueghel's famous large painting, is reported in a chapter of great compactness. The battle scene itself is typically brief; what interests the writer is only the outcome—the death of the king and his sons.

Sha'ul dies heroically. His decision to commit suicide stems not from depression or despair but from the desire to die with dignity and escape the humiliation which he fears would be his lot if the Philistines were to find him alive. As it is, his corpse is mutilated, with armor and torso taken as trophies for Philistine sites. In the end, however, the body and those of his sons are rescued by the men of Yavesh-Gil'ad, the very ones whom Sha'ul had saved from the Ammonites at the beginning of his career, and given proper burial.

At the same time as Sha'ul dies heroically, there is a sobering note. His suicide in battle recalls the death of a previous king, actually a usurper, Avimelekh, in Judg. 9. As with other foreshadowings of the reign of Sha'ul (see Judg. 19), the parallel does not do him honor.

◆ 22 but every evil and base man of the men who had gone with David
    spoke up
and said:
Because they did not go with me,
we will not give them any of the spoils that we rescued
except to each one his wife and his children;
let them drive [these] away and go!

23 David said:
You must not do thus, my brothers,
with what YHWH has given us!
—he watched over us and gave the band that came against us, into
    our hand.

24 For who would hearken to you in this matter?
Indeed, like the share of the one who goes down into battle is the
    share of the one who stays by the gear:
together they shall divide-shares.

25 So it was from that day and forward
that they made it a prescribed-law and a rule in Israel,
until this day.

26 David came back to Tziklag, and he sent off [some] of the spoils to
    the elders of Judah, to his fellows, saying:
Here, it is a blessing-gift for you, from the spoil of YHWH's enemies:

27 for those in Bet-El, for those in Ramot-Negev, for those in Yattir,

28 for those in Aro'er, for those in Sifmot, for those in Eshtemoa,

29 for those in Rakhal, for those in the Yerahme'elite towns, for those
    in the Kenite towns,

30 for those in Horma, for those in Bekhor-Ashan, for those in Atakh,

31 for those in Hevron,
and for all the places that David went around in, he and his men.

31:1 Now the Philistines were waging battle against Israel,
and the men of Israel fled before the Philistines;
the slain fell on Mount Gilboa.

---

22 **drive [these] away:** The verb is typically used of animals, hence it may have a derogatory tone here (as
in Gen. 31:26, as Alter 1999 notes).

27 **for those in Bet-El . . . :** The towns mentioned are
in the Negev region.

29 **Rakhal:** LXX has "Carmel."

31:1 **Now the Philistines . . . :** The text picks up the
action in mid-battle. The previous chapter, detailing
David's whereabouts, seems more important to the
text than military details.

2 And the Philistines caught up with Sha'ul and with his sons,
   and the Philistines struck down Yehonatan and Avinadav and Malki-
      Shua, Sha'ul's sons.

3 The battle was heavy around Sha'ul;
   the shooters, the men of the bow, found him,
   and he was seriously wounded by the shooters.

4 So Sha'ul said to his weapons bearer:
   Draw your sword and run me through with it,
   lest these Foreskinned Ones come and run me through and
      deal wantonly with me!
   But the weapons bearer would not, because he was exceedingly
      afraid,
   so Sha'ul took the sword and fell on it.

5 And his weapons bearer saw that Sha'ul was dead,
   so he too fell on his sword, and died with him.

6 Thus died Sha'ul, and his three sons and his weapons bearer,
   indeed, all his men, on that day, together.

7 The men of Israel saw, those across the Valley and those across the
      Jordan,
   that the [other] men of Israel had fled,
   and that Sha'ul and his sons had died,
   so they abandoned the towns and fled,
   and Philistines came and settled in them.

8 Now it was on the morrow,
   that the Philistines came to strip the slain,
   and they found Sha'ul and his three sons, fallen on Mount Gilboa.

9 They cut off his head and stripped off his armor,
   and sent [word] throughout the land of the Philistines, all around,
   to bring-the-news into the house of their carved-idols and among
      the people.

10 They placed his armor in the Temple-House of Ashtarot,
   and his corpse they thrust into the wall of Bet-She'an.

---

2 **caught up with:** Other forms of the verb (Heb. d-b-k) mean "stick to, cling to."

4 **deal wantonly with:** Mutilate the body, for the sake of humiliating their enemy.

7 **the towns:** Ancient versions read "their towns."

10 **Ashtarot:** A plural form of the goddess rendered here as "Astarte" (Heb. Ashtoret).

11 But the settled-folk of Yavesh-Gil'ad heard
about what the Philistines had done to Sha'ul,

12 so all the men of valor arose and went all night
and took down Sha'ul's corpse and the corpses of his sons from the
wall of Bet-Shan,
and brought them to Yavesh, and burned them there;

13 then they took their bones and buried them beneath the tamarisk in
Yavesh,
and fasted for seven days.

11 **the settled-folk of Yavesh-Gil'ad:** Whom Sha'ul
had rescued in his first great victory, in Chap. 11.

II Samuel

Chapter 1. *David's Reaction to Sha'ul's Death:* The news from the battle reaches David, though we wait to see how he will react. An Amalekite messenger, bringing some of Sha'ul's royal ornaments with him, reports a version of Sha'ul's death which some interpreters take at face value but which may well be a fabrication. In the latter case, his motive is likely greed or some other form of self-interest; as an Amalekite, he belongs to the group that David had defeated in the town of Tziklag where the present conversation takes place, and he may be seeking mercy. In any event, the ruse does not work, and the messenger is put to death. David's condemnation and execution of the man may serve to further support David's claim that he had no evil designs against Sha'ul.

What follows (vv.17–27) is one of the most famous poems in the Bible, whose key line, "How have (or: how are [KJV]) the mighty fallen," occurring three times in the poem, is still quoted when public figures fall from grace. It is the first example of David as poet in the Bible. At the end of his life, he will recite two longer ones (II Sam. 22 and 23), and many of the Psalms will be attributed to him, either by the Bible itself (if indeed that is what "a Psalm of David" means) or by later tradition. This poem is also at the center of Samuel, usually an indication of an important moment in a chapter or a book.

Notably, Yehonatan's name appears here as much as does Sha'ul's. Much has been made of the words ". . . my brother Yehonatan, / you were very delightful to me; / more wonderful was your love to me / than the love of women" (v.26). Once again, is this deep friendship or something more? In any case, the bond with Yehonatan seems to be the most deeply felt of all of David's human relationships, a phenomenon which, as we noted earlier, is not unusual in a warrior culture.

II Samuel

1:1 It was after the death of Sha'ul
—David had returned from striking the Amalek[ites]—
that David stayed in Tziklag for two days.

2 And it was on the third day,
that here, a man was coming from the camp, from Sha'ul,
with his garments torn and earth on his head;
and it was, when he came to David, that he flung himself on the
ground and bowed low.

3 David said to him:
Where are you coming from?
He said to him:
From the camp of Israel have I escaped!

4 David said to him:
How did the matter go? Now tell me!
He said:
[It was] that the fighting-people fled from the battle,
and also many fell of the fighting-people, and they died;
and also Sha'ul and Yehonatan his son died.

5 David said to the lad, the one telling him:
How do you know that Sha'ul and Yehonatan his son are dead?

6 The lad, the one telling him, said:
I chanced, yes, chanced upon Mount Gilboa,
and here, Sha'ul was leaning on his spear,
and here, the charioteers and the horsemen were pressing-him-
hard.

7 He faced about behind him and saw me;
he called out to me,
and I said: Here I am.

1:1 **after the death of Sha'ul:** The books of Joshua and Judges each begin with a similar phrase about Moshe and Yehoshua, suggesting that here too a new phase begins in Israel's history (Hamilton). **the Amalek[ites]:** MT appears to be missing a letter here.

2 **his garments torn and earth on his head:** Unmistakable signs of mourning.

4 **How did the matter go?:** Exactly Eli's question (I 4:16) in parallel circumstances. **[It was] that:** An odd Hebrew construction that occasionally occurs at the beginning of a quotation. **and also Sha'ul . . . :** The messenger leaves the ultimate blow for last, again as with Eli.

6 **chanced:** Casting doubt on his story; people do not usually happen upon battles.

◆

8 He said to me:
Who are you?
I said to him:
I am an Amalekite.

9 He said to me:
Now stand over me and dispatch me,
for dizziness has come upon me,
though there is still life in me!

10 So I stood over him and dispatched him,
since I knew that he could not live after his having fallen;
then I took the diadem that was on his head
and the bracelet that was on his arm,
and have brought them to my lord here.

11 David took hold of his clothes and tore them,
and likewise all the men that were with him;

12 they beat [the breast] and wept and fasted until sunset
over Sha'ul and over Yehonatan his son,
over the fighting-people of YHWH and over the House of Israel,
since they had fallen by the sword.

13 Then David said to the lad, the one telling him:
Where are you from?
He said:
I am the son of a sojourner man, an Amalekite.

14 David said to him:
How were you not afraid
to stretch out your hand to bring YHWH's anointed one to ruin?

15 And David called to one of the serving-lads
and said:
Approach, attack him!
And he struck him down, so that he died.

16 David said to him:
Your blood be on your head!
For your mouth bore witness against you, saying:
I myself dispatched YHWH's anointed one!

---

10 **diadem . . . bracelet:** These constitute Sha'ul's "royal insignia" (McCarter 1984), and hence would have served as proof that the Amalekite had encountered the king.

12 **YHWH:** LXX reads "Judah" (Heb. consonants *yhwdh*).

13 **sojourner:** A resident alien; a foreigner.

14 **not afraid:** In contrast to the arms bearer in the narrated account of the last chapter, v.4 (Fokkelman 1993).

17 Now David sang-dirge with this dirge
    over Sha'ul and over Yehonatan his son,

18 he said:
    To teach the Children of Judah the bow,
    here, it is written in the Record of the Upright:

19   O beauty of Israel, on your heights are the slain:
        how have the mighty fallen!

20   Tell it not in Gat,
        spread not the news in Ashkelon's streets,
        lest they rejoice, the daughters of the Philistines,
        lest they exult, the daughters of the Foreskinned Ones!

21   O hills of Gilboa, let there be no dew, no rain upon you,
        or surging of the [watery] deeps,
        for there lies-soiled the shield of the mighty, the shield of Sha'ul,
        no more anointed with oil.

22   From the blood of the slain, from the sword of the mighty,
        Yehonatan's bow never turned back, Sha'ul's sword never
            returned empty.

23   Sha'ul and Yehonatan, those beloved and delightful ones—
        in their lives and in their deaths they were not parted;
        they were swifter than eagles, they were mightier than lions!

24   O daughters of Israel, weep over Sha'ul,
        who clothed you in scarlet together with luxuries,
        who with golden ornaments decked your apparel!

25   How have the mighty fallen, in the midst of battle,
        Yehonatan slain on your heights—

---

18 **To teach . . . the bow:** The Hebrew phrase is difficult. It may refer to some kind of poem or performance method. **the Record of the Upright:** An ancient collection of poems or songs, to which Josh. 10:13 also refers. Along with the "Record of Yearly Events of the Kings of Judah," cited frequently in Kings, it seems to indicate that the Bible is actually a deliberate selection of the literature that existed in ancient Israel.

19 **beauty:** Or "gazelle."

21 **surging of the [watery] deeps:** Suggested by Greenstein, private communication, following an emendation by H. L. Ginsberg (*shera' tehomot* for *sedei terumot*). **anointed with oil:** To make the shield slippery and hence more effective in turning blows away. Alter (1999) notes the irony in the use of "no more anointed" in a poem about King Sha'ul.

22 **sword of the mighty:** Reading, with ancient versions, *herev* for *helev*, "fat."

◆ 26 I am distraught over you, my brother Yehonatan,
you were very delightful to me;
more wonderful was your love to me
than the love of women!
27 How have the mighty fallen,
yes, perished the weapons of battle!

27 **weapons of battle:** Referring to Sha'ul and Yehonatan.

PART IV

DAVID'S RULE CONSOLIDATED

(II 2–8)

THREE STAGES NOW CHARACTERIZE DAVID'S ASCENSION TO POWER AS ISRAEL'S second king: the elimination of rivals, principally from the house of Sha'ul; the establishment of a capital; and the subduing of external enemies. The accomplishment of the first goal is marred by three violent deaths: one in battle (David's nephew Asa'el), one standing by a gate (Sha'ul's general Avner), and one in a bed (Sha'ul's son Ish-Boshet). All of them, curiously, are struck "in the abdomen," a notably gory death. While David absolves himself of all this bloodshed, one conclusion is inescapable: as Polzin (1993) notes, kingship in Israel is "a major cause of frequent fratricide on a tribal or national level." It is a pattern that will be repeated within the royal house itself in the second half of the book.

The second part of this section relates the capture of Jerusalem, a previously unconquered and hence politically neutral site which had the advantages of central location and natural defenses. In a small fortified town, whose entirety would today be enveloped by the Arab village of Silwan directly south of the Old City, David establishes his capital, builds a palace, and brings the holy Coffer to its final and fitting resting place. At the last, his great moment of triumph and a remarkable blend of the political, the religious, and the personal, we see David in all his complexity: a conqueror who can bring the ancient tablets of God to the seat of royal power, a believer uninhibitedly religious enough to leap and whirl before God, and a man allied to Sha'ul's house by marriage, who nevertheless acts on his own instincts. And it is to "house" that the text turns in the long, climactic Chap. 7 (see Bar-Efrat), with its emphasis on the seeming permanence of Temple and dynasty. It is punctuated by God's use of the adjectives "secure" and "firm," with David's use of the root "great/greatness" in reply, and by the refrain "for the ages" resounding in both speeches. The David who emerges from this section is king of a dominant and unified nation, centered around a royal city and a dynasty that enjoy the blessing of God.

Finally, there is the matter of defeating surrounding military threats. The Bible sees David as Israel's most successful military leader since Yehoshua (Joshua). He at long last subdues the Philistines, who have plagued the Israelites for generations, and establishes for his son Shelomo (Solomon) a territorial sphere of influence which far exceeds that of any previous or subsequent Israelite ruler. If historically accurate on some level, this would not be totally surprising, as the classic powerful empires of the ancient Near East, Egypt and Assyria, were at a temporary low ebb in the tenth century B.C.E. If, on the other hand, the boundaries set forth here do not reflect actual fact, they nevertheless represent an ancient longing, appropriately tied to the most loved and admired of Israel's kings.

The section ends with a list of David's court officials, as does Chap. 20. As mentioned in the Introduction, this may delineate an ancient unit of the text, yet another indication that biblical books such as Samuel may have a complicated textual history behind them.

Jerusalem, the city conquered by David in Chap. 5, is as topographically striking as it is famous in history. Built on two ridges that rose over three valleys in antiquity (the middle one was later to be filled in), with the only true access from the north, David's Jerusalem was a hill sloping up to a kind of saddle, itself surrounded by a circle of slightly higher hills. It sat on the watershed, in a location that lay on a convergence of north-south and east-west axes. For all that, it was off the main ancient trade routes and had few natural resources, and so its choice as a capital city probably stemmed from the fact that it was readily defensible and could not be easily claimed by any Israelite tribe. It was thus relatively immunized from internal rivalries.

Despite its fame throughout history, furthered by artists' imaginations in innumerable drawings and paintings, David's Jerusalem would have actually been quite small, covering only the limited area of the southern slope and housing only a few thousand inhabitants. The westward expansion that would give the city its more familiar shape would not come until two centuries later, under the impetus of Assyrian invasion, when the Judeans needed to reinforce its fortifications and make room for refugees from both the surrounding communities and the besieged north.

The name of the city has come under much speculation, but most likely its original meaning was "Foundation of Shalem," that is, belonging to a local deity. The popular etymology, "City of Peace," probably reflects deeply held wishes more than linguistic accuracy, and is, to say the least, ironic, given Jerusalem's history. Although the Bible terms its former inhabitants *Yevusim* (Jebusites), that group is not thought to have occupied the site for very long previously.

Chapter 2. *Unresolved Political Tensions:* The Death of Sha'ul and several of his sons in battle does not assure David of an easy transition to the throne. While his fellow Judahites anoint him as king, the bulk of the country, to both the north and the northeast, throws in its lot with Sha'ul's son Ish-Boshet, who is backed by the powerful military commander Avner. A fierce battle ensues between soldiers loyal

◆ 2:1 It was [some time] after this
that David inquired of Yhwh, saying:
Shall I go up into one of the towns of Judah?
Yhwh said to him:
Go up!
David said:
To where shall I go up?
He said:
To Hevron.

2 So David went up there,
and also his two wives,
Ahinoam the Yizre'elite, and Avigayil the wife of Naval the
Carmelite.

3 As for his men who were with him, David brought them up, each
one and his household,
and they settled in the towns of Hevron.

4 And the men of Judah came and anointed David there as king over
the House of Judah . . . .

They told David, saying:
The men of Yavesh-Gil'ad have buried Sha'ul.

5 So David sent messengers to the men of Yavesh-Gil'ad;
he said to them:
Blessed are you of Yhwh,
in that you did this act-of-loyalty to your lord, to Sha'ul,
by burying him!

6 So-now,
may God show you loyalty and faithfulness,
and I too will do this act-of-good to you,
in exchange for your having done this thing!

7 And now,
let your hands be strengthened
and be valiant ones,
for your lord Sha'ul is dead,
and already it is I [whom] the House of Judah has anointed as king
over them.

2:3 **the towns of Hevron:** Those in the vicinity of the
city.

6 **do . . . good:** Another term for loyalty, found in
ancient treaties.

to David, led by Yoav, and the partisans of Sha'ul, led by Avner. In the process, the conflict gets personal, as Yoav's brother is unavoidably slain by Avner, who then manages to obtain a cease-fire in the interests of preventing further bloodshed and civil war. But in a world often marked by blood vengeance, it is most unlikely that matters will stand the way they are.

The narrative is marked by an unusual echoing word: "after." It resounds with both spatial and abstract meanings, fourteen times in twelve verses (19–30), and expresses well the concept of pursuit that is so central to the story. In the end, Avner's "Do you not know that it will be bitter *afterward*?" (v.26; italics mine) summarizes the need to resolve the civil war.

8 But Avner son of Ner, commander of the armed-forces that
    belonged to Sha'ul,
  had taken Ish-Boshet son of Sha'ul, and had had him cross over to
    Mahanayim;

9 he had made him king over Gil'ad, over the Geshurites, and over
    Yizre'el,
  over Efrayim and over Binyamin—over Israel, all of it.

10 Forty years old was Ish-Boshet son of Sha'ul when he began to
    reign as king over Israel,
  and for two years he reigned as king.
  But the House of Judah was [following] after David.

11 And the number of days that David was king in Hevron, over the
    House of Judah,
  was seven years and six months.

12 Now Avner son of Ner went out, along with the servants of Ish-
    Boshet son of Sha'ul, from Mahanayim to Giv'on,

13 while Yoav son of Tzeruya and David's servants went out [as well].
  They met them by the Pool of Giv'on together,
  and they sat down, these by the pool on this-side,
  and those by the pool on that-side.

14 Avner said to Yoav:
  Let the fighting-lads arise and hold-a-contest before us!
  Yoav said:
  Let them arise!

15 So they arose and crossed over by number:
  twelve for Binyamin and for Ish-Boshet son of Sha'ul,
  and twelve of David's servants.

---

8 **Ish-Boshet:** Trad. English "Ishbosheth." The original name was "Ish-Baal," "Man of Baal"; scribal
tradition, uncomfortable with the pagan overtones,
has changed it (and similar names—see 11:21, which
originally read "Yerubbaal") to a name meaning
"Man of Shame." **Mahanayim:** On the east bank
of the Jordan, east of Shekhem.

9 **Gil'ad:** The region in which Mahanayim is located,
east of the Jordan, between the Dead Sea and the Sea
of Galilee. **Geshurites:** MT has "Ashurites," but
Geshur, east of the Sea of Galilee, fits the geography
here. **Israel:** The future Northern Kingdom.

11 **number of days:** Or "number of years," "amount of
time."

12 **went out:** With a military connotation; JPS:
"marched out." **Giv'on:** Northwest of Jerusalem;
trad. English "Gibeon."

14 **hold-a-contest:** This seems to indicate a ritual
winner-take-all combat. The Hebrew verb (*s-h-k*) is
the same as that used in Judg. 16:25 to describe the
blind Shimshon's "providing amusement" for the
Philistines; B-R translate both with "dance" (here,
"do a war dance").

◆ 16 And each one took hold of his neighbor's head,
with his sword [thrust] into his neighbor's side,
and they fell together.
So that place was called: Helkat Ha-Tzurim/Field of the Sword-
Edges, which is in Giv'on.

17 Now the battle was rough—exceedingly so—on that day,
and Avner and the men of Israel were defeated before David's
servants.

18 Now three of the sons of Tzeruya were there: Yoav, Avishai, and
Asa'el;
and Asa'el was swift of feet, like one of the gazelles that is in the
open-field.

19 Asa'el pursued after Avner;
he did not swerve to go to the right or to the left from after Avner.

20 But Avner faced about after him
and said:
Is this you, Asa'el?
He said:
[It is] I.

21 Avner said to him:
Swerve you to your right or to your left,
and seize for yourself one of our fighting-lads [instead], and take
yourself his armor!
But Asa'el would not turn aside from [going] after him.

22 Once again Avner said to Asa'el:
Turn you aside from [going] after me;
why should I strike you to the ground—
for how could I lift my face to Yoav your brother?

23 But he refused to turn aside,
so Avner struck him with the afterpart of the spear, in the
abdomen,
so that the spear came out after him;
he fell there and died on the spot.
And it was: all who came to the place where Asa'el had fallen and
died, stopped,

16 **Sword-Edges:** Or "flints."
18 **Asa'el:** Trad. English "Asahel." The name means
"God Acts."
23 **afterpart:** The butt of the spear, often sharpened for
sticking into the ground (as in I 26:7). **after him:**
Behind him, through his back. **on the spot:** Lit.,
"under him."

24 but Yoav and Avishai pursued after Avner.
Now when the sun had come in,
they came to the Hill of Amma, that faces Gi'ah,
on the way to the Wilderness of Giv'on.

25 And the Children of Binyamin gathered themselves [to follow] after
Avner;
they became a single group
and stopped at the top of a hill.

26 And Avner called out to Yoav;
he said:
Is it forever that the sword must devour?
Do you not know
that it will be bitter afterward?
Until when will you not bid the fighting-people to turn back from
[going] after their brothers?

27 Yoav said:
By the life of God,
indeed, had you only spoken,
indeed, already in the morning the people would have gone up,
each one from [going] after his brother!

28 Then Yoav gave-a-blast on the *shofar,* and all the people stopped;
they no longer pursued after Israel,
and no longer continued to do battle.

29 Now Avner and his men went through the Plain all that night;
they crossed the Jordan
and went through the whole canyon, and came to Mahanayim.

30 Now when Yoav returned from [going] after Avner,
he gathered all the people,
and there were counted-missing of David's servants nineteen men
along with Asa'el,

31 while David's servants struck down some of Binyamin, among
Avner's servants—
three hundred and sixty men died.

---

24 **Amma . . . Gi'ah:** The meaning may be "water channel . . . spring," but the location is unknown.
26 **afterward:** Others, "in the end." **Until when:** Others, "How long."

28 *shofar:* The ram's horn, often used in the Bible for signaling.
29 **the Plain:** The Aravah or Jordan Valley. **the whole canyon:** Others, "all morning."

Chapter 3. *Civil War; the Death of Avner:* The report on the ongoing civil war is interrupted by the birth notice of David's sons, six by six different wives. Indeed, sexual politics begins the chapter, with Avner sleeping with Sha'ul's concubine Ritzpa, to the chagrin of Sha'ul's son Ish-Boshet. This classic demonstration of political power enables Avner to negotiate with David, which obviously needs to be done, but the king will agree to a treaty only if his own former wife Mikhal, Sha'ul's daughter, is returned to him. So, sandwiched in between the violence of the last chapter and the violence that is to come, the first half of this chapter is punctuated by strong words and strong emotions, from Ish-Boshet's complaints, Avner's retort and negotiating statements, to the weeping of Paltiel, Mikhal's second husband, who helplessly walks behind her as she is returned to David. The result of the negotiations is a carefully wrought agreement that the northern region, Israel, will acknowledge David as king, and that Ish-Boshet's life will not be threatened.

The "peace" described in v.21 cannot last, however, because Yoav, as we will continuously encounter him in these stories, is a "rough" man (v.39) who does not forgive and who constantly looks out for and unhesitatingly acts on David's interests. He cannot permit the man who killed his brother to live, even though we saw in the previous chapter that Avner tried his best to avoid killing Asa'el. And it does not seem coincidental that Avner's death would obviously have the effect of quashing David's northern opposition.

At this point, from v.28 on, the text goes to great lengths to clear David of Avner's brutal murder. Not only does he put a curse on the house of Yoav, but he gets the entire people to mourn over Avner, composing a brief dirge for the occasion (vv.33–34).

32 And they carried Asa'el away and buried him in the burial-place of
his father, which is in Bet-Lehem.
Then they went all night, Yoav and his men,
with light breaking upon them in Hevron.

3:1 And the war was long-lasting between the House of Sha'ul and the
House of David;
David went on becoming stronger, while the House of Sha'ul went
on becoming weaker.

2 Now sons were born to David in Hevron:
his firstborn was Amnon, by Ahinoam the Yezre'elite,

3 and his second was Kil'av, by Avigayil wife of Naval, the Carmelite,
and the third was Avshalom son of Maakha, daughter of Talmai,
king of Geshur,

4 and the fourth was Adoniyya son of Haggit,
and the fifth was Shefatya son of Avital,

5 and the sixth was Yitre'am, by Egla wife of David.
These were born to David in Hevron.

6 And it was,
when there was war between the House of Sha'ul and the House
of David,
that Avner was gaining strength in the House of Sha'ul.

7 Now Sha'ul had a concubine, her name was Ritzpa daughter of Aya.
And [Ish-Boshet] said to Avner:
For-what-reason did you come in to my father's concubine?

8 Avner became exceedingly agitated over the words of Ish-Boshet;
he said:
Am I the head of a dog belonging to Judah?
Today I do an act-of-loyalty to the House of Sha'ul your father,

---

3:1 **war:** Elsewhere, I use "battle." **went on becom-ing:** Hebrew idiom uses "to go" as an auxiliary here; idiomatically, one might say "became progressively . . ."

2–4 **Amnon . . . Avshalom . . . Adoniyya:** The three sons who will struggle for succession to David from II Sam. 13 to I Kings 2. None will ultimately survive to become king; that will fall to Shelomo (Solomon). Avshalom (*ahv-shah-LOME*) is trad. English "Absalom," while Adoniyya (*ah-doe-nee-YAH*) is "Adonijah."

3 **Talmai:** Avshalom will flee to this maternal grand-

father in Chap. 13. He rules over a northern realm east of the Jordan (and thus David's marriage to his daughter Ma'akha was a political act, as many have noted).

6 **war:** See note to v.1 above. **gaining strength:** Or political power.

7 **concubine:** A second-level wife, often a slave woman. The institution does not seem to have been widely practiced in ancient Israel. **Ritzpa:** Trad. English "Rizpah." Some understand the meaning as "glowing coal." **come in to:** Sleep with.

for his brothers and for his friends,
and have not let you come into David's hand—
yet you account me with a fault concerning a woman today!

9 Thus may God do to Avner, and thus may he add to him;
indeed, [just] as Y<small>HWH</small> swore to David,
indeed, thus I will do to him—

10 to have the kingship cross over from the House of Sha'ul,
to establish the throne of David over Israel and over Judah,
from Dan to Be'er-Sheva!

11 He was not able to answer Avner another word, out of his fear
of him.

12 And Avner sent messengers to David on his behalf, saying:
Whose is [the] land?
Cut your covenant with me,
Here, my hand is with you, to bring all Israel around to you!

13 He said:
Good,
I myself will cut a covenant with you;
but one thing I will require of you, namely:
you are not to see my face
unless you first bring Mikhal daughter of Sha'ul, when you come to
see my face.

14 So David sent messengers to Ish-Boshet son of Sha'ul, saying:
Give over my wife, Mikhal,
whom I betrothed to myself for a hundred Philistine foreskins!

15 Ish-Boshet sent and took her from [her] husband, from Paltiel son
of Layish.

16 And her husband went with her, going along and weeping behind
her, as far as Bahurim.
Then Avner said to him:
Go, turn back! And he turned back.

17 Now the word of Avner was with the elders of Israel, saying:
Even yesterday, even [the] day-before, you have been seeking [to
set] David as king over you.

---

13 **require:** The same verb, *shaal,* rendered "request" or "inquire" elsewhere. **namely:** Lit., "saying."
16 **Bahurim:** Just south of Jerusalem.

17 **Even yesterday, even [the] day-before:** See note to I 4:7.

◆ 18　So-now, do it!
For Yhwh has said of David, saying:
By the hand of David my servant
I will deliver my people Israel from the hand of the Philistines and
from the hand of all their enemies!

19　Avner spoke likewise in the hearing of Binyamin,
and Avner went likewise to speak in the hearing of David in
Hevron
all that was good in the eyes of Israel and in the eyes of all the
House of Binyamin.

20　And Avner came to David in Hevron,
—with him were twenty men—
and David made a drinkfest for Avner and for the men who were
with him.

21　Then Avner said to David:
Let me arise, let me go,
and let me gather all Israel to my lord king,
that they may cut a covenant with you
and that you may become king according to all that your appetite
craves.
So David sent Avner away,
and he went off in peace.

22　Now here, David's servants and Yoav came back from raiding, and
abundant spoils they brought with them—
but Avner was not with David in Hevron,
for he had sent him off, and he had gone away in peace.

23　When Yoav and all the forces that were with him came, [someone]
told Yoav, saying:
Avner the son of Ner came to the king,
but he sent him off and he went away in peace!

24　So Yoav came to the king and said:
What have you done?
Here, Avner came to you—
why now did you send him off,
so that he has gone, yes, gone?

18　**I will:** From manuscript readings; MT has "he will."

Chapter 4. *The Death of Ish-Boshet:* In the course of the ongoing civil war, another assassination is committed. This time the victim is Sha'ul's son Ish-Boshet (or, in uncensored form, Ish-Baal). The chapter begins with several brief notes: Sha'ul's son is terrified to hear about Avner's recent death; we are introduced to two of his chieftains; and we are informed that a grandson scion of Sha'ul is alive, albeit a lame young man. The story proper starts in v.5, where Ish-Boshet is killed, Mafia-style, in his bed. Initially, no motive is given, especially as the assassins are from Ish-Boshet's own circle, but it soon becomes clear that the two men are seeking compensation from David. He, however, reacts the same way he had to the Amalekite messenger in Chap. 1, even referring back to that incident himself, and the culprits are executed. In addition, they are mutilated, with their bodies put on public display. Much as in the classic period of sixteenth-century England, "treason" gets its very public reward. And once again, David is portrayed as indignant at the commission of violent deeds from which, however, he ultimately profits.

25 You know Avner the son of Ner:
indeed, to dupe you he came,
to gain knowledge of your going out and your coming in,
and to gain knowledge of all that you are doing!

26 So Yoav went out from David,
and he sent messengers after Avner;
they returned him from the cistern of Sira,
but David did not know [about it].

27 Avner returned to Hevron,
and Yoav took him to the inner-part of the gate, to speak with him
quietly,
but he struck him in the abdomen, so that he died,
[in exchange] for the blood of Asa'el his brother.

28 David heard [of it], after this,
and said:
Clear-of-blame am I and my kingdom by Yʜwʜ, for the ages,
from the blood of Avner son of Ner—

29 may it alight on the head of Yoav and on all his Father's House;
may there never be cut off from the House of Yoav
[anyone] with a flow, or with *tzaraat*,
or [a male] taking hold of a spindle, or one falling by the sword, or
one lacking food!

30 Now Yoav and Avishai his brother had killed Avner
on account that he had caused the death of Asa'el their brother at
Giv'on, in battle.

31 And David said to Yoav and to all the people that were with him:
Tear your garments and gird yourselves with sackcloth,
and beat [the breast] before Avner!
Now King David [himself] walked after the bier.

---

26 **the cistern of Sira:** North of Hevron.

27 **inner-part of the gate:** The space between the two walls of the casemate gate. **quietly:** Others, "in private."

29 **[anyone] with a flow:** A bodily excretion rendering the person ritually polluted; see Lev. 13. **tzaraat:** A skin disease (*not* leprosy) which in the Bible usually indicates some wrongdoing on the part of the victim. Its physical appearance suggested deterioration and hence death, although it was probably not a serious condition in and of itself. **[a male] taking hold of a spindle:** That is, doing work not usually associated with a warrior.

31 **sackcloth:** Another standard biblical sign of mourning.

32 They buried Avner in Hevron,
and the king lifted up his voice and wept upon the burial-place of
Avner,
and all the people wept.

33 And the king intoned-a-dirge over Avner; he said:
Like the death of a vile one, should Avner have died?

34 Your hands were not bound,
your feet were not put in double-bronze;
like one falling before the corrupt you fell!
And all the people continued to weep over him.

35 Then all the people came to nourish David with bread while it was
daylight,
but David swore, saying:
Thus may God do to me, and thus may he add,
if before the coming in of the sun I taste bread or anything [else]!

36 All the people took note, and it was good in their eyes;
like all that the king did, in the eyes of the people it was good.

37 So all the people and all Israel knew on that day
that it had not been from the king to cause the death of Avner son
of Ner.

38 The king said to his servants:
Do you not know
that a commander and a great [man] has fallen in Israel this day?

39 As for me, today I am softhearted, though anointed as king,
while these men, the sons of Tzeruya, are too rough for me!
May YHWH pay back the doer of evil in accordance with his evil-
deed!

4:1 The son of Sha'ul heard that Avner was dead in Hevron,
and his hands grew slack,
while all Israel were terrified.

2 Now two men, commanders of raiding-bands, belonged to the son
of Sha'ul;
the name of the one was Baana, and the name of the second was
Rekhav,

---

35 **if . . . I taste:** David fasts as a sign of his grief.
4:1 **his hands grew slack:** Others, "he/his heart lost courage."

2 **Be'erotite:** Be'erot was northwest of Jerusalem and a former Hivvite town that had been absorbed by the tribe of Binyamin.

◆ sons of Rimmon the Be'erotite, of the Children of Binyamin.
  —For Be'erot too was reckoned to Binyamin:

3 the Be'erotites had got away to Gittayim,
  and they have continued sojourning there, until this day.—

4 Now Yehonatan son of Sha'ul had a son, stricken in the feet;
  he had been five years old when the tidings had come of Sha'ul and
    Yehonatan, from Yizre'el,
  and his caretaker had lifted him up and fled.
  It was in her haste to flee that he had fallen and been made lame.
  —His name was Mefiboshet.

5 So the sons of Rimmon the Be'erotite, Rekhav and Baana, went
  and came, at the heat of the day, to the house of Ish-Boshet,
  while he was lying down for the noonday nap.

6 And here, when they came into the midst of the house, as fetchers
    of wheat,
  they struck him in the abdomen;
  then Rekhav and Baana his brother escaped.

7 —They had come into the house
  while he was lying on his couch, in his bedroom,
  and had struck him down and caused his death,
  and had removed his head.—
  They took his head
  and went off, by way of the Plain, all night,

8 and they brought the head of Ish-Boshet to David at Hevron,
  and said to the king:
  Here is the head of Ish-Boshet son of Sha'ul your enemy, who
    sought your life—
  Yhwh has granted vengeance to my lord king this day on Sha'ul
    and on his seed!

---

3 **Gittayim:** Further west of Be'erot. The name means "Double-Winepress."

4 **Now Yehonatan . . . had a son:** This verse is parenthetical. Despite the events of this chapter, the text apparently wishes to establish that someone from Sha'ul's line has survived (McCarter 1984). **stricken:** Crippled. **feet:** Or "legs"; biblical Hebrew does not make the distinction. **tidings:** Of their death. **Mefiboshet:** Pronounced *meh-fee-BO-shet;* trad. English "Mephibosheth." The name means "from the Mouth of Baal/Boshet."

The original form of the name, mentioned in I Chron. 8:34 and 9:40, is "Merib-baal."

5 **nap:** Heb. *mishkav,* from the same root (*sh-k-b*), "to lie down," that echoes in this chapter, emphasizing the heinousness of the murder.

6–7 **And here . . . :** The Hebrew passage is confusing; I follow B-R.

6 **as fetchers of wheat:** Pretending to be farmhands, and thus with access to the house. In these verses, LXX has a longer text, in which a woman guarding the house falls asleep, enabling the assassins to enter.

445

Chapter 5. *Major Victories for David:* A number of episodes are strung together here, all demonstrating David's ascendancy as king and as military leader. First (vv.1–5) he receives the throne of all Israel, at the request of the northern tribes. Following on the heels of Ish-Boshet's assassination, this seems both surprising and logical.

In vv.6–9, David conquers Jerusalem, which had thus far resisted takeover by the Israelites (despite Judg. 1:8). The text is incredibly brief, despite the great importance of the deed. We are not initially told why David decides to attack the Jebusite enclave, but the subsequent chapters make clear that he desires to make it the new capital of a united Israel, a politically ingenious move, since the city was quite defensible and situated close to the border between the northern and southern sections of the country.

The text continues at v.10, with several passages befitting a king: vv.10–11 trace the beginnings of an important alliance, with King Hiram of Tyre in Phoenicia, resulting in the building of a palace for David—a step beyond Sha'ul's chieftain-style rule. This seems to produce proof of divine favor (v.12), a theme which will be at the forefront of Chap. 7. Then (vv.13–16) we are given a list of children born to David in Jerusalem. In summary, we now have a king over all Israel, with a major alliance, a palace, and numerous heirs—a good recipe for political stability.

The chapter concludes with a larger story (vv.17–25) in which it is clear that having become king has not softened David the warrior. He is able to decisively defeat the Philistines, with the assistance of God. The victory cements his military accomplishments, as it was the long-lasting superiority of the Philistines that had led to the people's request for a king in I Sam. 8 in the first place.

9 David answered Rekhav and Baana his brother, the sons of
   Rimmon the Be'erotite;
   he said to them:
   By the life of YHWH,
   who has saved my life from every trouble:
10 indeed, the one telling me, saying: Here, Sha'ul is dead!,
   though he was like a bearer-of-[good]-news in his [own] eyes,
   I seized him and killed him in Tziklag,
   one to whom I might have given [reward for the] news!
11 More so, when guilty men have killed an innocent man in his
   house, in his bedroom!
   So-now,
   should I not seek-satisfaction for his blood at your hand,
   and eradicate you from the land?
12 So David commanded the fighting-lads,
   and they killed them and chopped off their hands and their feet
   and hung them up by the pool in Hevron,
   while the head of Ish-Boshet they took
   and buried in the burial-place of Avner in Hevron.

5:1 All the staff-bearers of Israel came to David in Hevron;
   they said, saying:
   Here we are—your bone and your flesh are we!
2 Even yesterday, even the day-before, when Sha'ul was king over us,
   it was you who took out and brought back Israel [in battle],
   and YHWH said to you:
   You shall shepherd my people Israel,
   you shall be *Nagid* over Israel!
3 So all the elders of Israel came to the king at Hevron,
   and King David cut a covenant with them at Hevron, in the
   presence of YHWH,
   and they anointed David as king over Israel.

---

10 **the one telling me . . . Sha'ul is dead!:** The Amalekite messenger of II 1.
11 **seek-satisfaction:** To hold responsible; premedi-
tated murder is punishable in the Bible by death. See
the classic statement in Gen. 9:5. **eradicate you
from the land:** JPS: "rid the earth of you." In Deu-

teronomy this phrase appears often as a refrain (e.g.,
13:6, 17:7) referring to serious offenses.
5:1 **staff-bearers:** McCarter (1984) here understands
shevatim (usually "tribes") thus, parallel to "elders"
in v.3.

◆

4 Thirty years old was David when he became king;
for forty years he reigned as king:

5 in Hevron he reigned as king over Judah for seven years and six
months,
and in Jerusalem he reigned as king for thirty-three years, over all
Israel and Judah.

6 Now the king and his men went to Jerusalem, to the Yevusites, the
settled-folk of the region,
but they said to David, saying:
You are not to enter here!
—For the blind and the lame had incited them, saying:
David is not to enter here!—

7 But David captured the Fortress of Zion—that is the city of David.

8 And David said on that day:
Whoever strikes down a Yevusite
and reaches the water-shaft . . . ,
since the lame and the blind are hated by David's very self;
therefore they say:
The blind and the lame are not to enter the Temple-House!

9 David settled in the fortress,
and he called it the City of David;
and David built all around, from the Earthfill and inward.

10 And David went on and on becoming great;
YHWH, God of the Forces-On-High, was with him.

11 Hiram king of Tyre sent messengers to David,
along with cedar wood and wood carvers and stone wall carvers;
they built a palace-house for David.

---

4 **Thirty years . . . forty years:** Patterned numbers, which in the Bible tend to signify perfection or rounded-out periods, rather than exact totals.

6 **the blind and the lame:** Possibly used here as a taunt—namely, even those unfit to fight were able to turn back enemies because of Jerusalem's impregnability. **had incited them:** In this difficult passage, read (with McCarter 1984, following 4QS^a) *hesit* for *hesir.*

7 **Zion:** Heb. *tziyyon,* the Jerusalem hill just north of David's city which became the Temple Mount; not the present Mount Zion.

8 **reaches the water-shaft:** That is, conquering the city through its water supply. B-R and McCarter (1984) read "should attack at the windpipe," but such

a usage is not attested elsewhere. In any event the passage is difficult, and words appear to be missing.

9 **Earthfill:** Probably a structure which was there previously. Some identify it as the archaeologically famous "Stepped Stone Structure" just south of the present Old City walls.

10 **God:** Missing in some ancient versions.

11 **Hiram king of Tyre:** Pronounced *hee-RAHM.* He provides both David and his son Shelomo with building materials, principally cedar wood. The name, known in Phoenician, means "My [Divine] Brother Is Exalted." As for Tyre, along with Sidon, the other great port city in Phoenicia, it was a major base for the sailor/traders of the eastern Mediterranean.

12   And David knew that YHWH had established him as king over Israel,
         and that he had exalted his kingdom for the sake of his people
             Israel.

13   David took more concubines and wives in Jerusalem, after his
             coming back from Hevron,
         and more [children] were born to David, sons and daughters.

14   And these are the names of those born to him in Jerusalem:
         Shammua and Shovav,
         Natan and Shelomo,

15   Yivhar and Elishua, Nefeg and Yafi'a,

16   Elishama, Elyada and Elifelet.

17   The Philistines heard that they had anointed David as king over
             Israel,
         so all the Philistines went up to seek out David.
         David heard, and he went down to the fortress.

18   Now the Philistines had come
         and had spread out in the Valley of the Shades.

19   So David inquired of YHWH, saying:
         Shall I go up against the Philistines?
         Will you give them into my hand?
         YHWH said to David:
         Go up,
         for I will give, yes, give the Philistines into your hand!

20   David came to Baal-Peratzim / Master of Bursting Forth,
         and David struck them there;
         he said:
         YHWH has burst my enemies before me like a bursting forth of
             water!
         Therefore they called the name of that place Baal-Peratzim / Master
             of Bursting Forth.

21   They abandoned their idols there,
         and David and his men carried them off.

---

14   **Natan:** Pronounced *nah-TAHN;* trad. English "Nathan." This is not the important court prophet who appears first in Chap. 7. The name is notable in its echoing of David's dear friend Yehonatan.   **Shelomo:** Trad. English "Solomon."
17   **they had anointed:** The Israelites.
18   **Valley of the Shades:** "Shades" refers to the *Refa'im,* ancestral spirits who were also understood to be primeval giants. The location of the valley is today a residential neighborhood in the southern part of West Jerusalem.
20   **Baal-Peratzim:** Southwest of Jerusalem.
21   **David and his men carried them off:** A common ancient Near Eastern practice, demonstrating ultimate victory (McCarter 1980).

Chapter 6. *Jerusalem Taken; the Coffer's Journey:* The account of how Jerusalem is consecrated, and its preeminent political status assured, by the bringing of the Coffer (others, "Ark") to reside there, has some unexpected twists. From David's point of view, this momentous religious and political act should be filled with joy, and the text (vv.5 and 13–14) indeed stresses the unfettered jubilation of the occasion through music and David's leaping and dancing. But the positive emotions of the moment are marred by two incidents, one public and one private. As the Coffer initially travels by wagon, it begins to slip, and the Israelite who tries to steady it is struck dead by God. This "carelessness" of physical contact, which might baffle modern readers since its intention is pure, nevertheless violates the sanctity of the object, and we are reminded that the Coffer represents God and is thus separated from normal human contact. It is a boundary that, in ancient cultures, must not be breached. At the same time, Uzza's death leads David to despair of ever attaining his royal goals.

The second incident in the chapter is colorful and very telling. Mikhal, the nouveau princess, is unable to stomach the mundane and, to her, undignified sight of her husband jumping and dancing for joy at the Coffer's entry to the city. She seems not to understand his strong emotions—or, possibly, his near nakedness reminds her of her father's prophetic moments, which had caused people to whisper (see I Sam. 19:24). At any rate, David counters her accusation that he is acting lewdly with a sexual threat of his own (v.22, "with the serving-maids of whom you spoke . . . I'll get honor!"). After several chapters that have contained two long lists of David's progeny, this one ends with the sober notice that Mikhal remained childless to the end of her days. So for multiple reasons, there will ultimately be no merging of the houses of Sha'ul and David. Biologically as well as militarily and politically, David's victory is now complete. We can now proceed to God's long and firm promises to the new king.

22 But the Philistines went up again,
and spread out in the Valley of the Shades.
23 So David inquired of Y_HWH,
and he said:
You are not to go up;
lead [your men] around, behind them,
and come at them in front of the balsam-trees.
24 And let it be:
when you hear the sound of marching on the tops of the balsam-
trees, then you are to act-decisively,
for then Y_HWH will go out before you, to strike down the camp of
the Philistines.
25 David did thus, as Y_HWH had commanded him;
he struck the Philistines from Geva until where-you-come to Gezer.

6:1 David continued [gathering] every hand-picked [man] in Israel,
thirty thousand.
2 And David arose and went, along with all the fighting-people who
were with him, from Baala in Judah,
to bring up from there the Coffer of God, over which was called the
name of Y_HWH of the Forces-On-High, [The One] Seated on the
Winged-Sphinxes.
3 They mounted the Coffer of God on a new wagon
and transported it from the house of Avinadav, which is in Giv'a,
while Uzza and Ahyo, the sons of Avinadav, were driving the new
wagon.
4 They transported it from the house of Avinadav that is in Giv'a,
with the Coffer of God,
with Ahyo walking in front of the Coffer.

---

23 **balsam-trees:** Others take Heb. *bekha'im* as a place-
name.
25 **Gezer:** David drives the Philistines well to the northwest.
6:1 **thirty thousand:** Some understand Heb. *elef* as a
military unit or division, thus making for more realistic numbers.
2 **Baala:** Identical to Kiryat-Ye'arim (see Josh. 15:9).
the name: The text is jumbled and perhaps a scribal
error; MT reads "the Name, the Name." Adding to

the problems with that word, *shem,* is *sham,* "there,"
earlier in the verse. **[The One] Seated on the
Winged-Sphinxes:** A title of Y_HWH, enthroned as
king, as in I Sam. 4:4.
3 **new wagon:** See note to I 6:7, above.
3–4 **transported it . . . Giv'a:** The repetition and resulting confusion here are probably the result of scribal
error. **Ahyo:** Either a proper name or a noun
meaning "his brother."

◆

5   Now David and the whole house of Israel were dancing in the
           presence of YHWH,
     with all the fir wood [instruments],
     with lyres and with lutes and with timbrels,
     with rattles and with cymbals.
6   They came to the threshing-floor of Nakhon,
     and Uzza stretched out [his hand] to the Coffer of God and took
           hold of it,
     for the oxen had let it slip.
7   YHWH's anger flared up at Uzza,
     and God struck him down there because of [his] carelessness, so
           that he died there,
     beside the Coffer of God.
8   And David was agitated over [the fact] that YHWH had burst forth, a
           bursting forth against Uzza,
     so that place is called Peretz Uzza / Bursting Forth [at] Uzza,
     until this day.
9   And David was fearful of God on that day;
     he said:
     How will the Coffer of YHWH [ever] come to me?
10   And David would not remove the Coffer of YHWH from him to the
           City of David,
     so David turned it aside to the house of Oved-Edom the Gittite.
11   The Coffer stayed at the house of Oved-Edom the Gittite for three
           months,
     and YHWH blessed Oved-Edom and all his household.
12   It was told to King David, saying:
     YHWH has blessed the house of Oved-Edom and all that is his, on
           account of the Coffer of God;
     so David went and brought up the Coffer of God from the house of
           Oved-Edom to the City of David, with rejoicing.

---

5   **with all the fir wood [instruments]:** I Chron. 13:8
    reads "with all their might and with songs" ('*oz ve-*
    shirim; here it is '*atzei veroshim*).
6   **Nakhon:** 4QS^a reads "Nadon."
7   **YHWH's anger flared up:** In Israelite thinking, holy
    objects were "removed" from everyday use, and
    hence coming into contact with them posed an ele-
    ment of danger for laypeople. **because of [his**

carelessness: Following some ancient witnesses;
others indicate a longer text (I Chron. 13:10: "he
stretched out his hand to the Coffer").
8   **burst forth:** The same verb had been used to
    describe God's power in 5:20.
10 **Oved-Edom the Gittite:** Interestingly, it is a foreign-
    er's house that is blessed. His name means "Servant
    of Edom, native of Gat."

◆

13　It was,

　　when those transporting the Coffer of Yhwh had stepped forward
　　　six steps,

　　that he sacrificed an ox and a fatling.

14　And David was whirling with all [his] might in the presence of
　　　Yhwh;

　　David was girded with an *efod* of linen.

15　Now David and all the House of Israel were bringing up the Coffer
　　　of Yhwh with shouting and with the sound of the *shofar*;

16　and as the Coffer of Yhwh was coming into the City of David,

　　Mikhal daughter of Sha'ul was looking out through the window:

　　she saw King David leaping and whirling in the presence of Yhwh,

　　and she despised him in her heart.

17　They brought the Coffer of Yhwh

　　and set it in its place, in the middle of the tent that David had
　　　spread out for it.

　　And David offered up offerings-up in the presence of Yhwh, and
　　　shalom-offerings.

18　[When] David had finished offering up the offering-up and the
　　　shalom-offerings,

　　he blessed the people in the name of Yhwh of the Forces-On-High,

19　and divided up [food] for the whole people, for the whole throng of
　　　Israel, from man to woman

　　—for each: one cake of bread, one roll, and one raisin-cake—

　　and all the people went off, each one to his house.

20　Then David returned to bless his household;

　　but Mikhal daughter of Sha'ul went out to meet David

　　and said:

　　How he has gotten honor today, the king of Israel,

　　who has exposed himself today before the eyes of his servants'
　　　maids—

　　like one of [those] empty-men exposes himself!

13　**an ox and a fatling:** McCarter (1984) takes this as a hendiadys, where two nouns in sequence connected by "and" are understood as a noun and an adjective, hence "a fatted bull."

14　**an *efod* of linen:** A common loincloth, not a priestly vestment (McCarter 1984).

16　**leaping and whirling:** I could not find an adequate English equivalent for the aurally dynamic *mefazzez um'kharker*.

19　**roll:** Others, "date cake."

20　**empty-men:** Heb. *rkym*. LXX, adding a letter, reads "dancers" (*rkdym*) here.

Chapter 7. *The Davidic Covenant:* Now that David's throne is secure (God has "given-him-rest," v.1), he logically seeks to build the one thing that his kingdom lacks: a temple. In the ancient Near East, such a desire would have been prompted not merely by piety; temples were political statements as well, symbolizing a god's approval and protection of the regime. The king's plea prompts a new character, Natan the court prophet, to encourage him, only to be overruled by YHWH: his son Shelomo (Solomon), not David, will get to build it. In the process, the text switches to a Deuteronomistic style, and we encounter what many would characterize as a masterpiece of royal propaganda. It is distinguished by, among other traits, wordiness, both in YHWH's promises and in David's grateful response.

The basic message of the chapter is that YHWH will be with David, and that he will establish both "my people" and the Davidic throne in perpetuity. The speeches are punctuated by several key words, first of all "name," here referring most often to God, whose fame will be augmented by what he does with Israel and by the future temple. "House," in the multiple senses of Temple and dynasty, appears fifteen times, and the encouraging "for the ages" eight times. Not surprisingly, the verb meaning "to make firm" appears five times, to stress God's commitment. And David's response to divine generosity contains the formal marker of submission: ten times in vv.19–29 he uses the expression "your servant" in speaking to God.

21 David said to Mikhal:
In the presence of YHWH, who chose me over your father and over
    all his house, to commission me as *Nagid* over the people of
    YHWH, over Israel:
I'll dance in the presence of YHWH,
22 and will hold-myself-lightly more than this;
I'll be lowly in my own eyes—
with the serving-maids of whom you spoke,
with *them* I'll get honor!
23 And Mikhal daughter of Sha'ul had no child
until the day of her death.

7:1 Now it was
when the king sat in his house
—YHWH had given-him-rest, round about, from all his enemies—
2 that the king said to Natan the prophet:
Now see:
I stay in a house of cedars,
while the Coffer of God stays in the midst of a curtained-shrine!
3 Natan said to the king:
All that is in your heart, go, do,
for YHWH is with you.
4 But it was on that very night
that the word of YHWH [came] to Natan, saying:
5 Go and say to my servant, to David:
Thus says YHWH:
Will *you* build me a house to stay in?
6 For I have not stayed in a house
from the day of my bringing up the Children of Israel from Egypt
    until this day;
but I have been going about in Tent and in Dwelling.

---

21 **in the presence of YHWH:** As in vv.3–4, the doublet in this verse suggests a scribal mistake.
22 **with *them* I'll get honor:** A sarcastic sexual reference.
7:1 **house:** The first occurrence in the chapter of the "house" motif, leading to a focus on David's dynastic "house."

2 **curtained-shrine:** The tapestries were a notable feature of the desert tabernacle; see Exod. 26–27, where this aspect of the structure is described.
5 **to stay in:** Lit., "for my staying in/inhabiting."
6 **in Tent and in Dwelling:** See the second half of the book of Exodus, from Chap. 25 onward.

◆

7   Wherever I have been going about among all the Children of Israel,
have I ever spoken a word with one of the judge-leaders of Israel
    whom I commisioned to shepherd my people Israel, saying:
Why have you not built me a house of cedars?

8   So-now,
thus are you to say to my servant, to David:
Thus says Yhwh of the Forces-On-High:
I myself took you from the pasture, from [following] after the flock,
to be *Nagid* over my people, over Israel.

9   I have been with you wherever you have gone,
and have cut off all your enemies from before you.
And I will make you a great name,
like the name of the great-ones who are on the earth,

10   and I will make a place for my people, for Israel:
I will plant them,
and they will dwell beneath it,
so that they will shudder no more,
so that malicious ones will not continue to afflict them, as in
    former-times,

11   from the day that I commisioned judges over my people Israel.
And I will give-you-rest from all your enemies.
Yhwh has told you that Yhwh will make you a house:

12   when your days are fulfilled
and you lie beside your fathers,
I will raise up your seed after you,
one who comes out from your body,
and I will make his kingdom firm.

13   *He* will build a house to my name,
and I will make his kingly throne firm for the ages;

14   I will be to him as a father,
and he will be to me as a son.
When he commits-iniquity,
I will rebuke him with the staff of men, and with the blows of
    humans;

---

7 **judge-leaders:** Reading *shivtei* ("tribes") as *shofetei;* see I Chron. 17:6 and v.11 below.

11 **Yhwh . . . Yhwh:** The repetition is strange, probably a scribal error.

12 **lie beside your fathers:** A common expression for the death of kings in the Bible; it was not used when

a king died in battle. **body:** Literally, "innards," ancient seat of both generation and emotion.

14 **father . . . son:** See the note to I 17:55. **the staff of men:** Referring to corporal punishment, applied by parents.

15   but my loyal-love I will not turn aside from him,
      as I turned aside from Sha'ul, from whom I turned aside before
         you.

16   Secure will be your house and your kingdom for the ages before
         me;
      your throne will be firm for the ages!

17   According to all these words and according to all this vision,
      thus did Natan speak to David.

18   King David came and sat in the presence of Yhwh;
      he said:
      Who am I, my Lord Yhwh,
      and who is my household,
      that you have brought me this far?

19   And still this was too small in your eyes, my Lord Yhwh—
      you have also spoken of your servant's house in a distant-time!
      This is the rule for a man-of-status, my Lord Yhwh!

20   And what more can David speak further to you,
      since you yourself know your servant, my Lord Yhwh?

21   For the sake of your word and in accordance with your heart
      you have done all this greatness,
      to make it known to your servant.

22   Therefore you are great, my Lord Yhwh;
      indeed, there is none like you
      and no God beside you
      according to all that we have heard with our ears.

23   And who is like your people, like Israel,
      a singular nation on earth,
      whom God went forth to redeem for himself as a people,
      to make for himself a name
      and to do for you great things, and awe-inspiring [acts] for your
         land,
      before your people whom you redeemed for yourself from Egypt,
      [driving out] nations and their gods?

24   You have made your people Israel firm, as a people for yourself for
         the ages,
      and you, O Yhwh, you have become God for them.

---

19 **This is the rule for a man-of-status:** The text is difficult; I follow Kimhi here.

23 **[driving out]:** As per I Chron. 17:21. This is likewise a verse with odd wording.

Chapter 8. *Warrior King; Bureaucracy:* Resuming the activities reported at the end of Chap. 5, David makes short order of Philistines, Moabites, and Arameans, with the result that he acquires a large amount of gold, silver, and bronze. These are "hallowed to Yhwh" (v.11), in line with the portrayal of the king as faithful servant in the mode of Deuteronomy. And the text emphasizes how David's victories are attributable to Yhwh's presence "wherever he went" (vv.6 and 14). This theological thrust, however, is accompanied by a more secular note about political strategy: Israelite garrisons are established throughout conquered Aramean territory.

The chapter ends with the initial part of a textual bracket (as noted by Brettler 1995), a list of David's officials, which will recur at the end of Chap. 20. Their functions include such royal, military, and religious duties as would have been found in many ancient Near Eastern states—proof either of David's historical power or of a later generation's desire to see him in their own terms.

◆ 25 So-now, O YHWH God,
as for the word that you have spoken about your servant and about
his house—
establish [it] for the ages,
and do as you have spoken.

26 And may your name be great for the ages, saying:
YHWH of the Forces-On-High is God over Israel,
and the house of your servant David—may it be firm before you!

27 For you, O YHWH of the Forces-On-High, God of Israel,
have bared your servant's ear, saying:
A house will I build for you;
therefore your servant has found his heart to pray to you this
prayer.

28 So-now, my Lord YHWH,
you are God, and your words are truth;
you have spoken this good [thing] to your servant.

29 So-now,
be pleased and bless the house of your servant,
to be in your presence for the ages,
for you, my Lord YHWH, you have spoken it,
and through your blessing may the house of your servant be
blessed for the ages!

8:1 It was [some time] after this
that David struck the Philistines and humbled them,
and David took Meteg Amma from the hand of the Philistines.

2 Then he struck Moav,
and he measured them with a rope, making them lie down on the
ground—
he measured two rope-lengths for putting to death
and a full rope-length for letting [them] live.
And Moav became servants to David, bearers of tribute.

---

27 **found his heart to pray:** Speech originates in the heart (Greenstein, written communication).

28 **spoken this good [thing]:** Not merely "good words"; this is covenant language in Israel and elsewhere in the ancient Near East (McCarter 1984 and others).

8:1 **Meteg Amma:** Following recent translations. The Hebrew is obscure; reading it as *mgt h'amh* would yield "from Gat to Amma."

2 **he measured them:** That is, he decided which of the prisoners were to die.

3   Then David struck Hadad'ezer/Hadad is Help, son of Rehov, king
      of Tzova,
      as he was going to restore his monument at the River;

4   David took from him a thousand and seven hundred horsemen and
      twenty thousand men, foot-soldiers,
      and David maimed all the chariot-horses, and left of them [only] a
      hundred chariot-horses.

5   And Arameans from Damascus came, to help Hadad'ezer king of
      Tzova,
      and David struck down from Aram twenty thousand men.

6   David put standing-garrisons at Aram of Damascus,
      and Aram became servants to David, bearers of tribute.
      Thus YHWH delivered David wherever he went.

7   And David took the gold bow cases that were upon Hadad'ezer's
      servants
      and brought them to Jerusalem,

8   while from Betah and from Berotai, Hadad'ezer's towns,
      King David took an exceedingly great [amount of] bronze.

9   And To'i king of Hamat heard that David had struck down
      Hadad'ezer's entire army,

10   so To'i sent Yoram his son to King David,
      to inquire of his welfare and to give-him-blessing
      on account of his waging battle against Hadad'ezer, and [that] he
      had struck him down,
      —for a man waging battle with To'i was Hadad'ezer—
      and in his hand were objects of silver and objects of gold and
      objects of bronze.

11   These too David hallowed to YHWH,
      with the silver and the gold that he had hallowed from all the
      nations that he had subdued:

---

3 **Hadad:** Pronounced *hah-DAHD.* An ancient
Near Eastern storm god, usually identified with
Baal. **the River:** The Euphrates.

4 **maimed:** Often translated as "hamstrung," but the
intent here was probably only to temporarily put
the enemy's horses out of commission. They would
have been too valuable to destroy (Cantrell).

7 **bow cases:** See McCarter (1984) for an extended discussion of the meaning of this term, traditionally
rendered "shields." Some use "quivers."

9 **Hamat:** The region northeast of Tzova, itself above
Damascus. It was the idealized northern border of
Israel, which controlled it in David's time, according
to the Bible.

10 **a man waging battle with To'i:** Experienced in conflict with him.

11 **hallowed:** Set aside.

◆

12　from Edom and from Moav, and from the Children of Ammon,
　　　　from the Philistines and from Amalek,
　　　　and from the spoil of Hadad'ezer son of Rehov, king of Tzova.

13　And David made a name [for himself] on his return from striking
　　　　Edom in the Valley of Salt, eighteen thousand [dead].

14　He put garrisons in Edom—throughout all Edom he put
　　　　garrisons—
　　　and all Edom became servants to David.
　　　Thus Yhwh delivered David wherever he went.

15　David reigned as king over all Israel,
　　　and David instituted justice and equity for all his people.

16　Now Yoav son of Tzeruya was [The One] Over the Armed-Forces,
　　　and Yehoshafat son of Ahilud was Herald,

17　and Tzadok son of Ahituv and Avimelekh son of Evyatar were
　　　　priests,
　　　and Seraya was scribe,

18　and Benayahu son of Yehoyada was [The One Over] the Kereitites
　　　　and the Peleitites,
　　　while the sons of David—they were priests.

12　**Edom:** Following ancient versions. MT has "Aram," which is visually similar in Hebrew.
13　**Valley of Salt:** Just south of the Dead Sea (biblically, the "Sea of Salt").
16　**[The One] Over the Armed-Forces:** The title of the commander in chief.
17　**Tzadok:** Pronounced *tzah-DOKE;* trad. English

"Zadok." Ancestor of the predominant priestly family under the Davidic dynasty. **Seraya:** "Sh'va" in 20:5, below.
18　**Kereitites and . . . Peleitites:** David's personal bodyguard, recruited from foreigners. The Kereitites were probably from Crete.

PART V

DAVID IN CONTROL AND OUT OF CONTROL

(II 9–12)

THIS SECTION BEGINS WITH DEMONSTRATIONS EVERYWHERE OF DAVID'S POWER: he reduces the rival house of Sha'ul to one physically challenged adult who depends on him for his daily bread, and, amid a campaign against the neighboring Ammonites, he manages to win peace from the powerful Arameans. As the ruler of a small empire and the central figure in a military and political success story, David seems to be the king with everything, including the blessing of God, multiple wives, and sons to succeed him.

It is precisely at this moment of triumph that the Bible inserts the turning point of II Samuel and one of the greatest of all biblical tales: the story of David and Bat-Sheva (Chaps. 11–12). The king, absent from battle for unknown reasons, acts like a typical monarch throughout history: he takes what is not his, in this case a married woman. While in the king's mind his lust for a woman is a personal matter, it is not hidden from God, who makes sure that David understands its wider ramifications (see Commentary to those chapters). The punishment will not be wrought only on the offending couple, but will extend through the generation of heirs to the throne and ultimately to the very stability of the state. From this point on, the private life of David and the public life of Israel will never be the same. In that sense, the book of Samuel, with its portrayal of how individuals affect the nation as a whole, is a fitting lead-in to the book of Kings.

It is notable that the parallel section of the much later book of Chronicles does not contain either this story or most of the subsequent chapters, which trace the revolt of David's son Avshalom. That would not have suited the Persian-era Jewish community, which on some level longed for the restoration of the Davidic line. But the Samuel account, by then undoubtedly considered authoritative, could not be expunged, and remains as one of the Bible's great acts of self-criticism.

Chapter 9. *Mefiboshet:* David's consolidation of power now makes it feasible for him to be magnanimous. As was noted previously in II 4, a descendant of Sha'ul has survived the civil war. As a man who is lame, Mefiboshet poses no threat to David, since such a condition would naturally have made it impossible for him to lead troops against the king, and so David allows him to both maintain a large laboring household and have a regular seat at the royal table. This arrangement recurs at the end of Kings, and hence at the end of the entire four-book sequence of the Early Prophets, where the surviving Davidic king, Yehoiakhin, is released from captivity in Babylon and boarded at state expense. His status as a favored but impotent royal figure is as telling there as Mefiboshet's is here.

The House of Sha'ul seems to have survived for centuries, at least in memory; inclusion of passages sympathetic to Sha'ul indicate a later desire to be sensitive to ongoing northern traditions. This kind of attachment to past loyalties can still be seen in many countries and cultures, as witnessed in the ethnic and religious conflicts of recent times.

9:1 David said:
Is there yet anyone that remains from the House of Sha'ul?
—so that I may show him loyalty for the sake of Yehonatan.

2 Now the House of Sha'ul had a servant, his name was Tziva,
and they called him to David.
The king said to him:
Are you Tziva?
He said:
Your servant.

3 The king said:
Is there no one still [alive] from the House of Sha'ul,
that I may show him the loyalty of God?
Tziva said to the king:
There is still a son of Yehonatan, stricken in the feet.

4 The king said to him:
Where is he?
Tziva said to the king:
Here, he is at the house of Makhir son of Ammiel, in Lo-Devar.

5 So King David sent and had him taken from the house of Makhir
son of Ammiel, from Lo-Devar.

6 And Mefiboshet son of Yehonatan son of Sha'ul came to David,
and he flung himself on his face and bowed low.
David said: Mefiboshet!
He said:
Here is your servant.

7 David said to him:
Do not be afraid,
for I will show, yes, show you loyalty for the sake of Yehonatan
your father;
I will return to you all the lands of Sha'ul your [grand]father,
and you, you will eat bread at my table regularly.

8 He bowed low and said:
What is your servant,
that you have turned your face toward a dead dog like me?

9:2 **Tziva:** Pronounced *tzee-VAH;* trad. English "Zibah."
4 **Lo-Devar:** Northeast of Bet-She'an, on the east
bank of the Jordan, and not far from Yavesh Gil'ad.

7 **return:** Or "restore." **the lands:** Lit., "the field."
8 **a dead dog:** Once again we encounter the canine
imagery that is so pervasive in the book.

Chapter 10. *War with Ammonites and Arameans:* At the start of Sha'ul's reign, he had rescued a town from the Ammonite king Nahash (I Sam. 11). Seeking now to cement ties with the Ammonites, David is met with suspicion and bad behavior—the humiliation of his emissaries—by the son of this same Nahash. David's subsequent attack overcomes mainly Arameans who had been hired as mercenaries by the Ammonites. The latter now realize their mistake. By the end of the chapter it is clear that the Ammonites' days as an effective enemy of Israel are numbered. Before their defeat at the hands of the Israelites can occur, however, the text turns to a contemporary incident which will reverberate far beyond the context of a local war.

9 The king called Tziva, Sha'ul's serving-lad, and said to him:
All that belonged to Sha'ul and to all his household, I give to your
      lord's [grand]son;

10 you are to work the ground for him, you and your children and
      your servants,
and you are to bring in [the produce], so that it may be food for
      your lord's grandson, and he may eat it,
while Mefiboshet, your lord's grandson, shall eat bread regularly at
      my table.
—Now Tziva had fifteen sons and twenty servants.—

11 Tziva said to the king:
According to all that my lord king commands his servant,
thus will your servant do.
So Mefiboshet was eating at David's table, like one of the king's
      sons.

12 Now Mefiboshet had a young son, his name was Mikha,
while all those dwelling in Tziva's house were servants to
      Mefiboshet.

13 And Mefiboshet stayed in Jerusalem,
for at the king's table he ate regularly.
Now he was lame in his two feet.

10:1 It was [some time] after this
that the king of the Children of Ammon died,
and Hanun his son became king in his stead.

2 David said:
I will show loyalty to Hanun son of Nahash,
as his father showed loyalty to me.
So David sent to comfort him by the hand of his servants, for his
      father,
and David's servants came to the land of the Children of Ammon.

---

9 **[grand]son:** Biblical Hebrew makes no verbal distinction between "son" and "grandson" (or between "father" and "forefather").

11 **was eating:** Some manuscripts of the Vulgate read this way; MT had "ate." **David's table:** MT has "my table," while a manuscript reads "our table."

12 **Mikha:** Pronounced *mee-KHAH*; trad. English "Micah." The previous bearer of this name was the morally compromised protagonist of Judg. 17–18.

10:1 **Ammon:** The region around today's Amman, capital of Jordan.

2 **as his father showed loyalty:** See I 20:14–16, above.

◆ 3 But the officials of the Children of Ammon said to Hanun their
lord:
Is David [really] honoring your father in your eyes,
when he sends you comforters?
Isn't it for the sake of spying out the town, to explore it and to
overthrow it
that David has sent his servants to you?

4 So Hanun took David's servants,
he shaved off half their beards
and cut their clothes in half, as far as their buttocks,
and then he sent them off.

5 They told David,
and he sent [men] to meet them,
for the men were exceedingly humiliated.
The king said:
Stay at Jericho until your beards have grown;
then you may return.

6 The Children of Ammon saw that they had made-themselves-reek
to David,
so the Children of Ammon sent and hired Arameans from Bet-
Rehov and Arameans from Tzova, twenty thousand foot-soldiers,
the king of Maakha, [with] a thousand men,
and men of Tov, twelve thousand men.

7 David heard,
and he sent Yoav and all the armed-forces, the mighty-men.

8 And the Children of Ammon went out and arranged-ranks for
battle, at the entrance to the gate,
while the Arameans from Tzova and Rehov and the men of Tov
and Maakha were alone in the open-field.

9 And Yoav saw that the face of battle was upon him, in front and in
back,
so he chose from all the choice-warriors in Israel
and arranged-ranks to meet the Arameans,

3 **officials:** Elsewhere the Hebrew word is translated "commanders."
4 **shaved off half their beards . . . :** This act of humili-ation is mentioned in the prophets (see Isa. 15:2, Jer. 41:5) as well.

10 while the rest of the fighting-people he placed in the hand of
    Avishai his brother,
and arranged-ranks to meet the Children of Ammon.

11 He said:
If Aram is too strong for me,
you will be deliverance for me,
and if the Children of Ammon are too strong for you,
I will go to deliver you!

12 Be strong and let us be strengthened, on behalf of our people and
    on behalf of the towns of our God,
while Yhwh—may he do what is good in his eyes!

13 And Yoav approached, and the fighting-people who were with him,
    for battle against Aram,
and they fled before him.

14 Now when the Children of Ammon saw that Aram had fled,
they fled before Avishai and came back to the town.
Then Yoav turned from [attacking] the Children of Ammon, and
    came back to Jerusalem.

15 And Aram saw that they were defeated before Israel,
so they gathered together,

16 and Hadad'ezer sent and brought out the Arameans who were
    across the River, so that they came to Helam,
with Shovakh commander of Hadad'ezer's forces in front of them.

17 It was told to David,
so he gathered all Israel and crossed the Jordan, and came to
    Helam,
and the Arameans arrayed-ranks to meet David, and waged battle
    with him.

18 And the Arameans fled before Israel;
David killed seven hundred charioteers and forty thousand
    horsemen from Aram,
while Shovakh, the commander of Hadad'ezer's forces, he struck
    down, so that he died there.

12 **Be strong and let us be strengthened:** This phrase was later adopted by Jews to be chanted whenever a book of the Torah is completed in the cycle of weekly synagogue readings.

16 **Helam:** Well south of Damascus, due east of the Sea of Galilee.

Chapters 11–12. *David's Double Crime and God's Response:* After a slew of political successes—eliminating his rivals, unifying the country, establishing a new centralized capital and bringing the Coffer there, and subduing foreign enemies—David makes a fateful and fatal error. He behaves as kings throughout the ages have done, taking what is not his and overstepping the bounds of both private morality and Israel's covenant with God. That later generations were uncomfortable with this story is clear already in the Bible: the book of Chronicles, wishing to focus on David as the ideal king (out of hope, perhaps, for restoration of the monarchy in the Persian period), simply omitted it and the troubling Avshalom episodes that follow. Equally, later Jewish tradition as represented in the Talmud (Ketubot 9b) sought to exonerate David at least from adultery, on the grounds that warriors of the time were required to give their wives conditional divorces.

The book of Samuel, however, will have none of such whitewashing, and features this tale as the root of subsequent events in David's life, lavishing a considerable amount of artistic skill upon it. Like so many central biblical tales, it is constructed on a foundation of leading words—in this case, "lie" and "send." Rather than functioning as mere signposts, however, these words undergo what Trible suggestively calls a "pilgrimage"; they are transformed within the story, and bring us along on the journey. From the initially neutral "lying-place," David's rooftop couch, we are taken to the crime itself, where he "lies" with Bat-Sheva (11:4). The verb next appears in Uriyya's righteous refusal to go back home in the midst of the war: "and I, I should come into my house / to eat and to drink and to lie with my wife?" (11:11). It subsequently becomes part of David's punishment: "I will take away your women . . . your fellow . . . will lie with your women" (12:11). The concluding scenes of the story trace David's movement back into the realm of forgiveness and resolution, with his "lying on the ground" (12:16), pleading for his newborn son's life, and then his final, legitimate "lying" with Bat-Sheva, which results in the conception of the promised heir, Shelomo. Thus an initially neutral term becomes the vehicle for a well-trodden biblical journey of sin and repentance.

The other key word, "send," has a parallel function. Eleven times in twenty-six verses, messages and people are sent, almost always by David, the master manipulator. The long arm of royal power reaches into the home of a private citizen and abroad to the public arena of the battlefield, with the king seemingly able to move his subjects around like chess pieces. Much of his sending is successful, but it is dramatically countered by the divine hand in 12:1 ("and Yhwh sent Natan to David"). Despite David's well-thought-out plans, in the end he cannot stand up to God's sending—a verb that in the Bible is almost always used in connection with prophets. And the prophet Natan's mission is a classic one, with the man of God pitted against the king. It will be structurally repeated, along with parallel circumstances, in the great encounter between Eliyyahu (Elijah) and Ah'av (Ahab) in I Kings 21. In the present story, it is only when David's repentance is accepted, and his punishment doled out, that we encounter the last "sending" of the sequence, in which God approves of the new son (12:25).

19 And all the kings, Hadad'ezer's servants, saw that they had been
defeated before Israel,
so they made-peace with Israel and served them,
for the Arameans were afraid to deliver the Children of Ammon
any longer.

11:1 Now it was at the turning of the year, at the time of kings' going
forth,
that David sent Yoav and his servants with him, and all Israel:
they wrought-ruin to the Children of Ammon and besieged Rabba,
while David stayed in Jerusalem.

2 Now it was around the time of sunset
that David arose from his lying-place and went-for-a-walk on the
roof of the king's house,
and he saw a woman washing herself, from on the roof—
the woman was exceedingly fair of appearance.

3 David sent and inquired after the woman,
and they said: Is this not Bat-Sheva daughter of Eliam, wife of
Uriyya the Hittite?

4 David sent messengers, and he had her taken:
she came to him and he lay with her
—now she had just purified herself from her state-of-*tum'a*—
and then she returned to her house.

5 The woman became pregnant;
she sent [word] and had it told to David, she said:
I am pregnant!

11:1 **the turning of the year:** In the spring, when the winter rains have stopped. **kings:** The MT consonants look like "messengers," but are vocalized as "kings," clearly the meaning here, to suggest David's inactivity and its unfortunate results. **Rabba:** Rabbat Benei Ammon, today Amman, the capital of Jordan.

2 **his lying-place:** More simply, "his bed," but I have sought to retain the key verb "lie" in the translation. Evidently David has been sleeping, or resting, from the time of the early afternoon nap on. **fair:** Lit., "good/goodly." The other biblical characters who are described as "fair to look at" are Rivka (Rebecca) and Ester (Esther).

3 **David . . . inquired:** Previously, he had inquired of God in different situations (2:1, 5:19, 23), but not, of course, here (Hamilton). **Bat-Sheva:** pronounced *bot-SHEH-vah;* trad. English "Bathsheba." **Uriyya**

the Hittite: Pronounced *oo-ree-YAH;* trad. English "Uriah." He was a high-ranking soldier in David's army. The name is ironically a pious Israelite one, meaning "YHWH Is My Light." The Hittites mentioned here are not to be confused with the earlier great empire in Anatolia (modern Turkey); as in Gen. 23, the term probably refers to a local Canaanite group.

4 **purified herself:** The verb *kiddeish* in other contexts denotes "hallowing"; here it is simply the non-priestly word for purification. **her state-of-tum'a:** Bat-Sheva's washing occurs at the end of her menstrual period, during which intercourse would have been forbidden because of ritual pollution (*tum'a;* see Lev. 18:19). It means that the forthcoming child could not be Uriyya's. Bat-Sheva is here also at her most fertile, twelve days or so after the onset of menstruation.

One might also note the text's repetition of "eat," a possible sexual metaphor, and "dead," with the illegitimate child's demise echoing Uriyya's as a kind of payback. Additionally, the story uses various meanings of the term "house," in an even broader spread than what we observed in Chap. 7. Indeed, the whole narrative here seems to be structured upon the movement of various characters from house to house—the palace, Uriyya's home, the sanctuary ("YHWH's House"), and the domicile of the prophet Natan. Looming over all the physical movement is the eventual fate of David's household and his dynastic house.

The story finds additional uses for the sound of words. Natan's little parable in Chap. 12, which some scholars feel does not fit the situation very well, is profoundly connected to its referent by the prophet's description of the poor man's lamb in 12:3: "from his morsel it would eat, from his cup it would drink, in his bosom it would lie— / it became to him like a daughter/*bat*." As literary critics have long pointed out (see, for instance, Simon 1967), the "eat/drink/lie" sequence echoes Uriyya's earlier refusal of 11:11, quoted above, and the coincidence of *Bat-Sheva*'s name is surely nothing of the kind. So when the unwitting king angrily condemns the rich man of the parable, the audience, its ears tuned aright, can sense the springing of the trap.

Also significant, and almost unprecedented in biblical poetry, is God's message in 12:11. It is noteworthy in its rhetoric and unprecedented in its use of rhyme, here represented in English by six consecutive lines that echo "your . . ." It is as if God's words, thus delivered, cannot be ignored, if only because the rhyme makes them reverberate throughout the throne room.

A final stylistic point has been noted by Brueggemann (1990). There are three dramatic two-word phrases in Hebrew, impossible, at least for me, to reproduce in English: "I am pregnant" (11:5), "You are the man!" (12:7), and "I have sinned against YHWH!" (12:13). The brevity of biblical language, here as elsewhere, makes for heightened emotional impact.

The David and Bat-Sheva story is an intimate look at David's many moods, and shows what he is capable of, for good and for ill, in a variety of situations. As presented in II Samuel, it is a moment from which David, despite the relatively happy endings of this chapter (Shelomo's birth and David's capture of Rabba), can never fully recover. From this point forward in his life, the misfortunes of Israel will be identical with those of the House of David.

6 So David sent [word] to Yoav:
  Send me Uriyya the Hittite.
  And Yoav sent Uriyya to David.
7 Uriyya came to him,
  and David asked after the welfare of Yoav, the welfare of the
    fighting-people, and the welfare of the battle;
8 then David said to Uriyya:
  Go down to your house and wash your feet!
  Uriyya went out of the king's house,
  and after him went out a portion from the king,
9 but Uriyya lay down at the entrance to the king's house, with all his
    lord's servants;
  he did not go down to his house.
10 They told David, saying:
  Uriyya has not gone down to his house.
  David said to Uriyya:
  Isn't it from a [long] journey that you have come?
  For-what-reason have you not gone down to your house?
11 Uriyya said to David:
  The Coffer and Israel and Judah are staying at Sukkot,
  my lord Yoav and my lord's servants are camping on the surface of
    the open-field—
  and I, I should come into my house
  to eat and to drink and to lie with my wife?
  By your life and by your [very] self: If I were to do this thing . . . !
12 David said to Uriyya:
  Stay here today as well; tomorrow I will send you off.
  So Uriyya stayed in Jerusalem on that day.
13 Now on the morrow David had him called, and he ate and drank in
    his presence,
  and he made him drunk.
  He went out in the evening to lie down in his lying-place with his
    lord's servants,
  but to his house he did not go down.

8 **wash your feet:** Possibly a euphemism for intercourse; "feet" sometimes signifies "genitals" in the
Bible. **portion:** Of food.
11 **at Sukkot:** Another location on the east bank of the
Jordan. Some alternatively read this as "in huts."

13 **but to his house he did not go down:** Reversal of
the usual word order underlines Uriyya's refusal.

◆ 14 So it was in the morning
that David wrote a letter to Yoav and sent it by the hand of Uriyya,

15 and he wrote in the letter, saying:
Put Uriyya facing the strongest [point of] battle,
and turn back behind him, so that he is struck down and dies.

16 So it was
when Yoav had observed the city,
that he placed Uriyya at the place where he knew that there were
men of valor;

17 the men of the city went out and did battle with Yoav,
and there fell some of the fighting-people, of David's servants,
and there died also Uriyya the Hittite.

18 Yoav sent and had David told all the details about the battle;

19 he charged the messenger, saying:
When you have finished reporting everything about the battle to
the king,

20 it will be:
if the king's anger starts up and he says to you:
For-what-reason did you draw near the city to do battle?
Did you not know that they would shoot down from on the wall?

21 Who struck down Avimelekh son of Yerubboshet—
did not a woman throw down on him a riding millstone from on
the wall,
so that he died at Tevetz?
Why did you approach the wall?—
Then you are to say:
Also your servant Uriyya the Hittite is dead.

22 The messenger went off, he came and told David all that Yoav had
sent him [to say];

23 the messenger said to David:
Indeed, the men were mightier than we, they went out at us in the
open-field;
we were upon them, up to the entrance to the gate,

14 **letter:** Heb. *sefer*, signifying a written document (which I usually render as "record").

21 **Avimelekh son of Yerubboshet:** Pronounced *ah-vee-MEH-lekh;* trad. English "Abimelech." The reference is to a son of Gid'on who in Judg. 9 proclaims himself king over the men of Shekhem and, not sur-prisingly, meets an untoward end. Yoav's message, if delivered, would be a not-so-subtle dig at David's behavior, by citing another well-known royal disaster involving a woman. **riding millstone:** The rolling portion of a millstone apparatus, thus a reasonably heavy stone.

24 but the shooters shot down at your servants from on the wall,
so that there died some of the king's servants,
and also your servant Uriyya the Hittite is dead.

25 David said to the messenger:
Say thus to Yoav:
Do not let this thing be evil in your eyes,
for like this and like that the sword devours!
Strengthen your battle against the city and destroy it!
And [you] strengthen him!

26 Uriyya's wife heard that her husband was dead,
so she beat [the breast] for her lord.

27 But when the mourning-period was past, David sent and had her
brought to his house;
she became his wife, and she bore him a son.
But the thing that David had done was evil in the eyes of Yhwh,

12:1 and Yhwh sent Natan to David;
he came to him and said to him:
There were two men in a certain town,
one rich and one poor.

2 The rich one had flocks and herds, exceedingly many,

3 while the poor one had nothing at all except for one little lamb
which he had bought;
he kept-it-alive, and it grew up with him, together with his children:
from his morsel it would eat, from his cup it would drink, in his
bosom it would lie—
it became to him like a daughter / bat.

4 A journey-walker came to the rich man,
but he thought-it-a-pity to take from his flocks or from his herds, to
make ready for the wayfarer who had come to him,
so he took the poor man's lamb and made it ready for the man who
had come to him.

---

24 **shooters:** Archers.
25 **like this and like that the sword devours:** Equivalent to "That's the way it goes." The focus on eating imagery recurs throughout the story (see 11:13, 12:16–17, 20). **[you] strengthen him:** Encourage him.
26 **Uriyya's wife:** She is not called "Bat-Sheva" again

until David's crime has been punished by the death of their child (12:24).
12:3 **eat . . . drink . . . lie:** Ironically recalling Uriyya's words to David in 11:11 above. **bat:** Echoing the leading lady's name.
4 **journey-walker . . . took:** Probably echoing "went-for-a-walk" and "had her taken" from 11:2, 4.

◆ 5 David's anger flared up exceedingly against the man,
and he said to Natan:
By the life of YHWH,
indeed, a son of death is the man who does this!

6 And for the lamb he shall pay fourfold,
because he did this thing, and since he had no pity!

7 Natan said to David:
You are the man!
Thus says YHWH, the God of Israel:
I myself anointed you king over Israel,
I myself rescued you from the hand of Sha'ul,

8 I gave you the house of your lord, and the women of your lord into
your bosom,
I gave you the House of Israel and Judah—
and as if [that were] too little, I would have added yet this and that
to you.

9 For-what-reason have you despised the word of YHWH, to do what
is evil in my eyes?
Uriyya the Hittite you have struck down by the sword,
and his wife you have taken for yourself as a wife—
while him you have killed by means of the sword of the Children
of Ammon!

10 So-now—
the sword shall not depart from your house for the ages,
because you despised me and took the wife of Uriyya the Hittite to
be a wife for you!

11 Thus says YHWH:
Here, I will raise up against your [person]
evil from your house;
I will take away your women
from before your eyes,
I will give them to your fellow

---

5 **son of death:** Deserving death (although
McCarter 1984 reads it as signifying something like
"scoundrel").

6 **fourfold:** In keeping with the law in Exod. 21:37. On
the other hand, LXX's reading "sevenfold" fits in
nicely with the other sevens in the story, including
the one suggested by the *Sheva* part of the female
character's name.

7 **You are the man!:** Or "The man is you!"

8 **your lord:** Sha'ul.

11 **[person]:** As mentioned above, the words of this
verse rhyme, somewhat unusually for biblical
poetry, so I have sought to have each line end with
"your ___." **under the eyes of this sun:** In broad
daylight.

and he will lie with your women,
    under the eyes of this sun.
12   For you, you did it in secret,
    but I, I will do this thing in front of all Israel and in front of the sun.
13   David said to Natan:
    I have sinned against Yhwh!
    Natan said to David:
    As for Yhwh, he has transferred your sin—
    you will not die;
14   nevertheless, because you have scorned, yes, scorned "Yhwh's
      enemies" by this thing,
    as for the son who is born to you: he must die, yes, die!
15   Natan went back to his house.
    And Yhwh attacked the child that Uriyya's wife had borne to
      David, so that he became sick.
16   David besought God on behalf of the boy,
    and David fasted a fast;
    he would come and spend-the-night lying on the ground.
17   And the elders of his house arose about him to raise him up from
      the ground,
    but he was unwilling and would not be nourished with food with
      them.
18   Now it was on the seventh day that the child died.
    David's servants were afraid to tell him that the child was dead, for
      they said:
    Here, while the child was alive, we spoke to him, but he did not
      hearken to our voice;
    so how can we say to him: The child is dead? He might do evil!
19   David saw that his servants were whispering [among themselves];
    and David understood that the child was dead.
    David said to his servants:
    Is the child dead?
    They said:
    [He is] dead.

---

12 **you did it in secret:** Heb. *asita va-sater*.
14 **"Yhwh's enemies":** Later scribes were not comfortable with the phrase "scorned Yhwh," so they added the "enemies" to blunt the sense.

18 **evil:** Harm (to himself).

20 Then David arose from the ground;
   he washed, and poured [oil on himself], and changed his clothes,
   and he came into the house of YHWH and bowed down;
   then he came back to his house, requested that they put food before
      him, and ate.

21 His servants said to him:
   What [kind of] thing is this that you have done?
   For the sake of the living child, you fasted and wept,
   but now that the child is dead, you arise and eat food!

22 He said:
   As long as the child was still alive, I fasted and wept,
   for I said [to myself]: Who knows, perhaps YHWH will be gracious
      to me, and the child will live!

23 But now he is dead—why, then, should I fast?
   Can I make him return again?
   I may go to him,
   but he will not return to me.

24 David comforted Bat-Sheva his wife;
   he came to her and lay with her,
   and she bore a son and called his name Shelomo / Peace.

25 Now YHWH loved him, and he sent by the hand of Natan the
      Prophet;
   he called his name Yedidya, by the grace of YHWH.

26 Yoav waged battle against Rabba of the Children of Ammon and
      captured the royal city;

27 then Yoav sent mesengers to David
   and said:
   I have waged battle against Rabba;
   I have also captured the water city.

---

20 **arose ... washed ... :** Kwitkin-Close (written communication) notes the breathlessness of David's actions here, via a long string of consecutive verb forms. **poured [oil on himself]:** See 14:2, below. Omitting this practice earlier indicated mourning; the Jewish holy day of Yom Kippur, which mimics a situation of death, still includes "anointing" on the list of forbidden actions.

24 **comforted:** The same verb applied to David (unknowingly, by himself) in v.6, meaning "pitied." **Peace:** Perhaps short for "YHWH's Peace." Alternatively, it may signify "Replacement" (for the dead child).

25 **Yedidya:** The name signifies "Beloved of YHWH," rather like the meaning of "David," and thus hints at a resolution to the story.

27 **water city:** Heb. unclear; a JPS note conjectures "perhaps the source of the water supply."

478

28   So-now,
      gather the rest of the fighting-people and encamp against the city,
         and capture it,
      lest I myself take the city, and my own name be called over it!

29   So David gathered all the fighting-people and went to Rabba;
      he waged battle against it and captured it.

30   Then he took their king's crown from off his head
      —its weight was a talent of gold, with a precious stone—
      and it was [put] on David's head,
      while the spoils of the city he brought out, exceedingly much.

31   As for the people who were in it, he brought them out and set
         [them to work] with the saw, and with picks of bronze, and with
         axes of bronze,
      and had them pass through the brick-kiln.
      Thus he would do with all the towns of the Children of Ammon.
      Then David and all the fighting-people returned to Jerusalem.

---

28 **lest . . . my own name be called over it:** In that case
David would miss out on the credit, which would be
politically inappropriate.

31 **pass through:** Or, with a slight letter change, "put to
work at."

PART VI

THE GREAT REBELLION

(II 13–20)

WHAT COULD NOT HAVE BEEN IMAGINED ABOUT THE DAVID WHO SLEW GOLYAT, outmaneuvered Sha'ul, conquered Jerusalem, and received God's spirit and blessing now comes to pass. Beginning with an episode in which sexual transgression and violence immediately reappear, family ties are betrayed and destroyed, and David's once "firm" kingdom—his "house"—totters. Jerusalem is no longer safe for him, and he is forced into exile across the very Jordan which had been the entry point for the Israelites at the time of the Conquest. Only intervention by God and continuing vigorous action by David's ruthless general Yoav prevent the king from being permanently overthrown or assassinated.

This cycle of stories about his son Avshalom's revolt concerns both David's decline, which had begun pointedly in Chap. 11 with the Bat-Sheva episode, and the portrait of his rebel son. Avshalom is many things, but none so much as his father's son, with his good looks, worldly wisdom, and charisma. It is as if David, in his maturity, is forced to relive what Sha'ul had experienced of him in his youth.

The rebellion account proper spans Chaps. 15–20, and, as Fokkelman (1999) has shown, it is arranged concentrically, like many biblical stories and cycles. In the weighty center is 17:24–18:18, the account of battle preparations, the battle itself, and the death of Avshalom.

The vocabulary of the cycle is striking and effective. The ebb and flow of David's flight and restoration are traced through the repeated use of "cross" and "return" in Chaps. 15 and 19. The Amnon and Tamar story with which the cycle opens recalls some of the echoing words of the David and Bat-Sheva episode ("lie," "nourish," "dead"), but also introduces the leading wordplay of the entire cycle, consistent with the book's concentration on body parts which I noted in the Introduction: variations on the word "heart." A fuller explanation is appropriate here.

The tone is set already in the opening episode, the rape of Avshalom's sister Tamar. Amnon, the crown prince, pretends to be ill and requests that his half sister make *levivot,* usually translated as "cakes," for him. The noun occurs four times, and the root appears twice more in verbal form. But as some interpreters have noticed, the homonym (*levav*) means "heart," and the verbal form of *l-b-b* (the biblical *v* and *b* are the same letter) occurs in the Song of Songs 4:9, "You have captured my heart" (NJPS). So a word connected in love poetry with seduction is appropriate enough in the mouth of the lovesick Amnon, and on this and other grounds (see Notes below) we are justified in understanding *levivot* as something like "heartcakes."

From the opening culinary salvo we are prepared for permutations of the word throughout the story. Avshalom, on hearing that Amnon has raped Tamar, counsels his sister not to "take this thing to heart" (13:20); when the moment is right—Amnon's "heart is merry with wine" (13:28)—Avshalom has his hench-men murder Amnon; King David, misled by the resulting outcry into thinking that all of his sons have been killed, is corrected by Yonadav, who informs him that Amnon alone is dead and tells him not to "take the matter to heart" (13:33); Yoav, David's chief of staff, notices that the king's "heart [is] toward Avshalom" (14:1), and reconciliation is therefore necessary; but eventually, of course, Avsha-lom rebels against David, and then meets his end at the hand of Yoav, who drives three rods "into Absalom's heart" as he swings in "the heart of the oak" (18:14). There are several more idiomatic uses of the word in the story (14:13, 15:10, 16:3, 19:8, 20), but the significant ones occur in 15:6, where Avshalom "stole away the heart" of the men of Israel; in 19:8, where Yoav urges David to "speak to the hearts" of those same men; and in 19:15, where the king "inclined the heart of all the men of Judah" toward him.

This key word, which is usually translated out for idiomatic reasons (in NJPS it is variously rendered as "cakes . . . keep in mind . . . merry . . . think . . . mind . . . chest . . . hearts . . . placate . . . hearts," respectively), is undoubtedly a "lead-ing word" in Martin Buber's definition, that is, one used thematically to point to a major message in the narrative. Its function here seems to be to highlight the issue of who will exercise leadership over Israel, David or Avshalom. In the language of the text, this comes down to who will command the hearts of the people—the king chosen by God or the upstart who has driven his own father out of Jerusalem, and who in words, at least, has sanctioned his murder. By present-ing varying connotations of the leading word while retaining the repeated sound link between different passages, the text encourages readers themselves to "take to heart" the painful lessons of a narrative, a narrative that begins with a lovesick prince but whose roots lie in another affair of the heart, the Bat-Sheva incident.

To return to other uses of meaningful language in this section, Avshalom's name ("Father is Peace") undergoes significant development in the narrative. The king, after their initial reconciliation, tells his son to "go in peace" (15:9); Ahitofel advises Avshalom that he will personally kill the king, and thus bring about peace (17:3); David's anxious question about his son, "Is there peace with the lad?" (18:29, 32, the conventional idiom for "Is he well?"), plays up the irony of what we know but he does not—that his "peaceful" Avshalom is dead. The king is finally able to return to his throne "in peace" (19:25, 31), but it is only through decisive, violent acts by Yoav and the "wise woman" of Avel (20:9, 19), cloaked in words of "peace" (20:9), that the kingdom will be secured at last.

It is worth noting that, just as the book opened with a woman, Hanna, as the character who expressed central emotions and ideas, this section, and much that has preceded it, turns on the deeds done to and by women. The Bat-Sheva incident is followed immediately by the rape of Tamar, which in turn gives way to the words of the "wise woman" of Tekoa as a vehicle for seeming reconciliation between David and Avshalom. It will take another such woman to bring the rebelling to a close in Chap. 21. Her counsel leads to the last of the book's beheadings, a symbolic comment, perhaps, on the perils of leadership.

It is also notable that the story of the revolt is fleshed out by a large supporting cast of colorful characters: rebels, advisers, adherents, crafty men and women, and concubines. There are two clusters here, with some overlap, with one connected to David's flight from Jerusalem and another to his return to power. Some of these characters have names that recall "brothers" (*Ahitofel*, *Ahimaatz*), while others' names betray their function (Ittai, the "accompanier," and Hushai, the adviser who causes Avshalom to make a "hasty" and fatal decision). The words and deeds of all these secondary characters help to throw the protagonists' sometimes impulsive, often agonized decisions into relief.

In the end, as Flanagan has perceptively noticed, the rebellion story is not about succession, despite the fact that for decades scholars have referred to Chaps. 9–20 as "The Succession Narrative," but rather about survival—notably, David's. As Fokkelman (1981) reminds us, David, not Avshalom, occupies the bulk of space and concern in these chapters. And in this extended story, David resembles no other biblical character so much as Yaakov (Jacob) in Genesis. Like the patriarch, David is heavily involved with women; he is unable to control his sons' behavior, which reflects some of his own; and his passivity in the face of impending disaster (13:21–39) strangely echoes that of Yaakov in Gen. 37. Both men, who are younger sons, experience exile and the threat of death, and neither, bereaved of beloved younger sons in their declining years, attains anything but the Bible's ideal of the "fullness of days" typified by Avraham and Moshe.

Chapter 13. *Amnon and Tamar:* If the previous story constituted the great divide in David's life as king, the next one immediately launches into its consequences. David's desire for a woman, culminating in a tale of adultery and murder, is followed by his son Amnon's obsession with his own half sister, which leads him to rape and then spurn Tamar. He is subsequently cut down in an act of revenge by her full brother Avshalom. The fact that Amnon is the heir to the throne well illustrates the fateful mixing of private and public spheres that is characteristic of many narratives on biblical leadership.

In further emphasizing the connection between the two texts, several words recur here. The story picks up on the "nourishment" that David had refused in Chap. 12 and makes it into a major motif, resounding six times in six verses. "Lying/lying down" also returns, understandably. What is new, though, is the intensity of speech between the central characters. Not only do terrible things occur, but they are haggled over, and we are brought into the realm of extreme emotions: obsession, desperation, shame, rejection, and vengefulness.

Amid the personal details, this narrative also opens the Avshalom cycle, as noted in the Introduction to Samuel above, with the repetition of the theme word "heart." In addition to its use as a descriptor of Tamar's prepared food, it appears in Avshalom's ironic statement to his sister in v.20, "Don't take this thing to heart!"

The sequence of events leading to the murder of Amnon is telling. In a move that suggests elements of the opening of the Yosef story in Genesis, a father sends his son into a situation of certain conflict (note too Amnon's "Have everyone go out from me" in v.9, recalling the moment before Yosef reveals himself to his brothers in Gen. 45:1, and the mention of Tamar's "ornamented tunic," a phrase used to describe Yosef's famous article of clothing in Gen. 37:3). The fact that the king at first believes the rumor that all of his sons have been murdered (vv.30–31) is perhaps indicative of a suddenly fragile state of mind. The first part of God's recent statement of punishment for David's crimes, "So-now— / the sword shall not depart from your house for the ages" (12:10), has received its first fulfillment.

This part of the chapter structurally balances the earlier rape scene, encompassing refusal, the appearance of Yonadav, eating, and grief marked by the usual tearing of clothing (Polzin 1989). It also suggests what will be more fully developed subsequently, namely, Avshalom's reprising of some of his father's traits and experiences. Here, he flees for a time, as David had fled from Sha'ul.

13:1   It was [some time] after this:

      now Avshalom son of David had a beautiful sister—her name was
         Tamar,

      and Amnon son of David fell in love with her.

2   And Amnon was distressed to [the point of] being sick because of
         Tamar his sister

      —indeed, she was a nubile-girl—

      and it seemed impossible in Amnon's eyes to do anything to her.

3   Now Amnon had a friend—his name was Yonadav son of Shim'a,
         David's brother,

      and Yonadav was an exceedingly worldly-wise man.

4   He said to him:

      For-what-reason are you so haggard, O son of the king, morning
         after morning?

      Won't you tell me?

      Amnon said to him:

      Tamar—the sister—of Avshalom—my brother—I love!

5   Yehonadav said to him:

      Lie down on your lying-place and feign-sickness,

      and when your father comes to see you, say to him:

      Now let Tamar my sister come

      and nourish me with some food;

      let her make the nourishment ready before my eyes, in order that I
         may see it,

      and I will eat from her hand.

13:1 **Avshalom:** Pronounced *ahv-shah-LOM*. The name combines "Father" (figuratively God, or actually David) and "Peace/Well-being." **Tamar:** Pronounced *tah-MAHR*. Her name means "date-palm." **Amnon:** Pronounced *ahm-NOHN*. Tamar and Avshalom's half brother and heir to the throne. His name ironically connotes "faithful."

2 **nubile-girl:** As with Jephthah's daughter in Judg. 12, the word *betula* here probably refers to a young woman of marriageable age rather than to a virgin per se; the reason for Tamar's being forbidden to Amnon appears to lie elsewhere (Wenham). **to do anything:** To have sexual contact.

3 **Yonadav:** Pronounced *yo-nah-DAHV*; trad. English "Jonadab." In v.5 the name has the alternate "Yehonadav." **worldly-wise:** Heb. *h-k-m* connotes not only intellectual but also practical wisdom. See also 14:2ff. and 20:16 below.

4 **Tamar—the sister . . . :** McCarter (1984) notes how each word in this verse begins with the same letter (*alef*), producing "a series of gasping sighs," and Rendsburg (1998–99) includes it as an example of (emotionally) "confused language."

6 So Amnon lay down and feigned-sickness,
and when the king came to see him, Amnon said to the king:
Now let Tamar my sister come
and heat two heartcakes before my eyes,
that I may be nourished from her hand.

7 David sent [word] to Tamar, in the palace-house, saying:
Pray go to the house of Amnon your brother
and make him some nourishment.

8 So Tamar went to the house of Amnon her brother, while he was
lying down.
She took some dough, kneaded it, heated it before his eyes, and
boiled the heartcakes;

9 then she took the pot and placed it before him,
but he refused to eat.
Amnon said:
Have everyone go out from me!
And everyone went out from him.

10 Amnon said to Tamar:
Bring the nourishment into the inner-room, so that I may be
nourished from your hand!
So Tamar took the heartcakes that she had made, and brought
them to Amnon her brother into the inner-room.

11 She brought them close to him to eat,
but he overpowered her and said to her:
Come, lie with me, sister!

12 She said to him:
No, brother, don't force me,
for such is not to be done in Israel—
don't do this vile thing!

13 As for me, where would I take my disgrace?
And as for you, you would be like one of the vile ones in Israel!

6 **heat . . . heartcakes:** Heb. *u-tlabbev levivot.* The verb appears also in the Song of Songs (4:9), to indicate sexual arousal. **heartcakes:** Heb. *levivot;* others, simply "cakes," but the "heart" (Heb. *leiv, leivav*) motif is central to the Avshalom stories, as I have argued in the Introduction to this section. Shaped foods were known in the ancient Near East (Prof. Chaim Cohen, personal communication).

9 **Have everyone go out:** The equivalent of "Clear the room!"

11 **overpowered:** Or "took hold of."

12–13 **such is not to be done . . . disgrace:** The same language is used in Gen. 34, the rape of Dina narrative. **vile thing . . . vile ones:** As in I Sam. 25; others understand as "foolishness . . . fools." **he will not withhold me:** In order for her plea to have any force, such a thing must have been possible in royal society. Yet, as Sasson shows, it does not appear much outside of Egypt. He makes the intriguing conjecture that Tamar may have in fact been Avsha-

So-now, just speak to the king—indeed, he will not withhold me
    from you!
14 But he would not hearken to her voice;
    he overpowered her and forced her, and lay with her.
15 Then Amnon hated her with an exceedingly great hatred—
    indeed, greater was the hatred with which he hated her than the
        love with which he had loved her.
    Amnon said to her:
    Get up! Go!
16 She said to him:
    About this great evil—more than the other thing that you did to
        me—sending me away . . . !
    But he would not hearken to her;
17 he called to his attending lad
    and said:
    Just send this one away from me, outside,
    and lock the door behind her!
18 —Now on her was an ornamented tunic,
    for thus were the king's nubile daughters clothed in robes.—
    So his attendant brought her outside, and locked the door behind
        her.
19 And Tamar put ashes on her head,
    while the ornamented tunic that was on her she tore;
    she put her hands on her head
    and went along, going along and crying out.
20 Avshalom her brother said to her:
    Has Amnon your brother been with you?
    For now, sister, be silent—he is your brother;
    do not take this thing to heart!
    So Tamar stayed, desolate, in the house of Avshalom her brother.
21 Now when King David heard about all these things,
    he was exceedingly agitated.

lom's daughter (see 14:27) and therefore Amnon's niece, which would solve a number of the story's problems.

15 **Get up! Go!:** With the force of "Get lost!" The wording is close to the horrifying "Get up! Let's go!" that the Levite of Judg. 19:28 barks at his gang-raped and unconscious (if not dead) concubine.

16 **About this great evil . . . :** The halting syntax here may be less a function of a defective text, as some

have maintained, and more of Tamar's emotional state (Kwitkin-Close, written communication, and Rendsburg 1998–99).

17 **this one:** Note how the phrasing suggests contempt.

18 **ornamented tunic:** Like Joseph's famous one in Gen. 37:3.

20 **For now:** Following Alter (1999).

21 **agitated:** Yet he apparently does not act further.

22 And Avshalom would not speak with Amnon, [anything] from evil
   to good,
   for Avshalom hated Amnon over the fact that he had forced Tamar
   his sister.

23 Now it was at two-years' time
   that they were shearing [sheep] for Avshalom in Baal Hatzor that is
   near Efrayim,
   and Avshalom invited all the king's sons.

24 Avshalom came to the king
   and said:
   Now here, your servant is having shearing [done];
   now let the king and his servants go with your servant.

25 The king said to Avshalom:
   No, my son, now we cannot go, all of us;
   let us not weigh-heavily on you!
   He pressed him, but he would not go,
   and he gave him farewell-blessing.

26 Avshalom said:
   If not, now let Amnon my brother go with us.
   The king said to him:
   Why should he go with you?

27 But Avshalom pressed him,
   so he sent Amnon with him, along with all the king's sons.

28 And Avshalom charged his serving-lads, saying:
   Now take note: when Amnon's heart is merry with wine,
   and I say to you: Strike down Amnon!,
   then put him to death—do not be afraid!
   Have not I myself charged you?
   Be strong, be valiant ones!

29 So Avshalom's lads did to Amnon as Avshalom had charged,
   and all the king's sons arose and mounted each on his mule, and
   they fled.

30 It was, when they were on the way,
   that the rumor came to David, namely:
   Avshalom has struck down all the king's sons;
   not one of them is left!

23 **Baal Hatzor:** Well north of Jerusalem. **Efrayim:**   28 **merry:** Elsewhere I use "in good-humor."
Presumably the name of another town; McCarter
(1984) suggests an original name of "Ofra."

488

31 The king arose and tore his garments, and lay down on the ground,
while all his servants stood [over him] with torn garments.

32 But Yonadav son of Shim'a, David's brother, spoke up and said:
Let not my lord think that all the lads, the king's sons,
have been put-to-death,
for Amnon alone has died;
for by Avshalom's mouth it has been determined since the time of
his forcing Tamar his sister.

33 So-now,
do not let the king take the matter to heart, saying: All the king's
sons have died,
for Amnon alone has died,

34 and Avshalom has gotten away.
And the serving-lad standing watch lifted up his eyes and saw:
now here, many people were going away on the road behind him,
from the side of the hill.

35 Yonadav said to the king:
Here, the king's sons have come;
exactly as your servant's word, so it was!

36 And it was, when he finished speaking,
that here, the king's sons came;
they lifted up their voices and wept,
and also the king and all his servants wept, an exceedingly great
weeping.

37 —Now Avshalom had gotten away;
he had gone to Talmai son of Ammihud, king of Geshur.—
And he mourned for his son all the days.

38 Now Avshalom had gotten away and gone to Geshur,
and he was there for three years.

39 Then the king's spirit was spent for going out against Avshalom,
for he was consoled concerning Amnon, for he was dead.

---

32 **mouth:** Or, as elsewhere, "order."
37 **Talmai:** His maternal grandfather.
39 **the king's spirit was spent for going out against:**
MT has "David the King longed for," but the verb is
feminine, like "spirit" (*ru'ah*) in Hebrew, and "David"
(Heb. *d-w-d*) could easily be an orthographic error
for "spirit" (*r-w-h*). Some interpreters feel that David

really is pining for Avshalom, but, as Alter (1999)
points out, in the next chapter the king refuses to see
him. **for he was dead:** Perhaps another indication
of David's ability to "move on" (see his reaction to
his illegitimate son's death in Chap. 12)—not necessarily an admirable trait, in this case.

Chapter 14. *The Wise Woman of Tekoa; Avshalom Returns:* After some time passes, David's commander Yoav, who throughout II Samuel acts in what he believes are the king's best interests, now perceives that David is ripe for Avshalom to return to Jerusalem. But knowing David as he does, he apparently feels that the reconciliation cannot occur without some kind of subterfuge, or at least teaching the king a lesson. So, like Natan had done in Chap. 12, he concocts a story to draw David into the emotional heart of the situation. Enlisting a "worldly-wise woman," Yoav lays out the fictional case of a sole surviving son, who, should he die at the hand of an angry family member, will by his death eradicate his father's name and line from the world. David of course promises to protect the helpless woman and her son, but eventually comes to realize that the story is really about himself—as he had not perceived in the case of Natan's little parable in Chap. 12.

The ultimate irony of the narrative is that father and son are brought together by the hardened warrior Yoav, yet it is he who will ultimately separate them forever, four chapters hence.

14:1 And Yoav son of Tzeruya knew
    that the king's heart was toward Avshalom,
2 so Yoav sent to Tekoa;
    he fetched from there a worldly-wise woman
    and said to her:
    Pray feign-mourning, pray clothe yourself in garments of mourning;
    do not pour oil [on yourself],
    but be like a woman [who] these many days has been mourning
      over the dead.
3 You are to come to the king
    and are to speak to him according to these words . . .
    And Yoav put the words in her mouth.
4 So the Tekoite woman talked to the king:
    she flung herself on her nostrils to the earth and bowed low,
    and said:
    Deliver [me], O king!
5 The king said to her:
    What [ails] you?
    She said:
    Alas, I am a widow woman—my husband died.
6 Now your handmaid had two sons,
    but the two of them scuffled in the open-field, with no rescuer
      between them;
    the one struck down the other-one and caused his death.
7 And here, the whole clan has arisen against your handmaid and has
      said:
    Give over the one who struck down his brother,
    that we may put him to death for the life of his brother, whom he
      killed;
    we want to destroy [him]! Even the heir!
    So they will extinguish my ember that remains,

14:2 **Tekoa:** South of Bet-Lehem, or about ten miles south of Jerusalem, on the border between farmland and the desert. **a worldly-wise woman:** Another one appears at the end of the stories concerning Avshalom, Chap. 20. The Bible uses this kind of bracketing structure fairly often. **pour oil:** The application of oil was considered a part of personal hygiene in the ancient world. See note on 12:20, above.

6 **your handmaid:** Showing suitable deference, by the speaker's referring to herself in the third person.

7 **Even the heir!:** Implying either that they don't care that he *is* his father's heir, or that they want to kill him for the property as well (Alter 1999). **my ember that remains:** In a memorable image, the last one left to carry on the family name. **survivor:** Or "remnant."

providing no name or survivor for my husband on the face of the
earth.

8 The king said to the woman:
Go back to your house,
and I myself will issue-a-command regarding you.

9 The Tekoite woman said to the king:
On me, my lord king, be the iniquity, and on my Father's House,
but the king and his throne are clear [of blame].

10 The king said:
The one who speaks [amiss] to you, have him brought to me—
he will not continue to harm you!

11 She said:
Pray let the king be mindful of YHWH your God
—too much might the blood redeemer bring-ruin—
so that they do not destroy my son!
He said:
By the life of YHWH,
if a hair of your son should fall to the ground . . . !

12 Then the woman said:
Pray let your handmaid speak a word to my lord king.
He said:
Speak.

13 The woman said:
Now why have you planned in this way against God's people?
By the king speaking this word, [he is] as one guilty,
by not letting his banished one return.

14 For we will die, yes, die,
like water running on the ground, which cannot be gathered up.
But God will not carry a life away;
he will plan plans, to not keep the banished one banished from him.

15 So-now,
[the reason] that I have come to speak this word to the king, my
lord,

---

11 **too much:** The Hebrew is difficult here. **blood redeemer:** A member of a family or clan whose duty it was to avenge the death of a kinsman. **a hair of your son:** Avshalom's own abundant hair will ultimately prove his undoing.

14 **he will plan plans:** JPS understands the phrase to mean that God will not punish David, the one who "plans plans."

is that the people made me afraid.
Your handmaid said [to herself]: Let me now speak to the king;
perhaps the king will act on his maidservant's word.
16   Indeed, the king will hearken
to rescue his maidservant from the grasp of the [avenging] man,
from destroying me and my son together, away from God's
    inheritance.
17   And your handmaid said [to herself]:
Now may the word of my lord king be for [my] rest,
for like a messenger of God, so is my lord king,
to hear out the good and the evil—
may YHWH your God be with you!
18   The king answered, he said to the woman:
Do not conceal from me a thing that I ask of you!
The woman said:
Pray let my lord king speak.
19   The king said:
Is the hand of Yoav with you in all this?
The woman answered and said:
By your life, my lord king,
there is no turning-right or turning-left from all that my lord king
    has spoken;
indeed, your servant Yoav himself commanded me—
he himself put in the mouth of your handmaid all these words.
20   In order to reverse the face of the matter
did your servant Yoav do this thing;
but my lord is wise,
like the wisdom of a messenger of God,
to know all that is on earth!
21   Then the king said to Yoav:
Here now, I have done this thing.
So go, return the lad Avshalom!

16 **God's inheritance:** Unlike the "YHWH's inheritance" in I Sam. 26:19 and II Sam. 20:19 and 21:3, this expression appears to refer to the ancestral estate (Lewis), or "the hereditary-property" from God.

20 **my lord is wise:** Yet David's ambiguous actions vis-à-vis Avshalom indicate that royal wisdom and control are in the process of unraveling.

Chapter 15. *David Driven from the Throne:* With Chap. 13, the narrative came full circle from the violence of Judges, as that book's chaos in a sense reappeared in the family sphere of David's house (Fishbane). Yet now it will expand again to the nation as a whole, with Avshalom's revolt against his father.

As frequently occurs in biblical narrative, this chapter is connected to the previous one by means of reprised words: "call," "come," "bow down," and "kiss," all in the first five verses (Bar-Efrat). More important, from the outset of the chapter it becomes clear that at this point Avshalom is seeking the throne itself. His strategy is the personal touch: he intercepts those people who come to Jerusalem for justice, assuring them of his personal concern, which he contrasts to David's supposed disinterest. Thus he begins the process of "[stealing] away the heart of the men of Israel" (v.6). He does this cleverly, without vocally laying claim to the throne (see Ehrlich).

A second stage in Avshalom's plan is to go, on a pretext, to Hevron, the original stronghold of David's political power. Here he is able to marshal his public relations machine by sending "spy-runners" throughout the land to proclaim his accession to the throne, by successfully recruiting David's adviser Ahitofel, and by increasing the number of his followers.

From here the chapter switches its focus to David. He is shown leading the flight from Jerusalem, and, rather pathetically, leaving ten of his concubines to symbolically guard the palace. Moreover, throughout this part of the story, David expresses an unusual tone of resignation. To his friend Ittai he describes his fate as "I am going wherever I am going" (v.20), and he has the precious Coffer returned to Jerusalem, not knowing whether he will ever see it and the city again.

Yet amid all the weeping for the king's fate (vv.23 and 30), David the crafty politician reemerges, plotting to win back his throne. He prays to YHWH to bring Ahitofel's advice to naught, and instructs Hushai how to frustrate the evil designs of Ahitofel and his master.

22 Yoav flung himself on his face to the ground and bowed low, and he
     blessed the king;
   Yoav said:
   Today your servant knows that I have found favor in your eyes, my
     lord king,
   [given] that the king has acted upon your servant's word!
23 And Yoav arose and went to Geshur,
   and he brought Avshalom to Jerusalem.
24 The king said:
   Let him turn round to his house,
   but my face he is not to see!
   So Avshalom turned to his house,
   but the king's face he did not see.
25 Now like Avshalom there was no man as beautiful throughout all
     Israel, so exceedingly to be praised;
   from the sole of his foot to his crown,
   there was no defect in him.
26 When he shaved his head
   —it used to be that at the end of the year, [every] year,
   he would shave it, for it was heavy upon him and [he had] to
     shave it—
   he would weigh the hair of his head: two hundred *shekel*-weights,
     by the king's [weighing-]stone.
27 And there were born to Avshalom three sons and one daughter,
     whose name was Tamar;
   she was a woman beautiful of appearance.

28 And Avshalom stayed in Jerusalem for two-years' time,
   but the king's face he did not see.
29 So Avshalom sent to Yoav, to send him to the king,
   but he would not come to him.
   He sent again, a second-time,
   but he would not come.

---

25 **no defect:** The language describes an animal
fit for sacrifice, or a priest qualified to serve in the
sanctuary.

27 **Tamar:** Strikingly, Avshalom names his only daughter after his raped sister.
28 **time:** Lit., "of days."

◆

30 So he said to his servants:
See, Yoav's plot is near me, and he has barley there;
go, kindle it with fire!
And Avshalom's servants kindled the plot with fire.

31 And Yoav arose and came to Avshalom at the house;
he said to him:
Why did your servants kindle the plot that belongs to me with fire?

32 Avshalom said to Yoav:
Here, I had sent [word] to you, saying:
Come here, I wish to send you to the king, to say:
Why did I come back from Geshur?
It would have been better for me [if] I were still there!
So-now,
let me see the king's face,
and if there be any iniquity in me, let him put me to death!

33 So Yoav came to the king and told him,
and he called for Avshalom;
he came to the king and bowed low to him, on his nostrils to the
    earth, before the king,
and the king kissed Avshalom.

15:1 It was, [some time] after this,
that Avshalom prepared himself a chariot and horses,
with fifty men running before him.

2 And Avshalom would start-early;
he would stand by the road of the main-gate,
and it was that everyone who had a case-for-quarrel coming before
    the king, for judgment,
Avshalom would call to him, and would say:
From what town are you?
And he would say:
From a certain one of the tribes of Israel is your servant.

3 Then Avshalom would say to him:
See, your words are good and correct,
but you have no one to hear on the part of the king!

32 **any iniquity:** Yet in just a few verses, Avshalom will begin the process of usurping his father's throne.
15:1 **fifty men running before him:** Usually taken as a sign of his pretensions to the throne, this may also have the function of keeping the horses calm in the face of a crowd (Cantrell).
3 **you have no one to hear:** McCarter (1984): "You will get no hearing."

4 And Avshalom said:
O who would make me judge in the land,
[that] every man might come to me who had a case-for-quarrel or a
matter-for-judgment
—I would declare him in the right!

5 So it would be, when a man would come near, to bow low to him,
that he would stretch out his hand and take hold of him, and kiss
him.

6 And Avshalom did according to this matter for all Israel who would
come for adjudication to the king;
thus Avshalom stole away the heart of the men of Israel.

7 It was at the end of four years, that Avshalom said to the king:
Now let me go, that I may pay my vow that I vowed to Yhwh in
Hevron,

8 for your servant vowed a vow when I stayed at Geshur in Aram,
saying:
If Yhwh will let me return, yes, return to Jerusalem,
I will serve Yhwh!

9 The king said to him:
Go in peace.
So he arose and went to Hevron.

10 And Avshalom sent spy-runners throughout all the tribes of Israel,
saying:
When you hear the sound of the *shofar,* you are to say:
Avshalom reigns as king in Hevron!

11 Now with Avshalom went two hundred men from Jerusalem,
invited-guests, going in their innocence—
they did not know anything.

12 And Avshalom sent for Ahitofel the Gilonite, David's adviser, from
his town, from Gilo,
when he was sacrificing sacrifices.
Now the banding-in-conspiracy was powerful,
and the people with Avshalom went on [and on] becoming many.

---

7 **four:** Following some LXX manuscripts; MT has "forty."
10 **spy-runners:** Following B-R; from Heb. *regel,* "foot" (see Gen. 42:9).
12 **Ahitofel:** Pronounced *ah-hee-TOE-fel.* The meaning of the name is unclear, but it seems a bit like the word for "folly" (Heb. *t-p-l*). **Gilo:** A town probably to the southwest of Hevron. **went on . . . becoming many:** Their number increased.

13 And a message-teller came to David, saying:
    The heart of the men of Israel [inclines] after Avshalom!

14 So David said to all his servants who were with him in Jerusalem:
    Arise, let us get away,
    for we will have no remnant [left] before Avshalom!
    Hurry and go,
    lest he hurry and overtake us and push evil upon us
    and strike the city with the mouth of the sword!

15 The king's servants said to the king:
    Just as my lord king chooses, here are your servants!

16 So the king and all his household went off on foot,
    and the king left ten concubine women to guard the palace-house.

17 And when the king and all the fighting-people went off on foot,
    they stopped at the Far House.

18 Now all his servants were crossing over next to him,
    while all the Kereitites and all the Peleitites and all the Gittites,
    six hundred men who came on foot from Gat,
    were crossing over in front of the king.

19 The king said to Ittai the Gittite:
    Why will you go, even you, with us?
    Return and stay with the king,
    for you are a foreigner, and also you are an exile from your [own]
        place.

20 [Just] yesterday was your coming,
    so today, should I make you wander with us, in [our] going-forth?
    I am going wherever I am going;
    return, and have your brothers return with you,
    in loyalty and faithfulness!

21 Ittai answered the king, he said:
    By the life of YHWH lives and by the life of my lord king,

---

14 **push evil:** The same Hebrew verb translated by "banished" in the previous chapter. The Hebrew here is probably corrupt; LXX reads *ha-raa* ("the evil/misfortune") as *ha-'ir* ("the city"), thus "push the city down upon us," following McCarter (1984).
15 **here are your servants:** We are ready to do your bidding.
17 **the Far House:** Presumably at the edge of the city.

18 **Kereitites . . . Peleitites . . . Gittites:** See note to 8:18, above.
19 **Ittai:** Pronounced *ee-TIE*. It sounds like the phrase "with me" (Heb. *itti*), appropriate in a passage about loyalty (Garsiel 1985, Polzin 1993).
20 **in loyalty:** The text appears to be defective. Others, including ancients, add "May YHWH show you loyalty . . ."

only in the place where my lord king is, whether for death or for
    life—
indeed, there your servant will be!

22 David said to Ittai:
Go, cross over!
So Ittai the Gittite and all his men and all the families who were
    with him crossed over.

23 Now the entire region was weeping in a great voice while all the
    fighting-people were crossing over,
while the king was crossing Wadi Kidron,
and while all the fighting-people were crossing over, facing the road
    to the wilderness.

24 And here: also Tzadok and all the Levites with him were carrying
    the Coffer of the Covenant of God;
they set down the Coffer of God, and Evyatar also went up,
until all the people had completed crossing away from the city.

25 The king said to Tzadok:
Return the Coffer of God to the city;
if I find favor in Yhwh's eyes,
he will let me return and let me see it, along with his abode.

26 If thus he says: I am not pleased with you,
here I am—
let him do with me as is good in his eyes.

27 And the king said [further] to Tzadok the priest:
Are you a seer?
Return to the city in peace,
along with Ahimaatz your son and Yehonatan son of Evyatar
—your two sons with you [both].

28 See, I myself will tarry at the plains in the wilderness
until word comes from you, telling me [something].

29 So Tzadok and Evyatar returned the Coffer of God to Jerusalem,
and they stayed there.

---

22 **families:** Elsewhere, "little-ones," but Heb. *taf* may include children and old people—namely, stragglers or dependents.
23 **in a great voice:** Loudly.   **Wadi Kidron:** The valley separating the (old) city of Jerusalem from the Mount of Olives.

24 **set down:** Reading *va-yatzigu* for MT *va-yatziku,* "poured out" (see McCarter 1984).
27 **Are you a seer?:** Heb. unclear; some take this as a sarcastic remark.
28 **from you:** Plural.

Chapter 16. *David in Exile; Avshalom and the Concubines:* As David crosses a natural border, reaching the far side of the Mount of Olives east of Jerusalem, he is met by two men whose behavior demonstrates the king's vulnerability. The first, Mefi-boshet's servant Tziva, uses a lie—that his master is supporting the rebellion out of the hopes of regaining the throne for his family—to try to obtain wealth for himself. The second, another relative of Sha'ul, Shim'i son of Gera, both curses and throws stones at David, yet the king's response is to accept the abuse, as if to suggest that he has reached a nadir of power and self-respect.

At the same time, David's plans for a return to power are bearing fruit, with the acceptance of his counselor Hushai by Avshalom toward the end of the chapter. This occurs amid Avshalom's symbolic act of sleeping with his father's concubines, always a sign of attempted or actual succession in biblical Israel (see Re'uven's actions in Gen. 35:22 and Avner's in II Sam. 3:7). But as Clines has noted, Avshalom's move, given that it involves multiple women, may additionally be an exaggerated act of masculine bravado, beyond the merely symbolic political aspect.

30 But David was going up the Ascent of Olives, going up and
    weeping;
his head was covered and he was walking barefoot,
while all the people who were with him covered each one his head,
and were going up, going up and weeping.

31 Now David was told, saying:
Ahitofel is among those banding together with Avshalom!
David said:
Pray make-foolish Ahitofel's advice, O YHWH!

32 Now it was, when David was coming to the summit, where [they]
    would bow down to God,
that here, [coming] to meet him was Hushai the Arkite, his tunic
    torn and earth on his head.

33 David said to him:
If you cross over with me,
you will be a burden to me,

34 but if you return to the city
and say to Avshalom: Your servant O king, will I be—
servant to your father was I formerly,
but now I am your servant!—
then you may annul Ahitofel's advice for me.

35 Will not Tzadok and Evyatar, the priests, be with you there?
It will be
that all the words that you hear from the king's house, you are to
    tell to Tzadok and Evyatar the priests;

36 here, their two sons, Ahimaatz of Tzadok and Yehonatan of
    Evyatar, are there with them;
you are to send by their hand to me any word that you hear.

37 So Hushai the Friend of David entered the city
[just] as Avshalom was about to enter Jerusalem.

---

30 **the Ascent of Olives:** The Mount of Olives, with a clear view of royal Jerusalem.
31 **David was told:** MT: "David told."
32 **Hushai:** Polzin (1993) notes the connection between the name and the verb "to hurry." **Arkite:** From the southernmost territory of Efrayim, northwest of Rama.
34 **annul:** Or "defeat."

16:1 Now David had crossed a little beyond the summit
when here: Tziva, Mefiboshet's retainer, [was coming] to meet him,
along with a brace of saddled donkeys,
and on them were two hundred bread-loaves, a hundred raisin-
cakes, a hundred fig-cakes, and a skin of wine.

2 The king said to Tziva:
What do you [mean] with these?
Tziva said:
The donkeys are for the king's household, for riding,
the bread and the figs are for eating by the lads,
and the wine is for drinking by those weary in the wilderness.

3 The king said:
And where is your lord's son?
Tziva said to the king:
Here, he is sitting in Jerusalem,
for he says [to himself]: Today the House of Israel will return my
father's kingdom to me!

4 The king said to Tziva:
Here, yours is all that was Mefiboshet's.
Tziva said:
I bow down!
May I find favor in your eyes, O my lord king!

5 Now when King David came to Bahurim,
here, a man was going out from there, from the clan of the House
of Sha'ul;
his name was Shim'i son of Gera.
He was going out, going out and cursing—

6 and he pelted David with stones, and all of King David's court-
servants,
along with all the fighting-people and all the mighty-men to his
right and to his left.

7 And thus did Shim'i say when he cursed him:
Get out, get out, [you] bloodguilty man, [you] base man!

16:1 **retainer:** Heb. *naar,* elsewhere "serving-lad" or "fighting-lad," but here signifying someone older.
5 **Bahurim:** A village on the east side of the Mount of Olives. **Shim'i:** Pronounced *shim-EE;* trad. English "Shimei."
6 **along with all the fighting-people:** Shim'i's dis-

regard of the heavily armed force accompanying David shows the depth of his hatred for the king (Ehrlich).
7 **bloodguilty man:** "Blood" here is in an expanded form (Heb. *damim* instead of *dam*); B-R translate as "man of bloody deeds."

8 YHWH has returned upon you all the bloodguilt of the House of
    Sha'ul, in whose place you reign as king,
  and YHWH has given the kingdom into the hand of Avshalom
    your son,
  for here, you are in your evil-fate,
  for you are a bloodguilty man!

9 Avishai son of Tzeruya said to the king:
  Why should this dead dog curse my lord king?
  Now let me cross over and take off his head!

10 But the king said:
  What is there [in common] between me and you, O sons of
    Tzeruya?
  Let him curse, for if YHWH says to him: Curse David,
  who is to say: For-what-reason do you do thus?

11 And David said to Avishai and to all his servants:
  Here, my [own] son, who came out of my body, is seeking my life;
  how much more, then, the Binyaminite!
  Let him be, that he may curse,
  for YHWH told him to.

12 Perhaps YHWH will look on my affliction
  and YHWH will return me good in place of his curses on this day!

13 David and his men went on the way;
  but Shim'i was going along the side of the hill, next to him,
  going along and cursing and pelting [him] with stones next to him
  and dumping dust [on him].

14 And the king and all the people that were with him came back
    weary,
  and they paused-for-breath there.

15 Now Avshalom and all the people, the men of Israel, came to
    Jerusalem,
  and Ahitofel was with him.

---

8 **you are in your evil-fate:** That is, you are experiencing misfortune.

11 **who came out of my body:** A rather male point of
view.   **the Binyaminite:** Shim'i.

12 **affliction:** Following ancient versions.

13 **dumping dust:** Lit., "bedusting (him with) dust"
(Heb. *'ippar be-'afar*).

Chapter 17. *Hushai's Advice; the Worm Turns:* Avshalom now seeks counsel as to the right move in the burgeoning rebellion. The first opinion he solicits is that of Ahitofel, of whose reputation for solid advice in the past we have just learned (16:23). The plan is a sound one: to isolate and kill David, thus avoiding mass bloodshed and providing for a quick restoration of the peace. Inexplicably, however, the usurper instead accepts the advice of Hushai, which is to be wary of the experienced and tough old king and to amass an army and attack the town where he is to be found. Only at the end of Hushai's proposal do we learn that Avshalom's acceptance of the old man's advice is actually YHWH's doing (v.14). In practical terms, it gives David time to solidify his own plans and marshal his forces (Sweeney 2007).

David must be informed of the possibilities, and this is accomplished by means of two messengers, whose escape from Avshalom's men in vv.18–21 is reminiscent of the story of Yehoshua's spies slipping away in Josh. 2. The king subsequently decides to cross to the east bank of the Jordan to assure his safety.

The upshot of this episode is that Ahitofel kills himself, a rather rare event for the Bible, at least in a nonmilitary setting, and David begins to prepare for the coming battle by feeding his troops.

16 And it was, when Hushai the Arkite, David's Friend, came to
    Avshalom,
 that Hushai said to Avshalom:
 May the king live! May the king live!
17 Avshalom said to Hushai:
 Is this your loyalty to your friend?
 Why didn't you go with your friend?
18 Hushai said to Avshalom:
 No—
 rather, the one whom YHWH and his people, all the men of Israel,
    have chosen,
 for him I will be, and with him I will stay!
19 And second, whom should I serve, if not in the presence of his son?
 As I served in the presence of your father,
 so I will serve in your presence.
20 Avshalom said to Ahitofel:
 Give advice, [both of] you—
 what should we do?
21 Ahitofel said to Avshalom:
 Come in to your father's concubines, whom he left to guard the
    palace-house;
 when all Israel hears that you have made yourself reek to your father,
 then the hands of all who are with you will be strengthened.
22 So they spread out a tent for Avshalom on the roof,
 and Avshalom came in to his father's concubines, before the eyes of
    all Israel.
23 Now the advice of Ahitofel which he advised
 was in those days like inquiring of the word of God;
 thus was all of Ahitofel's advice, so for David, so for Avshalom.

17:1 Ahitofel said to Avshalom:
 Pray let me choose twelve thousand men,
 and let me arise and pursue after David tonight.

16 **David's Friend:** This may be a title/office, that is, "Companion of the King."
21 **Come in to your father's concubines:** As suggested previously, usurping the sexual bed of the father appears elsewhere as a method of symbolically taking power by the son; see Gen. 35:22. Here it is the fulfillment of Natan's prophecy of 12:11, above.
23 **like inquiring of the word of God:** Like an oracle.

◆ 2   When I come upon him
and he is weary and slack of hands,
I will alarm him,
so that all the people that are with him will flee.
Then I will strike down the king alone,

3   and I will return all the people to you,
[so that] when all are returned
—the man whom you seek and all the fighting-people—
there will be peace.

4   The word was right in Avshalom's eyes
and in the eyes of all the elders of Israel.

5   But Avshalom said:
Pray call as well Hushai the Arkite;
we will hear what is in his mouth, his as well.

6   And Hushai came to Avshalom, and Avshalom said to him, saying:
In accordance with this word did Ahitofel speak;
shall we act on his word?
Or not? *You* speak!

7   Hushai said to Avshalom:
Not good is the advice that Ahitofel has advised this time.

8   And Hushai said [further]:
You yourself know your father and his men,
that they are mighty ones,
and that they are bitter of feelings,
like a bear bereaved in the open-field,
and your father is a man of battle—
he will not spend-the-night with the people.

9   Here now,
he is hiding in one of the pits or in one of the halting-places;
and it will be
when fighting-people fall at the start [of battle],
and a hearer hears and says:
There has been a defeat for the people who [follow] after
Avshalom—

17:2 **slack of hands:** See 4:1 above.
  3 **[so that] when . . . :** The Hebrew is unclear; LXX
adds after "return": "to you as a bride returns to her
husband; you seek only one man's life . . ." **peace:**
Again playing on Avshalom's name.
  4 **The word:** Of advice.

  8 **a bear bereaved:** Bar-Efrat and others see the mention of the bear here and the lion in v.10 as recalling
the youthful David (see I 17:34–37).
  9 **fighting-people fall:** According to some ancient versions; MT has "fall in them."

10 that even if he be a valiant one,
   whose heart is like the heart of a lion,
   he will melt, melt away [in fear].
   For all Israel knows that your father is a mighty-man,
   and valiant ones are with him!
11 So I advise:
   let all Israel be gathered, yes, gathered to you, from Dan to Be'er-
      Sheva,
   like the sand that is by the sea in abundance,
   with your presence walking among them.
12 We will come upon him
   in one of the places where he can be found,
   and light upon him as dew falls upon the ground;
   there will not be left to him, or to all the men that are with him,
      even one.
13 Now if he gathers himself into a town,
   then let all Israel bring ropes into that town
   and let us drag it, as far as the wadi, until even a pebble cannot be
      found there!
14 Avshalom and all Israel said:
   Better is the advice of Hushai the Arkite than the advice of
      Ahitofel!
   —Now YHWH had ordained to nullify the good advice of Ahitofel,
   in order that YHWH might bring an evil-fate upon Avshalom.
15 And Hushai said to Tzadok and to Evyatar, the priests:
   Like this and like that, Ahitofel advised Avshalom and the elders of
      Israel,
   and like this and like that, I myself advised.
16 So-now,
   send quickly and tell David, saying:
   Do not lodge tonight at the wilderness crossings,
   by-all-means cross over, yes, cross over,
   lest they be swallowed up, the king and all the people who are
      with him!

---

11 **among them:** So ancient versions; MT reads "in battle," i.e., leading the troops.

12 **light . . . as dew:** This is usually an image of peace; here it smells of death (Alter 1999).

Chapter 18. *Avshalom's Death:* As the rebellion narrative moves toward its inevitable conclusion, David will not be present at the climactic moment, just as he was not present at the moment of Sha'ul's death. His exclusion from the battle by his own soldiers, while couched in concern for his welfare, also suggests that he is no longer perceived as an effective military leader. It has the added effect of setting up the dramatic scene in which David learns the news about his son's death, which in fact comprises the bulk of this chapter.

The battle scene itself, as usual, is brief, with the striking note that the forest swallowed up the rebels (v.8). More significant is the mode of Avshalom's death, with its unforgettable image of the prince accidentally hanging from a tree. The two great theme words of the whole cycle, "head" and "heart," come into play once again: he who had sought to become head of Israel, during his royal father's lifetime, winds up hanging from his head, totally vulnerable to attack; and from having initially swayed the hearts of the people, he is struck "in the heart" as he hangs "in the heart" of a tree. Once again it is a son of Tzeruya, Yoav, who acts decisively and violently, to resecure the throne for David.

V.18 stands alone, perhaps as a postscript to Avshalom's death, to at least provide a tangible memory of the charismatic prince. The monument mentioned here, known to the writer or final editor of Samuel, should not be confused with the "Absalom's Tomb" that still stands in Jerusalem, in the valley east of the Old City. That structure dates from the much later Hellenistic period (second to first century B.C.E.).

For the narrator, the portrayal of how the bad news is brought to David is almost of equal weight to the relating of Avshalom's actual death. In the Bible we have previously encountered a number of imagined and real battle messenger scenes, most notably with Sisera's mother (Judg. 5) and Eli (I Sam. 4). Here, however, the drama is even more extreme. The king has repeatedly ordered his commanders and soldiers not to harm Avshalom, but we know that "the lad" is already dead. After some jockeying for the privilege of delivering the news—Ahimaatz, the usual messenger, is rejected by Yoav—the narrative speaks through the king's perspective. Three pieces of information are passed by the watchman to David, who sits anxiously awaiting news of his son: the existence of one runner, then two, and then the identification of Ahimaatz. We know, but the king initially does not, that this time Ahimaatz will pass, and the fateful message will be delivered by the unnamed Cushite (foreigners have previously delivered bad news to David in I Sam. 30:1ff. and II Sam. 1:2ff.). Note that David's only concern is for his son, not for his troops or the disposition of the rebellion. The actual news is delivered elliptically; unlike the earlier "also your servant Uriyya the Hittite is dead" (II 11:24), the messenger sees fit to say what he needs to by a circumlocution, although an obvious one: "May they be like that lad, my lord king's enemies . . ." (v.32).

17 Now Yehonatan and Ahimaatz were staying at En-Rogel,
and a handmaid would go and tell them,
and they would go and tell King David,
for they could not be seen coming to the town.

18 But a serving-lad saw them and told Avshalom,
so the two of them went quickly and came to the house of a man
in Bahurim;
he had a well in his courtyard,
and they went down there.

19 And the woman fetched and spread a screen over the mouth of the
well,
and she scattered some groats over it,
so that nothing was noticeable.

20 So when Avshalom's servants came to the woman in the house,
and they said: Where are Ahimaatz and Yehonatan?
the woman said to them:
They have [already] crossed the pond of water.
They sought but did not find [them],
so they returned to Jerusalem.

21 Now it was, after their going away,
that they came up out of the well, and went and told King David;
they said to David:
Arise and quickly cross the water,
for thus-and-so has Ahitofel advised concerning you.

22 So David arose, and all the people who were with him;
they crossed the Jordan, till the light of daybreak,
until there was no one left behind who had not crossed the Jordan.

23 Now when Ahitofel saw that his advice had not been acted upon,
he saddled a donkey, and arose and went to his house, to his town;
and he gave charge regarding his household, and then he strangled
himself, so that he died.
He was buried in the burial-place of his father.

---

17 **En-Rogel:** Pronounced *ayn ro-GAYL,* a spring south
of Jerusalem's main Gihon Spring. The name means
"Fuller's/Washer's Spring," referring to a person
whose task it is to clean, dye, shrink, or expand
cloth.

19 **noticeable:** Lit., "known."

20 **pond:** The Hebrew word (*mikhal*) is obscure.

23 **strangled himself:** By hanging, in anticipation of
his execution when the rebellion inevitably fails
(Alter 1999).

◆ 24 When David had come to Mahanayim, Avshalom crossed the
Jordan, he and all the fighting-men of Israel with him.

25 As for Amasa, Avshalom put him in place of Yoav, [The One] Over
the Armed-Forces
—Amasa was the son of a man whose name was Yitra the
Yizre'elite,
who had come in to Avigayil daughter of Nahash, sister of
Tzeruya, Yoav's mother.

26 Now Israel and Avshalom encamped in the region of Gil'ad.

27 And it was, when David came to Mahanayim,
that Shovi son of Nahash from Rabba of the Children of Ammon
and Makhir son of Ammiel from Lo-Devar and Barzillai the
Gil'adite from Rogelim

28 brought forward couches and basins and potter's vessels,
and wheat and barley and meal and parched-grain,
and beans and lentils,

29 and honey and curds and sheep and cheese from cattle for David
and for the people that were with him, to eat,
for they had said:
The people are hungry and weary and thirsty in the wilderness!

18:1 And David counted [for battle] the fighting-people who were
with him;
he put over them commanders of thousands and commanders of
hundreds.

2 And David sent out the fighting-people:
a third in the hand of Yoav,
a third in the hand of Avishai son of Tzeruya, Yoav's brother,
and a third in the hand of Ittai the Gittite.
The king said to the fighting-people:
I will go out, yes, go out, even I myself, with you!

---

24 **Mahanayim:** Yet another connection to the patriarch Yaakov (see Gen. 32). It is a fateful spot on Yaakov's journey back to both his father and his brother, where he encounters angels.

25 **Yizre'elite:** Following Levenson/Halpern (1980) as an indication that Avshalom was seeking to restore to Amasa his father's position. This Yizre'el was near Hevron. LXX and I Chron. 2:17 read "Yishmaelite"; MT has the puzzling "Israelite." **come in to:** Here denoting marriage.

28 **brought forward:** The verb actually occurs at the end of the sequence, in v.29. **beans and lentils:** MT's odd repetition of "parched grain" at the end of the verse is undoubtedly a scribal error.

3 But the people said:
  You are not to go out,
  for if we have to flee, yes, flee,
  they will not take us to heart,
  and [even] if half of us die,
  they will not take us to heart;
  but *you* are like us ten thousandfold!
  So-now, it is better if you are [there] for us in the town, to provide-
    help.
4 The king said to them:
  Whatever is good in your eyes, I will do.
  So the king stood by the gate,
  while all the fighting-people went out by the hundreds and by the
    thousands.
5 And the king charged Yoav and Avishai and Ittai, saying:
  Go-gently for me on the lad, on Avshalom!
  And all the people heard the charge of the king to all the
    commanders on the matter of Avshalom.
6 The fighting-people went out into the open-country to meet Israel;
  the battle occurred in the forest of Efrayim.
7 And the fighting-people of Israel were defeated there, before
    David's servants;
  there occurred there a great defeat on that day—twenty thousand
    [dead].
8 And the battle there was scattered over the face of all the ground;
  more did the forest devour among the fighting-people than the
    sword devoured on that day.

18:3 **take us to heart:** Pay any attention to us, set their mind to us. **but *you*:** The reading of LXX; MT has "for now" (a difference of one Hebrew letter).

4 **Whatever is good in your eyes, I will do:** The David of old would not have reacted so passively. **hundreds . . . thousands:** Ehrlich understands this as referring to military units ("companies and regiments"), not numbers per se.

5 **Go-gently:** McCarter (1984): "protect." **all the**

people heard . . . : To make responsibility for Avshalom's fate absolutely clear; the command will be repeated by the anonymous soldier in v.12.

6 **Israel:** I.e., Avshalom's partisans. **the forest of Efrayim:** Northwest of Mahanayim on the east side of the Jordan.

8 **more did the forest devour . . . :** An ominous note, reminiscent of folktales.

◆

9 And Avshalom chanced upon David's servants:
Avshalom was riding on a mule,
and the mule came under the thick-boughs of a great oak,
and his head became held fast in the oak,
so that he was left hanging between heaven and earth,
while the mule that was under him crossed on.

10 A man saw it and told Yoav;
he said:
Here, I saw Avshalom hanging from an oak!

11 Yoav said to the man, the one telling him:
Now here, you saw [him]—
so for-what-reason didn't you strike him down there to the ground?
I would have to have given you ten pieces-of-silver and a belt!

12 The man said to Yoav:
Even if I were feeling-the-weight in my palms of a thousand pieces-
of-silver,
I would not stretch out my hand against the king's son,
for it was in our ears that the king charged you and Avishai and
Ittai, saying:
Guard the lad, Avshalom, for me!

13 Else I would have been dealing falsely with my own life,
for nothing is hidden from the king—
yet you, you were standing aloof!

14 Yoav said:
I will not wait around like this before you!
So he took three rods in his palm
and thrust them into Avshalom's heart
—he was still alive in the heart of the oak.

15 And ten fighting-lads, Yoav's weapons bearers, surrounded him;
they struck Avshalom and put him to death.

9 **mule:** The customary animal for royal persons to ride. Many interpreters view its loss here as symbolic of Avshalom's loss of the throne. **oak:** A tree often connected to a holy place in the Bible; here it may have a connotation of judgment. **his head:** We would expect "his hair" because of the earlier emphasis on that feature (see 14:26, above). But Polzin's (1993) focus on "head," as signifying "head of state," is well taken. **left hanging:** Following versions; MT: "put, placed." **between heaven and** earth: In the sense of "between the sky and the ground."

12 **for me:** So ancient versions; MT has "who[ever]."

14 **like this:** Or "thus"; Yoav doesn't wish to hear about the king's command. **rods:** Heb. *shevet* carries two usual meanings: the rod of parental discipline and the scepter of royalty. Both have their echoes here.

14–16 **thrust . . . sounded a thrusting-blast:** The Hebrew verb (*t-k-'*) is the same.

16   Then Yoav sounded a thrusting-blast on the *shofar,*
      so that the fighting-people turned back from pursuing after Israel,
      for Yoav held back the people.

17   They took Avshalom
      and threw him in the forest, into a great pit,
      and set up over him a heap of stones, exceedingly large,
      while all Israel fled, each to his tent.

18   Now Avshalom had undertaken to set up for himself, during
         his lifetime, the standing-stone that is in the King's Valley,
      for he had said [to himself]: I have no son through whom to have
         my name recalled.
      So he called the standing-stone by his name—
      it is called Avshalom's Monument until this day.

19   Now Ahimaatz son of Tzadok said:
      Pray let me run and bring-the-news to the king
      that Yнwн has wrought justice for him from the hand of his
         enemies!

20   Yoav said to him:
      You are not to be a man of news on this day;
      you may bring-news on another day,
      but on this day, you are not to bring-news,
      since the king's son is dead.

21   Yoav said to a Cushite:
      Go, tell the king what you have seen.
      The Cushite bowed low to Yoav and ran off.

22   But once again Ahimaatz son of Tzadok said to Yoav:
      Come what may, pray let me run, me too, after the Cushite.
      Yoav said:
      Why should you run, my son,
      when you have no news [that] will find [you favor]?

---

17   **heap of stones:** Recalling the end of another law-breaker, Akhan, in Josh. 7.
18   **I have no son:** This seems to contradict 14:27; per-haps it is an indication that no male heirs survived Avshalom.   **standing-stone:** Some read "heap of stones." In any event, the contrast with the stones of the previous verse could not be more wrench-ing.   **Avshalom's Monument:** See Commentary.

19   **wrought justice:** Ironic, given 15:2ff.
20   **since:** The Hebrew contains the phrase *al ken,* which makes no sense. Here, as others do, I omit.
21   **Cushite:** An Ethiopian or Nubian.
22   **find [you favor]:** Following a suggestion by Alter (1999).

Chapter 19. *David Shaken and Restored to Power:* Few scenes of grief in literature are as affecting as the one with which this chapter opens. The king's emotions are conveyed largely through the use of sound (see note to v.1); the multiple repetitions of "my son" ring true, since grieving is by nature an obsessive process. While the reader's sympathy is with the king, Yoav brings us back to brutal reality by emphasizing that this is no time for David to appear weak. With stinging words he reprimands the king for putting his own emotions above those of political necessity; in Yoav's view, by excessively mourning his (unworthy) son, David is compromising his leadership and indeed ignoring his subjects' own needs.

After finally composing himself, David attempts to repair the fractures in his kingdom. In order to placate the northerners, he appoints Avshalom's erstwhile commander Amasa to replace Yoav. There may well be other motives at play here, given the troubled history between king and general; David must be aware that Yoav had dealt the initial blows to Avshalom as he hung from the tree. He assures Shim'i ben Gera, who had cursed him as a "bloodguilty man" in Chap. 16, that he will not be executed. Sha'ul's grandson Mefiboshet appears, unkempt, and excuses his absence during the rebellion by pointing to his servant Tziva's deception (see 16:1–4); subsequently, David reverses his earlier decision and restores to Mefiboshet at least some of his property. And a last piece of resolution takes place when Barzillai, the king's faithful friend who had supported him materially during his flight, elects to remain at home rather than come to Jerusalem, citing his advanced age. His fatigue perhaps reflects the king's own.

Yet the chapter still ends with conflict, at least of a verbal kind. The northerners are miffed at not being the ones to conduct David back across the Jordan. As the majority of Israel's population, they feel entitled, but in the end, the Judahites' "rougher" words prevail.

23   . . . Come what may, I want to run!
       So he said to him: Run!
       And Ahimaatz ran by way of the Oval, and passed the Cushite.

24   Now David was sitting between the two gateways,
       and the watchman on the roof of the gate went over to the [city]
           wall;
       he lifted up his eyes and saw: here, a man was running alone.

25   The watchman called out and told the king,
       and the king said:
       If he is alone, [there is] news in his mouth.
       And he went, going along and coming nearer,

26   but the watchman saw another man running;
       the watchman called out to the gatekeeper
       and said:
       Here, [another] man is running alone!
       The king said:
       This one too is bringing-news.

27   The watchman said:
       I see [that] the running of the first-one is like the running of
           Ahimaatz son of Tzadok.
       The king said:
       He is a good man, and with good news he comes!

28   Ahimaatz called out and said to the king: Peace!
       And he bowed low to the king, his nostrils to the ground,
       and said:
       Blessed is YHWH your God,
       who has turned over the men who lifted their hand against my lord
           king!

29   The king said:
       Is there peace with the lad, with Avshalom?
       Ahimaatz said:

23   **. . . Come what may:** It appears that a few words
     are missing, on the order of "He said / replied."   **the
     Oval:** The lower Jordan Valley.
24   **between the two gateways:** Fokkelman (1981) takes
     this as a symbol of David's ambivalence regarding
     Avshalom. It also recalls, as many have noted, one of
     the early scenes in Samuel, Eli awaiting news of the
     Coffer (I 4:13ff.).

29   **Is there peace . . . ?:** Or "Is he well? Is it well with
     him?," but, as the reader recalls, "peace" is part of
     the young man's name.   **when Yoav sent off the
     king's servant . . . :** The Hebrew appears garbled
     here; it could be "to send off the king's servant
     Yoav and your servant." Alter (1999) suggests that it
     reflects emotional confusion in the messenger.

I saw a great commotion when Yoav sent off the king's servant and
your servant,
but I do not know what [it was].

30   The king said:
Turn around, station yourself here.
He turned around and stopped.

31   And here, the Cushite came,
and the Cushite said:
Let my lord king receive-the-news
that Y<small>HWH</small> has wrought justice for you today from the hand of all
those rising against you!

32   The king said to the Cushite:
Is there peace with the lad, with Avshalom?
The Cushite said:
May they be like that lad, my lord king's enemies and all those who
have risen against you for evil!

19:1   The king was shaken;
he went up to the upper-part of the gate and wept,
and thus he said as he went:
My son Avshalom,
my son, my son Avshalom!
Who will grant my dying, myself, in your place?
Avshalom, my son, my son!

2   And it was told to Yoav:
Here, the king is weeping and mourning over Avshalom.

3   Now the victory became mourning on that day for all the people,
for the people heard on that day, saying:
The king is in pain over his son.

4   So the people stole away on that day, while coming into the city
as humiliated fighting-people steal away when they flee in battle.

5   Now the king wrapped his face,
and the king cried out in a loud voice:
My son Avshalom,
Avshalom, my son, my son!

19:1 **My son Avshalom, / my son, my son, Avshalom!:**
The sound of the phrase is more memorable in
Hebrew than in the usual English: Hebrew uses long
vowels (*benEE avshaLOM / benEE benEE avshaLOM*),
with last syllables accented, to echo the grief.   **Who
will grant my dying:** I.e., "if only I had died."

4 **the people stole away:** Earlier (15:6), Avshalom had
"stolen away" their hearts.

6 Yoav came to the king in the palace-house,
and said:
Today you have shamed the face of all your servants
who helped you escape with your life today
and the life of your sons and your daughters, and the life of your
wives, and the life of your concubines—
7 by loving those-who-hate-you, and by hating those-who-love-you!
For you have declared today that you have no commanders or
servants;
for today I know that if Avshalom were alive, and all of us today
were dead,
indeed, then it would be right in your eyes!
8 So-now, get up, go out
and speak to the heart of your servants,
for by Yhwh I swear, that [if] you do not go out,
no man will lodge with you tonight,
and this will be more evil for you
than all the evils that have come upon you from your youth
until now!
9 So the king got up and sat at the gate,
while to all the people they declared, saying:
Here, the king is sitting at the gate!
And all the people came before the king.
Now Israel had fled, each one to his tent;
10 and it was that all the people were in strife throughout all the tribes
of Israel, saying:
The king rescued us from the hand of our enemies,
and he himself helped us escape from the hand of the Philistines;
but now he had to run away from the land, from Avshalom,
11 while Avshalom, whom we anointed over us, has died in battle!
So-now,
why are you keeping silent about having the king return?
12 Now King David sent to Tzadok and Evyatar the priests, saying:
Speak to the elders of Judah, saying:
Why should you be the last to return the king to his house?
—For the words of all Israel had come to the king, to his house.—

8 [**if**]: So ancient versions; MT omits.
9 **sat:** McCarter (1984) suggests that the action is a
kind of re-enthronement.

13 You are my brothers, you are my bone and my flesh;
   so why should you be the last to return the king?

14 And to Amasa, say:
   Are you not my bone and my flesh?
   Thus may God do to me, and thus may he add,
   if you do not become commander of the armed-forces before me
      all the days [to come], in place of Yoav.

15 Thus he inclined the heart of all the men of Judah, as one man;
   they sent [word] to the king:
   Return, you and all your servants!

16 So the king returned and came to the Jordan,
   while Judah came to Gilgal to go and meet the king,
   to conduct the king across the Jordan.

17 And Shim'i son of Gera, the Binyaminite who was from Bahurim,
      hurried out;
   he went down with the men of Judah to meet King David,

18 and a thousand men were with him from Binyamin,
   along with Tziva, the retainer from the House of Sha'ul,
   and his fifteen sons and his twenty servants with him;
   they advanced to the Jordan ahead of the king,

19 while the river-crossing was being crossed, in order to conduct the
      king's household across,
   to do what was good in his eyes.
   Now Shim'i son of Gera flung himself down before the king, as he
      was crossing the Jordan;

20 he said to the king:
   Do not impute iniquity to me, my lord,
   do not call-to-mind what your servant iniquitously-did on the day
      that my lord king went out from Jerusalem,
   that the king should take it to heart!

21 For your servant knows that I myself sinned,
   but here: I have come today, as the first of the entire House of
      Yosef,
   going down to meet my lord king!

---

15 **inclined the heart:** The last appearance of the
"heart" motif in the Avshalom cycle.

22 Avishai son of Tzeruya spoke up and said:
For that, should not Shim'i be put to death?
Indeed, he cursed Yhwh's anointed one!

23 David said:
What is there between me and you, O sons of Tzeruya,
that you have become an adversary to me?
Today should a man be put to death in Israel?
Indeed, do I not know that today I am king over Israel?

24 The king said to Shim'i:
You will not die!
And the king swore-an-oath to him.

25 Now Mefiboshet [grand]son of Sha'ul went down to meet the king
—he had not done his toenails, he had not done his mustache,
and his garments he had not scrubbed,
from the day of the king's going away until the day that he came
     back in peace—

26 and it was, when he came from Jerusalem to meet the king
that the king said to him:
Why did you not go with me, Mefiboshet?

27 He said:
My lord king, my servant deceived me;
for your servant said [to himself]:
I will have my donkey saddled and ride it, and I will go to the king—
though your servant is lame.

28 But he slandered your servant to my lord king;
yet my lord king is like a messenger of God—
so do as is good in your eyes.

29 For all my father's household were nothing but men [deserving]
     death from my lord king;
yet you have set your servant among those eating at your table!
So what right do I still have to cry out to the king?

30 The king said to him:
Why are you still speaking your words?
I have decided:
you and Tziva are to divide the fielded-property.

---

25 **toenails:** Lit. "feet."
27 **my servant:** Tziva.
28 **your servant:** Mefiboshet.

30 **Why are you still speaking:** As Alter (1999) notes, this "still" impatiently picks up on Mefiboshet's words in the last verse.

Chapter 20. *Second Rebellion:* Avshalom's revolt has once again exposed the historic rift between north and south, a divide which does not end with his death. A Binyaminite named Sheva starts another rebellion; when David asks his new commander Amasa to call the Judahites together to respond, he acts slowly, which is enough to convince his predecessor Yoav that he is betraying the king. Yoav's brutal murder of Amasa dominates this chapter: the picture of the general wallowing in his blood by the side of the road is the first of two graphic images here strongly making the point that rebellion against David will not be countenanced, at least not by Yoav. The second example made of a rebel begins in v.14, and finds Sheva taking refuge up north in the town of Avel of Bet-Maakha. As Avshalom's return to Jerusalem, and hence the seeds of the revolt, had begun with a story about a "wise woman" (Chap. 14), so the cycle of rebellion ends with one. Here the woman is able to fend off Yoav's destructive urges and save her town by killing the rebel. What originated as an assault on the head of Israel draws to a close with the sight of a head flying off the ramparts of an Israelite town.

As the chapter ends, there is a second list of David's officials (the first had capped Chap. 8). This time, in addition to a new Herald, we have a brand-new office: "[The One] Over the Labor-Gangs." With the introduction of large-scale planning, Israel is moving from a fledgling state to something closer to the real thing, with institutions of centralized control. And with this "bureaucratic book-end" (Hamilton), we come to the end of the central account of David's tenure as king.

31 Mefiboshet said to the king:
Let him just take all of it,
seeing that my lord has come back in peace to his house!

32 Now Barzillai the Gil'adite had come down from Rogelim
and had crossed the Jordan with the king, to send him off at the
Jordan.

33 And Barzillai was exceedingly old, at eighty years;
he had provided for the king when he had stayed at Mahanayim,
for he was a man of exceedingly great-wealth.

34 The king said to Barzillai:
You, cross over with me, and I will provide for you beside me in
Jerusalem.

35 But Barzillai said to the king:
How many [more] are the days and years of my life,
that I should go up with the king to Jerusalem?

36 I am eighty years old today;
do I know between good and evil?
Or does your servant taste what I eat or what I drink?
Or do I still hearken to the voice of male-singers or female-singers?
So why should your servant still be a burden to my lord king?

37 Scarcely could your servant cross the Jordan with the king,
so why does the king reward me with this reward?

38 Now let your servant return, that I may die in my town,
beside the burial-place of my father and my mother.
But here is your servant Kimham—
let him cross over with my lord king,
and then do for him that which is good in your eyes.

39 The king said:
With me, Kimham shall cross,
and I myself will do for him what is good in your eyes;
whatever you choose for me, I will do for you!

40 So all the fighting-people crossed the Jordan,
and when the king was about to cross over,
the king kissed Barzillai and blessed him,
and he returned to his place.

---

38 **Kimham:** Pronounced *kim-HAHM*; trad. English "Chimham." This gentleman, who has the distinc-tion of being one of the most briefly mentioned characters in the Bible, may have been Barzillai's son.

41 Then the king crossed over to Gilgal, and Kimham crossed over
   with him.

   Now all the fighting-people of Judah had conducted the king across,
   and also half the fighting-people of Israel.

42 And here, all the men of Israel were coming to the king;
   they said to the king:
   Why have our brothers, the men of Judah, stolen you away
   and conducted the king and his household across the Jordan,
   and all of David's men with him?

43 All the men of Judah answered the men of Israel:
   Because the king is closely-related to me!
   Why are you so agitated about this matter?
   Have we eaten, yes, eaten any of the king['s food]?
   Or has any been carried, yes, carried off to us?

44 The men of Israel answered the men of Judah, they said:
   I have ten shares in the king,
   yes, in David, I more than you;
   so why do you insult me?
   Was not my word, mine, the first for having my king return?
   But the words of Judah's men were rougher than the words of
   Israel's men.

20:1 Now there chanced to be a base man there—his name was Sheva
   son of Bikhri, a Binyaminite man;
   he gave-a-blast on the *shofar* and said:
      We have no portion in David,
      nor inheritance for us in the son of Yishai;
      everyone to his tents, O Israel!

2 So all the men of Israel went up from [following] after David, [to
   following] after Sheva son of Bikhri,
   while the men of Judah clung to their king, from the Jordan to
   Jerusalem.

---

41 **Gilgal:** Site of Sha'ul's official coronation (Alter 1999).
43 **the men of Judah answered:** And the king does not, a sign of his breakdown (Fokkelman 1981).
44 **ten shares:** Representing one for each of the northern tribes. **rougher:** Or "more stubborn" (McCarter 1984), so they prevail.

20:1 **Sheva:** Trad. English "Sheba." The name echoes an earlier trouble-ridden story, that of David and Bat-Sheva (II 11–12). **Binyaminite:** Like Shim'i, and, of course, Sha'ul.

3 And David came to his palace-house in Jerusalem.
The king took the ten concubine women whom he had left to
   guard the house
and put them in a house under guard and provided for them,
but he did not come in to them,
for they were tied off until the day of their death in living
   widowhood.

4 Then the king said to Amasa:
Summon to me the men of Judah, in three days,
then you—stop here.

5 Amasa went to summon Judah,
but he delayed from the appointed-time that he had appointed.

6 And David said to Avishai:
Now,
Sheva son of Bikhri will be more evil for us than Avshalom!
So you, take your lord's servants and pursue after him,
lest he find himself fortified towns, and cast-shadows over our eye!

7 So Yoav's men went out after him,
with the Kereitites and the Peleitites and all the mighty-men;
they went out of Jerusalem to pursue after Sheva son of Bikhri.

8 When they were beside the great rock that is in Giv'on,
Amasa came up in front of them.
Now Yoav was girded in his garb, his [military] dress,
and on him was a girded sword bound on his loins, in its sheath;
when he went out, it fell down.

9 And Yoav said to Amasa:
Are you in peace, my brother?
And Yoav's right hand took hold of Amasa's beard, to kiss him,

10 but Amasa did not guard himself from the sword that was in Yoav's
   [other] hand,

---

3 **tied off . . . living widowhood:** Some see this as a reminder of Avshalom's usurpation, but it may also be another indication that David is not the man he once was.

5 **delayed:** Heb. *va-yoher* echoes *ahar, aharei,* "after," a theme word in this chapter, tied to the pursuit of the rebel Sheva. **he had appointed:** Referring to the king.

6 **cast-shadows over our eye:** Heb. difficult; it seems to imply Sheva's escape. This translation presupposes different vowels than MT.

8 **Giv'on:** The rebellion narrative ends where the conflict between the houses of David and Sha'ul had its bloody beginning in II 2:13 (Exum 1996). The assassination here plays out like scenes from the *Godfather* movies.

9 **took hold . . . to kiss him:** Parallel to Avshalom's approach to his legal supplicants in 15:5.

◆

and he struck him with it in the abdomen, so that his innards
poured out on the ground;
—he did not [have to] do it to him a second-time—and so he died.
Now Yoav and Avishai his brother pursued after Sheva son of
Bikhri,

11 while a man was standing by him from the serving-lads of Yoav;
he said:
Whoever desires Yoav, and whoever is for David—[follow] after
Yoav!

12 Now Amasa was rolling in blood in the middle of the road;
and the man saw that all the people were stopping,
so he turned Amasa over from the road into the open-field, and
threw a garment over him
—when anyone who came by saw him, he would stop.

13 When he had pushed him out of the road,
all the men who were [following] after Yoav crossed over to pursue
after Sheva son of Bikhri.

14 They crossed throughout all the tribes of Israel to Avel of Bet-
Maakha, to all the Bikhrites,
and assembled and came just after him.

15 They came and besieged him, in Avel of Bet-Maakha:
they cast up a mound against the town, and stopped at the rampart,
while all the fighting-people who were with Yoav were bringing-
ruin, to cause the wall to fall.

16 But a wise woman called out from the town:
Hearken! Hearken!
Now say to Yoav:
Come near to here—I would speak with you!

17 He came near to her.
The woman said:
Are you Yoav?
He said:

11 **Yoav . . . David:** Yoav's servant in a sense restores
his master's standing by mentioning David in the
same breath, even though Yoav has technically been
replaced (Alter 1999). **he said:** Yoav's man.
14 **Avel of Bet-Maakha:** Pronounced *ah-VAYL bayt
mah-ah-KHAH;* trad. English "Abel of Beth Maa-
cah." **Bikhrites:** So LXX; MT reads "Be'eirites."

15 **bringing-ruin:** Others, "battering." Alter (1999)
connects this with 14:11 above, "too much might the
blood redeemer bring ruin"; similarly, he sees v.19's
"Why would you swallow YHWH's inheritance?"
as echoing 14:16, "from destroying me and my son
together, [away] from God's inheritance."

◆ I am.

She said to him:

Hearken to the words of your maidservant.

He said:

I am hearkening.

18 She said, saying:

They used to speak, yes, speak formerly, saying:

When they inquired, yes, inquired in Avel,

thus they ended [the matter]!

19 *I* [am of] those most at peace, most trustworthy in Israel;

you seek to deal death to a town, a mother-city in Israel!

Why would you swallow up YHWH's inheritance?

20 Yoav answered and said:

[Heaven] forbid, forbid for me, if I cause it to be swallowed up, if I bring-ruin!

21 Not so is the matter,

but a man from the highlands of Efrayim, Sheva son of Bikhri his name,

has lifted his hand against the king, against David.

Give up him alone, and I will go from the town!

The woman said to Yoav:

Here, his head will be thrown to you by way of the wall.

22 And the woman came to all the people with her wisdom,

and they cut off the head of Sheva son of Bikhri and threw it to Yoav;

then he sounded-a-blast on the *shofar,*

and they scattered from the town, each one to his tents,

while Yoav returned to Jerusalem, to the king.

23 Now Yoav was [The One] Over All the Armed-Forces of Israel,

while Benaya son of Yehoyada was [The One] Over the Kereitites and Over the Peleitites,

18 **When they inquired . . . :** That is, one received a good answer in Avel.

19 *I* **[am of] those . . . :** The woman appears to be speaking for the whole town. **a town, a mother-city:** Lit., "town and mother."

24 and Adoram was [The One] Over the Labor-Gangs,
and Yehoshafat son of Ahilud was the Herald,
25 and Sh'va was Scribe,
and Tzadok and Evyatar were priests,
while also 'Ira the Ya'irite was priest to David.

PART VII

FINAL MATTERS

(II 21–24)

THE BOOK OF SAMUEL DOES NOT END WITH DAVID'S DEATH. THAT, AND THE complex and once again violent machinations which accompany the accession of his son Shelomo to the throne, have been placed in the two opening chapters of the book of Kings, perhaps as the first throne succession story in a long sequence to follow in that book. Nevertheless, the final section of Samuel has its own integrity and sense. As has long been noted, Chaps. 21–24 are chiastic (ring-shaped) in structure: David's two last poems (22:1–23:7) are surrounded first by accounts of his heroes' exploits, and then by two stories of disaster (famine and plague) and resolution, in which God finally "lets-himself-be-entreated" (21:14, 24:25). This structure has been created by some chronological shifting, since Chap. 21 would have more properly fit with the battle scenes of Chap. 9.

The long poem in Chap. 22, of which a parallel text exists as Ps. 18, may be one of the oldest pieces in the Bible, as attested by its spelling and grammatical forms. It also uses ideas found both in other early Israelite poems (for example, Exod. 15 and Deut. 32–33) and in the literature of Ugarit, a city north of and flourishing earlier than Israel: a god's impressive appearance and a king's victory song (see Cross/Freedman for an extended treatment of our text). As with the poems at the end of Deuteronomy, the book thus moves toward its conclusion on a note of heightened rhetoric.

Likewise, David's "last words" at the beginning of Chap. 23 present the picture of a king, not in decline, but supremely confident in his God and in himself. This short poem counterbalances the increasingly weakening figure of David, who, as the next book (Kings) opens, will be literally impotent and largely overshadowed by others in the palace.

The final narrative moments of Samuel bring some resolution to the issue of monarchy, as David accepts responsibility for the people's suffering. They also portend a glorious future: like Avraham acquiring the Cave of Makhpela and hence a legal foothold in the land in Gen. 23, David acquires the site of the future Temple, which he had so fervently desired to build in II Sam. 7. The institution of kingship, whose rocky road the narratives of the book of Samuel have traced, seems finally to be accepted as part of the landscape, however grudgingly.

Chapter 21. *Revenge on the House of Sha'ul; Battles with the Philistines:* After all the bloodshed that has occurred in Samuel, one piece of unfinished business remains. The text chooses this point to recount a symbolic execution—that of seven sons of Sha'ul—and uses the men of Giv'on (Gibeon) as the means to that end. In a story that does not appear elsewhere in the Bible, we are informed that Sha'ul, in contravention of the treaty with the Giv'onites that had been concluded in Josh. 9:15, had sought to destroy them. Now they demand a kind of blood vengeance, which David permits in order to stay the famine that is ravaging the land. One must again wonder at bloody deeds which benefit David but in which he does not wield the sword, and at the fact that he uses an oracle to shift the responsibility.

In an opposite vein, a final demonstration of David's magnanimity concerns the bodies of the executed men. The action of Sha'ul's concubine Ritzpa, who protects the corpses of both her own two sons and those of Sha'ul's daughter Merav, is a deed of compassion and heroism, stretching as it does from spring to fall in the heart of the hot, dry season, and is met by David's realization that all of Sha'ul's family should be interred together in the family plot. This provides a closure which had been lacking since Sha'ul's death, since he and the sons who had fallen in battle with him had remained buried under a tree in Yavesh-Gil'ad since I Sam. 31. But in truth, the burial is the final nail in the Saulide coffin.

The chapter concludes with four brief accounts of battle with the Philistines which appear to look back chronologically. In the first, David is actually taken captive, only to be rescued by Yoav's brother Avishai. This episode is followed by Israelite victories over various foes—huge warriors with sometimes unusual physical characteristics (see v.20). Golyat is mentioned again; in this version he is slain not by the youthful David but by a certain Elhanan (see the Comments to I Sam. 17, above).

◆ 21:1 Now there was a famine in David's days, for three years, year after
year,
and David besought the face of Yhwh.
Yhwh said:
Because of Sha'ul and because of the House of Bloodguilt,
because he caused the death of the Giv'onites . . . !

2 So the king called for the Giv'onites and said to them
—now the Giv'onites were not from the Children of Israel,
but rather from the remnant of the Amorites,
yet the Children of Israel had sworn [an oath] to them;
but Sha'ul had sought to strike them down, in his zeal for the
Children of Israel and Judah—

3 David said to the Giv'onites:
What shall I do for you?
In what [way] may I effect-atonement,
so that they may bless Yhwh's inheritance?

4 The Giv'onites said to him:
We have no [wish for] silver or gold with Sha'ul or with his house,
and we have no [wish to] put any man to death in Israel!
He said:
Whatever you say, I will do for you.

5 They said to the king:
The man who [wanted to] destroy us,
who intended for us [that] we should be wiped out from remaining
in all the territory of Israel:

6 let there be given to us seven men of his descendants,
and we will impale them to Yhwh at Giv'a of Sha'ul, the chosen
one of Yhwh!
The king said:
I myself will give [them over].

21:1 **the House of Bloodguilt:** Sha'ul's house. **the
death of the Giv'onites:** Trad. English "Gibeon-
ites." God's words refer to an event not previously
mentioned in the Bible. Apparently Sha'ul, in contravention of the treaty between Israel and the
Giv'onites recorded in Josh. 9:15, had killed some of
them.

2 **remnant of the Amorites:** Left over from the conquest of Canaan, again in violation of divine injunc-
tion.
6 **impale them to Yhwh:** In open court, as it were; see
v.9. **the chosen one:** The phrase suggests a sarcastic tone (Alter 1999).

7 But the king spared Mefiboshet son of Yehonatan son of Sha'ul,
because of the sworn-oath of YHWH that was between them,
between David and Yehonatan son of Sha'ul.

8 So the king took the two sons of Ritzpa daughter of Aya, whom
she had borne to Sha'ul, Armoni and Mefiboshet,
and the five sons of Merav daughter of Sha'ul, whom she had
borne to Adriel son of Barzillai the Meholatite,

9 and gave them into the hand of the Giv'onites;
they impaled them on the hill, in the presence of YHWH,
and the seven of them fell together.
—Now they were put to death at the time of the harvest, the first
days, at the start of the barley harvest.—

10 And Ritzpa daughter of Aya took sackcloth
and spread it out for herself on a rock
from the start of the harvest until water poured out on them from
the heavens;
she did not allow the birds of the heavens to alight on them by day
or the wildlife of the open-field by night.

11 And David was told what Ritzpa daughter of Aya, Sha'ul's
concubine, had done,

12 so David went
and took the bones of Sha'ul and the bones of Yehonatan his son
from the inhabitants of Yavesh-Gil'ad,
who had stealthily-taken them from the square of Bet-Shan,
where the Philistines had hung them up at the time that the
Philistines struck down Sha'ul at Gilboa;

13 he brought up from there the bones of Sha'ul and the bones of
Yehonatan his son,
and they gathered the bones of the impaled ones.

14 Then they buried the bones of Sha'ul and of Yehonatan his son
in the land of Binyamin, in the side-chamber of the burial-place of
Kish his father.

8 **Aya:** Pronounced *ah-YAH,* the name of a bird of prey, perhaps a kind of falcon, mentioned in Lev. 11:14 (and Deut. 14:13). It is appropriate to the action here (Garsiel 1991). **Merav:** So ancient versions; MT has "Mikhal."

9 **the start of the barley harvest:** The beginning of spring.

10 **until water poured out:** In the fall, when the rainy season in Israel begins.

14 **God let-himself-be-entreated:** And the famine ended.

And when they had done all that the king had commanded them,
God let-himself-be-entreated for the land after that.

15 Now there were battles again by the Philistines with Israel;
David went down, his servants with him,
and they did battle with the Philistines.
But David was weary,

16 and he was taken captive by Benov, who was of the descendants of
the Shades
—the weight of his lance was three hundred *shekel*-weights of
bronze,
while he was girded in new [armor]—
he intended to strike David down,

17 but Avishai son of Tzeruya came to his help:
he struck down the Philistine and put him to death.
Then David's men swore [an oath] to him, saying:
You must not go out with us again into battle;
you must not extinguish the lamp of Israel!

18 It was [some time] after this
that there was battle again, in Gov, with the Philistines.
And Sibbekhai the Hushatite struck down Saf, who was of the
descendants of the Shades.

19 And there was battle again in Gov, with the Philistines,
and Elhanan son of Yaarei-Oregim the Bet-Lehemite struck down
Golyat the Gittite
—now the shaft of his spear was like a weavers' beam.

20 And there was battle again in Gat:
and there was an immense man—
the fingers of his hands and the toes of his feet were six and six
[apiece], twenty-four in number,
and he too was descended from the Shades.

---

15 **battles:** Or "war."

16 **and he was taken captive:** Following B-R. Others
read, with the *Qere,* the name Yishbi here. **Benov:**
McCarter (1984) and others suggest that this difficult
text has lost the correct name of the hero, Dodo.

18 **Gov:** I Chron. 20:4 has "Gezer"; perhaps "Gov" was

anticipating the next verse. In any event, its location
is unknown.

19 **weavers':** Earlier in the verse, "Oregim" is a homonym (perhaps the result of a scribal error).

20 **toes:** The text uses the same word as the one for
"fingers," as is customary in biblical Hebrew.

Chapter 22. *David's Song of Deliverance:* The placement of poetry toward the end of a long section or book occurs a number of times in the Bible (see, for instance, Gen. 49 and Exod. 15). This chapter also serves as a bracket for the entire book, as noted in the Comments to II 1, above. In fact, it echoes both vocabulary and themes from the earlier Song of Hanna (Fokkelman 1999), down to the detail that both conclude with mention of "his anointed one" (v.51 and 2:10) (Fishbane).

Additionally, this "song" is a virtual compendium of Israelite poetic ideas. The writer takes the time to build up the impressive manifestation of God in a manner that would have been familiar to many groups in the region; David's God thunders in much the same manner as the Canaanite/Phoenician Baal. The divine appearance is in response to a beleaguered and despairing protagonist, who is so often the focus of biblical poetry from Jeremiah, Psalms, Lamentations, and Job, to cite just a few outstanding examples. Whether David was the writer or not, the poem's imagery seems to fit him and his struggles nicely: from a state of being surrounded by enemies, he is able to triumph, especially militarily; he keeps faith with God in wholeness of heart (conveniently, the Bat-Sheva incident is ignored); and he is assured of God's perpetual favor in the end.

Fishbane rightly stresses the "rock" imagery used here for God, and notes that, while it is used frequently in the Psalms, its appearance in this chapter focuses on hope rather than on a desperate plea for rescue.

◆

21　He mocked Israel,
　　　but Yehonatan son of Shim'a, David's brother, struck him down.

22　These four were descended from the Shades, in Gat;
　　　they fell by the hand of David and by the hand of his servants.

22:1　And David spoke forth to YHWH the words of this song
　　　at the time that YHWH rescued him from the hand of all his
　　　　　enemies and from the hand of Sha'ul;

2　he said:
　　　YHWH is my crag and my fortress, one helping me escape!

3　My God is my rock, in whom I seek-refuge,
　　　my shield, the horn of my deliverance,
　　　my secure-height, my place-of-retreat,
　　　my deliverer—from treachery you deliver me!

4　Praised One I call YHWH,
　　　from my enemies I am delivered.

5　For they encompassed me, the breakers of death,
　　　the torrents of Belial tormented me;

6　the ropes of Sheol surrounded me,
　　　they confronted me, the snares of death.

7　In my distress I called YHWH!
　　　to my God I called.
　　　He heard my voice from his Great-Hall,
　　　my cry-for-deliverance in his ears.

8　The earth did quake and shake,
　　　the foundations of the heavens shuddered,
　　　they quaked, because he was agitated;

9　smoke arose from his nostrils;
　　　fire from his mouth, devouring,
　　　coals burned forth from him.

10　He spread the heavens and came down,
　　　a heavy-cloud beneath his feet,

11　he mounted a winged-sphinx and flew,
　　　he darted upon the wings of the wind.

22:1FF. **And David spoke forth to** YHWH **. . . :** In this chapter I have been guided by the work of Cross/Freedman, with advice from Greenstein (written communication).

3 **horn of my deliverance:** See note to I 2:1. **place-of-retreat:** Following Goldman.

5 **Belial:** Another term (Heb. *beliyyaal*) for the underworld or the powers thereof.

11 **darted:** Reading, as is customary, *va-yid'eh* for *va-yera*.

◆ 12 He set darkness all around him as his hut,
the [heavenly] sieve of water, in masses of clouds;

13 from the brightness in front of him
burned forth coals of fire.

14 He thundered from the heavens, did Yhwh,
the Most-High gave forth his voice.

15 He sent forth arrows and scattered them,
lightning and he panicked them.

16 Then appeared the sources of the sea,
revealed, the foundations of the earth,
at your rebuke, O Yhwh,
at the breath of his nostrils' rush.

17 He stretched out [his hand] from on high and took me,
he drew me out of mighty waters.

18 He rescued me from my enemies so fierce,
from those hating me, for they were mightier than I.

19 They confronted me on the day of my calamity,
but Yhwh became support for me.

20 He brought me out to a wide-place,
he saved me because he was pleased with me.

21 Yhwh rewarded me according to my righteousness,
according to the purity of my hands, he paid me back.

22 For I have kept the ways of Yhwh,
and have done no wrong in the presence of my God.

23 For all his regulations are before me,
his laws I have not turned aside from me;

24 I have been wholehearted with him,
I have kept myself from iniquity.

25 Yhwh has paid me back according to my innocence,
according to my purity before his eyes.

26 With the loyal ones you are loyal,
with the wholehearted mighty-man you are whole,

27 with the pure one you are pure,
but with the crooked you are devious.

---

13 **from the brightness . . . coals:** The text is quite problematic here; perhaps "coals" has dropped down from v.9.

14 **his voice:** Often in the Bible, thunder is imagined as "Yhwh's voice" (see, for a powerful example, Ps. 29).

16 **your:** Missing here, but in Ps. 18:16.

25 **my innocence:** In the legal sense.

27 **you are devious:** Following McCarter's (1984) suggestion, based again on Ps. 18.

28 An afflicted people you will deliver,
but the haughty-eyed you will bring low.

29 Yes, you are my lamp, O Yhwh,
my God brightens my darkness.

30 Yes, with you I assault a troop,
with my God I can leap over a wall.

31 This God, whole is his way,
the word of Yhwh is tested,
a shield is he for all who take refuge in him.

32 For who is God besides Yhwh?
Who is a rock besides our God?

33 God encompasses me with might,
he makes wholeness his way.

34 He sets my feet like [those of] deer,
on my heights he makes me stand.

35 Training my hands for battle,
my arms to stretch a bow of bronze.

36 You have given me your shield of deliverance,
your battle-cry makes-me-many.

37 You have widened my steps under me,
my ankles do not slip.

38 I pursue my enemies, I destroy them,
I do not turn back until they are finished.

39 I batter them and shatter them, so that they rise no more,
they fall beneath my feet.

40 You have armed me with might for battle,
bowed my adversaries beneath me.

41 As for my enemies, you have given me their necks,
those hating me—I annihilate them.

42 They cried-for-help, but there was no deliverer,
to Yhwh, but he did not answer them.

---

28 **the haughty-eyed:** Cross/Freedman's reading, derived from combining this verse and Ps. 18.

29 **my God:** Suggested by manuscripts; MT has "Yhwh."

30 **troop:** JPS, on the basis of later Hebrew, reads "barrier," paralleling "wall."

33 **he makes:** Heb. *va-yittein,* from Ps. 18:33 and LXX, as opposed to MT's *va-yatteir.*

34 **He sets my feet like [those of] deer:** Able to leap from hill to hill.

35 **my arms to stretch a bow:** Cross/Freedman emend to "together with the javelin and the bow of bronze."

36 **your battle-cry:** Heb. *'annotekha;* some emend, following 4QSam[a], to *'ezratekha,* "your help."

39 **I batter them and shatter them:** Heb. *va-akhalleim va-emtza'eim.*

41 **their necks:** In a classic pose of subjugation; see Gen. 49:8 for another poetic use of the image, which specifically refers to the back of the neck.

Chapter 23. *David's "Last Words"; His Warriors:* A much briefer poem opens this chapter (vv.1–7). Strikingly, its initial words recall the prophet Bil'am's inspired vision of a peaceful, secure Israel in Num. 22–24. The poem touts the theme of God's reassurance, presenting mainly the natural imagery of light and growth for David himself, and concluding with a fiery portrayal of his enemies' demise. The latter is a frequent theme in the book of Psalms.

The rest of the chapter concentrates on the names and exploits of David's choice warriors, returning as it were to the end of Chap. 21. Some of the passages are difficult to interpret, but the intent is apparently to celebrate David as warrior king. The whole section would logically fit much earlier in the book, but it has probably been placed here because these final chapters of Samuel function to collect various traditions about David which are best served in isolation from the main narrative flow. They also have the effect of recovering some of David's earlier heroic stature: he is a selfless military leader who refuses to profit from his soldiers' fanatical loyalty (vv.13–17), and he heads a formidable group of warriors (vv.18–38) who are, significantly, remembered by name.

43 I crush-them-fine like the dust of the ground,
    like the dirt of the streets I pulverize them, I pound them!
44 You have saved me from my people's strife,
    you have guarded me as the head of nations;
    a people unknown to me serves me,
45 foreigners come-fawning to me,
    hearing by the ear, they hearken to me.
46 Foreigners crumble,
    they emerge from their enclosures.
47 By the life of Yhwh, blessed is my rock,
    exalted is my God, the rock of my deliverance;
48 the God giving me vengeance,
    bringing down peoples under me,
49 taking me out from my enemies.
    Over my adversaries you have exalted me,
    from the man of violence you have rescued me.
50 Therefore I praise you, O Yhwh, among the nations,
    and to your name I sing-melodies,
51 [the One] who magnifies the victories of his king,
    [the One] who shows loyalty to his anointed one,
    to David and to his seed,
    for the ages!

23:1 Now these are David's last words:
    Utterance of David the son of Yishai,
    utterance of one on high raised up,
    anointed one of Yaakov's God,
    favored one of Israel's Strength:
2 the spirit of Yhwh speaks through me,
    his discourse is on my tongue.
3 The God of Israel talks,
    to me the Rock of Israel speaks:
    A ruler over humans, a righteous one,
    a ruler with the awe of God,

---

43 **I pulverize them, I pound them:** Heb. *adikkeim erka'eim.*
44 **my people's strife:** LXX has "strife of peoples."
45 **hearken:** With the connotation of obedience.
49 **from the man of violence:** Cross / Freedman and others find this line strange and out of place.
51 **who magnifies:** Heb. *magdil,* following the written text (*ketiv*) of MT and Ps. 18:51. **for the ages!:** repeating the important refrain from II Sam. 7:13ff.

23:1 **Utterance ... :** The tone resembles that of Bil'am in Num. 24, using the vocabulary of prophecy. **favored one of Israel's Strength:** Understanding *zimra* (here in the plural) as in Exod. 15:2. Others, famously, "the sweet singer of Israel."

◆

4 is like the light of daybreak as the sun rises,
  a daybreak without clouds,
  by dint of brightness, by dint of rain,
  the herbage of the earth.

5 —Yes, is not so my house before God?
  For he has made me a covenant for the ages,
  arranged in all and guarded!
  Yes, all my deliverance, all my desire,
  yes, will he not cause it to sprout?

6 But base ones:
  like a thorn tossed away are all of them,
  for not by [one's] hand [alone] can they be taken up;

7 the man who touches them must fill [his hand] with iron or the
   shaft of a spear,
  but with fire they will burn, yes, burn where [they] stay!

8 These are the names of the mighty-men belonging to David:
  Yashav'am the Tahkemonite, head of the Three;
  he swung his ax over eight hundred slain at one time.

9 Now after him was El'azar son of Dodo son of Ahohi
  —among the three mighty-men with David when they made-
   mockery of the Philistines gathered there for battle,
  and the men of Israel went up.

10 He arose and struck down the Philistines, until his hand became
   weary,
  so that his hand stuck to the sword.
  And Yhwh wrought a great victory on that day:
  the fighting-people returned after him only to strip [the slain].

11 Now after him was Shamma son of Agei the Hararite;
  [once,] the Philistines gathered at Lehi,
  and there was a plot of open-field there full of lentils,
  and when the people fled before the Philistines,

12 he took a stand amid the plot and rescued it, and struck down the
   Philistines.
  Thus Yhwh wrought a great victory.

8 **Yashav'am the Tahkemonite:** The text is in difficult shape; I Chron. 11:11 reads the name as "Yashov'am son of Hakhmoni." **the Three:** Some understand as "the officers." **slain:** Or "wounded."

13 [Once,] three of the Thirty chiefs went down, and they came at
    harvest-time to David at the Cave of Adullam,
  while a troop of Philistines was encamped in the Valley of the
    Shades.
14 Now David was then at the fortress,
  while a garrison of Philistines was then at Bet-Lehem.
15 And David had a craving, he said:
  Who will give me water to drink from the cistern of Bet-Lehem
    that is at the gate?
16 The three mighty-men broke through into the camp of the
    Philistines
  and drew water from the cistern of Bet-Lehem that is at the gate,
  and carried it away and brought it to David.
  But he would not drink it—he poured it out to Yhwh
17 and said:
  [Heaven] forbid for me, by Yhwh, doing this;
  is it the blood of men who were going forth [at risk] of their lives?!
  And he would not drink it.
  These [deeds] did the three mighty-men do.

18 Now Avishai brother of Yoav son of Tzeruya was the head of the
    Thirty
  —he swung his spear over three hundred slain,
  and so he had a name among the Thirty.
19 Among the Thirty he was honored, so that he became a
    commander for them,
  but to the [status of the] Three he did not come.

20 Now Benayahu son of Yehoyada, the son of a valiant man, was
    abundant in valiant-deeds, from Kavtze'el;
  it was he [who] struck down the two [sons of] Ariel of Moav.
  And he went down and struck a lion in the midst of a cistern, on a
    day of snow.
21 It was he [who] struck an Egyptian man, a man of [giant]
    appearance,
  —now in the Egyptian's hand was a spear,

17 **is it the blood . . . :** The Hebrew text seems to be missing a few words.
18 **Thirty:** Following manuscripts; MT has "three."
20 **[sons of]:** Supplied by LXX.

Chapter 24. *Plague and Purchase:* The final chapter of Samuel begins on a puzzling note. We are not told why YHWH is angry at Israel, but David becomes an unwitting accomplice in a new sin, that of taking a census. What precisely is wrong with this act is not made explicit. Guesses range from some kind of ancient reluctance to count, at least outside of a religious context (see Exod. 30, where the counted Israelites must be monetarily "redeemed"), to a feeling that taking a military census shows a lack of trust in God. Already in ancient times interpreters were uncomfortable with the passage, and in the later book of Chronicles (I 21), the idea of the census is portrayed as stemming not from God but from a shadowy figure called "the *satan*," whose literal meaning is "adversary" (and not the Devil figure of later times).

Be that as it may, by the midpoint of the chapter, it appears that the whole episode is functioning as an opportunity for David to exercise renewed leadership. First he gets to choose the form of punishment that Israel must undergo, and then he alone accepts blame for the plague, imploring God to have compassion on Israel. In that sense, both David and the very concept of kingship are at least partially redeemed as the book of Samuel draws to a close.

There is, however, a further reason for the existence of this narrative. In order to properly atone for the taking of a census, David is to purchase some property up the hill from his palace, so that he may build an altar. The location is none other than the future site of the Temple, which David had been desperate to build in Chap. 7 and which will be erected by his son Shelomo. The book of Samuel thus concludes on a note that looks forward to the establishing of a permanent dynasty, with its presence firmly anchored in the royal complex of Jerusalem, and draws attention away from David's decline, which had been the narrative focus since Chap. 13. The indignities of his old age are left for the next two chapters, at the beginning of the book of Kings.

but he went down at him with [only] a staff;
he snatched the spear from the Egyptian's hand, and killed him
   with his own spear.

22   These [things] did Benayahu son of Yehoyada;
he had a name among the Thirty mighty-men.

23   Among the Thirty he was honored,
but to the [status of the] Three he did not come.
And David put him over his bodyguard.

24   Asa'el brother of Yoav was among the Thirty,
[with] Elhanan son of Dodo of Bet-Lehem,

25   Shamma the Harodite,
Elika the Harodite,

26   Heletz the Paltite,
Ira son of Ikkesh the Tekoite,

27   Avi'ezer the Annatotite,
Mevunnai the Hushatite,

28   Tzalmon the Ahohite,
Mah'rai the Netofatite,

29   Helev son of Baana the Netofatite,
Ittai son of Rivai from Giv'a of the Children of Binyamin,

30   Benayahu [the] Pir'atonite,
Hiddai from the wadis of Gaash,

31   Avi-Almon the Arvatite,
Azmavet the Barhumite,

32   Elyahba the Shaalvonite,
the sons of Yashen, Yehonatan,

33   Ahi'am son of Sharar the Ararite,

34   Elifelet son of Ahasbai the Bet-Maakhatite,
Eli'am son of Ahitofel the Gilonite,

35   Hetzrai the Carmelite,
Paarai the Arbite,

36   Yig'al son of Natan of Tzova,
Bani the Gadite,

37   Tzeleg the Ammonite,
Nah'rai the Be'erotite, weapons bearer of Yoav son of Tzeruya,

32 **sons of Yashen, Yehonatan:** The syntax is garbled
and difficult to untangle.

38 Ira the Yitrite,
Garev the Yitrite,

39 Uriyya the Hittite—
altogether, thirty-seven.

24:1 Once again Yhwh's anger flared up against Israel,
and he incited David against them, saying:
Go, take-a-census of Israel and Judah.

2 So the king said to Yoav, commander of the army that was
with him:
Now roam throughout all the tribes of Israel, from Dan to
Be'er-Sheva,
and count the fighting-people,
that I may know the number of the people.

3 Yoav said to the king:
May Yhwh your God add to the people, as [many as] they are, as
[many as] they are, a hundredfold!
My lord king's eyes can see it;
so my lord king—why does he desire this thing?

4 But the king's word overpowered Yoav and the commanders of the
fighting-forces,
so Yoav and the commanders of the forces went out from the king's
presence to count the people, Israel;

5 they crossed the Jordan and encamped in Aro'er, to the right / south
of the town that is in the midst of the Wadi of Gad, toward
Ya'zer,

6 then they came to Gil'ad and to the region of Tahtim-Hodshi,
then they came to Dan-Yaan and around to Sidon,

7 then they came to the fortress of Tyre and all the Hivvite and
Canaanite towns,
and [finally] went out into the Negev of Judah, [toward] Be'er-
Sheva.

8 They roamed throughout the entire land
and came back at the end of nine months and twenty days to
Jerusalem.

24:5 **Aro'er:** A town east of the Jordan, that sits on the
border of the territory of Heshbon.

9   Yoav gave the number of the people thus-accounted to the king,
    and Israel was: eight hundred thousand mighty-men of valor,
      drawing the sword,
    and the men of Judah: five hundred thousand men.

10   But David's heart struck him after he had numbered the people,
    and David said to YHWH:
    I have sinned exceedingly in what I have done!
    So-now, O YHWH, pray transfer the iniquity of your servant,
    for I have been exceedingly foolish!

11   David arose at daybreak,
    and the word of YHWH [came] to Gad the prophet, David's
      visionary, saying:

12   Go, you are to speak to David:
    Thus says YHWH:
    I will hold three [things] over you;
    choose yourself one of them, and I will do it to you.

13   Gad came to David and told him;
    he said to him:
    Shall there come upon you seven years of famine in your land,
    or three months of your fleeing before your foe, while he
      pursues you,
    or shall there be three days of plague in your land?
    So-now, know and take-note: what kind of word shall I answer to
      the one sending me?

14   David said to Gad:
    I am in exceedingly great distress;
    now let us fall into YHWH's hand,
    for great is his compassion;
    but into human hands may I never fall!

15   So YHWH gave forth a plague among Israel, from morning until the
    appointed-time,
    and there died of the people, from Dan to Be'er-Sheva,
    seventy thousand men.

---

11 **visionary:** Another word for seer or prophet.

12 **hold three [things] over you:** That is, give you a choice of three different punishments.

14 **never fall:** LXX continues, "So David chose the plague . . ." The use of "falling" contrasts with the "fall" of Sha'ul at the end of I Samuel.

16 But when the [divine] messenger stretched forth his hand against
    Jerusalem, to bring-it-to-ruin,
  Yhwh relented concerning the evil,
  and he said to the messenger, the one bringing-ruin among the
    people:
  Enough now, slacken your hand!
  Now Yhwh's messenger was beside the threshing-floor of Aravna
    the Yevusite.

17 And David said to Yhwh, when he saw the messenger, the one
    striking down the people,
  he said:
  Here, it is I who have sinned,
  it is I who have done-iniquity,
  but these sheep, what have they done?
  Pray let your hand be against me and against my Father's House!

18 Gad came to David on that day
  and said to him:
  Go up, erect an altar to Yhwh
  at the threshing-floor of Aravna the Yevusite.

19 So David went up, according to the word of Gad, as Yhwh had
    commanded him.

20 And Aravna looked out
  and saw the king and his servants crossing over to him;
  Aravna went out and bowed low to the king, his nostrils to the
    ground,

21 and Aravna said:
  For-what-reason does my lord come to his servant?
  David said:
  To acquire the threshing-floor from you, to build an altar to Yhwh,
  so that the plague may be restrained from upon the people!

---

16 **threshing-floor:** A common feature of biblical life, a threshing floor was used to process grain. It would typically be located on a flat, hard outdoor surface, where the grain would be broken down by heavy weights such as stone rollers or even oxen. The site in the present story lay higher than David's palace at the top of Mount Zion, and eventually became the location of Solomon's Temple. It appears to be identical to the site of the Dome of the Rock, the Muslim monument that has stood atop the Temple Mount for more than thirteen centuries. **Aravna:** Pronounced *ah-RAHV-nah;* trad. English "Araunah." The name is spelled several ways in biblical passages; the confusion stems, according to some, from the fact that it may not be a name at all but a title, meaning "lord" in Hurrian, an ancient Near Eastern language. Aravna has also been thought to have been a priest, further indicating that the Temple Mount may have been a long-standing holy site.

22 Aravna said to David:
   May my lord king take and offer up whatever is good in his eyes!
   See, an ox is for the offering-up
   and the sledges and the gear of the oxen are for wood;

23 all [this] does Aravna give, O king, to the king!
   And Aravna said to the king:
   May Yhwh your God show-you-good-will!

24 The king said to Aravna:
   No,
   rather I will acquire, acquire it from you at fair-price;
   I will not offer up to Yhwh my God offerings-up [obtained] for
      nothing!
   So David acquired the threshing-floor and the ox for silver, fifty
      weights,

25 and David built there an altar to Yhwh;
   he offered up offerings-up and *shalom*-offerings.
   And Yhwh let-himself-be-entreated for the land,
   so that the plague was restrained from upon Israel.

---

23 **all [this] does Aravna give, O king:** The phrase could also be read as "all [this] does Aravna the king give to the king," identifying the former as a person of royal blood.

25 **he offered up offerings-up and *shalom*-offerings:** Foreshadowing the future role of the Jerusalem Temple—obtaining God's forgiveness and turning away his anger. Yhwh **let-himself-be-entreated:** Echoing the end of Chap. 21 and thus providing a nice bracket for the final section of Samuel (Alter 1999).

מלכים

KINGS

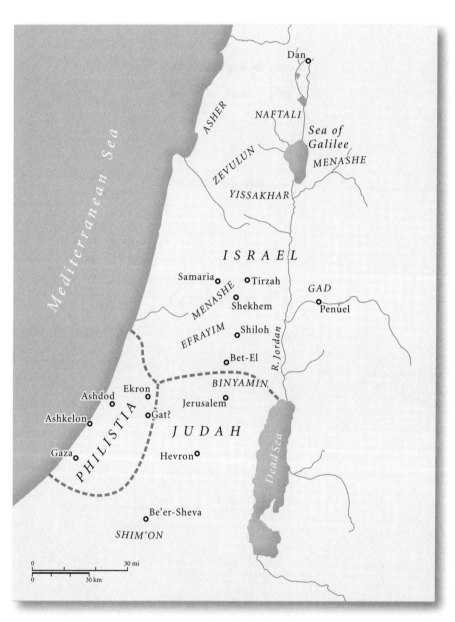

Israel and Judah

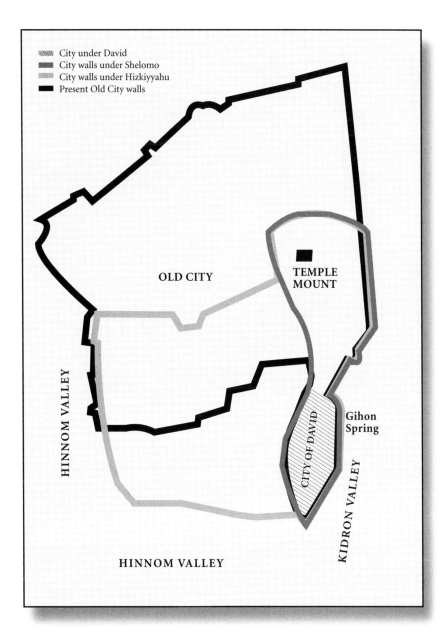

Jerusalem in the Times of David, Shelomo, and Hizkiyyahu

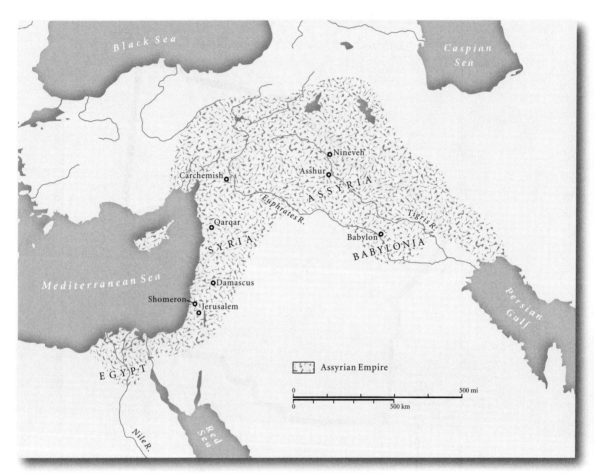

The Assyrian Empire

INTRODUCTION

A Grand Sweep

The book of Kings is the Early Prophets' most expansive meditation on Israel's past. Its narratives, ranging over forty-seven chapters, cover some four centuries, beginning with King Solomon's accession to the throne in the tenth century B.C.E. and concluding with his descendant Jehoiachin's release from a Babylonian prison in the sixth. And this chronological journey, far from being uniform, is composed of varied kinds of literature. The first quarter of the book includes a detailed description of Solomon's wealth, wisdom, and building accomplishments, including his fabled Temple, along with an interpretation of why the temporarily united kingdom of Israel split once and for all into two separate realms. This is followed by a long alternating narrative history of the two kingdoms, featuring a dizzying succession of rulers, which chronicles their interactions with both external enemies and internal challenges, and includes tales of renowned prophets who play important roles both nationally and internationally. Finally, the book relates how each kingdom fell to great empires. The north, Israel, was to virtually disappear from history, while the south, Judah, would survive exile and ultimately preserve the traditions recorded in Kings.

This large amount of text is not a history in the conventional sense of the term. It does not take pains to analyze events and trends by means of political, social, and economic analysis. Rather, it is best understood as an attempt, amid the turmoil of rebellions against imperial powers and ongoing tensions within Israelite society, to make emotional sense of traumatic historical experiences. The writers were concerned with fashioning an explanation of why the Northern Kingdom, Israel, fell to Assyria in 722 B.C.E., and why the Southern Kingdom, Judah, followed suit in 587. From beginning to end, the book of Kings consistently expresses the view that faithfulness to Israel's one God and loyalty to the divinely chosen Davidic dynasty in Jerusalem determine the survival and prosperity of the Israelite people. In the eyes of the final editors, it was the betrayal of the *covenant*, God's agreement with Israel, that best accounted for the fates of the two kingdoms.

Structure and Themes

In the simplest analysis, as indicated above, the book of Kings unfolds in three major parts: the reign of Solomon, accounts of northern and southern kings and prophets, and a narration of the last century and a half of the Southern Kingdom's existence. A more detailed look has been most fruitfully explicated by George Savran. He describes a chiastic or ring arrangement, with the important center segment focused on the ninth-century dynasty of Omri and the prophetic careers of Elijah and Elisha. And with Solomon's glory at one end of the book and the fall of his capital Jerusalem at the other, we are naturally led to the conclusion that it is sins such as those attributed to the Omrides—idolatry and oppression of the poor—that ultimately led to the disaster.

Savran's expanded scheme is as follows:

A Solomon/United Monarchy   I Kings 1:1–11:25

    B Jeroboam/Rehoboam; division of the kingdom   I Kings 11:26–14:31

        C Kings of Judah/Israel   I Kings 15:1–16:22

            D Omride dynasty; the rise and fall of Baal   I Kings 16:23–II 12
                 cult in the North/South

        C' Kings of Judah/Israel   II Kings 13–16

    B' Fall of Northern Kingdom   II Kings 17

A' Kingdom of Judah   II Kings 18–25

Overarching this scheme, Kings presents Israel's monarchic history as a pair of related struggles: YHWH versus the Canaanite storm god Baal and prophets versus kings. As I indicated in the General Introduction to this volume, such an approach is a prime example of "history with an attitude." And its formulation is somewhat unusual. Ancient Near Eastern kings typically presented themselves in their royal inscriptions as essentially great conquerors and builders, usually making use of the first person; while our book occasionally contains inscription-like material, especially as regards Solomon, the accounts are always narrated in the third person, by an omniscient narrator, and are generally subordinated to larger issues such as the covenant. So while "Kings" has been a serviceable title for many centuries, a better summation of the book's contents might be "A Prophetic Understanding of Israel's Monarchic Past." While not a very catchy title, it is closer to the nature of the material before us.

Another contribution made by Savran is his discussion of character and moral judgment in Kings. Despite the often stereotyped language found in the book—"X did what was evil in the eyes of YHWH," for example—the text presents characters and makes judgments that are surprisingly subtle and complex. King Ahab, for instance, is understood both as one of the worst kings in Israel's history and as a man capable of genuine regret. This breadth is, in fact, typical of most biblical narratives.

As many scholars have noted, a central theme in Kings can be summed up in the phrase "oracle and fulfillment." The book offers numerous examples of God's intervention in, or control of, history, with the particular twist that events are predicted by prophets. This may include individual acts such as Josiah's tearing down the rival northern altars of Bethel in II Kings 23:15–16, which is fore-told in the dramatic scene in I Kings 13:1–10, or events painted on an even larger canvas—the split of a united kingdom and the ultimate destruction of both north and south. This major theme of prophetic foresight not only informs the reader's understanding of Israel's past, but also forms a bridge to the next quarter of the Bible, the so-called Later Prophets, which is composed largely of poetic books of prophetic oracles, many of which address the same preexilic era that is portrayed in the book of Kings.

There is another theme of note. The book of Kings has been called "a book of two houses" (Knoppers), but it might make more to sense to think in terms of three: (1) the House of Judah, led by the dynasty of David; (2) the House of Israel, centered around Omri's, but actually encompassing multiple dynasties, which change regularly through palace coups and assassinations; and (3) the House of YHWH, the Temple in Jerusalem. The last of these holds particular significance. Not only is the detailed construction of Solomon's Temple the centerpiece of the first quarter of the book, but the building itself is the setting for the discov-ery of the Covenant Document (probably the core or more of Deuteronomy) in II Kings 22, a dramatic and hopeful moment but ultimately the last gasp of an attempt to set things right with Israel's God. In addition, the destruction of the Temple in II Kings 25, while swift and total, is presaged by a number of epi-sodes of the stripping, and occasional restoration, of its treasuries throughout the book:

> I Kings 14: The Egyptian king Shishak invades the country and takes
> Temple treasures
> I Kings 15: King Asa restores the Temple but sends some treasures as
> tribute to the north
> II Kings 12: The Temple is repaired but tribute is also sent to Aram
> II Kings 18: Temple tribute is sent to Assyria
> II Kings 24: The Babylonians invade in 597, and some Temple treasures
> are carried off
> II Kings 25: The Temple is destroyed in 587 by the Babylonians

The instances of invasion, the last two of which occur after ill-advised Judean revolts, along with the earlier examples of bribery and defilement, contribute strongly to an overall sense of decline in the book of Kings. It is not accidental that the first account of Temple stripping occurs around the time of Solomon's failures late in his reign. By the end of the book, the total razing of the Temple does not surprise us; it is as if it has been slowly dismantled along the way, inter-rupted only for occasional, and ultimately futile, repairs, just as Israel and Judah eventually crumble as the result of a broken covenant. That such decline and disaster historically had more to do with the rise of great empires in the ancient Near East is, from the Bible's point of view, rather beside the point (see Wright 2011 for a full discussion of the Temple stripping motif).

THEORIES OF COMPOSITION

GIVEN THE VARIETY OF THE MATERIALS IN KINGS, IT SEEMS CLEAR THAT THE book was compiled from a number of sources. More than any other book in the Early Prophets, multiple voices sound in the background here: pieces of royal chronicles, including works that have been lost, narratives in classical biblical style, and prophetic legends. The book also appears to have gone through at least several revisions. Lemaire is one of many who propose a multistage process of redaction; he theorizes fully seven stages of composition. Sweeney argues for a textual history in which early traditions about Solomon's glory have been combined with accounts of the fall of the House of Omri and the rise of that of Jehu in the north, culminating in primary editions under Hezekiah and Josiah. The last few chapters, with their portrayal of the fall of Jerusalem, would of course have to date from a later time. Much recent research is informed by a European model that sees in the books of Samuel and Kings a separate "History of the Kingdoms" of Israel and Judah; this History is said to have been originally transmitted separately from the "History of the People Israel," narrated in the books of Genesis–Joshua/Judges.

Regardless of the exact sequence, somewhere in the mix is a series of prophetic traditions, sharply focusing on the relationship between divine spokespersons and the throne. The dating and order of all these traditions is open to question. Some critics are convinced that the Solomonic sections are more or less contemporary with their subject, representing the product of a prosperous society, whereas others see it as a much later creation and argue that an actual tenth-century kingdom in Israel would not have had the resources or personnel to create such a sophisticated work.

A widely held scholarly approach, with which I basically agree, takes the position that, along with the Deuteronomistic History as a whole, there was a preexilic edition of Kings in Josiah's time (late seventh century B.C.E.), with possibly one during Hezekiah's reign a century earlier. This work would have served as a cautionary tale, given the destruction of the north, but also as a way to glorify the south, whose capital, Jerusalem, had miraculously survived the Assyrian ravaging of the Israelite countryside c. 701 B.C.E. and was reasserting its culture and its ambitions in the last decades of the seventh century. The present form of Kings, however, takes rather a dimmer view. Once editors added the final chapters, describing Judah's fall, and the ending paragraph about the imprisoned Judean king Jehoiachin's release in Babylon c. 561, the book took on a different, more depressing flavor. If, as many scholars think, a good portion of the biblical text was composed or edited in the Babylonian Exile, there may be good reason for this.

Recent studies (see Smith-Christopher) have sought parallels between twentieth- and twenty-first-century communal traumas and the biblical events of 722 and 587. The past century has witnessed not only numerous cases of devastating war and population displacement but also a good deal of research into these phenomena, using the tools of the social sciences. If we proceed with appropriate caution, we may assert that there are indeed insights to be gained into our texts. Clearly, the destruction of the Northern and Southern Kingdoms and the Babylonian Exile were central events in the life of Israel. In a pivotal article Wright (2009) argues that the Bible as a whole and its notion of a People of Israel owe themselves directly to catastrophic defeats (722 and 587) that resulted in Israel and Judah's loss of territorial sovereignty. More recently, Carr (2010) has called the Hebrew Bible "a Bible for exiles." This is manifested in the many biblical texts—not only portions of the Early Prophets, but also Lamentations, selected Psalms, passages from the prophets, and possibly Job—that express reactions akin to post-traumatic stress disorder. They reflect the need to constantly relive the trauma, as it were; they focus on blaming the Israelite community for its fate; and they at times give rise to feelings of intense nationalism, amid a glorification of the distant past. The Bible thus represents an Israel, or at least an influential group of Israelites responsible for its composition, trying to come to terms with catastrophe.

On the World Stage

KINGS IS SET IN THE TENTH TO SIXTH CENTURIES B.C.E., THE PERIOD THAT archaeologists call Iron Age II. It was an era that witnessed intense cultural and political activity in the ancient Near East, from Phoenicia in the northwest to Aram and Assyria in the northeast, and down to Babylonia and Egypt at each end of the southern regions. From the beginning of Kings, foreign rulers, craftsmen, and armies appear in the text as actors in events that have an impact on biblical civilization. Alliances, trade, hostilities, revolts, invasions, the spreading of languages and literatures throughout the wider region—these and more leave their imprint in the Bible.

More often than not, encounters with other cultures are understood in Kings in one particular way: as a reflection of Israel's behavior vis-à-vis the covenant with its God. Thus, the reader of Kings will encounter many interactions between Israel and its neighbors, but not necessarily for the sake of recounting diplomatic or military history. The great Assyrian Empire, for example, makes its presence felt in the book, but only as a backdrop for the greater divine-human drama the Bible understands to be playing out. The prophet Isaiah, a contemporary of eighth-century kings such as Hezekiah, thus speaks of Assyria as merely "the rod of God's anger" (10:5), not as the dreaded superpower whose expansion sent chills up and down the spines of the inhabitants of the ancient Near East.

At the same time as the Bible downplays the Assyrian and Babylonian civilizations, however, the pressing reality of international events in Iron Age II hovers in the background. I have therefore sought to provide some appropriate historical background in the Commentary to II Kings 15 below, where it will be more useful to the reader than here. The same holds for information about Babylonia, which can be found in the Commentary to II Kings 24. In any event, it seems incontrovertible that much of the Bible was created against the backdrop of these two great civilizations, both incorporating some of their modes of thinking and strongly responding to their claims to supremacy.

KINGS AND CHRONICLES

A NOTABLE FEATURE OF THE MONARCHIC PERIOD IN ISRAEL IS THAT IT IS REPRE-sented in not one but two separate accounts. As we have seen, the book of Kings presents one view of these centuries, but the later book of Chronicles, written perhaps around 400 B.C.E., goes over much of the same ground in vastly different fashion. After two chapters composed of genealogical lists beginning with Adam, the first human, Chronicles reaches King David, dynasty founder and father of Solomon, and stays with him for twenty-seven chapters. Solomon himself is then chronicled for nine more, and the book subsequently brings the history of Israel and Judah down to the destruction of Jerusalem in 587, some twenty-seven chapters later.

In addition to its pacing, Chronicles contains some other unusual features. It displays long lists of Israel's ancestors and names of David's warriors and court officials. It reports conversations and speeches that are not found in Kings. It ends, not with the notice of the long-exiled king of Judah, Jehoiachin, released from prison, but with the proclamation of a decree by Cyrus the Great, the first king of the Persian Empire, in 538 B.C.E., allowing exiled Judeans to return to their home-land. Most significant, Chronicles omits the troubling accounts of King David's sins and decline—the Bathsheba, Tamar, and Absalom narratives which take up a quarter of the book of Samuel.

Chronicles thus constitutes a revisionist history. Although it contains many passages that parallel or even match the wording of Kings, it clearly has its own agenda: to present the reigns of David and Solomon as the central moments in Israel's history and to stress the centrality of the Jerusalem Temple. More than a sweeping look back at the past amid an uncertain future, as in Kings, Chroni-cles longs for a Golden Age and hopes for some kind of restoration. That hope became part and parcel of Judaism, along with the relentlessly self-critical picture painted in Kings.

Scholars have debated whether Chronicles derives from (Samuel-)Kings, or whether they both used a common source. But regardless of origins, both read the past through a distinctive lens, and reveal a nation and culture in transition.

THE CULTURAL INFLUENCE OF KINGS

FOR THE HEIRS OF THE BIBLICAL TEXT—JEWS AND CHRISTIANS IN THE ROMAN period and their successors in the Middle Ages—the book of Kings became a rich source of ideas and imagery. Solomon was elevated even beyond his biblical glory, and numerous legends grew up around him, his city, and his Temple. Elijah was transformed from a powerful prophetic figure into an immortal guide and harbinger of the Messiah. Among the many monarchs mentioned in the book, several became role models at periods of European history (a potent example is the boy king of England, Edward VI [1537–1553], whose destruction of Catholic shrines and statues recalled the Judahite king Josiah's tearing down of pagan altars). Reading the biblical stories, audiences encountered familiar figures, and artists painted them as such, creating kings of Israel and Judah dressed in medieval armor and set against a landscape of rolling green hills and forests. The biblical text's portrayal of warfare, court intrigues, and assassinations, and the irruption of religious demands into the governing of nations, all had a familiar ring to later generations and provided them with a kind of mental script that could be drawn upon as situations arose. It is only in the modern postmonarchic period that the significance of the book for political discourse has faded somewhat, but it still remains compelling.

In the final analysis, the book of Kings, with its multiple voices, its prosaic formulas, its touches of the grandiose and the supernatural, and its ambiguous ending, serves to close out Israel's core story, which began in Genesis, completing what biblicist David Noel Freedman and others have called the "Primary History" in the Hebrew Bible. That what follows it chronologically in books such as Ezra and Nehemiah is somewhat sketchier only affirms that Kings, for the exiles in Babylonia and their successors, was meant to leave a lasting impression as an object lesson in national existence. On some level, ancient Jews took it to heart, as the book's dire warnings, combined with the memorable words of the Later Prophets, served as a springboard for cultural survival and restoration. Ultimately, despite the negativity of the book of Kings, those who transmitted it were able to use its concept of meaning in history to extrapolate a message of hope.

A NOTE ON THE TRANSLATION OF KINGS: I have profited greatly from the outstanding scholarship in Mordechai Cogan's two Anchor Bible volumes of Kings (II, 1985, with Hayim Tadmor, and I, 2001). If, at times, our translations appear similar, it is due to (1) his attention to some of the Buber-Rosenzweig principles, and (2) my acceptance of his philology in a number of cases.

The Kings of Israel in the Book of Kings

The exact chronology of kings in the Bible is not certain. There have been many detailed attempts to square the numbers of southern and northern rulers and fix their dates; these typically deal with such issues as when in a given year a king's reign began. Problems with the overall chronology of the kings have not been fully resolved, but a recent study by Hughes posits that this is due to there being essentially two kinds of chronologies in Kings: an earlier, fairly accurate one, based on existing chronicles, and later editorial reworkings, which may be termed "schematic." The latter, rather than attempting to reconstruct facts, present Israel's history as part of a divine plan, demonstrating through ordered chronology that history is meaningful. This mixture of chronologies reflects the complicated process through which the book came into being.

The chart below is for the reader's reference. Those who would like to pursue the matter further may consult the scholarly literature.

		Kingdom of Judah	Kingdom of Israel
tenth century	Shelomo		
		Rehav'am	Yorov'am
		Aviyyam (Aviyya)	Nadav
c. 900		Asa	Ba'sha
		Yehoshafat	Ela, Zimri
			Omri
			Ah'av
		Yehoram (Yoram)	Ahazyahu
		Ahazyahu (Yehoahaz)	Yehoram (Yoram)
		Atalya (Atalyahu; Queen)	Yehu
c. 800		Yehoash (Yoash)	Yehoahaz
		Amatzyahu (Amatzya)	Yehoash (Yoash)
		Azarya (Azaryahu/Uziyyahu)	Yorov'am II
			Zekharyahu; Shallum
			Menahem
			Pekahya
		Yotam	Pekah
		Ahaz	Hoshe'a
		Hizkiyyahu	

c. 700	Menashe
	Amon
	Yoshiyyahu
	Yehoahaz (Shallum)
	Yehoyakim (Elyakim)
c. 600	Yehoyakhin (Yekhonya)
	Tzidkiyyahu (Mattanya)

PART I

SHELOMO AND HIS KINGDOM

(I 1–11)

IN JEWISH AND CHRISTIAN TRADITION, SHELOMO (SOLOMON) IS A FABULOUS figure. Drawing not only from the Bible but also from the vast wealth of long-transmitted legends and folklore, later interpreters and the faithful masses saw in him the epitome of royal power, wealth, and, especially, wisdom. Volumes of legends were created to extol these virtues and to provide, especially for oppressed communities, a fabled past which they could dream about.

Yet it is not only this morphing of Shelomo in the postbiblical period with which the reader of the book of Kings has to contend. It is the biblical portrayal itself. Typically for ancient accounts of kings, for whom there rarely existed unofficial chronicles, the Bible makes it difficult if not impossible to extract a well-rounded historical personage from the text. Additionally, the very nature of the book of Kings as a composite text presents many difficulties. And its ideological thrust naturally gets in the way of a more "objective" portrait. In the Bible, Shelomo *is* the wisest of all kings, perhaps even of all men; the material splendor he creates and amid which he reigns is unparalleled; he is ruthless, appropriately for antiquity, but pious; and he erects the most celebrated and glorious of temples.

Despite the hyperbole, however, the writers of Kings have given us a picture that is at the same time somewhat balanced—perhaps not as much that of David, but evenhanded in its own way. In the spirit of Deuteronomistic writing, even this wisest of kings falters at the end, when it comes to women and idolatry. Magnifying the "good old days," whether real or imagined, does not blind the final compiler to a larger view of the monarchic period, and in his eyes, Shelomo, as much as any of his successors, bears royal responsibility for the eventual downfall of Israel. Even amid such demonstrations as the dazzling display put on for the benefit of the Queen of Sheba, we are reminded that an Israelite king's primary responsibility is to uphold the covenant with God. When Shelomo does this, in the earlier chapters of the book, he is praised beyond measure, but as soon as he neglects his covenantal role by worshipping gods other than YHWH, the result of his marrying foreign princesses, his kingdom is "torn apart." Ominously, this is the very verb that had been used to describe Sha'ul's losing the crown in I Sam. 15.

The reader would do well to bear in mind that Shelomo is more than simply the first fully described monarch in the book of Kings. Not only is he the son of the all-important David, but the account of his reign occupies over a quarter of the textual space of the book. So the Deuteronomistic editor(s) saw in his story a paradigm for those to come later and a reflection of both sides of kingship, the glorious and the regrettable.

Concrete historical evidence is hard to come by regarding the tenth century B.C.E., when Shelomo is portrayed as having lived. Those who seek a solidly historical figure have long pointed to the remains of three great gates at Hazor, Gezer, and Megiddo, indications of a relatively large population, and therefore an appropriately organized bureaucracy, in Israel, and to other aspects of the biblical account—expanded borders, reports of international trade, and descriptions of the trappings of a great court—to make their case. At the other end of the spectrum, those who deny Shelomo's historicity, whether completely or only partially, point to the difficulties of analyzing the textual and material evidence we have. Amid the general decline of Mediterranean civilizations during this time, shared also by the Near East, there is a scarcity of literary remains. The perishable nature of papyrus and parchment, which, regrettably, the Israelites tended to use rather than stone or clay, has probably rendered the possibility of discovering a written Solomonic text forever moot. At the same time, there is still some disagreement as to whether the massive building projects attributed to Shelomo belong in his century or slightly later. In any event, both the skeptics and the outright deniers see in the opening sections of Kings a projection of later generations' own concerns and fantasies back upon an earlier time, with little reflection of an authentic tenth-century history.

A possible breakthrough in the debate has recently occurred with the unearthing of a fairly sophisticated wall in the area of the Ophel in Jerusalem. This location, just above David's city and south of the present Old City, corresponds to where Shelomo would have built, and some preliminary reports date the site to the tenth century. Whether the identification holds up, or more will be found, remains to be seen; but it is unlikely at this point that an archaeologist will discover the basement of the First Temple, or the dining room of Shelomo's palace. And even digging at the presumed site of these buildings on the Temple Mount is so fraught with political explosiveness at present and into the foreseeable future that, should it ever occur, archaeology's gain would surely be drowned in violence between Arabs and Israelis.

We are therefore limited to our text. Like the book in which the account of Shelomo is embedded, our section in its present form, Chaps. 1–11, is arranged in a chiastic, ring arrangement. The king's youthful accession and elderly misbehavior sit at the outer ends, with his wisdom and wealth further in, but it is finally his crowning achievement—the building of the Temple—that is solidly placed at the all-important center. That is what the biblical writers, or at least editors, wanted to emphasize.

ON THE TEMPLE

DESPITE THE ABSENCE OF MATERIAL REMAINS, THE FAMOUS STRUCTURE WHICH the Bible attributes to Shelomo, known traditionally as Solomon's Temple or the First Temple, is of central importance in the book of Kings and in Israelite thought, both before and after the destruction of Jerusalem in 587 B.C.E. As encountered in I Kings 6–8 and elsewhere, the Temple had three main functions: *religious,* as a means for obtaining forgiveness and atonement from YHWH; *political,* as a visible symbol of Shelomo's grandeur; and *ideological,* as a locus for the important triad of God, king, and city.

The purely religious aspect of the Temple is an echo of the extended description of the Dwelling (or Tabernacle) and its attendant sacrificial cult in the central sections of the Torah, Exod. 25–Num. 10 and beyond. (See "On Animal Sacrifice" in my *The Five Books of Moses.*) As was the case with the earlier sanctuary, the symmetry of the Temple structure is significant, pointing to the perfection of God through its use of balanced measurements. The basic scheme of the Temple is also identical to that of the Dwelling: a large rectangle divided into two squares, with the innermost one being the "Holiest Holy-Place" or Shrine, housing either the Coffer (Ark) or later, apparently, nothing at all, in contrast to the divine statuary of surrounding cultures. The Temple's sacrificial system and priestly hierarchy also mirror the symbolism and function of the wilderness shrine. Our text contains a long prayer uttered by the king (I Kings 8), in which the rationale for the Temple's existence is spelled out. Even though much of this chapter may have been written considerably later, it does function to set the Temple apart from the Dwelling on a rhetorical level.

The key element in the Temple's religious function is Israel's relationship to its God through animal and grain sacrifice, with accompanying prayers. If not offered properly, or in their absence, the immediate result is understood to be the critical loss of communication between the human and divine. One can thus grasp the terrible despair experienced by the Israelites in the sixth-century B.C.E. Babylonian Exile, well expressed in books such as Lamentations, in which the community bewailed the loss of the Temple, seen as a chief means of contact with God.

The reader of these chapters in Kings will not fail to note the very large dimensions and sizes of the objects described. The two great columns flanking the entrance to the Temple, for instance, are portrayed as being over thirty feet tall; the winged-sphinx throne in the inner sanctum would have been fifteen feet in height. This reflects a well-known tendency in ancient societies to construct the earthly abode of the gods as befitting their power; famously, a pagan temple unearthed in 1976 at 'Ain Dara in Syria has a giant footprint, presumably belonging to the goddess Ishtar, in front of the portal.

Politically, Kings sets both the initial description of the building process and the Temple structure itself in the context of Shelomo's wealth and accomplishments. Just as his table is sumptuous, his provisions massive, his borders expansive, his bureaucrats numerous, his wisdom world-famous, and his overall building plans ambitious, so too his Temple is portrayed as memorable on all counts. Prized cedar wood has to be imported in great quantities from Lebanon; the structure is inlaid with gold throughout; and all Israel is impressed into building service, with crucial agricultural manpower being depleted in order to fuel the building project. Thus, as with kings in all societies, ancient and medieval, the expense and magnificence of a religious building also function as a symbol of royal power.

Perhaps most important in the larger ancient Near Eastern context is the Temple's anchoring function as a great ideological symbol of the bond among deity, dynasty, and capital city. The Temple makes the royal house and Jerusalem inseparable in their confirmation by YHWH. As Levenson (1987) has shown, the Temple Mount (Tziyyon/Zion) comes to substitute totally for Mount Sinai, where YHWH had come down in fire to speak to the Israelites and give them his laws. In other words, the city on a hill now takes the place of the sacred mountain of revelation, and the king in some sense takes the place of Moshe (alternatively, he serves as the earthly representative of the divine king). In smiling upon David's dynasty, located in Jerusalem, the city of the "House of YHWH," God re-creates the idealized situation portrayed at Sinai. There, receiving and keeping the covenant was to protect the Israelites in their wanderings; here, the existence and functioning of the Temple is to preserve them in their land, betokening divine protection from hostile neighbors and assurance of material prosperity.

Physically, the Temple as described in Kings would have been larger than any other contemporary building in the ancient Near East. Its size, combined with its central and elevated location in Jerusalem, must have given strong support to the idea that YHWH was overseeing the king and the people and allowing his presence to dwell among them. This certainly would have strengthened the existing institutions of monarchy and priesthood, both of which were understood to uphold the stability of society, and assured their own power in the political realm. A similar arrangement prevailed all over the ancient Near East.

With all the emphasis on the Temple as a potent, multifaceted symbol, some caution should be exercised as to its place in the hearts of average Israelites in the monarchic period. Some scholars have theorized that the Temple may have been quite secondary to these folk, focused as they were on the hardships of everyday existence on the not always fertile soil of Israel. Its version of the sacrificial cult may also not have been exactly what was done at local shrines, which, as the book of Kings and prophetic texts demonstrate, played an equally if not more significant role in daily life. Kings does not portray a centralized cult until the days of Hizkiyyahu's reform in the late eighth century, and the Northern Kingdom's appropriation of the Temple's function in new sanctuaries at Dan and Bet-El, after Shelomo's death, gives strong evidence of varied local traditions, identified in the Bible as pagan or at the very least syncretistic (combining gods from different systems). A stronger sense of common purpose probably obtained after the exiles returned from Babylonian Exile and rebuilt the Temple on a more modest scale, at the end of the sixth century. It was subsequently expanded into its more renowned form by Herod the Great in the late first century B.C.E. It is this "Second" Temple to which later, nascent Judaism and Christianity most readily related, especially after its destruction by the Romans in 70 C.E.

The detailed description of the construction of the Temple in I Kings 6–7 has proved somewhat of a puzzle to interpreters, including modern scholars. For traditionalists, it is an exact blueprint, with final details to be filled in by ancient and medieval authorities. However, many of the technical terms used in the text are no longer clear, and it is difficult to come up with any kind of exact rendering. Over the centuries, artists have striven to portray the Temple, but more often than not they have created it in the architectural image of their own era. More fruitfully, other interpreters have focused on what are taken to be symbolic aspects of the structure and its appurtenances, noting, for instance, that the molten "sea" of I Kings 7:23–26 is not only a giant basin for the priests' washing but may also be a representation of primeval cosmic waters, appropriate in a House of God. Others have connected such varied information as the conspicuous floral decorations, the winged-sphinxes on the Coffer (Ark), and the Gihon spring near Jerusalem to the appearance of these in the Garden of Eden story of Gen. 2–3, thus suggesting that the Temple recalls the "perfect" world before the expulsion of the First Parents.

Recent help in conceptualizing the Temple physically comes from archaeology. Several sites excavated in Syria have uncovered structures which, while considerably smaller, conform to the basic features of the biblical Temple. Dever (2001) has listed the similarities, which include a three-part, successive floor plan, so-called dressed stones, alternating courses of stone and wood (to provide extra earthquake protection), decorations such as lions, "cherubs," and pomegranates, and decorated braziers for providing light. These are but a few of the common features. Dever thus understands the Solomonic structure as strongly akin to regional Bronze and Iron Age temples, making it highly unlikely that it was "invented" in the fantasy of much later (i.e., Hellenistic) writers who, some have asserted, were seeking to restore Israel's lost glory.

But the Temple and its builder, as presented in the opening section of Kings, transcend whatever mundane realities may have existed in tenth-century Israel. The book has fixed them forever as potent symbols of a Golden Age, and, as such, they have fired the imagination of Jews and Christians for millennia.

Chapter 1. *Shelomo as Heir to the Throne:* Although many commentators such as Alter (1999) see Chaps. 1 and 2 as a continuation of the "Succession Narrative" that began in II Sam. 11, and thus as the natural conclusion to the David story, one could equally argue that these chapters have a life of their own. As the book of Kings opens, they form the beginning of the account of Shelomo's accession to the throne. Their link to what has gone before fits the pattern of "overlapping structures" that I noted in the General Introduction, but these chapters also have their own vocabulary and point of view.

In Chap. 1, several repeating phrases point the reader/hearer toward the central themes: "sit/seated on the/my throne" and "after" (denoting succeeding one's father as king, used similarly in Samuel). "Bowed low" graphically highlights both court etiquette and the desperate situation of Natan and Bat-Sheva advocating for Shelomo, who is not the firstborn, and also, at chapter's end, for reducing the status of the ambitious heir to the throne, Adoniyyahu. Above all, the repetition of the word "know," beginning with David's impotence in v.2, suggests that, while David may not be fully aware of what is going on around him, *we* surely are: Shelomo, and no other, will be the next king.

The older principals in the chapter are especially fascinating to watch. David is obviously a shadow of his former self, unable to navigate very well either sexually or politically; Walsh points out that there are no active verbs that accompany his name in this chapter. But when the time comes, he is able to summon some strength of will, and at least nominally ensure that Shelomo will be "firmly-established." We have not encountered either the prophet Natan or David's great love Bat-Sheva since the moral catastrophe of II Sam. 11–12, but both play key roles here in engineering Shelomo's ascent to power. Their interplay around persuading the king is a kind of strategic dance.

In general, the story laid out in Chap. 1 is a replaying of the national split that was in evidence already during Sha'ul's (Saul's) succession, as well as later in Avshalom's (Absalom's) revolt. These conflicts are a constant reminder of what will become an essential fact of life in the book of Kings, the great schism between the kingdoms of Israel and Judah.

◆   1:1   Now King David was old, advanced in days,
and they covered him with garments, but he could not get warm.

2   So his servants said to him:
Let them seek for my lord king a nubile girl,
that she may stand [in waiting] before the king
and be a caregiver for him;
she will lie in your bosom, and my lord king will be warm.

3   So they sought out a beautiful girl throughout all the territory of
Israel,
and they found Avishag the Shunammite
and brought her to the king.

4   Now the girl was beautiful, exceedingly so;
she became a caregiver for the king, and attended him,
but the king did not know her.

5   Meanwhile, Adoniyya son of Haggit was exalting himself, saying:
I will be king!
And he provided himself with chariotry and steeds,
with fifty men running ahead of him.

6   Now his father had never scolded him in [all] his days, saying:
For-what-reason did you do thus?
And he was also exceedingly goodly in form;
it was he to whom she gave birth after Avshalom.

7   Now his [private] words were with Yoav son of Tzeruya, and with
Evyatar the priest;
they provided help [to follow] after Adoniyya,

1:1   **David:** Pronounced *dah-VEED*.   **advanced in days:**
A usual biblical expression for old age. Heb. *yamim*
can sometimes mean "years."

2   **nubile:** Heb. *betula*, usually translated "virgin,"
means mainly one who has passed puberty, a marriageable young woman.   **caregiver:** Heb. *sokhenet;*
the masculine version appears in Isa. 22:15, as an old
term for "steward of the household."

3   **Avishag:** Pronounced *ah-vee-SHAHG;* trad. English
"Abishag."   **Shunammite:** From the town of Shu-
nem, near the Jezreel Valley in the north. It reso-
nates with the beginning of David's rule, since the
Philistines pitched camp there before the battle of
Mount Gilboa, where Sha'ul was killed.

4   **know her:** The Hebrew verb *y-d-'* most often indicates awareness or knowledge, but can also, as here,
be extended to include intimate, "biblical" knowledge: sexual relations.

5   **Adoniyya:** Pronounced *ah-do-nee-YAH;* trad. English "Adonijah." "YHWH Is My Lord" is an ironically pious name for David's son who will not get to
rule. The name sometimes appears in fuller form,
"Adoniyyahu."

6   **And he was also:** He is spoiled and handsome like
Avshalom (Absalom) his older brother.   **goodly:**
The good looks apparently run in the family,
but are no guarantee against disaster.   **it was
he to whom . . . :** The Hebrew is a bit strange
here.   **Avshalom:** Pronounced *ahv-shah-LOHM;*
trad. English "Absalom."

7   **Yoav:** Pronounced *yo-AHV;* trad. English "Joab." He
is David's fanatically loyal general.   **Tzeruya:** Trad.
English "Zeruiah."   **Evyatar:** Trad. English "Abiathar."   **provided help:** Supported his claim to the
throne.

8 while Tzadok the priest and Benayahu son of Yehoyada and Natan
   the prophet and Shim'i and Re'i and the mighty-men who
   belonged to David
were not with Adoniyyahu.

9 And Adoniyyahu sacrificed sheep and oxen and fatlings
   beside Even Ha-Zohelet / The Serpent Stone that is near En-Rogel,
   and he invited all his brothers, the king's sons,
   and all the men of Judah, the king's court-servants,

10 but Natan the prophet and Benayahu and the mighty-men and
    Shelomo his brother he did not invite.

11 So Natan said to Bat-Sheva mother of Shelomo, saying:
Have you not heard that Adoniyyahu son of Haggit has become
   king,
while our lord David does not know?

12 So-now,
go, pray let me advise you with some advice:
save your life and the life of your son Shelomo!

13 Come, go to King David and say to him:
Did not you yourself, my lord king, swear to your handmaid,
   saying:
Indeed, Shelomo your son will reign as king after me,
he will sit on my throne?
So for-what-reason has Adoniyyahu become king?

14 Here,
[while] you are still speaking there with the king,
I myself will come in after you
and will confirm your words.

---

8 **Tzadok:** Trad. English "Zadok." **Benayahu:** Trad. English "Benaiah." **Yehoyada:** Pronounced ye-ho-yah-DAH, with the meaning, central to the story, of "Yhwh Knows." Trad. English "Jehoiada." **Natan:** Pronounced nah-TAHN; trad. English "Nathan." He is David's influential court prophet (see II Sam. 7, 12). **Shim'i:** Pronounced shim-EE; trad. English "Shimei." He had cursed David in the Avshalom narrative (II Sam. 16), but thus far, David has spared him. **Re'i:** LXX reads *"re'av,"* "his friends."

9 **Serpent Stone:** Others, "the stone of Zoheleth," "the sliding stone." **En-Rogel:** Pronounced ayn ro-GAYL. The "Washer's [or Fuller's] Spring" in the Kidron Valley near Jerusalem, marking the boundary line between the territories of Benjamin and

Judah. It figured previously in the spy story of II Sam. 17. **invited:** Literally, "called."

10 **Shelomo:** Trad. English "Solomon." The accent is on the last syllable.

11 **Bat-Sheva:** Pronounced baht-SHEH-vah; trad. English "Bathsheba." David's beloved wife. The *Sheva* part of her name puns with the Hebrew word for "swear [an oath]," a theme in this chapter (Walsh).

13 **my lord king . . . Adoniyyahu become king:** Heb. adoni ha-melekh . . . malakh adoniyyahu, a wordplay that is another indication of the narrator's "mastery of intonation" (Fishbane). **your handmaid:** An appropriate way for Bat-Sheva to refer to herself in court etiquette.

14 **confirm:** Or literally "fill in" (Alter 1999).

◆ 15 So Bat-Sheva came to the king, into the [inner] room
—now the king was exceedingly old, and Avishag the Shunammite
was attending the king—

16 and Bat-Sheva prostrated herself, and bowed low to the king,
and the king said: What is your [business]?

17 She said to him:
My lord, you yourself swore by Y‌HWH your God to your handmaid:
indeed, Shelomo your son will reign as king after me,
he will sit on my throne!

18 But now,
here, Adoniyyahu has become king,
yet you, my lord king, you do not know!

19 He sacrificed oxen and fatlings and sheep in abundance,
and invited all the king's sons, and Evyatar the priest,
and Yoav Commander of the Armed-Forces,
but Shelomo your servant he did not invite.

20 As for you, my lord king, the eyes of all Israel are upon you,
to tell them who will sit on the throne of my lord king after him!

21 Else it will be,
when my lord king lies beside his fathers,
that I and my son Shelomo will be guilty ones!

22 Now here, while she was still speaking with the king,
Natan the prophet came,

23 and they told the king, saying:
Here is Natan the prophet!
He came before the king and bowed low to the king, on his nostrils
to the earth,

24 and Natan said: My lord king,
you must have said: Adoniyyahu will reign as king after me,
he will sit on my throne!—

25 for he went down today
and sacrificed oxen and fatlings and sheep in abundance,

16 **What is your [business]?:** The Heb. *ma-lakh* may be a pun on *malokh,* "reign as king" (Walsh).
17 **Y‌HWH:** As explained above in "On Using This Book," the name of God in the Hebrew Bible, whose pronunciation is not precisely known, is traditionally transcribed as "the Lord" and the like. Here it is printed according to the way it appears in the Hebrew text, and the reader may choose how to say it (for example, "The Eternal," *"Adonai"*).
21 **lies beside his fathers:** Indicating a peaceful death. **guilty ones:** Others, "offenders," "criminals."

and invited all the king's sons and army commanders and Evyatar
   the priest—
now here, they are eating and drinking before him,
and they said: May King Adoniyyahu live!
26 But as for me, myself your servant
   and Tzadok the priest and Benayahu son of Yehoyada and Shelomo
      your servant he did not invite.
27 Is it from my lord king that this matter has come,
   while you have not made known to your servant
   who will sit on my lord's throne after him?
28 King David answered and said:
   Call Bat-Sheva to me!
   She came before the king and stood before the king,
29 and the king swore and said:
   By the life of YHWH, who has redeemed my life from every trouble:
30 indeed, as I swore to you by YHWH, the God of Israel, saying:
   indeed, Shelomo your son will be king after me,
   he will sit on my throne in my place—
   indeed, thus will I do this very day!
31 And Bat-Sheva prostrated herself, nostrils to the earth, and bowed
      low to the king,
   and said:
   May my lord King David live, forever!
32 King David said:
   Call to me Tzadok the priest and Natan the prophet and Benayahu
      son of Yehoyada!
   They came before the king.
33 And the king said to them:
   Take your lord's servants with you
   and have Shelomo my son mount the mule that belongs to me,
   and bring him down to the Gihon;

30 **after me . . . in my place:** Heb. *aharai . . . tahtai.* The two parallel words provide a poetic rhythm, hinting at the importance of the thought (Walsh).
33 **mule:** The animal of choice for royal riders.   **the Gihon:** Pronounced *gee-HOHN,* "The Gusher," the important spring just outside of Jerusalem, not far from En-Rogel. Friedman (1999) notes that a similarly named river is found in the Garden of Eden story (Gen. 2:13), and thus posits that an "original core" of the first half of the Bible was bracketed by occurrences of this name.

34 Tzadok the priest is to anoint him there, along with Natan the
prophet,
as king over Israel.
Then you are to sound-a-blast on the *shofar*
and are to say: May King Shelomo live!

35 You are to go up after him,
and he is to come in and sit on my throne;
he will be king in my place,
him I have charged to be *Nagid* over Israel and over Judah!

36 And Benayahu son of Yehoyada answered the king and said: Amen!
So may YHWH, the God of my lord king, declare!

37 As YHWH has been with my lord king,
so may he be with Shelomo,
and he may make his throne greater than the throne of my lord
King David!

38 So he went down, Tzadok the priest, with Natan the prophet and
Benayahu son of Yehoyada,
and the Kereitites and the Peleitites;
they had Shelomo mount the mule of King David
and brought him to the Gihon.

39 Then Tzadok the priest took a horn of oil from the Tent
and anointed Shelomo,
and they sounded-a-blast on the *shofar;*
and all the people said:
May King Shelomo live!

40 And all the people went up after him;
the people were piping on pipes and rejoicing with great joy,
so that the earth split at their sound.

34 *shofar:* The ram's horn, sounded to summon people for military, official, or religious occasions. **May King Shelomo live!:** The Hebrew idiom for "Long live King Shelomo!"

35 *Nagid:* Pronounced *nah-GEED,* this is a term possibly indicating dynastic choice, but not identical with "king." Others, "prince, designate."

36 **Amen!:** From a verb meaning "to trust, to be certain," it is pronounced *ah-MAYN* in Hebrew. Later, of course, it enters prayer texts, even in English. **declare:** Or "say." Some ancient manuscripts have "do."

38 **the Kereitites and the Peleitites:** David's personal bodyguard, made up, it appears, of mercenaries from Crete and Philistia, although the latter identification is not certain.

39 **Tent:** Probably the "Tent of Appointment," the pre-Temple shrine, described in detail in the book of Exodus.

40 **pipes:** Or "flutes." The Hebrew word (sing. *halil*) is onomatopoetic, and comes from a root meaning "hollow."

Chapter 2. *Settling Scores, Securing the Throne:* For a brief moment—the first part of this chapter—the old David returns, although he is not the hero and Psalmist beloved by tradition or the chastened monarch with which the book of Samuel ended. It is the canny and ruthless politician who makes his appearance here. His opening words to his son (vv.2–4) use classic Deuteronomistic language ("be strong," "keep the keeping of YHWH," "the teaching," "prosper," "with all their heart/being"), and are seen by many as a passage inserted later to soften what follows. For David proceeds to use the word "know," which appeared in Chap. 1, as a prelude to political assassination. Even Yoav, David's trusted but violent commander in chief, is not to be spared, for the new king must settle scores and begin afresh. That this advice and behavior sound like those of a Mafia don should not surprise us, given the violent period in which they are set and the literature, succeeding the books of Judges and Samuel, in which they appear. In the end, in contrast to his victims, David simply "lay beside his fathers" (v.10)—but this description is rather pale compared to the deaths of patriarchs (Avraham) and prophets (Moshe), figures with whom one might expect David to be grouped. There is, notably, no public mourning mentioned; thus ends the life of Israel's greatest king and the measuring rod for all the Judean kings to come. In essence, the cheering we witnessed in I Sam. 18:7 has stopped. The only truly positive note in this chapter is that the dynasty will continue.

David's successor Shelomo now sheds his passive image from Chap. 1 and emerges as a powerful force on his own. His brother Adoniyyahu, who had expected to be king and had been acting accordingly, finds himself at a disadvantage, but instead of cleverly countering the palace intrigue, he walks into a trap of his own making. In a move reminiscent of a previous usurper, Avshalom, he seeks to sleep with a royal concubine, a move which in the Bible is less of purely sexual import and more an indication that a son seeks to replace his father in power.

In the subsequent action, Bat-Sheva once again appears, and, as Walsh notes, we may wonder about her motivations in interceding for Adoniyyahu. Is she trying to bring about reconciliation between the brothers, or is she, like the audience, fully aware of how Shelomo will react to his brother's request?

Shelomo's rule is "firmly-established" at both the beginning (v.12) and end (v.46) of this sequence, but it is disturbing that in the middle, such extreme violence has to take place. Like the stereotyped violence of assassination in Samuel (four uses of the rare word "abdomen" to specify where the victims are stabbed), the murders here are described by means of a single verb, "attack." Another key word provides one answer to the troubling question of whether the killing is justified: the bloodguilt and other crimes of Yoav and Shim'i "*return* [on their heads]" (vv.33 and 44; italics mine). And Adoniyyahu's death as well is a kind of payback for his acts of usurpation. So by the end of the chapter all the loose ends have been tied up, albeit that the new king, whose name suggests "peace,"

41 Adoniyyahu heard it, and all those invited who were with him
   —now they had just finished eating—
   and [when] Yoav heard the sound of the *shofar,*
   he said:
   For-what-reason is the sound of the city [one of] panic?

42 He was still speaking,
   when here: Yonatan son of Evyatar the priest came.
   Adoniyyahu said: Come in!
   For you are a man of valor,
   and you bring good news.

43 Yonatan spoke up and said to Adoniyyahu:
   But—our lord King David has made Shelomo king!

44 The king sent with him Tzadok the priest and Natan the prophet
      and Benayahu son of Yehoyada,
   and the Kereitites and the Peleitites,
   and they had him mount the king's mule,

45 and Tzadok the priest and Natan the prophet anointed him as king
      at the Gihon;
   they went up from there rejoicing,
   and the city was [as in a] panic!
   That is the sound that you heard.

46 And even more, Shelomo is seated on the throne of the kingdom,

47 and even more, the king's servants have come to bless our lord King
      David, saying:
   May your God make Shelomo's name better than your name,
   may he make his throne greater than your throne!
   And the king bowed low on the couch.

48 And even more, thus did the king say:
   Blessed is Yhwh, the God of Israel,
   who has given [one] today to sit on my throne, and my eyes see it!

49 Then they trembled and arose, all those invited who were for
      Adoniyyahu,
   and each one went on his way.

---

41 **city:** The word used here (*kirya*) is more frequently found in poetry.

42 **Yonatan:** Trad. English "Jonathan," not to be confused with the prince who dies at the end of I Samuel. **valor:** Or "character," "caliber." It can at times mean something closer to "value," i.e., wealth. **you bring good news:** Like David in II Sam. 18, where similar wording appears, his son Adoniyyahu will be disappointed and devastated by the news he hears (Alter 1999).

has achieved it through the usual and not very peaceful methods practiced by kings.

A nonviolent resolution of conflicts does occur in vv.26–27, where the last of the line of Eli the priest (see the opening chapters of Samuel) is relieved of a future priestly role. Thus the text has God's word in history fulfilled, beginning a major pattern in the book of Kings.

50 And Adoniyyahu was in fear before Shelomo,
so he arose and went and took hold of the horns of the sacrificial-
altar.

51 And it was told to Shelomo, saying:
Here, Adoniyyahu is in fear of King Shelomo,
and here, he has taken hold of the horns of the altar, saying:
Let King Shelomo swear to me this [very] day that he will not put
his servant to death by the sword!

52 So Shelomo said:
If he behaves like a valiant one,
not a hair of his will fall to the ground;
but if any evil be found in him, then he shall die!

53 King Shelomo sent, and they brought him down from the altar;
he came and bowed low to King Shelomo,
and Shelomo said to him:
Go back to your house!

2:1 Now David's days drew near to die,
so he charged Shelomo his son, saying:

2 I am about to go the way of all the earth.
You are to be strong, and be a man!

3 You are to keep the keeping of Yhwh your God,
walking in his ways, keeping his laws, his commandments, his
rules, and his testimonies,
as it is written in the Instruction of Moshe,
in order that you may cause to prosper all that you do
and wherever you face,

4 in order that Yhwh may fulfill his word that he spoke to me, saying:
If your sons will guard their way,
walking in my presence in truth,
with all their heart and with all their being,
no one will [ever] be cut off from you from the throne of Israel.

---

50 **took hold of the horns:** Biblical altars had projections at their four corners; as sacrificial blood was sprinkled there, they were considered the holiest part of the altar and thus were seized when people sought asylum (Walsh).

51 **King Shelomo:** Used four times in three verses, the phrase reveals Adoniyyahu's new point of view (Walsh).

52 **if any evil . . . :** Or "if he is caught in any wrongdoing" (Cogan 2001).

2:1 **David's days drew . . . die:** The Hebrew is not alliterative.

2 **the way of all the earth:** A euphemism for death.

3–4 **You are to keep the keeping . . . :** Probably a Deuteronomistic insertion into the text, which sounds a pious note at an otherwise bloodcurdling moment. "Keep the keeping" is a standard expression for holding to the covenant.

4 **in my presence:** Or "before my face."

5 Now even more, you yourself know what Yoav son of Tzeruya did
       to me,
   what he did to the two commanders of the armed-forces of Israel,
   to Avner son of Ner and to Amasa son of Yeter—he killed them,
   and he brought the blood of war into peacetime:
   he put the blood of war on his belt that is on his loins and on his
       sandal that is on his feet.
6 So you are to act according to your worldly-wisdom:
   you must not let his gray-hair go down in peace to Sheol!
7 But to the sons of Barzillai the Gil'adite you are to show loyalty;
   they should be among those eating at your table,
   for thus they came near to me [in friendship] when I ran away from
       Avshalom your brother.
8 And here, with you is Shim'i son of Gera, the Binyaminite from
       Bahurim:
   he cursed me with a grievous curse on the day of my going to
       Mahanayim.
   But when *he* went down to meet me at the Jordan,
   I swore to him by YHWH, saying:
   If I should put you to death by the sword . . . !
9 But now, do not hold him clear,
   for you are a worldly-wise man:
   you know what you must do to him,
   so that you bring down his gray-hair in blood to Sheol!
10 And David lay beside his fathers,
   and was buried in the City of David.

5 **Avner . . . Amasa:** Pronounced *ahv-NAYR* and *ah-mah-SAH;* David's perceived enemies, allied to Sha'ul. They are both killed by being stabbed in the abdomen (II Sam. 3, 20). **brought the blood of war into peacetime:** Hebrew difficult; perhaps it means "shedding blood outside the context of battle." **belt:** Recalling Yoav's most recent murder, that of Amasa.
6 **worldly-wisdom:** In the Hebrew Bible, "wisdom" is most often practical, not intellectual, and so can include political shrewdness, as here. **Sheol:** The underworld, as a little-defined place of repose—a concept similar to that of the Greek Hades, and

distinct from later Western notions of Heaven and Hell.
7 **Barzillai:** "Iron One," David's aged and loyal friend, who supported him during Avshalom's revolt (II Sam. 17:27–29). **came near to me [in friendship]:** Or "stood by me" (Sweeney 2007).
8 **If I should put . . . :** This form of declaration is common in biblical oaths, and has the force of "If so, may I be cursed."
9 **clear:** I.e., guiltless. **in blood:** Alter (1999) notes Shim'i's curse hurled at David in II Sam. 16:7 ("blood-guilty man . . . !").

11 Now the days that David reigned as king over Israel were forty
    years:
  in Hevron he reigned as king for seven years, while in Jerusalem he
    reigned as king for thirty-three years.

12 And Shelomo sat on the throne of David his father,
  and his kingdom was exceedingly firmly-established.

13 Adoniyyahu son of Haggit came to Bat-Sheva mother of Shelomo.
  She said:
  Is your coming in peace?
  He said:
  In peace.

14 And he said:
  I have a word for you.
  She said: Speak!

15 He said:
  You yourself know that mine was the kingdom,
  and that toward me all Israel had set their faces to be king.
  But the kingdom has been reversed and has become my brother's,
  since it was from YHWH that it became his.

16 So-now,
  there is one request that I request of you—
  do not turn away my face!
  She said to him: Speak!

17 He said:
  Pray talk to Shelomo the king
  —for he will not turn away your face—
  that he may give me Avishag the Shunammite as a wife.

18 Bat-Sheva said: Very well,
  I myself will speak regarding you to the king.

---

11 **forty . . . seven . . . thirty-three:** Such patterned numbers do not attempt to portray chronology accurately. The message that significant figures lived or reigned for "perfect" lengths of time (40, 70, 120 years) was perhaps more important to the audience than historical accuracy; nevertheless, such numbers were taken as factual by generations of readers. **Hevron:** Pronounced *hev-ROHN;* trad. English "Hebron."

13 **in peace:** Or "friendly."
15 **reversed:** The Hebrew verb *s-b-b* is used several times in these books to indicate a change of leadership (Machinist 1995). **from YHWH:** Intended by God.
16 **turn away my face:** Refuse me.

19 So Bat-Sheva came to King Shelomo, to speak to him regarding
    Adoniyyahu.
    And the king arose to meet her, and bowed low to her;
    then he sat down on his throne,
    and he prepared a throne for the king's mother, and she sat down at
      his right.
20 She said:
    There is one small request that I request of you;
    do not turn away my face.
    The king said to her:
    Make request, mother,
    for I will not turn away your face.
21 She said:
    Let Avishag the Shunammite be given to Adoniyyahu your brother
      as a wife.
22 King Shelomo answered and said to his mother:
    Now why are you requesting Avishag the Shunammite for
      Adoniyyahu?
    Request the kingdom [itself] for him,
    for he is my brother, the one older than I!
    —for him and for Evyatar the priest and for Yoav son of Tzeruya!
23 And King Shelomo swore by Yhwh, saying:
    Thus may God do to me, and thus may he add:
    indeed, at [the cost of] his life has Adoniyyahu spoken this word!
24 So-now, Yhwh, who has established-me-firmly and seated me on
      the throne of David my father,
    and who has made me a [dynastic] house, as he promised:
    indeed, today Adoniyyahu will be put to death!
25 So King Shelomo sent by the hand of Benayahu son of Yehoyada;
    he attacked him, so that he died.

---

20 **small:** Given the political implications of this request, it is not so small.

22 **for him . . . for Evyatar . . . for Yoav:** They will get the kingdom as well. The awkward phrasing here perhaps reflects Shelomo's emotions (Walsh).

24 **today:** A theme word in these chapters. "Adonijah's todays have run out" (Walsh).

25 **attacked:** The verb (Heb. *p-g-'*) is used four times in this chapter (parallel perhaps to the four occasions in Samuel when David's enemies are stabbed in the abdomen). It often means "come upon," but can also connote violence. Older translations use "smite," which I rejected as unnecessarily archaic.

26 Now to Evyatar the priest, the king said:
To Anatot, go to your fields!
For you are a man [deserving] of death,
but on this day I will not put you to death,
since you carried the Coffer of Yhwh before my father David,
and since you suffered all that my father suffered.

27 So Shelomo drove out Evyatar from being priest to Yhwh,
so as to fulfill the word of Yhwh that he had spoken regarding the
House of Eli at Shilo.

28 Now the report came to Yoav
—since Yoav had inclined after Adoniyya, though after Avshalom
he had not inclined—
and Yoav fled to the Tent of Yhwh and took hold of the horns of
the altar.

29 King Shelomo was told that Yoav had fled to the Tent of Yhwh,
and here: he was next to the altar,
so Shelomo sent Benayahu son of Yehoyada, saying:
Go, attack him!

30 Benayahu came to the Tent of Yhwh
and said to him:
Thus says the king:
Come out!
He said:
No, for here I will die!
Benayahu returned word to the king, saying:
Thus spoke Yoav, and thus he answered me.

31 The king said to him:
Do as he spoke—
attack him and then bury him,
so that you may remove the causeless blood that Yoav shed
from me and from my Father's House.

---

27 **the word:** See I Sam. 2:27–36, where an anony- mous prophet foretells the downfall of Eli's priestly line. **Eli:** Pronounced *ay-LEE;* the chief priest/ leader at the beginning of the book of Sam- uel. **Shilo:** Pronounced *shee-LO;* it was a major religious center in the north.

28 **inclined after:** supported.

29 **was next to:** LXX reads "had taken hold of," which makes more sense.

31 **the causeless blood:** Or "the (guilt of) innocent blood" (Cogan 2001).

32 May YHWH return his blood on his head—
[seeing] that he attacked two men more righteous and noble than
he, and killed them with the sword,
while my father David did not know:
Avner son of Ner, Commander of the Armed-Forces of Israel,
and Amasa son of Yeter, Commander of the Armed-Forces of
Judah.

33 Their bloodguilt will return on the head of Yoav and on the head of
his seed, into the ages,
while for David, and for his seed, and for his house, and for his
throne, there will be peace for the ages from YHWH!

34 So Benayahu son of Yehoyada went up and attacked him, and put
him to death;
he was buried in his house in the wilderness.

35 And the king put Benayahu son of Yehoyada in his place as [The
One] Over the Armed-Forces,
while Tzadok the priest, the king put in place of Evyatar.

36 Then the king sent and summoned Shim'i
and said to him:
Build yourself a house in Jerusalem and stay there;
you are not to go out of there, [either] here or there.

37 For it will be, on the day of your going out and crossing Wadi
Kidron:
know, yes, know that you will die, yes, die—
your blood will be on your [own] head!

38 Shim'i said to the king:
The word is good;
as my lord king has spoken, thus will your servant do.
And Shim'i stayed in Jerusalem for many days.

---

32 **noble:** Literally "good" (Heb. *tov*), which in the
Hebrew Bible carries a wide range of meanings,
physical and spiritual.

34 **house:** Some see this as denoting a kind of mauso-
leum. **in the wilderness:** Alter (1999), following
the medieval commentator Gersonides, raises the
possibility that Yoav, as a man of violence, is deliber-
ately buried off the beaten path.

36 **not to go out:** A difficult restriction, given the small
size of Jerusalem at the time (Walsh). It amounts to
house arrest.

37 **Wadi Kidron:** The valley on the east side of Jerusalem; crossing it would lead him to the Mount of
Olives and eventually to his estate at Bahurim.

38 **The word is good:** The sentence is fair (Walsh).

39 But it was at the end of three years
    that two of Shim'i's servants ran off to Akhish son of Maakha, king
        of Gat,
    and they told Shim'i, saying:
    Here, your servants are at Gat!
40 So Shim'i arose and saddled his donkey and went to Gat, to Akhish,
    to seek his servants.
    And Shim'i went and brought back his servants from Gat.
41 Shelomo was told that Shim'i had gone from Jerusalem to Gat, and
        had returned,
42 so the king sent and called for Shim'i;
    he said to him:
    Did I not have you swear by Yhwh
    —and I warned you—saying:
    On the day of your going out, if you should go [either] here or
        there,
    know, yes, know that you will die, yes, die!?
    And you said to me:
    The word is good—I hearken.
43 So why did you not keep the sworn-oath of Yhwh,
    and the command that I commanded you?
44 And the king said to Shim'i:
    You know all the evildoing that your heart knew,
    that you did to David my father.
    So Yhwh will return your evildoing on your head!
45 But King Shelomo is blessed,
    and the throne of King David will be firmly-established before
        Yhwh for the ages!
46 So the king commanded Benayahu son of Yehoyada,
    and he went out and attacked him, so that he died.
    And the kingdom was firmly-established in Shelomo's hand.

---

39 **Gat:** Pronounced *GOT;* trad. English "Gath," one of the five major Philistine cities near the Mediterranean coast. So Shim'i actually does not cross the Kidron, which lies in the opposite direction.
42 **I hearken:** With the connotation of "I accept" (Cogan 2001). The Heb. *shama'ti* perhaps puns on the name Shim'i (Fokkelman 1981).

44 *You* **know all the evildoing that your heart knew:** This odd phraseology calls upon Shim'i to remember the past; his previous "evildoing" to David will now bring down the ultimate evil (or "disaster") upon himself.   **heart:** In the Hebrew Bible, it is often close to our concept of "mind."

Chapter 3. *Shelomo the Wise:* The bulk of this chapter deals with Shelomo's acquisition of wisdom—the practical wisdom needed to govern—and a memorable demonstration of this quality (vv.16–28). Yet these accounts are preceded by three verses of a Deuteronomistic kind, in which two discordant themes are introduced: marriage to a foreigner (in this case, the Egyptian king's daughter) and Israel's continuing use of local sanctuaries. Since at the end of Shelomo's reign the worship of foreign gods and use of these local holy places are held to be responsible for the kingdom's permanent split, this chapter, which also introduces some of the glories of the king's rule, could be understood as yet another example of the Bible's complex feelings about kingship.

Similarly, the site of the story produces complex reactions. Giv'on, according to I Chron. 16:39 and 21:29, housed the altar and Tent used in Israelite worship, and so is appropriate for a scene of sacrifice. But it is also associated with two tales of violence in Samuel: the military contest between Yoav's and Avner's troops in II 2 and the killing of Sha'ul's remaining descendants in II 21 as revenge for his massacre of the Giv'onites. So it may reflect the dual image of Shelomo and his kingship that is presented in the book.

The dream sequence in vv.5–14 draws on well-established traditions in ancient lore: dreams as revelations of the divine and the folklore motif of the supernatural offering to grant a mortal's wish. As usual, the offer functions as a kind of test, and in this case the hero passes it with flying colors. Seven times we hear the word "request," which not only makes sense in context, but also harks back to the story of Israel's clamoring for a king in I Sam. 8. The general vocabulary of the dialogue between God and Shelomo lays out the idealized role of the monarch: he should be a man of "understanding," "wisdom," and "discernment," with "justice" as the ultimate goal.

The story of the two prostitutes and the contested baby follows immediately, a deeply human tale set amid a celebratory feast. It has become famous in Western art; the combination of a presumably opulent setting, the contrasting emotions of the two women, a baby (typically portrayed by artists as naked), and a fearsome sword have proven irresistible. That the women are prostitutes should not be surprising. In the ancient Near East, it was understood that ordinary folk should have access to the throne to air their grievances, and so the tale is the perfect test case for Shelomo's ability to govern his entire people wisely. He emerges as an astute assessor of human behavior, a ruler with "an understanding heart" (v.9) who, despite his inexperience, is now able "to discern between good and evil" (v.9) in people's actions and motivations. The story is also our first encounter in Kings with anonymous women, who will play a major role in the book by throwing issues of power and character into sharp relief.

3:1 Shelomo became the son-in-law of Pharaoh of Egypt:
he took Pharaoh's daughter [in marriage], and brought her to the
City of David,
until he had finished building his house, and the House of YHWH,
and the wall of Jerusalem, all around.

2 However, the people were sacrificing at the sanctuaries,
since no house had been built for the name of YHWH up until those
days.

3 And Shelomo loved YHWH,
walking in the practices of David his father;
however, at the sanctuaries he was offering-sacrifices and sending-
up-smoke.

4 And the king went to Giv'on, to sacrifice there,
for it was the great sanctuary;
a thousand offerings-up would Shelomo offer up on that altar.

5 At Giv'on, YHWH appeared to Shelomo in a dream of the night.
God said:
Make request: What shall I give you?

6 Shelomo said:
You yourself have shown great loyalty to your servant, David my
father,
as he walked before you in truth and in equity and in rightness of
heart beside you,
and you have kept this great loyalty toward him, by giving him a
son to sit on his throne, as is this day.

3:1 **Pharaoh:** As usual, we are not told which king of Egypt is meant here. **the City of David:** Referring to the area south of the present Old City; Shelomo expanded the royal precinct northward, with the Temple atop what the ancients called Mount Zion (today's Temple Mount). **his house:** The Hebrew word used for both "palace" and "Temple" are the same (*bayit*) in these texts. Note which of the two is mentioned first here—a possible suggestion as to their relative importance in Shelomo's eyes.

2 **the sanctuaries:** Traditionally rendered "high places," this is a technical term for shrines outside of Jerusalem (a more focused translation might be "platform shrines" or, according to some, "open-air

sanctuaries"). Given the strong slant of the book toward centralized worship in Jerusalem, every king who tolerates or sacrifices at them is to some extent condemned. **for the name of YHWH:** In Deut. 12 and I Kings 8, in contrast to earlier literature, the Temple becomes the residence of God's "name" rather than of the deity himself.

3 **sending-up-smoke:** The Hebrew verb, *k-t-r*, usually denotes incense (*ketoret*) offerings.

4 **Giv'on:** Trad. English "Gibeon," located about five miles northwest of Jerusalem. See Commentary for some of its resonances.

5 **dream:** A common form of revelation in the Bible, as attested many times in Genesis.

7 So-now, YHWH my God,
you yourself have made your servant king in place of David my
father,
but I am a young lad—
I do not know how to go out and to come in!

8 And your servant is in the midst of your people whom you have
chosen,
a people so many that it cannot be measured and cannot be
numbered in abundance.

9 So give your servant an understanding heart
to judge your people, to discern between good and evil.
For who is able to judge this your weighty people?

10 The word was good in the eyes of the Lord,
that Shelomo had requested this thing;

11 God said to him:
Because you requested this thing
and did not request for yourself many days
and did not request for yourself riches
and did not request the life of your enemies,
but requested for yourself discernment to understand justice,

12 here, I have done according to your words—
here, I am giving you a wise and discerning heart,
such that like you, none has been before you
and after you, none will arise like you.

13 And even what you did not request, I give you:
even riches, even honor,
such as none has been like you, as a man among kings, for all your
days.

14 And if you walk in my ways, keeping my laws and my
commandments,
as David your father walked,
I will prolong your days.

---

7 **to go out and to come in:** Meaning "to lead the
people in battle."

9 **an understanding heart:** Lit., "a listening heart."
As with the term "wisdom," here the point is not
merely intellectual capacity but the practical ability
to make wise decisions and administer justice.

10 **requested:** The verb pointed to a major theme in the
Sha'ul ("The Requested One") story; here, it comes
from the king himself and is obviously viewed favorably, since it occurs five times in v.11 alone.

15 Shelomo awoke, and here: [It was] a dream!
He came to Jerusalem and stood before the Coffer of the Lord's
     Covenant
and offered up offerings-up, and performed *shalom*-offerings,
and made a drinkfest for all his servants.

16 Then two whore women came to the king
and stood before him.

17 The one woman said:
Please, my lord, I and this woman dwell in one house,
and I gave birth alongside her in the house.

18 And it was, on the third day after my giving birth,
that also this woman gave birth
—now we were together, there was no outsider with us in the
     house,
only the two of us in the house.

19 And this woman's son died at night,
[seeing] that she had lain upon him,

20 so she arose in the middle of the night and took my son from next
     to me
while your handmaid was sleeping,
and laid him in her bosom,
while her son, the dead one, she laid in my bosom.

21 I arose at daybreak to nurse my son,
and here: he was dead!
But when I examined him at daybreak,
now here, he was not my son whom I had borne!

22 The other woman said:
No—indeed,
my son is the living one, and your son is the dead one!
And this one was saying:
No—indeed,
your son is the dead one, and my son is the living one!
Thus they spoke before the king.

15 *shalom*-**offerings:** A type of sacrifice that creates
reconciliation and solidarity within the community.
JPS and others use "offerings of well-being."

Chapter 4. *Shelomo's Bureaucracy:* This short chapter mirrors II Sam. 8:15–18, which enumerated the officials of King David's court. While it is impossible to verify the names historically (and, as Walsh says, they may be here simply to give the narrative a plausible flavor), the text does present both rulers as presiding over a developed bureaucracy, and thus suggests at least the beginnings of a centralized state. As we have noted above, the tensions that normally grow out of such a transition from a tribal to a cosmopolitan society are reflected throughout Samuel and Kings. In both this and the Samuel passage, "all Israel" is stressed, although the mention of "Judah and Israel" at the end here (v.20) does not allow us to forget that the strong identity of the two separate regions was the prevailing reality throughout most of Israelite history.

23 The king said:
This one says: This is my son, the living one, and your son is the
   dead one;
while this one says: No—indeed,
your son is the dead one, and mine is the living one!

24 So the king said:
Fetch me a sword!
And they brought a sword before the king.

25 And the king said:
Cut the living child in two
and give half to the one and half to the [other] one!

26 Then said the woman whose son was the living one to the king
—for her insides burned for her son—
she said:
Please, my lord, give her the living newborn,
but death, don't put him to death!
But this one was saying:
Not mine and not yours will he be;
cut [him] up!

27 The king spoke up and said:
Give her the living newborn;
but death, do not put him to death—
she is his mother!

28 And all Israel heard the judgment that the king had pronounced-as-
   judgment,
and they were in awe of the king,
for they saw that the wisdom of God was in him, to execute justice.

4:1 King Shelomo was king over all Israel.

2 And these were the ministers whom he had:
Azaryahu son of Tzadok the Priest,

---

26 **her insides burned:** The same description of strong family ties occurs when Yosef sees his younger brother Binyamin for the first time in many years (Gen. 43:30). Note that "insides" (*rahamim*) can also mean "compassion," and the singular form *rehem* also denotes "womb." **living newborn:** Manuscripts change the word to *yeled,* but MT has *yalud,* a term more intimately connected to "birthing" and hence a strong clue as to who the real mother is (see Walsh). **but death:** Brettler (private communication) notes that at first hearing one can also read *ve-ha-met* as "the dead one," contrasting to "the living" one in the line above.

27 **her:** The first speaker in v.26.

28 **judgment:** Or "decision."

4:2 **Azaryahu:** In the notes I omit English equivalents for this and lesser-known names.

Chapter 5. *Shelomo's Wealth, Wisdom, and Fame; Preparations for Building the Temple:*
The splendor of Shelomo's court now unfolds. The chapter is awash with details
about the extent of the king's territory, his provisions for a single day, and his
horses, interspersed with a note of peace and security such as we rarely hear in
this part of the Bible. Vv.9–14 describe Shelomo's wisdom in glowing terms, so
that in this account he surpasses other ancient sages and is universally admired.

From the sevenfold sounding of the root "wise/wisdom," which in its appearance above meant the ability to govern well, the text moves toward the central
aspect of Shelomo's reign, the building of the Temple, which must also be done
with wisdom of the practical kind—that is, with skill and craftsmanship. For the
initial stages, the king contacts his father's old northern ally, Hiram of Tyre, from
whom he will procure the needed building materials. But the on-site work will be
done by Israelites, who are now impressed into labor gangs. This massive organi-
zation of men, which would have been the only possible way to accomplish such
a project, well symbolizes the concept of a burgeoning state, with all its attendant
disruption, for thousands of men must be drawn from the fields where they normally toil. The text makes no direct complaints here, however. Its primary goal is
no doubt to impress the audience.

3 Elihoref and Ahiyya sons of Shisha, [royal] Scribes,
   Yehoshafat son of Ahilud, the Herald,

4 and Benayahu son of Yehoyada, [The One] Over the Armed-Forces,
   and Tzadok and Evyatar, priests,

5 and Azaryahu son of Natan, [The One] Over the Prefects,
   and Zavud son of Natan the priest, Friend of the King,

6 and Ahishar, [The One] Over the Household,
   and Adoniram son of Avda, [The One] Over the Labor-Gangs.

7 Now Shelomo had twelve prefects over all Israel.
   They provided for the king and for his household;
   for a month of the year it would be each one's duty to provide.

8 And these were their names:
   Son of Hur: in the highlands of Efrayim,

9 Son of Deker: in Makatz, in Shaalvim, in Bet-Shemesh and Elon
     Bet-Hanan,

10 Son of Hesed: in Arubbot
   —his [responsibility] was Sokho and all the region of Heyfer,

11 Son of Avinadav: all Nafat-Dor
   —Tafat daughter of Shelomo was his wife—

12 Baana son of Ahilud: in Ta'nakh and Megiddo, and in all of Bet-
     She'an that is near Tzaretan, below Yizre'el,
   from Bet-She'an to Avel-Mehola, to [the region] across from
     Yokmo'am,

13 Ben-Gever: in the Heights of Gil'ad
   —his were the Villages of Ya'ir son of Menashe, that were in
     Gil'ad—
   his was Hevel Argov that is in Bashan,
   sixty large towns, [each with] a wall and a bronze bar,

14 Ahinadav son of Iddo: Mahanayim,

15 Ahimaatz: in Naftali
   —he too took Bas'mat daughter of Shelomo as a wife—

16 Baana son of Hushai: in Asher and in Alot,

---

3 **[royal] Scribes:** They would have handled the king's correspondence and other record-keeping tasks. **Herald:** Possibly a royal spokesperson.

5 **Prefects:** Or "governors." **Friend of the King:** An official title, denoting the king's chief counselor. This office is only mentioned in conjunction with the reigns of David and Shelomo.

6 **[The One] Over the Household:** Royal Steward, with duties probably extending beyond the palace itself.

7 **Israel:** From the territories listed here, the term clearly means what it does after Shelomo's death: the northern region of the country (Walsh).

8 **highlands:** Or "districts," an educated guess based on the context (Cogan 2001).

◆ 17 Yehoshafat son of Paruah: in Yissakhar,
18 Shim'i son of Ela: in Binyamin,
19 Gever son of Uri in the land of Gil'ad, the land of Sihon king of the
       Amorites, and of Og king of Bashan,
       and one prefect who was in the land of . . .

20 Judah and Israel were abundant [in number],
    like the sand that is by the sea in abundance,
    eating and drinking and rejoicing.
5:1 Now Shelomo was ruling over all the kingdoms
     from the River [to] the land of the Philistines, to the border of Egypt;
     they were bringing tribute-gifts and were subservient to Shelomo
        all the days of his life.
2   And Shelomo's food for a single day was:
     thirty *cors* of flour and sixty *cors* of meal,
3   ten fattened cattle, twenty pastured cattle, and a hundred sheep,
     aside from gazelles and deer, roebucks, and well-fed geese.
4   For he had dominion over all [the land] Across the River,
     from Tifsah to Gaza,
     over all the kings Across the River,
     and peace was on his every side, round about.
5   So Judah and Israel dwelt in security,
     each one beneath his vine and beneath his fig tree,
     from Dan to Be'er-Sheva,
     all the days of Shelomo.

6   Now Shelomo had four thousand stalls of horses for his chariotry
     and twelve thousand steeds.
7   And these prefects provided for King Shelomo and for all those who
     came near the table of King Shelomo,

17 **Yissakhar:** Trad. English "Issachar."
18 **Binyamin:** Trad. English "Benjamin."
19 **Gil'ad:** Trad. English "Gilead." **in the land of . . . :**
    It appears that a name is missing, but is probably
    Judah, which begins the next verse. This would have
    been a fairly typical scribal error.
20 **Judah and Israel:** Owing to the reversed order,
    probably a later insertion (DeVries).
5:1 **all the kingdoms:** II Chron. 9:26 reads "kings." **the
    River:** The Euphrates.
2   *cors:* This measure, dry, equaled fourteen bushels,
    and is the equivalent of the *homer,* cited elsewhere.
4   **Tifsah:** Pronounced *tif-SAH,* a town on the Euphra-

tes, about four hundred miles from Gaza; it was on
a major trade route from Mesopotamia to the western lands.
5   **in security . . . :** The Bible's classic expression of
    peace and prosperity, especially when combined
    with the imagery of sitting "beneath one's vine and
    fig tree." **from Dan to Be'er-Sheva:** The phrase
    might be termed a "spatial merism" (Wazana 2003),
    citing important sites in the north and the south to
    express "the whole country." Be'er-Sheva is trad.
    English "Beersheba."
6   **four thousand:** Following Chronicles and LXX; MT
    has "forty," probably a mistake (Walsh).

each one for his [particular] month;
    they let nothing be wanting.
8 And as for the barley and the hay for the horses and for the pack-
      animals,
    they would bring it to the place where he would be,
    each one according to his turn.

9 And God gave wisdom to Shelomo,
    and discernment, exceedingly much,
    and breadth of mind
    like the sand that is on the shore of the sea,
10 so that much greater was Shelomo's wisdom than the wisdom of
      all the Children of the East,
    and than the wisdom of Egypt.
11 He was wiser than all [other] human beings—
    than Eitan the Ezrahite
    and Heiman and Kalkol and Darda, the sons of Mahol,
    and his fame was throughout all the nations, all around.
12 He spoke three thousand proverbs,
    and his songs were five and a thousand.
13 And he spoke of trees,
    from the cedar that is in the Levanon
    to the hyssop that grows out of the wall;
    and he spoke of animals, of birds, of crawling things, and of fish.
14 And they came from all the peoples to hear Shelomo's wisdom,
    from all the kings of the earth who had heard of his wisdom.

15 Hiram king of Tyre sent his servants to Shelomo,
    for he had heard that it was he who had been anointed as king in
      place of his father
    —for Hiram had loved David [in covenant] all the days.

---

8 **pack-animals:** In contrast to the faster horses. **his turn:** Following JPS.
10 **Children of the East:** Cogan (2001) understands the term as referring to desert Arabs.
11 **Eitan . . . :** These names appear in conjunction with the Psalms (see 89:1), suggesting to some scholars that they were court singers/musicians. **fame:** Heb. *shem,* most often translated "name."
12 **five and a thousand:** LXX reads "five thousand," but the phrase may simply mean "a thousand and more" (Walsh).

15 **Hiram:** Pronounced *hee-RAHM.* The Phoenician king's name is probably short for "Ahiram." **loved David [in covenant]:** The verb "love" in the Hebrew Bible can sometimes be a technical term for "be in treaty with," "be loyal to," as in Deut. 6:5, although Jews and Christians have traditionally taken that phrase to indicate the love of God. **all the days:** Indicating ongoing time.

◆ 16 And Shelomo sent word to Hiram, saying:

17 You yourself know [regarding] David my father
    that he was not able to build a House for the name of YHWH his
        God,
    because of the wars that surrounded him,
    until YHWH put them beneath the soles of my feet.

18 But now,
    YHWH my God has granted me rest round about;
    there is no adversary and no evil circumstance.

19 So here, I intend to build a House for the name of YHWH my God,
    as YHWH promised to David my father, saying:
    Your son whom I will put in your place on your throne,
    he will build the House for my name!

20 So-now,
    command that they cut down cedars for me from the Levanon;
    my servants will be beside your servants,
    and your servants' wage I will give you, according to whatever
        you say,
    for you yourself know that there is no one among us who knows
        how to cut down trees like the Sidonians.

21 It was, when Hiram heard Shelomo's words,
    that he rejoiced exceedingly;
    he said:
    Blessed is YHWH today,
    who has given David a wise son over this numerous people!

22 And Hiram sent to Shelomo, saying:
    I have heard [the message] that you sent to me;
    I myself will do whatever you desire
    regarding cedar trees and regarding juniper trees.

23 My servants will bring them down from the Levanon to the Sea,
    and *I* will make them into rafts at the Sea, for any place that you
        send to me;
    then I will break them up there, so that *you* may carry them away.
    As for you, you will do my desire, to give food for my household.

17 **them:** Israel's enemies. **beneath the soles of my feet:** The proper position of a defeated enemy in the ancient world.
20 **the Levanon:** The "white" Lebanon mountain range after which the modern country is named. In the Bible it is almost always accompanied by the definite article.

24 So Hiram would give Shelomo cedar trees and juniper trees,
> whatever he desired,

25 while Shelomo gave Hiram twenty thousand *cors* of wheat as food
> for his household,
> and twenty *cors* of pressed oil.
> Thus did Shelomo give Hiram, year by year.

26 And Yнwн gave wisdom to Shelomo, as he had promised him;
> there was *shalom*/peace between Hiram and Shelomo,
> and the two of them cut a covenant.

27 King Shelomo raised up labor-gangs from all Israel,
> and the labor-force was thirty thousand men.

28 He sent them to the Levanon,
> ten thousand per month, in shifts:
> one month they would be in the Levanon, [and] two months at
> home.
> And Adoniram was [The One] Over the Labor-force.

29 Now Shelomo had seventy thousand burden carriers
> and eighty thousand stone-cutters in the hill-quarry,

30 aside from the prefect commanders of Shelomo who were Over the
> Work,
> three thousand and three hundred, who supervised the people,
> those doing the work.

31 The king commanded that they transport [from the quarry] large
> stones, costly stones for setting-the-foundation of the House
> [with] hewn stones.

32 And Shelomo's builders and Hiram's builders and the Giblites
> carved them.
> Thus they prepared the timber and the stone for building the
> House.

---

25 **Shelomo gave Hiram . . . :** The payment for the trees of Lebanon amounts to a huge sum (Walsh). **twenty *cors*:** LXX reads "twenty thousand *bahts*," referring to the liquid measure (a tenth of a *cor*) mentioned in 7:26 below. **pressed:** By hand, and thus quite pure (see Exod. 27:20).

26 *shalom*/**peace:** The word is also used to indicate "treaty loyalty" (Fishbane). Here it links up with the Israelite king's name.

28 **at home:** Lit. "in his house."

32 **Giblites:** Men from Byblos, north of Hiram's region on the Mediterranean coast.

Chapter 6. *Building the Temple I:* The first chapter on the construction of the Temple concentrates initially on its outer dimensions and ends with a description of the walls and sacred "Rear-Chamber," along with their decorations. In between (vv.11–13) has been inserted a Deuteronomistic pledge by God that, contingent on Israel keeping the stipulations of the covenant, he will maintain his presence among the Israelites and not abandon them. The Bible understands this as a key goal of the Temple, which mimics the role of the Tabernacle ("Dwelling") in the presettlement period, as described especially in Exodus.

A more detailed description of the inner furnishings of the Temple has been left to the next chapter.

6:1 Now it was in year four hundred and eighty of the years of the
    Children of Israel's going out from the land of Egypt,
in the fourth year—in the month of Ziv, that is the second
    month—of Shelomo's reign as king over Israel,
that he [began] building the House to Yhwh.

2 And the House that King Shelomo built for Yhwh was:
sixty cubits its length, twenty its width, and thirty cubits its height.

3 As for the portico at the front of the Great-Hall of the House:
twenty cubits was its length, along the width of the House,
and ten by the cubit its depth, in front of the House.

4 And he made windows for the House, framed [and] latticed,

5 and he built an extension against the wall of the House, all around,
namely, along the walls of the House,
round about the Great-Hall and the Rear-Chamber,
and he made side-chambers all around.

6 The lowest side-chamber was five by the cubit its width,
with the middle one, six by the cubit its width,
and the third one, seven cubits its width,
for he placed offsets for the House, all around, on the exterior,
so as not to fasten [them] to the walls of the House.

7 And the House as it was being built,
of complete quarry stone it was built,
and [neither] hammers nor pickax—any tool of iron—
was heard in the House as it was being built.

6:1 **four hundred and eighty:** Interpreters have spent centuries trying to calculate the date of the Exodus from this, but it seems much more likely that this is another "meaningful" biblical number, equaling forty times twelve or four times ten times twelve, and indicating the orderliness of God's plan for Israel. **Ziv:** Pronounced *zeev*, the "Blossom Month," in the spring. This designation, from the Phoenician calendar, corresponds to the Jewish month of Iyyar.

2 **built:** Kimhi understands the verb as indicating "began to build." **sixty . . . twenty . . . thirty:** As with the Tabernacle in Exodus, the measurements are highly proportional, conveying a message of symbolic perfection.

3 **portico:** Or "forecourt." It seems to have been uncovered, and large, measuring about thirty feet by fifteen feet. **Great-Hall:** The word (*hekhal*),

cognate elsewhere in the ancient Near East, can indicate a large space, including also "palace" (see I Kings 21:2) and "temple."

5 **extension:** Or "layer" (Mulder). **Rear-Chamber:** Others, "adytum," "inner sanctuary," identical to the "Holiest Holy-Place." The word (*devir*) is sometimes linked to the "word" (*davar*) of God, but is probably an architectural rather than a theological term.

6 **offsets:** Some kind of retaining walls seem to be meant (Sweeney 2007). **so as not to fasten [them]:** That is, the offsets do not offer extra support to the walls of the Temple (Mulder).

7 **complete:** Others, "unhewn"; the term (*shalem*) echoes the name Shelomo, and is used elsewhere in these chapters as a verb. **tool of iron:** In the Torah, the altar was likewise forbidden to be made with iron tools (see Exod. 20:22, Deut. 27:5).

◆

8 The entrance to the lowest side-chamber was on the right shoulder
of the House,
while winding-stairs went up to the middle one from the lower one,
and from the middle one to the third one.

9 So he built the House and finished it:
he covered the House with hollow-squares and beam-projections,
of cedar.

10 He built the extension along the entire House, five cubits its height,
and secured the House with cedar wood.

11 Now the word of YHWH [came] to Shelomo, saying:

12 [Regarding] this House that you are building:
if you walk in my ways, and my practices you observe,
and you keep my commandments, walking in them,
I will fulfill my word with you which I promised to David your
father:

13 I will dwell in the midst of the Children of Israel,
and I will not abandon my people Israel!

14 So Shelomo built the House and finished it;

15 he built the walls of the House on the interior with cedar planks,
from the floor of the House up to the beams of the ceiling;
he overlaid it with wood on the interior,
and overlaid the floor of the House with juniper planks.

16 And he built twenty cubits from the flanks of the House with cedar
planks,
from the floor up to the beams,
and built it on the interior as a Rear-Chamber, the Holiest Holy-
Place.

17 Forty by the cubit [long] was the House—
that was the Great-Hall in front [of it].

---

8 **lowest:** LXX, more logically; MT reads "middle."
shoulder: Or "flank, side." **winding-stairs:** So
understood by LXX and Targum; Mulder: "spiral-
shaped decorations."

9 **covered:** The verb (*s-p-n*) means "to cover with
wood," the noun, "ceiling." **beam-projections:**
Heb. unclear; Mulder conjectures "drain pipes."

11 **the word of YHWH [came]:** As Fishbane notes, this
expression is used most often in connection with
prophets, not kings, and so is of special significance
here.

16 **the Holiest Holy-Place:** Others, "Holy of Holies."

17 **in front [of it]:** Hebrew odd; LXX has "in front of
the Rear-Chamber."

18 Now the cedarwork of the interior of the House was carving of
      gourds and open flowers;
    all was cedar, no stone was to be seen.

19 Now the Rear-Chamber within the House, in the interior, he
      prepared for placing there the Coffer of Yнwн's Covenant.

20 And in the forepart of the Rear-Chamber were twenty cubits of
      length, twenty cubits of width, and twenty cubits its height,
    and he overlaid it with refined gold.
    And he overlaid the sacrificial-altar with cedar.

21 And Shelomo overlaid the House on the interior with refined gold;
    he passed chains of gold across the front of the Rear-Chamber
    and overlaid it with gold,

22 and the entire House he overlaid with gold, until the entire House
      was done,
    while the entire altar that belonged to the Rear-Chamber he
      overlaid with gold.

23 And in the Rear-Chamber he made two winged-sphinxes of
      oleaster wood,
    ten cubits its height.

24 Five cubits was the wing of the one sphinx,
    and five cubits was the wing of the second sphinx—
    ten cubits from the tips of its wing to the tips of its [other] wing.

25 And ten by the cubit was the second sphinx,
    a single measure and a single shape for the two winged-sphinxes.

26 The height of the one sphinx was ten by the cubit,
    and thus for the second sphinx.

27 And he placed the winged-sphinxes in the middle of the inner
      House;
    the wings of the sphinxes were spread out

---

18 **gourds and open flowers:** The vegetation motif is often symbolic of life-giving in ancient Near Eastern architecture, and appeared already in conjunction with the sacred seven-branched lampstand in Exod. 25:31ff.

20 **the forepart:** The text seems confused here and at the beginning of v.17 ("in front [of it]"); some conjecture that vv.18–19 were inserted.   **it:** The Rear-Chamber.   **refined gold:** Gold that is beaten out, more commonly referred to in English as gold leaf.

23 **winged-sphinxes:** Trad. English "cherubim," not to be confused with the chubby baby angels familiar in Western art. The *keruvim* were a common symbol in the ancient Near East; imaginary, composite creatures, they appear as guardians to royal and sacred buildings. See also Exod. 25:18–20.   **oleaster wood:** Lit., "oil wood." Cogan (2001) understands it as pine-wood.   **its:** Referring to each sphinx.

24 **wing:** MT has "wings," but some versions read it in the singular.

Chapter 7. *The Palace; Building the Temple II:* Shelomo's palace, whose construction takes almost twice as long as that of the Temple, includes five structures, most notably the "House of the Forest of Levanon," an apt metaphor for a stunning, multicolumned structure. From v.13 on, the text returns to the Temple, beginning with an identification of Hiram, the chief craftsman—just as the account of the Tabernacle ("Dwelling") in Exodus had identified its own, Betzalel. It proceeds to provide descriptions of architectural features (such as the two great columns in front of the Temple, along with their capitals), ritual appurtenances (for example, the huge basin known as the "Sea," and the washing-stands for the priests), and the elaborate wall decorations.

As the chapter moves toward the completion of these buildings (vv.40–50), the pace quickens, again resembling the final chapters of Exodus. Significantly, the whole account ends with an emphasis on silver, gold, and vessels—which, as explained in the Introduction to Kings, will be systematically looted at moments throughout the book, culminating in the final despoiling in the last chapter of Kings.

so that the wing of the one touched the wall,
and the wing of the second sphinx was touching the second wall,
while their wings toward the middle of the house were touching,
wing to wing.

28 And he overlaid the winged-sphinxes with gold.

29 Now all the walls of the House, round about, he carved with
engraved carvings of winged-sphinxes and palmettes and open
flowers,
on the inside and out.

30 And the floor of the House he overlaid with gold,
inside and out.

31 Now the entrance to the Rear-Chamber he made as doors of
oleaster wood;
the jamb [and] the doorposts were a fifth [of the wall-length].

32 As for the two doors of oleaster wood,
he carved on them carvings of winged-sphinxes, palmettes, and
open flowers,
and overlaid them with gold,
and he hammered the gold over the winged-sphinxes and over the
palmettes.

33 And so [too] he made for the entrance to the Great-Hall: posts of
oleaster wood, a fourth [of the wall-length],

34 and two doors of juniper wood,
with two rib-leaves for the one door, folding,
and two rib-leaves for the second door, folding,

35 and he carved winged-sphinxes, palmettes, and open flowers,
and overlaid them with gold,
evenly over the chiseled-work.

36 And he built the interior courtyard of three rows of hewn-stones,
and a row of cut cedar.

37 In the fourth year
the House of YHWH was laid-in-foundation,
in the month of Ziv.

29 **palmettes:** The palm tree was another common symbol of life and prosperity.
31 **a fifth [of the wall-length]:** Sweeney (2007) understands *hamishit* as "five-sided," and thus bonded for strength.

36 **cut cedar:** Beams or the like. The alternation of stone and wood was common in the ancient Near East, where it helped to cushion structures in the event of earthquakes.
37 **the fourth year:** Of Shelomo's reign.

38 And in the eleventh year, in the moon of Bul—that is the eighth
    month—
    the House was finished, in all its details and in all its specifications;
    he had built it in seven years.

7:1 Now his [own] house Shelomo built in thirteen years;
    then he finished his entire house.

2 And he built the House of the Forest of the Levanon:
    a hundred cubits its length, fifty cubits its width, and thirty cubits
        its height,
    on four rows of cedar columns, with cut cedarwork atop the columns.

3 And it was covered with cedar from above, atop the planks that
        were on the columns,
    forty-five: fifteen per row.

4 And the window-frames were of three rows,
    with sight line toward sight line, three times.

5 And all the entrances and posts were square of frame, opposite,
    sight line toward sight line, three times.

6 And the Portico of Columns he made: fifty cubits its length
    and twenty cubits its width,
    with a portico in front of them,
    with columns and a cornice in front of them.

7 And the Portico of the Throne, where he would pronounce
        judgment, the Portico of Justice, he made;
    it was covered with cedar, from floor to floor.

8 And his housing where he would reside, in the other courtyard
        within the portico,
    was like this [same] pattern;
    and he was [also] to make a house for Pharaoh's daughter, whom
        Shelomo had taken [in marriage], like this portico.

---

38 **moon:** Heb. *yerah,* an older term for "month." **Bul:**
The "Rain Month," roughly October. It corresponds
to the Jewish month of Marheshvan. **seven years:**
Seven is usually the measure of perfection in the
Bible. Yet note that in the next verse, we are told
that Shelomo spent thirteen years on his own house
(palace), making this "seven" look less significant.
7:2 **House of the Forest of the Levanon:** Whatever its
function (probably for assembly), it must have been
quite impressive, judging from the image conjured
up by the name. **cut cedarwork:** Apparently these
were beams, placed to support the roof.

5 **sight line toward sight line:** The Hebrew is
obscure, perhaps indicating facing windows.
7 **pronounce judgment:** Others, "rule." **floor to
floor:** We would use "floor to ceiling," and ancient
versions have the latter.
8 **pattern:** Or "construction." The word comes from
the verb "to make," so frequently used in these chapters. **he was [also] to make:** This took place later,
but in Walsh's view has been placed here to emphasize that Shelomo built it before the Temple.

9 All these were of costly stones, hewn according to measure,
smoothed with a smoothing-tool, within and without,
from the foundation to the coping,
from outside to the Great Courtyard.

10 It was founded [on] costly stones, large stones,
stones of ten cubits and stones of eight cubits.

11 And above were costly stones, hewn to measure, and cedar.

12 Now the Great Courtyard, all around, was of three rows of hewn-
stones and a row of cut cedarwork;
[so] for the inner courtyard of the House of YHWH and for the
Portico of the Palace-House.

13 And King Shelomo sent and fetched Hiram from Tyre,

14 the son of a widow woman, from the tribe of Naftali,
while his father was a Tyrian man, an engraver in bronze;
he was filled with practical-wisdom, discernment, and technical-
knowledge
to make all kinds of work in bronze.
He came to King Shelomo and made all his work:

15 he fashioned the two columns, of bronze—
eighteen cubits the height of the one column,
with a cord of twelve cubits [able to] go around it, and so the
second column.

16 And two capitals he made
to put on the tops of the columns, cast in bronze—
five cubits the height of the one capital, and five cubits the height
of the second capital,

17 [with] networks made of netted making, twisted-decorations of
chain making,
for the capitals that were on top of the columns:
seven for the one capital and seven for the second capital.

---

13 **Hiram:** Not to be confused with King Hiram, who supplied building materials to Shelomo earlier in the text. In II Chron. 2:13, he is called Huram Avi, "My Father is [the god] Horon."

14 **Naftali:** Whose territory was next to that of Tyre. **engraver in bronze:** Others, "copper-smith." **he was filled . . . :** The description echoes that of the Tabernacle architect, Betzalel, in Exod.

31:3 and 35:31. **make:** Here, as in the Tabernacle accounts in Exodus, the verb recurs in this chapter in various forms.

15 **a cord . . . [able to] go around:** Describing the circumference. **and so:** Emending *et* to *oto ve-khen*, as suggested in ancient versions.

17 **networks:** Some suggest that the words "he made" are missing here.

◆ 18 And he made the pomegranates,
with two rows surrounding [each] one network, to cover the
capitals that were on the top of the columns,
and thus he made for the second capital.

19 And the capitals that were on the top of the columns
were a pattern of lilies, in the Portico,
four cubits.

20 And the capitals on the two columns were also above, close to the
bulging-section that was across from the netting,
and the pomegranates were two hundred in rows, all around the
second capital.

21 He set up the columns for the portico of the Great-Hall:
he set up the right column, and called its name *Yakhin*/He
Establishes,
and he set up the left column, and called its name *Boaz*/In Him,
Strength.

22 And on the top of the columns was a pattern of lilies.
Then the work of the columns was done.

23 He made the Sea-Basin, cast: ten by the cubit from its lip to its
[other] lip, circular, all around,
five cubits its height,
and a line of thirty cubits could surround it, all around.

24 And gourd-ornaments were beneath its lip, all around,
surrounding it,
ten in cubits, encompassing the Sea all around;
two rows of gourd-ornaments were cast at its casting.

18 **pomegranates . . . columns:** According to ancient versions, sensibly; MT reverses them (the words are *rimmonim* and *'ammudim*).

20 **bulging-section:** Lit., "belly."

21 **columns:** In the Roman period, the [Second] Temple's two columns became a central symbol of Judaism, and their image is found on coins made during the Bar Kokhba revolt (132–135 C.E.). Their origin may be Canaanite, with connotations of fertility, attributable to the phallic shape and the inclusion of pomegranates (Mulder). And the unusual names attached to them may also reflect ancient Near Eastern practice, where pillars were accompanied by inscriptions of prayers. The names here would have been the opening words of a phrase like "In strength He establishes (or: May He establish) [the earth]."

23 **Sea-Basin:** Scholars disagree on whether this object had mythic overtones, symbolizing the primeval waters of chaos brought under control by YHWH (see, for instance, Ps. 104:6–9), or was merely a place for the priests to wash. Perhaps it was both. JPS uses the inelegant "tank."

25 [It was] standing on twelve oxen: three facing north, three facing
    seaward, three facing south, and three facing sunrise,
    with the Sea upon them, from above,
    and all of their hindquarters inward.
26 Its thickness was a handbreadth,
    with its lip like the pattern of the lip of a cup, a lily flower.
    Two thousand *baht*-measures could it contain.

27 He made the stands, ten, of bronze,
    four by the cubit the length of each one stand,
    and four by the cubit its width,
    and three by the cubit its height.
28 And this was the pattern of the standwork:
    they had enclosures,
    and enclosures between the crosspieces—
29 and on the enclosures that were between the crosspieces
    were lions, oxen, and sphinxes,
    and on the crosspieces were thus;
    above and below the lions and the oxen were spirals of hammered
    making.
30 And four wheels of bronze were for each one stand, and axles of
    bronze,
    and its four legs had shoulder-pieces under the basin;
    the shoulder-pieces were cast across from each one in spirals.
31 And its mouth, within the capital, and above [it] for one cubit,
    its mouth was circular, in the pattern of a pedestal,
    a cubit and half a cubit,
    and even on the mouth there were carvings.
    Now their frames were square, not circular.
32 And four wheels were beneath the enclosures;
    the supports of the wheels were in the stand, with the height of the
    one wheel a cubit and half a cubit.

---

25 **inward:** Facing inside.
26 **handbreadth:** About three inches (Gray 1970).
    baht-measures: A fluid measure equal perhaps to
    six gallons. Most translations use "baths," to which
    English word this concept is unrelated.
27 **He:** Indicating Hiram, as Cogan (2001) points

out. **stands:** For worshippers to wash, etc. (Gray
1970).
28 **enclosures:** Apparently describing rims or frames.
30 **shoulder-pieces:** Or "supports."
32 **supports:** Lit. "hands"; Cogan (2001) renders "axle-
trees."

Chapter 8. *Shelomo's Prayer of Dedication:* This long speech, beginning with a statement about Shelomo's intent to build a Temple and culminating in a remarkable series of prayers, appears to have a complicated textual history. Some of it presupposes exile, while other parts hint at a later return; however, the bulk seems to belong to a time after the destruction of the Northern Kingdom in 722 (Sweeney 2007). Its wordiness is almost ceremonial, reminiscent of II Sam. 7, where God had made dramatic promises to David about his dynasty. And the opening fits well into an ancient Near Eastern pattern: a king solidifies his rule by dedicating or rededicating a temple in the name of the god who put him on the throne.

Beginning with v.31, the chapter enumerates seven cases in which people may petition God in the Temple. They involve mainly internal crises, but also shift, after v.44, to situations outside the land of Israel, such as war and captivity. These do not necessarily put this part of the chapter in a Babylonian Exile setting, although they undoubtedly came to be read that way. All square nicely with the Deuteronomistic view that Israel's security and prosperity come from keeping the covenant with YHWH.

As Sweeney (2007) points out, the blessing uttered by Shelomo (vv.54–60) likewise encapsulates Deuteronomistic ideas, including divine promises to the ancestors and emphasis on the covenant, encompassing both YHWH's faithfulness and Israel's need to obey. Indeed, the verb "promise" (literally, "speak") occurs eight times in the chapter, six in vv.15–26 and then twice at the end (v.56).

33 Now the pattern of the wheels was like the pattern of a chariot
   wheel,
   with their supports, their back-rims, their spokes, and their hubs—
   all were cast.

34 And the four shoulder-pieces were at the four corners of each one
   stand,
   from the stand [itself came] its shoulder-pieces.

35 And at the top of the stand, half a cubit its height, was a circular-
   band all around,
   and at the top of the stand, its handles and its enclosures [came]
   from itself.

36 And he engraved on the panels, its handles, and on its enclosures:
   sphinxes, lions, and palmettes, according to the bare space on each,
   with spirals all around.

37 Like this he made the ten stands,
   with one casting, one measure, one shape for all of them.

38 Then he made ten basins of bronze—
   forty *baht*-measures could each one basin contain;
   four by the cubit, for each one basin,
   one basin per one stand, for the ten stands.

39 And he placed the stands: five at the right shoulder of the House,
   and five at its left shoulder,
   while the Sea he [had] placed on the House's right shoulder,
   eastward, toward the south.

40 And Hiram made the pots, the shovels, and the sprinkling-bowls.

   So Hiram finished making all the work
   that he had made for King Shelomo for the House of YHWH:

41 the columns, two,
   and the bowl-shapes of the capitals that were at the top of the two
   columns, two,
   the netting-pieces, two, for covering the two bowl-shapes of the
   columns that were at the top of the columns;

---

34 **from . . . [itself came]:** Or idiomatically, "were of
one piece with." This formulation is used frequently
in the Tabernacle texts of Exodus.

36 **according to the bare space . . . :** Heb. obscure,
just like v.30's "cast across from each one in spirals"
(Cogan 2001).

38 **four by the cubit:** In diameter.

40 **pots:** LXX; MT has "basins." **finished:** A key word
in both the Creation (Gen. 2:1–2) and Tabernacle
(Exod. 40:33) accounts, undoubtedly meant to connect the two.

◆

42 the pomegranates, four hundred, for the two network-pieces,
two rows of pomegranates for each one network, for covering
the two bowl-shapes of the capitals that were on the top of the
columns;

43 and the stands, ten,
and the basins, ten, on the stands,

44 and the one Sea,
with the oxen, twelve, beneath the Sea;

45 and the pots, and the shovels, and the sprinkling-bowls—
all these vessels that Hiram made for King Shelomo, for the House
of Yʜwʜ,
were of polished bronze.

46 In the round-plain of the Jordan the king had cast them, in thick
soil,
between Sukkot and Tzaretan.

47 And Shelomo left all the vessels [unweighed], out of their
exceeding, exceeding abundance;
the weight of the bronze could not be ascertained.

48 And Shelomo made all the vessels that were for the House of
Yʜwʜ:
the golden sacrificial-altar,
and the table on which was the Bread of the Presence, of gold,

49 and the lampstands, with five to the right and five to the left,
in front of the Rear-Chamber, of refined gold,
and the flowerwork, the lamps, and the tongs, of gold,

50 and the bowls, the snuffers, the sprinkling-bowls, the ladles, and the
incense-pans, of refined gold,
and the hinge-pieces for the doors to the inner house, the Holiest
Holy-Place,
[and] for the doors of the House, for the Great-Hall, of gold.

51 And all the work that King Shelomo had made on the House of
Yʜwʜ was completed;
Shelomo brought the holy-objects of David his father:

---

46 **in thick soil:** Or "in clay molds."
47 **left . . . [unweighed]:** Following JPS.
50 **House . . . Great-Hall:** LXX omits "House."
51 **completed:** Here the text uses, not the usual "finished" (*k-l-h*), but *sh-l-m* again, as in 6:7. Cogan (2001)

notes that "finished" seems to be used here to designate parts of the work, as in vv.9, 14, and 38 (and 7:1
and 40). **holy-objects:** Spoils of war and gifts that
were deposited in the sanctuary.

the silver, the gold, and all the [other] vessels,
and he put them in the treasuries of the House of Yʜwʜ.

8:1 Then Shelomo assembled the elders of Israel,
all the heads of the tribes, the ancestral leaders of the Children of
Israel, to King Shelomo in Jerusalem,
to bring up the Coffer of Yʜwʜ's Covenant from the City of
David—that is Zion.

2 And every man of Israel assembled to King Shelomo, in the month
of Etanim/Ever-Flowing, at the Festival—that is the seventh
month.

3 And all the elders of Israel came,
and the priests carried the Coffer;

4 they brought up the Coffer of Yʜwʜ along with the Tent of
Appointment and all the holy vessels that were in the Tent;
the priests and the Levites brought them up.

5 Meanwhile, King Shelomo and the entire community of Israel who
were present with him before the Coffer
were offering-sacrifices of sheep and oxen
which could not be numbered or measured in abundance.

6 And the priests brought the Coffer of Yʜwʜ's Covenant to its place,
to the Rear-Chamber of the House, to the Holiest Holy-Place,
beneath the wings of the sphinxes.

7 For the sphinxes were spreading [their] wings to the place of the
Coffer,
so that the sphinxes were sheltering the Coffer and its poles from
above.

8 And the poles were so long that the heads of the poles could be
seen from the Holy-Place in front of the Rear-Chamber, but
could not be seen outside;
they have been there until this day.

8:1 **leaders:** Lit., "exalted ones." **Zion:** Heb. *Tziyyon*, the hill on which the Temple was built. What is today called Mount Zion is in fact located some distance southwest of the original Temple Mount.

2 **Ever-Flowing:** In the fall, the month at whose end it begins to rain in Israel. It was later (and still is today) called Tishre. **the Festival:** Sukkot ("Huts"), the pilgrimage festival that takes place after all the harvests are concluded. It was the most important of ancient Israel's agricultural holidays, and hence is referred to as "*The* Festival" in the Bible.

4 **the priests and the Levites:** The fact that they share the same duties may indicate a late date for this part of the chapter, since in the Exodus texts relating to the Tabernacle their tasks are quite separate (Gray 1970).

6 **sphinxes:** Elsewhere translated as "winged-sphinxes."

7 **spreading [their] wings:** Cogan (2001): "formed a canopy."

8 **heads:** Tips.

9   There is nothing in the Coffer

save the two stone tablets that Moshe had put there at Horev,

when YHWH had cut [a covenant] with the Children of Israel, at
their going out from the land of Egypt.

10   And it was, at the priests' going out from the Holy-Place,

that the cloud filled the House of YHWH,

11   and the priests were not able to stand to attend because of the
cloud,

for the Glory of YHWH had filled the House of YHWH.

12   Then Shelomo said:

YHWH has determined to dwell in thick darkness.

13   I have built, yes, built a lofty House for you,

a fixed-place for your [royal] seat, for the ages.

14   And the king turned his face and blessed the entire assembly of
Israel

while the entire assembly of Israel was standing;

15   he said:

Blessed is YHWH, the God of Israel,

who promised David my father with his own mouth,

and with his own hand confirmed, saying:

16   From the day that I brought out my people Israel from Egypt,

I have not chosen a city from all the tribes of Israel

[in which] to build a House, to have my name be there.

But I chose David to be over my people Israel,

17   and it was in the heart of David my father to build a House for the
name of YHWH, the God of Israel,

18   so YHWH said to David my father:

Because it was in your heart to build a House for my name,

you have done well, for it was in your heart.

---

9 **There is nothing:** Implying a popular belief that something else—perhaps of a miraculous nature—was there (Gray 1970). **Horev:** Another name for Mount Sinai.

10–11 **the cloud . . . the Glory of YHWH had filled the House of YHWH:** The language recalls Moshe, making Shelomo an idealized figure beyond his own time, the "Moses of the monarchy" (Fishbane).

11 **Glory:** Cogan (2001) prefers "essence, presence."

12 **determined:** Or "said." Heb. '-m-r can encompass a wide range of concepts beyond speaking, including thinking and intending.

13 **I have built:** The first of six occurrences of this phrase in the chapter, pointing to the king's "personal piety" (Zevit 2004).

15 **promised:** Usually rendered "spoke" in this translation, but as "promised," it is a key idea in this chapter. **confirmed:** Heb. "filled"; others, "fulfilled with his hand."

16 **I have not chosen a city:** Shelomo thus eliminates the claims of other locations for the Ark or a sanctuary (Sweeney 2007).

17 **in the heart:** Or "in the mind."

19 However: *you* shall not build the House,
rather, your son, the one going out of your loins,
he shall build the House for my name.

20 And Yhwh has fulfilled his word which he promised:
I have arisen in the place of David my father,
and have taken seat on the throne of Israel, as Yhwh promised;
I have built the House for the name of Yhwh, the God of Israel,

21 and I have put there a place for the Coffer, in which is Yhwh's
covenant
that he cut with our fathers, when he brought them out from the
land of Egypt.

22 Then Shelomo stood in front of the altar of Yhwh, opposite the
entire assembly of Israel,
and he spread his palms heavenward

23 and said:
O Yhwh, God of Israel,
there is none like you as a god
in the heavens above or on the earth beneath,
keeping the covenant, loyalty with your servants, those who walk
in your presence with all their heart,

24 who has kept regarding your servant David my father what you
promised him;
you promised with your own mouth and with your own hand
confirmed, as is this day.

25 So-now, Yhwh God of Israel,
keep for your servant David my father what you promised him,
saying:
There will never be a man cut off from you in my presence,
sitting on the throne of Israel—
if only your sons keep their way, walking in my presence
as you have walked in my presence!

26 So-now, O God of Israel,
pray let your word be confirmed that you promised to your servant
David my father.

---

20 **promised:** Others, "predicted." **I have arisen . . . and have taken seat:** LXX sets these words in the third person, undoubtedly out of a pious impulse. But perhaps we are meant to see Shelomo as self-centered here (Walsh).

27 But will God really reside on earth?
Here, the heavens and the heavenmost heavens cannot contain you,
how much less this House that I have built!

28 Yet turn your face to the prayer of your servant, and to his plea, O
YHWH my God,
to hearken to the cry-of-praise and to the prayer that your servant is
praying in your presence today,

29 that your eyes may be open toward this House, night and day,
toward the place about which you said: My name will be there,
to hearken to the prayer that your servant will pray toward this
place.

30 And when you hear the plea of your servant and of your people
Israel
that they will pray toward this place—
then may *you* hearken at the place of your [royal] seat in the
heavens;
may you hearken and may you forgive!

31 Should a person sin against his neighbor
and he lifts up an oath-curse upon him, to put him under a curse,
and he comes with the oath-curse before your altar, in this House—

32 then may *you* hearken in the heavens
and may you act and judge your servants,
to bring punishment on the guilty, by putting his way on his head,
and to vindicate the innocent, by giving him according to his
innocence.

33 When your people Israel is defeated before an enemy, because
they have sinned against you,
and then they return to you and praise your name,
and they pray and plead to you in this House,

34 then may *you* hearken in the heavens
and may you forgive the sin of your people Israel,
and return them to the soil that you gave to their fathers.

29 **toward the place:** Implying exile, and thus another
indicator of compositional layering in this chapter.

35 When the heavens are held back, and there is no early-rain,
   because they have sinned against you,
   and they pray toward this place, and praise your name,
   and from their sin they turn, since you afflicted them—
36 then may *you* hearken in the heavens,
   and may you forgive the sin of your servants, your people Israel,
   so that you instruct them the good way in which they should walk,
   and may you give rain upon your land which you gave to your
      people as heriditary-property.

37 A famine—if it should come upon the land;
   pestilence—if it should come;
   blight, green-mildew, ravaging locust, grasshopper—if it should
      come;
   if his enemy should put him in straits in one of his gates;
   whatever the affliction, whatever the sickness:
38 [for] any prayer, any plea that any person might have among any of
      your people Israel
   who knows the affliction in his heart, and spreads his palms toward
      this House—
39 then may *you* hearken in the heavens, the fixed-place of your [royal]
      seat;
   may you forgive and act, giving to each according to all his ways,
   [seeing] that you know his heart,
   for you yourself know the heart of every human being,
40 in order that they may hold you in awe all the days that they live on
      the face of the ground that you have given to our fathers.

41 And also to the foreigner, who is not from your people Israel,
   but comes from a land far off for the sake of your name,
42 for he hears of your great name
   and your strong hand and your outstretched arm,
   and comes and prays toward this House—

---

35 **early-rain:** The heavy rains of late fall, crucial for fertility. **you afflicted them:** Slightly emended from MT: "you answer them."
37 **one:** LXX; MT has "land."
38 **any prayer, any plea:** Heb. *kol ha-tefilla, kol ha-tehinna.* **spreads his palms:** In prayer. This posture is typically biblical, as opposed to the later, oft-drawn pose of clasped hands.
39 **your [royal] seat:** Or "your dwelling," which fits equally well here.

43 may *you* hearken in the heavens, the fixed-place of your [royal] seat,
and may you act,
in accordance with all that the foreigner calls out to you,
in order that all the peoples of the earth may know your name,
holding you in awe as your people Israel [does],
and acknowledging that your name is called over this House that I
have built.

44 When your people goes out to battle against its enemy, on the road
that you send them,
and they pray to Yhwh, toward the city that you have chosen
and the House that I have built for your name—
45 then may you hearken in the heavens to their prayer and to their
plea,
and may you act justly toward them.

46 When they sin against you
—for there is no human being who does not sin—
and you rage against them, and give them before the enemy,
and they lead them captive, their captors, to the land of their
enemy, far or near,
47 but then they turn their heart in the land to which they were led
captive,
and return and plead to you in the land of their captivity, saying:
We have sinned and we have done perversely, we have done
wickedly!,
48 and they return to you with all their heart and with all their being,
in the land of their enemies who led them captive,
and they pray to you toward their land that you gave their fathers,
the city that you chose and the House that I have built to your
name—
49 then may you hearken in the heavens, the fixed-place of your
[royal] seat,
to their prayer and to their plea;
may you act justly toward them

43 **may *you* hearken:** Some manuscripts and Chronicles read, as in earlier paragraphs, "Then may you hearken . . ."
44 **toward:** Heb. *derekh*, the same word as "the road" in the previous phrase.

47 **turn their heart:** As in "having a change of heart." The verse plays on *shuv*, "turn/return" and *shavoh*, "take-captive, deport."

50 and forgive your people who have sinned against you
>for all the rebellious acts through which they have rebelled
>>against you,
>and grant them compassion before their captors, that they may
>>have compassion on them.

51 For they are your people and your inheritance, whom you brought
>>out from Egypt, from amid the iron furnace,

52 so that your eyes may be open to the plea of your servant, and to
>>the plea of your people Israel,
>to hearken to them whenever they call out to you.

53 For *you* have set them apart for yourself as an inheritance
>from all the peoples of the earth,
>as you promised by the hand of Moshe your servant, when you
>>brought out our fathers from Egypt, O Yʜwʜ God!

54 Now it was, when Shelomo had finished praying to Yʜwʜ all this
>>prayer and plea,
>that he arose from in front of the altar of Yʜwʜ, from bending
>>down on his knees, with his palms spread toward the heavens,

55 and he stood
>and he blessed
>the entire assembly of Israel in a loud voice, saying:

56 Blessed is Yʜwʜ,
>who has given rest to his people Israel, exactly as he promised;
>not one thing has failed of all his good words which he promised by
>>the hand of Moshe his servant!

57 May Yʜwʜ our God be with us
>as he was with our fathers
>—may he not abandon us, may he not leave us!—

58 inclining our heart toward him
>to walk in all his ways and to keep all his commandments, his laws,
>>and his judgments
>which he commanded our fathers.

---

51 **iron furnace:** A furnace used for smelting iron; this symbolic image of Egyptian bondage is used elsewhere in the Bible (for instance, Deut. 4:20 and Jer. 11:4).

53 **Moshe your servant:** A description of Moshe found mainly in Deuteronomy and later texts.

56 **failed:** Lit., "fallen."

Chapter 9. *The Warning; Labor; Shelomo's Accomplishments:* Just as the building of the Temple was preceded by a description of forced labor and accompanying dealings with Hiram king of Tyre, these return in Chap. 9, with some subtle variations. Hiram is not fully content with his payment of twenty Galilee towns in vv.11–14, though in vv.26–28 he does give Shelomo gold from Ofir. In between we are told how Shelomo impressed into service remnants of the Canaanites, whom the Israelites had not been able to totally drive out (see both Joshua and Judges); this, combined with mention of his wife, Pharaoh's daughter, imparts to the chapter a slightly ominous tone, given that in the Bible Canaanite presence and intermarriage most often bring with them the danger of idolatry.

This feeling is further amplified by the opening section of the chapter (vv.2–9), in which the king, in a second dream at Giv'on, is given a classic Deuteronomistic warning: following in the faithful ways of David will lead to a permanent dynasty, but failing to do so will lead to destruction and exile, with the Temple, so central over the previous four chapters, in ruins. After the glorious description and prayer of Chaps. 6–8, it is a sobering ending—written, perhaps, from the perspective of Israel in exile.

59 And may these words of mine which I have pleaded in the presence
       of Yhwh
    be near to Yhwh our God, day and night,
    to render justice [for] his servant and justice [for] his people Israel,
    each day's need in its day,
60 in order for all the peoples of the earth to know
    that Yhwh, he is God, there is none else!
61 And may your heart be complete with Yhwh our God,
    to walk in his laws and to keep his commandments, as is this day!

62 Now the king and all Israel with him were sacrificing sacrifices in
       the presence of Yhwh,
63 and Shelomo sacrificed as the sacrifice of *shalom* that he sacrificed
       to Yhwh
    twelve thousand oxen and a hundred twenty thousand sheep;
    thus they inaugurated the House of Yhwh,
    the king and all the Children of Israel.
64 On that day
    the king hallowed the middle of the courtyard that was in front of
       the House of Yhwh,
    for he performed there the offerings-up and the grain-gifts
    and the fat parts of the *shalom*-offerings,
    since the bronze altar that was in the presence of Yhwh was too
       small for containing the offerings-up, the grain-gifts, and the fat
       parts of the *shalom*-offerings.
65 So Shelomo observed the Festival at that time, and all Israel with
       him, a great assemblage,
    [coming] from Levo-Hamat to the Wadi of Egypt,
    in the presence of Yhwh our God, for seven days and seven days
       [more],
    fourteen days.
66 On the eighth day he sent the people off,
    and they gave the king farewell-blessing and went back to their tents,
    rejoicing and [feeling] good at heart

59 **need:** Elsewhere translated "portion."
64 **hallowed:** Referring to ritual purification. **fat parts:** Considered the choicest parts of the sacrifice, and hence reserved for God (see Lev. 3:14–16, and also the story of Kayin and Hevel [Cain and Abel] in Gen. 4).

65 **Levo-Hamat:** The "Entrance of Hamat," some fifty miles north of Damascus. **Yhwh our God:** As Cogan (2001) points out, this phrase, common in Deuteronomy, is unprecedented here. "Our" has the effect of bringing the audience into the scene.

over all the good things that Y<small>HWH</small> had done for David his servant
and for Israel his people.

9:1 Now it was, when Shelomo had finished building the House of
Y<small>HWH</small>, and the House of the King,
and every desire of Shelomo that he wished to do,

2 that Y<small>HWH</small> appeared to Shelomo a second time, [just] as he had
appeared to him at Giv'on.

3 And Y<small>HWH</small> said to him:
I have hearkened to your prayer and to your plea which you have
pleaded before me—
I have hallowed this House that you have built in which to set my
name there throughout the ages;
my eyes and my heart will be there all the days [to come].

4 As for you, if you walk before me
as David your father walked—in wholeness of heart and in
uprightness,
doing exactly what I commanded you,
and if my laws and my judgments you will keep,

5 I will establish your kingly throne Israel for the ages,
as I promised regarding David your father, saying:
No one will be cut off from you on the throne of Israel!

6 [But] if you should turn, yes, turn, you and your children, from
[following] after me
and do not keep my commandments and my laws that I have
placed before you,
but go and serve other gods and bow down to them,

7 I will cut off Israel from the face of the ground that I have given
them,
while the House that I have hallowed to my name
I will send away from my presence,
and Israel will become a proverb and a reproach among all peoples.

8 And this House will become a ruin;
all who cross by it will be appalled and will whistle,

9:2 **at Giv'on:** See 3:4–14.
5 **as I promised regarding David:** See 2:4.
6 **if you should turn:** As elsewhere, the future exile
is here alluded to, probably a later addition. **you:**
Walsh points out that from here through v.9, "you"
is in the plural.

7 **reproach:** Heb. *shenina*, from a verb denoting
"sharp."
8 **a ruin:** MT has Heb. *'elyon*, "exalted," undoubtedly, even though it makes little sense, to substitute
a euphemism for what versions rightly read as *le-
'iyyin*. **whistle:** In amazement.

and they will say:
Why did YHWH do thus to this land and to this House?
9 And they will say:
Because they abandoned YHWH their God, who brought their
fathers out from the land of Egypt;
they held fast to other gods, they bowed down to them and served
them—
therefore has YHWH brought all this evil upon them!

10 Now it was at the end of twenty years during which Shelomo built
the two houses,
the House of YHWH and the House of the King,
11 —Hiram king of Tyre had supplied Shelomo with trees of cedar
and trees of juniper, and gold, as much as he desired—
[that] then King Shelomo gave Hiram twenty towns in the region
of the Galilee;
12 but when Hiram went out from Tyre, to see the towns that
Shelomo had given him,
they were not right in his eyes.
13 He said:
What are these towns that you have given me, brother?
So they called them the Region of Cavul / As Nothing, until this day.
14 And Hiram sent the king a hundred and twenty talents of gold.

15 Now this was the matter of the forced-labor that King Shelomo
raised
for building the House of YHWH, his own House, the Earthfill, the
wall of Jerusalem,
and Hatzor and Megiddo and Gezer:

---

13 **brother:** A treaty term for an equal partner.
14 **talents:** Heb. *kikkar,* a "round thing," the heaviest unit of weight in the Bible.
15 **Earthfill:** This reference, which occurs a number of times in Samuel and Kings, seems to be to a supporting structure used by Israel's kings in the building up of Jerusalem. It is often identified with the "Stepped Stone Structure" unearthed just south of the present Old City of Jerusalem. **Hatzor:** Pronounced *hah-TZOR;* trad. English "Hazor," a city north of the Sea of Galilee, on two major trade routes. Its ruins have recently been the site of considerable archaeological activity. **Megiddo:** Pronounced *meh-gee-DOE.* Situated at a pass which gives access to major movements of traders and troops from eastern empires down through the Coastal Plain, this was

the site of crucial battles throughout antiquity. Its name of the "Hill of Megiddo," *Har Megiddo,* has entered the English language as "Armageddon"— the Final Battle mentioned in the New Testament (Rev. 16:16) and a general catchword for the end of the world. **Gezer:** Pronounced *GEH-zer.* In the foothills west of Jerusalem, not far from modern Ramleh, it controlled yet another route of access: to the Coastal Plain from Jerusalem and the highlands. Thus the three cities mentioned in this verse were of signal strategic importance, and all three have left evidence of almost identical massive buildings, containing chambered gates with casemate walls. Many archaeologists connect these with the period of Shelomo (tenth century B.C.E.), although some date them later.

Chapter 10. *The Queen's Visit; Shelomo's Opulence:* In an encounter made famous through legend and art, Shelomo is now visited by the exotic Queen of Sheba. Interpreters have spent centuries speculating on the nature of their relationship, and the last emperor of Ethiopia, the colorful Haile Selassie (ruled 1930–1974), claimed descent from their union. But the text gives no hint of a romantic relationship, and focuses instead on how overwhelmed the queen is by the magnificence of Shelomo and his court. While the meeting (vv.4–9) cites "wisdom" as the thing that makes the greatest impression upon her, it is in fact "gold," mentioned ten times in vv.14–25, which dominates the chapter once she has departed. Thus material splendor threatens to overcome the wisdom motif. And the chapter ends with a description of Shelomo's holdings in horses, exactly the item whose acquisition was warned against in Deut. 17:16, along with a prohibition against amassing too much gold in the very next verse. What we may well have here, then, is a good example of how a tradition originally intended to be a positive one (Shelomo's splendor) comes, in the context of the next chapter and Deuteronomistic History (DH) overall, to take on a negative tone. The text has its own life, as it were.

The chapter abounds in numbers—not surprising, given that it seeks to impress both the royal visitor and the reader—and makes use mostly of multiples of three and six, beginning with 666 in v.14. Such patterned numbers in many ancient cultures point to the ideas of abundance and perfection. Also notable throughout the chapter is the repetition, from the very first verse, of the Hebrew letter *shin;* the *sh*-sounds punctuate the text, as if to echo the queen's feeling of being overwhelmed by King *Sh*elomo and his accomplishments.

16 —Pharaoh king of Egypt had gone up
and had taken Gezer and burned it with fire,
while the Canaanites who were settled in the city he had killed,
and he had given it as a sendoff-gift to his daughter, Shelomo's
wife—
17 Shelomo built Gezer and Lower Bet-Horon,
18 Baalat and Tadmor in the wilderness, in the land [of Judah],
19 and all the storage towns that belonged to Shelomo and the chariot
towns and the steeds' towns,
and the desirable things that Shelomo desired to build in Jerusalem
and in the Levanon,
and throughout all the land of his rule.
20 All the people left from the Amorites, the Hittites, the Perizzites,
the Hivvites, and the Yevusites,
who were not of the Children of Israel,
21 their children who were left after them in the land,
whom the Children of Israel were not able to devote-to-
destruction—
Shelomo raised them up for slave labor, until this day.
22 But from the Children of Israel Shelomo did not make a slave,
for they were the men of battle, namely, his servants, his
commanders, his officers, his chariot commanders, and his steed-
riders.
23 [And] these were the prefect commanders, Those Over Shelomo's
Work:
fifty and five hundred,
who were supervising the people who were doing the work.
24 Nevertheless, Pharaoh's daughter went up from the City of David
to her house which he had built for her;
then he built the Earthfill.

16 **sendoff-gift:** Some understand this as "dowry."
17 **Bet-Horon:** This town allows access to Jerusalem from the west; as Gray (1970) notes, it was strategically important in the later Hasmonean (second century B.C.E.) and Roman (first century C.E.) wars.
18 **Baalat . . . Tadmor:** The identification is uncertain, but it is likely, on the analogy of the previous verses, that these too were strategic sites. The rendering "Tadmor" for MT "Tamar" is based on ancient versions and II Chron. 8:4, and makes more sense, given that it is inside the land of Israel like the other

locations on the list (Cogan 2001). **[of Judah]:** The hanging "land of" in MT does not make sense.
20 **Amorites . . . :** Mentioned often in the Torah as a term for the indigenous peoples of Canaan.
21 **slave:** Heb. *'eved,* elsewhere rendered "servant" or "serf."
22 **steed-riders:** This might be a late text, or from a later perspective; cavalry seems not to have been in use at this point in Israel's history.
23 **these:** A list seems to be missing here.

◆ 25 Now Shelomo would offer up, three times a year, offerings-up and
   shalom-offerings
   on the altar that he had built to Y<small>HWH</small>,
   and would send up smoke with it, on the one in the presence of
   Y<small>HWH</small>;
   thus he kept the House [in] complete [repair].

26 Now Shelomo made a fleet-of-ships at Etzyon-Gever that is by Elat,
   next to the Reed Sea in the land of Edom.

27 And Hiram sent by ship his servants, the men for ships, those
   knowing the sea,
   along with the servants of Shelomo.

28 They came to Ofir and took away gold from there, four hundred
   and twenty talents,
   and they brought it to King Shelomo.

10:1 Now the Queen of Sheba had been hearing the reports of Shelomo,
   for the fame of Y<small>HWH</small>,
   and so she came to test him with riddles.

2 She came to Jerusalem with an exceedingly heavy array:
   camels carrying spices and gold, in exceeding abundance, and
   precious stones.
   She came to Shelomo and spoke to him all that was on her mind,

3 and Shelomo told her [the answer to] all her words;
   there was no matter so hidden from the king that he could not
   tell her.

4 And the Queen of Sheba saw all Shelomo's wisdom,
   and the House that he had built,

---

25 **kept . . . [in] complete [repair]:** It is not clear what
is meant here. Others: "paid [vows]." Kimhi understands the phrase as meaning "he completed the
arrangements for the Temple rituals." The Heb. *shil-
lem* also puns with "*shalom*-offerings" (*shelamim*) and
"Shelomo" (Walsh).
26 **Etzyon-Gever:** On the Gulf of Aqaba, and hence
an outlet for trade with Africa and/or India. **Reed
Sea:** Others, "Red Sea" (not the same as the famous
site in Exodus), "Gulf of Aqaba," or even "Endmost
Sea" (reading *sof* for *suf*).
28 **Ofir:** Possibly in southwest Arabia.
10:1 **Sheba:** Trad. English; Heb. "Sh'va." It is identified as
today's country of Yemen, in the southern part of
the Arabian Peninsula. **Sheba, Shelomo . . . she:**

The Hebrew is even more alliterative, with *u-malkat
sh'va shomaat et sheima shelomo le-sheim* Y<small>HWH</small>. I was
tempted to use "shining-reports" in the translation,
for that reason. **for the fame of Y<small>HWH</small>:** It is not
entirely clear what is meant here; it probably points
to Y<small>HWH</small> as the source of Shelomo's success (see
Cogan 2001). **riddles:** Cogan (2001) elevates this
to "difficult questions," since "riddles" may have too
light a connotation in modern culture.
3 **words:** Others, "problems," "questions." **hidden:**
Or "obscure."
4 **House:** Once again, the word could refer to either
the Temple or the royal palace; it appears logically
to be the latter.

5 and the food at his table, the seating of his court-servants, his
    attendants' standing and their attire, and his cupbearers,
and his offering[s]-up that he would offer up in the House of
    Yhwh,
and she was left breathless.

6 She said to the king:
True was the word that I heard in my land about your way-with-
    words, about your wisdom!

7 Now I did not believe the words until I came [here] and my own
    eyes saw it,
but here: I had not been told the half [of it]:
you have more wisdom and bounty than the report that I had
    heard!

8 O the happiness of your men, O the happiness of these your
    servants who stand [in attendance] before you regularly,
who hear your wisdom!

9 May Yhwh your God be blessed,
who has taken pleasure in you,
to place you on the throne of Israel.
Because of Yhwh's love for Israel, for the ages,
he has made you king, to render justice and equity!

10 And she gave the king a hundred and twenty talents of gold
and an exceeding abundance of spices, and precious stones;
such spices never came again in abundance
that the Queen of Sheba gave King Shelomo.

11 And also Hiram's ships, which carried gold from Ofir,
brought *almug* wood from Ofir, exceedingly much, and precious
    stones.

12 And the king made from the *almug* wood railings for the House of
    Yhwh and for the House of the King,
and lyres and harps for the singers;
no such *almug* wood had come [before],
and none has been seen until this day.

---

5 **she was left breathless:** Following JPS; it might also
be rendered, "It took her breath away." Curiously,
the same expression is used to describe the Canaanites in fear right before the conquest of Jericho (see
Josh. 5:1).
6 **way-with-words:** Following B-R.

7 **bounty:** Lit., "good things."
8 **men:** Some ancient versions read "women."
11 **almug wood:** The identification is not certain; some
surmise red sandalwood.
12 **railings:** Others, "paths," "steps," "materials for fur-
nishing" (Mulder).

◆ 13 Now King Shelomo gave the Queen of Sheba whatever she wished,
      that she had requested,
   aside from what had been given her according to the capacity of
      King Shelomo.
   Then she faced about and went back to her land, she and her
      servants.

   14 Now the weight of gold that came to Shelomo in a single year
      was six hundred sixty-six talents of gold,
   15 besides [what came] from the tradesmen and from the commerce
      of the merchants
      and all the kings of Arabia and governors of the land.
   16 And King Shelomo made two hundred [large] shields of hammered
      gold,
      —six hundred gold pieces would go for each one shield—
   17 and three hundred bucklers of hammered gold
      —three *minas* of gold would go for each one buckler—
      and the king put them in the House of the Forest of the Levanon.
   18 And the king made a great throne of ivory,
      and he overlaid it with refined gold.
   19 There were six steps for the throne,
      with a rounded top to the throne, on its back,
      with armrests on this-side and on that-side at the place of sitting,
      and two lions standing beside the armrests,
   20 and twelve male-lions standing there on the six steps, on this-side
      and on that-side;
      none such was made in any [other] kingdom.
   21 Now all of King Shelomo's drinking vessels were of gold,
      while all the vessels of the House of the Forest of the Levanon
      were of fine gold;
      there were none of silver—it was not reckoned of any [value] in the
      days of Shelomo.

---

13 **according to the capacity of:** Cogan (2001): "as befitted."

17 **bucklers:** Small forearm shields, designed primarily for mobile or hand-to-hand combat. ***minas:*** Weights of fifty *shekels*, according to Ezek. 45:12. As

with many biblical measures, an accurate modern equivalent is difficult to calculate.

18 **throne of ivory:** Most likely, inlaid with ivory.

19 **rounded top:** Some suggest a "calf's head."

22 For the king had a shipping-fleet of Tarshish on the sea,
   along with Hiram's ships;
   once out of every three years, a ship of Tarshish would come
   carrying gold and silver,
   tusks, monkeys, and peacocks.
23 So King Shelomo was greater than all the kings of the earth, in
      riches and in wisdom,
24 and all the earth was seeking Shelomo's face
   to hear his wisdom which God had put in his heart;
25 they brought, each one, his tribute:
   vessels of silver and vessels of gold,
   clothing and weaponry and spices,
   horses and mules—
   each year's due in its year.
26 And Shelomo gathered chariots and steeds:
   he had a thousand and four hundred chariots and twelve thousand
      steeds,
   and he put them in chariot towns and with the king in Jerusalem.
27 And the king made the silver in Jerusalem like stones,
   while the cedars he made like sycamores that are in the lowlands, in
      abundance.
28 And the import-source of horses for Shelomo was from Egypt and
      from Kue;
   the king's merchants would get them from Kue at a fixed-price.
29 So a chariot imported from Egypt would go for six hundred silver
      pieces, and a horse for fifty and a hundred.
   Thus it was for all the Hittite kings and the Amorite kings;
   by their [own] hand they exported them.

22 **Tarshish:** Either a geographic location, either Spain or somewhere further east in the Mediterranean, or else a general designation for the smelting of metals. In the latter case, "ships of Tarshish" would be large ships designed to transport metals (see Isa. 2:16, Ezek. 27:25). **tusks . . . :** The identification is not clear; perhaps exotic animals are purposely included (Walsh).
24 **all the earth:** versions add "the kings of," as in v.23.
26 **put:** MT reads "led," which is a bit strange.

27 **like stones . . . like sycamores . . . in abundance:** That is, as widespread as these common substances.
28 **Egypt:** Heb. *mitzrayim,* but some propose Mutzri, north of the Taurus Mountains. **Kue:** On the coast of today's Turkey, south of the Taurus Mountains, it was later known as Cilicia.
29 **chariot:** Or perhaps "chariot and team" (Gray 1970). **by their [own] hand:** That is, by the agency of Shelomo's traders.

Chapter 11. *Shelomo's Last Years: Foreign Wives and the Beginnings of Revolt:* Despite all the previous emphasis on the king's wisdom, the Temple, and the glory of the court, the biblical traditions about Shelomo end on an unabashedly negative note. As is usual in Deuteronomistic texts, the eventual collapse of Shelomo's unified kingdom is attributed to idolatry, brought on by his marriage to foreign women. This is in keeping with the warnings registered in Deut. 7 and 17.

Several motifs which will recur in Kings appear for the first time in this chapter. One is the postponement of punishment until the next generation (v.12), while another is the prophet's reporting of God's word to a king (although in this case it is a king-to-be, Yorov'am). That speech, in vv.31–39, is typical of the Deuteronomistic passages in Kings, concentrating as it does on the reason for specific future events.

So Shelomo dies, with his great accomplishments overshadowed for the moment by the imminent dissolution of his kingdom. The rebel Yorov'am waits in the wings, and Shelomo is powerless to eliminate him before his death, unlike the ruthless successes against potential rivals that had marked the beginning of his reign.

◆ 11:1 Now King Shelomo loved many foreign women, along with
       Pharaoh's daughter:
       Moavites, Ammonites, Edomites, Sidonians, and Hittites,
    2 from the nations of which YHWH had said to the Children of Israel:
       You are not to come among them and *they* are not to come among
         you—
       surely, they will incline away your heart after their gods.
       To them Shelomo clung in love.
    3 He had princess wives, seven hundred,
       and concubines, three hundred,
       and his wives inclined away his heart.
    4 So it was at the time of Shelomo's old age:
       his wives inclined away his heart after other gods,
       and his heart was not complete with YHWH his God,
       like the heart of David his father.
    5 Shelomo went [following] after Astarte godhead of the Sidonians
       and after Milkom the Detestable One of the Ammonites.
    6 So Shelomo did what was evil in the eyes of YHWH;
       he did not fully-follow after YHWH, like David his father.
    7 And Shelomo built a sanctuary to Kemosh the Detestable-One of
        Moav,
       on the hill that faces Jerusalem,
       and to Molekh, the Detestable One of the Children of Ammon.
    8 Thus did he do for all his foreign wives,
       those sending up smoke and offering-sacrifices to their gods.
    9 So YHWH was enraged at Shelomo,
       for he had inclined his heart away from YHWH, the God of Israel,
       who had appeared to him twice,

11:1 **foreign:** The word is omitted in LXX, along with v.3's "and his wives inclined away his heart."

2 **clung in love:** The phrase seems to point to the women, but "clung" is also used in the Bible to refer to the worship of gods (Walsh).

4 **complete:** Heb. *shalem*, playing on Shelomo's name as one whose heart was *not* "complete" with God.

5 **Astarte:** The name of a goddess or group of goddesses, found throughout the ancient Near East in various forms, and corresponding to the Greek Aphrodite and the planet Venus. The Hebrew form *Ash-*

toret uses the vowels of the word *boshet*, "shame," to fill out what may originally have been "Astart." Similarly constructed are a number of other biblical names for pagan gods—such as "the Molekh" (for Malik), and "Kemosh" (using the vowels of *be'osh*, "stench," for Kamish), both in v.7. **godhead:** Tellingly, biblical Hebrew has no word for "goddess."

7 **faces:** Others "east of." **Molekh:** Pronounced *MO-lekh*. Possibly a god, and often associated in Kings with child sacrifice. LXX, though, reads "Milkom" here.

◆ 10 and had commanded him about this matter, not to walk after other
     gods,
    but he had not kept what YHWH had commanded him.

11 And YHWH said to Shelomo:
    Because this was your [intention],
    namely, you have not kept my covenant and my laws which I
     commanded you,
    I will tear, yes, tear the kingdom away from you and give it to your
     servant!

12 However, in your own days I will not do it,
    for the sake of David your father;
    from the hand of your son I will tear it away.

13 Yet I will not tear away the entire kingdom:
    one tribe I will give to your son, for the sake of David my servant,
    and for the sake of Jerusalem, which I have chosen.

14 So YHWH raised up an adversary to Shelomo,
    Hadad the Edomite, who was from the royal seed in Edom.

15 Now it was, when David struck Edom, when Yoav Commander of
    the Armed-Forces had gone up to bury [all] the slain—
    he struck down all the males in Edom,

16 since for six months Yoav and all Israel stayed there, until he had
    cut off all the males in Edom—

17 that Hadad ran away, he and his fighting-men, Edomites from
    among his father's servants with him, to come to Egypt,
    and Hadad was [then] a young lad.

18 They proceeded from Midyan and came to Pa'ran,
    and took fighting-men with them from Pa'ran
    and came to Egypt, to Pharaoh king of Egypt;
    he gave him a house, and food he assigned for him,
    and land he gave him.

---

10 **him:** Added, following ancient versions.

11 **was your [intention]:** Or "in your mind." **tear . . .
away:** The same language used regarding Sha'ul's
forfeiting the kingship in I Sam. 15:28.

13 **one tribe:** Yehuda. Perhaps Binyamin is also understood as included, to make the overall tribal division
ten plus two.

14 **adversary:** The Hebrew word, *satan*, later developed

into familiar "Satan"; here it denotes only a human
being. **Hadad:** A theophoric name (containing the
name of a deity), using that of a well-known storm
god worshipped by the Arameans. **royal seed:** I.e.,
royal family.

15 **struck:** Following LXX; MT has "was."

17 **Hadad:** In this case, MT spells as "Adad."

19	And Hadad found exceeding favor in the eyes of Pharaoh,
	so that he gave him as wife the sister of his own wife, the sister of
		the *Tah'penes,* the queen-mother.
20	The sister of the *Tah'penes* bore him Genuvat his son, and the
		Tah'penes weaned him amid the house of Pharaoh.
	And Genuvat remained in the house of Pharaoh, amid Pharaoh's
		sons.
21	Now when Hadad heard in Egypt that David lay beside his fathers,
	and that Yoav Commander of the Armed-Forces was dead,
	Hadad said to Pharaoh:
	Send me off, that I may go back to my land.
22	Pharaoh said to him:
	What do you lack with me
	that here, you seek to go back to your land?
	He said:
	No[thing], but send, send me off!

23	And God raised up against him an[other] adversary,
	Rezon son of Elyada,
	who had run away from Hadad'ezer king of Tzova, his lord.
24	He gathered fighting-men to himself
	and became commander of a raiding-band,
	when David was killing them,
	and he went to Damascus and settled in it, and he became king in
		Damascus.
25	He was an adversary to Israel all the days of Shelomo, along with
		the evil that Hadad . . . ;
	he felt loathing at Israel,
	and he reigned as king over Aram.

19	**the *Tah'penes*:** Pronounced *tah-pe-NACE.* The meaning in Egyptian indicates a title, "wife of the king."
20	**Genuvat:** Pronounced *ge-noo-VAHT.* It possibly means "stranger" or "outsider," like Moshe's son Gershom (Exod. 2:22). The whole verse is reminiscent of the Moshe story. **weaned:** LXX reads "brought up."
23	**Rezon:** Possibly meaning "dignitary." **Elyada:** "God Knows"—an ironic allusion to the "know" theme in Chaps. 1–2, which were also concerned

with succession to the throne. **Tzova:** South of Damascus.
24	**when David was killing them:** Here, as in most translations, this phrase is understood as having been misplaced in v.24, where it stands in MT. The incident referred to occurs in II Sam. 8. **went . . . settled . . . became king:** Following LXX; MT has plural.
25	**that Hadad . . . :** Hebrew unclear; most translations add "did." **felt loathing at:** JPS: "repudiated."

26 Now Yorov'am son of Nevat the Efratite, from Tzereda,
—his mother's name was Tzerua, a widow woman—
was a servant of Shelomo,
but he raised a hand against the king.

27 And this is the matter in which he raised a hand against the king:
when Shelomo built the Earthfill,
he closed up the breach of the City of David his father.

28 Now the man Yorov'am was a mighty-man of valor;
Shelomo saw the lad,
that he was a [skilled] doer of work,
so he appointed him over all the burden-force of the House of
Yosef.

29 It was at [about] that time,
when Yorov'am went out of Jerusalem,
that Ahiyya the Shilonite, the prophet, encountered him on the
road
—he had covered himself with a new cloak—
and the two of them were alone in the open-field.

30 And Ahiyya seized the new cloak that was on him
and tore it into twelve torn-pieces;

31 he said to Yorov'am:
Take yourself ten torn-pieces,
for thus says YHWH, the God of Israel:
Here, I am about to tear away the kingdom from the hand of
Shelomo
and will give you the ten tribes,

32 while the one tribe will remain his,
for the sake of my servant David
and for the sake of Jerusalem,
the city which I have chosen from all the tribes of Israel—

---

26 **Yorov'am:** Some read as "Yarov'am"; trad. English "Jeroboam." It means either "May God [lit. 'the kinsman'] Be Great" or "May the People [kin] Increase." **Efratite:** From the northern tribe of Efrayim. **Tzerua:** The sound of the name echoes the skin disease *tzaraat*, which in the Bible is often seen as reflecting wrongdoing. So its use may be intentional here, given Yorov'am's low standing in the eyes of the author(s) of Kings. **raised a hand:** That is, rebelled.
28 **burden-force:** Walsh and others understand this to refer to porters or haulers. **the House of Yosef:**

The northern region, which was shortly to become the kingdom of Israel.
29 **Ahiyya:** Pronounced *ah-hee-YAH;* trad. English "Ahijah." It means "Yah (YHWH) Is My Brother." **Shilonite:** From the town of Shilo in the highlands of Efrayim, an important religious center in premonarchic days. **new:** Typically in folk literature and ancient religion, what is new has magical properties or can even be considered holy.
31–32 **ten . . . one:** See the note to v.13 above. LXX and other versions read "two" for the second number.

33 because he has abandoned me and bowed down to Astarte goddess
of the Sidonians,
to Kemosh god of Moav,
and to Milkom god of the Children of Ammon,
and has not walked in my ways,
to do what is right in my eyes—my laws and my judgments,
like David his father.

34 But I will not take away the entire kingdom from his hand;
indeed, I will make him exalted-leader all the days of his life,
for the sake of David my servant, whom I chose,
who kept my commandments and my laws.

35 But I will take away the kingdom from the hand of his son
and will give it to you,
the ten tribes.

36 Yet to his son I will give one tribe,
in order that there may be a lamp for David my servant all the days
[to come] in my presence in Jerusalem,
the city that I chose for myself to put my name there.

37 And you I will take,
that you may reign as king over all that you crave,
and you shall be king over Israel.

38 Now it will be:
if you hearken to all that I command you,
and walk in my ways,
and do what is right in my eyes,
keeping my laws and my commandments
as David my servant did,
then I will be with you;
I will build you a firm house, as I built for David,
and I will give you Israel.

39 And I will afflict the seed of David on account of this,
yet not for all the days [to come].

33 **he . . . :** Following ancient versions; MT has "they."
34 **exalted-leader:** Or "chief" (Heb. *nasi*). Since this old term is not exactly synonymous with "king," our verse may be a subtle demoting of Shelomo (Gray 1970).

36 **lamp:** Found also in 15:4 and II Kings 8:19, this term (Heb. *ner*) is taken to indicate either dynasty continuity or dominion (*nir*) in recent scholarship.
39 **this:** Presumably, Shelomo's deeds.

40 Shelomo sought to put Yorov'am to death,
so Yorov'am arose and ran away to Egypt, to Shishak king of
Egypt,
and remained in Egypt until Shelomo's death.

41 Now the rest of the events of Shelomo, and all that he did, and his
wisdom—
are they not written in the Record of the Events of Shelomo?

42 Now the days that Shelomo reigned as king in Jerusalem, over all
Israel, were forty years;

43 then Shelomo lay beside his fathers,
and he was buried in the City of David his father,
and Rehav'am his son reigned as king in his place.

---

40 **Shishak:** Pronounced *shee-SHOCK.* Shoshenq I (late
tenth century) was the founder of Egypt's Twenty-
Second Dynasty.

41 **Record of the Events:** Affairs of state; Cogan (2001),
"History." Shelomo is the only king to have his own
personal book of annals thus cited.

42 **forty:** The standard "magical" number again.

43 **Rehav'am:** Pronounced *reh-hav-AHM;* meaning
either "God [the Kinsman] Has Caused Expansion"
or "The People [Kin] Has Expanded"; trad. English
"Rehoboam." Cogan (2001) notes how both his and
Yorov'am's names may point to the prosperity of
the Solomonic era.

PART II

THE SPLIT: KINGS NORTH AND SOUTH

(I 12–16:22)

SHELOMO'S DEATH IS FOLLOWED BY AN EVENT THAT FLOWED FROM THE NATURAL geographical and economic conditions of the land of Israel: the splitting of his little empire into two independent kingdoms. While the Bible's overall explanation for this fateful event is Shelomo's idolatry in old age, the immediate impetus for the political fracture is his son Rehav'am's shortcomings as a ruler, following hard on the rigors of Shelomo's extensive building program. But the writers are also at pains to make clear that the new king of the north, Yorov'am, commits a grave act of rebellion against YHWH by establishing rival sanctuaries to the Jerusalem Temple and constructing molten calves of gold. Scholars note that, from the perspective of northern practice, these and other cultic acts of Yorov'am do not actually constitute idol worship, but the text is written from a southern point of view, and hence Yorov'am emerges as a kind of model sinner. From this point on in chronicling events in the north, the text will compare every one of its kings to this first one, emphasizing how virtually all of them continued in his nefarious tradition. And, as Cogan (2001) points out, only two of them will die a peaceful death: Omri and Yehu, both of whom will found dynasties. It is as if the Northern Kingdom is doomed from the start because of Yorov'am's deeds.

With the rift accomplished, the bulk of Israel's history on the land is presented in the form of two parallel accounts which alternate but are at the same time interwoven. As background it should be noted that the Northern Kingdom of Israel, large, fertile, and prosperous, lay closer to the eastern lands of the Fertile Crescent, and thus was involved in greater economic and cultural interaction with other civilizations. In contrast, the Southern Kingdom of Judah, with its rocky hills and relative isolation, was, at least corresponding to this point in the narrative, less prominent in both text and historical record.

The dynastic history of Israel recounted in Kings is a troubled one, marked by frequent changes in rulership brought about through coups and assassinations. While the standard Assyrian reference to the north by the name Bit Humri, "The House of Omri," does not reflect the complex picture that emerges from biblical texts, it does demonstrate the prominence of that particular dynasty, and Kings is at pains to describe its rise and fall.

This long middle section of the book, here encompassing Parts II–IV, is punctu-ated by so-called regnal formulas, the descriptions of kings' accessions and deaths by means of standardized expressions. Thus a typical king of Israel is said to come to the throne in Year X of a corresponding king of Judah's reign, and vice versa. We are given his age on accession, the length of his reign, and often his mother's name—an important element in a society where kings, at least, could be polyg-amous. More important, from the Bible's point of view, is the evaluation that usually follows: "He did what was evil/good in the eyes of YHWH" (always with either Yorov'am or David as the measuring rod), a phrase which lets us know up front how the text wishes us to evaluate the king's tenure. At the other end of a typical reign, three things are usually noted: first, mention is made of a mysteri-ous "Record of Yearly Events (or Annals) of the Kings of ____" for any further information we may require; second, the king's death, if peaceful, is described in the phrase "he lay beside his fathers"; and third, the name of his successor, usually his son, is noted. These formulaic phrases provide coherence to a long series of narratives, and also enable the text to occasionally moderate its black-and-white stance by deviating slightly from the standard phrasing. So, for example, there are passages such as II 14:3–4, where

> He [Amatzyahu] did what was right in the eyes of YHWH—
> however, not like David his father;
> exactly as Yoash his father had done, he did.
> However, the sanctuaries were not removed;
> the people still were offering-sacrifices and sending-up-smoke at the
> sanctuaries.

Chapter 12. *Rehav'am and the Split; Yorov'am and the Calves:* The division of the kingdom is recounted, not by a humdrum description of events, but by a dramatic narrative. We are presented with the age-old clash between the old, to whom experience has taught political wisdom, and the young, who think they know better. The text raises the issue of "serving," but the real problem is ironically posed here by the ten-time repetition of the word "return": Will the kingdom be returned to its previous state of wholeness?

In order to prevent the restoration of the newly independent north to the con-trol of Jerusalem, Yorov'am takes the fateful step of constructing two golden calves, in a move that textually echoes the Israelites' apostasy in Exod. 32. While it is possible, as mentioned above, that this action did not constitute idolatry—the calves, in this view, would have served simply as YHWH's symbolic footstool—it certainly was seen that way by subsequent biblical writers/editors, who trace all

12:1   Rehav'am went to Shekhem,
for to Shekhem all Israel came to make him king.

2   And it was, when Yorov'am son of Nevat heard—he was still in
    Egypt, where he had run away from before King Shelomo—
that Yorov'am returned from Egypt.

3   They sent and called for him, and Yorov'am and the entire assembly
    of Israel came
and spoke to Rehav'am, saying:

4   Your father made our yoke hard,
but *you* now, lighten your father's hard servitude
and the heavy yoke that he placed upon us,
and we will serve you!

5   He said to them:
Go off for three days, and [then] return to me.
So the people went off.

6   And King Rehav'am sought advice from the elders who had stood
    before Shelomo his father when he was alive, saying:
How do you advise returning word to this people?

7   They spoke to him, saying:
If today you would be servant to this people, and would serve
    them,
then answer them and speak good words to them,
and they will be servants to you all the days [to come].

8   But he abandoned the advice of the elders which they had advised
    him;
he sought advice from the youngsters who had grown up with him,
    who were standing [in service] before him.

9   He said to them:
What do you advise that we return as word to this people,
who spoke to me, saying:
Lighten the yoke that your father placed upon us!?

12:1 **Shekhem:** This city, today's Nablus, about sixty miles north of Jerusalem, is prominently featured in biblical narratives from Genesis through Judges, and was a major cultic center.

2 **returned:** MT has "lived in" (Heb. *va-yeshev*), but the "returned" (*va-yoshav*) reflected in LXX and II Chron. 10:2 better echoes the theme word of Chaps. 12–13.

7 **speak good words:** Often understood as "kind words," but in the language of the ancient Near East, including the Bible, this expression denotes concluding a covenant (Weinfeld 2000; see also the Comment to II Sam. 7:28, above).

8 **abandoned:** The same word used above in 11:33, to describe his father Shelomo's faithlessness toward God.

of the kingdom of Israel's troubles back to this moment. Thus every northern king will be compared to Yorov'am, "who made Israel to sin." To compound his central crime in the eyes of southern writers, Yorov'am makes priests of non-Levites and establishes a new holy day on the calendar. In Walsh's words, "he celebrates at the wrong time, in the wrong place, on the wrong altar, in honor of the wrong gods."

10 The youngsters who had grown up with him said:
Say thus to this people who spoke to you, saying:
Your father made our yoke heavy,
but you—lighten [it] from upon us!
Thus should you speak to them:
My little-thing is thicker than my father's loins!

11 So-now:
my father loaded a heavy yoke upon you,
but *I* will add to your yoke;
my father disciplined you with whips,
but *I* will discipline you with "scorpions"!

12 So when Yorov'am and the people came to Rehav'am on the
third day,
as the king had spoken to them, saying: Return to me on the
third day.

13 And the king answered the people roughly;
he abandoned the advice of the elders that they had advised

14 and spoke to them according to the advice of the youngsters, saying:
My father made your yoke heavy,
but *I* will add to your yoke;
my father disciplined you with whips,
but *I* will discipline you with "scorpions"!

15 Now the king did not hearken to the people,
for it was a reversal-of-events from YHWH,
in order that he might fulfill his word that YHWH had spoken by the
hand of Ahiyya the Shilonite to Yorov'am son of Nevat.

16 And all Israel saw that the king had not hearkened to them,
so the people returned word to the king, saying:
What portion do we have in David?
No inheritance in the son of Yishai!
To your tents, O Israel!
Now—see to your own house, O David!
And Israel went back to their tents.

10 **little-thing:** Others, "little finger," but the entire phrase makes equal sense as a sexual reference.
11 **"scorpions":** Perhaps more elaborate devices than the whips mentioned earlier in the verse.
15 **fulfill:** Or "confirm." **his word:** See 11:31ff., where Ahiyya the prophet foretells the split.

16 **What portion . . . :** Parallel to the words of the rebel Sheva son of Bikhri in II Sam. 20:1. Probably there had been an undercurrent of dissatisfaction with the rule of the Davidic dynasty all along (Gray 1970).

◆ 17 But as for the Children of Israel who were settled in the towns of Judah,
    Rehav'am reigned as king over them.

18 And King Rehav'am sent Adoram, [The One] Over the Forced-Labor,
    but all Israel pelted him with stones, so that he died,
    while King Rehav'am managed to go up into a chariot, to flee to Jerusalem.
19 So Israel rebelled against the House of David—until this day.

20 Now it was, when all Israel heard that Yorov'am had returned,
    that they sent and called him to the Community
    and made him king over all Israel;
    there was no one [following] after the House of David except for the tribe of Yehuda alone.
21 Rehav'am came to Jerusalem, and he assembled the entire House of Judah, along with the tribe of Binyamin,
    a hundred eighty thousand chosen ones, ready for battle,
    to do battle with the House of Israel,
    to return the kingship to Rehav'am son of Shelomo.
22 But the word of God [came] to Shema'ya, the man of God, saying:
23 Say to Rehav'am son of Shelomo, king of Judah, and to the entire House of Judah, and Binyamin
    and the rest of the people, saying:
24 Thus says YHWH:
    You are not to go up, you are not to do battle with your brothers, the Children of Israel;
    return, each one to his house, for from me is this matter!
    They hearkened to the word of YHWH,
    and they turned back, going in accordance with the word of YHWH.

---

18 **Adoram:** Pronounced *ah-doe-RAHM*. Earlier "Adoniram." As Gray (1970) points out, he is the wrong choice as envoy in this situation. **managed:** Others: "with effort."

19 **rebelled:** Cogan/Tadmor note that the verb used for rebellion here, Heb. *p-sh-'*, carries legal and religious overtones (a vassal rebelling against his lord), as contrasted with the more standard *m-r-d*, "revolt," used elsewhere. **until this day:** So this part of the text would predate the destruction of the Northern Kingdom in 722.

20 **Community:** Some kind of representative body, probably of nobles or tribal leaders.

22 **Shema'ya:** "YHWH Hearkens," which is ironic given the use of the verb in this chapter (vv.15, 16, 25).

24 **go up:** The verb often implies "to attack" (Cogan 2001).

25 Yorov'am built up Shekhem in the highlands of Efrayim, and held
     seat in it;
  then he went out from there and built up Penuel.
26 And Yorov'am said in his heart:
  Now the kingdom may [well] return to the House of David;
27 if this people should go up to make sacrifices at the House of
     YHWH in Jerusalem,
  the heart of the people will turn back to their lord, to Rehav'am
     king of Judah,
  and they will kill me
  and return to Rehav'am king of Judah!
28 So the king sought advice,
  and made two calves of gold.
  He said to them:
  Enough for you, going up to Jerusalem!
  Here are your gods, O Israel, who brought you up from the land of
     Egypt!
29 He put the one at Bet-El,
  while the [other] one he placed at Dan.
30 So this matter became a sin.
  And the people went before the one, as far as Dan.
31 He made a temple-house [for] the sanctuaries,
  and made priests from [all] quarters of the people who were not
     from the Sons of Levi.
32 And Yorov'am made a pilgrimage-festival in the eighth month, on
     the fifteenth day of the month,
  like the Festival that is in Judah,
  and he went up on the sacrificial-altar;
  thus did he make at Bet-El,
  to offer-sacrifices to the calves that he had made,

25 **Efrayim:** Although Shekhem was properly in the territory of Menashe. This may mean that "Efrayim" is more than merely a tribal designation (Gray 1970). **held seat:** Ruled. **Penuel:** On the Jabbok, east of the Jordan; so its fortification would have helped secure Yorov'am's control of the territory of Gil'ad (Gilead).

27 **Rehav'am king of Judah:** The full title reflects Yorov'am's insecurity (Walsh).

28 **sought advice:** The second instance of receiving bad counsel in this chapter. **to them:** To the Israelites.

29 **Bet-El . . . Dan:** The southern and northern reaches of the Northern Kingdom.

30 **went before the one, as far as Dan:** Presumably "before the one near Bet-El and" has dropped out in MT. Cogan (2001) suggests the present reading, demonstrating the people's enthusiasm for the new form of worship.

32 **eighth month:** A month after the usual New Year's festival. **the Festival:** See note to 8:2, above.

Chapter 13. *The North: Prophets and Predictions:* The Yorov'am story continues in an unprecedented and directly Deuteronomistic way: a prophet, here termed a "man of God," predicts that a purge conducted by King Yoshiyyahu (Josiah), fully three centuries hence, will undo the results of Yorov'am's terrible idolatry. When the king stretches out his hand against the prophet, it withers, and is restored (lit. "returned") only after the king requests the prophet's intercession. And the recurrence of the verb "return" is once again the key here. The man of God is told by God to go home by another route, and he refuses hospitality from both Yorov'am and another prophet living in Bet-El. But eventually he relents, eating and drinking with the old prophet, and the result is his death, seen as a punishment from God. The end (and, to my mind, the main point) of the matter is that Yorov'am does not "return" from his wicked path, but instead "returns" to the appointing of illegitimate priests. Things will not go back to the way they were. The north and the south have split forever.

Simon (1997) focuses on the other main theme in this chapter, which is a significant one in the Early Prophets: the divine word will be fulfilled, even if the messenger (the "man of God") does not obey as he is told. It may take centuries, but the "signs" and "portents" will come to pass. In v.26, the old prophet understands his colleague's death as fulfilling God's word; v.32 equally points ahead to Yoshiyyahu's time, when the earlier prophecy regarding the altar will also come to fruition.

The enduring image in the last section is reminiscent of fairy tales. We are treated to the sight of the man of God's corpse, the lion who has killed him, and his unharmed donkey standing in the road. Walsh sees the animals as a kind of "honor guard," and indeed, the whole story has a kind of tragic nobility. The old prophet recognizes the truth of the man of God's word, and seeks fellowship with his colleague (Walsh notes the play on *shuv,* "return," accomplished through multiple occurrences of *yashov,* "sit/settle") in death just as he had, with disastrous results, in life. For Walsh, the fate of the two prophets who have gone astray mirrors the eventual fate of the two kingdoms from which they hail.

and he had them stand at Bet-El [to officiate], the priests of the
   sanctuaries that he had made.

33 And he went up on the altar that he had made at Bet-El
on the fifteenth day of the eighth month, the month that he had
   devised of his own heart;
so he made a festival for the Children of Israel.
And he went up on the altar, to send-up-smoke,

13:1 when here, a man of God was coming from Judah by the word of
   YHWH to Bet-El.
As Yorov'am was standing by the altar to send up smoke,

2 he called over the altar with the word of YHWH,
he said:
O Altar! Altar!
Thus says YHWH:
Here, a son will be born to the House of David, Yoshiyyahu his
   name;
he will slay upon you
the priests of the sanctuaries who are sending up smoke upon you,
and human bones will he burn upon you!

3 And he gave a portent on that day, saying:
This is the portent that YHWH has spoken:
Here, the altar will be torn apart,
and spilled out will be the ash-heap that is on it!

4 And it was, when the king heard the word of the man of God
   which he called out over the altar at Bet-El,
that Yorov'am stretched out his hand from over the altar, saying:
Seize him!
But his hand dried up, the one that he stretched out against him,
and he was not able to return it to himself.

---

33 **went up:** Others, "offered whole offerings on." The
verb seems to indicate the king's direct participation
in the ritual. **heart:** Or "mind."

13:2 **he called:** The subject is the man of God. **O
Altar! Altar!:** This is the only time in the Bible
that an earthbound object is addressed (Walsh);
the effect is striking. **Yoshiyyahu:** Pronounced
yo-shee-YAH-hoo; trad. English "Josiah." The meaning of the name is uncertain; proposals range from
"YHWH Will Grant" and "YHWH Will Protect" to

"YHWH Makes Forget." Although not etymologi-
cally related, it also recalls "Yehoshua" (Joshua). The
prophecy will be fulfilled in II Kings 23:16. **human
bones will he burn:** Thus rendering the site ritually
polluted (*tamei*).

3 **spilled out:** In violation of the priestly obligation
to dispose of sacrificial ashes in a special place (see
Lev. 6:3–4).

4 **dried up:** That is, the hand was paralyzed or
withered.

5   And the altar was torn apart,
    and the ashes spilled from the altar,
       in accordance with the portent that the man of God had given him
          by the hand of YHWH.

6   Then the king spoke up and said to the man of God:
    Now soothe the face of YHWH your God,
       and pray on my behalf, that my hand may be returned-in-health
          to me!
    And the man of God soothed the face of YHWH,
       so that the king's hand was returned-in-health to him,
    and became as at the beginning.

7   The king spoke to the man of God:
    Come back with me to the house and be refreshed,
       so that I may give you a gift.

8   But the man of God said to the king:
    If you were to give me half your house
    I would not come back with you,
    I would not eat food, I would not drink water in this place,

9   for thus I was commmanded by the word of YHWH, saying:
    You are not to eat food, you are not to drink water,
       and you are not to return by the way that you went!

10 So he went off by another way,
       and did not return by the way that he had come to Bet-El.

11 Now an old prophet was settled at Bet-El.
    And his sons came and recounted to him all the doings that the
       man of God had done that day in Bet-El;
       the words that he had spoken to the king,
       they recounted them to their father.

12 Their father spoke to them:
    By which way did he go?
       —His sons had seen the way by which the man of God had gone,
          who had come from Judah.—

---

6 **soothe:** Appease. **pray:** Or "intercede." **returned-in-health:** Meaning "restored," but I have tried to keep the theme word of the chapter ("return") in translation.

11 **sons:** So LXX and other versions; MT uses the singular. The word may refer to disciples, not necessarily biological sons. **the man of God:** The anonymous prophet of the previous scene.

13 He said to his sons:
Saddle a donkey for me.
So they saddled a donkey for him, and he mounted it,

14 and he went after the man of God;
he found him sitting under an oak
and said to him:
Are you the man of God who came from Judah?
He said:
I am.

15 He said to him:
Go back with me to the house and eat [some] food.

16 He said:
I am not able to return with you, to come back with you,
and I will not eat food, I will not drink water with you in this place,

17 for the word [came to me] by the word of YHWH:
You are not to eat food, you are not to drink water there;
you are not to return, going by the way on which you went!

18 He said to him:
I too am a prophet like you,
and a messenger spoke to me by the word of YHWH, saying:
Have him return with you to your house,
that he may eat food and drink water!
—He was lying to him.

19 So he returned with him
and ate food in his house, and drank water.

20 Now it was:
as they were sitting at the table,
the word of YHWH [came] to the prophet who had had him return,

21 and he called out to the man who had come from Judah, saying:
Thus says YHWH:
Because you have revolted against YHWH's order
and have not kept the command that YHWH your God commanded,

22 but have returned and eaten food and drunk water in the place of
which he spoke to you:
Do not eat food and do not drink water!—
your corpse shall not come to the burial-place of your fathers!

---

16 **to come back with you:** Omitted in LXX and manuscripts.

19 **he returned:** LXX reads "he had him return."

21 **order:** Lit., "mouth."

Chapter 14. *Yorov'am and Rehav'am:* Instead of merely focusing on events and policies of the kings' reigns, the narrative now keeps the events on a personal level. As with the story of the "Wise Woman of Tekoa" in II Sam. 14, a deception is initially practiced through a female messenger, but the truth manages to come out. Ahiyya the prophet, using strident, colorful language that will recur in reference to King Ah'av (Ahab), foretells the downfall of Yorov'am's dynasty and the eventual exile of Israel. It is jarring to hear this so early in the book, but it has the effect of setting up a pattern of prophecy and fulfillment that is very much at the ideological center of the book of Kings (Walsh).

Almost nothing is attributed to Rehav'am's reign except for Judah's idolatrous practices. The Egyptian invasion that follows in vv.25ff. therefore feels not merely political but punitive. And Rehav'am's death notice departs from the usual formula in that his mother is mentioned again (see v.21), perhaps because she is an Ammonite—emphasizing Shelomo's sin of intermarriage once more.

23 And it was,
    after his eating food and after his drinking,
    that the donkey was saddled for him, belonging to the prophet who
        had had him return.

24 He went off, and a lion encountered him on the way, and caused his
        death,
    and his corpse was [left] thrown into the way,
    with the donkey standing near him,
    while the lion was standing near the corpse.

25 Now here, some men were crossing by,
    and they saw the corpse thrown into the way, with the lion standing
        near the corpse,
    so they came and spoke [of it] in the town where the old prophet
        was settled.

26 And he heard, the prophet who had had him return from the way,
        and he said:
    He is the man of God who revolted against YHWH's order,
    so YHWH gave him to the lion, so that he mangled him and put
        him to death,
    in accordance with the word of YHWH which he had spoken
        to him.

27 And he spoke to his sons, saying:
    Saddle me the donkey!
    And they saddled it.

28 He went and found the corpse thrown in the way,
    with the donkey and the lion standing near the corpse—
    the lion had not eaten the corpse, and had not mangled the donkey!

29 And the prophet lifted up the corpse of the man of God and put it
        on the donkey, and had him return;
    then he came to the town of the old prophet, to beat [the breast]
        and to bury him.

30 He put his corpse in his [own] burial-place
    and they beat [the breast] over him: Alas, my brother!

28 **the lion had not eaten the corpse . . . :** The lion
acted not out of hunger but as an agent of God
(Geneva Bible).

31 And it was, after he buried him, that he said to his sons, saying:
When I die, you are to bury me in the burial-place where the man
of God is buried;
near his bones put my bones.

32 For it will come, come-to-pass, the word that he called out by the
word of Yhwh
concerning the altar that is in Bet-El and concerning all the
sanctuary buildings that are in the towns of Shomeron.

33 After this matter, Yorov'am did not return from his evil way,
but he returned to making priests from [all] quarters of the people
for the sanctuaries;
[to] whoever desired, he would give mandate, and he became a
priest at the sanctuaries.

34 So this matter became a sin by the House of Yorov'am,
for effacing, for erasing [it] from the surface of the ground.

14:1 At [about] that time,
Aviyya son of Yorov'am became sick.

2 Yorov'am said to his wife:
Now arise and change your [appearance],
so that they will not know that you are Yorov'am's wife,
and go to Shilo
—there is Ahiyya the prophet; it was he [who] declared me as king
over this people—

3 and take in your hand ten bread-loaves and biscuits and a bottle of
honey
and come to him;
he will tell you what will happen to the lad.

4 Yorov'am's wife did thus:
she arose and went to Shilo, and came to the house of Ahiyya.
Now Ahiyyahu was not able to see,
for his eyes were set from his hoary-age.

---

32 **Shomeron:** Pronounced *sho-meh-ROHN;* trad. English "Samaria," the northern capital (which will not be named until Chap. 16!). Here it appears to refer to a region, rather unusually for the Bible.

33 **After this matter:** The earlier story from vv.6–10. **returned to making:** Or "kept on appointing" (Cogan 2001). **priest:** Following versions; MT has a defective plural form.

34 **effacing . . . erasing:** Heb. *le-hakhhid ul'hashmid.* **[it]:** The dynasty of Yorov'am.

14:1 **At [about] that time:** A formula that often serves to link different sections in the editing process. **Aviyya:** "Yhwh Is Father." Trad. English "Abijah."

4 **set:** Frozen, as it were. See the same description of the priest Eli in I Sam. 4:15.

5 But God had said to Ahiyyahu:
Here, Yorov'am's wife is coming
to search out a word through you concerning her son, for he is sick;
like this and like that you are to speak to her.
And it will be that when she comes, she will act-like-a-stranger.

6 Now it was, when Ahiyyahu heard the sound of her feet as she
came in at the entrance,
that he said:
Come in, Yorov'am's wife,
why now do you act-like-a-stranger?
I myself am sent to you with a hard [message]:

7 Go, say to Yorov'am:
Thus says YHWH, the God of Israel:
Because I exalted you from the midst of the people,
and made you *Nagid* over my people Israel,

8 and tore the kingdom away from the House of David and gave it
to you
—but you have not been like my servant David,
who kept my commandments and who walked after me with all his
heart,
doing only what was right in my eyes;

9 you have done evil, more than all who were before you,
you have gone and made yourself other gods, namely molten ones,
to provoke me,
and me you have thrown behind your back—

10 therefore:
here, I am bringing evil upon the House of Yorov'am:
I will cut off from Yorov'am he who pisses against the wall,
[even] those fettered and forsaken in Israel,
and I will eradicate after [you] the House of Yorov'am
as a ball of dung is burned, until it is gone.

---

5 **search out:** A technical term for consulting an oracle. **act-like-a-stranger:** Disguise herself.
9 **thrown behind your back:** Or, more idiomatically in English, "turned your back on."
10 **he who pisses against the wall:** A derisive term for "all the males," used previously in I Sam. 25:22. **[even] those fettered and forsaken:** Even the lowest members of society. Some see the phrase as connoting opposites, namely, "[whether] fettered or free." **as a ball of dung is burned:** Dung was used as fuel in the ancient world. "Burned" here is a homonym, or maybe even identical, to the verb "eradicate" earlier in the verse (Heb. *bi'er*).

◆

11 He who dies of Yorov'am in the city, the dogs will eat,
while he who dies in the open-field, the birds of the heavens
will eat;
for YHWH has spoken!

12 As for you, arise, go back to your house;
when your feet come into the city, the child will die.

13 And all Israel will beat [the breast] for him and will bury him,
for he alone of Yorov'am will come to a burial-place,
because some good toward YHWH, the God of Israel, has been
found in him [alone] of the House of Yorov'am.

14 And YHWH will raise up a king for himself over Israel, who will cut
off the House of Yorov'am, this very day and even now.

15 YHWH will strike Israel,
like a reed that sways in water,
and will uproot Israel
from this good ground that he gave their fathers,
and will scatter them across the River,
because they made their Ashera-poles,
provoking YHWH.

16 He will give Israel up, on account of Yorov'am's sins which he
sinned, and which he caused Israel to sin.

17 Yorov'am's wife arose
and went back to Tirtza;
[just as] she was coming in to the threshold of the house,
the child died.

18 They buried him and all Israel beat [the breast] for him,
according to the word of YHWH that he had spoken by the hand of
his servant Ahiyyahu the prophet.

19 Now the rest of the events of Yorov'am,
how he waged battle and how he reigned as king—

---

11 **dogs:** Wild, not domesticated ones. **dogs . . . birds . . . will eat:** Identical curses appear elsewhere in ancient Near Eastern treaties.
13 **because some good toward YHWH:** Following Gray (1970).
14 **this very day and even now:** Heb. obscure.
15 **the River:** As usual in the Bible, the Euphrates. **Ashera-poles:** The goddess was often worshipped through these objects.
16 **on account of:** Heb. *biglal,* perhaps a double pun with "dung" (*galal,* v.10) and "Illicit-Things" (*gillulim*) elsewhere. **which he caused Israel to sin:** Varia-

tions on this phrase (including "who caused Israel to sin") will occur subsequently some twenty times in the book, as an obsessive theme.
17 **Tirtza:** Trad. English "Tirzah," it was some six miles northeast of Shekhem, and for a time the capital of the Northern Kingdom.
19 **Record of Yearly Events:** Or "Matters"; this is a literal translation of what was traditionally rendered "Book of the Chronicles." The phrase occurs thirty-four times in Kings. Other documents in this vein have not been found in Israel, but the general designation was a common one in the ancient world.

here, they are written in the Record of Yearly Events of the Kings
  of Israel.

20 Now the days that Yorov'am reigned as king were twenty and two
    years;
   then he lay beside his fathers,
   and Nadav his son reigned as king in his place.

21 Now Rehav'am son of Shelomo reigned as king in Judah:
   forty-one years old was Rehav'am at his becoming king,
   and for seventeen years he reigned as king in Jerusalem,
   the city that YHWH had chosen to put his name there from all the
     tribes of Israel;
   his mother's name was Naama the Ammonite.

22 And Judah did what was evil in the eyes of YHWH:
   they aroused his zealous-indignation more than all their fathers had
     done, in the sins that they sinned.

23 They too built for themselves sanctuaries and standing-pillars and
     Ashera-poles
   on every lofty hill and under every luxuriant tree.

24 And there were even [male] prostitutes in the land;
   they did according to all the abominable deeds of the nations that
     YHWH had dispossessed before the Children of Israel.

25 Now it was
   in the fifth year of King Rehav'am,
   that Shishak king of Egypt came up against Jerusalem.

26 He took away the treasures of the House of YHWH and the
     treasures of the king's house
   —he took everything.
   He [even] took all the gold bucklers that Shelomo had made,

27 so King Rehav'am made, in their place, bronze bucklers;
   he would entrust them to the hand of the Commanders of the
     Outrunners, those on watch at the entrance to the king's house.

---

20 **Nadav:** "[God is] Noble."
21 **Now:** JPS understands as "meanwhile."
22 **Judah:** LXX and versions read "Rehav'am."
24 **[male] prostitutes:** Lit., "sacred ones." Despite older scholarly theories, it is now accepted that they were not performing religious rites of a sexual nature, but may have been engaging in prostitution

to pay back religious vows. However, the text is also polemical, so accuracy may not be the issue here.
25 **Shishak:** See note to 11:40, above. The invasion referred to here is mentioned on the wall of Amun-Re's temple at Karnak, and a victory stele of Sho-shenq has been found at Megiddo.

Chapter 15. *North and South: Warring Kings:* A uniformly depressing chapter, this text describes two kings for each kingdom, and is anchored in the center by a military intervention on the part of Aram (Syria). The accession of a relatively "good" king in the south, Asa, whose religious reforms mildly foreshadow the notable ones of later Judean kings, is tempered by his failure to remove the "sanctuaries," a serious shortcoming from the Deuteronomistic point of view, which advocates centralized worship in Jerusalem.

Two important messages come through by the end of the chapter: the introduction of assassination as a normal means of succession in the Northern Kingdom, and the concomitant end of Yorov'am's dynasty. We also hear, ominously, of a second siphoning off of Temple treasures, hard on the heels of the first one in the previous chapter.

28 It was, whenever the king entered Yнwн's House,
  that the outrunners would carry them
  and would return them to the outrunners' guardroom.
29 Now the rest of the events of Rehav'am, and all that he did—
  are they not written in the Record of Yearly Events of the Kings of
    Judah?
30 And there was war between Rehav'am and Yorov'am all the days.
31 Rehav'am lay beside his fathers;
  he was buried with his fathers, in the City of David.
  Now his mother's name was Naama the Ammonite.
  And Aviyyam his son reigned as king in his place.

15:1 In year eighteen of King Yorov'am son of Nevat, Aviyyam became
    king over Judah.
2 For three years he reigned as king in Jerusalem;
  his mother's name was Maakha daughter of Avishalom.
3 He walked
  in all the sins of his father which he had done before him;
  his heart was not complete with Yнwн his God,
  like the heart of David his father.
4 But for the sake of David,
  Yнwн his God gave him a lamp in Jerusalem,
  to establish his son after him and to let Jerusalem stand,
5 since David did what was right in the eyes of Yнwн:
  he did not turn aside from all that he had commanded him all the
    days of his life—
  save in the matter of Uriyya the Hittite.
6 And there was war between Aviyyam and Yorov'am all the days of
    his life.

---

30 **all the days:** Meaning "all those years."
31 **his mother's name . . . :** This sentence is missing in LXX and Chronicles. **Aviyyam:** Trad. English "Abijam." Possibly a variation on "Yнwн Is My Father" (the alternative explanation, that Yamm, the Canaanite god of the sea, is included here, is unlikely).
15:2 **Avishalom:** A variant form of the name Avshalom (Absalom). If he is identical to the celebrated son of David from II Samuel, a more appropriate rendering of *bat* (here, "daughter") would be "granddaughter."

3 **He walked / in all the sins . . . :** Here the usual formulaic evaluation of kings in the book of Kings first appears fully, making clear that the writer/editor is "more concerned over piety than politics" (Mann).
4 **stand:** Or "endure," "survive."
5 **save in the matter of Uriyya:** See II Sam. 11–12 for this key story of David's committing adultery and murder. Evidently the tradition was too well known to be ignored in our passage.
6 **there was war . . . :** LXX and others omit; clearly there has been a scribal mix-up (see 14:40 and 15:7).

7 Now the rest of the events of Aviyyam, and all that he did—
are they not written in the Record of Yearly Events of the Kings of
Judah?
And there was war between Aviyyam and Yorov'am.

8 Aviyyam lay beside his fathers;
they buried him in the City of David,
and Asa his son reigned as king in his place.

9 In year twenty of Yorov'am king of Israel,
Asa king of Judah became king.

10 For forty-one years he reigned as king in Jerusalem;
his mother's name was Maakha daughter of Avishalom.

11 And Asa did what was right in the eyes of YHWH,
like his father David:

12 he put away the [male] prostitutes from the land,
and removed all the Illicit-Things that his fathers had made.

13 And also Maakha his mother—he removed her from being queen-
mother,
since she had made the Horrid-Thing for Ashera;
Asa cut down her Horrid-Thing, and burned it at Wadi Kidron.

14 But the sanctuaries were not removed;
however, Asa's heart was complete with YHWH all his days.

15 He brought the holy-objects of his father and his own holy-objects
into the House of YHWH,
silver, gold, and vessels.

16 And there was war between Asa and Ba'sha king of Israel all their
days.

17 Ba'sha king of Israel came up against Judah and built Rama,
so as not to allow going out or coming in to Asa king of Judah.

---

10 **mother . . . Maakha:** This does not square with
the previous king, whose mother bears the same
name—so possibly "grandmother" or "Queen
Mother" is meant (Gray 1970).

12 **Illicit-Things:** Heb. *gillulim*, perhaps related to
Akkadian *gillatu* (crime), but also suggesting Hebrew
words for "dung," so that here, as is common in the
Bible, idolatry is understood pejoratively.

13 **Horrid-Thing:** Some kind of idol is meant here. In
modern Hebrew usage the word means "monster,"

and is the name of a well-known and playful metal
sculpture in contemporary Jerusalem.

14 **were not removed:** Gray (1970), quoting Noth, feels
that the text goes a bit easy on this southern king,
since he is not held personally responsible for failing
to removing the idols.

15 **his own holy-objects:** Reading according to the
Ketiv.

17 **Rama:** Five miles north of Jerusalem, in a strategic
location.

18 So Asa took all the silver and gold that was left in the treasuries of
the House of Y{\small HWH} and in the treasuries of the House of the
King

and gave them into the hand of his servants,

and King Asa sent them to Ben-Hadad son of Tavrimon son of
Hezyon, king of Aram, who had seat in Damascus, saying:

19 There is a covenant between me and you, as between my father and
your father;

here, I am sending you a bribe of silver and gold—

go, violate your covenant with Ba'sha king of Israel,

that he may go up away from me!

20 And Ben-Hadad hearkened to King Asa;

he sent the commanders of the soldiers who belonged to him
against the towns of Israel

and they struck Iyyon, and Dan, and Avel Bet-Maakha

and all the Kinneret-regions, next to all the region of Naftali.

21 It was, when Ba'sha heard, that he refrained from building up
Rama,

and returned to Tirtza.

22 Now King Asa mustered all Judah—there was no one clear [of
obligation]—

and they carried away the stones of Rama and its timber, which
Ba'sha had built up,

and King Asa built with them Geva / The Hill of Binyamin and
Mitzpa.

23 Now the rest of all the events of Asa, and all his mighty-deeds, and
all that he did,

and the towns that he built up—

are they not written in the Record of Yearly Events of the Kings of
Judah?

However: at the time of his old age, he became sick in his feet.

---

18 **and in:** A small emendation from "and," based on ancient versions.

20 **Iyyon . . . Dan . . . Avel Bet-Maakha:** Towns in the northern part of Israel. **Kinneret:** The "lyre-shaped" Sea of Galilee (known also as Lake Tiberias today).

21 **returned:** Following LXX and versions; MT has "settled in."

22 **mustered:** Lit., "had them hearken." **carried away the stones of Rama:** Thus moving his border two miles north into Israel (see Zevit 2004).

23 **sick in his feet:** LXX adds: "He did what was evil and became . . ."

Chapter 16. *Northern Kings:* Continuing the instability manifest in the last chapter, there are two coups subsequent to Ba'sha's twenty-four-year rule, a reign about which the text again reports next to nothing. The result is the accession of Omri, whose dynasty will last for four decades and will appear by name in Assyrian records. Ominously, v.25 characterizes him as the most evil king to date, but the same will later be said of his son Ah'av (twice, in vv.30 and 34). The latter's great offense consists in his marrying a Phoenician princess and thus greatly furthering the worship of the fertility god Baal in Israel.

24 And Asa lay beside his fathers;
 he was buried with his fathers, in the City of David his father,
 and Yehoshafat his son reigned as king in his place.

25 Now Nadav son of Yorov'am became king over Israel in year two
 of Asa king of Judah,
 and he reigned as king over Israel for two years.

26 He did what was evil in the eyes of YHWH:
 he walked in the way of his father and in his sin which he had
 caused Israel to sin.

27 And Ba'sha son of Ahiyya, of the House of Yissakhar, conspired
 against him;
 Ba'sha struck him down at Gibbeton that belonged to the
 Philistines,
 while Nadav and all Israel were besieging Gibbeton.

28 Ba'sha put him to death in year three of Asa king of Judah,
 and reigned as king in his place.

29 And it was, when he became king,
 that he struck down the entire House of Yorov'am;
 he did not leave anyone breathing who belonged to Yorov'am, until
 he had wiped it out,
 in accordance with the word of YHWH which he had spoken by the
 hand of his servant Ahiyya the Shilonite,

30 because of the sins of Yorov'am which he sinned and by which he
 had caused Israel to sin,
 in his provocation by which he provoked YHWH, the God of Israel.

31 Now the rest of the events of Nadav, and all that he did—
 are they not written in the Record of Yearly Events of the Kings of
 Israel?

32 And there was war between Asa and Ba'sha king of Israel all their
 days.

---

24 **Yehoshafat:** "YHWH Judges/Leads"; trad. English "Jehoshaphat," remembered in English chiefly through the mid-nineteenth-century exclamation "Jumpin' Jehosaphat!," which mercifully has no connection to any biblical events.

25 **Nadav:** Pronounced *nah-DAHV;* trad. English "Nadab."

27 **Ahiyya:** Obviously not the same as the prophet above, but his name serves to recall those prophecies (Walsh). **Gibbeton:** A town on the western edge of the hill-country of Judah, not far from Gezer. It was occupied by the tribe of Dan, and later by the Philistines.

◆ 33 In year three of Asa king of Judah,
    Ba'sha son of Ahiyya became king over all Israel in Tirtza, for
        twenty-four years.

34 He did what was evil in the eyes of YHWH:
    he walked in the way of Yorov'am and in his sin, by which he had
        caused Israel to sin.

16:1 And the word of YHWH [came] to Yehu son of Hanani regarding
    Ba'sha, saying:

2 Because I elevated you from the dust and made you *Nagid* over my
    people Israel,
    but you have walked in the way of Yorov'am and have caused my
        people Israel to sin,
    provoking me by their sins—

3 here, I will eradicate [those coming] after Ba'sha and after his
        House;
    I will make your house like the House of Yorov'am son of Nevat:

4 he who dies of Ba'sha in the city, the dogs shall eat,
    while he who dies of him in the open-field, the birds of the heavens
        shall eat!

5 Now the rest of the events of Ba'sha, and what he did, and his
        mighty-deeds—
    are they not written in the Record of Yearly Events of the Kings of
        Israel?

6 Ba'sha lay beside his fathers;
    he was buried in Tirtza,
    and Ela his son reigned as king in his place.

7 Then, too, by the hand of Yehu son of Hanani, the prophet,
    the word of YHWH [had come] concerning Ba'sha and concerning
        his house,
    regarding all the evil that he had done in the eyes of YHWH,
    provoking him with the doings of his hands, being like the House
        of Yorov'am,
    and because he had struck it down.

16:1 **Yehu:** Pronounced *yay-HOO;* trad. English "Jehu."
The name means "YHWH Is He," appropriate given
Yehu's purge of the idolatrous house of Omri.

3 **his:** The reading of LXX; MT has "your."

4 **of Ba'sha:** Of his family.

6 **Ela:** Pronounced *ay-LAH.*

7 **because he had struck it down:** Heb. unclear.

8   In year twenty-six of the years of Asa king of Judah,
     Ela son of Ba'sha became as king over Israel in Tirtza, for two
         years.

9   And his servant Zimri, commander of half the chariotry, conspired
         against him.
     Now he was in Tirtza, drinking himself drunk in the house of
         Artza, [The One] Over the Household in Tirtza,

10   and Zimri came and struck him down, putting him to death,
     in year twenty-seven of Asa king of Judah,
     and he became king in his place.

11   And it was, when he became king, as soon as he sat on his throne,
     that he struck down the entire House of Ba'sha
     —he did not leave him one pissing against the wall,
     either his blood-redeemers or his friends.

12   So Zimri wiped out the entire House of Ba'sha,
     in accordance with the word of YHWH which he had spoken
         regarding Ba'sha, by the hand of Yehu the prophet,

13   because of all of Ba'sha's sins and the sins of Ela his son
     which they had sinned and which they had caused Israel to sin,
     provoking YHWH, the God of Israel, with their futilities.

14   Now the rest of the events of Ela, and all that he did—
     are they not written in the Record of Yearly Events of the Kings of
         Israel?

15   In year twenty-seven of the years of Asa king of Judah,
     Zimri became king, for seven days in Tirtza.
     Now the fighting-people were encamped against Gibbeton, which
         belonged to the Philistines.

16   And the fighting-people who were encamped heard [tell], saying:
     Zimri has made a conspiracy, and he has even struck down the
         king!
     So all Israel made Omri, Commander of the Armed-Forces, king on
         that day in the camp.

---

9 **Zimri:** The narrative will now include three would-be kings: Zimri, Omri, and Tivni, all with the accent on the last syllable. Their deeds do not match their melodious sound.
11 **blood-redeemers:** That is, family members responsible for avenging the death of a relative.

13 **futilities:** Or "emptinesses," from *hevel*, "vapor," referring to other gods, who were viewed by the writers as insubstantial. The Heb. word *hevel* is used at the famous opening of Ecclesiastes, "Vanity of vanities" (KJV).

◆ 17 And Omri came up, and all Israel with him, from Gibbeton,
and they besieged Tirtza.

18 It was, when Zimri saw that the city was taken,
that he went to the citadel of the king's house,
and he burned down the king's house with fire over himself, and so
he died—

19 for the sins which he had sinned,
doing what was evil in the eyes of YHWH,
walking in the way of Yorov'am and in his sin which he did, to
cause Israel to sin.

20 Now the rest of the events of Zimri, and his conspiracy that he
conspired—
are they not written in the Record of Yearly Events of the Kings of
Israel?

21 Then the people Israel were split in half:
half of the people were [following] after Tivni son of Ginat, to
make him king,
while half were after Omri.

22 But the people who were [following] after Omri were stronger than
the people who were [following] after Tivni son of Ginat.
Then Tivni died, and Omri became king.

PART III

OMRIDES AND PROPHETS

(I 16:23–II 13)

THE HEART OF THE BOOK OF KINGS CONCERNS THE RISE AND FALL OF ONE northern dynasty, the House of Omri, and the careers of two great prophets, Eliy-yahu and Elisha, who rail against it. These events and personalities dominate the bulk of the narratives about the ninth century, a period of complex interactions among the kingdoms of Israel, Judah, Moav, and Aram (Syria) and their attempt to cope with the threat of Assyria to the northeast.

The biblical text at this point is filled with battles, assassinations, and other events which are, however, not always clearly set out; as an example, scholarly opinion is somewhat divided on the identity of the king known as Yehoram or Yoram (II Kings 8). The Bible seems more interested in the prophetic figures than in the royal ones, perhaps out of a desire to show how the later prophets such as Isaiah and Jeremiah have a long and distinguished spiritual lineage.

The House of Omri were singularly accomplished as builders. To Omri himself is attributed the founding and building up of Shomeron (Samaria) as the capital of the north, into a city which archaeology has revealed to have been quite impres-sive. His son Ah'av (Ahab), famous for his confrontations with Eliyyahu, probably built the palaces and stables at Megiddo, and is credited with having constructed an ivory palace in I 22:39. The Bible grudgingly mentions these accomplishments, which could not be entirely ignored, but places more emphasis on these kings' straying from the covenant, particularly so in the case of Ah'av, whose politically canny marriage with the Phoenician princess Izevel is condemned by the biblical text in the strongest possible terms. Thus Israel's relations with foreign powers, so natural and necessary in everyday political and economic reality, is seen instead by the Bible as the source of idolatry and hence of most of Israel's problems.

The narratives in this section are colorful and dramatic, and, amid all the male bravado, feature two powerful women as villainesses. Izevel, whose name (English, "Jezebel") came to be synonymous with a dangerous female, is the very personification of the Enemy in the Bible, as she brings into her marriage hun-dreds of priests of Baal and Ashera. Those deities become YHWH's chief rivals for the hearts of the Israelites. In a text that rarely gives space to queens, Izevel is more than a match for most of the Israelite kings, including her husband. The other female figure, Atalya, demonstrates that a Queen Mother could occasion-ally come to power. Her six-year reign in Judah ends in her execution, as had the Israelite career of Izevel.

ON ELIYYAHU AND ELISHA

(I KINGS 17–II KINGS 13)

IT IS SIGNIFICANT THAT ELIYYAHU AND ELISHA LITERALLY OCCUPY CENTER STAGE in the book of Kings. Central here too is the political setting, a plot which could be described as the Fall of the House of Omri (see Savran). The background is in fact both social and religious. This period of Israelite history has been described as a departure from the traditional control of Israelite society by small highland agrarian communities and clans in favor of a centralized urban elite seizing power. It is thus a story that, in one way or another, rings familiar in many societies up to the present day. Not surprisingly, in the biblical setting Eliyyahu and Elisha frequently represent the interests of the poor. Their stories are peopled with widows, the sick, and the mass of Israelites affected by famine and oppression (Rentería). In this sense they are most likely an authentic memory of a society in transition, and, rather than being a court-based narrative, may have their roots in a more popular reaction to events. Such accounts often feature miracle workers—the hallmark of what is sometimes called "popular religion"—who through their deeds stand in for the powerless peasants. One need only think of stories about saints in various cultures. In Kings, this intervention for the disenfranchised is always understood as coming from YHWH, whereas the powers that be, the kings and nobles, are usually linked to Baal and other Canaanite deities such as Ashera. So the bitter struggles undergone by Eliyyahu and Elisha are an indication that religion is not merely a matter of theological principles. And the thrust of these stories suggests that they may have originated in prophetic circles, to be later incorporated in archival and other types of material that appear in Kings.

At the same time, it should be noted that they have not merely been placed in the middle of a narrative unthinkingly. The tales around Eliyyahu and Elisha also provide backing for the revolt and dynasty of Yehu. As Rentería shows, Elisha not only champions the poor but, in his dealings with royalty, also acts as a middleman between classes, in a time of transition.

Of all the figures that appear in Kings, none is as powerful, or mysterious, as the prophet Eliyyahu. He appears as if from nowhere, mediates miraculous deeds, and inserts the word of YHWH into the political events of the region. Moreover, his final spectacular *dis*appearance leads ultimately to his transformation for generations of Jews, Christians, and Muslims into an even larger figure in religious literature and folklore.

In the text of Kings, the portrayal of Eliyyahu touches on a number of themes. As a personality, he is utterly devoted to his task as prophet and is therefore, not surprisingly, a deeply solitary figure. He is constantly on the move, argues with God, and almost succumbs to despair. He also stands up to royalty, at peril of his life, especially in Chap. 21, the story of Navot's vineyard. In all these aspects, he introduces the classic prophetic persona to Kings. While in this book we have previously encountered figures such as Natan and Ahiyya, they do not have the force of personality and stature we come to identify with the "literary" prophets such as Yirmiyahu (Jeremiah) and Yehezkel (Ezekiel). Eliyyahu, on the other hand, is clearly their forerunner.

At the same time, Eliyyahu belongs substantially to an earlier expression of prophecy well known in the ancient world, including in Greece. This takes the form not of long, inspired poetic speeches such as we find later in the Bible, but largely of ecstatic, "mantic" behavior. In the typical pattern, bands or guilds of holy men (see the last Eliyyahu chapter, II Kings 2, or the earlier accounts of Sha'ul in I Sam. 9 and 10) travel around and are frequently seized by the divine spirit, "ranting like prophets." Eliyyahu's sudden appearances and breathtaking travels, not to mention his other, often miraculous feats, likewise suggest mantic prophecy.

Looming in the background of the Eliyyahu stories is an earlier figure: Moshe. Especially toward the end of the cycle, in the prophet's sojourn at Sinai and his final crossing of the divided waters of the Jordan, the text clearly recalls Israel's great founder. Rather in the mode of modern political campaigns, the evoking of an earlier founding father appears intended to send a strong message to a generation in trouble.

The narratives about Eliyyahu give evidence of a memorable personality, solidly rooted in its early biblical setting. As noted above, in the Bible's after-history his larger-than-life persona expanded to greater roles in the three Western religions. In Judaism, Eliyyahu took on the function of guardian angel, messenger of God, and settler of disputes, especially to the Talmudic rabbis and, over a millennium later, to the Hasidic masters. He also became a ubiquitous figure at ritual occasions, including circumcision and the Passover meal. Following later biblical imagery (in Mal. 4), he came to be seen as the herald of the Messiah. Christianity, principally in the New Testament, honors Eliyyahu as one of the figures present at Jesus's Transfiguration; accompanied by Moshe, he is usually taken to represent the Prophets. Finally, Islam continues some of the biblical themes about Eliyyahu, and some traditions also identify him with Al-Khidr, "The Green One," who is a transformative figure.

The prophet Elisha, who does not quite share Eliyyahu's biblical and enduring charisma, nonetheless occupies more space than his master in the text of Kings. He does resemble Eliyyahu in his uncompromising nature; in addition, he works parallel miracles and similarly speaks truth to power. If anything, he is more stern than Eliyyahu, as witnessed by numerous episodes resulting in death—even of youngsters, if need be (II Kings 2:23–24). Despite all this, one could argue that Elisha has never fully taken root in postbiblical popular imagination. Perhaps this is due to the absence of scenes in which he is in dialogue with God, or to the plethora of other characters, major and minor, who draw attention away from him. Regardless, the stories about him in Kings deal with an important period in the history of the Northern Kingdom and further clarify prophetic concerns.

Elisha's career spans the reigns of several northern kings and sees the fulfillment of a number of Eliyyahu's tasks regarding royal succession. As Bergen points out, Elisha does not pose the threat to monarchy itself that his master does; rather, he serves to reinforce that monarchy is an acceptable system, within limits imposed by God. His miracles extend once again to the poor and even to prophetic guilds in trouble. A number of the narratives about him are quite brief but highlight desperate, life-and-death problems; the longer ones typically involve extended interactions with kings. Here too the prophet is depicted as a wonder worker and a master of symbolic actions.

The Elisha stories may have originated in the north (his and Elijah's tales are written in a northern accent, so to speak) and been brought to Judah after Israel's destruction in 722. In their present position, they certainly signal a strong prophetic presence in the overall stories of Kings.

Chapter 17. *Eliyyahu Makes His Appearance:* Once we have been introduced to the arch northern king, Ah'av, the great prophetic figure of Eliyyahu appears, as if from nowhere. This suddenness will characterize his persona throughout. Unlike previous prophets, he is thoroughly associated with the miraculous from the very beginning: ravens feed him, he produces an abundance of food from a skimpy amount, and he brings a child who has died back to life. In the larger context, it is the phrase and concept of the "word of God" that echoes here, and the chapter ends with the widow's ringing affirmation that Eliyyahu possesses it.

◆

23   In year thirty-one of the years of Asa king of Judah,
       Omri became king over Israel, for twelve years;
       in Tirtza he reigned as king for six years.
24   He acquired the Hill Shomeron from Shemer, for two talents of
            silver
       and built up the hill
       and called the name of the city that he built after the name of
            Shemer, owner of the Hill Shomeron.
25   And Omri did what was evil in the eyes of YHWH;
       he did evil more than all who were before him:
26   he walked in all the way of Yorov'am son of Nevat, and in his sin
            which he caused Israel to sin,
       provoking YHWH, the God of Israel, with their futilities.
27   Now the rest of the events of Omri that he did, and his mighty-
            deeds that he did—
       are they not written in the Record of Yearly Events of the Kings of
            Israel?
28   Omri lay beside his fathers;
       they buried him in Shomeron,
       and Ah'av his son reigned as king in his place.
29   Now Ah'av son of Omri became king over Israel
       in year thirty-eight of the years of Asa king of Judah;
       Ah'av son of Omri reigned as king over Israel in Shomeron for
            twenty-two years.
30   And Ah'av son of Omri did what was evil in the eyes of YHWH,
       more than all who were before him.
31   And as if it were a light matter, his walking in the sins of Yorov'am
            son of Nevat,
       he took as wife Izevel daughter of Etbaal king of the Sidonians,
       and he went and served Baal, bowing down to him;
32   he raised up a sacrificial-altar to Baal
       at the House of Baal, which he built in Shomeron.

---

24 **acquired:** Through purchase.
28 **Ah'av:** Pronounced *akh-AHV*; trad. English "Ahab."
The name combines two words that mean "father"
and "brother," or "kinsman," but which in proper
names often are taken to indicate a god.
30 **son of Omri:** The repetition highlights the evil
dynasty (Walsh).

31 **Izevel:** The name (pronounced *ee-ZEH-vel*), like
I-Khavod in I Sam. 4:21, may be a negative judg-
ment in Hebrew (lit., "Where is the Exalted One?").
Cogan (2001) understands it as a standard West
Semitic "Zebul [Baal] Exists." The trad. English is
"Jezebel." **Etbaal:** Phoenician "Ittobaal," "Baal
Exists."

◆
33 And Ah'av made the Ashera-pole.
    Ah'av continued to do [much] to provoke YHWH, the God of Israel,
    more than all the kings of Israel who were before him.
34 In his days, Hi'el the Bet-Elite rebuilt Jericho—
    with Aviram his firstborn he laid-its-foundation,
    and with Seguv his youngest he set up its doors,
    in accordance with the word of YHWH that he had spoken by the
        hand of Yehoshua son of Nun.

17:1 Eliyyahu/YHWH Is My God, the Tishbite, of the settled-folk of
        Gil'ad, said to Ah'av:
    By the life of YHWH, the God of Israel, before whom I stand,
    if there be dew or rain during these years
    except at my word . . . !
2   And the word of YHWH [came] to him, saying:
3   Go from here
    and face you eastward;
    you are to hide in Wadi Kerit/Cut Off which faces the Jordan.
4   And it will be: from the wadi you will drink,
    while I have charged ravens to sustain you there.
5   So he went and did according to the word of YHWH:
    he went and stayed in the Wadi Kerit which faces the Jordan.
6   And the ravens were bringing him bread and meat in the morning
    and bread and meat in the evening,
    while from the wadi he would drink.
7   But it was at the end of some days that the wadi dried up,
    for there had been no rain-showers in the land.
8   Then the word of YHWH [came] to him, saying:
9   Arise, go to Tzarefat that belongs to Sidon:
    you are to stay there,
    [for] here, I have charged a widow woman there to sustain you.

---

34 **with Aviram . . . Seguv:** That is, with the loss of his
sons. The reiteration and fulfillment of an old curse
(Josh. 6:26) puts Ah'av's reign in an even more negative light. **doors:** Of the gates. **Yehoshua:** Trad.
English "Joshua."
17:1 **Eliyyahu:** Pronounced *ay-lee-YAH-hoo;* trad. English
"Elijah." **Tishbite . . . Gil'ad:** The location of
Eliyyahu's hometown is cloudy, but Gil'ad (Gilead)
was the large area held by the Israelites to the east
of the Jordan and north of Ammon. *Tishbi* ("Tishbite") also resembles *toshavei,* the "settled-folk" of

the verse. **before whom I stand:** As faithful servant. **rain:** Specifically, the heavy rains of late fall
and early winter.
3 **Kerit:** East of the Jordan, opposite Jericho. **which
faces:** That is, from the east.
4 **ravens:** The trickster figures of folklore around the
world. Here they introduce a mysterious and miraculous element into the Eliyyahu cycle.
9 **Tzarefat:** Pronounced *tzah-re-FAHT.* A town located
a few miles south of Sidon, today in Lebanon.

10 So he arose and went to Tzarefat;
   he came to the entrance of the town,
   and here: a widow woman there was gathering [pieces of] wood.
   He called to her and said:
   Pray fetch me a little water in a vessel, that I may drink.

11 She went to fetch it,
   and he called to her and said:
   Pray fetch me a bit of bread in your hand.

12 She said:
   By the life of YHWH your God,
   if I have anything baked
   except a palmful of meal in a jar
   and a little oil in a jug . . . ,
   for here, I have been gathering two pieces-of-wood;
   I will come home and make it for me and for my son,
   and we will eat it and die.

13 Eliyyahu said to her:
   Do not be afraid;
   go, do according to your words,
   but make me a small baked-cake from there first, and bring it out
      to me,
   while for you and for your son, make [some] afterward.

14 For thus says YHWH, the God of Israel:
   The jar of meal will not be finished
   and the jug of oil will not be lacking
   until the day of YHWH's giving showers upon the face of the
      ground!

15 She went and did according to the word of Eliyyahu,
   and she ate, she and he and her household, for some days.

16 The jar of meal was not finished
   and the jug of oil was not lacking,
   according to the word of YHWH that he had spoken by the hand of
      Eliyyahu.

---

12 **a palmful of meal:** A similar lack of food is noted in the Ugaritic epic of Kirta, as Mann remarks. In our story in general, the question concerns which god, YHWH or Baal (who is featured in Ugaritic texts), will provide for the people. **two:** Or "a few."

Chapter 18. *Eliyyahu and Ovadyahu; The Contest at Mount Carmel:* The transition of Eliyyahu from a mysterious, isolated prophet to a significant public figure is facilitated by the introduction of a secondary character, Ovadyahu, literally "Servant of YHWH," who in an earlier persecution of YHWH's prophets had heroically hidden them. By v.17, Eliyyahu confronts the king, and sets up the famous contest between himself and the prophets of Baal—or, more properly, between YHWH and Baal.

The setting is striking: the great promontory overlooking the Mediterranean, the upper part of today's Haifa, still called the Carmel. Down the coast from Sidon, it continues to serve as the backdrop for Eliyyahu's mission in Baal country, so to speak. The contest itself is as theatrical as anything in the Bible. At the center are contrasts: the lone Eliyyahu against the 450 prophets of Baal; Eliyyahu's dialoguing with the people versus the purely ritual behavior of his opponents; and, most notably, his calm demeanor, contrasted with their "ranting" and self-mutilation. The latter, of course, produces no results, whereas Eliyyahu's heart-felt words in vv.36–37, punctuated by a twofold "know" (the motif of the public acknowledgment of God), lead to the miraculous descent of fire onto the altar. The special effects are spectacular: the fire consumes not only the sacrifice but the altar itself, *and* the stones and dust, *and* the water which Eliyyahu had previously poured over the altar. Moreover, the behavior of the prophets of Baal is mocked, mirroring a treatment of other religious systems that appears frequently in the Bible. In the end, therefore, after the slaughter of those prophets, we should not be surprised that the rains, which had been hitherto withheld, burst out of the sky. Their suddenness is not only reflective of Middle Eastern reality, but is also an indication of where the power really lies. Baal was worshipped in the region chiefly as a storm god, so the polemic is unmistakable.

17 Now after these events it was
   that he became sick,
   the son of the woman, the mistress of the house.
   And his sickness was exceedingly strong,
   until no breath was left in him.
18 She said to Eliyyahu:
   What have I to do with you, O man of God?
   You have come to me to bring my iniquity to mind, to cause the
      death of my son!
19 He said to her:
   Give me your son.
   And he took him from her bosom
   and brought him up to the upper room, where he was staying,
   and had him lie on his bed;
20 then he called out to YHWH, and said:
   O YHWH my God,
   upon the very widow with whom I am lodging
   will you bring evil, to cause the death of her son?
21 And he measured himself out upon the child, three times,
   and called out to YHWH, and said:
   O YHWH my God,
   pray let the life of this child return within him!
22 And YHWH hearkened to the voice of Eliyyahu;
   the life of the child returned within him, so that he lived.
23 Then Eliyyahu took the child
   and brought him down from the upper-room into the house,
   and gave him to his mother.
   Eliyyahu said:
   See, your son is alive!

---

17 **no breath was left in him:** The medieval commentators are split on the issue of whether the child is actually dead, but he certainly seems to be from the description. The wording is different from the Queen of Sheba's "breathless" reaction in 10:5, above (there the word for "breath" is *ru'ah;* here, it is *neshama*).

18 **What have I to do with you:** Or "What do you have against me?" (Sweeney 2001). **to bring my iniquity to mind:** In popular ancient belief, focusing

divine attention on an ordinary person was not necessarily good, but could be downright dangerous.

20 **lodging:** A different form of the verb (Heb. *g-w-r*) usually rendered "sojourn."

21 **measured himself:** A practice of putting a template, as it were, of a holy person over the sick one was thought to bring about a cure (a known ancient Near Eastern practice; see Gaster for examples in world folklore). **life:** In the sense of "life force."

22 **life:** See note to v.21 above.

◆ 24 The woman said to Eliyyahu:
Now indeed I know
that you are a man of God,
and that the word of YHWH in your mouth is truth!

18:1 Now it was many days [later]
that the word of YHWH [came] to Eliyyahu
in the third year, saying,
Go, appear to Ah'av,
that I may give rain upon the face of the ground.
2 So Eliyyahu went to appear to Ah'av.
—Now the famine was strong in Shomeron.—
3 And Ah'av called for Ovadyahu/Servant of YHWH, [The One] Over
the Household,
—now Ovadyahu held YHWH in awe exceedingly;
4 it was, when Izevel cut off the prophets of YHWH,
that Ovadyahu had taken a hundred prophets
and had hidden them, fifty men in a cave, and sustained them with
bread and water—
5 and Ah'av said to Ovadyahu:
Come, let us cross through the land, to all the springs of water and
to all the wadis.
Perhaps we will find some green grass, that we may keep horse and
mule alive,
and will not have to cut off [any] of the animals.
6 So they divided the land between them, to cross through it:
Ah'av went on one road alone,
and Ovadyahu went on another road alone.
7 Now when Ovadyahu was on the road:
here was Eliyyahu, [coming] to meet him!
He recognized him, flung himself on his face and said:
Is it really you, my lord Eliyyahu?

18:1 **in the third year:** Perhaps of the drought.
3 **Ovadyahu:** Pronounced *o-vahd-YAH-hoo;* trad. English "Obadiah." **Household:** Or "Palace-House."
5 **Come, let us cross through:** As emended by Cogan (2001), who notes that the MT here ("Go through")

is ungainly, and so follows LXX. **cut off:** Ah'av worries about the animals, when Izevel has just "cut off" the prophets—a strong clue as to his priorities (Walsh). **animals:** Understood as domestic animals.

◆

8 He said to him:
[It is] I.
Go, say to your lord: Eliyyahu is here!

9 But he said:
How have I sinned,
that you are giving your servant into the hand of Ah'av, to cause
my death?

10 By the life of YHWH your God,
if there be a nation or a kingdom where my lord has not sent there
to seek you . . . ,
and when they say: He is not [here],
he makes the kingdom or the nation swear that they did not
find you.

11 But now *you* say:
Go, say to your lord: Eliyyahu is here!

12 It will be
that *I* will go from you,
and the rushing-spirit of YHWH will carry you to I know not where,
and I will come to tell Ah'av, and he will not find you—
so he will kill me!
Yet your servant has held YHWH in awe since my youth.

13 Has it not been told to my lord what I did
when Izevel was killing the prophets of YHWH:
how I hid a hundred men of the prophets of YHWH,
fifty men, fifty men [each] in a cave,
and sustained them with bread and water?

14 But now *you* say:
Go, say to your lord: Eliyyahu is here!
So he will kill me!

15 Eliyyahu said:
By the life of YHWH of the Forces-On-High, before whom I stand,
indeed, today I will appear to him!

---

8 **[It is] I:** Heb. simply has "I"; the repeated word has the effect of "yes" here (see Greenstein 1989).

11 **Eliyyahu is here!:** This could also be understood, tellingly in the mouth of the faithful Ovadyahu, as "Here, YHWH is my God!" (Walsh).

12 **rushing-spirit:** Heb. *ru'ah* can mean both "spirit" and "wind," so the concept is quite a physical one.

Eliyyahu appears to move about quickly, "like the wind."

15 YHWH **of the Forces-On-High:** This title appears frequently in Samuel, and seems to suggest both the Lord of the heavenly bodies (or of the heavenly court) and the divine commander in chief of Israel's armies.

16 So Ovadyahu went to meet Ah'av, and he told him,
and Ah'av went to meet Eliyyahu.

17 And it was, when Ah'av saw Eliyyahu,
that Ah'av said to him:
Is this you, bringer-of-disaster on Israel?

18 He said:
I have not brought-disaster on Israel,
but rather you and your Father's House,
in that you have abandoned Yнwн's commandments
and have walked after the Baals!

19 So-now,
send [messengers], gather all Israel to me at Mount Carmel,
along with the prophets of Baal, four hundred and fifty, and the
   prophets of Ashera, four hundred,
those eating at Izevel's table.

20 Ah'av sent [messengers] among all the Children of Israel
and gathered the prophets at Mount Carmel.

21 And Eliyyahu came close to all the people and said:
How long will you hop on two branches?
If Yнwн is God, walk after him,
and if Baal, walk after him!
But the people did not answer him a word.

22 Eliyyahu said to the people:
I am left of the prophets of Yнwн, myself alone,
while the prophets of Baal are four hundred and fifty men.

23 Let two bulls be given us,
and let them choose one bull for themselves,
and let them section it and put it atop the wood,
but fire they shall not put [on it].
I will prepare the other bull
and place it atop the wood,
but fire I will not put [on it].

17 **bringer-of-disaster:** Evoking the image of Akhan, whose greed after the fall of Jericho caused Israel's initial defeat at Ai in Josh. 7. Note the threefold use of "disaster" there (vv.24–26).
18 **you have abandoned:** The Hebrew "you" is plural.
19 **those eating at Izevel's table:** And thus they are her royal dependents.

21 **hop on two branches:** As usual, the Bible presents its ideas in concrete imagery; thus the oft-seen translation, "halt between two opinions" (King James et al.), is not adequate. Another possibility for the verb is "hobble"; see Lev. 21:18, where the root means "lame." Then the translation here might read "limp on two crutches."

24 And you are to call on the name of your god,
while *I* will call on the name of Yhwh.
And it will be:
the god who answers with fire, he is God.
All the people answered, they said: The matter is good!

25 Then Eliyyahu said to the prophets of Baal:
Choose yourselves the one bull and prepare [it] first, for you are the many,
and call upon the name of your god,
but fire you are not to put [on it].

26 So they took the bull that he gave them and prepared [it],
and they called upon the name of Baal, from daybreak until noon, saying:
O Baal, answer us!
But there was no voice, and no one answering.
And they hopped all around the altar that they had prepared.

27 Now it was at noon, that Eliyyahu taunted them; he said:
Call out in a great voice, for he is a god!
Maybe he is busy—maybe "doing his business"—or maybe on the road for himself;
perhaps he is asleep and will wake up!

28 So they called out in a great voice
and gashed themselves after their practice with swords and lances,
until blood spilled out over them.

29 And it was, when noon had passed, that they ranted on until the [time of the] offering up of the grain-gift,
but there was no voice, no one answering, and no attention.

26 **O Baal, answer us!:** A prayer of such brevity would have seemed rude to Hebrew-speaking audiences. Eliyyahu's address beginning in v.36 is more formally correct.

27 **Maybe he is busy—maybe "doing his business"—:** Following some, Heb. *ki si'ah ki sig lo* is thus understood as scatological, and fits nicely with the rest of the taunt.

28 **after their practice:** Such cutting of the flesh is attested elsewhere in the ancient world, with a variety of meanings. Gaster connects it with fertility rites designed to revive a dying god, among other interpretations.

29 **ranted on:** As mentioned in the Commentary, this form of prophecy, sometimes called "mantic" or "ecstatic," was known throughout antiquity (for instance, in the case of the Greek followers of Dionysus); see I Sam. 10, where it applies to Sha'ul. Forms of religious enthusiasm are, of course, still practiced in the modern world. **until the [time of the] . . . grain-gift:** Late afternoon, so a good many hours have passed. **no voice:** Heb. *kol* is also used as the conventional word for thunder (see the "voice of Yhwh" in Ps. 29), and since Baal was worshipped as a storm/rain god, the wording here may be sarcastic (Fishbane).

30 Then Eliyyahu said to all the people:
Come close to me!
And all the people came close to him.
He mended the wrecked altar of YHWH;

31 then Eliyyahu took twelve stones, like the number of tribes of the
Children of Yaakov,
to whom the word of YHWH had [come], saying:
Israel shall be your name!,

32 and he built the stones [into] an altar, to the name of YHWH,
and made a channel [big enough] to house two *sei'as* of seed all
around the altar;

33 then he arranged the wood
and sectioned the bull
and placed it atop the wood,

34 and said:
Fill four jugs with water
and pour it on the offering-up and on the wood.
And he said:
Double it! And they doubled it.
And he said:
Triple it! And they tripled it,

35 so that water went all around the altar,
and also the channel filled up with water.

36 And it was, at the [time of] offering-up the grain-gift,
that Eliyyahu the prophet came close and said:
YHWH, God of Avraham, Yitzhak, and Yisrael,
today let it be known
that you are God in Israel, and that I am your servant,
and that it is by your word that I have done all these things.

37 Answer me, O YHWH, answer me,
that this people may know that you, O YHWH, are God,
that you yourself have reversed their heart!

---

30 **mended:** Lit., "healed," hence my use of "mended" rather than the more conventional "repaired."

32 *sei'as:* The *sei'a* was a fairly large dry measure.

34 **Double it!:** That is, do it a second time.

36 **Eliyyahu the prophet:** The use of his full title, reinforcing his stature as the "real" prophet and setting up the drama that now follows.

38 And fire of YHWH fell
and consumed the offering-up and the wood
and the stones and the dust,
and the water that was in the channel it licked up.

39 All the people saw,
and they fell upon their faces, and said:
YHWH, he is God! YHWH, he is God!

40 Eliyyahu said to them:
Seize the prophets of Baal!
Let not one of them escape!
They seized them,
and Eliyyahu brought them down to Wadi Kishon
and slaughtered them there.

41 Then Eliyyahu said to Ah'av:
Go up, eat and drink,
for hark! Roaring showers!

42 So Ah'av went up to eat and to drink,
while Eliyyahu went up to the top of the Carmel and crouched
    down to the ground
and put his face between his knees.

43 Then he said to his serving-lad:
Now go up and look in the direction of the sea.
He went up and looked, and said:
There is nothing.
He said:
Again, seven times.

44 And it was, at the seventh, that he said:
Here, a small cloud like a man's palm is coming up from the sea!
He said:

38 **fire of YHWH:** Lightning; or an "incredible fire."
39 **fell:** Elsewhere in such cases I use "flung them-selves," but Walsh points out the connection with the "fell" of the previous verse here. **YHWH, he is God!:** The phrase has been taken over into Jews' Yom Kippur prayers, moments before the end of the long day of fasting and prayer, when God is acknowledged as supreme.
40 **slaughtered:** A word usually connected to animal sacrifice; see Gen. 22:10.
41 **Go up:** In contrast to his speech to the servant in

v.43, where he uses "pray," Eliyyahu is more "con-frontative" with Ah'av (Walsh). **hark!:** Under-standing Heb. *kol* here as in the Kayin and Hevel (Cain and Abel) story in Gen. 4:10, and elsewhere.
42 **So Ah'av went up ... :** He seems to have no reaction to the slaughtering of the Baalite priests! **crouched . . . and put his face between his knees:** In concentration (Montgomery).
43 **seven times:** As we have encountered it previously, this is a folkloric number, usually indicating per-fection.

Chapter 19. *Eliyyahu's Flight to Sinai; Elisha Appointed:* At the moment of his greatest triumph, Eliyyahu has to take to flight. God's stunning victory over the prophets of Baal, while it wins over the hearts of the people for the moment, cannot prevent the pagan queen Izevel from forcing the prophet into a long journey. It takes place in miraculously quick fashion, and he winds up where he began in Chap. 17: alone in the wilderness, fed at divine command. But this time there is a sense of deep despair which we have not seen previously. The theme of death echoes through Eliyyahu's multiple negative references to the Hebrew term *nefesh,* here meaning "life" (Fishbane). In the midst of his torment, the prophet finds himself at Sinai, in "the cave," perhaps the site where Moshe had communed with God in Exod. 33. In one of the Bible's greatest revelation scenes, God speaks to Eliyyahu, but not by means of the usual Sinai pyrotechnics which were so characteristic of the Exodus stories, and which in Ugaritic literature are often connected to the god Baal. Instead, after wind, earthquake, and fire, God addresses the prophet in a "still small voice." The message is both consoling (he is to be relieved of duty, so to speak) and concentrated: he must go back into the world and set up future events, by appointing his successor and anointing not only the next king of Israel but the king of Aram as well.

The portrait of a prophet as an isolated, persecuted, and self-doubting figure is characteristic of the Hebrew Bible's understanding of the role. Moshe begins the pattern in his initial refusal to serve (Exod. 3) and continues in the many moments when he alone stands between an angry God and the erring people. But the pattern continues elsewhere, especially in the person of Yirmeyahu (Jeremiah) (see, for instance, Jer. 1 and 20). The nature of the prophet's role is to stand against "nations and kingdoms: / to uproot and to pull down, / to destroy and to overthrow, / to build and to plant" (Jer. 1:10). Despite the terrible personal price to be paid by the prophet in his personal and communal life, however, he is exhorted, "Do not break down before them, / lest I break you before them. . . . They will attack you, / but they shall not overcome you; / for I am with you—declares YHWH—to save you" (Jer. 1:17, 19).

There is pathos in Eliyyahu's loneliness, which stands out in contrast to his mastery of the miraculous elsewhere; the wonder-worker cannot overcome his destiny. And so it is that he finds one over whom he can literally throw his mantle, a successor (Elisha) who will surpass his master in textual space and miraculous deeds, but not in force of personality.

Go up, say to Ah'av:
Get harnessed and go down,
so that the showers do not stop you!

45 And it was by then, by then
that the heavens became gloomy with clouds and wind,
and there were heavy showers;
so Ah'av mounted up and went to Yizre'el.

46 And the hand of YHWH was upon Eliyyahu:
he bound up his loins and ran ahead of Ah'av
as far as where you come to Yizre'el.

19:1 And Ah'av told Izevel
all that Eliyyahu had done,
and above all, that he had killed all the prophets with the sword.

2 So Izevel sent a messenger to Eliyyahu, saying:
Thus may the gods do, and thus may they add,
for by this time tomorrow I will make your life like the life of one
of them!

3 He was afraid, so he arose and went away for his life,
and he came to Be'er-Sheva that belongs to Judah,
and left his serving-lad there,

4 while he himself went into the wilderness, a day's journey.
He came and sat down under a broom tree,
and wished for his life to die;
he said:
Enough!
Now, O YHWH,
take my life,
for I am no better than my fathers!

---

46 **ran ahead of Ah'av:** Medieval commentators, and Cogan (2001), see this as a mark of respect for the king, with Eliyyahu acting like one of the outrunners. But it should also be noted that from Carmel to Yizre'el is a hefty run, perhaps eighteen miles. So Eliyyahu outraces the king's chariot horses, again acting almost supernaturally (Cantrell).

19:1 **and above all:** Following ancient versions; MT has "and all that," which makes no sense.

3 **He was afraid:** Ancient versions and manuscripts; MT has "he saw." **Be'er-Sheva that belongs to Judah:** Some two hundred miles from Eliyyahu's usual haunts in the north.

4 **a broom tree:** Others, "a single/lone broom tree," but Heb. *ahat* may simply be the indefinite article in northern biblical speech. As for the tree, commentators differ over whether this is a different bush than the one above, or some kind of textual error.

5 He lay down and fell asleep under a broom tree.
And here, there was a messenger touching him!
He said to him:
Get up, eat!

6 He looked,
and here, at his head was a cake [baked on] glowing coals, and
a jug of water.
So he ate and drank, and returned to lie down.

7 And the messenger of YHWH returned a second-time and
touched him,
and said: Arise, eat!
For the journey is too much for you.

8 So he arose and ate and drank,
and walked in the strength of that eating for forty days and forty
nights,
as far as the Mountain of God, Horev.

9 He came there, to a cave, and spent the night there.
And here, the word of YHWH [came] to him;
he said to him:
What [brings] you here, Eliyyahu?

10 He said:
I have been zealous, yes, zealous for YHWH, the God of the Forces-
On-High,
for the Children of Israel have abandoned your covenant:
your altars they have wrecked
and your prophets they have killed with sword—
while *I* am left, myself alone,
and they have sought my life, to take it!

11 He said:
Go out and stand on the mountain, in the presence of YHWH.
And here, YHWH was crossing by:

---

5 **messenger:** From God; our "angel" is derived from Greek *angelos*, "messenger." **touching:** Perhaps even with the nuance of "punching" (Mann) or "poking."

7 **too much:** Or "more than enough" (Walsh).

9 **a cave:** The definite article in biblical Hebrew can often be understood as indefinite in English. Nevertheless, some take it as *the* cave of revelation to Moshe (see the "cleft of the rock" in Exod. 33:22).

11 **YHWH was not in the . . . :** The unusual form here seems to break out of narrative and belong almost to the realm of incantation, or at least oral performance, making the scene even more vivid. Before each phrase, virtually all translations insert "but," which, however, is not in the text.

now a great and strong wind was crushing mountains and
    smashing boulders in the presence of YHWH—
YHWH was not in the wind;
and after the wind, an earthquake—
YHWH was not in the earthquake;

12   and after the earthquake, fire—
YHWH was not in the fire;
but after the fire,
a still, small voice.

13   It was, when Eliyyahu heard,
that he wrapped his face in his mantle
and went out and stood at the entrance to the cave.
And here, there [came] to him a voice;
it said: What [brings] you here, Eliyyahu?

14   He said:
I have been zealous, yes, zealous for YHWH, God of the Forces-On-
    High,
for the Children of Israel have abandoned your covenant:
your altars they have wrecked
and your prophets they have killed with the sword—
while *I* am left, myself alone,
and they have sought my life, to take it!

15   YHWH said to him:
Go, return on your way, toward the Wilderness of Damascus;
when you come [there], you are to anoint Hazael as king over
    Aram,

16   and Yehu son of Nimshi you are to anoint as king over Israel,
while Elisha son of Shafat, from Evel-Mehola, you are to anoint as
    prophet in your place.

---

12 **a still, small voice:** Heb. *kol demama dakka.* Levine suggests a usage of *d-m-m* that describes mourning or the like, and Simon (1997) notes a similar meaning in ancient versions; I therefore contemplated using "a mild murmuring voice." But the King James Version's "a still, small voice" has never been surpassed, and retains much of the mystery and ambiguity of the Hebrew, in which the prophetic experience encompasses both awestruck silence and speech. The genius of the King James translators is also on display here, since what they inherited from their great predecessor, William Tyndale (whose translation informs the bulk of their text), was "a small, still voice."

15 **way:** Translated as "journey" in v.7. **the Wilderness of Damascus:** East of Lake Tiberias, and a region well-known as a place of refuge (Gray 1970). **anoint Hazael:** This action will actually be done by Eliyyahu's disciple Elisha, so Eliyyahu will accomplish it only indirectly (Fishbane).

16 **Elisha:** Pronounced *eh-lee-SHAH.* The name means "My God Delivers." **Evel-Mehola:** Southeast of Bet-She'an, near the Jordan River. **anoint:** In the case of Elisha, some commentators see the act as indicating "appointing," and not literally pouring oil on his head.

Chapter 20. *Ah'av/Israel and Aram:* The book of Kings is highly interested in neighboring nations, as in Aram here; but typically that interest stems less from a desire to report detailed historical events and more from a need to teach about God, kings, and prophets. And so this chapter presents Ah'av as defiant of the Aramean king—a stance that is supported by God through a prophet—but he also releases the defeated Ben-Hadad following the battle, much to the chagrin of YHWH. This last is perhaps a hint of the historical record as found outside the Bible; Assyrian sources characterize Israel and Aram as close allies in the Battle of Qarqar in 853 B.C.E.

Aram covers the large area to the northeast of Israel, substantially today's Syria. It thus became, in the early centuries of the first millennium B.C.E., a border or buffer state between Assyria and those peoples living on the Mediterranean coast. Aram was not destined to become a great empire like those to the east and southeast, although it attained some prominence in the ninth century; throughout much of its history it was in fact disunified, never possessing a central government. Its chief contributions to the world were, first, its adaptation of Phoenician writing into a more functional alphabet, with the innovation of several letters coming to serve as vowels; and, second, its status as the birthplace of the Aramaic language, which first served as a major diplomatic language in the ancient Near East and later became the daily tongue of Jews for well over a thousand years, including of Jesus and of the Roman-period Rabbis.

From the vantage point of narrative continuity, this chapter would be most fruitfully paired with Chap. 22, and indeed, in LXX the chapter order is 21–20–22.

17 Now it shall be: he who escapes from the sword of Hazael, Yehu
   will put to death,
   and he who escapes from the sword of Yehu, Elisha will put to
   death!

18 But I will allow seven thousand to remain in Israel—
   every [one of] the knees that has not bent to Baal
   and every mouth that has not kissed him!

19 He went from there and found Elisha son of Shafat,
   —now he was plowing with twelve teams [of oxen] in front of him,
   while he was with the twelfth—
   and Eliyyahu crossed over to him and threw his mantle over him.

20 He left the oxen
   and ran after Eliyyahu,
   and said:
   Now let me kiss my father and my mother [good-bye];
   then I will go after you.
   He said to him:
   Go, turn back!
   For what have I done to you?

21 He turned back from [going] after him
   and took a team of oxen and slaughtered it,
   and in the vessel [intended] for the oxen he boiled them, the meat;
   he gave it to the people and they ate it.
   Then he arose and went after Eliyyahu, and attended him.

20:1 Now Ben-Hadad king of Aram gathered his entire army
   —thirty-two kings with him, and horses and chariots—
   and went up and besieged Shomeron, and did battle against it.

2 He sent messengers to Ah'av king of Israel in the city;

3 he said to him:
   Thus says Ben-Hadad:
   Your silver and your gold—it is mine,
   your women and your children, the best ones—they are mine!

---

17 **Yehu:** He is not to be confused with the prophet
Yehu, whom we encountered in 16:1.

19 **twelve:** Undoubtedly representing the idealized,
united twelve tribes of Israel. **threw his mantle
over him:** The mantle or cloak was a symbol of self-
hood and authority; see David's cutting off of the
edge of Sha'ul's mantle in I Sam. 24:5.

20 **what have I done to you?:** The tone and force of
Eliyyahu's question are unclear. It sounds like a
rebuke.

21 **slaughtered . . . boiled . . . ate:** The meal has the
aura of a ritual of parting and is, in fact, a dramatic
moment in Elisha's life.

4 The king of Israel answered, he said:
According to your word, my lord king:
I am yours and all that I have.

5 The messengers returned and said:
Thus says Ben-Hadad, saying:
Indeed, I sent to you, saying:
Your silver and your gold, your women and your children, to *me*
you must give them!

6 But at this time tomorrow I will send my servants to you;
they will search your house and the houses of your servants,
and it will be: everything delightful in your eyes
they will put in their hand and they will take.

7 The king of Israel called for all the elders of the land
and said:
Now know and take-note
that this one is seeking evil,
for he sent to me for my women and for my children, for my silver
and for my gold,
yet I kept back nothing from him!

8 Then all the elders and all the people said to him:
Do not listen,
you must not consent!

9 So he said to the messengers of Ben-Hadad:
Say to my lord king:
Every matter about which you first sent to your servant, I will do,
but this matter I am not able to do!
So the messengers went off, and returned word to him.

10 And Ben-Hadad sent to him
and said:
Thus may the gods do to me, and thus may they add,
if the dust of Shomeron suffices for handfuls for all the fighting-
people who are behind me!

20:6 **your eyes:** Some versions read "their eyes."
7 **know and take-note:** Following Cogan's (2001) suggestion; Heb. *u-d'u u-r'u.* **sent:** Or even "demanded" (Long).

10 **dust:** Or "rubble." **suffices for handfuls:** According to Kimhi, the army will be so large that the dust of the destroyed Shomeron will not even fill up their hands.

◆   II   The king of Israel answered,
        he said: Speak on;
        let not the one who buckles on boast like the one who strips off!

    I2   Now it was, when he heard this word
        —he was drinking, he and the [other] kings at Sukkot—
        that he said to his servants: Set [the attack]!
        So they set upon the city.

    I3   Now here, a prophet came close to Ah'av king of Israel, and said:
        Thus says Yhwh:
        Do you see all this great throng?
        Here, I am giving it into your hand today,
        so that you may know that I am Yhwh!

    I4   Ah'av said:
        Through whom?
        He said:
        Thus says Yhwh:
        Through the squire-lads of the district commanders.
        He said:
        Who will bind up the battle-array?
        He said:
        You.

    I5   So he counted [for war] the squire-lads of the provincial
        commanders
        —they were two hundred two and thirty—
        and after them he counted all the fighting-people, all the Children
        of Israel: seven thousand.

    I6   And they went out at noon.
        Now Ben-Hadad was drinking himself drunk at Sukkot,
        he and the kings, thirty-two kings helping him.

II **Speak on:** The time for politeness has passed (Walsh, Long). **let not the one who buckles on . . . :** A military metaphor about dressing in armor, perhaps the equivalent of "Don't count your chickens before they're hatched" (Walsh). **strips off:** Equivalent to "unbuckles," after the battle.

I2 **Sukkot:** Used as a base of operations east of the Jordan, but some read simply as "in booths." **Set [the attack]!:** Following Cogan (2001).

I4 **squire-lads:** Not as heavily armed as the regular troops, and so less easy to detect (Gray 1970). **bind up the battle-array:** The verb is usually used regarding horses and chariots. It has parallels in Akkadian (Cogan 2001).

I5 **Children of Israel:** Heb. *benei yisrael,* which LXX understands as *benei hayil,* "valiant ones." **seven thousand:** Here and elsewhere in the verse, versions differ on the numbers (here the LXX reads "sixty thousand").

I6 **helping:** or "allied with" (Walsh).

17 And the squire-lads of the provincial commanders went out first;
they sent [to] Ben-Hadad
and told him, saying:
Men have gone out from Shomeron!
18 He said:
If they have gone out for peace, seize them alive,
and if it is for battle that they have gone out, alive seize them [too]!
19 But these went out from the city, the squires of the provincial
commanders,
along with the army that was behind them;
20 each man struck his man down,
and they fled to Aram, while Israel pursued them.
And Ben-Hadad king of Aram escaped on a horse, with cavalry.
21 The king of Israel went out and struck down horse and chariot;
he struck Aram, a great striking-down.
22 And the prophet came close to the king of Israel and said to him:
Go, strengthen yourself;
know and take-note of what you must do,
for at the turn of the year, the king of Aram will go up against you.
23 Now the servants of the king of Aram said to him:
A god of the hills is their god,
therefore they were stronger than we;
but we should do battle with them in the plain
[and see] if we aren't stronger than they!
24 And this thing, do:
Remove the kings, each one from his place,
and put governors in their steads;
25 while you, you are to number yourself an army
like the army fell away from you,
horse like horse, chariot like chariot,
that we may battle them in the plain,
[and see] if we aren't stronger than they!
He hearkened to their voice, and did thus.

17 **they sent [to] Ben-Hadad:** MT has, confusingly, "he
sent Ben-Hadad."
18 **alive seize them [too]:** An incoherent answer which
betrays Ben-Hadad's drunken state (Walsh).
22 **the prophet:** Mentioned in v.13. **the turn of the
year:** Probably in late spring.

23 **A god of the hills:** Alternatively, "mountain gods"
(Cogan 2001).
24 **governors:** A loan word from Assyrian.
25 **fell away from:** Deserted.

26   So it was, at the turn of the year,
     that Ben-Hadad counted Aram [for war],
     and he went up to Afek for battle with Israel,

27   while the Children of Israel were mustered and provided [with food]
     and went to meet them;
     the Children of Israel encamped over against them
     like two bare flocks of goats,
     while Aram filled up the land.

28   And the man of God came close and said to the king of Israel, he
         said:
     Thus says YHWH:
     Because Aram said: A god of the hills is YHWH,
     he is not a god of the valleys—
     I will give all this great throng into your hand,
     so that you may know that I am YHWH!

29   They encamped, these opposite those, for seven days,
     and it was on the seventh day, that the battle came near;
     the Children of Israel struck down of Aram a hundred thousand
         foot-soldiers in one day.

30   Those left fled to Afek, to the town,
     and the wall fell upon the twenty-seven thousand fighting-men who
         were left.
     Ben-Hadad [too] had fled, and he came into the town, into a room
         within a room.

31   His servants said to him:
     Now here, we have heard that the kings of the House of Israel—
         indeed, they are kings [who keep] loyalty;
     now let us put sackcloth on our loins and cords on our heads,
     and let us go out [to surrender] to the king of Israel
     —perhaps he will spare your life.

26 **Afek:** Pronounced *ah-FAKE*. The name of several towns in the Bible. Gray (1970) understands this particular reference as a place east of Lake Tiberias, on the road to Damascus.
27 **bare:** Hebrew unclear; ancient versions read as "little." Clearly, a sense of vulnerability is central.
28 **so that you may know that I am YHWH!:** Echoing a common theme in the Exodus, Conquest traditions, and the book of Ezekiel.
30 **a room within a room:** "Deeper and deeper into

the maze of buildings" (Walsh), or even "a closet" (Mann).
31 **kings [who keep] loyalty:** Not "merciful," as in some translations. The point is that these kings keep their agreements ("covenants"). **cords:** Koehler/Baumgartner see these as "a sign of surrender"; a kind of leash is attested in Assyrian depictions of prisoners. **your life:** MT; ancient versions have "our lives."

Chapter 21. *Navot's Vineyard:* This story, which might be titled "The Framing of Navot," appears to have been inserted in the middle of two accounts of Israel's relationship with Aram. It has been made to connect to the first by means of an aural association: the description of Ah'av's mood in 20:43 as "sullen and enraged" is repeated verbatim in v.4. The story is a high point in the biblical narrator's art, and tells us more about a situation and an ideology than it does about the prophet himself. Eliyyahu's ringing condemnation of Ah'av is a classic prophetic trope, rather removed from his usual miracle-working behavior. Indeed, structurally the story is almost a clone of the David and Bat-Sheva tale of II Sam. 11–12. In both instances, a king takes what is rightfully another's; he has the owner murdered; as he is about to get away with the dual crime, a prophet confronts and condemns him; the king immediately repents; and aspects of the punishment are deflected or put off until the next generation. A message beyond specific historical circumstances is presented here, namely, that the king may not trespass on certain sacred rights, especially regarding the family inheritance of land. And Mann notes that the king and queen even break most of the Ten Commandments in this brief story. In a broader sense, then, the story exposes the unresolved tension between small community and monarchy, a tension which applies not only to Eliyyahu's era but probably to an extended period of change, whenever it may have occurred historically. It is all the more ironic that Izevel makes use of the social mechanisms of small community, a council of elders and freemen, to bring about Navot's murder.

Of particular interest are the portraits of Izevel and Ah'av painted in the text. The Phoenician princess who becomes queen of Israel is the epitome of connivance and control, more paralleling the David of the Bat-Sheva story than her husband does. Upon hearing Ah'av's complaint, without missing a beat she uses her power to get what he cannot, as if she has a plan already drawn up. He, on the other hand, appears utterly tentative—whether out of weakness of character or respect for ancient institutions, we are not told. But when confronted by Eliyyahu, Ah'av is transformed into the model sinner, repenting even more strongly than did his predecessor David.

The chapter gives the writer the opportunity to include a Deuteronomistic note (vv.24–26) about how terrible Ah'av was, and sets up the next major section of Kings, which will recount how the Omride dynasty (and Izevel) meets its downfall. The narrative will take its time getting there; the prophecy's fulfillment will occur only during the career of Eliyyahu's successor Elisha. The fact that this chapter seems to be modeled on the earlier story from Samuel may indicate that the writers/editors felt so strongly about the theme of kingly usurpation that they made sure to include a separate parallel story about the north, whenever our chapter was actually written.

The narrator makes use of several key words in repetition. Five times in vv.13–16 we hear the root "die," which hammers in the seriousness of the crime (just as both David's murder of Uriyya and the finality of David's punishment, the death

32 So they girded sackcloth on their loins and cords on their heads
and came to the king of Israel
and said:
Your servant Ben-Hadad says:
Pray spare my life!
He said:
Is he still alive? He is my brother!

33 Now the men were practicing divination and quickly seized upon it,
and said:
Ben-Hadad is your brother!
And he said:
Come, fetch him!
So Ben-Hadad went out to him, and he pulled him up into the
   chariot.

34 He said to him:
The towns that my father took from your father, I return,
and you may put bazaars in operation for yourself in Damascus,
just as my father put in operation in Shomeron;
while I, under [this] covenant I will send you free.
So he cut a covenant with him, and sent him off.

35 Now a man from the Sons of the Prophets said to his neighbor:
By the word of Yнwн, pray strike me!
But the man refused to strike him,

36 so he said to him:
Because you did not hearken to the voice of Yнwн,
here, when you go from me, a lion will strike you down!
He went from beside him, and a lion found him and struck him
   down.

37 Then he found another man and said: Pray strike me!
And the man struck him, striking and wounding [him].

38 Then the prophet went and stood [waiting] for the king, by the road,
and he disguised himself with a covering over his eyes.

---

32 **brother:** In the sense of an equal, a treaty partner.
33 **practicing divination:** Or looking for an omen (Cogan 2001). **seized upon it:** Following Cogan. **Ben-Hadad is your brother!:** They seem to be surprised.
34 **He said:** That is, Ben-Hadad. **bazaars:** That is,

streets, with the specific connotation of market stalls. **while I:** Apparently, Ah'av is now the speaker.
35 **Sons of the Prophets:** Members of prophetic guilds, not loners, as Eliyyahu seems to be.
38 **covering:** Or "bandage" (Gray 1970).

of his newborn child, are stressed through the same root in II Sam. 11:17–24 and 12:18–19). The fourfold "take possession" later in the story turns our attention to the second stage of Ah'av's crime. Above all, however, is the signal use of the commonplace verb "give," occurring fully nine times in the first seven verses of the story. If the David/Bat-Sheva narrative was about "sending," the present story is about who has the power to give over what is not theirs. And the dynasty is condemned in just those terms—v.22's "I will *give* your house to be" like the other defunct dynasties of the Northern Kingdom. While the Hebrew verb *n-t-n* in such passages usually signifies "make" or "place," here it may be meant to echo the earlier theme word "give." The same verb can also connote "to sell," so we have here a rich use of language.

39   It was, as the king was crossing by,
that he cried out to the king;
he said:
Your servant went out into the midst of the battle,
when here, a man turned aside and brought a man to me,
and he said: Guard this man—
if he is counted-missing, yes, missing [later],
it will be your life in place of his life,
or else you will have to weigh out a talent of silver!

40   Now it was: your servant was facing here and there,
and then he was no more!
The king of Israel said to him:
Correct is your judgment: you yourself have decided.

41   Quickly he removed the covering from over his eyes,
and the king of Israel recognized him,
that he was of the prophets.

42   He said to him:
Thus says YHWH:
Because you sent free the man, one devoted-to-destruction by me,
    from [your] hand,
it will be your life in place of his life,
and your people in place of his people!

43   The king of Israel went back to his house sullen and enraged;
thus he came to Shomeron.

21:1   Now after these events it was:
A vineyard belonged to Navot the Yizre'elite that was in Yizre'el,
next to the Great-House of Ah'av king in Shomeron.

2   And Ah'av spoke to Navot, saying:
Give me your vineyard, that it may be a garden of greens for me
—for it is nearby, next to my house—

---

39 **a talent of silver:** Gray (1970) notes that this is a hundred times the price of a slave in Exod. 21:32, and therefore a huge amount of money. It may be an indication that, at least in this case, prisoners of war were given over to the sanctuary.

40 **judgment:** Or "sentence."

42 **Because you sent free . . . :** The king is condemned here for sparing his enemy, which violated certain biblical views on warfare. In this, he is paralleled to Sha'ul (King Saul), who lost his throne over this issue in I Sam. 15. **devoted-to-destruction:** Others, "under the ban," reserved for YHWH.

21:1 **Navot:** Pronounced *nah-VOTE;* trad. English "Naboth." It may mean "shoot" (of a plant). The Bible frequently compares human mortality to the transitory nature of plant growth. **Great-House:** Palace.

2 **Give me:** Here, as in some other biblical passages, the verb has the connotation of "sell." **my house:** Likewise, the palace.

◆
and I will give you, in its place, a vineyard better than it;
[or] if it is better in your eyes,
I will give you silver for the price of this one.

3 But Navot said to Ah'av:
Yhwh forbid for me
from my giving over the inheritance of my fathers to you!

4 Ah'av came back to his house sullen and enraged
over the word that Navot the Yizre'elite had spoken to him
when he said: I will not give you the inheritance of my fathers!
He lay down on his couch and turned away his face
and would not eat food.

5 And Izevel his wife came to him
and spoke to him:
Now why is your spirit so sullen
that you do not eat food?

6 He spoke to her:
Because I spoke to Navot the Yizre'elite;
I said to him:
Give me your vineyard for silver,
or, if you like,
I will give you a vineyard in its place—
yet he said: I will not give you my vineyard!

7 Izevel his wife said to him:
Do *you*, now, exercise kingship over Israel?
Arise, eat food, that your heart may be in good-humor;
I will give you the vineyard of Navot the Yizre'elite!

8 So she wrote letters in Ah'av's name
and sealed [them] with his seal,
and sent the letters to the elders and the freemen who were in his
    town, those settled with Navot.

9 And she wrote in the letters, saying:
Proclaim a fast
and seat Navot at the head of the people;

---

4 **turned away his face:** In II Kings 20:2, Hizkiyyahu (Hezekiah) is similarly described, indicating that he is ready to die (Walsh).

6 **I will not give you my vineyard!:** Not surprisingly, Ah'av omits Navot's emphasis on "the inheritance of my fathers."

7 **Do *you*, now, exercise kingship over Israel?:** JPS reads, "Now is the time to show yourself king," but the Hebrew seems to imply a more sarcastic tone.

8 **freemen:** A different root than the one used as "free" in v.21. Others, "nobles."

10 then seat two base men in front of him;
   have them testify against him, saying:
   You cursed God and the king!
   Then bring him out and pelt him, so that he dies.

11 So they did, the men of his town
   —the elders and the freemen that were settled in his town—
   as Izevel had sent to them,
   as was written in the letters that she had sent to them:

12 they proclaimed a fast
   and seated Navot at the head of the people,

13 and the two base men came and sat in front of him;
   the base men testified against Navot, in front of the people,
   saying:
   Navot cursed God and the king!
   So they took him outside the town
   and pelted him with stones, and he died.

14 Then they sent to Izevel, saying:
   Navot has been pelted, and has died.

15 Now it was, when Izevel heard that Navot had been pelted, and had
      died,
   that Izevel said to Ah'av:
   Arise, take possession
   of the vineyard of Navot the Yizre'elite
   which he refused to give to you for silver,
   for Navot is not alive,
   for he is dead!

16 It was, when Ah'av heard that Navot was dead,
   that Ah'av arose to go down to the vineyard of Navot the
      Yizre'elite, to take possession of it.

17 But the word of YHWH [came] to Eliyyahu the Tishbite, saying:

18 Arise, go down
   to meet Ah'av king of Israel who is in Shomeron:
   here, [he is] at the vineyard of Navot,
   where he has gone down to take possession of it.

---

10 **cursed:** Lit. "blessed"; ancient scribes did not wish
to use the direct word for "cursed" in reference to
God. The same construction occurs in the first two
chapters of Job. **pelt him:** With stones.
13 **pelted him:** The mention of the incident in II Kings

9:25–26 includes Navot's sons as well, thus solving
Ah'av's problem of heirs surviving to claim the
property.
18 **meet:** Or "confront."

Chapter 22. *War with Aram and the Death of Ah'av:* In an earlier stage of the development of Kings, this chapter undoubtedly followed Chap. 20. In addition, the use of the term "king of Israel" instead of "Ah'av" or "King Ah'av" has led some scholars to theorize that the figure described here originally referred to another monarch. This is further supported by v.40's description of Ah'av's death in normal terms, as opposed to his falling in battle.

In our discussion of the structure of Kings above (p. 551), we noted that this section of the book is concerned with the relationship between kings and prophets. Chap. 22 introduces a whole new cast of the latter, both in plural and in singular, and poses a question that is raised a number of times in the Bible: How does one know if a prophet is a "true" one or a false one? The Judahite king Yehoshafat's initial query about the outcome of the imminent battle meets with enthusiastic predictions from a large group of professional prophets, but their answer somehow does not satisfy the king; perhaps he understands their function as "yes men." He summons instead a prophet known to be contrary—not Eliyyahu, but a certain Mikhayhu—who proceeds first to lie, but finally reveals that Ah'av will die in the battle. The result of this revelation is Mikhayhu's receiving a slap from one of the onlooking court prophets, and then his imprisonment.

In the second part of the chapter (vv.29ff.), Ah'av meets his fate. Despite a desperate attempt to outwit the enemy by discarding his royal garb while encouraging his Judahite ally not to do so, he is hit by an Aramean arrow. Propped up in the chariot in the heat of the battle, he bleeds to death.

The Ah'av who may be teased from history appears to have been more accomplished than the Bible gives him credit for. While the text hints at some building projects (v.39), archaeology credits him with more, including probably the so-called stables at Megiddo. Of equal significance is the fact that he was a participant in the important battle at Qarqar, where the burgeoning Assyrian Empire apparently suffered a temporary setback. For the book of Kings, however, the account of Navot's framing is of much greater import, and there is no hint there of Qarqar, in an excellent example of the Bible's attitude toward what we call history. Thus Ah'av is judged by standards other than political ones, and, regardless of his actual accomplishments, he has been effectively frozen for all time as the Baal-tolerating king of Israel, Izevel's husband, and Eliyyahu's opponent. It is intriguing, but not entirely unexpected, that Melville appropriated his name for the captain of the *Pequod,* who makes a virtual idol of his desire for revenge.

19 You are to speak to him, saying:
Thus says YHWH:
Murdered have you, and dispossessed too?
And you are to speak to him, saying:
Thus says YHWH:
In the place where the dogs have licked up the blood of Navot
the dogs will lick up your blood, even yours!

20 Ah'av said to Eliyyahu:
Have you found me, my enemy?
He said:
I have found [you]!
Because you have sold yourself
to do what is evil in the eyes of YHWH,

21 here, I will bring evil upon you
and will eradicate [those coming] after you
and will cut off from Ah'av he who pisses against the wall,
[even] the fettered and forsaken in Israel!

22 I will give your house to be
like the House of Yorov'am son of Nevat,
like the House of Ba'sha son of Ahiyya,
because of the provocation by which you have provoked [me]
and caused Israel to sin.

23 And also about Izevel YHWH has spoken, saying:
The dogs will eat Izevel
at the rampart of Yizre'el!

24 He who dies of Ah'av in the town
the dogs shall eat,
while he who dies in the open-field
the birds of the heavens shall eat!

---

19 **Murdered have you, and dispossessed too?:** Heb. *ha-ratzahta ve-gam yarashta.* I could not find a compact rhyme to echo the Hebrew. Note that *y-r-sh,* connoting possession, is a key root in the narrative (vv.15, 16, 18, and 26 as well).

20 **sold yourself:** In legal language, "alienated your-self," that is, effected a transfer of ownership or affection.

21 **he who pisses against the wall:** All males; see note to I Sam. 25:22.

23 **at the rampart:** Others read MT's *be-hel* as *be-helek,* "in the district," with ancient versions.

25 —Surely there was never [another] like Ah'av,
who sold himself to do what was evil in the eyes of YHWH,
whom Izevel his wife incited;

26 he did exceedingly abominably in walking after the Illicit-Things,
exactly as the Amorites had done,
whom YHWH had dispossessed before the Children of Israel.—

27 Now it was, when Ah'av heard these words,
that he tore his garments
and put sackcloth upon his flesh
and fasted,
and lay down in sackcloth,
and went around softly.

28 And the word of YHWH [came] to Eliyyahu the Tishbite, saying:

29 Do you see that Ah'av is humbling himself before me?
Because he is humbling himself before me,
I will not bring the evil in his days;
in the days of his son I will bring the evil on his house.

22:1 They stayed put for three years,
[since] there was no war between Aram and Israel.

2 But it was in the third year
that Yehoshafat king of Judah went down to the king of Israel.

3 The king of Israel said to his servants:
Do you know that Ramot-Gil'ad is ours?
Yet we keep silent about taking it from the king of Aram!

4 So he said to Yehoshafat:
Will you go with me in battle to Ramot-Gil'ad?
Yehoshafat said to the king of Israel:
I am as you are: my fighting-people as your fighting-people,
my horses as your horses!

5 And Yehoshafat said to the king of Israel:
Pray inquire of the word of YHWH here-and-now.

---

27 **tore his garments . . . :** Typical signs of mourning.
22:2 **Yehoshafat:** Last mentioned in 15:24.
3 **Ramot-Gil'ad:** The "Heights of Gilead," equivalent to the present-day Golan Heights, overlooking the eastern part of the Jezreel Valley.

4 **I am . . . :** Namely, I am ready, at your disposal. The Hebrew uses "as, like" before each pronoun and noun.

6 So the king of Israel gathered the prophets, some four
    hundred men,
and said to them:
Shall I go against Ramot-Gil'ad in battle, or shall I refrain?
They said:
Go up—Yhwh will give it into the hand of the king!

7 Yehoshafat said:
Is there not a prophet of Yhwh here, yet another, that we may
    inquire through him?

8 The king of Israel said to Yehoshafat:
There is yet another man through whom one may inquire of Yhwh,
but I myself hate him,
for he never prophesies for good concerning me, but only for evil:
Mikhayhu son of Yimla.
Yehoshafat said:
Let not the king say thus!

9 So the king of Israel called an officer and said:
Quickly! Mikhayhu son of Yimla!

10 Now the king of Israel and Yehoshafat king of Judah were sitting,
    each one on his throne
clothed in [royal] garments,
at the threshing floor at the entrance to the Gate of Shomeron,
while all the prophets were prophesying before them.

11 And Tzidkiyya son of Kenaana made himself horns of iron
and said:
Thus says Yhwh:
With these you shall gore Aram, until they are finished off!

12 And all the prophets prophesied thus, saying:
Go up to Ramot-Gil'ad, and triumph,
for Yhwh will give [it] into the hand of the king!

---

6 **Yhwh:** Following ancient manuscripts and versions; MT has "the Lord."

8 **never . . . for good . . . only for evil:** Mann notes a similar situation in the *Iliad*, with Agamemnon complaining about Calchas's prophecies. **Mikhayhu son of Yimla:** Pronounced *mee-KHAI-hoo;* trad. English "Micaiah son of Imlah." His name means "Who Is Like Yhwh?"

11 **Tzidkiyya son of Kenaana:** A curious name that seems to mix cultures ("Yhwh Is Righteous" and "Canaanite") (Walsh). The trad. English is "Zedekiah," also the name of Judah's last king.

13 Then the messenger who had gone to call Mikhayhu spoke to him,
     saying:
Now here, the words of the prophets are as one mouth for good
     regarding the king;
pray may your word be like the word of one of them, so that you
     speak for good!

14 But Mikhayhu said:
As YHWH lives!
Indeed, whatever YHWH says to me, that [alone] may I speak.

15 He came to the king, and the king said to him:
Mikhayhu, shall we go to Ramot-Gil'ad in battle,
or shall we refrain?
He said to him:
Go up and triumph;
YHWH will give it into the hand of the king.

16 The king said to him:
How many times must I make you swear
that you are not to speak to me anything but truth in the name of
     YHWH?

17 So he said:
I saw all Israel scattered on the hills
like sheep that have no herder,
and YHWH said: There are no masters for these.
Let each return to his house in peace!

18 The king of Israel said to Yehoshafat:
Did I not say to you:
He never prophesies for good concerning me, but only for evil?

19 He said:
Therefore, hearken to the word of YHWH:
I saw YHWH sitting on his throne,
with all the Forces of the Heavens standing over against him, on his
     right and on his left;

---

14 **that [alone] may I speak:** The classic prophet's retort, so central to the Bil'am (Balaam) story in Num. 22–24.

19 **He said:** Mikhayhu. **Forces of the Heavens:** I also use "Forces-On-High" for this phrase, Heb. *tzeva'ot.*

The image of a heavenly council is alluded to many times in the Bible; here it is somewhat spelled out. Elsewhere in the ancient world it would have referred to a council of the gods themselves.

◆ 20   and YHWH said:
Who will entice Ah'av
so that he will go up and fall at Ramot-Gil'ad?
And this one said thusly, while that one said thusly.

21   Then a spirit came out and stood in the presence of YHWH
and said:
I will entice him.
YHWH said to him:
In what [way]?

22   He said:
I will go out and be a false spirit
in the mouth of all his prophets.
He said:
You will entice [him], aye, you will prevail.
Go out and do thus!

23   So-now, here: YHWH has placed a false spirit
in the mouth of all these your prophets,
for YHWH has spoken evil regarding you!

24   Then Tzidkiyyahu son of Kenaana approached and struck
Mikhayhu on the cheek,
and said:
Which way did the spirit of YHWH cross over from me to speak
with you?

25   Mikhayhu said:
Here, you will see on that day,
when you enter a room within a room to hide!

26   The king of Israel said:
Take Mikhayhu
and turn him over to Amon, commander of the town, and to
Yoash, the son of the king;

20 **fall:** A double entendre, connoting both "die" and
"attack" ("fall upon") (Walsh).
25 **a room within a room:** See 20:30 above and note.

26 **Yoash:** Pronounced *yo-AHSH;* trad. English "Joash."
son of the king: Possibly a title (Gray 1970).

◆

27   you are to say:
Thus says the king:
Put this one in the prison house
and have him eat meager bread and meager water,
until I return in peace.

28   Mikhayhu said:
If you return, yes, return in peace,
Yhwh has not spoken through me!
And he said:
Hearken, O peoples, all of them . . .

29   The king of Israel and Yehoshafat king of Judah went up to Ramot-Gil'ad.

30   And the king of Israel said to Yehoshafat:
[I] will disguise [myself] and come to battle,
but you, clothe yourself in your [royal] garments.
So the king of Israel disguised himself and came to battle.

31   Now the king of Aram had charged the chariot officers belonging to him,
thirty-two, saying:
You are not to engage in battle with anyone from small to great,
except with the king of Israel alone!

32   And it was, when the chariot officers saw Yehoshafat,
that they said:
Surely he is the king of Israel!
So they turned toward him, to do battle,
and Yehoshafat cried out [for help].

33   But it was, when the chariot officers saw that he was not the king of Israel,
that they turned away from him.

---

27 **in peace:** Or "safely."
28 **Hearken, O peoples . . . :** Apparently an editor understood Mikhayhu to be the later prophet Micah (Heb. Mikha), and thus has quoted the opening of the latter's prophetic book (1:2) here.

30 **[I] will . . . come:** So LXX; MT has imperatives here.

34 Now a man drew his bow in his innocence
and struck the king of Israel between the connecting-plates and the
armor.
He said to his chariot driver:
Reverse your hand and take me out of the camp,
for I have been wounded!

35 The battle heightened on that day,
and the king was stood up in the chariot, facing Aram.
He died at sunset, with the blood of his wound pouring into the lap
of the chariot.

36 And a ringing-cry passed through the camp as the sun was coming
in, saying:
Each one to his town! Each one to his land!

37 So the king died and was brought to Shomeron,
and they buried the king in Shomeron.

38 The chariot was rinsed off by the Pool of Shomeron;
the dogs licked up his blood,
and whores bathed [in it],
according to the word of YHWH which he had spoken.

39 Now the rest of the events of Ah'av, and all that he did,
and the house of ivory that he built
and all the towns that he built—
are they not written in the Record of Yearly Events of the Kings of
Israel?

40 Ah'av lay beside his fathers,
and Ahazyahu his son reigned as king in his place.

34 **in his innocence:** Others, "at random." Another possibility is "to the limit," namely, drawing the bow all the way back for a powerful shot. **Reverse your hand:** That is, turn the reins, equivalent to "Put the chariot in reverse." **camp:** Heb. *mahaneh,* but others read as *milhama,* "battle," which makes more sense. Walsh suggests that Ah'av's wounds have made him disoriented.

35 **was stood up:** Or "propped up." Walsh points up the irony: "a king who pretended not to be a king is now a corpse pretending not to be dead." **facing Aram:** Facing the enemy troops, as if the commander of Israel is still at the helm. Something similar happens in the medieval account of the Spanish hero El Cid.

37 **was brought:** Reflecting LXX; MT has "came."

38 **whores bathed:** Some read "washed his armor," which pales in comparison to the traditional reading adopted here.

39 **the house of ivory:** Presumably a palace, with ivory inlays (Gray 1970).

40 **lay beside his fathers:** This oft-repeated image is an indication here that we may have different traditions about Ah'av—one violent, one peaceful—that have been spliced together. **Ahazyahu:** Trad. English "Ahaziah."

41 Now Yehoshafat son of Asa became king over Judah
in year four of Ah'av king of Israel.

42 Yehoshafat was thirty-five years old at his becoming king,
and for twenty-five years he reigned as king in Jerusalem;
his mother's name was Azuva daughter of Shilhi.

43 And he walked in all the way of Asa his father;
he did not turn aside from it, doing what was right in the eyes of
YHWH.

44 However, the sanctuaries were not removed—
the people were still offering-sacrifices and sending-up-smoke at the
sanctuaries.

45 And Yehoshafat made peace with the king of Israel.

46 Now the rest of the events of Yehoshafat and his mighty-deeds that
he did, and how he waged battle—
are they not written in the Record of Yearly Events of the Kings of
Judah?

47 And the rest of the [male] prostitutes who were left in the days of
Asa his father
he eradicated from the land.

48 Now king there was none in Edom;
a prefect reigned as king.

49 And Yehoshafat had made ships of Tarshish for going to Ofir, for
gold,
but they did not go,
because the ships broke apart at Etzyon-Gever.

50 It was then that Ahazyahu son of Ah'av had said to Yehoshafat:
Let my servants go with your servants aboard the ships!
But Yehoshafat had not consented.

51 Yehoshafat lay beside his fathers;
he was buried with his fathers
in the city of David his father,
and Yehoram his son reigned as king in his place.

---

44 **removed:** Following ancient versions; MT has
"turned aside," the simpler form of the verb.
48 **Edom:** Probably mentioned here because the
events of the next verse take place at an Edomite
port. **reigned as king:** Reading *malakh* for *melekh*.

50 **It was then:** or "At that time" (Walsh).
51 **Yehoram:** Pronounced *ye-ho-RAHM;* trad. English
"Jehoram."

◆

52   Ahazyahu son of Ah'av became king over Israel in Shomeron
       in year seventeen of Yehoshafat king of Judah;
       he reigned as king over Israel for two years.

53   And he did what was evil in the eyes of Yhwh:
       he walked in the way of his father and in the way of his mother,
       and in the way of Yorov'am son of Nevat,
       who had caused Israel to sin;

54   he served Baal and bowed down to him
       and provoked Yhwh the God of Israel,
       exactly as his father had done.

II KINGS

Chapter 1. *Eliyyahu and Ahazyahu:* The text returns to Eliyyahu and his marvelous powers. It begins with a king who is ill and thus in need of an oracle; quickly the issue becomes, as previously in Chap. 18, whether to rely upon YHWH or upon Baal. King Ahazyahu unhesitatingly turns to the pagan god, and as a result he is condemned to die on his sickbed.

Beyond the prophetic word, we are given another demonstration of Eliyyahu's ability to call down fire from heaven. In this case, the "sacrifice" is two army commanders and their bands of fifty soldiers (tellingly, we recall that Eliyyahu serves "YHWH of the Forces-On-High"); the third commander, like Ovadyahu in Chap. 17 above, successfully pleads with the prophet. It is all a continuation of Eliyyahu's (really, God's) power over life and death, a theme that permeates the entire cycle of stories.

The repetition of refrains relating to the king ("Is it because there is no God in Israel whose word [one] can consult?"; "the bed into which you climbed up," etc.) serves to underscore the prophet's condemnation of idolatry, which even more than the folktale/miraculous aspect is the key to the stories here.

Interestingly, in v.8 we are given one of the few physical descriptions of a central biblical character: Eliyyahu is "a hairy man, / with a girded-belt of leather girded about his loins." The description befits his folkloristic character. He is an elemental figure who in his very appearance brings out the struggle between the powerless and those who rule.

II KINGS

1:1 And Moav rebelled against Israel after the death of Ah'av.

2 Now Ahazya fell through the lattice of his upper-chamber that was
    in Shomeron,
    and he became sick [from his injuries].
    So he sent messengers, and said to them:
    Go, inquire of Baal Zevuv/Master of Flies, the god of Ekron,
    whether I will live through this sickness!

3 Now a messenger of YHWH spoke to Eliyya the Tishbite:
    Arise, go up to meet the messengers of the king of Shomeron,
    and speak to them:
    Is it because there is no God in Israel
    [that all of] you go to inquire of Baal Zevuv, the god of Ekron?

4 So therefore, thus says YHWH:
    The bed into which you climbed up,
    you will not come down from it,
    but you will die, yes, die!
    And Eliyya went off.

5 The messengers returned to him, and he said to them:
    Now why have you returned?

6 They said to him:
    A man came up to meet us,
    and he said to us:
    Go, return to the king who sent you,
    and speak to him:
    Thus says YHWH:
    Is it because there is no God in Israel
    [that] you send to inquire of Baal Zevuv, the god of Ekron?
    Therefore,
    the bed into which you climbed up,

1:1 **rebelled:** See note to I Kings 12:19, above. Moav's rebellion will resurface in Chap. 3.

2 **became sick [from his injuries]:** Biblical Hebrew does not make a distinction between illness and injury, the latter of which is clearly meant here. **Baal Zevuv/Master of Flies:** Pronounced *ze-VOOV*. The name is a nasty pun on "Baal Zevul," "Baal the Exalted," commonly found in Ugaritic texts. See the name "Izevel" in I Kings 16:31, for a possible similar usage. The trad. English for the name is "Baal-zebub," which in later Jewish and then Christian tradition became Beelzebub, a significant demon and eventually a nickname for the Devil. **Ekron:** Pronounced *eh-KROHN*. One of the five major Philistine towns.

3 **Eliyya:** A shortened variant of Eliyyahu.

5 **to him:** To the king.

◆   you will not come down from it,
                but you will die, yes, die!

    7   He spoke to them:
                What is the manner of the man who came up to meet you
                and spoke these words to you?

    8   They said to him:
                A hairy man,
                with a girded-belt of leather girded about his loins.
                He said:
                It is Eliyya the Tishbite!

    9   So he sent to him a captain of fifty, with his [unit of] fifty.
                He went up to him,
                and here, he was sitting on top of a hill;
                and he spoke to him:
                O man of God, the king has spoken:
                Come down!

    10   Eliyyahu answered
                and spoke to the captain of fifty:
                Now if I am a man of God,
                let fire come down from the heavens
                and consume you and your fifty!
                And fire came down from the heavens
                and consumed him and his fifty.

    11   He sent again to him—another captain of fifty and his fifty;
                he went up and spoke to him:
                O man of God,
                thus says the king:
                Come down quickly!

    12   Eliyya answered and spoke to them:
                If I am a man of God,
                let fire come down from the heavens

---

8 **hairy:** Heb. *baal se'ar,* "possessing (much) hair," echoing "Baal Zevuv" (Cohn 2000). It is not clear whether the text means a hairy man or merely one wearing animal skins. **leather:** Lit. "[animal] skin."

9 **captain of fifty:** Head of a defined military unit. The term was common in the ancient Near East.

10 **man . . . fire:** Martin notes the sound play here, which continues throughout the chapter: *ish* and *esh.* **heavens:** In the usual biblical sense of "the sky" (and not the abode of the blessed dead, as in later concepts).

12 **fire of God:** The phrase "X of God" is frequently used to express the superlative in the Bible (as in Gen. 35:5, I Sam. 26:12).

◆
and consume you and your fifty!
And fire of God came down from the heavens
and consumed him and his fifty.

13 He sent again—a third captain of fifty and his fifty;
he went up and came, the third captain of fifty,
but he bowed on his knees in front of Eliyyahu
and pleaded with him
and spoke to him:
O man of God, now may my life and the life of these your fifty
servants be precious in your eyes!

14 [For] here, fire came down from the heavens
and consumed the previous captains of fifty and their fifties;
but now, may my life be precious in your eyes!

15 Then a messenger of God spoke to Eliyyahu:
Go down with him; do not be afraid before him.
So he arose and went down with him to the king.

16 And he spoke to him:
Thus says YHWH:
Because you sent messengers to inquire of Baal Zevuv, the God of
Ekron,
—Is it because there is no God in Israel whose word can be inquired
of?—
therefore,
the bed into which you climbed up,
you will not come down from it,
but you will die, yes, die!

17 And he died, in accordance with the word of YHWH that Eliyyahu
had spoken,
and Yehoram reigned as king in his place,
in year two of Yehoram son of Yehoshafat, king of Judah,
for he had no son.

18 Now the rest of the events of Ahazyahu, [and] what he did—
are they not written in the Record of Yearly Events of the Kings of
Israel?

---

13 **went up:** Heb. *va-yaal*, following LXX; MT has *va-yaan*, "spoke up."

17 **Yehoram:** Some versions insert "his brother" after the name. Note that the text cites two kings with the same name, north and south.

Chapter 2. *Eliyyahu's Ascent and Elisha's Succession:* With a majesty that foreshadows such legendary heroes as King Arthur (Gaster), Eliyyahu's end is one of the most memorable in the Bible. It is fully fitting for one whose life has been consistently mysterious and majestic.

In a somewhat surprising narrative move, the manner of his death is revealed in the chapter's opening verse. This has the effect of shifting the reader's focus from the fantastic to what the text regards as key: first, the relationship between the prophet and his forerunner Moshe, and second, the one between him and his successor Elisha. The former has already been strongly suggested by Eliyyahu's Sinai experience in Chap. 19 above, and is strengthened in our chapter by his splitting of the waters of the Jordan and his disappearance. (Cohn [2000] notes how the site of Moshe's grave is unknown as well.) Eliyyahu's relationship to Elisha—in particular, his passing of the literal mantle of authority—takes up most of the chapter. And this is the only place in the Hebrew Bible where a prophet gets to appoint his successor. As Cohn points out, the narrative is arranged chiastically, with Eliyyahu's ascent at the center, but with Elisha prominent on either side. The reader is thus assured (along with Elisha's immediate performing of Eliyyahu-like miracles) that the younger man will be the worthy successor to the older one. This is further supported by the final episode, where the prophet brings down a terrible curse on his young tormentors, parallel to what Eliyyahu had done to King Ahazyahu's soldiers. Burnett has suggested that the traditional understanding of the taunters as little children may well be wrong, sadly for artists over the centuries; instead, he argues, they are like the "youngsters" in I Kings 12, Rehav'am's immature counselors, in this case probably young men attached to the royal or even religious establishment at the previously delegitimized shrine at Bet-El. In this reading, the taunt "Go up . . . Go up!" might also be reflecting Eliyyahu's death, suggesting that Elisha should go the way of his master. So the episode demonstrates not only that the prophet possesses or at least represents powers that are not to be tampered with, but also sets him against the powers that be, a scenario that was central to the Eliyyahu stories and which occurs frequently in the Hebrew Bible.

Regardless of the age of the victims, however, already in Roman times Jews and Christians found this story troubling.

◆　2:1　Now it was,
　　　　when Yhwh was about to bring up Eliyyahu in a storm to the
　　　　　　heavens,
　　　　that Eliyyahu went with Elisha from Gilgal.

　　2　And Eliyyahu said to Elisha:
　　　　Pray stay here,
　　　　for Yhwh has sent me as far as Bet-El.
　　　　Elisha said:
　　　　By the life of Yhwh and by your own life, if I should leave
　　　　　　you . . . !
　　　　So they went down to Bet-El.

　　3　And the Sons of the Prophets who were in Bet-El came out to
　　　　　　Elisha
　　　　and said to him:
　　　　Do you know
　　　　that today Yhwh is going to take your lord from your head?
　　　　He said:
　　　　Certainly I know; be silent!

　　4　Eliyyahu said to him:
　　　　Elisha, pray stay here,
　　　　for Yhwh has sent me to Jericho.
　　　　But he said:
　　　　By the life of Yhwh and by your own life, if I should leave
　　　　　　you . . . !
　　　　So they came to Jericho.

　　5　And the Sons of the Prophets who were in Jericho came close to
　　　　　　Elisha
　　　　and said to him:
　　　　Do you know
　　　　that today Yhwh is going to take your lord from your head?
　　　　He said:
　　　　Certainly I know; be silent!

2:1 **storm:** Others, "whirlwind." This phenomenon is often associated with the appearance of God in the Bible, most famously and dramatically in Job 38:1. **Gilgal:** The term for a "round place" of stones or a round platform, this particular one is probably not the significant one near Jericho (see Josh. 4:19), but a site in a central location of the Northern Kingdom.

3 **Sons of the Prophets:** See note to I Kings 20:35. **from your head:** The phrase describes the master-servant relationship here (Cogan/Tadmor).

◆ 6 Then Eliyyahu said to him:
Pray stay here,
for Yhwh has sent me to the Jordan.
But he said:
By the life of Yhwh and by your own life, if I should leave you . . . !
Thus the two of them walked on.

7 Now fifty men of the Sons of the Prophets went
and stood opposite, at a distance,
while the two of them stood by the Jordan.

8 And Eliyyahu took his mantle, folded it up, and struck the waters,
and they split in half, to here and to there,
and the two of them crossed over on dry-ground.

9 It was when they crossed that Eliyyahu said to Elisha:
Make-request: what may I do for you before I am taken from beside
you?
Elisha said:
Pray let a twofold measure of your spirit be upon me!

10 He said:
You have made a difficult request.
If you see me being taken from you, it will be thus for you,
but if not, it will not be.

11 And it was, as they were walking, walking along and speaking,
that here, a chariot of fire and horses of fire:
they parted the two of them,
and Eliyyahu went up in the storm to the heavens.

12 When Elisha saw [it],
he kept crying out: Father! Father!
Israel's chariotry and its horsemen!
But he saw him no more.
So he took hold of his garments and tore them into two torn-
pieces,

---

6 **Thus the two of them walked on:** Reminiscent of the pregnant "Thus the two of them walked on together" in the Avraham/Yitzhak (Abraham/Isaac) story of Gen. 22.
8 **folded:** A rare biblical word, meaning more precisely "wrapped."
11 **walking:** Also in the sense of an auxiliary verb that conveys repetition—for example, "going along and speaking," meaning "continuing to speak."
12 **Israel's chariotry and its horsemen!:** Elisha appears to be equating Eliyyahu with the entire army, as if to suggest that the prophet is the people's true strength.

13   and picked up the mantle of Eliyyahu that had fallen from him;
then he returned and stood at the bank of the Jordan.

14   And he took the mantle of Eliyyahu that had fallen from him
and struck the waters,
and said:
Where is YHWH, the God of Eliyyahu, indeed?
He struck the waters
and they split in half, to here and to there,
and Elisha crossed over.

15   And the Sons of the Prophets who were in Jericho saw him
opposite;
they said:
The spirit of Eliyyahu has come to rest upon Elisha!
They came to meet him and bowed low before him to the ground,

16   and they said to him:
Now here, there are fifty men among your servants, valiant ones;
pray let them go and seek your lord,
lest the rushing-spirit of YHWH has carried him off
and has thrown him onto one of the mountains or into one of the
valleys!
But he said:
You are not to send!

17   But they pressed him until he was ashamed,
so he said: Send.
They sent fifty men
and searched for three days,
but they did not find him.

18   They returned to him
—he was staying in Jericho—
and he said to them:
Did I not say to you: Do not go?

19   The men of the town said to Elisha:
Now here, the site of the town is good, as my lord can see,
but the water is bad, and the land causes miscarrying!

---

14 **Where is YHWH:** He equates the disappearance of his master with a rupture in divine-human communication. **indeed:** An oft-used emendation from *'af hu*, "even he," to *efo*. No good solution has been found to this awkward sentence.

Chapter 3. *Israel and Moav:* This is a classic Kings text, with international events—in this case, the political and military interactions of three territories—understood in the light of prophecy. As if three kings were not enough participants in the events, the prophet serves as mediator, and is (in v.11) immediately identified as Eliyyahu's disciple. We are even given insight into the prophetic process, at least in one manifestation: it is induced by string music (v.15). As in the Eliyyahu stories, water also plays a role here, but with the striking twist that, through the illusion of the rising sun's reflection, the water is taken to be blood.

It has long been noted that while the prophet predicts Moav's defeat, this did not happen historically. Modern commentators therefore see in the chapter's strange and ambiguous end an attempt to square the discrepancy.

◆ 20 He said:
Fetch me a new bowl and put salt there.
They fetched [it] for him.
21 He went out to the outflow of the waters
and threw salt in it,
and he said:
Thus says YHWH:
I have healed these waters;
there will no longer be death and miscarrying from there!
22 And the waters were healed, until this very day,
in accordance with the word of Elisha which he had spoken.

23 He went up from there to Bet-El.
And as he was going up on the road, some young lads went up out
of the town;
they jeered at him and said to him:
Go up, baldhead! Go up, baldhead!
24 He faced about behind him and saw them
and cursed them in the name of YHWH,
and two she-bears came out of the forest
and ripped up forty-two youngsters from them.
25 He went from there to Mount Carmel,
and from there he returned to Shomeron.

3:1 Now Yehoram son of Ah'av became king over Israel in Shomeron
in year eighteen of Yehoshafat king of Judah;
he reigned as king for twelve years.
2 And he did what was evil in the eyes of YHWH,
although not like his father or like his mother:
he removed the standing-stone of Baal that his father had made
3 —although he clung to the sins of Yorov'am son of Nevat, who had
caused Israel to sin,
and did not turn aside from them.

---

20 **new:** See note to I Kings 11:29. **bowl:** Others, "dish," "pot."
21 **outflow:** Source.
22 **the waters were healed:** See Exod. 15:22–25, where God "heals" bitter water by having Moshe throw a piece of wood into it.
23 **baldhead:** Others, more colloquially, "baldy."

24 **ripped up:** Are they killed, or "mauled," as most translations have it? **forty-two:** The number is used later to count Yehu's victims in 10:14; it looks like another "special" biblical number (forty plus two, or seven times three times two).
3:2 **standing-stone:** A cultic image.

4   Now Mesha king of Moav was a sheep-dealer;
    he would supply the king of Israel with a hundred thousand he-
        lambs and a hundred thousand rams in wool.

5   But it was, at the death of Ah'av,
    that the king of Moav rebelled against the king of Israel.

6   And King Yehoram went out on that very day from Shomeron
    and counted all Israel [for war];

7   he went and sent to Yehoshafat king of Judah, saying:
    The king of Moav has rebelled against me.
    Will you go with me to Moav in battle?
    He said:
    I will go up!
    [For] I am as you are:
    my people as your people,
    my horses as your horses!

8   He said:
    By which road shall we go up?
    He said:
    The Road of the Wilderness of Edom.

9   So they went, the king of Israel, the king of Judah, and the king of
        Edom;
    they [traveled] round about the road for seven days.
    Now there was no water for the camp or for the animals that were
        behind them,

10 so the king of Israel said:
    Alas,
    for YHWH must have called these three kings together
    to give them into the hand of Moav!

11 Yehoshafat said:
    Is there no prophet of YHWH here
    that we may inquire of YHWH through him?
    One of the servants of the king of Israel answered and said:
    Here is Elisha son of Shafat,
    who poured water over the hands of Eliyyahu.

---

4 **Mesha:** Pronounced *may-SHAH*. See the reference
to Moav in the Commentary. **he would supply:**
As tribute. Others, "had to supply," implying a one-
time payment (Martin).

7 **I am . . . :** See I Kings 22:4 for the same phraseology.

8 **The Road of the Wilderness of Edom:** So they take
a long route, coming up from the south.

11 **poured water over the hands:** As servant; a sign of
deference.

◆ 12 Yehoshafat said:
With him is the word of YHWH!
And so they went down to him,
the king of Israel, and Yehoshafat, and the king of Edom.

13 Elisha said to the king of Israel:
What have I to do with you?
Go to your father's prophets and to your mother's prophets!
The king of Israel said to him:
No—
for YHWH has called these three kings together
to give them into the hand of Moav!

14 Elisha said:
By the life of YHWH of the Forces-On-High, in whose presence I
stand,
indeed: were it not that I hold up the face of Yehoshafat king of
Judah [in respect],
I would not look at you, I would not see you!

15 So-now, fetch me a [lyre] strummer!
For it was, when the strummer strummed,
that the hand of YHWH would [come] upon him—

16 and he said:
Thus says YHWH:
This wadi will produce ditches upon ditches,

17 for thus says YHWH:
You will not see wind, you will not see showers,
yet that wadi will be filled with water,
and you and your cattle and your animals will drink!

18 And this is [but] a light matter in YHWH's eyes;
he will give Moav into your hand.

19 You will strike every fortified town and every choice town,
every good tree you will fell,
and every spring of water you will stop up,
and every good plot-of-land you will mar with stones!

---

13 **What have I to do with you?:** Or, "What business
do we have?" When "Go" follows in the next line,
we get the striking Heb. *Ma li va-lakh? Lekh!*

15 **when the strummer strummed:** Biblical Hebrew
uses *n-g-n* to specifically describe playing stringed

instruments; a more general musical verb would
have been *z-m-r*.

17 **wind . . . showers:** Which would be necessary for
filling up the wadi with water.

19 **mar:** Lit., "cause pain."

Chapter 4. *Tales of Elisha:* Elisha's status is further enhanced by a series of stories, long and short, that typify miracle tales and directly parallel his master Eliyyahu's deeds. The text starts with another food multiplication story (see I 17). The variation is that this time the food is to be used not to feed the hungry but to pay off a debt. The "revival of the son" account that follows (vv.8–37) includes the familiar motif of a childless couple and an unexpected birth. Like Yitzhak (Isaac) in Genesis, the son is immediately in peril, and in fact dies. The story here is a much fuller one than the parallel episode involving Eliyyahu in I Kings 17; we get a sense of extended interaction between the woman and the prophet, and the addition of his servant (who, somewhat unexpectedly, is named). This time, when the child is brought back to life, there is no need for the woman to verbally confirm that Elisha is a man of God, for that, by now, is obvious to characters and readers alike. Amid the human interactions, however, it should not be forgotten that Elisha, through his life-giving actions in this story, continues the polemic against Baal that had begun with the tales of his master (Sweeney 2007).

Returning to the theme of food, the next story (vv.38–41) utilizes a motif found previously with Moshe (Exod. 16:22–26) and Elisha himself (2:19–22), with the variation that here it is stew which is "healed," whereas previously it had been naturally occurring water.

As usual, the different episodes are not strung together randomly. As Fishbane notes, they are linked by means of props, personae, and the child and by actions: shutting the door and the fulfillment of the prophet's request, "What can I/we do for you?" He also points out a series of untranslatable puns, such as *mi-neshei* ("from the wives") and *ha-nosheh* ("a creditor") in v.1. All this is evidence of possible oral folk composition, and the chapter simultaneously presents aspects of what scholars term "popular religion," such as the consulting of a holy man on matters of bodily or economic well-being.

The chapter ends much as it began, with another account of "stretching" food, this time to feed not only a family but a large group.

20 It was at daybreak, at about the [time of] offering up the grain-gift,
that here, water was coming from the direction of Edom,
and the land filled up with water.

21 Now all Moav had heard
that the kings were coming up to do battle against them,
and they were summoned,
from all those belting on a sword-belt and upward,
and they stood at the border.

22 They started early in the morning,
when the sun rose over the water,
and Moav saw, from a distance, water red as blood.

23 So they said:
This is blood!—
the kings have been put-to-the-sword, yes, the sword,
each one has struck down his fellow!
So-now, to the spoils, O Moav!

24 They came to the camp of Israel,
but Israel arose and struck Moav, so that they fled before them;
they came against it, to strike down Moav:

25 the towns they wrecked,
and into every good plot-of-land each one threw his stone, and
filled it up,
while every source of water they stopped up
and every good tree they felled,
until [only] its stones in Kir-Hareset were left—
but the slingers surrounded [it] and struck it down.

26 And the king of Moav saw that the battle was too strong for him,
so he took with him seven hundred men drawing the sword,
to break through to the king of Edom,
but they could not prevail.

---

21 **all those belting on . . . and upward:** Everyone of
military age (twenty) and skill.

22 **red:** Reflecting the rising sun, and also the reputation of the mountains of Edom; note Heb. *adom*,
"red."

24 **they came against it . . . :** The text here is in disarray; "strike" appears in the Hebrew three times in
quick succession, so many interpreters read the second one as "came," as I do here.

25 **Kir-Hareset:** Some identify the site with the later
ruins of a Crusader castle, Kerak, situated in an
elevated area east of the Dead Sea. It is strategically
located on the north-south King's Highway.

26 **with him:** Emending *oto* to *itto*, as some manuscripts
have. **to . . . Edom:** Some emend to "against . . .
Aram" (Hebrew *d* and *r* letters are similar in
appearance).

◆ 27 So he took his firstborn son, who was to become king in his place,
and offered him up as an offering-up on the wall.
And a great wrath was upon Israel,
so that they had to march away from him and return to the land.

4:1 Now a woman from the wives of the Sons of the Prophets cried
out to Elisha, saying:
Your servant, my husband, is dead.
You yourself know
that your servant held Yнwн in awe.
But a creditor has come to take away my two children as slaves for
himself!

2 Elisha said to her:
What can I do for you? Tell me, what do you have in the house?
She said:
Your handmaid has nothing at all in the house
except for a cruse of oil.

3 He said:
Go, borrow vessels for yourself from outside, from all your
neighbors, empty vessels
—do not skimp—

4 and come in, close the door behind you and behind your children,
and pour [oil] into all these vessels,
while the full ones set aside.

5 So she went from him and closed the door behind her and behind
her sons;
as they were bringing them to her, she kept on pouring.

6 And it was, when the vessels were filled up, that she said to her son:
Bring me another vessel.
He said:
There is no other vessel!
And the oil stopped.

---

27 **wrath:** The situation is unclear, since the text seems to slip into a Moabite perspective, namely that the human sacrifice works and the Moabite god triumphs. The effect of the passage is to deny the Israelites a complete victory under an Omride king (Cogan/Tadmor, quoting D. N. Freedman).

4:1 **cried out:** Lodged a formal appeal. **take away . . . as slaves:** The practice of indentured servitude was widespread in the ancient Near East, and it is this, rather than chattel slavery (such as later existed in America and elsewhere), that is the more common form in the Bible.

7 Then she came and told the man of God.
He said:
Go, sell the oil
and pay off your debt;
you and your children will live on the rest.

8 Now it was, one day, that Elisha traveled to Shunem.
There was a prominent woman there,
and she urged him strongly to eat food [with her].
So it would be, whenever he traveled by, he would turn aside there
to eat food.

9 She said to her husband:
Now here, you know
that he is a holy man of God,
passing by us regularly.

10 Now let us make him a little walled upper-chamber
and let us put a bed, a table, a chair, and a lamp there for him,
so that it may be, whenever he comes to us, he may turn aside
there.

11 And it was one day that he came there,
and he turned aside to the upper-chamber and lay down there.

12 He said to Gehazi his serving-lad:
Call this Shunammite!
He called her, and she stood before him.

13 He said to him:
Now say to her:
Here, you have taken the trouble for us, all this trouble;
what can be done for you?
Might you be spoken about to the king, or to the commander of
the armed-forces?
She said:
Among my own kinspeople I reside.

---

8 **Shunem:** Below the slopes of the Hill of Moreh, about fifteen miles from Mount Carmel. **prominent:** Heb. *gadol*, usually rendered here as "great."
12 **Gehazi:** Pronounced *gay-ha-ZEE*. The meaning of the name is not certain, but Gray links it to an Arabic verb that means "to be greedy," appropriate here.
13 **trouble:** Lit., "trembling." The concept is of "solicitous deference" (Gray 1970).

♦ 14 He said:
So what can be done for her?
Gehazi said:
Well, she has no son, and her husband is old.

15 He said:
Call her.
And he called her, and she stood in the entrance.

16 Then he said:
At this set season, when time revives,
you will embrace a son!
She said:
Do not, my lord, O man of God,
do not lie to your handmaid!

17 But the woman became pregnant and gave birth to a son,
at that set season, when time revived,
as Elisha had spoken to her.

18 And the boy grew.
Now it was one day, that he went out to his father, to the reapers,

19 and he said to his father: My head, my head!
He said to a serving-lad:
Carry him to his mother!

20 So he carried him and brought him to his mother;
he sat on her knees until noon,
and then he died.

21 She went up and lay him down upon the bed of the man of God,
closed [the door] on him, and went out.

22 Then she called to her husband and said:
Now send me one of the lads and one of the she-asses,
that I may run out to the man of God and then return.

23 He said:
For-what-reason must you be going to him today?
It is not New-Moon, it is not the Sabbath.

---

16 **when time revives:** Next year. The phrase recalls the
Sara story in Gen. 18; there, too, the woman scoffs
at the idea that she will have a son, and there, too,
the child comes close to death at one point. **you:**
In the text as written (the *ketiv*), this common word
is spelled out as *atti* (instead of the usual *atta*), suggesting a northern origin of this tale.

23 **New-Moon:** In biblical Israel, the New Moon was
a significant religious occasion, involving a sacred
meal with family and a visit to a holy man (such as
I Sam. 20:6) and/or a shrine (I Sam. 1).

She said:

[All] is well.

24 But she saddled the she-ass and said to her serving-lad:

Lead and go,

do not stop me from riding unless I say [so] to you.

25 So she went

and came to the man of God, to Mount Carmel.

It was, when the man of God saw her at a distance,

that he said to Gehazi his serving-lad:

Here is that Shunammite.

26 So-now, pray run to meet her and say to her:

Is it well with you?

Is it well with your husband?

Is it well with the child?

She said: It is well.

27 She came to the man of God, to the mountain,

and she took hold of him by the feet;

Gehazi approached to push her away,

but the man of God said:

Leave her be, for her feelings are bitter within her,

yet Yhwh has concealed it from me and has not told me.

28 She said:

Did I request a son from my lord?

Did I not say: Do not set me [too much] at ease?

29 He said to Gehazi:

Gird up your loins,

take my rod in your hand, and go.

If you encounter a man, you are not to bless him [in greeting];

you are to answer no man,

and if any man blesses you [in greeting],

you are not to answer him.

But put my rod on the face of the lad.

---

25 **Mount Carmel:** The scene of Eliyyahu's great victory over the prophets of Baal in I Kings 18.

27 **feelings:** Frequently (and wrongly) translated as "soul," Heb. *nefesh* can mean "being," "essence," or "life" (as Cohn 2000 renders it here), or even "throat," that is, "life-breath."

28 **set me [too much] at ease:** Or "give me false hopes" (JPS: "mislead me").

29 **put my rod on the face of the lad:** We might expect a miracle from a holy man's staff, but none will be forthcoming until Elisha shows up and bodily revives the child.

◆ 30 The mother of the lad said:
As Yʜwʜ lives and as you live, if I should leave you . . . !
He arose and went after her.

31 Meanwhile Gehazi crossed over ahead of them and put the rod on
the face of the lad,
but there was no sound and no attention,
so she returned to meet him and said to him, saying:
The lad did not wake up!

32 Elisha came into the house,
and here, the lad was dead, lying on his bed.

33 He came in and closed the door behind the two of them
and prayed to Yʜwʜ,

34 then he climbed up and lay down atop the child;
he put his mouth on his mouth, his eyes on his eyes, and his palms
on his palms,
and bent over him,
and the flesh of the child became warm.

35 He turned away and went through the house, once here and once
there,
then he climbed up and bent over him;
the lad sneezed seven times
and the lad opened his eyes!

36 He called Gehazi and said:
Call this Shunammite!
He called her and she came to him,
and he said:
Lift up your son!

37 She came and flung herself at his feet, and bowed low to the
ground;
then she lifted up her son and went out.

38 When Elisha returned to Gilgal,
there was famine in the land.
Now the Sons of the Prophets were sitting before him.

---

34 **he put his mouth on his mouth . . . :** Recalling
exactly Eliyyahu's "measuring himself out" over a
similarly dead boy in I Kings 17:21 (note also the parallel in "no sound . . . no attention" in v.31 and the
expanded phrase in I Kings 18:29).

35 **bent over:** Long, quoting Jonas Greenfield, suggests "panted/breathed heavily over." **sneezed:** A
clear sign of life, with the "magical" number seven
attached for good measure. This is the only sneeze
mentioned in the Hebrew Bible.

And he said to his serving-lad:
Set on the large pot,
and cook stew for the Sons of the Prophets.

39 One [of them] went out into the field to gather herbs,
and he came across a field vine
and gathered field gourds from it, [enough] to fill his garment.
Then he came back and split them into the pot of stew,
for he did not know [what they were].

40 Now they were poured out for the men to eat,
but it was, just as they ate them from the stew,
that they cried out and said:
There is death in the pot, O man of God!
and they could not eat it.

41 He said:
Then fetch some meal! . . .
And he threw it into the pot
and said:
Pour some for the people, so that they may eat!
And then there was nothing evil in the pot.

42 A man came from Baal Shalisha;
he brought to the man of God bread of the firstfruits:
twenty bread-loaves of barley and ears of fresh grain.
And he said:
Give some to the people, that they may eat!

43 His attendant said:
How can I give this before a hundred persons?
He said:
Give some to the people, so that they may eat!
For thus says YHWH:
They will eat and have some left over.

---

39 **field gourds:** Cogan/Tadmor identify these as "bitter apples," consumption of which could be fatal. The "field" part can be understood as "wild" (Gray). **[enough] to fill his garment:** Cogan/Tadmor: "a skirt-full."

40 **poured out . . . cried out:** Heb. *va-yitzku . . . tzaaku.*

41 **meal:** Regular, as opposed to fine, flour. **evil:** Or "harmful."

42 **Baal Shalisha:** Probably located in the hill-country of Efrayim, in Binyaminite territory. **ears of fresh grain:** Others, "fresh grain in his bag," but a Ugaritic cognate supports the present rendering (Cogan/Tadmor).

43 **How can I give this:** How will it last? More elegant here and in the next verse would be "place," but the Hebrew root usually rendered "give" forms a refrain here.

Chapter 5. *Elisha and Naaman:* The Bible revels in stories in which a foreigner acknowledges or comes to acknowledge the God of Israel (for example, Bil'am [Balaam] in Num. 22–24 and Rahav in Josh. 2:6), and the present chapter is another example. Elisha's initial motive in curing Naaman's disease is "that he may know that there is a prophet in Israel" (v.8), but here, as elsewhere in these stories, recognizing the prophet's power is basically the same as acknowledging God's, as Naaman confirms in vv.15 and 17.

The second part of the story, in which Elisha's servant Gehazi attempts to obtain for himself Naaman's present of gratitude, which the prophet had refused, again demonstrates Elisha's power. The prophet somehow knows what Gehazi has done, despite the latter's denial, and the disease that had been removed from Naaman now cleaves to Gehazi—not temporarily, as is usual in the Bible (see Lev. 13), but, ominously, "for the ages," down through the family line.

44 So he gave it before them and they ate, and they had some left over,
in accordance with the word of YHWH.

5:1 Now Naaman, commander of the armed-forces of the king of
Aram, was a man prominent before his lord, one lifted up of face,
for through him, YHWH had given victory to Aram.
But the man, [though] a mighty-one of valor, was stricken-with-
tzaraat.

2 Once Aram had gone out in raiding-bands,
and they had taken a young girl captive from the land of Israel;
she was [in service] before Naaman's wife.

3 She said to her mistress:
Would that my lord were [standing] before the prophet who is in
Shomeron—
then he would cure him of his *tzaraat!*

4 He came back and told his lord, saying:
Like this and like that spoke the girl who is from the land of Israel.

5 The king of Aram said:
Go, come [then]—I will send a letter to the king of Israel.
He went and took in his hand ten talents of silver and six thousand
pieces of gold, and ten sets of garments,

6 and he brought the letter to the king of Israel [which] said:
So-now, when this letter reaches you,
here, I am sending you Naaman my servant,
so that you may cure him of his *tzaraat.*

7 But it was, when the king of Israel read the letter, that he tore his
garments
and said:
Am I God, to deal death and bestow life,
that this one sends [a message] to me to cure a man of his *tzaraat?*
Indeed, just know and take-note
of how he is seeking a pretext against me!

5:1 **Naaman:** Pronounced *nah-ah-MAHN.* From a common Semitic root meaning "pleasant." **lifted up of
face:** Respected, "high in his favor" (JPS). **mighty-
one of valor:** Omitted in LXX. *tzaraat:* For centuries translated as "leprosy," the dreaded Hansen's
disease, but modern scholars understand it as some
sort of unsightly but not contagious or serious skin
rash. The strong negativity it invokes (see Lev. 13–14)
may be due to the common visual deterioration and

hence the suggestion of death, which was the great
ritual pollutant in the Bible.
3 **She said ... he would cure him:** A young girl
knows what the great general does not. **cure him:**
Lit., "gather him back" into society.
6 **[which] said:** Lit., "saying."
7 **this one:** With the force of "this guy" (Cohn
2000). **pretext:** See, similarly, Judg. 14:4.

8 Now it was, when Elisha the man of God heard
  that the king of Israel had torn his garments,
  he sent to the king of Israel, saying:
  Why have you torn your garments?
  Just have him come to me,
  that he may know
  that there is a prophet in Israel!

9 So Naaman came with his horses and with his chariot,
  and stood at the entrance to the house belonging to Elisha.

10 And Elisha sent a messenger to him, saying:
   Go and wash seven times in the Jordan;
   then your flesh will be restored to you, and you will be purified.

11 But Naaman became furious and went away;
   he said:
   Here, I had said to myself:
   He will come out, yes, out, and stand [there] to call on the name of
       YHWH his god,
   then he will raise his hand over the diseased-spot, and take away the
       tzaraat.

12 Are not the Amana and the Parpar, the rivers of Damascus, better
       than all the waters of Israel?
   Could I not wash in them and be purified?
   He turned and went away in hot-anger.

13 But his servants approached and spoke to him, they said:
   If it were a hard thing that the prophet spoke to you, would you
       not do it?
   How much more so, when he said to you: Wash and be purified!

14 So he went down and dipped in the Jordan seven times, in
       accordance with the word of the man of God,
   and his flesh was returned-to-health like a young lad's flesh,
   and he was purified.

15 Then he returned to the man of God, he and all his camp,
   and he came and stood before him and said:
   Now here, I know

---

8 **know:** Or "acknowledge."
10 **purified:** And thus able to return to the company of society. For priestly rules regarding *tzaraat,* see Lev. 13–14.

13 **If:** I follow ancient versions here in eliminating MT's "Father, . . ." which seems out of place in addressing a general. Some, however, understand it as "Sir." **hard:** Lit., "great, large."

◆ that there is no god in all the earth except in Israel!
So-now, pray accept a blessing-gift from your servant!

16 He said:
As Yhwh lives, before whom I stand,
if I should accept [anything] . . . !
Now he pressed him to take [it], but he refused.

17 So Naaman said:
If not, let there be given to your servant
a mule team's load of earth—
for never again will your servant prepare an offering-up or a
sacrifice to other gods,
except to Yhwh!

18 In this [one] matter, may Yhwh pardon your servant:
when my lord comes to the House of Rimmon, to bow down
there,
and he leans on my arm, so that I bow down in the House of
Rimmon—
when I bow down in the House of Rimmon,
may Yhwh pardon your servant in this matter!

19 He said to him:
Go in peace.
And he went from him, a stretch of land [in distance].

20 And Gehazi, the serving-lad of Elisha the man of God, said [to
himself]:
Here, my lord spared this Naaman the Aramean by [not] accepting
what he brought from his hand;
by the life of Yhwh, I will surely run after him and accept
something from him!

21 So Gehazi pursued Naaman;
when Naaman saw him running after him, he got down from the
chariot to meet him,
and said:
Is [all] well?

---

16 **if I should accept [anything] . . . !:** Typically, there is to be no profit for the prophet.

17 **If not:** Or "at least." **load of earth:** From his own soil (Martin).

18 **House of Rimmon:** The temple of the god Ramman (Baal-Haddad), the "Thunderer," punned on and denigrated here as *rimmon*, "pomegranate."

20 **accepting:** Or "getting."

Chapters 6–7. *More Elisha Tales; Israel and Aram:* The text continues with the usual pattern of a combination of long and short episodes (Cohn 2000). In the first, Elisha solves a mundane problem, the loss of an ax head in the river, by means of what feels like magic—throwing something (in this case, a piece of wood) into the water.

In the next, longer episode, the miraculous becomes more full-blown, with Elisha able to divine the king of Aram's private conversations, and subsequently his revealing, in v.17, a mountain "full of horses and chariots of fire." We are reminded, of course, of Eliyyahu's end, but equally significant is the image of the prophet as one who, countering the armies of nations, can summon up an army of his own. In fact, all throughout the Elisha cycle, the stories, which are ostensibly about kings, tend to magnify the prophet's role (see Cohn 2000).

V.24 introduces a more complex narrative, which ominously introduces a note of familial cannibalism in the midst of a siege. The king of Israel reacts by threatening the life of Elisha, who had previously advised him on military matters concerning Aram. Through a long story within a story, a strange tale of four diseased men and the empty camp of Aram, God saves Israel, and the king's officer, who had doubted Elisha's promise of relief, is trampled in the rush for food by the townspeople of the besieged Shomeron. Once again, things happen "as the man of God had spoken" (7:17).

All of the above stories are visually vivid (as Cohn 2000 points out, both "seeing" and blindness are prominent), and one can easily imagine them as subjects in classical art, as indeed some of them have been. I can only fantasize about what Pieter Brueghel the Elder, painter of the memorable *Parable of the Blind,* might have done with the incident concerning the men stricken with *tzaraat* (7:3–10).

22 He said:
    [All] is well.
    My lord sent me, saying:
    Here, now two lads from the highlands of Efrayim, from the Sons
        of the Prophets, just came to me.
    Pray give them a talent of silver and two sets of garments.
23 Naaman said:
    Consent [to] accept two talents!
    He pressed him, and he wrapped up two talents of silver in two
        purses, with two sets of garments,
    and gave them to his two lads,
    and they carried them ahead of him.
24 He came to the Ofel/The Bulge,
    and he took them from their hand, and deposited them in the
        house.
    Then he sent the men off, and they went away,
25 while he himself came and stood opposite his lord.
    Elisha said to him:
    From where, Gehazi?
    He said:
    Your servant has gone neither here nor there.
26 He said to him:
    Did not my heart go along, when a man reversed [course] from his
        chariot to meet you?
    [Is this] the time to take silver, to take garments, or olive-groves or
        vineyards, or flocks or herds, or servants or handmaids?
27 So Naaman's *tzaraat*—it will cleave to you and to your seed, for the
        ages!
    And he went out from before him, afflicted with *tzaraat* like snow.

6:1 [Once] the Sons of the Prophets said to Elisha:
    Now here, the place where we are residing before you is too
        narrow for us.
  2 Pray let us go to the Jordan, and let each one take a log from there,
        and let us construct ourselves there a place to reside.
    He said: Go.

---

24 **Ofel/The Bulge:** The raised section of ancient Jeru-   26 **Did not my heart go along:** Burney: "Wasn't I pres-
    salem, probably including the palace and Temple   ent in spirit?"
    complexes.

◆

3   One [of them] said:
Pray consent to go with your servants!
Elisha said:
I will go.

4   So he went with them, and they came to the Jordan,
where they felled some trees.

5   And it was, as one was felling a log, that the iron [ax head] fell into
the water;
he cried out and said: Alas, my lord, for it was borrowed!

6   The man of God said: Where did it fall?
He showed him the place.
Then he carved out some wood and threw it in there, and it made
the iron float,

7   and he said: Pick it up for yourself.
So he stretched out his hand and took it.

8   Now the king of Aram was waging battle against Israel.
He sought advice from his servants, saying:
Descend on thus and such a place [to attack]!

9   But the man of God sent to the king of Israel, saying:
Be careful when crossing by this place,
for there Aram descends [to attack].

10 The king of Israel sent to the place about which the man of God
had spoken to him and warned him, so that he took care there,
not [only] once and not [only] twice.

11 And the king of Aram's heart was in turmoil over this matter,
so he called his servants and said to them:
Will you not tell me:
who from among us is for the king of Israel?

12 One of his servants said to him:
No, my lord king;
but Elisha the prophet, who is in Israel,
tells the king of Israel
the words that you speak in your [very] bedroom!

6:5 **that the iron [ax head]:** Heb. unclear; LXX adds "here, . . ."

6   **some wood:** Others, "a stick." B-R understand it as "the [ax] handle."

8   **Descend on:** Reading MT's *tahanoti* as *tinhatu,* derived from *n-h-t* with Cogan/Tadmor, to link up with v.9.

10 **not [only] once and not [only] twice:** Rather, again and again.

11 **was in turmoil:** Elsewhere the root connotes "storming," as in the divine whirlwind that takes Eliyyahu in Chap. 2.

13 He said:
Go and see where he is,
and I will send and fetch him!
It was told to him, saying:
Here, in Dotan.

14 So he sent there horses and chariots, a weighty army;
they came at night and encircled the town.

15 And the attendant of the man of God started-early to rise and
went out,
and here, an army was surrounding the town, with horse and
chariotry!
His serving-lad said to him:
Alas, my lord, what shall we do?

16 He said:
Do not be afraid,
for many more are those who are with us than who are with them.

17 Now Elisha prayed and said:
O Yhwh, now open his eyes, that he may see!
So Yhwh opened the eyes of the lad, and he saw:
now here, the mountain was full of horses and chariots of fire
surrounding Elisha!

18 They went down against him, but Elisha prayed to Yhwh and said:
Now strike this nation with dazzling-light!
And he struck them with dazzling-light, in accordance with the
word of Elisha.

19 Elisha said to them:
This is not the way and this is not the town!
Go along after me, and I will lead you to the man whom you seek.
And he led them to Shomeron.

20 It was, when they came to Shomeron,
that Elisha said: O Yhwh,
open the eyes of these [people], that they may see!
So Yhwh opened their eyes, and they saw:
now here, [they were] in the midst of Shomeron!

---

13 **Dotan:** North of Shekhem, strategically placed on
the way to the Jezreel Valley.
18 **dazzling-light:** Just as the evildoers of Sodom were
struck by God in Gen. 19:11.

19 **This:** Instead of *zeh,* the standard word for "this"
in biblical Hebrew, the text makes use of *zo,* an Ara-
maism.

◆ 21 The king of Israel said to Elisha when he saw them:
Shall I strike, strike them down, Father?
22 He said:
You are not to strike.
Those whom you have taken captive with your sword, with
your bow,
would you strike [them] down?
Put food and water before them, that they may eat and drink and
go back to their lords.
23 And he spread out for them a great spread,
so that they ate and drank;
then he sent them off, and they went back to their lords.
And the raiding-bands of Aram no longer came into the land of
Israel.

24 Now it was, [some time] after this,
that Ben-Hadad king of Aram collected all his camp;
he went up and besieged Shomeron.
25 And there was a great famine in Shomeron;
here, they were besieging it
until [the price of] a donkey's head was eighty silver-pieces,
and a quarter of a *kav* of "pigeons' dung," five silver-pieces.
26 Now it was that the king of Israel was crossing on the wall when a
woman cried out to him, saying:
Save [me], my lord king!
27 He said:
No; let YHWH save you—
from where can I save you?
From the threshing-floor or from the winepress?

---

21 **Father:** A term of respect; Elisha had employed it in addressing Eliyyahu in Chap. 2.
23 **a great spread:** Or "feast," based on the Akkadian *kiretu*. The Hebrew word (*kera*) occurs only here in the Bible.
25 **until . . . :** Spelling out the anticipated effects of the siege. **donkey's head:** They would be forced by circumstances to eat ritually forbidden animals (Kimhi). **"pigeons' dung":** Usually understood as the name of a plant.
26 **on the wall:** The double (casemate) wall of the city, and hence wide enough to walk on top of (as one can on the present, Ottoman-period wall of Jerusalem's Old City). **cried out:** The technical legal term for lodging an appeal with the king (Cogan/Tadmor), also used in 8:3. **Save:** Others, "help."

28 And the king said to her:
   What [ails] you?
   She said:
   This woman said to me:
   Give over your son, that we may eat him today,
   and my son we will eat tomorrow!
29 So we boiled my son, and ate him;
   then I said to her on the next day:
   Give over your son, that we may eat him
   —but she hid her son.
30 Now it was, when the king heard the woman's words,
   that he tore his garments;
   and as he was crossing by the wall,
   the people saw that here, the sackcloth was on his flesh, on the
      inside.
31 He said:
   Thus may God do to me, and thus may he add,
   if the head of Elisha son of Shafat is left standing upon him today!
32 Now Elisha was sitting in his house, and the elders were sitting
      with him,
   and he had sent a man from his presence;
   but before the messenger came to him, he had said to the elders:
   Do you see that this son of a murderer has sent to remove my
      head?
   See, when the messenger comes, close the door and press him
      against the door;
   is not the sound of his lord's footsteps behind him?
33 He was still speaking with them
   when here, the king came down to him
   and said:
   Here now, this evil-fate is from YHWH;
   what more hope in YHWH can I have?

28 **What [ails] you?:** The king calms down after his blowup (Cohn 2000).
30 **tore his garments . . . sackcloth was on his flesh:** As a sign of mourning or repentance.

32 **he had sent:** Referring to the king.   **press him against the door:** Or "restrain him at the door" (Sweeney 2007).
33 **evil-fate:** Or "calamity" (JPS).

◆ 7:1 Then Elisha said:
Hear the word of YHWH:
Thus says YHWH:
Around this time tomorrow,
a *sei'a* of flour [will go] for a *shekel*
and two *sei'as* of barley for a *shekel*, at the gate of Shomeron.

2 Then the officer upon whose arm the king leans spoke up to the
man of God
and said:
Here, were YHWH to make hatches in the sky,
could this thing happen?
He said:
Here, you will it see with your eyes,
but from there you shall not eat!

3 Now there were four men with *tzaraat*, at the entrance to the
[town] gate.
They said, each one to his neighbor:
Why are we sitting here until we die?

4 If we say, Let us go into the town,
there is a famine in the town,
and we will die there,
and if we sit here, we will die.
So-now, let us go and fall away to the camp of Aram—
if they let us live, then we will live,
and if they put us to death, then we will die.

5 So they arose at twilight-breeze, to enter the camp of Aram.
They had entered the edge of camp of Aram,
and here, there was no one there!

6 —For YHWH had made the camp of Aram hear
the sound of chariots, the sound of horses,
the sound of a great army,
so that each one said to his brother:
Here, the king of Israel has hired against us the kings of the
Hittites and the kings of Egypt, to come against us!

7:1 **for a *shekel*:** Food commodities will be incredibly expensive because of the siege. **gate:** That is, the marketplace (Cogan/Tadmor).

2 **were YHWH to make hatches . . . :** The officer does not believe the prophet's words.

4 **fall away:** That is, desert.

7 So they arose and fled at twilight-breeze,
and abandoned their tents and their horses and their donkeys,
[with] the camp as it was,
and they fled for their lives.—

8 And those with *tzaraat* came to the edge of the camp,
and they entered a tent, and ate and drank,
and carried off from there silver and gold and garments,
and went away and hid them;
then they returned and entered another tent,
and carried off [things] from there
and went away and hid them.

9 Then they said, each one to his neighbor:
It is not proper, what we are doing;
this day—it is a day of [good] news,
and we are keeping silent!
If we wait until the light of daybreak,
iniquity will find us!
So-now, let us go, let us enter, and let us inform the king's house.

10 So they went and called out to the gatekeepers of the town
and told them, saying:
We entered the camp of Aram,
and here, no one was there, or even a human voice,
but the horses were tied up and the donkeys were tied up,
[with] the tents as they were.

11 The gatekeepers called out and informed the king's house within,

12 and the king arose at night and said to his servants:
Now let me inform you what Aram has done to us:
they knew that we were famished,
so they went out of the camp to hide in the open-field, saying:
When they have gone out of the town,
we will seize them alive, and the town we will enter!

8 **entered . . . ate . . . entered . . . :** The string of verbs, as so often in the Bible, emphasizes "speed and purpose" (Cohn 2000).

9 **iniquity will find us:** We will be punished for delaying delivering the news to the king. **find:** Or "overtake."

Chapter 8. *Elisha, Past and Present; On the Regional Stage:* The opening of this chapter is a summing up, "as if the prophet were already dead" (Cohn 2000). Elisha's act of reviving the child in Chap. 4 is recalled, and then the mother shows up; the king of Israel and the servant Gehazi, who previously had been vilified, here appear in a positive light: Gehazi is truthful, while the king carries out proper justice for the mother.

With v.7 the scene shifts to Aram and another sick king. While Elisha seems to be lying to the king about his recovery (he tells Hazael that the monarch will, in fact, die), Cohn (2000) notes that Ben-Hadad asks for Elisha's own opinion and does not make inquiry through the proper oracular channels. He also points out the way in which the story shows how Elisha's wide influence is not confined to Israel alone. Additionally, Elisha's anointing of Hazael foreshadows the rise of Yehu in the next chapter.

V.20 introduces an important historical note. The Edomites, inhabiting the territory east of the Negev, now achieve independence from Judah (see Gen. 27:40 for the patriarch Yitzhak's prophecy regarding these events). This is a serious blow to Judah's control of southern trade.

A last point, of considerable significance, is the lineage of King Ahazyahu of Judah, who makes his appearance in v.25. His mother, Atalyahu, is the granddaughter of King Omri of Israel. Thus, as Sweeney (2007) notes, every Davidic king from this point forward will also be a descendant of the house of Omri. While this might be diplomatically savvy, from the text's point of view it is yet another fact pointing toward the inevitable fall of both houses.

13 Then one of his servants spoke up and said:
Now let them take five of the remaining horses, the ones that
   remain in it;
here, they are like the whole throng of Israel that remain in it,
here, they are like the whole throng of Israel that is done for.
Let us send them and let us see!

14 So they picked two chariots of horses,
and the king sent them after the camp of Aram, saying:
Go and see.

15 They went after them, as far as the Jordan,
and here, the whole road was filled with garments and vessels
which Aram had thrown away in their fearful-haste.
The messenger returned and told the king.

16 And the people went out and despoiled the camp of Aram;
and it was that a *sei'a* of flour [went for] a *shekel,* and two *sei'as* of
   barley for a *shekel,* in accordance with the word of Yhwh.

17 Now the king had appointed the officer upon whose arm he leans
   to the town gate,
and the people trampled him at the gate, so that he died,
as the man of God had spoken,
as he had spoken when the king had come down to him.

18 For it was when the man of God had spoken to the king, saying:
Two *sei'as* of barley [will go] for a *shekel,* and a *sei'a* of flour for
   a *shekel* will go at around this time tomorrow at the gate of
   Shomeron—

19 that the officer had answered the man of God and said:
Now here, were Yhwh to make hatches in the sky,
could this thing happen?
And he had said:
Here, you will see it with your eyes,
but from there you shall not eat!

20 And thus it happened to him:
the people trampled him at the gate, and he died.

13 **five:** The number sometimes indicates "a few" (JPS). **they are like the whole throng . . . :** The verse is garbled, with an entire phrase virtually repeated. **see:** Or "find out" (JPS).

15 **their fearful-haste:** MT has an extra letter *het* here; the *Qere* reads correctly.

◆ 8:1 Now Elisha had spoken to the woman whose son he had restored
to life, saying:
Arise and go, you and your household,
and sojourn where you wish to sojourn,
for YHWH has proclaimed a famine
—indeed, it has come upon the land—for seven years.
2 So the woman arose and did in accordance with the word of the
man of God;
she went, she and her household, and sojourned in the land of the
Philistines, for seven years.
3 It was at the end of the seven years
that the woman returned from the land of the Philistines,
and she went out to cry out to the king about her house and about
her fields.
4 Now the king had been speaking to Gehazi, the servant of the man
of God, saying:
Pray recount to me all the great things that Elisha has done.
5 And it was, as he was recounting to the king how he had restored
the dead one to life,
that here, the very woman whose son he had restored to life was
crying out to the king about her house and about her fields.
So Gehazi said:
My lord king,
this is the woman and this is her son whom Elisha restored to life!
6 The king inquired of the woman, and she recounted it to him;
so the king gave her over to an official, saying:
Return everything that is hers, along with all the revenue from the
fields,
from the time that she left the land until now.

7 Elisha came to Damascus
when Ben-Hadad, king of Aram, was sick,
and it was told to him, saying:
The man of God has come here.

8:1 **the woman:** See Chap. 4. **to sojourn:** To take up
temporary residence.
3 **fields:** Heb. *sadeh* can be understood as a collective
plural here.

6 **revenue:** From the crop yield (Cogan/Tadmor).

8 The king said to Hazael:
Take a gift in your hand
and go to meet the man of God.
Inquire of God through him, saying:
Will I live through this sickness?

9 Hazael went to meet him,
he took a gift in his hand—namely, all the best-goods of Damascus,
forty camel loads,
and he came and stood before him, and said:
Your son, Ben-Hadad king of Aram, has sent me to you, saying:
Will I live through this sickness?

10 Elisha said to him:
Go, say to him:
You will live, yes, live—
but Yhwh has shown me that he will die, yes, die.

11 He kept his face still, setting it [thus] until he was ashamed,
and then the man of God wept.

12 Hazael said:
Why does my lord weep?
He said:
Because I know what you will do to the Children of Israel—evil:
their fortified places you will set on fire,
their young men you will kill with the sword,
their babies you will dash-to-pieces,
and their pregnant women you will split open!

13 And Hazael said:
Indeed, what is your servant, a [mere] dog,
that he could do such a great thing?
Elisha said:
Yhwh has shown you to me as king over Aram.

---

9 **Your son:** A term indicating respect. **live through:** I.e., recover from.

10 **to him:** / **You will live:** Ancient versions and manuscripts read this as "not"—"You will not live"—showing that later transmitters of the text were uncomfortable with the idea that a prophet might practice deception.

11 **He kept his face still:** The text here may mean that Elisha stares at the king. **until he was ashamed:** It seems to be the king who is embarrassed by the stare. The phrase may also be idiomatic for "a long while." Similarly, Moshe is "shamefully-late" coming down from Sinai in Exod. 32:1.

13 **such a great thing:** Such major devastation.

Chapter 9. *Yehu's Coup:* A memorable and bloody account of how Ah'av's son and wife meet their deaths, this chapter introduces the figure of Yehu, who carries out divine vengeance on the House of Ah'av for its crimes. Both of the deaths are gruesome in their details (note the similarity between Ah'av's demise in a chariot and his son's death). While Homer routinely describes such matters in cinematic detail, the Bible is usually reticent, unless it is trying to make a point, as here, in "a tale of conspiracy, deception, irony, and murder . . ." (Cohn 2000). The greatest irony is the repetition of the word *shalom* (vv.17–19, 22), here rendered "peace," in a story that is shot through with violence. By the end, Eliyyahu and Navot's vineyard are recalled, and the double crime of that story in I Kings 21 is well on the way to being expiated.

Yehu dominates Chaps. 9 and 10. His personality (which centers on his zeal for YHWH) is hinted at by his driving a chariot "like-a-madman" (9:20). Unlike many northern kings, he establishes a dynasty which lasts for several generations. But the text also notes (10:29 and 31) how he does not remove Yorov'am's golden calves, and thus the Bible's final judgment on him is decidedly mixed.

A curious historical note is sounded in this chapter. V.15 introduces a certain Yonadav son of Rekhav. This family, known to scholars as Rechabites, seem to have constituted a separatist group that lived in a strict religious manner and so allied themselves with the anti-Ah'av faction headed by Yehu.

14 He went out from Elisha and came back to his lord,
    and he said to him:
    What did Elisha say to you?
    He said:
    He said to me:
    You will live, yes, live.

15 But it was on the morrow
    that he took meshed-cloth and dipped it in water;
    he spread it over his face, and he died.
    And Hazael reigned as king in his place.

16 In year five of Yoram son of Ah'av king of Israel—Yehoshafat was
        king of Judah—
    Yehoram son of Yehoshafat king of Judah became king.

17 Thirty-two years old was he at his becoming king,
    and for eight years he reigned as king in Jerusalem.

18 He walked in the way of the kings of Israel,
    as the House of Ah'av had done,
    for the daughter of Ah'av was a wife for him;
    and he did what was evil in the eyes of YHWH.

19 But YHWH was not willing to bring ruin upon Judah
    for the sake of David his servant,
    as he had said to him,
    to give him a lamp for his children, for all the days [to come].

20 In his days Edom rebelled from under the hand of Judah,
    and they kinged themselves a king.

21 So Yoram crossed over to Tza'ir, and all the chariotry with him;
    it was that he set out in the night
    and struck Edom, who was surrounding him and the chariot
        commanders,
    and the fighting-people fled to their tents.

---

15 **he took:** Questions abound here. Is "he" Hazael or the king? Is this an act of succor or murder? (Cogan/ Tadmor).

16 **Yehoshafat was king of Judah:** This odd phrase is missing in many versions. **Yehoram:** A variation on "Yoram," "YHWH Is Exalted."

18 **walked in the way of the kings of Israel:** He is the first king of Judah to be so described (Mann).

19 **a lamp:** If the word refers to descendants, then "for his children" here (Heb. *le-vanav*) might better be read *le-fanav* ("before him").

21 **Tza'ir:** The site is not certain. Some have proposed southeast of the Dead Sea.

22 And Edom has been rebelling from under the hand of Judah,
until this day.
Then Livna [too] rebelled at that time.

23 Now the rest of the events of Yoram, and all that he did,
are they not written in the Record of Yearly Events of the Kings of
Judah?

24 Yoram lay beside his fathers;
he was buried with his fathers in the City of David,
and Ahazyahu his son reigned as king in his place.

25 In year twelve of the years of Yoram son of Ah'av king of Israel,
Ahazyahu son of Yehoram king of Judah became king.

26 Twenty-two years old was Ahazyahu at his becoming king,
and for one year he reigned as king in Jerusalem;
his mother's name was Atalyahu [grand]daughter of Omri king of
Israel.

27 He walked in the way of the House of Ah'av:
he did what was evil in the eyes of YHWH, like the House of Ah'av,
for he was a son-in-law of the House of Ah'av.

28 He went out with Yoram son of Ah'av to do battle with Hazael
king of Aram, at Ramot-Gil'ad,
and the Arameans struck Yoram.

29 And Yoram the king returned to be healed in Yizre'el
from the wounds that the Arameans had struck him at Rama
when he engaged in battle with Hazael king of Aram.
And Ahazyahu son of Yehoram king of Judah went down
to see Yoram son of Ah'av in Yizre'el,
for he was sick [from his wounds].

9:1 Now Elisha the prophet called one of the Sons of the Prophets
and said to him:
Gird up your loins,
take this flask of oil in your hand,
and go to Ramot-Gil'ad.

---

22 **Livna:** A location somewhere in the territory of
Judah.

25 **Ahazyahu:** "YHWH Seizes [to protect]."

26 **Atalyahu:** With a possible meaning of "YHWH
Has Declared His Nobility," but this is uncertain.
Trad. English "Athaliah." **[grand]daughter:** The
Hebrew will admit both meanings.

27 **son-in-law:** The word may also mean simply "relative" (Gray 1970).

28 **Ramot-Gil'ad:** On the border between Israelite-
controlled Gil'ad and Aram.

29 **Yoram the king:** A rare construction in biblical
Hebrew.

2 When you come there, look there for Yehu son of Yehoshafat son
    of Nimshi;
  when you come, you are to take him up from the midst of his
    brothers
  and are to bring him into a room within a room.
3 Then you are to take the flask of oil and you are to pour it on his
    head
  and say: Thus says YHWH:
  I am anointing you as king over Israel!
  Then you are to open the door and are to flee; you are not to wait.
4 So the lad, the prophet lad, went to Ramot-Gil'ad.
5 He came there, and here, the commanders of the army were sitting
    around;
  he said:
  I have a message for you, O Commander!
  Yehu said:
  For whom of all of us?
  He said:
  For you, O Commander.
6 He arose and entered the house,
  then he poured the oil on his head
  and said to him:
  Thus says YHWH, the God of Israel:
  I anoint you as king over the people of YHWH, over Israel!
7 You are to strike down the House of Ah'av, your lord,
  that I may avenge the blood of my servants the prophets
  and the blood of all the servants of YHWH at the hand of Izevel.
8 All the House of Ah'av will perish;
  I will cut off from Ah'av he who pisses against the wall,
  [even] the fettered and forsaken in Israel!
9 And I will make the House of Ah'av like the House of Yorov'am
    son of Nevat,
  and like the House of Ba'sha son of Ahiyya.

9:2 **a room within a room:** Here connoting a secure
place.

4 **lad ... prophet:** MT is garbled here, and it is
unclear what is meant.

10 And Izevel the dogs will eat in the plot of Yizre'el,
with no one to bury [her]!
Then he opened the door and fled.

11 Now Yehu went out to the servants of his lord;
they said to him:
Is [all] well?
For-what-reason did this madman come to you?
He said to them:
You know the man and his talk!

12 They said:
A lie!
Now tell us!
He said:
Like this and like that he said to me, saying:
Thus says Yнwн:
I anoint you as king over Israel!

13 Quickly each one took his garment
and put it under him, on the steps themselves;
then they sounded a blast on the *shofar*
and said:
Yehu reigns as king!

14 So Yehu son of Yehoshafat son of Nimshi bound himself [in
conspiracy] against Yoram
—now Yoram had been protecting Ramot-Gil'ad, he and all Israel,
from Hazael king of Aram.

15 But King Yehoram had returned to be healed at Yizre'el from the
wounds with which the Arameans had wounded him,
when he had engaged in battle with Hazael king of Aram.—
Yehu said:
If this be your desire,
do not let any escaped-one out of the town, to go tell in Yizre'el!

16 And Yehu mounted up and went to Yizre'el,
for Yoram was laid up there,
while Ahazya king of Judah had gone down to see Yoram.

---

13 **on the steps themselves:** The Hebrew is unclear; I
follow Cogan/Tadmor's suggestion of a literal reading. JPS has "on the top step."

14 **bound himself [in conspiracy]:** In an oath. This is
the usual phrase for conspiracy in the Bible.

◆

17 Now the lookout was standing on the tower in Yezre'el;
he saw Yehu's horde as he was coming,
and said:
I see a horde!
Yehoram said:
Take a rider and send him to meet them, that he may say: Is [all]
well?

18 The horse rider went to meet him and said:
Thus says the king: Is [all] well?
Yehu said:
What is it to you if [all] is well?
Turn in behind me!
So the lookout reported, saying:
The messenger coming to them does not return.

19 So he sent a second horse rider,
and he came to them and said:
Thus says the king: [Is all] well?
Yehu said:
What is it to you if [all] is well?
Turn in behind me!

20 So the lookout reported, saying:
He came to them but does not return.
Now his driving is like the driving of Yehu son of Nimshi—
for he drives like-a-madman!

21 Then Yehoram said:
Harness up!
They harnessed his chariot,
and Yehoram king of Israel went out, with Ahazyahu king of
Judah, each one in his chariot;
they went to meet Yehu,
and they encountered him in the plot of Navot the Yizre'elite.

---

17 **Is [all] well?:** Alternately, "Is there peace?"
19 **[Is all]:** Not in MT, but found in manuscripts and
versions.

20 **like-a-madman:** Lit., "with madness."
21 **Navot:** See I Kings 21.

22 And it was, when Yehoram saw Yehu,
that he said:
Is [all] well, Yehu?
He said:
What is "well," as long as the many whorings of Izevel your
    mother and her sorceries [continue]?
23 Yehoram reversed his hands and fled,
and said to Ahazyahu: Treason, Ahazya!
24 But Yehu filled his hand with the bow
and struck Yehoram between his shoulder-blades,
so that the arrow stuck out of his heart,
and he collapsed in his chariot.
25 Then he said to Bidkar his officer:
Pick [him] up! Throw him
into the plot of field of Navot the Yizre'elite,
for keep in mind—I and you were riding, each with a team, behind
    Ah'av his father,
when YHWH pronounced this pronouncement upon him:
26 Did I not see the blood of Navot and the blood of his sons
    yesterday?
—the Utterance of YHWH;
so I will pay you back in this very plot
—the Utterance of YHWH.
So-now, pick [him] up, throw him into the plot, in accordance with
    the word of YHWH!
27 Now when Ahazyahu king of Judah saw [it], he fled by the road to
    Bet-Ha-Gan,
and Yehu pursued after him and said:
Him too—strike him down!
. . . in the chariot at the ascent of Gur, which is near Yivle'am.
He fled to Megiddo, and died there.

---

22 **whorings:** The sexual metaphor is a common one in the Bible, referring to Israel's worshipping of idols; see its use especially in the prophetic book of Hosea.
23 **reversed his hands:** See note to I Kings 22:34.
24 **filled his hand with the bow:** Meaning either simply "drew the bow" (so JPS) or "to full stretch" (so Gray 1970).
25 **Bidkar:** Ironically here, Heb. *d-k-r* means "to pierce," so this officer is perhaps the original Captain Pierce. **pronouncement:** Gray (1970): "oracle."

26 **the Utterance of YHWH:** A common prophetic formula.
27 **Bet-Ha-Gan:** Probably modern Jenin, a few miles south of Jezreel. **. . . in the chariot . . . :** In MT, the accents connect this phrase with "He struck him down." In any event, there are clearly words missing here; Cogan/Tadmor add "They shot him." **Yivle'am:** A fortified, strategically important site guarding the southern end of the Jezreel Valley. Trad. English "Jibleam."

28 His servants drove him to Jerusalem,
   and they buried him in his burial-place, beside his fathers,
   in the City of David.

29 In year eleven of the years of Yoram son of Ah'av, Ahazya became
   king over Judah.

30 And Yehu came to Yizre'el;
   when Izevel heard,
   she put kohl on her eyes and prettied her hair
   and looked out through the window.

31 When Yehu came to the gate, she said:
   Is [all] well, [you] Zimri, killer of his lord?

32 He lifted up his face toward the window
   and said:
   Who is with me? Who?
   And two [or] three officials looked out at him.

33 He said:
   Hurl her down! And they hurled her down;
   some of her blood was sprinkled on the wall and on the horses,
   and he trampled her.

34 Then he came in, and ate and drank,
   and he said:
   Take care of this doomed one, and bury her,
   for she is the daughter of a king.

35 But when they went to bury her, they could not find [anything]
   of her
   except for the skull, the feet, and the palms of the hands.

36 They returned and told him,
   and he said:
   It is the word of YHWH
   that he spoke by the hand of his servant Eliyyahu the Tishbite,
   saying:
   In the plot of Yizre'el
   the dogs will eat the flesh of Izevel!

---

30 **kohl:** Others, "antimony." This powder was commonly used in eye makeup throughout the region. **hair:** Lit., "head."

31 **[you] Zimri:** A strong insult, given that Zimri had only ruled for a week, and as the result of treachery.

33 **Hurl her down!:** Or "Let her drop!"

36 **the word of YHWH / that he spoke:** See I Kings 21:23.

Chapter 10. *Yehu Consolidates Power:* Whereas the last chapter described individual deaths in the House of Ah'av, this one moves to not one but three large-scale killings. The triple massacre involves a good deal of deception, and implicates both soldiers and the general population. Given that the dead are the heirs to Ah'av and are Baal-worshippers, it is not surprising that Yehu, whose name mimics God's own (YHWH), is rated positively as a king by the text. Yet the chapter closes with some reservations about him, namely, that he is not guiltless of the sins of Yorov'am. In fact, Yehu is less a heroic figure and more a vehicle for divine punishment of those judged by the Bible to be wrongdoers. Even though they are set in a ruthless age, the accounts of his violent and underhanded behavior might well have caused discomfort among ancient readers as they do among modern ones.

37 And the corpse of Izevel will be like dung on the surface of the
        ground, in the plot of Yizre'el,
    so that they will not [be able to] say: This is Izevel!

10:1 Now Ah'av had seventy sons in Shomeron.
    And Yehu wrote letters and sent [them] to Shomeron,
    to the commanders of Yizre'el, the elders,
    and to those raising Ah'av's [sons], saying:
2 So-now, when this letter comes to you,
    —since with you are your lord's sons,
    and since with you are the chariotry and the horses,
    and the fortified city and the weapons—
3 select the best and the brightest one of your lord's sons
    and put him on the throne of his father,
    and do battle for the house of your lords!
4 They became exceedingly afraid, exceedingly, and said:
    Here, two kings could not stand against him,
    so how will we stand, we ourselves?
5 [The One] Over the House, and [The One] Over the City, and the
        elders, and the child-rearers, sent to Yehu, saying:
    We are your servants!
    Now whatever you say to us, we will do!
    We will not make anyone king;
    what is best in your eyes, do!
6 He wrote to them a second letter, saying:
    If you are for me,
    and to my voice you would hearken,
    then fetch the heads of the men, your lord's sons,
    and bring them to me around this time tomorrow, to Yizre'el.
    Now the king's sons, seventy men,
    were with the great-ones of the city, the ones rearing them.

10:1 **those raising:** Or "guardians of" (Cohn 2000).
    [sons]: In MT the word is missing, and seems to
    have dropped out. Some take it in the sense of
    "descendants."
2 **city:** Ancient versions and manuscripts read the
    word in the plural.
3 **select:** Another meaning of Heb. *r-'-h,* usually

translated here as "to see." A notable example is
Gen. 22:8, "God will see-for-himself to [or: select]
the lamb for the offering-up." **brightest:** Heb. is
literally "rightest."
6 **heads:** A double meaning, leaders and physical
    heads, might be suggested here. **bring them:** So
    versions; MT has "come."

7 And it was, when the letter came to them,
that they took the king's sons
and slaughtered them, seventy men,
and put their heads in baskets;
then they sent them to him in Yizre'el.

8 A messenger came and told him, saying:
They have brought the heads of the king's sons!
He said:
Put them in two piles at the entrance to the city-gate until
daybreak.

9 Now it was at daybreak that he went out and stood
and said to all the people:
You are innocent.
—Here, I conspired against my master, and I killed him,
but who struck down all of these?

10 Know, therefore,
that no word of YHWH will fall to the ground
that YHWH promised concerning the House of Ah'av;
YHWH has done
what he promised through the hand of his servant Eliyyahu.

11 Then Yehu struck down all who remained of the House of Ah'av in
Yizre'el,
along with all his great-ones, his intimates, and his priests,
until he had left him no survivor.

12 Then he arose and came, that he might go to Shomeron.
He was at a binding house for shepherds on the way,

13 when Yehu came upon brothers of Ahazyahu king of Judah.
He said:
Who are you?
They said:
We are brothers of Ahazyahu;
we have come down [to see] the welfare of the sons of the king and
the sons of the queen [mother].

---

10 **fall:** That is, remain unfulfilled.
11 **great-ones:** Nobles. LXX reads Heb. *gedolav* as *go'alav,* "blood-redeemers" or relatives. **intimates:** So JPS, Cogan/Tadmor. Others, "acquaintances."
12 **binding house:** Or "meeting house," or even simply a place-name, "Bet-'Eked."

13 **brothers:** With the meaning, often found in the Bible, of "kin." **[to see] the welfare of:** Or "pay respects to" (JPS).

◆   14   He said:
Seize them alive!
They seized them alive
and slaughtered them at the cistern of the binding-house,
forty-two men;
he did not leave out one of them.

15   He went from there and came upon Yehonadav son of Rekhav
[coming] to meet him;
he blessed him [in greeting] and said to him:
Is your heart straight-and-true, as my heart is with your heart?
Yehonadav said:
It is, yes, it is!
[He said]:
Give me your hand!
He gave him his hand, and he pulled him up to him in the chariot.

16   He said:
Go with me, and see my zeal for Yhwh!
And he had him ride in his chariot.

17   He came to Shomeron
and struck down all who were left to Ah'av in Shomeron, until he
had wiped it out,
in accordance with the word of Yhwh which he had spoken to
Eliyyahu.

18   Then Yehu collected all the people
and said to them:
Ah'av served Baal a little;
Yehu will serve him much!

19   So-now, all the prophets of Baal, all those serving him and all his
priests, call together to me—
let no man be unaccounted for,
for I have a great sacrifice for Baal;
anyone who is unaccounted for shall not live!

15   **Yehonadav:** A variation on "Yonadav." The name links Yhwh with the idea of generosity (*n-d-b*). **Rekhav:** The Hebrew root *r-k-b* plays on the sounds of "bless" (*b-r-k*) and "chariot" (*rekhev*), significant in this chapter (Martin). Note that *b* and *v* are orthographically the same letter in Hebrew. **Give me your hand!:** MT doesn't specify the speaker,

but most read it as implying Yehu, as does the "he pulled" that follows.
17   **it:** A little awkward here, rather than "them."
18   **Yehu will:** Manuscripts and LXX imply "but" at the beginning of the phrase.
19   **those serving:** With the connotation of "worshippers" here and in v.23.

◆ —Now Yehu was acting with cunning,
in order to annihilate those serving Baal.—

20 Yehu said:
Hallow an *atzara*-festival for Baal!
And they proclaimed it.

21 And Yehu sent throughout all Israel,
and all those serving Baal came—
there was not left one who did not come;
they came to the House of Baal, and filled the House of Baal from
end to end.

22 Then he said to [The One] Over the Wardrobe:
Bring out apparel for all those serving Baal!
and he brought them out apparel.

23 And Yehu and Yehonadav son of Rekhav came into the House of
Baal,
and he said to those serving Baal:
Search out and see, lest there be with you some of the servants of
YHWH,
rather than those serving Baal alone!

24 They came in to perform sacrifices and offerings-up;
meanwhile, Yehu had placed eighty men for himself outside
and had said:
The man who lets [anyone] escape from the men whom I am
bringing into your hand—
his life in place of his life!

25 So it was, when he was finished performing the offering-up,
that Yehu said to the outrunners and to the officers:
Come in, strike them down! Let no one get away!
So they struck them down with the mouth of the sword,
and the outrunners and the officers [left them] thrown [there],
and went on to the rear-chamber of the House of Baal.

---

20 *atzara*-festival: A term used in relation to a holy day, the eighth day of the pilgrimage festival of Sukkot (see Lev. 23:36). Its meaning is unclear; some propose "restraint" or "a solemn gathering" (JPS).
21 **end to end:** Lit., "mouth to mouth."
22 **apparel:** With the possible implication of special clothing.

25 **[left them] thrown [there]:** Left their corpses lying there exposed (Cogan/Tadmor). **rear-chamber:** August Klostermann (quoted in Cogan/Tadmor) emends '*ir*, "city," to *devir* here, signifying the interior of the temple of Baal.

◆ 26 They took out the standing-pillar of the House of Baal,
and then they burned it.

27 And they demolished the standing-pillar of Baal,
and they demolished the House of Baal
and made it into a latrine, until today.

28 Thus Yehu wiped out Baal from Israel.

29 —However, as for the sins of Yorov'am son of Nevat, which he had
caused Israel to sin,
Yehu did not turn aside from [following] after them,
the golden calves that were at Bet-El, and that were at Dan.

30 Yhwh said to Yehu:
Because you have acted well, doing what is right in my eyes,
—according to all that was in my heart, you have done to the
House of Ah'av—
sons of four [generations] from you shall sit on the throne of Israel.

31 Yet Yehu did not take care to walk according to the Instruction of
Yhwh, the God of Israel, with all his heart;
he did not turn aside from the sins of Yorov'am, who had caused
Israel to sin.

32 In those days, Yhwh began to truncate Israel:
Hazael struck them throughout the entire territory of Israel,

33 from the Jordan toward the rising of the sun,
all the land of Gil'ad: the Gadite, the Re'uvenite, and the
Menashite,
from Aro'er which is by Wadi Arnon, including the Gil'ad and the
Bashan.

34 Now the rest of the events of Yehu, and all that he did, and all his
mighty-deeds—
are they not written in the Record of Yearly Events of the Kings of
Israel?

35 Yehu lay beside his fathers;
they buried him in Shomeron,
and Yehoahaz his son reigned as king in his place.

---

26 **standing-pillar:** MT has plural here.
32 **truncate:** Or "cut away at."
33 **Aro'er:** A fortified site on the Arnon River east of
the Dead Sea, and a traditional border with Moav.

35 **Yehoahaz:** See note on "Ahazyahu," a variant form
of the name, at 8:25.

Chapter 11. *The Orderly Coup in Judah:* In contrast to the last few chapters, the change of rule in Judah that now takes place occurs without extensive violence. Indeed, the text emphasizes protection more than killing: the royal child Yoash is hidden in a bedroom with his nurse, and guard details are placed around him; the wicked Atalya is escorted into the palace to her doom in an orderly fashion; and the young king is brought down from the Temple to the palace, to take his place on the throne. Notably, from v.14 through v.20, "the House of YHWH" and "the House of the King" repeat, eight and four times, respectively; the single occurrence of "the House of Baal" serves to herald its destruction.

36 Now the days that Yehu had reigned as king over Israel
were twenty-eight years in Shomeron.

11:1 Now when Atalya, Ahazyahu's mother, saw that her son was dead,
she set out to annihilate all the seed of the kingdom.

2 But Yehosheva daughter of King Yoram, sister of Ahazyahu, took
Yoash son of Ahazya
and stole him from the midst of the king's sons who were being put
to death
—him and his nurse—in the bedchamber,
and they hid him from Atalyahu, so that he was not put to death.

3 And he was with her in the House of YHWH, in hiding, for six years,
while Atalyahu was reigning over the land.

4 But in the seventh year, Yehoyada sent and took the commanders
of hundreds of the Carites, and of the outrunners,
and brought them to him in the House of YHWH;
he cut them a covenant and had them swear [fealty] in the House
of YHWH,
and showed them the king's son.

5 And he charged them, saying:
This is the thing that you are to do:
a third of you coming [on your watch] for the Sabbath,
those who guard the guarding of the king's house,

6 and a third at the Sur Gate,
and a third at the gate behind the Outrunners' [Gate]—
you are to guard the guarding of the House. . . .

7 The [other] two units among you,
all those going off-duty for the Sabbath,
are to guard the guarding of YHWH's house, over the king.

11:2 **Yehosheva:** "YHWH Is Perfection/Abundance."
Yoash: "YHWH Has Given/Rewarded." **stole:** In
this case meaning "kidnapped."

4 **Yehoyada:** The name, significantly, means "YHWH
Knows." **Carites:** Possibly identical to the "Kereitites," mercenaries from the Aegean who served the
House of David as far back as the book of Samuel
(e.g., I 30:14, II 8:18). **cut them a covenant:** Not the
usual "cut . . . with them," which would indicate a

reciprocal agreement; here the phrase indicates a
one-way "grant" (Cogan/Tadmor).

5–7 **guard the guarding:** An idiom for "keep guard."

6 **Sur Gate:** Location unknown. **Outrunners'**
[Gate]: See v.19, where the gate leads into the palace. It would be used by the king (see I Kings 14:28
[Fishbane]). **of the House. . . . :** MT then has the
enigmatic word *massah,* which I (and others) have
omitted here.

8 You are to encircle the king, all around, each one with his weapons
in his hand,
so that whoever comes through to the rows is to be put to death.
And be with the king in his going out and in his coming in!

9 So the commanders of hundreds did exactly as Yehoyada the priest
had charged:
they took, each one, his fighting-men,
those coming on duty on the Sabbath and those going off-duty on
the Sabbath,
and came to Yehoyada the priest.

10 And the priest gave to the commanders of hundreds the spear-
arsenal and the bow cases that had belonged to King David
that were in the House of YHWH,

11 and the outrunners took a stand, each one with his weapons in his
hand,
from the right shoulder of the House to the left shoulder, at the
sacrificial-altar and at the House, all around the king.

12 Then he brought out the king's son
and placed on him the diadem and the insignia;
they made him king—they anointed him,
and they struck their hands together and said:
May the king live!

13 Atalya heard the sound of the outrunners [and] of the fighting-
people,
so she came to the People in the House of YHWH.

14 And she saw: here, the king was standing by the standing-column,
as was the custom,
with the commanders and their trumpets by the king,

8 **rows:** Or "ranks."
9 **the priest:** Here he functions as both religious and
military chief (Cohn 2000).
10 **that had belonged to King David:** Appropriate in a
story about legitimate rule.
11 **right . . . left:** South . . . north.
12 **the insignia:** In their discussion, Cogan / Tadmor lay
out the spectrum from "jewels" to the usual "testimony"; clearly some kind of symbolic object connected to the covenant is meant.
14 **Landed People:** An oft-debated term, Heb. *am*

ha-aretz is found frequently in this literature, perhaps indicating landholders, or what we might call
citizens. Their function in Kings seems to include
choosing the king in unstable circumstances such as
a coup. In later centuries the phrase came to signify
the "salt of the earth," the working poor, and eventually, the ignorant. **tore . . . called out:** Heb. *va-
tikra'*, with the first word ending with *ayin* and the
second with *alef*, so an analogy (but not a repetition)
of sound is meant to catch the ear (Cohn 2000).

and all the Landed People were rejoicing and sounding a blast on
 the trumpets.
Then Atalyahu tore her garments and called out: Conspiracy!
 Conspiracy!
15 And Yehoyada the priest charged the commanders of hundreds,
 those accountable for the army,
and said to them:
Bring her out within the rows,
and anyone who comes after her, put to death with the sword!
For the priest said [to himself]:
Let her not be put to death in the House of Yhwh!
16 So they laid hands on her
and she came in by way of the Horses' Entrance to the House of
 Yhwh,
and was put to death there.
17 Then Yehoyada cut a covenant between Yhwh and the king and the
 people,
to be Yhwh's people,
and [one] between the king and the people.
18 And all the Landed People came to the House of Baal and
 demolished it:
its sacrificial-altars and its images they smashed to bits,
and Mattan, the priest of Baal, they killed in front of the altars.
Then the priest set accountable men over the House of Yhwh,
19 and he took the commanders of hundreds and the Carites and the
 outrunners and all the Landed People,
and they brought the king down from the House of Yhwh;
they entered by way of the Outrunners' Gate, into the House of
 the King,
and he took his seat on the kings' throne.
20 And all the Landed People rejoiced, and the city was quiet,
while Atalyahu they put to death with the sword in the House of
 the King.

---

15 **within:** Or "through" (Cogan/Tadmor). **comes after:** Follows.
16 **Horses' Entrance:** East of the Ofel, and leading to the royal area (Cogan/Tadmor).

18 **House of Baal:** Not mentioned elsewhere in the Bible. **accountable men:** Or "guards" (Cogan/Tadmor).
20 **quiet:** Or "tranquil."

Chapter 12. *Yehoash and the Temple:* After two chapters in which the tearing down of Baal's temple and altars figured prominently, the description of the long reign of Yoash/Yehoash, who in fact grows up in the Temple, is limited mainly to what he did regarding the "House of YHWH" in Jerusalem. The leisurely description of the repairs there, and how money was raised for them, is a welcome contrast to the bloody changes of government that have recently characterized the text. As Zevit (2004) notes, income from good deeds goes to the repair, while that from guilt, etc., is given to the priests.

Two ironies spring out at the reader at the end of the chapter: after fifteen occurrences of the word "silver" in eleven verses, holy vessels and gold are quickly given over to the king of Aram, to avert an attack on Jerusalem. And after all the care that the king has lovingly lavished on the Temple's repair, which would seem to make him deserve only praise and long life, Yehoash is assassinated.

◆ 12:1 Seven years old was Yehoash when he became king.

2 In year seven of Yehu, Yehoash became king,
and for forty years he reigned as king in Jerusalem;
his mother's name was Tzivya, from Be'er-Sheva.

3 And Yehoash did what was right in the eyes of Yhwh, all his days,
as Yehoyada the priest had instructed him.

4 However, the sanctuaries were not removed;
the people were still offering-sacrifices and sending-up-smoke at the
sanctuaries.

5 Yehoash said to the priests:
All the silver for holy-purposes that is brought to the House of
Yhwh,
silver of one's counting [in the census],
—silver of the valuation of persons,
[or] any silver that goes up in a man's heart to bring to the House
of Yhwh—

6 let the priests take it for themselves, each one from his
acquaintance,
and they themselves shall strengthen the breaches in the House,
wherever a breach is found there.

7 But it was in year twenty-three, that year of King Yehoash:
the priests had not strengthened the breaches in the House.

8 So King Yehoash called for Yehoyada the priest and for the [other]
priests
and said to them:
Why are you not strengthening the breaches in the House?
Now,
do not keep silver from your acquaintances,
but rather for the breaches in the House you are to give it over.

9 The priests agreed not to take silver from the people,
and not to strengthen the breaches in the House.

12:2 **Yehoash:** Trad. English "Jehoash." **Tzivya:** Trad.
English "Zibeah." The name means "[female]
gazelle."

5 **that goes up in a man's heart:** That is, which he
donates of his own volition.

6 **strengthen the breaches:** JPS and others render less
literally, "repair the damage."

9 **and not:** In the sense of "nor," "neither."

Chapter 13. *Northern Kings; The Death of Elisha:* The reigns of two "evil" northern kings lead up to the death of Elisha. The first, Yehoahaz, is notable for entreating YHWH (v.4), with the result that God sends an unnamed "deliverer"—phraseology that recalls Judges (Cogan/Tadmor). The second king, Yehoash, has his sixteen-year reign compressed into four verses, yet another example of the approach to history writing taken in the book of Kings.

Elisha's final act, while not as memorable as his predecessor's, is striking nevertheless. The prophet, on his sickbed, has the king shoot an arrow through the window, and then exhorts him to strike the ground with more arrows. When the king stops at three blows, the prophet expresses his disappointment and prophesies that Israel will now not be able to defeat Aram decisively (although Yehoash is able to recover some Israelite territory). Thus ends Elisha's career, with his powers undiminished, still affecting the course of international affairs.

Integrated into this account is a tiny, two-verse story about Elisha's grave that gives further evidence of his involvement in the miraculous, even after his death. It recounts how his bones resurrect a dead man who is in the process of being buried. This is the kind of motif that we find in world folklore but which is fairly uncommon in the Hebrew Bible. Such a typical saint story would have been unthinkable regarding Moshe, but, as we have seen, the Elisha (and Eliyyahu) narratives preserve a kind of folk religion in which almost anything can happen, especially as it relates to life and death.

◆ 10 Then Yehoyada the priest took a coffer
and bored a hole in its lid,
and gave it near the sacrificial-altar,
on the right as one entered the House of Yнwн;
the priests, the guardians of the threshold, would give there
all the silver that was brought to the House of Yнwн.

11 So it was, whenever they saw that there was much silver in the
coffer,
that the king's scribe and the Great Priest would go up,
they would tie up and count the silver that was found in the House
of Yнwн.

12 Then they would give the silver that was measured out into the
hands of those doing the work, those accountable in the House
of Yнwн,
and they would pay it out to the carvers of wood and to the
builders who were doing [tasks] in the House of Yнwн,

13 and to the wall-builders and to the stone-cutters,
for purchasing wood and quarried stones
to strenghen the breaches in the House of Yнwн,
and for everything [else] that was paid out for the House, to
strengthen it.

14 But there would not be made for the House of Yнwн
silver basins, snuffers, sprinkling bowls, trumpets,
any kind of vessels of gold or vessels of silver,
from the silver that was brought to the House of Yнwн;

15 rather, to those doing the work they would give it,
so that with it they would strengthen the House of Yнwн.

16 And they did not have to reckon [exactly] with the men into whose
hand they gave the silver,
to give [payment] to those doing the work,
for in trustworthy-fashion they dealt.

---

10 **coffer:** Cogan/Tadmor note that "cash boxes" situated next to temples were common in the ancient Near East.
11 **Great Priest:** High Priest.   **tie up:** In a bag.
12 **those accountable:** Those "in charge of the work"

(Cogan/Tadmor). "Doing" in this verse is closer to "supervising."
13 **wall-builders:** Masons.
16 **trustworthy-fashion:** Or "integrity, honesty."

◆   17   Silver from *asham*-offerings and silver from *hattat*-offerings was not
            brought into the House of YHWH;
        it was for the priests.

     18   Then Hazael king of Aram went up and waged battle against Gat,
            and took it,
        and [afterward] Hazael set his face to go up against Jerusalem.

     19   So Yehoash king of Judah took all the hallowed things that
            Yehoshafat, Yehoram, and Ahazyahu, his fathers, the kings of
            Judah, had hallowed,
        and his own hallowed things,
        and all the gold that was found in the treasuries of the House of
            YHWH and in the House of the king,
        and sent [them] to Hazael king of Aram,
        so that he went up away from Jerusalem.

     20   Now the rest of the events of Yoash, and all that he did—
        are they not written in the Record of Yearly Events of the Kings of
            Judah?

     21   His servants arose and conspired a conspiracy;
        they struck Yoash down at Bet-Millo, which leads down to Silla.

     22   Now it was Yozakhar son of Shim'at and Yehozavad son of Shomer
            his servants who struck him down, so that he died;
        they buried him beside his fathers, in the City of David,
        and Amatzya his son reigned as king in his place.

     13:1 In year twenty-seven of the years of Yoash son of Ahazyahu king of
            Judah,
        Yehoahaz son of Yehu became king in Shomeron,
        for seventeen years.

---

17 *asham*-offerings: Sacrifices designed to make reparations for sin (sometimes with the meaning of
"penalty"); see Lev. 5. *hattat*-offerings: These
were decontamination or purification sacrifices,
intended to effect atonement for sin. A major feature was the sprinkling of the slaughtered animal's
blood by the priest (see Lev. 4).

19 hallowed things: Donations to the sanctuary. hallowed: Or "dedicated" (Cogan / Tadmor).

21 Bet-Millo . . . Silla: The first term is possibly part
of the defense works of the city, the second, less
clear—perhaps a street or district close by.

22 Yozakhar: Trad. English "Jozakar." The name
means "YHWH Has Called to Mind." This is the
reading of manuscripts, since MT has "Yozavad"—
improbable given that "Yehozavad" is the other
person's name here. Yehozavad means "YHWH Has
Given." servants: It is not clear whether courtiers
or soldiers are meant here (Gray 1970). Amatzya:
"YHWH Is Strong"; trad. English "Amaziah."

13:1 Yehoahaz: Pronounced *ye-ho-ah-HAZ;* it means
"YHWH Has Grasped." Trad. English "Jehoahaz."

2 He did what was evil in the eyes of YHWH:
he walked after the sin of Yorov'am son of Nevat, who had caused
    Israel to sin;
he did not turn aside from it.

3 So YHWH's anger flared up against Israel,
and he gave them into the hand of Hazael king of Aram
and into the hand of Ben-Hadad son of Hazael, for all the days.

4 But Yehoahaz soothed the face of YHWH,
and YHWH hearkened to him,
for he saw the oppression of Israel,
for the king of Aram had oppressed them.

5 So YHWH granted Israel a deliverer, so that they came out from
    under the hand of Aram,
and the Children of Israel could sit in their tents, as yesterday [and]
    the day-before.

6 However, they did not turn aside from the sins of the House of
    Yorov'am, who had caused Israel to sin—
in them they walked;
even an Ashera-pole stood in Shomeron.

7 For no fighting-people were left to Yehoahaz
except for fifty riders, ten chariots, and ten thousand foot-soldiers,
for the king of Aram had annihilated them;
he had made them like dust for trampling.

8 Now the rest of the events of Yehoahaz, and all that he did, and all
    his mighty-deeds—
are they not written in the Record of Yearly Events of the Kings of
    Israel?

9 Yehoahaz lay beside his fathers;
they buried him in Shomeron,
and Yoash his son reigned as king in his place.

10 In year thirty-seven of the years of Yoash king of Judah,
Yehoash son of Yehoahaz became king of Israel in Shomeron,
for sixteen years.

---

2 **sin:** MT has plural "sins," but that conflicts with the subsequent "it."
3 **for all the days:** For a long time.
5 **in their tents:** The Israelites certainly dwelt in houses by this period; the phrase may simply be an older idiom for "peacefully" (Cogan/Tadmor). **as yesterday [and] the day-before:** A biblical idiom for "in the past." "Day-before" is literally "day three [ago]," where today is the first in the sequence, and yesterday the second.

11 And he did what was evil in the eyes of YHWH:
he did not turn aside from all the sins of Yorov'am son of Nevat,
who had caused Israel to sin;
in them he walked.

12 Now the rest of the events of Yoash, and all that he did, and his
mighty-deeds when he did battle with Amatzya king of Judah—
are they not written in the Record of Yearly Events of the Kings of
Israel?

13 Yoash lay beside his fathers,
and Yorov'am sat on his throne,
and Yoash was buried in Shomeron, beside the kings of Israel.

14 Now Elisha fell sick with the sickness from which he was to die.
Yoash king of Israel went down to him
and wept upon his face, he said:
Father! Father! Israel's chariotry and its horsemen!

15 Elisha said to him:
Take a bow and some arrows.
So he took him a bow and some arrows.

16 He said to the king of Israel:
Have your hand mount the bow.
He had his hand mount it.
Then Elisha put his hands on the king's hands,

17 and said:
Open the east-facing window.
And he opened it.
Then Elisha said:
Shoot.
And he shot.
He said:
An arrow of victory for YHWH, and an arrow of victory over Aram;
you will strike down Aram at Afek, until [they are] finished off!

18 And he said:
Take the arrows.
So he took them.

---

14 **Father! Father! . . . :** Elisha's own words to his master Eliyyahu at their parting in 2:12.

16 **Have your hand mount:** A technical term for grasping a bow.

17 **Afek:** Cogan/Tadmor identify this particular Afek with a site east of the Sea of Galilee (see I Kings 20:26ff.).

18 **Strike the ground:** With the arrows.

◆ Then he said to the king of Israel:
Strike the ground.
So he struck three times, and then stopped.

19 The man of God became furious with him and said:
Striking five or six times—
then you would have struck down Aram until [they would have
been] finished off!
But now
you will strike Aram [only] three times.

20 Elisha died, and they buried him.
Now raiding-bands from Moav would come into the land at the
coming of the year.

21 And [once] it was, they were burying a man,
and here, they saw such a band,
so they threw the man into the burial-place of Elisha and went off.
And [when] the man touched the bones of Elisha, he lived [again],
and he arose and stood on his feet.

22 Now Hazael king of Aram oppressed Israel all the days of
Yehoahaz.

23 But YHWH was gracious to them
and had compassion on them
and turned his face toward them
for the sake of his covenant with Avraham, Yitzhak, and Yaakov;
he was not willing to bring them to ruin
and has not cast them out from his presence until now.

24 Hazael king of Aram died,
and Ben-Hadad his son reigned as king in his place.

25 And Yehoash son of Yehoahaz once again took the towns from the
hand of Ben-Hadad son of Hazael
which he had taken from the hand of Yehoahaz his father, in battle:
three times Yehoash struck them,
and recovered the towns of Israel.

19 **Striking five or six times:** Ancient versions read,
"Would that you had struck . . ."
20 **at the coming of the year:** JPS reads "every year"; I
emend, with others, from *ba'* to *b-vo'*.

21 **they were burying:** The natives. **went off:** MT
has singular.
23 **until now:** Indicating that this text came into being
before the time of the Babylonian Exile.

PART IV

SOUTHERN AND NORTHERN KINGS: DESTRUCTION I

(II 14–17)

WITH THE DEATH OF ELISHA AND THE FALL OF THE OMRIDE DYNASTY, THE TEXT settles into narrating a depressing succession of rulers in both kingdoms, culminating with the fall of the Northern Kingdom after a revolt against Assyria in 722. Prominently featured are the formulas mentioned previously—dates, age at accession, length of reign, mother's name, and, most important, whether or not the king did "what was good in the eyes of YHWH." The chief events reported are military ones, with occasional forays into palace coups. But there is not much material on the actual lives of the Israelites, or even of the kings themselves. This is striking, considering that for the first half of the eighth century, both Israel and Judah were ruled over for long periods of time by a single king apiece, Azarya in the south and Yorov'am II in the north. At the beginning of Chap. 15, the account of Azarya's fifty-two-year reign mentions only two facts: that he did not remove the oft-condemned local sanctuaries, and that, as a result, he was stricken with a plague and confined to the royal palace for an untold period of time. Regarding Yorov'am as well, a king whose reign witnessed economic prosperity (for the rich, at any rate), there are only a few verses, mentioning his military exploits but, more important, condemning him for doing evil in God's sight.

The pattern of synchronic, alternating histories such as we find in these chapters has a parallel in Assyrian records; just as there, Assyria takes primacy over Babylonia, so here Judah predominates over Israel (Cogan/Tadmor). And the events reported in this part of Kings are for the most part corroborated by other ancient Near Eastern sources.

The bulk of this section is devoted to Chap. 17, which, after a cursory description of the fall of Shomeron, goes on at great length about the meaning and aftermath of the Northern Kingdom's demise (see Commentary to that chapter).

Historically speaking, for several decades preceding the middle of the eighth century, Assyria had been in decline, but beginning with the reign of Tiglath-Pileser III in 742, there was a resumption of its military aggressiveness. As Hallo/ Simpson note, it was not unusual for a revolt to follow a change of rulers, and this may have provided some impetus for the king's western campaigns. The result would have been destruction of much of the Israelite Northern Kingdom before Tiglath-Pileser's final act, the siege of Shomeron (Samaria).

———————

Chapter 14. *Kings North and South I:* We begin a sequence of kings with the Judahite Amatzyahu, who is judged rather favorably by the writers. Unlike Yehu, he is careful to observe the law, even in the midst of taking vengeance. On the other hand, he unsuccessfully defies Yehoash of Israel, and the result is another despoiling of the Temple. One cannot help feeling that a process is at work that will lead to disaster by the book's end.

In the midst of such foreboding, a strong king (Yorov'am II) comes to the throne of the north. Despite his bad rating, for the usual reasons, it is noted that he "restored the border of Israel" (v.25)—a recollection implying an earlier chronicle as a source text for the writers here, one that is not as harsh on his forty-two-year reign as we normally get in this book (Cogan/Tadmor). Once again, God takes pity on the Israelites, promising to let them survive. Yet we are just a few chapters from the fall of this Northern Kingdom.

14:1 In year two of Yoash son of Yehoahaz king of Israel,
Amatzyahu son of Yoash became king of Judah.

2 Twenty-five years old was he on his becoming king,
and for twenty-nine years he reigned as king in Jerusalem;
his mother's name was Yehoaddan, from Jerusalem.

3 He did what was right in the eyes of YHWH—
however, not like David his father;
exactly as Yoash his father had done, he did.

4 However, the sanctuaries were not removed;
the people still were offering-sacrifices and sending-up-smoke at the
sanctuaries.

5 Now it was
when the kingdom was strong in his hand,
that he struck down [those of] his servants who had struck down
the king his father.

6 But the sons of those who had struck [him] down he did not put to
death,
as is written in the Record of the Instruction of Moshe which
YHWH commanded, saying:
Fathers are not to be put to death for sons, and sons are not to be
put to death for fathers;
rather, each for his own sin is to be put to death!

7 It was he who struck down Edom in the Valley of Salt, ten thousand,
and took the Boulder in battle;
he called its name Yokte'el, until this day.

8 Then Amatzya sent messengers to Yehoash son of Yehoahaz son of
Yehu king of Israel, saying:
Come, let us see each other's face [in battle]!

9 Yehoash king of Israel sent [word] to Amatzyahu king of Judah,
saying:
The briar that is in the Levanon sent [word] to the cedar that is in
the Levanon, saying:
Give your daughter to my son as a wife!

14:1 **Amatzyahu:** Trad. English "Amaziah."
2 **Yehoaddan:** meaning "YHWH Has Delight."
4 **removed:** LXX; MT has "turned aside."
6 **as is written:** In Deut. 24:16. **the Record of the
Instruction of Moshe:** Heb. *sefer torat moshe.* The
reference is probably to the core of the book of Deu-

teronomy, either in its reality or in the perspective of
a later redactor of Kings.
7 **Valley of Salt:** Identification unclear. **the Boulder:** Thought by LXX to refer to the famous site
of Petra in today's Jordan, its location is not known
with certainty.

◆ But a beast of the open-field that is in the Levanon crossed by and
trampled the briar.

10 You struck, yes, struck down Edom,
but your heart lifts you up [in arrogance]!
Keep your glory and stay at home!
Why should you stir up evil for yourself
and fall, you and Judah with you?

11 But Amatzyahu would not hearken,
so Yehoash king of Israel went up, and they saw one another's faces
[in battle], he and Amatzyahu king of Judah,
at Bet-Shemesh that belongs to Judah.

12 And Judah was defeated before Israel,
and they fled, each to his tent.

13 And Amatzyahu king of Judah, son of Yehoash son of Ahazyahu,
Yehoash king of Israel seized at Bet-Shemesh;
then he came to Jerusalem and breached the wall of Jerusalem,
from the Efrayim Gate to the Corner Gate, four hundred cubits,

14 and he took all the gold and the silver and all the vessels that were
found in the House of YHWH and in the treasuries of the king's
house, along with hostages.
Then he returned to Shomeron.

15 Now the rest of the events of Yehoash, [and] what he did, and his
mighty-deeds, and how he engaged in battle with Amatzyahu
king of Judah—
are they not written in the Record of Yearly Events of the Kings of
Israel?

16 Yehoash lay beside his fathers;
he was buried at Shomeron, beside the kings of Israel,
and Yorov'am his son reigned as king in his place.

17 And Amatzyahu son of Yehoash king of Judah lived after the death
of Yehoash king of Israel for fifteen years.

18 Now the rest of the events of Amatzyahu—

---

10 **at home:** Lit., "in your house." **stir up evil:** Or
"flirt with disaster" (Cohn 2000).
11 **Bet-Shemesh that belongs to Judah:** Cogan/Tad-
mor cite earlier scholars who see this phrase as indicating a northern origin for the passage.
13 **Efrayim Gate:** In the center of Jerusalem's northern

wall, the main spot of Jerusalem's vulnerability historically. **Corner Gate:** In the northwest corner of
the city wall.
16 **Yorov'am:** The Second.
17 **fifteen years:** The chronology does not work here,
given the twenty-nine-year figure for Ahazyahu's

are they not written in the Record of Yearly Events of the Kings of
	Judah?

19	They conspired a conspiracy against him in Jerusalem, and he fled
	to Lakhish;
	they sent [men] after him to Lakhish, and they put him to death
	there.

20	Then they carried him back on horses,
	and he was buried in Jerusalem, beside his fathers, in the City of
	David.

21	And all the people of Judah took Azarya
	—he was sixteen years old—
	and made him king in place of his father Amatzyahu.

22	It was he who rebuilt Elat and restored it to Judah,
	after the king lay beside his fathers.

23	In year fifteen of the years of Amatzyahu son of Yehoash king of
	Judah,
	Yorov'am son of Yoash became king over Israel at Shomeron,
	for forty-one years.

24	He did what was evil in the eyes of YHWH:
	he did not turn aside from all the sins of Yorov'am son of Nevat,
	who had caused Israel to sin.

25	It was he who restored the border of Israel
	from Levo-Hamat to the Sea of the Plain,
	in accordance with the word of YHWH the God of Israel
	which he had spoken by the hand of his servant Yona son of
	Amittai the prophet, who was from Gat Ha-Heyfer,

26	for YHWH saw the affliction of Israel, exceedingly bitter [as it was],
	with none but the fettered, none but the forsaken—
	and no one to help Israel.

reign. This is another indication of the difficulties
in squaring the historical record in Kings, perhaps
because of differing source material.
19	**Lakhish:** Trad. English "Lachish," the great fortified
city in the lowlands of Judah, west of Jerusalem.
21	**all the people:** An exaggeration; perhaps equal to
"the Landed People."
22	**Elat:** Pronounced *ay-LAHT*. The Etzyon-Gever of
I Kings 9:26 and 22:49, and II Kings 16:6, and today a
popular resort city on the Gulf of Aqaba.

23	**king over Israel:** Emending MT's "Yorov'am king
of Israel," with ancient versions.
25	**the Sea of the Plain:** The Dead Sea (so understood
by Josh. 3:16 and 12:3). The "Plain" is the Jordan/Rift
Valley.	**Gat Ha-Heyfer:** A town in Lower Galilee,
on the eastern border of Zevulun's tribal territory
(not far from Sepphoris).

Chapter 15. *Kings North and South II:* In this remarkable chapter, eight separate reigns are subsumed. But they are constructed with the book of Kings' standard building blocks: a king's illness, a conspiracy and several assassinations, bloody warfare, tribute paid in silver to Assyria, and an exile of Israelite townspeople. As is typical, the northern kings are judged as evil and the southerners as good, except for the latter's failure to destroy the local sanctuaries.

Equally notable is the sudden appearance, in v.29, of the premier power of the ancient Near East at the time, Assyria. Although Kings has thus far ignored the growing strength of the Assyrian Empire, it will break out in full force in the chapters to come. Some background is thus in order.

Throughout a good part of the period covered in Kings, Assyria, situated around the Tigris River in the northern part of Mesopotamia, today's Iraq, was the first of the great ancient empires to dominate Israel after Egypt some centuries before. By the ninth century they had extended their reach westward to the Mediterranean, and in the ensuing centuries one can speak of "Neo-Assyria," which for the first time established an empire that encompassed most of the Middle East. Its scope has been revealed by modern archaeological exploration, which has turned up extensive written documents and fine examples of monumental architecture as well, including some memorable pieces currently in the British Museum, such as the large "cherubim" (winged sphinxes) that guarded the palace at Nineveh, and the moving reliefs depicting the conquest of the Judean city of Lachish. These sources convey a vivid picture of both splendor and warfare: elaborate portraits of kings on their thrones, surrounded by gods, servants, and subject kings; scenes of royal hunting of lions; soldiers with battering rams and siege ladders. In all of these, distinctive rectangular curly beards appear, along with the pointed helmets that struck dread throughout the ancient Near East.

Assyrian war policy included two memorable features, the impaling of captured peoples on tall stakes (as illustrated in the Lachish reliefs) and the deportation of subject populations, sometimes replacing them with others (as in II Kings 17). The former may have been done to set an example to the constantly rebelling provinces under Assyria's domination, while the latter would have both depleted the local leadership and talent and supplied Assyria herself with new blood for administrative and commercial purposes.

Certainly the daily political life of the Israelites was profoundly affected by the Assyrian threat, but that threat also had long-term cultural influences. Assyria's destruction of the Northern Kingdom terrified the south, but probably also effected the fleeing of northern refugees, who may well have brought with them texts and traditions that were later incorporated into the Bible. In addition, the language and concepts used in Assyrian inscriptions and treaties appear to have been mimicked, or rather co-opted, by biblical writers in texts such as Deuteronomy, Kings, and Isaiah. So, in a very real sense, eighth-century Assyria had a major if indirect hand in the creation of the Hebrew Bible.

27 But YHWH had not resolved to wipe out the name of Israel from
    under the heavens,
    so he delivered them by the hand of Yorov'am son of Yoash.

28 Now the rest of the events of Yorov'am and all that he did, his
    mighty-deeds when he waged battle,
    how he recovered Damascus and Hamat for Israel—
    are they not written in the Record of Yearly Events of the Kings of
    Israel?

29 Yorov'am lay beside his fathers, beside the kings of Israel,
    and Zekharyahu his son reigned as king in his place.

15:1 In year twenty-seven of the years of Yorov'am king of Israel,
    Azarya son of Amatzya king of Judah became king.

2 Sixteen years old was he at his becoming king,
    and for fifty-two years he reigned as king in Jerusalem;
    his mother's name was Yekholyahu, from Jerusalem.

3 He did what was right in the eyes of YHWH,
    exactly as Amatzya his father had done.

4 However, the sanctuaries were not removed;
    the people were still offering-sacrifices and sending-up-smoke at the
    sanctuaries.

5 And YHWH afflicted the king, so that he had *tzaraat* until the day of
    his death;
    he had to stay in the Separate House,
    while Yotam the king's son was [The One] Over the House,
    leading the Landed People.

6 Now the rest of the events of Azaryahu, and all that he did—
    are they not written in the Record of Yearly Events of the
    Kings of Judah?

---

28 **mighty-deeds:** Yorov'am is the last king of Israel (the Northern Kingdom) whose accomplishments are so judged, perhaps indicating Israel's impotence in the face of Assyria from this point forward. **for Israel:** Omitting MT's "for Yehuda and," along with most scholars.

29 **Zekharyahu:** "YHWH Has Called to Mind"; trad. English "Zechariah."

15:1 **Azarya:** Short for "Azaryahu," meaning "YHWH Helps." He is sometimes also called Uzziya (Uzziah), from a similar root meaning "YHWH Is Strong." Trad. English "Azariah."

2 **Yekholyahu:** "YHWH Prevails"; trad. English "Jecoliah."

5 **Separate House:** Many interpreters read as "House of Separation," while Kimhi understands the phrase as indicating that Azarya was now "free" of the burdens of office. If the former, the text is pointing to the practice of quarantining those with the skin disease *tzaraat,* which was thought to convey serious ritual impurity (see Lev. 13–14). **Yotam:** Pronounced *yo-TAHM;* trad. English "Jotham," with the meaning "YHWH Is Perfect." See Judg. 9:5–21 for a more famous bearer of the name.

◆ 7 Azarya lay beside his fathers;
they buried him beside his fathers, in the City of David,
and Yotam his son reigned as king in his place.

8 In year thirty-eight of the years of Azaryahu king of Judah,
Zekharyahu son of Yorov'am became king over Israel in Shomeron,
for six months.

9 He did what was evil in the eyes of YHWH, as his fathers had done:
he did not turn aside from the sins of Yorov'am son of Nevat, who
had caused Israel to sin.

10 And Shallum son of Yavesh conspired against him;
he struck him down at Yivle'am, and put him to death, and became
king in his place.

11 Now the rest of the events of Zekharya—
here, they are written in the Record of Yearly Events of the Kings
of Israel.

12 That is the word of YHWH which he spoke to Yehu, saying:
Sons to the fourth generation shall have seat for you on the throne
of Israel.
And thus it was.

13 Shallum son of Yavesh became king in year thirty-nine of the years
of Uziyya king of Judah;
he reigned as king for a month of days in Shomeron.

14 And Menahem son of Gadi, from Tirtza, went up and came to
Shomeron;
he struck down Shallum son of Yavesh in Shomeron, and put him
to death, and became king in his place.

15 Now the rest of the events of Shallum, and his conspiracy which he
conspired—
here, they are written in the Record of Yearly Events of the Kings
of Israel.

---

10 **Shallum:** Pronounced *shah-LOOM* and mean- ing perhaps "payback" for a vow (so Gray 1970, who also notes that this king is called "Son of a Nobody" in Assyrian records—confirming his status as usurper). **Yivle'am:** MT is garbled here, look- ing somewhat like an Aramaic phrase for "before the people." I follow LXX, given that another political assassination took place in that location in II Kings 9:27.

12 **the word of YHWH . . . :** See 10:30.

14 **Menahem:** "Comforter." **Gadi:** Meaning either "Gadite" or "[YHWH Is] My Fortune." **Tirtza:** See note to 14:17, above.

◆ 16   Then Menahem struck Tappuah and all who were in it, and its
        territory, [proceeding] from Tirtza, since it would not open [its
        gates];
       he struck it, and all its pregnant women he split open.

17   In year thirty-nine of the years of Azarya king of Judah,
       Menahem son of Gadi became king over Israel,
       for twenty years in Shomeron.

18   He did what was evil in the eyes of YHWH:
       he did not turn aside from the sins of Yorov'am son of Nevat, who
        had caused Israel to sin.

19   In his days, Pul king of Assyria came against the land,
       and Menahem gave Pul a thousand talents of silver to have his
        hands be with him, to keep the kingdom strong in his hand.

20   And Menahem imposed a silver [payment] on Israel, from all the
        mighty-men of value, to give [as payment] to the king of Assyria:
       fifty *shekels* of silver for [each] one man.
       So the king of Assyria turned back,
       and did not stay there in the land.

21   Now the rest of the events of Menahem, and all that he did—
       are they not written in the Record of Yearly Events of the Kings of
        Israel?

22   Menahem lay beside his fathers,
       and Pekahya his son reigned as king in his place.

23   In year fifty of the years of Azarya king of Judah,
       Pekahya son of Menahem became king over Israel in Shomeron,
       for two years.

24   He did what was evil in the eyes of YHWH:
       he did not turn aside from the sins of Yorov'am son of Nevat, who
        had caused Israel to sin.

---

16 **Tappuah:** One manuscript of LXX has this, while another reads it as Tirtza; MT has "Tifsah." Tappu'ah is fourteen miles southwest of Tirtza, on the Menashe-Efrayim border.

19 **In his days:** In its present place at the end of v.18 in printed Bibles, this phrase (Heb. *kol yamav*) breaks the usual formula associated with Yorov'am. Better, here, is to put it at the beginning of v.19 and to emend slightly to "in his days" (*be-yamav*), which it resembles orthographically, and which is a common archival phrase in this literature.   **Pul:** A nickname for Tiglat Pil'eser III (see note to v.29) in late sources (Cohn 2000).   **to have his hands be with him:** I.e., to support him.

22 **Pekahya:** "YHWH Has Opened [the eyes or the womb]."

Chapter 16. *Ahaz and Assyria:* From the breakneck chronological speed of the previous chapter, the text now slows down to concentrate on an "evil" Judean king, Ahaz. His crimes consist not only of the oft-repeated act of allowing the people to worship at the local shrines, but also of child sacrifice. In addition, he appeals to the king of Assyria for military help against Aram, cementing his request with a gift/bribe of treasures from the Temple. As a result of the despoiling, which this time is self-imposed, Ahaz comes to build an Assyrian-style altar—that is, he does Assyrian-like renovations in Jerusalem—on which the text spends more time than on any other aspect of his sixteen-year reign.

25 And Pekah son of Remalyahu, his officer, conspired against him;
   he struck him down in Shomeron, in the citadel of the king's
      house, with [men from] Argov and the Aryei
   —and along with him were fifty men of the Children of the
      Gil'adites—
   and he put him to death and became king in his place.
26 Now the rest of the events of Pekahya, and all that he did—
   here, they are written in the Record of Yearly Events of the Kings
      of Israel.

27 In year fifty-two of the years of Azarya king of Judah,
   Pekah son of Remalyahu became king over Israel in Shomeron,
   for twenty years.
28 He did what was evil in the eyes of YHWH:
   he did not turn aside from the sins of Yorov'am son of Nevat, who
      had caused Israel to sin.
29 In the days of Pekah king of Israel,
   Tiglat Pil'eser king of Assyria came;
   he took Iyyon and Avel Bet-Maakha and Yanoah and Kedesh and
      Hatzor
   and the Gil'ad and the Galilee,
   all the region of Naftali,
   and he exiled them to Assyria.
30 Then Hoshe'a son of Ela conspired a conspiracy against Pekah son
      of Remalyahu;
   he struck him down and put him to death, and became king in his
      place,
   in year twenty of Yotam son of Uziyya.
31 Now the rest of the events of Pekah, and all that he did—
   here, they are written in the Record of Yearly Events of the Kings
      of Israel.

25 **Remalyahu:** Possibly meaning "YHWH Has Adorned." **Argov and the Aryei:** The Hebrew is obscure; the fact that *aryei* means "lion" does not help much.
29 **Tiglat Pil'eser:** Akkadian *Tukulti-apil-Esharra*, "My Help is the Son of Esharra [the god Ashur]," the third Assyrian king by that name, who ruled from 745 to 727 B.C.E. During his active military career, the Neo-Assyrian Empire reached its maximum expansion. The Hebrew is pronounced *tig-LAHT pil-EH-ser*. **Iyyon:** At the base of Mount Hermon. **Avel Bet-Maakha:** South of the previous town. **Yanoah:** Of uncertain location. **Kedesh:** Ten miles north of Hatzor. **Iyyon . . . Hatzor:** The five towns mentioned here appear to form a straight north-south line, just to the west of the Jordan River.
30 **Hoshe'a:** Short for "YHWH Delivers."

32 In year two of Pekah son of Remalyahu king of Israel,
Yotam son of Uziyyahu became king, king in Judah.

33 Twenty-five years old was he when he became king,
and for sixteen years he reigned as king in Jerusalem;
his mother's name was Yerusha daughter of Tzadok.

34 He did what was right in the eyes of YHWH:
exactly as Uziyyahu his father had done, he did.

35 However, the sanctuaries were not removed;
the people were still offering-sacrifices and sending-up-smoke at the
sanctuaries.
It was he who built the Upper Gate of the House of YHWH.

36 Now the rest of the events of Yotam, which he did—
are they not written in the Record of Yearly Events of the Kings of
Judah?

37 In those days
YHWH first sent out against Judah
Retzin king of Aram and Pekah son of Remalya.

38 Yotam lay beside his fathers;
he was buried with his fathers in the City of David, his father,
and Ahaz his son became king in his place.

16:1 In year seventeen of the years of Pekah son of Remalyahu,
Ahaz son of Yotam, king of Judah became king.

2 Twenty years old was he at his becoming king,
and for sixteen years he reigned as king in Jerusalem.
He did not do what was right in the eyes of YHWH his God, like
David his father,

3 but he walked in the way of the kings of Israel,
and even had his son cross through the fire,
[just] like the abominations of the nations whom YHWH had
dispossessed before the Children of Israel.

---

32 **Uziyyahu:** "YHWH Is My Strength"; trad. English "Uzziah."

33 **Yerusha:** "Possession"; trad. English "Jerushah."

35 **Upper Gate:** It is not clear where this was.

37 **sent out:** Others, "let loose." Cogan/Tadmor note that the verb is usually used in connection with divine punishment. **Retzin:** Probably meaning "Desirable."

16:3 **had his son cross through the fire:** It is not clear whether this was an actual sacrifice or some kind of milder ritual.

4   He offered-sacrifices and sent-up-smoke at the sanctuaries and on
      the hilltops,
    and under every luxuriant tree.

5   Then Retzin king of Aram and Pekah son of Remalyahu king of
      Israel went up to Jerusalem for battle;
    they besieged Ahaz, but could not overcome [him] in battle.

6   —At that time Retzin king of Aram restored Elat to Edom:
    he expelled the Judahites from Elat,
    while Edomites came to Elat and settled there, until this day.—

7   So Ahaz sent messengers to Tiglat Pil'eser king of Assyria, saying:
    Your servant and your son am I!
    Come up and deliver me from the hand of the king of Aram
      and from the hand of the king of Israel, who have risen up
      against me!

8   And Ahaz took the silver and the gold that were found in the House
      of YHWH and in the treasuries of the king's house,
    and sent a bribe to the king of Assyria.

9   And the king of Assyria hearkened to his [plea];
    the king of Assyria went up to Damascus, seized it, and exiled it
      to Kir,
    while Retzin he put to death.

10 Then King Ahaz went to meet Tiglat Pil'eser king of Assyria at
      Damascus,
    and he saw the sacrificial-altar that was in Damascus,
    so King Ahaz sent to Uriyya the priest a likeness of the altar and its
      pattern, including all [the details for] its making.

11 And Uriyya the priest built the altar;
    exactly as King Ahaz had sent from Damascus, so did Uriyya the
      priest make,
    by the time King Ahaz came back from Damascus.

12 The king came back from Damascus,
    and the king looked over the altar.
    Then the king drew near to the altar, and went up on it;

---

6 **Judahites:** Cogan/Tadmor see this as a late usage
(late seventh century). Several centuries later, the
term came to designate "Jews," a name which barely
appears in biblical texts.   **from Elat:** MT has "Elot"
here.   **until this day:** Also in 8:22 and 14:7 in reference to territorial changes, this refers to the time of
Josiah, not the exile (Cogan/Tadmor).

9 **Kir:** Location unknown; it is referred to in Amos 9:7
as the Arameans' point of origin.

10 **likeness:** Or "model."

Chapter 17. *First Catastrophe: The Fall of Israel:* Readers who are accustomed to the detailed battle scenes in Homer and elsewhere will be disappointed by the long-awaited account of Israel's destruction, which takes up a mere handful of words in two verses. While the Assyrian relief commemorating the somewhat later destruction of the Judean city of Lachish lays out the contemporary particulars of siege, execution, and exile in gripping and poignant artistic terms, the biblical writers in our chapter are content to describe Israel's demise, which had such a major influence on biblical thinking, in the sparsest way possible.

The reason for this laconic approach becomes clear beginning in v.7: "So it was, / because . . . ," which then continues at great length, first, to recall God's warnings to Israel through the prophets, and then, to recount through a long string of verbs how the people turned away from the right path into idolatry. Only in v.18 does the text finally inject God's reaction, as it were. Vv.21–23 provide an additional interpretation of the downfall, citing Yorov'am's primal sin of idolatry.

Beginning in v.24, we are additionally told how, in consonance with what we now know of Assyrian practice, the conquerors place some of their own citizens in the vanquished land. When the new settlers are attacked by lions, which the Bible understands as punishment for their not acknowledging YHWH, they are given an exiled priest to teach them how to worship him. But the result, ranging far from idealized Israelite practice, is syncretism, a combination of religions. In this section, which again takes up much more textual space than the fall of Israel itself, the key word is "awe"; that is, the settlers are supposed to worship God correctly, but do not, "until this day" (v.41). So from the perspective of a southern writer, the north has lost its identity, and thus is lost to history. In fact, the northern exiles blended into the Assyrian population, and for all practical purposes disappeared. The romantic notion of the "Ten Lost Tribes," which envisioned them in distant lands awaiting discovery by later explorers, has no historical currency, despite its being a legend beloved in the Western world. On the other hand, those northerners who fled in the opposite direction, into Judah, may have brought with them their own traditions about Israel's past, and this contribution to the process of the Bible's development is of the greatest significance. It may even have been the beginning of the long sequence of adaptation which ultimately led to the canonization, the final form, of the text.

This chapter gives evidence of a complex history, mixing condemnations of both the north and the south, and inserting several verses (18b–21) that bring the chapter up to date with the Babylonian Exile (see Brettler 1995 for a full analysis). As we have seen elsewhere in Kings and indeed throughout Deuteronomistic History (DH), such a practice is not unusual, and supports the idea of an evolving biblical text that is a testimony to Israel's creative memory.

13 he sent-up-in-smoke his offering-up and his gift-offering, and
        poured out his poured-offering,
    and he sprinkled the blood of the *shalom*-offerings that he had
        against the altar.
14 As for the bronze altar that was in the presence of YHWH,
    he brought it near from in front of the House, from between the
        [new] altar and the House of YHWH,
    and placed it on the flank of the [new] altar, northward.
15 And King Ahaz commanded Uriyya the priest, saying:
    On the large altar, send-up-in-smoke the morning offering-up, the
        evening gift, the offering-up of the king and his grain-gift,
    and the offering-up of all the Landed People and their gifts, along
        with their poured-offerings;
    and all the blood of the offerings-up and all the blood of the
        [*shalom*-]sacrifice, you are to sprinkle against it,
    while the bronze altar is to be mine to frequent.
16 So Uriyya the priest did
    just as King Ahaz had commanded.
17 And King Ahaz stripped the rims of the stands
    and removed the basin from them,
    while the Sea he took down from the bronze oxen that were
        beneath it,
    and placed it on the pavement of stones;
18 and the covered-passage for the Sabbath which they had built in
        the House and the king's outer entrance, he removed from the
        House of YHWH,
    on account of the king of Assyria.
19 Now the rest of the events of Ahaz, [and] what he did—
    are they not written in the Record of Yearly Events of the Kings of
        Judah?

13 **he sent-up-in-smoke . . . :** The king is able to act as priest on this occasion, since he is presenting a one-time dedication sacrifice, not a daily one (Cogan/Tadmor).

15 **his grain-gift:** Elsewhere "gift-offering," but I have tried to cut down on the repetition of "offering" here, since it is not in the Hebrew per se. "His" refers to the king's sacrifice to God.   **frequent:** Following Cogan/Tadmor.

18 **the covered-passage for the Sabbath:** A difficult phrase which could, alternately, mean "the cast-metal seat" which "he removed" (Mulder).   **on account of . . . :** Because of Tiglat Pil'eser's plundering (Cogan/Tadmor).

◆ 20 Ahaz lay beside his fathers;
he was buried with his fathers, in the City of David,
and Hizkiyyahu his son reigned as king in his place.

17:1 In year twelve of Ahaz king of Judah,
Hoshe'a son of Ela became king in Shomeron, over Israel,
for nine years.

2 He did what was evil in the eyes of YHWH—
however, not like the kings of Israel who were before him.

3 Against him Shalman'eser king of Assyria came up,
and Hoshe'a became servant to him
and rendered him tribute.

4 But the king of Assyria found conspiracy in Hoshe'a,
in that he sent messengers to So king of Egypt
and did not send up tribute to the king of Assyria as year after year.
So the king of Assyria arrested him and bound him over to the
prison house.

5 And the king of Assyria went up throughout all the land;
he went up to Shomeron and laid siege to it, for three years.

6 In the ninth year of Hoshe'a, the king of Assyria captured
Shomeron,
and he exiled Israel to Assyria;
he settled them in Halah and on the Havor, the River Gozan, and
the towns of Media.

7 So it was,
because the Children of Israel had sinned against YHWH their God,
the one bringing them up from the land of Egypt, from under the
hand of Pharaoh king of Egypt,
and had held other gods in awe,

---

20 **Hizkiyyahu:** Pronounced *hiz-kee-YAH-hu*, meaning
"YHWH Was Strong." The name Ezekiel (Yehezke'el)
derives from the same Hebrew root. The trad. English is "Hezekiah."

17:3 **Against him . . . came up:** Heb. *'alav 'ala*, suggesting perhaps a heightened rhetoric, fitting for
the introduction to such a dramatic moment in
Israel's history. **Shalman'eser:** Assyrian *Shalmanu
asharedu*, "[The God] Shalman Is Exalted." Sargon II
is also mentioned in Assyrian records as the con-

queror of Shomeron. **servant:** More of a technical term here connoting "vassal."

4 **to So:** The name is not otherwise attested as the
name of an Egyptian king; Cogan/ Tadmor conjecture "To Sais (a place name) [to] the king of
Egypt." **arrested . . . bound . . . over:** Heb. *va-
ya'tzereihu . . . va-ya'asreihu.*

6 **Halah . . . the Havor . . . Gozan:** Known locations
in Assyria.

8 and had walked in the customs of the nations which YHWH had
dispossessed before the Israelites
and of the kings of Israel, which they had observed;
9 and the Children of Israel had imputed things which are not so to
YHWH their God,
and had built themselves sanctuaries throughout all their towns,
from guards' tower to fortified town;
10 and had set up standing-pillars and Ashera-poles for themselves, on
every lofty hill and beneath every luxuriant tree,
11 and had sent-up-smoke there, at all the sanctuaries, like the nations
whom YHWH had exiled before them,
and had done evil things, to provoke YHWH,
12 and had served Illicit-Things
about which YHWH had said to them:
You are not to do this thing!
13 And YHWH had warned Israel and Judah by the hand of every
prophet, every seer, saying:
Turn back from your evil ways and keep my commandments and
my regulations,
according to all the Instruction that I commanded your fathers
and which I sent to them by the hand of my servants the prophets.
14 But they had not hearkened;
they had hardened their neck, like the neck of their fathers,
who had not trusted in YHWH their God,
15 and they had rejected his rules and his covenant which he had cut
with their fathers,
and his warnings by which he had warned them;
and they had walked after futility and became futile [themselves],
and after the nations that were around them, about whom YHWH
had commanded them to not do like them;
16 they had abandoned all the commandments of YHWH their God
and had made for themselves something molten—two calves,
and had made an Ashera-pole

13 **every prophet:** MT spelling of "prophet" is garbled; this may be a gloss.
14 **hardened their neck:** See Exod. 32:9, where God characterizes the Israelites by the same image.
15 **rejected:** With the flavor of "despised."

16 **the Forces of the Heavens:** Or "Armies of the Heavens," here denoting the planets and stars. The worship of heavenly bodies was common throughout the ancient Near East.

and bowed down to all the Forces of the Heavens
and served Baal;

17 and they had made their sons and their daughters cross through the
fire,
and they had augured augury and practiced divination,
and had sold themselves to do what was evil in the eyes of Yʜᴡʜ,
provoking him—

18 so Yʜᴡʜ became exceedingly angry at Israel, and he removed them
from his presence;
none remained, save the tribe of Judah alone.

19 But even Judah did not keep the commandments of Yʜᴡʜ their
God;
they walked in the customs of Israel which they had observed.

20 And so Yʜᴡʜ rejected all the seed of Israel;
he afflicted them and gave them into the hand of pillagers,
until he had cast them out from his presence.

21 When he had torn Israel away from the House of David
and had made Yorov'am son of Nevat king,
Yorov'am had led Israel away from [following] after Yʜᴡʜ
and had caused them to sin a great sin.

22 And the Children of Israel had walked in all the sins of Yorov'am
son of Nevat which he wrought,
and had not turned aside from it,

23 until Yʜᴡʜ removed Israel from his presence,
as he had promised by the hand of all his servants the prophets.
So Israel was exiled from its soil to Assyria,
until this day.

24 And the king of Assyria brought [people] from Babylon, from Kuta,
from Avva, from Hamat, and from Sefarvayim,
and settled them in the towns of Shomeron, in place of the
Children of Israel;
they took possession of Shomeron, and settled in her towns.

---

23 **removed:** Heb. *hesir,* punning on *saru,* "turn aside,"
in the previous verse.

24 **from Babylon . . . :** Apparently from all over the
empire—a known Assyrian practice.

25 Now it was:
at the start of their settlement there, they did not hold YHWH
in awe,
so YHWH sent out lions against them,
and they were killing [some] among them.

26 So they said to the king of Assyria, saying:
The nations whom you exiled and resettled in the towns of
Shomeron
do not know the practices of the god of the land,
so he has sent out lions against them;
here, they are causing their death,
as they do not know the practices of the god of the land.

27 So the king of Assyria commanded, saying:
Have one of the priests whom I exiled from there go there,
let him go and settle there, and instruct them in the practices of the
god of the land.

28 So one of the priests whom they had exiled from Shomeron came
and settled at Bet-El,
and he was instructing them how they should hold YHWH in awe.

29 But each-nation, each-nation went on making their own gods;
they put them in the sanctuary buildings that the Shomeronites had
made,
each-nation, each-nation in their towns in which they had settled:

30 the men of Bavel made Sukkot Benot,
and the men of Kut made Nergal,
and the men of Hamat made Ashima,

31 and the Avvites made Nivhaz and Tartak,
and the Sefarvites were burning their children in fire to
Adrammelekh and to Anammelekh, the gods of Sefarvayim.

25 **sent out:** or "let loose." **lions:** As earlier in the book (I 13:24), sent by God to punish people in the Bible. The Hebrew word, *arayot*, echoes the key verb *y-r-'*, "hold in awe," as well as the term "instruct" (*y-r-h*) in v.27.

26 **practices:** In the sense of "religious practices." Cogan/Tadmor translate as "rites."

29 **Shomeronites:** The Assyrians designated the entire province as Shomeron (Gray 1970).

30 **Sukkot Benot . . . :** Some of these gods are known, while others seem to be fragments of names. **Ashima:** Gray (1970) theorizes that this is the goddess Ashera, transformed into an Aramaic word for "guilt."

31 **Adrammelekh . . . Anammelekh:** The rhyme is striking, but the names are so far not known in ancient Near Eastern pantheons.

32 Now they went on holding Yнwн in awe,
    but they [also] made for themselves, from [all] their quarters, priests
       for the sanctuaries;
    they went on making [worship] for them at the sanctuary buildings.
33 Now Yнwн they held in awe,
    while their gods they went on serving,
    according to the practice of the nations from among whom they
       had been exiled.
34 To this day they do, according to their earlier practices:
    they do not hold Yнwн in awe;
    they do not do according to their laws, according to their practice,
    or according to the Instructions and the commandments that
       Yнwн commanded the Children of Yaakov, whose name he
       appointed Israel.
35 But Yнwн had cut a covenant with them and had commanded
       them, saying:
    You are not to hold other gods in awe,
    you are not to bow down to them,
    you are not to serve them,
    and you are not to sacrifice to them!
36 Rather, Yнwн,
    who brought you up from the land of Egypt with great power and
       an outstretched arm,
    him you are to hold in awe,
    to him you are to bow down, to him you are to sacrifice!
37 The laws and the practices, the instruction and the commandment
       that he wrote down for you,
    you are to keep, observing it all the days [of your life];
    you are not to hold other gods in awe!
38 The covenant that I cut with you, you are not to forget;
    you are not to hold other gods in awe!
39 Rather, Yнwн your God you are to hold in awe—
    and *he* will rescue you from the hand of all your enemies.
40 But they did not hearken,
    rather, according to their former practice they went on doing.

34 **whose name he appointed:** See note to Judg. 8:31.

41 So these nations have been holding YHWH in awe,
but their idols they have gone on serving,
and also their children and their children's children:
as their fathers did, [so] they go on doing,
until this day.

41 **until this day:** Here, as often in this book, the phrase
appears to refer to a time before the destruction of
Judah.

PART V

JUDAH AS VASSAL AND REBEL: DESTRUCTION II

(II 18–25)

AT THIS POINT, AS IS OBVIOUS FROM THE PREVIOUS CHAPTER, INTERNATIONAL power politics play a dominant role in the history of ancient Israel. From 722 to 587 B.C.E., the time period that covers all but the last paragraph of the book of Kings, Judah's every political move is scrutinized and reacted to by the great empires of the ancient Near East. On the one hand, this means that the reader must pay close attention to whether a particular Judean king is cooperating with Assyria/Babylonia (or Egypt, also flexing its power) or trying to break free. On the other hand, the biblical text's chief concern is still the degree to which a given Judean king is faithful to the covenant.

The historical setting at the beginning of this section is the Neo-Assyrian empire in its last century. Under its powerful kings Sargon II, Sennacherib, Esarhaddon, and Ashurbanipal, Assyria extended its grip over much of the Near East, including what today is Iraq, Egypt, Israel, Lebanon, Syria, Jordan, and parts of Iran, Turkey, and Armenia. Its spectacular capital at Nineveh, near modern Mosul in northern Iraq, which included one of the great libraries of antiquity, gave further evidence of its power; palace reliefs and sculptures testify to a high level of artistic accomplishment. Many of these pieces can be viewed today in the British Museum.

The book of Kings, for its own purposes, reflects both the language and the psychological force of Assyrian power in the speeches attributed to their officials before the gates of a besieged Jerusalem in II 18–19. But it also counters it with its own weapons, divine words, and action in the subsequent rescue of Jerusalem.

Kings chooses to remain largely silent on Assyria over the decades that follow the destruction of the Northern Kingdom, preferring instead to concentrate on the deeds of the three kings described below. But we know from Assyrian records that the seventh century saw both the zenith of their power and, after the death of Ashurbanipal in 627, a descent into internal chaos and external fragmentation. The Babylonians to the south, who held traumatic memories of the Assyrian capture of Babylon in 689, found their revenge in the sacking of Nineveh in 612.

Following the demise of the Assyrian Empire in 605 at the Battle of Carchemish, Babylonia succeeded to the role of dominant power in the area, lasting until its fall in turn to Persia two-thirds of a century later. Neo-Babylonian civilization was the heir to millennia of high culture, manifested in great literature such as the Epic of Gilgamesh, as well as in law, science, and architecture. It was quite possibly Babylonia where at least some of biblical literature was compiled, including the book of Kings.

True to type, the biblical account in these chapters is laced with reports of how one Judean king or another paid tribute to Babylonia or revolted against it. The result of the revolts was two fateful sieges of Jerusalem: a first one in 597, which resulted in both the exile of elite sections of the population and despoliation of Temple treasures, and a second one a decade later, which saw the Temple's and the city's destruction and thus the end of biblical Israel as a continuous independent entity.

The entire book ends with a postscript, openly dated a quarter of a century after the fall of Jerusalem. Its description of a Davidic king released from prison but not from exile holds open many possibilities, negative and positive, in keeping with the double-edged thrust of the book of Kings.

ON THREE KINGS OF JUDAH

ALTHOUGH THE BOOK OF KINGS COVERS THE REIGNS OF THIRTY-NINE KINGS AND one queen, three of Judah's rulers who appear toward the end of the book occupy disproportionate space and thus have particular importance: Hizkiyyahu (Hezekiah), Menashe (Manasseh), and Yoshiyyahu (Josiah). While recovering precise historical information about these kings is difficult, given the ideological thrust of the biblical text and the vagueness of some passages, the way in which the Bible presents them has great interest for the overall narrative. Their portrayal in Kings posits that, despite the extensive reforms (especially the eradication of idol worship) enacted by Hizkiyyahu in the late eighth century and Yoshiyyahu in the late seventh, it is Menashe's evil deeds which ultimately could not be overlooked or overcome, and Judah inevitably met its horrible fate of destruction and exile. In these texts one can feel a later historian, if not the wider culture itself, attempting to grapple with the question, "If Hizkiyyahu and Yoshiyyahu were so faithful and zealous in their observance of the covenant, why was Jerusalem destroyed in 587?"

Historically, things may well not have been this cut and dried. Scholars note that the presentation of the three kings might be said to follow a classic ancient Near Eastern literary pattern, where good kings alternate with bad. Then, too, it is unclear how much the first reform under Hizkiyyahu has influenced the telling of the second under Yoshiyyahu, and possibly vice versa. We are thus left with, as usual, a series of memories that have been processed. The book of Chronicles, written later and perhaps using other sources, sees the history differently. It gives many more details on Hizkiyyahu's reform, and presents a startling view of Menashe, absent in Kings, as an evildoer who, after being exiled, repented and restored his father's covenantal loyalty.

The reign of Hizkiyyahu, dated by many scholars from c. 715 to 687, encompasses at least two events of major importance to the biblical text: his attempt at wide-ranging religious reform and his rebellion against Assyria, which Jerusalem survived but which decimated much of the rest of Judah.

The reform, outlined briefly at the beginning of Chap. 18, is described as involving the destruction of pagan altars around the country and the concentration of the sacrificial cult in the Jerusalem Temple. Since these ideas are central to the book of Deuteronomy, some scholars have been inclined to identify the period of Hizkiyyahu's reign as the time of origin of much of the Deuteronomistic History (DH), which, as the reader will recall, is often bunched together with that fifth book of the Torah. This conclusion is buttressed by the undoubted emigration of northern refugees from the destruction of Israel in 722, a population which might well have brought with them the kind of northern-based traditions found in both Deuteronomy and portions of DH. In any event, it is not clear how successful Hizkiyyahu's policy was; its accomplishments may have been played down by Josianic editors a century later, who sought to claim greater credit for their own reformer king, Yoshiyyahu (Rosenbaum).

Hizkiyyahu revolted against Assyria, as did some other sections of the empire such as Babylonia after the death of Sargon II in 705. This led to a ruthless campaign by the new king of Assyria, Sennacherib, who destroyed numerous Judean towns, as enduringly attested to in an astounding frieze, now displayed in the British Museum, which portrays the successful siege of the fortress city of Lachish. Assyrian texts compare Hizkiyyahu's subsequent entrapment in a besieged Jerusalem to the situation of "a bird in a cage." That the king and the city unexpectedly survived this potentially catastrophic situation seems to have been taken as a sign of divine favor, and may have contributed to Jerusalem's false sense of security a century later under similarly trying circumstances.

Another archaeological remnant of Hizkiyyahu's kingship comprises many storage jars stamped *lmlk,* "belonging to the king," which have been recovered at the northern and western borders of ancient Judah and dated to this period. They give evidence of preparations for the Assyrian invasion, as well as supporting the extent of the king's control of the country, an element necessary for a major reform.

Most intriguing, and historically valuable, are the two major material remains of the period: the Siloam water tunnel with its famous inscription describing the two teams of workers finally meeting (although some scholars have now dated this to Menashe's reign), and the remnant of the so-called Broad Wall of Jerusalem, over twenty feet wide. It is clear that the defense preparation and expansion of the capital city are among the truly enduring of Hizkiyyahu's accomplishments. Jerusalem as we come to know it in the Bible, substantially expanded up the western hill from the small city of David and Solomon, is basically Hizkiyyahu's city.

As indicated above, in Menashe the writers of Kings found their last great villain (earlier ones in the book had been Yorov'am and Ah'av). His reign encompasses most of the first half of the seventh century, in a time of relative quiet in the Assyrian Empire (the destruction of Babylon in 689 notwithstanding). Our book goes to great lengths to excoriate Menashe's restoration of pagan worship in Jerusalem. This was undoubtedly a return to earlier popular forms of religion in Judah and not an attempt to curry favor with the Assyrians, who normally did not impose their religion on their foreign subjects. Whatever the historical realities, Menashe as we encounter him in Kings is, covenantally speaking, a monster; the fact that he also "filled Jerusalem with blood" seems almost to be an afterthought. From DH's standpoint, he is the inheritor of the heretical mantle of Ah'av, and seals Jerusalem's fate, which will not be played out until over a half century after his death, just as Ah'av's punishment was postponed onto the next generation. In both cases, one senses a writer or writers struggling to understand the meaning of historical events. The destruction of Jerusalem in 587 urgently needed an explanation, especially after Yoshiyyahu's striking reform, and the memory of Menashe, sandwiched between that of the two great reformer kings, provided a focus. As mentioned above, the later book of Chronicles, with its own agenda, presents Menashe in a much better light, and lays the blame for the fall of Jerusalem on the generation of the destruction (see II Chron. 36:14–16).

With Yoshiyyahu, we encounter a figure whose importance in Israelite thought and history transcends his own time. The text has him come to the throne as a child, around 640; although he does not reach the age of forty, his reign witnesses a momentous historical shift in the entire region, including the fall of the Assyrian capital Nineveh and the rise of the Neo-Babylonian Empire. But the biblical text is most interested in Yoshiyyahu's reform, which is described as sweeping and is studded with dramatic events: the destruction of pagan shrines, the observance of Passover after a centuries-long hiatus, and the cleaning up of the Temple, which includes the finding of the document termed "the Record of the Instruction of Moshe."

The reform itself seems ultimately to have failed; in any case, the great hopes pinned on Yoshiyyahu as the revived David were cut short by his ill-advised military move up to Megiddo, where the book of Kings reports that he was slain by the Egyptian king in an attempt to inject himself into international power politics.

In Kings, Yoshiyyahu is the Last Great Hope of Judah. The praise heaped on him may reflect a new and strongly nationalistic energy in the wake of Assyria's decline and fall, a development which has led many scholars to view his reign as the occasion for compiling the book of Joshua. Seen by the text as the incomparable echo of David, Yoshiyyahu is faithful to YHWH in the extreme, in fulfillment of a prophecy which we encountered earlier (I Kings 13:2); his ruthless purging of non-YHWH sanctuaries as the text describes it made a lasting impression on later Western culture as well. Equally important, the "discovery" of what may well have been the core of Deuteronomy (22:8ff.) suggests for many scholars that a good deal of what came to be the Early Prophets was written or edited during his reign. The debate rages on as to whether the writing/editing began under Hizkiyyahu, as I hinted at above, but the general circumstances favorable to the production of much of the text appears, in the mind of many scholars, to fit well in the waning days of monarchic Judah. Assessing the later contribution of the exilic period in this regard remains a matter of vigorous discussion among scholars.

Chapter 18. *Hizkiyyahu: Reform and Revolt:* As the text shifts for its remaining eight chapters to the Southern Kingdom, Judah, three will now be devoted to one king. Hizkiyyahu (Hezekiah) is lauded above all his predecessors, and we are immediately told why: he destroys the pagan sanctuaries and their attendant cult objects. Most of Chap. 18, however, is taken up with the problem of the threat from Assyria. The king is forced to strip more wealth from the Temple, but that does not prevent King Sanheriv (Sennacherib) of Assyria from sending a large army to menace Jerusalem.

What ensues is one of the Bible's most memorable scenes, which is retold beginning in Isa. 36, with Chap. 37 paralleling our Chap. 19. High Assyrian officials, speaking within earshot of the city walls, taunt the Jerusalem delegation, haughtily suggesting that YHWH himself has commissioned them to come against the city, and that they have overcome many other gods in their military sweep through that part of the world. The tension in their speech, outside of its sarcasm and constant insulting of YHWH, arises from the fact that it is delivered in "Judean," that is, Hebrew, and thus can be understood by the onlooking soldiers who are seemingly destined to die in the siege. As for the people's silence, while it is mandated by Hizkiyyahu (v.36), it is a hollow one, and has more dismay than defiance in it.

Cohn likens the scene to a showdown in a Western movie, and notes how, by mentioning names and titles of the participants, the writer renders the action more serious and more vivid. Its historicity is impossible to verify, but its use of typical Assyrian diplomatic language (Sweeney 2007) makes it realistic. More important, as explicated by Machinist (2000), the speech at first poses a serious challenge to Israelite theology, perhaps voicelessly joined by those Judeans who must have urged capitulation; but this makes the end result in the next chapter— the precipitous withdrawal of the Assyrian army—all the more proof of YHWH's supreme power over earthly empires.

18:1   Now it was in year three of Hoshe'a son of Ela, king of Israel:
        Hizkiyya son of Ahaz, king of Judah, became king.

2   Twenty-five years old was he at his becoming king,
        and for twenty-nine years he reigned as king in Jerusalem;
        his mother's name was Avi daughter of Zekharya.

3   He did what was right in the eyes of Yhwh,
        exactly as David his father had done:

4   it was he who removed the sanctuaries
        and smashed the standing-pillars
        and cut down the Ashera-pole
        and crushed to bits the Viper of Copper that Moshe had made,
        for until those days, the Children of Israel used to send-up-smoke
            to it
        —it was called Copperviper.

5   On Yhwh the God of Israel did he rely;
        after him there was no one like him among all the kings of Judah,
        [nor] of those who were before him.

6   He clung to Yhwh,
        and did not turn aside from [following] after him,
        but he kept his commandments, which Yhwh had commanded
            Moshe.

7   So Yhwh was with him;
        wherever he went out, he prospered.
        He rose-in-revolt against the king of Assyria, and would not
            serve him.

8   It was he who struck the Philistines as far as Gaza and its territories,
        from guards' tower to fortified town.

9   Now it was in the fourth year of King Hizkiyyahu
        —that is the seventh year of Hoshe'a son of Ela king of Israel—
        Shalman'eser king of Assyria came up against Shomeron and laid
            siege to it,

18:4 **Viper of Copper:** Literally, a snake of bronze, Heb. *nehash ha-nehoshet*. Biblical Hebrew does not differentiate between copper and its alloys (Zevit 2004). See Num. 21:4–9, where Moshe is commanded to counter a plague of snakes by hanging one made out of bronze on a standard, for those afflicted to look at and be healed. According to our passage, it had been preserved and was apparently worshipped.

7 **wherever he went out:** Equivalent to "in all that he did."

◆ 10 and he took it at the end of three years;
    in year six of Hizkiyyahu—that is year nine of Hoshe'a king of
        Israel—
    Shomeron was captured.

11 The king of Assyria exiled Israel to Assyria;
    he led them off to Halah and Havor, the River Gozan and the
        towns of Media,

12 because they had not hearkened to the voice of YHWH their God,
    but had crossed his covenant,
    all that he had commanded Moshe, the servant of YHWH—
    they had not hearkened, they had not done [it.]

13 In the fourteenth year of King Hizkiyya,
    Sanheriv king of Assyria came up against all the fortified towns of
        Judah and seized them.

14 And Hizkiyya king of Judah sent to the king of Assyria at Lakhish,
        saying:
    I have sinned—turn back from me;
    whatever you place upon me, I will bear.
    So the king of Assyria imposed upon Hizkiyya king of Judah
    three hundred talents of silver and thirty talents of gold;

15 and Hizkiyya gave over all the silver that was found in the House of
        YHWH
    and in the treasuries of the king's house.

16 At that time,
    Hizkiyya stripped the doors of YHWH's Great-Hall,
    and the posts which Hizkiyya king of Judah had overlaid,
    and gave them to the king of Assyria.

17 But the king of Assyria sent the Field-Marshal and the Chief
        Official and the Chief Cupbearer from Lakhish to King
        Hizkiyyahu with a weighty army to Jerusalem;
    they went up and came to Jerusalem,

---

11 **led them off:** Some versions read "settled them."
12 **crossed:** Violated.
13 **Sanheriv:** Pronounced *sahn-hay-REEV*; trad. English "Sennacherib," Assyrian *Sin-ahhe-eriba*, "[The God] Sin Compensated for [Dead] Brothers."
14 **sinned:** Or "given offense."
16 **posts:** A rare Hebrew word, probably from the root

'-m-n, denoting "firmness" or "support" (Cogan/Tadmor). **king of Judah:** The inclusion of the title and name seem unnecessary here.
17 **Field-Marshal:** The Heb. *tartan* probably derives from the Assyrian *turtanu*. **weighty:** Or "massive." **Washer's Field:** See note to I 1:9. It is usually translated as "Fuller's Field"; at this location, near

and when they had gone up and come, they stopped at the channel
    of the Upper Pool that is by the road of the Washer's Field

18 and called for the king.
And Elyakim son of Hilkiyyahu, [The One] Over the House,
and Shevna the [Royal] Scribe
and Yoah son of Asaf the Herald went out to them.

19 The Chief Cupbearer said to them:
Now say to Hizkiyyahu:
Thus says the Great King, the king of Assyria:
What is this reliance on which you rely?

20 Do you really think that [mere] words from lips
are counsel and might for battle?
Now, on whom do you rely, that you have risen-in-revolt
    against me?

21 Now here, you have relied for yourself on this snapped shaft
    of a reed, on Egypt,
which when a man leans on it, it enters his palm and punctures it!
That is Pharaoh king of Egypt to all who rely on him!

22 And if you say to me:
On Yʜᴡʜ our God we rely—
is it not he whose sanctuaries and whose altars Hizkiyyahu
    removed
and said to Judah and to Jerusalem:
Before this sacrificial-altar [alone] you are to bow down, in
    Jerusalem!?

23 So-now, pray make a wager with my lord, with the king of Assyria:
I will give you two thousand horses
if you are able to place riders upon them!

24 So how will you turn away the face of a single governor of the least
    of my lord's servants?
Yet you rely for yourself on Egypt for chariotry and horsemen!

---

the spring of En-Rogel at the southern tip of Jerusalem, sheep's wool would be cleaned.

18 **Elyakim:** "Yʜᴡʜ Will Fulfill." **Shevna:** Trad. English "Shebna." **Yoah:** Pronounced *yo-AH;* "Yʜᴡʜ Is Kinsman."

19 **Hizkiyyahu:** The omission of "King" here feels like a deliberate insult (Cohn 2000). **the Great King:** The usual title for the king in Assyrian usage.

22 **is it not he . . . :** Cohn (2000) sees this verse as a retrojection from the time of Yoshiyyahu (Josiah); see Chap. 23 below.

24 **governor:** The construction of the whole phrase is awkward, and so this Akkadian word, *pahat,* may be considered a gloss (Cogan/Tadmor), and is often omitted.

Chapter 19. *Jerusalem Saved:* From the low points at the beginning of the chapter, where Hizkiyyahu clothes himself in sackcloth (the garment of mourning) and the text repeats at least part of Assyria's taunting (vv.10–13), the audience is assured in just two verses (6–7) that not only will the mighty conqueror fail in his designs, but he himself will also fall. It is the prophet Yesha'yahu (Isaiah) who makes this confident pronouncement, and his appearance provides the perfect counter to military force. Here, as so often in the book of Kings, politics is overcome by the divine Word.

Literarily, this is accomplished in two passages. First comes Hizkiyyahu's heartfelt prayer (vv.15–19), mimicking an old cuneiform model (Hallo / Simpson). It ends with the familiar theme of universal acknowledgment of YHWH. More pointed is Yesha'yahu's pronouncement of the word of YHWH, beginning in v.21. Breaking into poetry, while unusual in Kings, is perfectly in keeping with the Bible's practice of inserting verse at climactic moments (see, for instance, Exod. 15 and I Sam. 2). Picking up on the "mocking" motif (v.16), the prophet sends the Assyrian king packing. Significantly, he opens with the ironic reversal of an image that will be familiar a bit later in the Bible. "The Nubile Daughter of Zion" (Jerusalem), so often an object of pity and derision in the literature that postdates the destruction of Jerusalem, here gets to do a little deriding of her own. In other imagery, the poem alternates visions of agricultural growth and plenty with ones of destruction. Thus the rescue of Jerusalem is artistically adorned, as it were, and the theological challenge has been overturned (Machinist 2000).

◆ 25 And now [too],
is it without Yhwh that I have come up against this place, to bring
   it to ruin?
It is Yhwh who said to me:
Go up against this land and wreak ruin upon it!

26 Then Elyakim son of Hilkiyyahu and Shevna and Yoah to the Chief
   Cupbearer said:
Pray speak to your servants in Aramaic, for we understand it,
but do not speak with us in Judean within earshot of the fighting-
   people who are on the wall!

27 But the Chief Cupbearer said to them:
Is it to your lord and to you that my lord has sent me to speak these
   words?
Is it not to the men sitting on the wall,
[who will have] to eat their filth and drink the "water of their legs"
   with you?

28 And the Chief Cupbearer stood forth and called out in a loud voice
   in Judean,
he spoke and said:
Hearken to the word of the Great King, the king of Assyria:

29 Thus says the king:
Do not let Hizkiyyahu deceive you,
for he is not able to rescue you from my hand,

30 and do not let Hizkiyyahu make you rely on Yhwh, saying:
Yhwh will rescue, yes, rescue us;
this city will not be given into the hand of the king of Assyria!

31 Do not hearken to Hizkiyyahu,
for thus says the king of Assyria:

25 **And now:** The "and," part of the usual construction, is in some manuscripts but not in MT.
26 **Aramaic:** Beginning around this time, Aramaic
became the diplomatic language of the western
Near East, lasting for centuries. It later became the
main language of Jews (through the Roman era),
and survived in classical Jewish texts such as the
Talmud and some prayers, as well as the standard
form of the marriage contract. It is also still actively
spoken, independent of Jews, in some areas of the
Middle East. **Judean:** The language later known as
Hebrew.
27 **filth . . . "water of their legs":** *Qere* euphemisms
for excrement and urine.

29 **my:** According to ancient versions, including LXX;
MT has "his."
31 **Make me a blessing-gift:** Heb. *berakha,* most often
"blessing," can sometimes mean "gift," as in Gen.
33:11. Cogan/Tadmor see the construction here
(with "make") as deriving from Akkadian usage,
and others have remarked on the Assyrian flavor of
the speech. **vine . . . fig tree:** Ironically playing
on the ultimate description of peace and security
in I Kings 5:5 (under Shelomo). At the same time,
Cogan/Tadmor point out that, as part of their reset-
tlement policy, the Assyrians had to treat their captives well.

◆ Make me a blessing-gift, and come out to me [in surrender],
and each will eat of his vine, each of his fig tree,
and each will drink waters of his cistern,

32 until my coming to take you away to a land like your land,
a land of new-wine and grain, a land of bread and vineyards, a land
of shining olive oil and honey,
that you may live and not die.
So do not hearken to Hizkiyyahu
when he incites you, saying:
Yhwh will rescue us!

33 Did the gods of the [other] nations rescue, yes, rescue their land
from the hand of the king of Assyria?

34 Where are the gods of Hamat or Arpad?
Where are the gods of Sefarvayim, Heina, and Ivva?
Indeed, did they rescue Shomeron from my hand?

35 Who is it among all the gods of these lands that rescued their land
from my hand,
that Yhwh should rescue Jerusalem from my hand?

36 But the people were silent, and did not answer him a word,
for it was the king's command, saying:
You are not to answer him!

37 Then Elyakim son of Hilkiyya, [The One] Over the Household,
and Shevna the Scribe, and Yoah son of Asaf the Herald, came to
Hizkiyyahu, with torn garments,
and they told him the words of the Chief Cupbearer.

19:1 It was, when King Hizkiyyahu heard,
that he tore his garments
and covered himself in sackcloth
and came into the House of Yhwh.

2 Then he sent Elyakim, [The One] Over the Household, and Shevna
the Scribe, and the elders of the priests, covered in sackcloth,
to Yesha'yahu the prophet, son of Amotz;

---

34 **Hamat . . . Arpad . . . Shomeron:** In fact, these cities were conquered earlier in the century, by other kings (Cogan/Tadmor). Based on the LXX and Isa. 36:19, a phrase ("And where are the gods of the region of Shomeron?") may be missing here.

19:2 **Yesha'yahu:** Pronounced *ye-shah-YAH-hu*, "Yhwh Has Delivered," the great prophet (English: Isaiah) whose book follows Kings in the Hebrew Bible.

3　they said to him:
Thus says Hizkiyyahu:
A day of distress, rebuke, and scorn is this day,
for children have come to the womb-breaking,
but strength there is none for giving birth!

4　Perhaps Yhwh your God will hear all the words of the Chief
Cupbearer with which the king of Assyria, his lord, sent him to
mock the Living God
and will give rebuke because of the words that Yhwh your God has
heard—
so lift up a prayer on behalf of the remnant that is found!

5　So the servants of King Hizkiyyahu came to Yesha'yahu,

6　and Yesha'yahu said to them:
Thus are you to say to your lord:
Thus says Yhwh:
Do not be afraid before the words that you have heard,
with which the serving-lads of the king of Assyria have
blasphemed me!

7　Here, I will put a spirit in him,
so that he hears some hearsay and has to return to his land,
and I will cause him to fall by the sword in his land!

8　The Chief Cupbearer returned and found the king of Assyria
engaging in battle against Livna,
for he had heard that he had marched on from Lakhish.

9　He heard [a report] about Tirhaka king of Kush, saying:
Here, he has gone out to engage in battle with you!
So he sent messengers back to Hizkiyyahu, saying:
Thus are you to say to Hizkiyyahu king of Judah, saying:

10　Do not let your God on whom you rely beguile you, saying [to
yourself]:
Jerusalem will not be given into the hand of the king of Assyria!

4　**to mock the Living God:** The language echoes the
David and Golyat (Goliath) story in I Sam. 17—or
was that one perhaps cast in Assyrian costume? See
the Commentary there, and also v.16 here.　**give
rebuke:** Or "punish" (Gray 1970).　**lift up a prayer:**
Or "make intercession."　**the remnant:** Jerusalem.
7　**hearsay:** Or "rumor."

8　**returned:**　Cogan / Tadmor　have　"withdrew."
Livna: Somewhere in the lowlands of Judah (see
8:22).
9　**He heard:** The king of Assyria.　**Tirhaka:** According to Assyrian records, he actually succeeded to the
throne a bit later, in 690.　**Kush:** Ethiopia.

◆   11   Here, *you* have heard what the kings of Assyria did to all the [other]
              lands, devoting-them-to-destruction—
          so will *you* be rescued?

     12   Did the gods of the nations whom my fathers brought to ruin
              rescue them:
          Gozan and Harran,
          Retzef and the Children of Ehden who were in Telassar?

     13   Where is he, the king of Hamat, or the king of Arpad, or the king
              of La'ir, of Sefarvayim, Heina, and Ivva?

     14   Hizkiyyahu took the letter from the hand of the messengers and
              read it;
          then he went up to the House of YHWH,
          and Hizkiyyahu spread it out in the presence of YHWH.

     15   And Hizkiyyahu prayed in the presence of YHWH, he said:
          O YHWH, God of Israel, [Who is] Seated on the Winged-Sphinxes,
          you are God, you alone, of all the kingdoms of the earth;
          you made the heavens and the earth.

     16   Incline, O YHWH, your ear and hearken;
          open, O YHWH, your eyes and see,
          and hear the words of Sanheriv which he sent to mock the
              Living God!

     17   In truth, O YHWH, the kings of Assyria have laid waste to nations
              and their land[s],

     18   and they have put their gods to the fire
          —for they are not gods,
          but the work of human hands, wood and stone—
          so they have demolished them.

     19   But now, O YHWH our God,
          pray deliver us from his hand,
          so that all the kingdoms of the earth may know that you, YHWH,
              are God, you alone!

     20   And Yesha'yahu son of Amotz sent [word] to Hizkiyyahu, saying:
          Thus says YHWH, the God of Israel:

---

12 **Gozan . . . :** The places mentioned here are all areas
    of Assyria.   **Harran:** The famous crossroads town
    (its literal meaning) from where Avraham (Abra-
    ham) and his family depart for Canaan in Gen. 11.
14 **letter:** MT has plural, which does not fit the second
    half of the sentence; I follow ancient versions.

18 **put their gods to the fire:** Not a reflection of the
    usual Assyrian practice, which was to tolerate other
    religions; so the verse is probably a polemic (Cogan/
    Tadmor).

◆ That which you prayed to me concerning Sanheriv king of Assyria,
    I have heard.

21 This is the word that Yʜwʜ speaks concerning him:
    She despises you, she derides you,
    the Nubile Daughter of Zion;
    after you, she shakes her head after you,
    the Daughter of Jerusalem:

22   Whom have you mocked and blasphemed?
    Against whom have your raised [your] voice?
    You have lifted up your eyes on high
    against the Holy One of Israel!

23   By the hand of your messengers you have mocked Yʜwʜ,
    you said: With my vast chariotry
    I have gone up the loftiest mountains,
    the flanks of the Levanon;
    I cut down the highest of its cedars,
    the choicest of its junipers.
    And I came to its farthest lodge,
    its garden-like forest.

24   It was I who dug and drank
    the water of strangers,
    and I dried up with the soles of my feet
    all the Nile-streams of Egypt.

25   Have you not heard? From of old I did it,
    in former days I fashioned it;
    now I bring it to pass,
    and it is:
    crashing into wrecked heaps
    fortified towns,

26   while their settled-folk, short-armed,
    were dismayed and confounded.
    They were [like] the herbage of the field,
    the green grass,
    the straw of the rooftops, blasted
    before the east wind;

---

21 **concerning:** Heb. *'al* can also be understood as "against" (Cohn 2000).

26 **short-armed:** Powerless. **straw of the rooftops:** Grain was usually processed on the flat Israelite rooftops. **before the east wind:** Heb. *qdym,* the reading in the Dead Sea Isaiah Scroll, which is clearly more correct than MT's *qmh,* "standing grain."

Chapter 20. *Hizkiyyahu and the Prophet Yesha'yahu:* In a twist from what by now seems like a well-worn motif, a sick king is given a reprieve. As Hizkiyyahu's praying worked previously, so it does here as well. The chapter abounds in interesting images: on the positive side, the king is shown a sundial going backward, confirming that his disease has indeed been reversed, while negatively, Hizkiyyahu's displaying of Jerusalem's treasures is used by the prophet to remind the king (and the reader) that within a few generations, treasures and princes alike will be exiled to Babylon. So the clock cannot be turned back after all.

Hizkiyyahu's reign comes to an end with the barest of mentions of what modern historians of Jerusalem remember him for: the crucial step of making the city's water supply from the Gihon Spring more accessible. Not cited at all is what is of equal or greater importance: the considerable expansion of the city to the so-called Western Hill (today's Jewish and Armenian Quarters of the Old City). From this period of history on, at the very least, Jerusalem is a city of consequence.

27 your staying, your going, and your coming I know,
[yes], and your raging against me.

28 Because you have raged against me,
and your roaring has ascended to my ears,
I will put my hook in your nostrils
and my bridle in your lips,
and I will turn you back on the way
by which you came.

29 And this shall be the sign for you:
eat this year the wild-growth,
and in the second year, the aftergrowth,
and in the third year, sow and harvest and plant vineyards,
and eat their fruit.

30 And the survivors of the House of Judah, the remaining ones,
will add rootgrowth below,
and will produce fruit above;

31 for from Jerusalem shall go forth a remnant,
and the survivors from Mount Zion
—the zeal of Yʜᴡʜ of the Forces-On-High will do this!

32 Therefore, thus says Yʜᴡʜ concerning the king of Assyria:
He shall not enter this city,
he shall not shoot an arrow there,
he shall not advance upon it [with a] shield,
he shall not pile up a siege-mound against it!

33 By the way that he came, he shall return,
but this city he shall not enter
—the Utterance of Yʜᴡʜ!

34 And I will shield this city to deliver it, for my sake and for the sake
of David my servant.

---

27 **[yes], and your raging against me:** Probably a dittography, where a scribe erroneously repeated a phrase that he had just written down.

28 **roaring:** This according to ancient versions and later commentators, who read Heb. *shaanankha*, "complacency," as *she'onkhato*. **hook . . . bridle:** A form of humiliation depicted on Assyrian monuments (Cogan/Tadmor).

29 **the sign:** Namely, Yʜᴡʜ will still provide food, despite the devastating Assyrian invasion.

35 It was on that very night
that the messenger of YHWH went forth
and struck down in the camp of Assyria a hundred and eighty-five
thousand;
they started-early at daybreak,
and here, all of them were corpses, dead men!

36 So Sanheriv king of Assyria marched off and went away and
returned [home],
and stayed in Nineveh.

37 Now it was, when he was bowing down in the house of Nisrokh
his god,
that Adrammelekh and Sar'etzer his sons struck him down with the
sword.
They escaped to the land of Ararat,
and Esar-haddon his son became king in his place.

20:1 In those days,
Hizkiyyahu became sick, to [the point of] death.
And Yesha'yahu son of Amotz, the prophet, came to him and said
to him:
Thus says YHWH:
Charge your household,
for you are about to die, and will not live!

2 He turned his face to the wall
and prayed to YHWH, saying:

3 Please, O YHWH,
pray recall how I have walked about before you with truthfulness
and with a whole heart,
and what was good in your eyes, I have done!
And Hizkiyyahu wept with a great weeping.

35 **struck down:** Apparently in a plague.
36 **marched off:** Lit. "pulled up [stakes]," the physical act of pulling out the tent pegs for travel.
37 **Nisrokh:** Not a known divine name, so possibly a miscopying of another name. It may be intentional (Cogan/Tadmor). **Adrammelekh and Sar'etzer:** Ironic Hebraized names ("Glorious King" and "Protect the Ruler"). According to Assyrian records, Sanheriv was assassinated by another individual, some twenty years after the siege of Jerusalem. The Bible

nevertheless closely connects the two events, in classic Deuteronomistic fashion. **Ararat:** Armenia. **Esar-haddon:** Akkadian *Ashur-ah-iddina*, "[The god] Ashur Has Given a Brother."
20:1 **Charge your household:** That is, give them final instructions.
2 **turned his face to the wall:** See note to I Kings 21:4.
3 **walked about before you:** Followed God's will; see the same expression regarding Avraham in Gen. 17:1.

◆ 4 Now Yesha'yahu had not yet gone out of the middle courtyard
when the word of Y<small>HWH</small> [came] to him, saying:

5 Return, you are to say to Hizkiyyahu, *Nagid* of my people:
Thus says Y<small>HWH</small>, the God of David your father:
I have heard your prayer,
I have seen your tears.
Here, I am healing you;
on the third day, you will go up to the House of Y<small>HWH</small>.

6 I will add fifteen years to your days,
and from the grasp of the king of Assyria I will rescue you, along
with this city;
I will shield this city
for my sake and for the sake of David my servant.

7 Then Yesha'yahu said:
Fetch a cake of figs.
They fetched it and placed it on the boil,
and he lived.

8 And Hizkiyyahu said to Yesha'yahu:
What is the sign that Y<small>HWH</small> will heal me,
so that I may go up by the third day to the House of Y<small>HWH</small>?

9 Yesha'yahu said:
This will be for you the sign from Y<small>HWH</small>
that Y<small>HWH</small> will do the thing that he has promised:
the shadow has gone forward ten steps;
can it return ten steps?

10 He said:
It is easy for the shadow to lengthen ten steps;
not so, that the shadow can return backward ten steps.

11 So Yesha'yahu the prophet called out to Y<small>HWH</small>,
and he made the shadow return by the steps by which it had gone
down on the step-dial of Ahaz, backward by ten steps.

---

4 **middle courtyard:** Between the palace and the Temple.

5 *Nagid:* See note to I Kings 1:35. Since the term has not been used from I Kings 14:7 until now, it is clear that Hizkiyyahu is being singled out in a positive way. **the third day:** Either because he was healed or because he was now ritually purified.

7 **figs . . . boil:** It was widely believed that figs had curative properties. **lived:** Recovered.

9 **shadow:** On a sundial.

10 **easy for the shadow:** Heb. *nakeil la-tzeil.*

Chapter 21. *Evil Kings: Menashe and Amon:* The long reign of Menashe is the last straw in YHWH's toleration of Judah's idolatry. We know what is to come immediately, as the usual formula, "he did what was evil in the eyes of YHWH," is amplified by the ominous phrase "according to the abominations of [the Canaanites]." From v.12 on, a sentence of doom is pronounced over Jerusalem and Judah.

Of Menashe's successor Amon, it is only necessary for the text to note, first, how he continues in his father's idolatrous footsteps, and second, how both he and those who assassinate him are done away with. His death may have come at the hands of an anti-Assyrian faction who were themselves killed by the "Landed People." Their actions, which resulted in installing his eight-year-old son Yoshiyyahu on the throne, may have held off the Assyrians.

12 At [about] that time,
    Merodakh Bal'adan son of Bal'adan king of Babylon sent letters
        and a gift to Hizkiyyahu,
    for he had heard that Hizkiyyahu was sick.
13 And Hizkiyyahu was pleased with them,
    and he had them see his whole storehouse—the silver, the gold, the
        spices, and the fine oil,
    his weapons house,
    and all that was to be found in his treasuries.
    There was not a thing that Hizkiyyahu did not have them see in his
        house or in all his kingdom.
14 Then Yesha'yahu the prophet came to King Hizkiyyahu and said to
        him:
    What did these men say,
    and from where do they come to you?
    Hizkiyyahu said:
    From a land far away they came, from Babylon.
15 He said:
    What did they see in your house?
    He said:
    Everything that is in my house they saw;
    there was not a thing that I did not have them see in my treasuries.
16 Then Yesha'yahu said to Hizkiyyahu:
    Hear the word of YHWH:
17 Here, days are coming
    when everything in your house will be carried off,
    [all] that your fathers amassed-as-treasure up until this day, to
        Babylon;
    there will not be a thing left, says YHWH!

12 **At [about] that time:** Scholars have noted that this phrase is an editorial device, connecting originally independent sections. **Merodakh Bal'adan:** According to some versions and manuscripts; MT has "Berodakh Bal'adan." The name in Akkadian is *Marduk-apla-iddina*, "[The God] Marduk Gave the Inheriting Son." This foe of Assyria reigned from 722 to 710 and again from 704 to 703.

13 **was pleased with them:** Following versions and Isa. 39:2, with *s-m-h* replacing MT's *sh-m-'*, "heard about them." **them:** Presumably the messengers from the Babylonian king. **storehouse:** Heb. *[bet] nekhot*, a loan word from Akkadian.

◆ 18 And some of your sons who have issued from you, whom you have
  begotten, will be taken away,
  and they will become officials in the Great-Hall of the king of
  Babylon.
19 Hizkiyyahu said to Yesha'yahu:
  Good is the word of YHWH that you have spoken.
  For he said [to himself]:
  Will there not [at least] be trustworthy peace in my days?
20 Now the rest of the events of Hizkiyyahu, and all his mighty-deeds,
  —how he made the pool and the channel, and brought the waters
  into the city—
  are they not written in the Record of Yearly Events of the Kings of
  Judah?
21 Hizkiyyahu lay beside his fathers,
  and Menashe his son reigned as king in his place.

21:1 Twelve years old was Menashe at his becoming king,
  and for fifty-five years he reigned as king in Jerusalem;
  his mother's name was Heftzi-va.
2 He did what was evil in the eyes of YHWH,
  according to the abominations of the nations that YHWH had
  dispossessed before the Children of Israel:
3 he once again built the sanctuaries that Hizkiyyahu his father had
  demolished,
  and erected sacrificial-altars to Baal,
  and made an Ashera-pole, just as Ah'av king of Israel had made,
  and bowed down to all the Forces of the Heavens, and served them;
4 he built sacrificial-altars in the House of YHWH
  about which YHWH had said: In Jerusalem I will set my name!,

---

18 **sons who have issued from you:** Idiomatically, "your offspring" (Cogan/Tadmor).
19 **trustworthy:** Secure.
20 **the pool and the channel:** The famous Siloam Tunnel, in which workers dug a third of a mile through rock from the Gihon Spring (outside of Jerusalem's city wall to the east) to a pool which would supply water to the city in time of siege. A contemporary inscription chronicling the completion of the work has survived, and was uncovered in 1880.
21:1 **Menashe:** Pronounced *meh-nah-SHEH;* trad. English "Manasseh." The meaning seems to be "He

Who Makes Forget" (the name of one of Yosef's [Joseph's] sons; see Gen. 41:51). **Heftzi-va:** Pronounced *hef-tzee-VAH.* It means "My Delight Is in Her"; trad. English "Hephzibah."
3 **sacrificial-altars:** LXX has the singular here.
4–6 **he built . . . he had his son cross . . . made:** The form of the Hebrew verbs here points to archival style; to indicate a difference from the customary phraseology, I have omitted some "and"s before these verbs (see Gray 1970, following Montgomery).
4 **he built sacrificial-altars:** To whom? Perhaps something is missing here; JPS adds "to them."

5 and he built sacrificial-altars to all the Forces of the Heavens
in the two courtyards of the House of YHWH;
6 he had his son cross through the fire
and practiced soothsaying and divination, made [contact with]
ghosts and all-knowing ones—
he did much that was evil in the eyes of YHWH, to provoke him.
7 And he placed the statue of Ashera that he had made
in the House about which YHWH had said to David and to Shelomo
his son:
In this House in Jerusalem, which I have chosen from all the tribes
of Israel,
I will set my name for the ages,
8 and I will not continue to make Israel's foot wander from the soil
that I gave to their fathers;
if only they take care to observe according to all that I have
commanded them,
including all the Instruction that my servant Moshe commanded
them.
9 But they did not hearken,
and Menashe led them astray to do what was evil, more than the
nations that YHWH had wiped out before the Children of Israel.
10 So YHWH spoke by the hand of his servants the prophets, saying:
11 Because Menashe king of Judah has done these abominations,
practicing more evil than all that the Amorites did who were
before him,
and has caused Judah too to sin with his Illicit-Things,
12 therefore,
thus says YHWH, the God of Israel:
Here, I am about to bring such evil upon Jerusalem and Judah
that all who hear of it, their two ears will ring!

6 **son:** LXX has "sons." **divination:** Foretelling the future, often through use of techniques involving shapes in water or metal. **ghosts:** The Hebrew word (sing. *'ov*) derives from a pit where ghosts are summoned. It and "all-knowing ones" are used to describe both them and those who deal with them. **all-knowing ones:** Spirits.

11 **Amorites:** Often used as a general designation for Canaanites.
12 **ring:** See I Sam. 3:11 for the same disaster terminology.

Chapter 22. *Yoshiyyahu's Accession; The Finding of the Scroll:* Having been told a few chapters previously about how Judah's greatest king since the United Monarchy was Hizkiyyahu, the text introduces a new hero, Yoshiyyahu, another one who "did what was good in the eyes of YHWH," and innocuously goes on to describe some Temple repairs and the payment for them, a motif which we encountered earlier. In the midst of the repairs, however, a "Record of the Instruction" is found. When it is read before the king, he breaks down, realizing that this divine Instruction, whatever its exact identity, has not been heeded for generations. In typical Kings fashion, this is confirmed by prophetic speech, this time from a female member of the profession (Hulda), and the news is not good: Judah and Jerusalem will indeed eventually fall, and Yoshiyyahu's only consolation is that he himself will not live to see it. Similar thoughts had been addressed to Hizkiyyahu in 20:16–18.

It has long been asserted that the newly found scroll is the book of Deuteronomy, or at least its core. Among that book's major goals, after all, are the extirpation of idolatry and the centralization of the sacrificial cult in Jerusalem, and the language applied to Yoshiyyahu is a reprise of Deuteronomic phrases (see 23:25 below). Further, the discovery fits a known pattern in the ancient world, where a king's desire to promulgate new laws is often accompanied by the publication of an authoritative document. If that scroll is represented as being of hoary lineage, as in this case, so much the better.

Amid the dramatic scenario of the newly found scroll and national revival, an odd note can be heard. Three of Yoshiyyahu's court officials have names of animals that live in concealed areas: the rock badger (*shafan*), the mouse (*'akhbor*), and the mole (*hulda*). This is possibly a coincidence, but it may also be slyly purposeful in a narrative that describes the unearthing of a long-lost document in the bowels of the Temple. I am not prepared, however, to declare this chapter the Bible's version of *The Wind in the Willows.*

13 I will stretch out over Jerusalem the measuring-line of Shomeron
    and the plumb-bob of the House of Ah'av,
  and I will wipe Jerusalem clean as one wipes a dish clean,
    wiping and turning it over on its face.
14 And I will forsake the remnant of my inheritance
    and give them into the hand of their enemies,
  so that they become spoil and pillage for all their enemies,
15 because they have done what was evil in my eyes, and have been
    provoking me
  from the day that their fathers went out of Egypt until this day.
16 —Now even more, Menashe spilled innocent blood, exceedingly
    much,
  until he filled Jerusalem from one end to the [other] end,
  aside from his sin by which he caused Judah to sin,
  by doing what was evil in the eyes of YHWH.
17 Now the rest of the events of Menashe, and all that he did,
  and the sins that he sinned—
  are they not written in the Record of Yearly Events of the Kings of
    Judah?
18 Menashe lay beside his fathers;
  he was buried in the garden of his house, in the garden of Uzza,
  and Amon his son reigned as king in his place.

19 Twenty-two years old was Amon at his becoming king,
  and for two years he reigned as king in Jerusalem;
  his mother's name was Meshullemet daughter of Harutz, from Yotva.
20 He did what was evil in the eyes of YHWH, as Menashe his father
    had done:
21 he walked in all the way that his father had walked,
  and served the Illicit-Things that his father had served, and bowed
    down to them;
22 he abandoned YHWH, the God of his fathers,
  and did not walk in the way of YHWH.

13 **measuring-line . . . plumb-bob . . . as one wipes a dish clean:** Cogan/Tadmor note the irony of using images of construction and satiation to point to ruin and disaster.
16 **end:** See note to 10:21. **his sin by which he caused Judah to sin:** A measure of Menashe's low "rating" is this verbal comparison to the much-vilified northern king Yorov'am I.

18 **in the garden:** After Hizkiyyahu, Judean kings were no longer buried in the City of David, for lack of space (Cogan/Tadmor). **the garden of Uzza:** Benjamin Mazar takes this to be Siloam (Cogan/Tadmor). **Amon:** Ironically, the name means "Faithful."
19 **Yotva:** A town in Galilee, some nine miles north of Nazareth.

23 And Amon's [court-]servants conspired against him,
and put the king to death in his house.

24 But the Landed People struck down all those who had conspired
against Amon,
and the Landed People made Yoshiyyahu his son king in his place.

25 Now the rest of the events of Amon, [and all] that he did—
are they not written in the Record of Yearly Events of the Kings of
Judah?

26 He was buried in his burial-place in the garden of Uzza,
and Yoshiyyahu his son became king in his place.

22:1 Eight years old was Yoshiyyahu at his becoming king,
and for thirty-one years he reigned as king in Jerusalem;
his mother's name was Yedida daughter of Adaya, from Botzkat.

2 He did what was right in the eyes of YHWH,
and walked in all the way of David his father;
he did not turn aside to the right or to the left.

3 Now it was in the eighteenth year of King Yoshiyyahu:
the king sent Shafan son of Atzalyahu son of Meshullam the Scribe
to the House of YHWH, saying:

4 Go up to Hilkiyyahu the Great Priest and have him sum up the
silver that has been brought to the House of YHWH,
which the guardians of the threshold have gathered from the people,

5 and let them give it into the hand of those doing the work, those
accountable in the House of YHWH;
they shall give it over to those doing the work who are in the House
of YHWH, to strengthen the breaches in the House of YHWH—

6 to the carvers, to the builders, and to the wall-masons,
and for purchasing wood and hewn stone, to strengthen the House.

7 But there need not be reckoning with them for the silver that is
given into their hand,
for in trustworthy-fashion they deal.

---

25 **[and all]:** Inserted by ancient manuscripts and LXX.
26 **Yoshiyyahu:** Pronounced *yo-shee-YAH-hu*, and possibly meaning "YHWH Will Grant."
22:1 **Botzkat:** East of Lakhish, in the Judean Lowlands.
3 **Shafan:** Pronounced *shah-FAHN*. The hyrax or the rock badger, an animal mentioned in Lev. 11:5 (see Commentary to this chapter).
4 **Hilkiyyahu:** Pronounced *hil-kee-YAH-hu*. "YHWH Is My Portion"; trad. English "Hilkiah." Some have

suggested that he is identical to the father of the prophet Jeremiah, although the latter's family came from Anatot, and seem not to have been serving as priests any longer. **Great Priest:** High Priest.
5 **accountable:** Those who hired the actual workers (Cogan/Tadmor).
6 **to strengthen:** Ancient manuscripts and LXX add "the cracks of."
7 **reckoning:** Or "auditing," in the financial sense.

8   Then Hilkiyyahu the Great Priest said to Shafan the Scribe:
    I have found a [written] Record of the Instruction in the House of
       Yнwн!
    And Hilkiyyahu gave the record to Shafan, and he read it.

9   Then Shafan the Scribe came to the king
    and returned word to the king;
    he said:
    Your servants have melted down the silver that was found in the House
    and have given it over to the hand of those doing the work, those
       accountable in the House of Yнwн.

10   And Shafan the Scribe told the king, saying:
    Hilkiyya the priest has given me a [written] record.
    And Shafan read it before the king.

11   It was, when the king heard the words of the Record of the
       Instruction,
    that he tore his garments;

12   and the king commanded Hilkiyya the priest and Ahikam son of
       Shafan and Akhbor son of Mikhaya and Shafan the Scribe and
       Asaya Servant of the king, saying:

13   Go, inquire of Yнwн on my behalf, on behalf of the people, and
       on behalf of all Judah
    concerning the words of this Record that has been found,
    for great is the wrath of Yнwн that has been kindled against us
    because our fathers did not hearken to the words of this Record,
    to observe all that is written concerning us!

14   So Hilkiyyahu the priest and Ahikam and Akhbor and Shafan and
       Asaya
    went to Hulda the prophetess, wife of Shallum son of Tikva son of
       Harhas, Guardian of the [Royal] Garments
    —now she was dwelling in Jerusalem, in the Second [District]—
    and they spoke to her.

---

8 **Record of the Instruction:** See Commentary.
9 **melted down:** Lit., "poured out."
12 **Ahikam:** "My Brother Has Risen [for battle]." **Akhbor:** "Mouse." **Mikhaya:** "Who Is Like Yнwн?" **Asaya:** "Yнwн Has Made/Created."
13 **wrath:** Or "venom" (Meir Gruber, quoted in Cogan/Tadmor). **written:** Others, "prescribed."

concerning: Alternatively, "against."
14 **Hulda:** Pronounced *hool-DAH,* and meaning "Mole." Female prophets are likewise attested in seventh-century Assyria (Cogan/Tadmor). **Second [District]:** West of the Temple and palace, today's Jewish and Armenian Quarters in the Old City.

Chapter 23. *Yoshiyyahu's Reform; His Death:* After a great public ceremony in vv.1–3, in which, as Mann notes, the word "all" is used for emphasis, and during which the newly found document, now significantly called the "Record of the Covenant," is read before the people, the text turns (v.4) to a rapid-fire and detailed recounting of the religious purge initiated by Yoshiyyahu. There is no dialogue to interrupt the violence or to oppose the king's actions, and the verbs used are in the singular, as if to personalize the action (Cohn 2000).

Except for the burial site of the prophet who had foretold the purge all the way back in I Kings 13:2–3, and that of another prophet, everything not tied to YHWH is not only physically destroyed but rendered ritually polluted as well. One positive act is the re-observance of the Passover offering, which the text portrays as having been neglected for centuries. Something similar had taken place in Chap. 5 of Joshua, as an affirmation of the invaders' peoplehood. Here too it is a fitting symbol of a utopian attempt to reorder society.

Despite the superlatives applied to Yoshiyyahu, surpassing the description of Hizkiyyahu a century earlier, the decree against the Southern Kingdom is not canceled, and the king himself is overtaken by the events of international politics. On a mission northward to stop Egyptian aid to Assyria, he is killed by the Pharaoh; interestingly, the exact details are not given. So dies the last hope of Judah. His great reform as described by the text appears as too little, too late. The reign of his son Yehoahaz lasts for only three months, and is succeeded by an Egyptian-appointed puppet king, Yehoyakim. Both are rated by the text as "evil."

15 She said to them:
   Thus says Yhwh, the God of Israel:
   Say to the man who sent you to me:
16 Thus says Yhwh:
   Here, I am about to bring evil upon this place and upon its
       inhabitants,
   all the words of the Record that the king of Judah has read,
17 because they have abandoned me and sent-up-smoke to other
       gods,
   in order to provoke me with all the works of their hands—
   so my wrath will be kindled against this place, and will not be
       extinguished!
18 But to the king of Judah, the one sending you to inquire of
       Yhwh,
   thus you are to say to him:
   Thus says Yhwh, the God of Israel:
   As for the words that you have heard,
19 because your heart was tender and you humbled yourself before
       Yhwh
   when you heard what I spoke concerning this place and concerning
       its inhabitants,
   to become a desolation and a curse,
   and you tore your garments and wept before me,
   I too have heard
   —Yhwh's Utterance.
20 Therefore,
   here, I will gather you to your fathers;
   you will be gathered to your burial-place in peace,
   so that your eyes will not see all the evil that I am about to bring
       upon this place.
   And they returned word to the king.

16 **evil:** Or "disaster." **words:** B-R gloss as "words of exhortation."
19 **a desolation and a curse:** Echoing Deut. 28:37.

20 **in peace:** Yoshiyyahu's end in 23:29–30 belies this prediction, a clear indication of separate traditions or editions.

23:1 The king sent
    and had all the elders of Judah and Jerusalem gathered to him.
   2 Then the king went up to the House of YHWH,
    and all the men of Judah and all the inhabitants of Jerusalem
      with him,
    and the priests and the prophets and all the people, great and small,
    and he read in their ears all the words of the Record of the
      Covenant that had been found in the House of YHWH.
   3 And the king stood by the standing-column
    and cut a covenant in the presence of YHWH
    to walk after YHWH, to keep his commandments, his testimonies,
      and his laws
    with all [one's] heart and with all [one's] being,
    to fulfill the words of this covenant that were written in this
      Record.
    And all the people took a stand in the covenant.
   4 Then the king charged Hilkiyyahu the Great Priest and the priests
      of second rank and the guardians of the threshold
    to take out of the Great-Hall of YHWH
    all the vessels that had been made for Baal and for Ashera and for
      all the Forces of the Heavens,
    and he burned them outside Jerusalem, on the terraces of Kidron,
    and carried their ashes to Bet-El.
   5 And he put an end to the clerics whom the kings of Judah had
      given-license to send-up-smoke at the sanctuaries in the towns of
      Judah and in the [sacred] places around Jerusalem,
    namely, those who sent-up-smoke to Baal, to the sun, to the moon,
      and to the constellations,
    and to all the Forces of the Heavens.
   6 And he brought out the Ashera-pole from the House of YHWH,
      outside Jerusalem, to the Wadi Kidron,

23:2 **men of Judah:** Cogan / Tadmor see this as an anachronistic term inserted here; it could thus be rendered "fighting-men of Judah." **great and small:** Lit., "from small to great"; others, "from oldest to youngest."

   3 **the king stood by the standing-column:** See, similarly, 11:14. Perhaps this was a symbolic act of some kind. **took a stand in:** Possibly meaning "agreed to."

5 **clerics:** A term (Heb. *komer*) used only of foreign (pagan) priests in the Hebrew Bible. **given-license:** Or "appointed." **constellations:** Or "planets."

6 **the Wadi Kidron:** The valley to the east of Jerusalem. **burned . . . crushed . . . dust:** Directly evoking the fate of the Golden Calf in Exod. 32:20.

and burned it in the Wadi Kidron;

then he crushed it into dust

and threw its dust over the burial-ground of the [common] people.

7 And he demolished the houses of the [male] prostitutes that were
in the House of YHWH,

where the women had been weaving coverings for the Ashera-pole.

8 And he brought in all the priests from the towns of Judah,

and he rendered *tamei* the sanctuaries where the priests had sent-
up-smoke

from Geva to Be'er-Sheva,

and he demolished the sanctuaries at the gates that were at the
entrance to the gate of Yehoshua, commander of the city,

which were at a person's left [entering] the gate of the city.

9 However, the priests of the sanctuaries did not go up to the
sacrificial-altar of YHWH in Jerusalem,

although they ate unleavened-bread among their brothers.

10 And he rendered *tamei* the *Tofet*/Hearth that is in the Valley of Ben
Hinnom,

so that no [one could] cross his son or his daughter through the fire
to the Molekh.

11 And he put an end to the horses that the kings of Judah had
dedicated to the sun at the entrance to the House of YHWH,

near the chamber of Natan-Melekh the Official that was in the
[Temple] colonnade,

and the chariots of the sun he burned with fire.

---

7 **[male] prostitutes:** See note to I Kings 14:24.
women . . . weaving: Coverings for statues of gods
are known elsewhere in the ancient Near East. This
is apparently one of the few tasks which actively
included women at Israelite sanctuaries.

8 **rendered *tamei*:** That is, ritually polluted, and so
permanently unfit for sacred use. **Geva:** Possibly Giv'a (Gibeah), a few miles north of Jerusalem, although some have suggested a site farther
north. **gate of Yehoshua:** Trad. English "Gate of
Joshua"; identity unclear. **left:** South.

9 **However, the priests . . . :** Their rights are somewhat restricted here.

10 **Valley of Ben Hinnom:** Pronounced *ben hee-NOHM*.
It was directly south of the present Old City walls.
Heb. *Gei Hinnom* (also in the Aramaic form *Gehenna*),
because of the terrible deeds done in this location,
became the term for Hell in later Jewish literature.

11 **horses . . . sun:** The connection between the two,
including in worship, is known in both Mesopotamia and Assyria. **entrance:** Following versions,
whereas MT has an erroneous vowel. **colonnade:**
A loan word from Persian (*parvarim*).

12 And as for the sacrificial-altars that were on the roof of the upper
    chamber of Ahaz, which the kings of Judah had made,
and the sacrificial-altars that Menashe had made in the two
    courtyards of the House of Yhwh,
the king demolished them;
he hastened them from there and threw their rubble into the Wadi
    Kidron.

13 And the sanctuaries which were facing Jerusalem, which were to
    the right/south of the Mount of the Ruinbringer,
which Shelomo king of Israel had built to Astarte, the Detestable-
    One of the Sidonians,
to Kemosh the Detestable-One of Moav,
and to Milkom the Abominable-One of the Children of Ammon,
the king rendered *tamei*.

14 And he smashed the standing-pillars,
and cut down the Ashera-poles
and filled in their sites with human bones.

15 And also the sacrificial-altar that was at Bet-El, the sanctuary that
    Yorov'am son of Nevat made, [the one] who had caused Israel
    to sin,
also that altar and the sanctuary, he demolished,
and he burned the sanctuary and crushed it fine, into dust,
and he burned the Ashera-pole.

16 And Yoshiyyahu faced about
and saw the burial-places that were there on the hill,
so he sent and had the bones taken from the burial-places and
    burned on the altar, rendering it *tamei*,
in accordance with the word of Yhwh which the man of God had
    proclaimed,
who had proclaimed these things.

17 Then he said:
What is this marker that I see?
The men of the town said to him:
It is the burial-place of the man of God who came from Judah,

---

12 **hastened:** Following Cogan/Tadmor's emendation
from *vayyarotz* to *vayyeritzem*.
13 **facing:** To the east of.
14 **with human bones:** Since, in ancient Israel, death
was the ultimate ritual pollutant (see Num. 19 for an
elaborate purification ritual).

16 **the man of God:** In I Kings 13:2. **who had proclaimed:** The repetition in this verse may be due to
a scribal error.
17 **this marker that I see:** Apparently one of the grave
markers stood out.

who proclaimed these things that you have done against the
    sacrificial-altar of Bet-El.

18   He said:

Let it rest;

let no one disturb his bones!

So they let his bones be,

along with the bones of the prophet who had come from
    Shomeron.

19   And also all the sanctuary buildings that were in the towns of
    Shomeron

which the kings of Israel had made to provoke [Yhwh], Yoshiyyahu
    removed;

he dealt with them in accordance with all the deeds that he had
    done in Bet-El.

20   And he slew all the priests of the sanctuaries who were there, on
    the sacrificial-altars,

and burned human bones on them.

Then he returned to Jerusalem.

21   And the king commanded all the people, saying:

Observe the Passover to Yhwh your God,

as is written in this Record of the Covenant!

22   —For no such Passover had been observed

since the days of the judge-leaders who led Israel,

and all the days of the kings of Israel and the kings of Judah.

23   But in the eighteenth year of King Yoshiyyahu

such a Passover was observed to Yhwh in Jerusalem.

24   And also the ghosts and the all-knowing ones, the *terafim* and the
    Illicit-Things,

and all the Detestable-Things that could be seen in the land of
    Judah and in Jerusalem,

Yoshiyyahu eradicated,

in order to fulfill the words of the Instruction, the ones written in
    the Record that Hilkiyyahu the priest had found in the House of
    Yhwh.

---

18 **rest:** The only peace amid a chapter of dismantling and destruction.   **from Shomeron:** But the man of God had come from Bet-El, not the as yet unbuilt Shomeron. Here, as often in the Bible, the story is told from the perspective of the (later) writers.

19 **to provoke** [Yhwh]: Ancient versions, undoubtedly correctly, add what is missing in MT: the divine name.

24 *terafim:* Pronounced *te-rah-FEEM*. Household idols, notable in Gen. 31:19 and I Sam. 19:13–16.

Chapter 24. *The First Exile:* All of a sudden a new dominant power, Babylon, appears in the text. The Bible is chiefly interested in how several Judean rebellions bring down the wrath of the Babylonian king, Nevukhadnetzar, upon the Southern Kingdom, leading to disaster. The destruction of Jerusalem takes place in two stages in the two remaining chapters. The first is triggered by a revolt against Babylon by Yoshiyyahu's son Yehoyakim; this is followed by Aramean, Moabite, and Ammonite attacks (attributed, however, not to the king's wrongdoings but to those of Menashe, decades earlier). During Yehoyakhin's brief reign, the Babylonians themselves invade. The resulting exile, dated to 597 B.C.E., involves the remaining Temple treasures and the military and elite of the country. Those left, according to the text, are simply the poor and the new puppet king, Yehoyakhin's uncle Tzidkiyyahu.

Amid the narratives of destruction, it will be useful for the reader to have a sense of who the Babylonians were. By the mid-seventh century, Assyria began to falter. Several decades later, civil war provided the opportunity for the Neo-Babylonians to throw off the Assyrian yoke, and in 612, Nineveh, the capital, was sacked.

Based around the Euphrates in southern Mesopotamia, Babylonia arose on a hoary foundation of language (Sumerian and Akkadian), law, literature, and architecture. By the ninth century, the Chaldeans (anachronistically mentioned in Gen. 11:31) had taken over the area, although within a century, the Assyrians to the north conquered Babylonia and established a dual monarchy which lasted for a long period. With the fall of Nineveh, the Neo-Babylonian Empire came to dominate the Middle East for the next seven decades, until the rise of Persia.

The accomplishments of Babylonian civilization were considerable. Nebuchadnezzar built the fabulous Hanging Gardens in his capital city. The country abounded in ziggurats, the pyramid-shaped temples whose ruins still dot the Iraqi landscape. As befitted an old civilization, the Babylonians made signal advances in astronomy, astrology, and mathematics, and already possessed an advanced irrigation system. They also contributed or transmitted some of the world's earliest surviving great literature, including the immortal Epic of Gilgamesh.

In the Hebrew Bible, all this is barely hinted at, but many biblical narratives, especially those that appear early on (such as aspects of the Creation, Flood, and Tower of Babel stories in the first section of Genesis), may well be reacting to, or against, some of its ideas and institutions. There may even be an element of parody in some of these stories. Once again, then, the Bible comes across as a kind of counter-text, a text which, as the prophet Jeremiah himself was characterized, was "appointed against nations and kingdoms, / to uproot and to pull down" (Jer. 1:10), despite the seeming insignificance of ancient Israel in the context of the region.

25 Now like him there was none before him as king,
who turned back to YHWH with all his heart, with all his being, and
with all his substance,
in accordance with all the teaching of Moshe,
and after him there arose none like him.

26 Yet YHWH did not turn back from his great flaming-anger, whose
anger flared up against Judah,
on account of all the provocations with which Menashe had
provoked him.

27 So YHWH said:
Judah too I will remove from my presence,
just as I removed Israel,
and I will reject this city which I chose, Jerusalem,
along with the House about which I said: My name will be there!

28 Now the rest of the events of Yoshiyyahu, and all that he did—
are they not written in the Record of Yearly Events of the Kings of
Judah?

29 In his days, Pharaoh Nekho king of Egypt came up to the king of
Assyria, to the River Euphrates,
and King Yoshiyyahu marched out to meet him,
but he put him to death at Megiddo when he saw him.

30 His servants conveyed him dead from Megiddo, and brought him
to Jerusalem,
and they buried him in his burial-place.
And the Landed People took Yehoahaz son of Yoshiyyahu
and anointed him, making him king in place of his father.

31 Twenty-three years old was Yehoahaz at his becoming king,
and for three months he reigned as king in Jerusalem;
his mother's name was Hamutal daughter of Yirmeyahu, from
Livna.

---

25 **heart . . . being . . . substance:** Echoing the famous
passage in Deut. 6:5, and, in the subsequent "none
arose like him," likewise connected to Moshe himself in Deut. 34:10 (Cogan/Tadmor).

29 **Nekho:** Pharaoh Neco II, ruled 610–595. **to . . .
Assyria:** That is, to aid the Assyrians, something
Yoshiyyahu wished to prevent.

30 **Yehoahaz:** Pronounced *ye-ho-ah-HAZ*, "YHWH Has
Seized"; trad. English "Jehoahaz." The name is
another form of the previously encountered "Ahaz-

yahu." Apparently this was a regnal name, since formerly his name was Shallum. **anointed:** Said of
only two other kings, Shelomo in I Kings 1:45 and
Yehoash in II Kings 11:12. In Kimhi's view, this was
necessary because of the abnormality of succession
in each case.

31 **Yirmeyahu:** "YHWH Has Founded." It is the same
name as that of the famous prophet (Jeremiah) who
was alive at the time.

◆ 32 He did what was evil in the eyes of YHWH,
exactly as his fathers had done.

33 And Pharaoh Nekho imprisoned him at Rivla, in the region of
Hamat, from reigning as king in Jerusalem,
and placed a fine on the land of a hundred talents of silver and a
talent of gold.

34 Pharaoh Nekho made Elyakim son of Yoshiyyahu king in place of
Yoshiyyahu his father,
and changed his name to Yehoyakim,
while Yehoahaz he took away, so that he came to Egypt and died
there.

35 Now the silver and the gold, Yehoyakim gave [as payment] to
Pharaoh,
but he had to assess the land, in order to give the silver by order of
Pharaoh:
from each one according to his assessment he exacted the silver and
the gold, from the Landed People, to give to Pharaoh Nekho.

36 Twenty-five years old was Yehoyakim at his becoming king,
and for eleven years he reigned as king in Jerusalem;
his mother's name was Zevuda daughter of Pedaya, from Ruma.

37 He did what was evil in the eyes of YHWH,
exactly as his fathers had done.

24:1 In his days, Nevukhadnetzar king of Babylon came up.
And Yehoyakim was servant to him for three years,
but then he turned and rose-in-revolt against him.

2 So YHWH sent loose against him raiding-bands of Chaldeans, bands
of Aram, bands of Moav, and bands of the Children of Ammon;
he sent them loose against Judah, to annihilate it,

---

33 **imprisoned:** Foreshadowing the fate (in 25:5–6) of Tzidkiyyahu, Judah's last king (Cohn 2000). **Rivla, in the region of Hamat:** On the Orontes River in western Syria, a wide area used as headquarters for both Pharaoh Nekho and the Babylonian king Nevukhadnetzar.

34 **Elyakim:** "May God Establish." **Yehoyakim:** Trad. English "Jehoiakim"; "May YHWH Establish." The change of name upon accession is not unusual.

36 **Ruma:** A site in the north.

24:1 **Nevukhadnetzar:** The Second (605–562), founder of the Neo-Babylonian Empire; pronounced *ne-*

voo-khad-ne-TZAR; trad. English "Nebuchadnezzar." Among his other accomplishments was the construction of the Hanging Gardens of Babylon, renowned as one of the Seven Wonders of the ancient world. In Akkadian his name is *Nabu-kudurru-utzur,* "[The god] Nabu Has Protected the Inheriting Son." **came up:** To attack.

2 **Chaldeans:** A southern subgroup of the Babylonians, by this time the dominant one in the country. They are referred to anachronistically in Gen. 11:31. **annihilate:** A verb (*'-b-d*) which in this form appears as part of the future curses against Israel in

in accordance with the word of Yʜwʜ which he had spoken by the
hand of his servants the prophets.
3   Yes, at the order of Yʜwʜ did all this [come] against Judah,
to remove them from his presence,
for the sins of Menashe, in accordance with all that he did,
4   and also [because of] the innocent blood that he shed
—for he filled Jerusalem with innocent blood—
so Yʜwʜ was not willing to forgive.
5   Now the rest of the events of Yehoyakim, and all that he did—
are they not written in the Record of Yearly Events of the Kings of
Judah?
6   Yehoyakim lay beside his fathers,
and Yehoyakhin his son became king in his place.
7   Now the king of Egypt no longer went out [to war] from his land
any more,
for the king of Babylon had taken away, from the Wadi of Egypt to
the River Euphrates,
all that had belonged to the king of Egypt.

8   Eighteen years old was Yehoyakhin at his becoming king,
and for three months he reigned as king in Jerusalem;
his mother's name was Nehushta daughter of Elnatan, from
Jerusalem.
9   He did what was evil in the eyes of Yʜwʜ,
exactly as his father had done.
10   At [about] that time, the servants of Nevukhadnetzar king of
Babylon went up to Jerusalem,
and the city came under siege.
11   Nevukhadnetzar king of Babylon came to the city
while his servants were besieging it,
12   and Yehoyakhin king of Judah went out [in surrender] to the king
of Babylon,
he and his mother, his court-servants, his officers, and his officials,
and the king of Babylon took him [prisoner] in year eight of his
being king.

Deut. 28:51 and 63 (Cogan/Tadmor), and is also used
regarding Baal worshippers in 10:19 above.
5   **Record of Yearly Events:** The last time it is mentioned in the book (Cogan/Tadmor).

6   **Yehoyakhin:** Trad. English "Jehoiachin"; "Yʜwʜ
Has Established."
7   **Wadi of Egypt:** Usually identified as Wadi El-Arish.

Chapter 25. *Final Catastrophe: The Fall of Judah:* As in Chap. 17, the account of the final battle here is extraordinarily brief; the narrator clearly has little interest in military details. More central, once the city wall is breached, are the capture and treatment of Tzidkiyyahu, the king, and the destruction of the Temple. After, once again, a brief description of the fate of the buildings and people of Jerusalem, the text becomes expansive, dwelling longingly (and not surprisingly) on the destroyed or despoiled vessels and columns of the Temple.

Some key political details remain. The Babylonians appoint a governor, ironically named Gedalyahu ("God has done great things"), to administer what is left of Judah. He counsels cooperation with the conquerors, but is assassinated by those Judahites who are still in a rebellious frame of mind.

The entire narrative of Kings then fast-forwards and comes to an end (vv.27–30) with what amounts to an extended note, precisely dated in the spring of 561 B.C.E., describing the treatment of the surviving Davidic king, Yehoyakhin, who had been exiled thirty-six years before. The captive king's fate—he is taken out of prison and allowed to eat at the Babylonian king's table for the rest of his days— could be read in two ways: either he is highly favored in his limited circumstances (his throne is "set above the thrones of the [other] kings" who have been taken to Babylon), thus providing a shred of hope for the exiles, or the text is reaffirming that his power is quite limited, since he is supported not by his own subjects but at the whim of the king of Babylon. This subdued, even depressing ending leaves us in a kind of limbo; as McKenzie (2010) puts it, both Kings and the DH overall are "strangely silent about the future." In any event, with the end of the book, Israel embarks on centuries of control by others or other forces (Babylonians, Persians, Greeks, and Romans), which would lead ultimately to both a wider exile and the creation of the Hebrew Bible in its final form.

13 And he brought out from there all the treasuries of the House of
YHWH and the treasuries of the king's house;
he cut-to-pieces all the vessels of gold that Shelomo king of Israel
had made in the Great-Hall of YHWH,
as YHWH had promised.

14 He exiled all of Jerusalem:
all the officers and all the mighty-men of valor,
ten thousand exiles,
and all the carvers and the smiths;
none remained, save the poorest of the people of the land.

15 And he exiled Yehoyakhin to Babylon,
while the king's mother and the king's wives and his officials and
the "rams" of the land he made go into exile, from Jerusalem to
Babylon,

16 along with all the men of valor, seven thousand,
and the carvers and the smiths, a thousand,
all mighty-men, trained for battle;
the king of Babylon brought them into exile, to Babylon.

17 And the king of Babylon installed Mattanya his uncle as king in his
place,
and changed his name to Tzidkiyyahu.

18 Twenty-one years old was Tzidkiyyahu at his becoming king,
and for eleven years he reigned as king in Jerusalem;
his mother's name was Hamutal daughter of Yirmeyahu, from
Livna.

19 He did what was evil in the eyes of YHWH,
exactly as Yehoyakim had done.

20 Indeed, [it was] because of YHWH's anger that it happened in
Jerusalem and in Judah,
until he cast them out from his presence.
And Tzidkiyyahu rose-in-revolt against the king of Babylon.

---

14 **people of the land:** Now either just a neutral term
or else a composite phrase from II Kings 25:12 and
Jer. 52:15 (Shemaryahu Talmon, cited in Cogan/
Tadmor).

15 **"rams":** Prominent men or nobles; see Exod. 15:15.

17 **Mattanya:** "Gift of YHWH." **his uncle:** Yehoyakhin's. **Tzidkiyyahu:** "YHWH Is My Righteous-

ness," a rather ironic name given the circumstances
(Cohn 2007).

20 **Indeed, [it was]:** Heb. not entirely clear. **them:**
Heb. is singular. **rose-in-revolt:** Against the advice
of the prophet Yirmeyahu (Jeremiah), who encourages the king to submit to the yoke of Babylon and
avoid disaster.

◆ 25:1 So it was in the ninth year of his being king,
         in the tenth month, on the tenth of the month:
         Nevukhadnetzar king of Babylon, he and all his army, came against
             Jerusalem;
         they set up camp against it and built a bulwark against it, all
             around.
    2   And the city came under siege until the eleventh year of King
             Tzidkiyyahu.
    3   On [day] nine of the [fourth] month, hunger became strong in the
             city;
         there was no food [even] for the Landed People.
    4   The city-wall was broken through,
         [and Tzidkiyyahu] and all the men fit for battle [fled] at night
             through the gate between the double-walls that are near the
             king's garden,
         with the Chaldeans all around the city;
         he went by the Road of the Plain.
    5   But the Chaldean army pursued after the king
         and overtook him in the Plains of Jericho,
         with all his army having scattered from him.
    6   They seized the king and brought him up to the king of Babylon, at
             Rivla,
         and pronounced judgment upon him.
    7   The sons of Tzidkiyyahu were slain before his eyes,
         and Tzidkiyyahu's eyes were blinded;
         then they bound him with double-bronze and brought him to
             Babylon.

25:1 **bulwark:** A siege tower.
   2 **eleventh year:** Making for a siege of almost a year
      and a half.
   3 **[fourth]:** See Jer. 52:6, filling out the date. **[even]:**
      Following Cogan/Tadmor.
   4 **[fled]:** See Jer. 39:4. **he went:** Presumably, the
      king. **Road of the Plain:** Or "Arava Road," which
      goes through the Jordan Valley. To get to this north-
      south route, the king had to descend eastward to
      Jericho, which he barely reached before being cap-
      tured.
   5 **the Plains of Jericho:** Thus the last king of Israel/
      Judah is captured in the same vicinity that the Isra-

elites had entered the land at the beginning of the
Early Prophets, in Joshua (Sweeney 2007).
   7 **blinded:** The normal punishment for a rebellious
      slave throughout the ancient Near East (Cogan/
      Tadmor). **they bound him with double-
      bronze:** The same fate, along with the blinding,
      was meted out to Shimshon by the Philistines in
      Judg. 16:21. **brought him to Babylon:** So the last
      king of Israel/Judah does not receive the dignity
      of the usual death formula in Kings (Cohn 2000).
      According to Jer. 52:11, he remains in prison until his
      death, unlike his nephew Yehoyakhin (see vv.27–30).

◆ 8 Now in the fifth month, on [day] seven of the month—that is the
        nineteenth year of King Nevukhadnetzar, king of Babylon,
     Nevuzar'adan, Captain of the Guard, servant to the king of
        Babylon, came to Jerusalem;
   9 he burned down the House of Yʜᴡʜ and the king's house
     and all the houses of Jerusalem,
     and every house of a great-one he burned with fire.
  10 As for the walls of Jerusalem, all around,
     they were demolished by all the Chaldean army that belonged to
        the Captain of the Guard.
  11 And the rest of the people who remained in the city,
     and those falling away who had fallen away to the king of Babylon,
     the rest of the masses,
     Nevuzar'adan the Captain of the Guard exiled;
  12 but from the poor of the land, the Captain of the Guard allowed
        some to remain,
     as vine-dressers and as husbandmen.

  13 Now the bronze columns that were in the House of Yʜᴡʜ,
     and the bases and the Bronze Sea that were in the House of Yʜᴡʜ,
        the Chaldeans smashed,
     and brought their bronze to Babylon.
  14 And the pots and the shovels and the snuffers and the ladles
     and all the bronze vessels with which they attended, they took.
  15 And the fire-pans and the forks that were of gold, [each of] gold,
        and of silver, [each of] silver—
     the Captain of the Guard took.
  16 Now the columns, two, the Sea, one, and the bases that Shelomo
        had made for the House of Yʜᴡʜ,
     were beyond weighing for bronze, all these vessels.

---

8 **Nevuzar'adan:** Pronounced *ne-vu-zar-ah-DAHN;*
Akkadian *Nabu-zer-iddina,* "Nabu has given me
offspring." **Captain of the Guard:** Lit., "Chief
Cook," a title like "Chief Cupbearer," whose duties
went well beyond their original named function.
9 **he burned down:** Some archaeological evidence
for this celebrated destruction remains, despite the
heavy rebuilding of Jerusalem throughout the ages.

11 **falling away:** Deserted.
13 **bronze columns . . . :** Based on I Kings 7, where the
building of the Temple is described.
16 **were beyond weighing:** The amount was simply
too large.

17 Eighteen cubits was the height of the one column,
   with a crowning-capital for it of bronze,
   and the height of the capital three cubits,
   with a lattice-work and pomegranates on the capital, all around,
   —all of it was bronze—
   and like these for the second column, along with the lattice-work.

18 And the Captain of the Guard took Seraya the Head Priest and
      Tzefanyahu the Second Priest
   and the three guardians of the threshold;

19 and from the city he took an official who was [The One]
      Accountable for the Men of War,
   and five men from Those [Who] See the King's Face who were
      found in the city,
   and the Scribe of the Commander of the Armed-Forces who
      mustered the forces of the Landed People,
   and sixty men from the Landed People who were found in the city;

20 Nevuzar'adan the Captain of the Guard took them
   and brought them to the king of Babylon at Rivla.

21 And the king of Babylon struck them down and put them to death
      at Rivla, in the land of Hamat.
   So Judah was exiled from its soil.

22 Now as for the people who remained in the land of Judah,
   whom Nevukhadnetzar king of Babylon allowed to remain—
   he appointed over them Gedalyahu son of Ahikam son of Shafan.

23 And all the commanders of the soldiers heard, they and their men,
      that the king of Babylon had appointed Gedalyahu,
   so they came to Gedalyahu at Mitzpa—
   Yishmael son of Netanya, Yohanan son of Kare'ah, Seraya son
      of Tanhumet the Netofatite, and Yaazanyahu son of the
      Maakhatite,
   they and their men.

---

17 **three cubits:** According to Jer. 52:22, it was five cubits.
19 **Those [Who] See the King's Face:** His attendants.
21 **struck them down:** Not necessarily personally, but at his command.
22 **Gedalyahu:** "YHWH Has Done Great Things"; trad. English "Gedaliah." Cohn (2000) notes that this man is the grandson of Yoshiyyahu's scribe, a meaningful connection to a better era.

23 **Mitzpa:** Eight miles north of Jerusalem—but according to the archaeological record, it was unscathed by the capital's fall (Cogan/Tadmor). Zevit (2004) notes the irony of this site being associated with the very beginnings of the monarchy, in Sha'ul's territory. **Yishmael:** "God Has Hearkened." Trad. English "Ishmael." Note the connotation of all the personal names in this verse. **Yohanan:** "YHWH Was Gracious." **Tan-**

24 And Gedalyahu swore to them and to their men;
    he said to them:
    Do not be afraid of serving the Chaldeans;
    stay in the land and serve the king of Babylon, and it will go well
        with you!

25 But it was in the seventh month
    that Yishmael son of Netanya son of Elishama, one of the royal
        seed, and ten men with him, came
    and struck down Gedalyahu, so that he died,
    along with the Judeans and the Chaldeans who were with him at
        Mitzpa.

26 Then all the people, great and small, and the commanders of the
        soldiers, arose and went to Egypt,
    for they were afraid of the Chaldeans.

27 Now it was in the thirty-seventh year of the exile of Yehoyakhin
        king of Judah,
    in the twelfth month, on the twenty-seventh of the month,
    that Ehvil-Merodakh, king of Babylon, in the year of his becoming
        king, lifted up the head of Yehoyakhin king of Judah, from the
        prison house.

28 He spoke kind-words with him
    and set his throne above the thrones of the kings who were with
        him in Babylon.

29 So he changed his prison garments
    and ate food regularly before him,
    all the days of his life;

30 his allowance, a regular allowance, was given to him by the king,
        each day's amount in its day,
    all the days of his life.

---

humet: "Consolation." **Netofatite:** From a town near Bet-Lehem. **Yaazanyahu:** "Yнwн Has Given-Ear." **Maakhatite:** Either from a town way in the northeast corner of Israel, or from a clan mentioned in I Chr. 2:48 (Cogan/Tadmor).

24 **of serving:** See Jer. 40:9; MT has "the servants of."

27 **Ehvil-Merodakh:** Pronounced *eh-VEEL mero-DAKH;* Akkadian *Amel-marduk,* "Worshipper of [the god] Marduk." The son of Nevukhadnetzar, he reigned only from 562 to 560 B.C.E. Trad. English translations render the name as "Evil Merodach," with

unintentional negative connotations. In biblical Hebrew, though, *ehvil* does happen to mean "foolish." **lifted up the head:** Pardoned, as happened to Pharaoh's chief cupbearer in Gen. 40:13. LXX adds "and brought him out." **from the prison house:** Preceded in LXX and Jer. 52:32 by "and took him out of."

28 **spoke kind-words:** The Babylonian phrase which is translated here signals a legal agreement reached through negotiation. **thrones:** MT singular; the plural appears in Jer. 52:32.

Recurring Names in
The Early Prophets

"Ay" is pronounced as in "hay," "ah" as in the English "ah," "oh" as in the English "oh."

The Hebrew letter *khaf* (*kh*) is pronounced like the *ch* in Johann Sebastian Bach. The Hebrew letter *het,* which is pronounced with a lighter gutteral than the letter *khof,* is not indicated separately. As a result, Hebrew words ending in *heh* are generally rendered without a final *h* in transliteration.

All dates are B.C.E.

Names are listed first in the Hebraic forms in which they appear in the text, followed by an approximate pronunciation in parentheses, and then by their traditional English equivalent in brackets. Place-names are underlined.

Adoniyya/Adoniyyahu (*ah-doh-ni-YAH/YAH-hu*) [Adonijah]: David's son and rival to Shelomo for the throne.

Agag (*ah-GAHG*) [Agag]: Amalekite king whom Sha'ul spares, leading to rejection by God as king of Israel. Agag is slain by Shemuel.

Ah'av (*ah-AHV*) [Ahab]: King of Israel and husband of Izevel, opposed by the prophet Eliyyahu.

Ahaz (pronounced closer to *akh-AHZ*) [Ahaz]: Judean king; father of Hizkiyyahu.

Ahazyahu (*ah-haz-YAH-hu*) [Ahaziah]: 1) Son of Ah'av, and briefly king of Israel; 2) son of Atalyahu, and briefly king of Judah.

Ahimaatz (*ah-hee-MAH-atz*) [Ahimaaz]: Son of King David's priest Tzadok; one of the messengers who bears news of Avshalom's death to David.

Ahitofel (*ah-hee-TOH-fel*) [Ahitophel]: Adviser of King David who sides with Avshalom. Upon the latter's rejection of his advice, he hangs himself.

Akhan (*ah-KHAN*) [Achan]: He violates the ban against taking spoils in Josh. 7, and is subsequently put to death.

Akhish (*ah-KHEESH*) [Achish]: Philistine king during the time of David, who serves as his mercenary.

Akhsa (*akh-SAH*) [Achsah]: Forthright wife of Calev in Joshua and Judges.

Amalek (*ah-mah-LAYK*) [Amalek]: Enemy of Israel in Exodus; Sha'ul is commanded to exterminate them.

Amasa (*ah-mah-SAH*) [Amasa]: Avshalom's commander in chief during his rebellion against David; slain by Yoav.

<u>Ammon</u> (*ah-MOHN*) [Ammon]: Neighboring and often hostile nation to Israel's northeast (east of Gil'ad).

Amnon (*ahm-NOHN*) [Amnon]: David's eldest son, who rapes his half sister Tamar and is killed by her brother Avshalom.

<u>Aram</u> (*ah-RAHM*) [Aram]: Ancient Syria, involved in battles and treaties in the period of Kings.

Aravna (*ah-RAHV-nah*) [Araunah]: Owner of a threshing floor on Mount Zion in Jerusalem. He sells it to King David; it becomes the site of the future Temple.

Asa (*ah-SAH*) [Asa]: Great-grandson of Shelomo and king of Judah.

Asa'el (*ah-sah-AYL*) [Asahel]: Brother of Yoav, David's commander in chief; he is killed by Sha'ul's general Avner.

Asher (*a-SHAYR*) [Asher]: Northern tribe whose territory occupied the northwest strip of Israel.

Ashkelon (*osh-ke-LOHN*) [Ashkelon]: One of the five Philistine cities. It lies on the Mediterranean coast, north of Gaza.

Atalyahu (*ah-tahl-YAH-hu*) [Athaliah]: Northern princess who marries into the royal family of Judah and is the mother of King Ahazyahu. She reigns alone for six years, and murders the Judahite heirs, of whom Yoash survives. She herself is later killed.

Avigayil (*a-vee-GAH-yil*) [Abigail]: Wife of wealthy landowner Naval, she becomes David's wife after her husband's sudden death.

Avimelekh (*a-vi-MEH-lekh*) [Abimelech]: Illegitimate son of the judge Gid'on, he kills his brothers and has himself proclaimed king.

Avishag (*ah-vee-SHAHG*) [Abishag]: A young woman who is brought to Jerusalem to attend to the aged King David.

Aviyya (*ah-vee-YAH*) [Abijah]: 1) A son of Rehav'am and king of Judah; 2) A son of Yorov'am I and king of Israel.

Avner (*av-NAYR*) [Abner]: Sha'ul's commander in chief, assassinated by Yoav.

Avshalom (*av-sha-LOHM*) [Absalom]: David's rebel son and full brother of Tamar.

Baal (*BAH-al*) [Baal]: A major Canaanite god, associated with thunder and fertility. He is the chief rival of YHWH for the hearts of the Israelites in the Early Prophets.

Baana (*bah-ah-NAH*) [Baanah]: One of two brothers who assassinate Sha'ul's son Ish-Boshet. See also *Rekhav*.

Barak (*bah-RAHK*) [Barak]: General under Devora.

Barzillai (*bar-zee-LIE*) [Barzillai]: Aged friend of King David who remains loyal to him during Avshalom's revolt.

Bat-Sheva (*baht-SHEH-va*) [Bathsheba]: David's beloved wife, obtained through the murder of her husband Uriyya. She is the mother of Shelomo, the next king.

Be'er-Sheva (*beh-AYR SHEH-vah*) [Beersheba]: Town in the territory of Shim'on, regarded in the Bible as the southernmost inhabited place in Israel.

Ben-Hadad (*ben hah-DAHD*): Name of several Aramean kings mentioned in the book of Kings.

Bet-El (*bayt AYL*) [Bethel]: Important religious site on the southern border of the Northern Kingdom.

Bet-Lehem (*bayt LEH-hem*) [Bethlehem]: Town south of Jerusalem; David's birthplace.

Bet-She'an (*bayt she-AHN*) [Beth Shan]: Canaanite city south of the Kinneret (Sea of Galilee), where Sha'ul's body is hung by the victorious Philistines.

Binyamin (*bin-ya-MEEN*) [Benjamin]: Tribe straddling the border between north and south; home of Sha'ul and location of Jerusalem.

Calev (*kah-LAYV*) [Caleb]: Along with Yehoshua, a "faithful" spy in the book of Numbers; he receives choice southern territory after the Conquest.

Dagon (*dah-GOHN*) [Dagon]: Philistine god, adopted from local Canaanite culture.

Dan (*don*): [Dan]: Tribe whose territory west of Jerusalem later moved to the north of Israel.

David (*dah-VEED*) [David]: Second king of Israel; a central figure of the book of Samuel and of the Bible in general.

Delila (*de-lee-LAH*) [Delilah]: Philistine lover, and betrayer, of Shimshon.

Devora (*de-voh-RAH*) [Deborah]: The only female judge-leader.

Efrayim (*ef-RAH-yim*) [Ephraim]: Major northern tribe, located north of Philistia, Judah, and Binyamin.

Eglon (*egg-LOHN*) [Eglon]: King of Moav; assassinated by the early judge Ehud.

Ehud (*ay-HUDE*) [Ehud]: See *Eglon*.

Ekron (*eh-KROHN*) [Ekron]: One of the five Philistine cities.

Eli (*ay-LEE*) [Eli]: Priest at Shilo and mentor of the young Shemuel.

Elisha (*e-li-SHAH*) [Elisha]: Prophet; disciple of Eliyyahu.

Eliyyahu (*ay-li-YAH-hu*) [Elijah]: Noted prophet and foe of King Ah'av and his queen Izevel.

Elkana (*el-kah-NAH*) [Elkanah]: Husband of Hanna and father of Shemuel.

Evyatar (*ev-yah-TAHR*) [Abiathar]: Priestly descendant of Eli and follower of King David, he is ultimately banished by Shelomo for having sided with the latter's rival Adoniyyahu.

Gad (*god*) [Gad]: Tribe whose territory lay due east of the Jordan River.

Gat (*got*) [Gath]: Philistine city and home of Golyat.

Gedalyahu (*geh-dal-YAH-hu*) [Gedaliah]: Judean governor after the destruction of Jerusalem. He is assassinated by dissident groups in Judah.

Gehazi (*gay-ha-ZEE*) [Gehazi]: Servant of the prophet Elisha.

Gid'on (*gid-OHN*) [Gideon]: Northern Judge who throws off the Midyanite yoke.

Gil'ad (*gil-AHD*) [Gilead]: The large area east of the Jordan River, containing the territory of the two and a half Israelite tribes (Re'uven, Gad, and half of Menashe) not located in the traditional land of Canaan.

Giv'a (*giv-AH*) [Gibeah]: Town north of Jerusalem, notorious as the site of the rape of the Levite's concubine in Judg. 19, and also connected with the career of Sha'ul.

Giv'on (*giv-OHN*) [Gibeon]: An important military and religious site northwest of Jerusalem.

Golyat (*gol-YAHT*) [Goliath]: The imposing Philistine warrior slain by the young David.

Hadad'ezer (*hah-DAHD EH-zer*) [Hadadezer]: Aramean king who engages in war with King David.

Hanna (*hah-NAH*) [Hannah]: Mother of Shemuel and wife of Elkana.

Hatzor (*hah-TZOR*) [Hazor]: Major fortress city in northern Israel.

Hazael (*hah-zah-AYL*) [Hazael]: Powerful king of Aram in the second half of the ninth century.

Hevron (*hev-ROHN*) [Hebron]: Southern town and David's base of support.

Hilkiyya / hu (*hil-kee-YAH*) [Hilkiah]: High priest during King Yoshiyyahu's reform.

Hiram (*hee-RAHM*) [Hiram]: Phoenician king who is allied with both David and Shelomo. He provides cedar wood for the building of the Jerusalem Temple.

Hizkiyyahu (*hiz-kee-YAH-hu*) [Hezekiah]: Reformer king of the late eighth century; expands Jerusalem.

Hofni (*hof-NEE*) [Hofni]: One of the priest Eli's wicked sons in I Samuel.

Hulda (*hul-DAH*) [Huldah]: Prophetess during the time of King Yoshiyyahu's reform.

Hushai (*hoo-SHY*) [Hushai]: King David's loyal adviser who pretends to defect to Avshalom in order to give him faulty counsel.

Ish-Boshet (*eesh BO-shet*) [Ish-Bosheth]: Son of Sha'ul who is king of Israel for a short period; he is assassinated.

Ittai (*ee-TIE*) [Ittai]: Friend of David who sticks by him during the rebellion of Avshalom.

Izevel (*ee-ZEH-vel*) [Jezebel]: Phoenician princess and wife of Ah'av, notorious in Kings for bringing hundreds of pagan priests with her to Israel.

Lakhish (*lah-KHEESH*) [Lachish]: Judean city destroyed by Assyria in 701.

Levanon (*leh-vah-NOHN*) [Lebanon]: The "white" mountain range to the north of Israel. The area is known for its cedar trees.

Levi (*lay-VEE*) [Levi]: Tribe of priests, which receives no territory of its own.

Mahanayim (*mah-ha-NAH-yim*) [Mahanaim]: Town in the tribal territories east of the Jordan, on the border between Gad and Menashe.

Mefiboshet (*meh-fee-BOH-shet*) [Mephibosheth]: Lame grandson of Sha'ul, he is kept alive and supported by David, based on the latter's covenant with Yehonatan.

Megiddo (*meh-gee-DOE*) [Megiddo]: A high mound overlooking a crucial western pass to the coastal plain, and hence the site of many major battles throughout history.

Menashe (*meh-na-SHEH*) [Menasseh]: 1) Northern tribe; 2) vilified king of Judah, son of Hizkiyyahu.

Merav (*may-RAHV*) [Merab]: Daughter of Sha'ul, married initially to David.

Midyan (*mid-YAHN*) [Midian]: Area in the western Arabian Peninsula, connected by some to the birth of Israelite religion.

Mikha (*mee-KHAH*) [Micah]: Efrayimite man whose household is a focus in stories toward the end of Judges.

Mikhal (*mee-KHAL*) [Michal]: Daughter of Sha'ul and wife of David. She does not bear him children.

Mikhayhu (*mee-KHIGH-hu*) [Micaiah]: Prophet during time of King Ah'av.

Mitzpa (*mitz-PAH*) [Mizpah]: Important fortified settlement in Binyamin, in the border area between the two kingdoms.

Moav (*mo-AHV*) [Moab]: Israel's neighbor and frequent enemy, situated east of the Dead Sea.

Moshe (*mo-SHEH*) [Moses]: Central human figure of biblical books of Exodus through Deuteronomy; leader, prophet, and lawgiver.

Naaman (*nah-ah-MAHN*) [Naaman]: Aramean king stricken with skin disease; healed by the prophet Elisha.

Naftali (*naf-ta-LEE*) [Naphtali]: Tribe in the northern inland part of Israel.

Natan (*nah-TAHN*) [Nathan]: Prophet at the court of David.

Naval (*na-VAHL*) [Nabal]: Rich farmer who refuses hospitality to David's band and subsequently dies. His wife is Avigayil.

Navot (*nah-VOTE*) [Naboth]: Farmer whose land is seized by Ah'av and Izevel following his murder.

Nekho (*neh-KHO*) [Necho]: Pharaoh of Egypt in late seventh century. He is responsible for the death of Yoshiyyahu.

Nevukhadnetzar (*neh-voo-khad-neh-TZAR*) [Nebuchadnezzar]: Babylonian king; conquers Jerusalem in 587.

Og (*OHG*) [Og]: King of Bashan, fertile region to the east of the Kinneret. He figures in traditions about Israel's approach to Canaan in the waning days of Moshe and the book of Numbers.

Omri (*ohm-REE*) [Omri]: Founder of a prominent northern dynasty (including his son Ah'av), which is eventually snuffed out by Yehu.

Ovadyahu (*o-vahd-YAH-hu*) [Obadiah]: Courtier and ally of Eliyyahu.

Peninna (*pe-nee-NAH*) [Peninah]: Wife of Elkana and rival of Hanna, Shemuel's mother.

Pin'has (*pee-ne-HASS*) [Phineas]: The other wicked son of the priest Eli in I Samuel.

Rama (*rah-MAH*) [Ramah]: Town north of Jerusalem, known as the home base of Shemuel.

Rehav'am (*re-hav-AHM*) [Rehoboam]: Son of Shelomo and first king of Judah after the split of the kingdom.

Rekhav (*ray-KHAV*) [Rechab]: One of two brothers who assassinate Sha'ul's son Ish-Boshet. See also *Baana*.

Re'uven (*reh-oo-VAYN*) [Reuben]: Tribe whose territory lies east of the northern part of the Dead Sea.

Ritzpa (*ritz-PAH*) [Rizpah]: Concubine of Sha'ul, who figures in two stories after the king's death.

Sanheriv (*san-hay-REEV*) [Sennacherib]: King of Assyria, 704–681. He invades Judah and besieges Jerusalem, c. 701.

Sha'ul (*sha-OOL*) [Saul]: First king of Israel; succeeded by David.

Shekhem (*sheh-KHEM*) [Shechem]: Important northern city, today's Nablus.

Shelomo (*sheh-loh-MOH*) [Solomon]: Son of David and third king of Israel.

Shemuel (*sheh-moo-AYL*) [Samuel]: Prophet and in a sense the last of the Judges. He anoints both Sha'ul and David as king.

Sheva (*SHEH-va*) [Sheba]: Leader of revolt against King David; subsequently killed.

Shilo (*shee-LOH*) [Shiloh]: Major religious center in the north.

Shim'i (*shim-EE*) [Shimei]: Northern sympathizer who curses David on his flight from Avshalom. Later executed by Shelomo.

Shim'on (*shim-OHN*) [Simeon]: Southern tribe whose territory is subsumed in that of Yehuda.

Shimshon (*shim-SHOHN*) [Samson]: A Danite and last of the named judges; a hero of immense strength.

Shomeron (*sho-meh-ROHN*) [Samaria]: Capital of the Northern Kingdom, including at the time of its destruction by Assyria.

Sihon (*see-HOHN*) [Sihon]: Amorite king who denies passage to the Israelites after the Exodus (see *Og* as well).

Tamar (*tah-MAHR*) [Tamar]: David's daughter, who is raped by her half brother Amnon.

Tirtza (*tir-TZAH*) [Tirzah]: A capital of the Northern Kingdom until Yorov'am establishes Shomeron as his capital.

Tzadok (*tzah-DOHK*) [Zadok]: Loyal priest under King David, he is made chief priest by Shelomo.

Tzidkiyyahu (*tzid-kee-YAH-hu*) [Zedekiah]: Last king of Judah; defeated and captured by the Babylonians.

Tziva (*tzee-VAH*) [Ziba]: Servant of Mefiboshet, Sha'ul's grandson, who manipulates David to get property during Avshalom's revolt.

Uriyya (*oo-ree-YAH*) [Uriah]: One of David's lieutenants and husband of Bat-Sheva.

Ya'el (*ya-AYL*) [Jael]: Heroine at the time of Devora who kills the enemy Canaanite general.

Yavesh-Gil'ad (*yah-VAYSH gil-AHD*) [Jabesh Gilead]: A town across the Jordan River in Gil'ad; southeast of Bet-She'an. It is the site of one of Sha'ul's early victories.

Yehoahaz (*ye-ho-ah-HAHZ*) [Jehoahaz]: 1) King of Israel at the end of the ninth century; 2) king of Judah after his father Yoshiyyahu.

Yehoash (*ye-ho-AHSH*) [Jehoash]: 1) Son of Judahite king, Ahazya, who begins his reign as the only survivor of a bloody purge by Atalya; 2) king of Israel around 800; present at Elisha's death.

Yehonatan/Yonatan (*ye-ho-nah-TAHN*/*yo-nah-TAHN*) [Jonathan]: Son of Sha'ul and heir to the throne of Israel, who dies in battle along with his father and brothers.

Yehoshafat (*ye-ho-shah-FAHT*) [Jehoshaphat]: King of Judah during the era of Eliyyahu and Elisha.

Yehoshua (*ye-ho-SHU-a*) [Joshua]: Moshe's successor and conqueror of Canaan.

Yehoyada (*ye-ho-yah-DAH*) [Jehoiadah]: High Priest and kingmaker for Yehoash.

Yehoyakhin (*ye-ho-ya-KHEEN*) [Jehoiachin]: King of Judah at the time of the first Babylonian deportation in 597; exiled and released from prison over three decades later.

Yehoyakim (*ye-ho-ya-KEEM*) [Jehoiakim]: King of Judah around 600, in the years just before successive Babylonian invasions.

Yehu (*yay-HOO*) [Jehu]: Leader of a purge against the Omri dynasty, and later king of Israel.

He is mentioned, and depicted, on the "Black Obelisk" of Shalmaneser III of Assyria (c. 841).

Yehuda (*ye-hu-DAH*) [Judah]: Principal southern tribe; home base of David. Also used as the name of the Southern Kingdom.

Yerub-baal (*ye-ru-BAH-al*) [Jerubaal]: Alternate name for Gid'on.

Yesha'yahu (*yeh-sha-YAH-hu*) [Isaiah]: Prophet during the late eighth century in Judah. His long book begins the Later Prophets.

Yiftah (*yif-TAH*) [Jephthah]: The son of a concubine, he is one of the last Judges, and famous for a rash vow.

Yishai (*yee-SHY*) [Jesse]: Father of David.

Yissakhar (*yi-sa-KHAR*) [Issachar]: Tribe occupying territory to the east of Zevulun and bordering on Lake Kinneret.

Yizre'el (*yiz-re-AYL*) [Jezreel]: Fertile valley in the north.

Yoash (*yo-AHSH*) [Joash]: 1) Judean king who survives Atalyahu's purge as a child. He is cited as repairing the Jerusalem Temple, and also for his conflicts with Aram; 2) an Israelite king who also fights the Arameans.

Yoav (*yo-AHV*) [Joab]: David's fanatically loyal commander in chief.

Yonadav (*yo-nah-DAHV*) [Jonadab]: Avshalom's cousin and friend.

Yoram/Yehoram (*yo-RAHM/ye-ho-RAHM*) [Joram/Jehoram]: 1) Judean king who marries Atalyahu. The Edomites break away from Israel during his rule; 2) king of Israel and son of Ah'av.

Yorov'am (*yo-rov-AHM*) [Jeroboam]: 1) First king of the north (Israel), who is vilified for setting up alternative worship at Dan and other towns; 2) king of Israel during the prosperous period of the eighth century (first half).

Yosef (*yo-SAYF*) [Joseph]: Sometimes used as a name for the Northern Kingdom; Yosef was the father of Efrayim and Menashe, whose names are used for two of the largest northern tribes.

Yoshiyyahu (*yo-shee-YA-hu*) [Josiah]: Reformer king in Judah's waning days. He recaptures much northern territory but ultimately is killed at Megiddo.

Yotam (*yo-TAHM*) [Jotham]: Surviving son of Gid'on after Avimelekh's massacre of his brothers.

Zevulun (*ze-vu-LUN*) [Zebulun]: Northern tribe, located mostly in the Yizre'el (Jezreel) Valley.

BIBLIOGRAPHY

In the wake of several decades of intense scholarly interest in the books of the Early Prophets, a proper listing of books and articles would comprise a thick volume of its own. I have therefore had to content myself here with citing those works, predominantly in English, of either general interest or those which I think are particularly helpful or simulating. There will necessarily be unfortunate omissions, for which I apologize. Fine bibliographies can be found in the books and articles cited. I have also included in this list works referred to specifically in the Introductions, Commentary, and Notes in this volume. Robert Alter's translation and commentary on Joshua through Kings has not been consulted; my manuscript was handed in before its appearance. At the same time, I was able to get a preview of Jacob L. Wright's *King David: His Reign Revisited,* which appears in 2014 in printed form; this is an important work which treats the composition of Samuel and the place that war commemoration plays in the creation of biblical literature.

Three recent general introductions to the Hebrew Bible include judicious discussions of the books of the Early Prophets: Michael Coogan's *Old Testament: A Historical and Literary Introduction to the Hebrew Scriptures,* 2nd ed.; David Carr's *An Introduction to the Old Testament: Sacred Texts and Imperial Contexts for the Hebrew Bible;* and Marvin A. Sweeney's *Tanak: A Theological and Critical Introduction to the Jewish Bible.* Another valuable resource for readers with a particular interest in history is *The Oxford History of the Biblical World,* edited by Coogan.

A single alphabetical list has been provided. Each entry is labeled to indicate its primary focus, as follows: general source on the books of the Early Prophets or on biblical narrative and history (Gen'l.), the book of Joshua (Josh.), the book of Judges (Judg.), the book of Samuel (Sam.), and the book of Kings (Kings).

Aberbach, David. 1993. *Imperialism and Biblical Prophecy: 750–500 BCE.* New York. (Kings)

Ackerman, Susan. 1998. *Warrior, Dancer, Seductress, Queen: Women in Judges and Biblical Israel.* New York. (Judg.)

———. 2005. *When Heroes Love: The Ambiguity of Eros in the Stories of David and Gilgamesh.* New York. (Sam.)

Aharoni, Yohanan. 1979. *The Land of the Bible: A Historical Geography.* Revised and enlarged ed. Philadelphia. (Gen'l.)

Alter, Robert. 1981. *The Art of Biblical Narrative.* New York. (Gen'l.)

———. 1988. "Language as Theme in the Book of Judges." In *Eleventh Annual Rabbi Louis Feinberg Memorial Lecture in Judaic Studies.* University of Cincinnati, February 22. (Judg.)

———. 1999. *The David Story: A Translation with Commentary of 1 and 2 Samuel.* New York. (Sam.)

Amit, Yairah. 1999a. *The Book of Judges: The Art of Editing.* Leiden. (Judg.)

———. 1999b. *History and Ideology: An Introduction to Historiography in the Hebrew Bible.* Sheffield, England. (Gen'l.)

———. 2004. "Judges." In *The Jewish Study Bible,* ed. Adele Berlin and Marc Zvi Brettler. New York. (Judg.)

Arnold, Bill T., and H. G. M. Williamson, eds. 2005. *Dictionary of the Old Testament: Historical Books.* Downers Grove, IL. (Gen'l.)

Assis, Eliyahu. 2005. *From Moses to Joshua and from the Miraculous to the Ordinary: A Literary Analysis of the Conquest Narrative in the Book of Joshua* (Hebrew). Jerusalem. (Josh.)

Auld, A. Graeme. 1998. *Joshua Retold: Synoptic Perspectives* (Old Testament Studies). Edinburgh, Scotland. (Josh.)

———. 2011. *I & II Samuel* (Old Testament Library). Louisville, KY. (Sam.)

Bar-Efrat, Shimon. 1989. *Narrative Art in the Bible.* Sheffield, England. (Sam.)

Ben-Dov, Jonathan. 2011. "Some Precedents for the Religion of the Book: Josiah's Book and Ancient Revelatory Literature." In *Constructs of Prophecy in the Former and Latter Prophets and Other Texts,* ed. Lester L. Grabbe and Martti Nissinen. Atlanta. (Kings)

Bergen, Wesley J. 1992. "The Prophetic Alternative: Elisha and the Israelite Monarchy." In *Elijah and Elisha in Socioliterary Perspective,* ed. Robert B. Coote (The Society of Biblical Literature Semeia Studies). Atlanta. (Kings)

Bloch-Smith, Elizabeth. 2002. "Solomon's Temple: The Politics of Ritual Space." In *Sacred Time, Sacred Place: Archaeology and the Religion of Israel,* ed. Barry M. Gittlen. Winona Lake, IN. (Kings)

Boling, Robert. 1975. *Judges* (Anchor Bible, vol. 6A). Garden City, NY. (Judg.)

———. 1982. *Joshua* (Anchor Bible, vol. 6). Garden City, NY. (Josh.)

Borgman, Paul. 2008. *David, Saul and God: Rediscovering an Ancient Story.* New York. (Sam.)

Borowski, Oded. 1998. *Every Living Thing: Daily Use of Animals in Ancient Israel.* Walnut Creek, CA. (Gen'l.)

Brauner, Ronald A. 1974. " 'To Grasp the Hem' and Samuel 15:27." *Journal of the Ancient Near Eastern Society* 6. (Sam.)

Brettler, Marc Zvi. 1995. *The Creation of History in Ancient Israel.* London. (Gen'l.)

———. 2001a. *The Book of Judges.* New York. (Judg.)

———. 2001b. "Memory in Ancient Israel." In *Memory and History in Christianity and Judaism,* ed. Michael A. Signer. Notre Dame, IN. (Gen'l.)

Brueggemann, Walter. 1990. *First and Second Samuel* (Interpretation: A Bible Commentary for Teaching and Preaching). Louisville, KY. (Sam.)

———. 2009. *Divine Presence amid Violence: Contextualizing the Book of Joshua.* Eugene, OR. (Josh.)

Buber, Martin. 1967. *The Kingship of God.* New York. (Gen'l.)

———. 1994. *Scripture and Translation.* Translated by Lawrence Rosenwald with Everett Fox. Bloomington, IN. (Gen'l.)

Buber, Martin, and Franz Rosenzweig. 1956. *Buecher der Geschichte.* Cologne. (Gen'l.)

Burnett, Joel S. 2010. " 'Going Down' to Bethel: Elijah and Elisha in the Theological Geography of the Deuteronomistic History." *Journal of Biblical Literature* 129:2 (Summer). (Kings)

Burney, C. F. 1920. *The Book of Judges.* 2nd ed. London. (Judg.)

Campbell, Edward F., Jr. 1998. "A Land Divided: Judah and Israel from the Death of Solomon to the Fall of Samaria." In *The Oxford History of the Biblical World,* ed. Michael D. Coogan. New York. (Kings)

Cantrell, Deborah O'Daniel. 2011. *The Horsemen of Israel: Horses and Chariotry in Monarchic Israel (Ninth–Eighth Centuries B.C.E.).* Winona Lake, IN. (Gen'l.)

Carr, David M. 2005. *Writing on the Tablet of the Heart: Origins of Scripture and Literature.* New York. (Gen'l.)

———. 2010. *An Introduction to the Old Testament: Sacred Texts and Imperial Contexts for the Hebrew Bible.* Malden, MA. (Gen'l.)

Clines, David J. A. 1995. "David the Man: The Construction of Masculinity in the Hebrew Bible." In *Interested Parties: The Ideology of Writers and Readers of the Hebrew Bible* (JSOT Supplement Series 205). Sheffield, England. (Sam.)

Cogan, Mordechai. 1998. "Into Exile: From the Assyrian Conquest of Israel to the Fall of Babylon." In *The Oxford History of the Biblical World*, ed. Michael D. Coogan. New York. (Kings)

———. 2001. *I Kings* (Anchor Bible, vol. 10). New York. (Kings)

———. 2008. *Inscriptions from Assyria and Babylonia Relating to Ancient Israel*. Jerusalem. (Kings)

Cogan, Mordechai, and Hayim Tadmor. 1998. *II Kings* (Anchor Bible, vol. 11). New York. (Kings)

Cohn, Robert L. 1982. "The Literary Logic of 1 Kings 17–19." *Journal of Biblical Literature* 101:3. (Kings)

———. 2000. *2 Kings* (Berit Olam). Collegeville, MN. (Kings)

Cohn, Robert L., and Trude Dothan. 1994. "Before Israel: The Canaanites as Other in Biblical Tradition." In *The Other in Jewish Thought and History*, ed. Laurence J. Silberstein and Robert L. Cohn. New York. (Josh.)

Coogan, Michael. 2010. *Old Testament: A Historical and Literary Introduction to the Hebrew Scriptures*. 2nd ed. New York. (Gen'l.)

———. 2011. *The Oxford Encyclopedia of the Books of the Bible*. New York. (Gen'l.)

———, ed. 1998. *The Oxford History of the Biblical World*. New York. (Gen'l.)

Cross, Frank Moore. 1973. *Canaanite Myth and Hebrew Epic: Essays in the History of the Religion of Israel*. Cambridge, MA. (Gen'l.)

Cross, Frank Moore, Jr., and David Noel Freedman. 1975. *Studies in Ancient Yahwistic Poetry*. Grand Rapids, MI. (Sam.)

Dever, William G. 2001. *What Did the Biblical Writers Know, and When Did They Know It?: What Archaeology Can Tell Us About Ancient Israel*. Grand Rapids, MI. (Gen'l.)

———. 2003. *Who Were the Early Israelites and Where Did They Come From?* Grand Rapids, MI. (Josh.)

DeVries, Simon J. 1985. *1 Kings* (Word Biblical Commentary, vol. 12). Waco, TX. (Kings)

Dietrich, Walter. 2007. *The Early Monarchy in Israel: The Tenth Century B.C.E.* Atlanta. (Sam.)

Dothan, Trude. 1982. *The Philistines and Their Material Culture*. New Haven, CT. (Gen'l.)

Dothan, Trude, and Robert L. Cohn. 1994. "The Philistine as Other: Biblical Rhetoric and Archaeological Reality." In *The Other in Jewish Thought and History*, ed. Laurence J. Silberstein and Robert L. Cohn. New York. (Gen'l.)

Dothan, Trude, and Moshe Dothan. 1992. *People of the Sea*. New York. (Gen'l.)

Driver, Samuel Rolles. 1890. *Notes on the Hebrew Text of the Books of Samuel*. Oxford, England. (Sam.)

Ehrlich, Arnold B. 1969. *Mikra ki-Pheschuto. Vol. 2: Divrei Soferim*. New York. (Gen'l.)

Exum, J. Cheryl. 1990. "The Centre Cannot Hold: Thematic and Textual Instabilities in Judges." *Catholic Bible Quarterly* 52. (Judg.)

———. 1993. "On Judges 11." In *A Feminist Companion to Judges*, ed. Athalya Brenner. Sheffield, England. (Judg.)

———. 1996. *Tragedy and Biblical Narrative*. Cambridge, England. (Gen'l., Sam.)

———. 2012. *Plotted, Shot, and Painted: Cultural Representations of Biblical Women*. Sheffield, England. (Sam.)

Fewell, Danna Nolan. 2010. "A Broken Hallelujah: Remembering David, Justice, and the Cost of the House." In *The Fate of King David: The Past and Present of a Biblical Icon*, ed. Todd Linafelt, Claudia V. Camp, and Timothy Beal. New York. (Sam.)

Finkelstein, Israel, and Amihai Mazar. 2007. *The Quest for the Historical Israel,* ed. Brian B. Schmidt. Atlanta. (Gen'l.)

Finkelstein, Israel, and Nadav Na'aman. 1994. *From Nomadism to Monarchy: Archaeological and Historical Aspects of Early Israel.* Jerusalem/Washington, DC. (Gen'l.)

Fishbane, Michael. 2002. *The JPS Bible Commentary: Haftarot.* Philadelphia. (Gen'l.)

Flanagan, James W. 1988. *David's Social Drama.* Sheffield, England. (Sam.)

Fokkelman, J. P. 1981. *Narrative Art and Poetry in the Books of Samuel. Vol. 1: King David.* Assen, The Netherlands. (Sam.)

———. 1993. *Narrative Art and Poetry in the Books of Samuel. Vol. 4: Vow and Desire.* Assen, The Netherlands. (Sam.)

———. 1999. *Reading Biblical Narrative: An Introductory Guide.* Louisville, KY. (Gen'l.)

Fox, Everett. 1995. *The Five Books of Moses.* New York. (Gen'l.)

———. 1999. *Give Us a King!* New York. (Sam.)

Fried, Lisbeth. 2002. "The High Places (*bāmôt*) and the Reforms of Hezekiah and Josiah: An Archaeological Investigation." *Journal of the American Oriental Society* 122:3. (Kings)

Friedman, Richard Elliott. 1998. *The Hidden Book in the Bible.* San Francisco. (Gen'l.)

Frontain, Raymond-Jean, and Jan Wojcik, eds. 1980. *The David Myth in Western Literature.* West Lafayette, IN. (Sam.)

Gaposchkin, M. C. 2008. "Louis IX, Crusades and the Promise of Joshua in the Holy Land." *Journal of Medieval History* 34:3 (September). (Josh.)

Garsiel, Moshe. 1985. *The First Book of Samuel: A Literary Study of Comparative Structures, Analogies and Parallels.* Translated by P. Hacket. Ramat Gan, Israel. (Sam.)

———. 1991. *Biblical Names: A Literary Study of Midrashic Derivations and Puns.* Ramat Gan, Israel. (Gen'l.)

Gaster, Theodor H. 1970. *Myth, Legend, and Custom in the Old Testament.* Vol. 2. New York. (Gen'l.)

Geoghegan, Jeffrey C. 2006. *The Time, Place, and Purpose of the Deuteronomistic History: The Evidence of "Until This Day."* Providence, RI. (Gen'l.)

Goldman, Solomon. 1949. *Samuel* (Soncino Books of the Bible). London. (Judg.)

Grabbe, Lester L. 2007. *Ancient Israel: What Do We Know and How Do We Know It?* New York. (Gen'l.)

Gray, John. 1970. *I and II Kings: A Commentary.* 2nd ed. Philadelphia. (Kings)

———. 1986. *Joshua, Judges, Ruth* (New Century Bible Commentary). Grand Rapids, MI. (Judg.)

Greenberg, Moshe. 1957. "The Hebrew Oath Particle Hay/Hē." *Journal of Biblical Literature* 76:1.

———. 1969. *Understanding Exodus.* New York. (Sam.)

Greenstein, Edward L. 1981. "The Riddle of Samson." *Prooftexts* 1:3 (September). (Judg.)

———. 1989. "The Syntax of Saying 'Yes' in Biblical Hebrew." *Journal of the Ancient Near Eastern Society* 19. (Gen'l.)

———. 1990. "The Formation of the Biblical Narrative Corpus." *AJS Review* 15:2 (Autumn). (Gen'l.)

Greenstein, Edward L., and David Marcus. 1976. "The Akkadian Inscription of Idrimi." *Journal of the Ancient Near Eastern Society* 8. (Judg.)

Gunn, David. 2005. *Judges* (Blackwell Bible Commentaries). Malden, MA. (Judg.)

Hallo, William W., and William Kelly Simpson. 1998. *The Ancient Near East: A History.* 2nd ed. Fort Worth, TX. (Gen'l.)

Halpern, Baruch. 1988. *The First Historians: The Hebrew Bible and History.* San Francisco. (Gen'l.)

Hamilton, Victor P. 2004. *Handbook on the Historical Books.* Grand Rapids, MI. (Gen'l.)

Hancock, Rebecca. 2011. "1 and 2 Samuel." In *The Oxford Encyclopedia of the Books of the Bible,* ed. Michael D. Coogan. New York. (Sam.)

Hareuveni, Nogah. 1984. *Tree and Shrub in Our Biblical Heritage.* Kiryat Ono, Israel. (Judg.)

Hawk, L. Daniel. 2000. *Joshua (Berit Olam).* Collegeville, MN. (Josh.)

———. 2010. *Joshua in 3-D: A Commentary on Biblical Conquest and Manifest Destiny.* Eugene, OR. (Josh.)

Hess, Richard S. 2008. *Joshua* (Tyndale Old Testament Commentaries). Downers Grove, IL. (Josh.)

Hoerth, Alfred J., Gerald L. Mattingly, and Edwin M. Yamauchi, eds. 1994. *People of the Old Testament World.* Grand Rapids, MI. (Gen'l.)

Hurowitz, Victor Avigdor. 2005. "Yнwн's Exalted House—Aspects of the Design and Symbolism of Solomon's Temple." In *Temple and Worship in Ancient Israel,* ed. John Day. London. (Kings)

Jeffrey, David Lyle, ed. 1992. *A Dictionary of Biblical Tradition in English Literature.* Grand Rapids, MI. (Gen'l.)

Keller, Brad, Frank Ritchel Ames, and Jacob L. Wright, eds. 2011. *Interpreting Exile: Displacement and Deportation in Biblical and Modern Contexts.* Atlanta. (Kings)

Killebrew, Ann E. 2005. *Biblical Peoples and Ethnicity.* Atlanta. (Gen'l.)

King, Philip J., and Lawrence E. Stager. 2001. *Life in Biblical Israel.* Louisville, KY. (Gen'l.)

Klein, Lillian R. 1988. *The Triumph of Irony in the Book of Judges* (JSOT Supplement Series 68). Sheffield, England. (Judg.)

Knoppers, Gary N. 1994. *Two Nations Under God: The Deuteronomistic History of Solomon and the Dual Monarchies,* vol. 2. Atlanta. (Kings)

Koehler, Ludwig, and Walter Baumgartner. 1994–2000. *The Hebrew and Aramaic Lexicon of the Old Testament.* 5 vols. Leiden. (Gen'l.)

Lemaire, André. 2000. "Toward a Redactional History of the Book of Kings." In *Reconsidering Israel and Judah: Recent Studies on the Deuteronomistic History,* ed. Gary N. Knoppers and J. Gordon McConville. Winona Lake, IN. (Kings)

Levenson, Jon D. 1978. "I Samuel 25 as Literature and History." *Catholic Bible Quarterly* 40. (Sam.)

———. 1981. "From Temple to Synagogue: I Kings 8." In *Traditions in Transformation: Turning Points in Biblical Faith,* ed. Baruch Halpern and Jon D. Levenson. Winona Lake, IN. (Kings)

———. 1987. *Sinai and Zion: An Entry into the Jewish Bible.* San Francisco. (Kings)

Levenson, Jon D., and Baruch Halpern. 1980. "The Political Import of David's Marriages." *Journal of Biblical Literature* 99:4 (December). (Sam.)

Levine, Baruch A. 1993. "Silence, Sound, and the Phenomenology of Mourning in Biblical Israel." *Journal of the Ancient Near Eastern Society* 22. (Kings)

Lewis, Theodore J. 1991. "The Ancestral Estate (*nhlt 'lhym*) in 2 Samuel 14:16." *Journal of Biblical Literature* 110. (Sam.)

Linafelt, Tod, Claudia V. Camp, and Timothy Beal, eds. 2010. *The Fate of King David.* New York. (Sam.)

Long, Burke O. 1991. *2 Kings* (The Forms of the Old Testament Literature, vol. 10). Grand Rapids, MI. (Kings)

Machinist, Peter. 1994. "Outsiders or Insiders: The Biblical View of Emergent Israel and Its Contexts." In *The Other in Jewish Thought and History,* ed. Laurence J. Silberstein and Robert L. Cohn. New York. (Gen'l.)

———. 1995. "The Transfer of Kingship: A Divine Turning." In *Fortunate the Eyes That See:*

Essays in Honor of David Noel Freedman in Celebration of His Seventieth Birthday, ed. A. B. Beck, A. H. Bartelt, C. A. Franke, and P. R. Raabe. Grand Rapids, MI. (Gen'l.)

———. 2000. "The *Rab Shaqeh* at the Wall of Jerusalem: Israelite Identity in the Face of the Assyrian 'Other.'" *Hebrew Studies* 41. (Kings)

Malamat, Abraham. 1976. "Charismatic Leadership in the Book of Judges." In *Magnalia Dei: The Mighty Acts of God: Essays on the Bible and Archaeology in Memory of G. Ernest Wright,* ed. Frank Moore Cross et al. Garden City, NY. (Judg.)

Mann, Thomas W. 2011. *The Book of the Former Prophets.* Eugene, OR. (Kings)

Marcus, David. 1986. *Jephthah and His Vow.* Lubbock, TX. (Judg.)

———. 1989. "The Bargaining Between Jephthah and the Elders (Judges 11:4–11)." *Journal of Near Eastern Studies* 19. (Judg.)

Martin, Charles G. 1986. "1 and 2 Kings." In *The International Bible Commentary,* ed. F. F. Bruce. Grand Rapids, MI. (Kings)

McCarter, P. Kyle. 1980. *I Samuel* (Anchor Bible, vol. 8). Garden City, NY. (Sam.)

———. 1984. *II Samuel* (Anchor Bible, vol. 9). Garden City, NY. (Sam.)

McCarthy, D. J. 1971. "The Theology of Leadership in Joshua 1–9." *Biblica* 52. (Josh.)

McKenzie, Steven L. 2000. *King David: A Biography.* New York. (Sam.)

———. 2010. *Introduction to the Historical Books.* Grand Rapids, MI. (Gen'l.)

Meyers, Carol. 1987. "The Israelite Empire: In Defense of King Solomon." In *Backgrounds for the Bible,* ed. Michael Patrick O'Connor and David Noel Freedman. Winona Lake, IN. (Kings)

———. 1998. "Kinship and Kingship: The Early Monarchy." In *The Oxford History of the Biblical World,* ed. Coogan. (Gen'l., Kings)

———. 2004. "Joshua." In *The Jewish Study Bible,* ed. Adele Berlin and Marc Zvi Brettler. New York. (Josh.)

Miller, Alan. 1977. "Claude Levi-Strauss and Gen. 37–50." In *Shiv'im,* ed. Ronald Brauner. Philadelphia. (Gen'l.)

Miscall, Peter D. 1986. *1 Samuel: A Literary Reading.* Bloomington, IN. (Sam.)

Mitchell, Gordon. 1993. *Together in the Land: A Reading of the Book of Joshua* (JSOT Supplement Series 134). Sheffield, England. (Josh.)

Mobley, Gregory. 2005. *The Empty Men: The Heroic Tradition of Ancient Israel.* New York. (Judg.)

———. 2011. "Judges." In *The Oxford Encyclopedia of the Books of the Bible,* ed. Coogan. (Judg.)

Montgomery, James A. 1951. *A Critical and Exegetical Commentary on the Books of Kings* (The International Critical Commentary). New York. (Kings)

Moore, George Foote. 1923. *A Critical and Exegetical Commentary on Judges* (The International Critical Commentary). New York. (Judg.)

Mulder, Martin J. 1998. *I Kings. Vol. 1: I Kings 1–11* (Historical Commentary on the Old Testament). Leuven, Belgium. (Kings)

Na'aman, Nadav. 1994. "The 'Conquest of Canaan' in the Book of Joshua and in History." In *From Nomadism to Monarchy: Archaeological and Historical Aspects of Early Israel,* ed. Finkelstein and Na'aman. (Josh.)

———. 1996. "Sources and Composition in the History of David." In *The Origins of the Ancient Israelite States,* ed. Volkmar Fritz and Philip R. Davies. Sheffield, England. (Sam.)

———. 2005. *Ancient Israel and Its Neighbors: Interaction and Counteraction* (Collected Essays, vol. 1). Winona Lake, IN. (Gen'l.)

Nelson, Richard D. 1997. *Joshua: A Commentary* (Old Testament Library). Louisville, KY. (Josh.)

Niccacci, Alviero. 1990. "The Syntax of the Hebrew Verb in Classical Hebrew Prose." *Journal for the Study of the Old Testament: Supplement Series,* 86. (Gen'l.)

Niditch, Susan. 1993. *War in the Hebrew Bible: A Study in the Ethics of Violence.* New York. (Gen'l.)

———. 2008. *Judges: A Commentary* (Old Testament Library). Louisville, KY. (Judg.)

Noth, Martin. 1981. *The Deuteronomistic History.* Winona Lake, IN. (Gen'l.)

Olyan, Saul M. 1988. *Asherah and the Cult of Yahweh in Israel.* Atlanta. (Gen'l.)

The Oxford History of the Biblical World. 1998. Edited by Michael Coogan. New York. (Gen'l.)

Parpola, Simo. 2003. "Assyria's Expansion in the Eighth and Seventh Centuries and Its Long-Term Repercussions in the West." In *Symbiosis, Symbolism, and the Power of the Past,* ed. William J. Dever and Seymour Gitin. Winona Lake, IN. (Kings)

Perry, Menakhem. 2007. "Counter-stories in the Bible: Rebekah and Her Bridegroom, Abraham's Servant." *Prooftexts* (March). (Sam.)

Polak, Frank H. 1998. "The Oral and the Written: Syntax, Stylistics, and the Development of Biblical Prose Narrative." *Journal of the Ancient Near Eastern Society* 26. (Gen'l.)

Polzin, Robert. 1980. *Moses and the Deuteronomist: A Literary Study of the Deuteronomistic History. Part I: Deuteronomy, Joshua, Judges.* New York. (Josh.)

———. 1989. *Samuel and the Deuteronomist.* San Francisco. (Sam.)

———. 1993. *David and the Deuteronomist.* Bloomington, IN. (Kings)

Rainey, Anson F., and R. Steven Notley. 2006. *The Sacred Bridge: Carta's Atlas of the Biblical World.* Jerusalem. (Gen'l.)

Reinhartz, Adele. 1994. "Anonymous Women and the Collapse of the Monarchy: A Study in Narrative Technique." In *A Feminist Companion to Samuel and Kings,* ed. Athalya Brenner. Sheffield, England. (Kings)

Rendsburg, Gary. 1986. *The Redaction of Genesis.* Winona Lake, IN. (Sam.)

———. 1998–99. "Confused Language as a Deliberate Literary Device in Biblical Hebrew Narrative." *Journal of Hebrew Scriptures* 2; electronic version on the Web at www.jhsonline.org. (Gen'l.)

———. 2003. "A Comprehensive Guide to Israelian Hebrew: Grammar and Lexicon." *Orient* 38. (Gen'l.)

Rentería, Tamis Hoover. 1992. "The Elijah/Elisha Stories: A Socio-cultural Analysis of Prophets and People in Ninth-Century B.C.E. Israel." In *Elijah and Elisha in Socioliterary Perspective,* ed. Robert B. Coote. Atlanta. (Kings)

Römer, Thomas. 2007. *The So-Called Deuteronomistic History: A Sociological, Historical, and Literary Introduction.* London. (Gen'l.)

Rösel, Hartmut N. 2011. *Joshua* (Historical Commentary on the Old Testament). Leuven, Belgium. (Josh.)

Rosenbaum, Stanley Ned. 2002. *Understanding Biblical Israel: A Reexamination of the Origins of Monotheism.* Macon, GA. (Kings)

Rosenberg, Joel. 1986. *King and Kin: Political Allegory and the Hebrew Bible.* Bloomington, IN. (Sam.)

Rost, Leonhard. 1926. *Die Überlieferung von der Thronnachfolge Davids.* Stuttgart. (Sam.)

Rowlett, Lori L. 1996. *Joshua and the Rhetoric of Violence: A New Historicist Analysis* (JSOT Supplement Series 226). Sheffield, England. (Josh.)

Sasson, Jack M. 2001. "Absalom's Daughter: An Essay in Vestige Historiography." In *The Land That I Will Show You: Essays in the History and Archaeology of the Ancient Near East in Honor of J. Maxwell Miller,* ed. J. Andrew Dearman and M. Patrick Graham. Sheffield, England. (Sam.)

Savran, George. 1987. "1 and 2 Kings." In *The Literary Guide to the Bible,* ed. Robert Alter and Frank Kermode. Cambridge, MA. (Kings)

Schneider, Tammi J. 2000. *Judges (Berit Olam).* Collegeville, MN. (Judg.)

Schniedewind, William. 1996. "The Problem with Kings: Recent Study of the Deuteronomistic History." *Religious Studies Review* 22:1 (January). (Kings)

———. 2004. *How the Bible Became a Book: The Textualization of Ancient Israel.* Cambridge, England. (Gen'l.)

Simon, Uriel. 1967. "The Poor Man's Ewe-Lamb: An Example of a Juridical Parable." *Biblica* 48. (Sam.)

———. 1997. *Reading Prophetic Narratives.* Translated by Lenn J. Schram. Bloomington, IN. (Gen'l.)

Smith, Mark S. 2004. *The Memoirs of God: History, Memory, and the Experience of the Divine in Ancient Israel.* Minneapolis. (Gen'l.)

Smith-Christopher, Daniel L. 2002. *A Biblical Theology of Exile.* Minneapolis. (Kings)

Soggin, J. A. 1981. *Judges: A Commentary* (Old Testament Library). Philadelphia. (Judg.)

Spina, Frank Anthony. 1994. "Eli's Seat: The Transition from Priest to Prophet in I Samuel 1–4." *Journal for the Study of the Old Testament* 62. (Sam.)

Stager, Lawrence E. 1989. "The Song of Deborah." *Biblical Archaeology Review* (January / February). Reprinted in *Approaches to the Bible: The Best of Bible Review,* vol. 2, ed. Harvey Minkoff. Washington, DC. (Judg.)

Steussy, Marti J. 1999. *David: Biblical Portraits of Power* (Studies on Personalities of the Old Testament). Columbia, SC. (Sam.)

Stone, Lawson G. 2009. "Eglon's Belly and Ehud's Blade: A Reconsideration." *Journal of Biblical Literature* 128:4. (Judg.)

Stulman, Louis. 1990. "Encroachment in Deuteronomy: An Analysis of the Social World of the D Code." *Journal of Biblical Literature* 109. (Josh.)

Sweeney, Marvin A. 1997. "Davidic Polemics in Judges." *Vetus Testamentum* 47:4 (October). (Judg.)

———. 2001. *King Josiah of Judah: The Lost Messiah of Israel.* New York. (Kings)

———. 2007. *I & II Kings: A Commentary* (Old Testament Library). Louisville, KY. (Kings)

———. 2012. *Tanak: A Theological and Critical Introduction to The Jewish Bible.* Minneapolis. (Gen'l.)

Trible, Phyllis. 1984. *Texts of Terror: Literary-Feminist Readings of Biblical Narratives.* Philadelphia. (Gen'l.)

Tsevat, Matityahu. 1980. "The Biblical Account of the Formation of the Monarchy in Israel." In *The Meaning of the Book of Job and Other Biblical Studies.* New York. (Sam.)

Tyndale, William. 1992. *Tyndale's Old Testament,* ed. David Daniell. New Haven, CT. (Gen'l.)

Ussishkin, David. 2003. "Jerusalem as a Royal and Cultic Center in the Tenth–Eighth Centuries B.C.E." In *Symbiosis, Symbolism, and the Power of the Past,* ed. William G. Dever and Seymour Gitin. Winona Lake, IN. (Kings)

Van der Toorn, Karel, Bob Becking, and Peter W. Van Der Horst, eds. 1999. *Dictionary of Deities and Demons in the Bible.* 2nd ed. Leiden, The Netherlands. (Gen'l.)

Walsh, Jerome T. 1996. *I Kings (Berit Olam).* Collegeville, MN. (Kings)

Waltke, Bruce K., and Michael O'Connor. 1990. *An Introduction to Biblical Hebrew Syntax.* Winona Lake, IN. (Gen'l.)

Walton, John H., Victor H. Matthews, and Mark W. Chavals, eds. 2000. *The IVP Bible Background Commentary.* Downers Grove, IL. (Gen'l.)

Wazana, Nili. 2003. "From Dan to Beer-Sheba and from the Wilderness to the Sea: Literal and

Literary Images of the Promised Land in the Bible." In *Experiences of Place,* ed. Mary N. MacDonald. Cambridge, MA. (Josh.)

———. 2011. "Joshua." In *The Oxford Encyclopedia of the Books of the Bible,* ed. Coogan. (Josh.)

Weinfeld, Moshe. 1993. *The Promise of the Land: The Inheritance of the Land of Canaan by the Israelites* (Taubman Lectures in Jewish Studies). Berkeley, CA. (Josh.)

———. 2000. "The Counsel of the 'Elders' to Rehoboam and Its Implications." In *Reconsidering Israel and Judah: Recent Studies on the Deuteronomistic History,* ed. Gary N. Knoppers and J. Gordon McConville. Winona Lake, IN. (Kings)

Wenham, Gordon J. 1972. "Betulah 'A Girl of Marriageable Age,'" *Vetus Testamentum* 22, Fasc. 3 (July). (Gen'l.)

Willis, John T. 1984. *First and Second Samuel.* Austin, TX. (Sam.)

Woudstra, Marten H. 1981. *The Book of Joshua* (The New International Commentary on the Old Testament). Grand Rapids, MI. (Josh.)

Wright, Jacob L. 2009. "The Commemoration of Defeat and the Formation of a Nation in the Hebrew Bible." *Prooftexts* 29. (Gen'l.)

———. 2011. "The Deportation of Jerusalem's Wealth and the Demise of Native Sovereignty in the Book of Kings." In *Interpreting Exile: Displacement and Deportation in Biblical and Modern Contexts,* ed. Keller, Ames, and Wright. (Kings)

Yadin, Yigael. 1955. "Goliath's Javelin and the *menor 'origim.*" *Palestine Exploration Quarterly* 86. (Sam.)

Yee, Gale A. 2007. *Judges and Method: New Approaches in Biblical Studies.* 2nd ed. Minneapolis. (Judg.)

Younger, K. Lawson, Jr. 1990. *Ancient Conquest Accounts: A Study in Ancient Near Eastern and Biblical History Writing* (JSOT Supplement Series 98). Sheffield, England. (Josh.)

Zakovitch, Yair. 1983. "The Associative Arrangement of the Book of Judges and Its Use for the Recognition of Stages in the Formation of the Book." In *The Isaac Leo Seligmann Volume,* ed. Yair Zakovitch and Alexander Rofé. Jerusalem. (Judg.)

Zevit, Ziony. 1983. "Archaeology and Stratigraphy in Joshua 7–8." *Bulletin of the American Society of Oriental Research* 251. (Josh.)

———. 2004. "First Kings" and "Second Kings." In *The Jewish Study Bible,* ed. Berlin and Brettler. (Kings)